Foundations and Frameworks for AI in Education

Viktor Wang
California State University, San Bernardino, USA

IGI Global
Scientific Publishing
Publishing Tomorrow's Research Today

Vice President of Editorial — Melissa Wagner
Director of Acquisitions — Mikaela Felty
Director of Book Development — Jocelynn Hessler
Production Manager — Mike Brehm
Cover Design — Jose Rosado

Published in the United States of America by
IGI Global Scientific Publishing
701 East Chocolate Avenue
Hershey, PA, 17033, USA
Tel: 717-533-8845
Fax: 717-533-7115
Website: https://www.igi-global.com E-mail: cust@igi-global.com

Library of Congress Cataloging-in-Publication Data

Names: Wang, Viktor editor http://id.loc.gov/authorities/names/n2020055940 http://id.loc.gov/rwo/agents/n2020055940
Title: Foundations and Frameworks for AI in Education / edited by: Viktor Wang.
Other titles: Transformational artificial intelligence tools for use in education and learning
Description: Hershey, PA : IGI Global Scientific Publishing, [2026] | Includes bibliographical references and index. | Summary: "This book aims to explore the transformative potential of artificial intelligence (AI) tools in education, focusing on their application to enhance teaching, learning, and administrative processes. It seeks to bridge the gap between theoretical advancements in AI and their practical implementation in educational settings"-- Provided by publisher.
Identifiers: LCCN 2025004360 (print) | LCCN 2025004361 (ebook) | ISBN 9798337323978 hardcover | ISBN 9798337323985 paperback | ISBN 9798337323992 ebook
Subjects: LCSH: Artificial intelligence--Educational applications http://id.loc.gov/authorities/subjects/sh87006783
Classification: LCC LB1028.43 .T733 2025 (print) | LCC LB1028.43 (ebook) | DDC 371.33/4--dc23/eng/20250530
LC record available at https://lccn.loc.gov/2025004360
LC ebook record available at https://lccn.loc.gov/2025004361

British Cataloguing in Publication Data
A Cataloguing in Publication record for this book is available from the British Library.

Table of Contents

Detailed Table of Contents

complex collaboration (Co-Construction), personalized learning (Learning), and transformative instructional redesign (Evolution). This chapter emphasizes the importance of iterative, practice-based approaches to AI integration, ensuring that technology augments rather than replaces human expertise, ultimately enhancing cognitive performance and supporting more personalized, impactful learning experiences.

The integration of artificial intelligence (AI) in curriculum development is transforming education by enabling personalized learning, adaptive assessments, and data-driven decision-making. This paper explores how AI-driven technologies enhance curriculum design, ensuring that educational programs remain relevant, future-oriented, and responsive to evolving workforce demands. Key advancements such as machine learning algorithms, AI-powered learning analytics, and automated content generation are examined for their impact on curriculum planning, instructional strategies, and learner engagement. Additionally, the authors discuss ethical considerations, challenges in AI adoption, and the role of educators in guiding AI-enhanced curriculum development. By properly embracing AI, providing the needed infrastructure and professional development alongside addressing ethical dimensions of AI in education institutions can foster innovation, inclusivity, and lifelong learning, preparing students for a rapidly changing digital landscape.

Artificial Intelligence (AI) is transforming higher education by enhancing teaching, learning, and administrative processes. AI-driven technologies, such as intelligent tutoring systems, personalized learning platforms, and automated grading, provide educators with new tools to improve student engagement and learning outcomes. Additionally, AI streamlines administrative tasks, increases accessibility for diverse learners, and supports data-driven decision-making. However, integrating AI into higher education also presents challenges, including ethical concerns, data privacy risks, faculty adaptation, and the potential displacement of human roles. Institutions must address these issues through responsible AI governance, professional development programs, and policies that ensure AI serves as a complement to, rather than a replacement for, human educators. This paper explores the evolving role of AI in higher education, examining both its transformative potential and the critical considerations that must be navigated to ensure equitable and effective implementation.

By enabling individualized and flexible educational experiences, artificial intelligence (AI) is revolutionizing lifelong learning. AI can help identify learning gaps and provide access to tools and resources for skill improvement in real time, which is crucial in the ever-changing job market. This chapter reviews how AI can support lifelong learning through recommendation systems, adaptive learning platforms, and intelligent tutoring systems—all of which help to increase access to education. Emphasizing personalized learning and skill development, the application of AI in corporate training and micro-credentialing is also covered. However, integrating AI into educational settings still presents ethical questions regarding algorithmic biases and data privacy. Stakeholders must engage in ongoing conversations about future educational systems that merge technology with human understanding to establish ethical and inclusive strategies that promote empowerment and equal access to lifelong learning through AI.

Students with disabilities make up a notable portion of today's classrooms. To address their varied educational, social, and life skill needs, schools utilize high leverage practices. One of these strategies is the use of technology and assistive technology. Artificial intelligence technology may meet the definition of assistive technology in increasing the functioning capabilities of individuals with disabilities. Research finds support for the use of extended reality, robot assisted, smart eyewear, health monitoring wearables, captioning, text creation, speech-to-text, and text-to-speech. This artificial intelligence can personalize the learning experience, increase motivation and engagement, and improve academic knowledge. Challenges of implementing artificial intelligence among students with disabilities include the lack of teacher knowledge, access, and costs. Additional concerns noted in the research are ethics, privacy, data, and security. Nonetheless, the use of artificial intelligence by students with disabilities holds promise to meet the diverse needs of students.

This article explores how AI-powered tutoring systems are transforming student support across K–12, higher education, corporate training, and lifelong learning. Leveraging machine learning, natural language processing, and data analytics, these systems offer personalized, scalable, and interactive alternatives to traditional tutoring. The shift from human-led to AI-enabled tutoring is examined, along with benefits such as adaptive learning paths, immediate feedback, accessibility, and engagement. Challenges like data privacy, bias, and the role of human mentors are addressed. The article identifies trends such as predictive analytics in global tutoring networks and smart corporate systems. Ethical concerns—transparency, fairness, and access—are discussed as essential to responsible AI use. Recommendations emphasize a hybrid model that integrates AI tools with human-centered pedagogy, ensuring meaningful learning and future workforce readiness.

This chapter explores the impact of an in-person AI training workshop on Chilean in-service teachers across a network of four schools. Through a mixed-methods approach—including pre- and post-surveys with qualitative and quantitative data—the study examines shifts in teacher attitudes, knowledge, and intentions to use AI in educational practice. Results show increased confidence, pedagogical alignment, and ethical awareness, particularly regarding inclusion and differentiated instruction. The chapter also highlights the importance of contextualized training, gender representation, and long-term support to ensure equitable and meaningful AI integration in Latin American classrooms

This chapter pursues two primary objectives. First, it aims to guide teachers new to AI game design, from the essentials to their initial steps in exploring deeper prompting. Second, it evaluates the effectiveness of AI-generated games based on three factors: their artistic merit (analyzed via Aristotelian drama structure), adherence to the provided sociological theory, and students' quiz performance and lesson engagement. For the sake of demonstration, two AI-generated game demos are explored: a Role-Playing Game (RPG) and a branching narrative game, whose plots are developed based on Strain Theory and Max Weber's concepts.

Artificial Intelligence (AI) is rapidly transforming academic research by streamlining literature reviews, data collection, statistical analysis, and academic writing. This chapter traces the evolution of AI in research, from early rule-based systems to current machine learning and deep learning applications. It explores key areas where AI enhances research productivity and insight, while also addressing pressing ethical and methodological concerns such as algorithmic bias, data privacy, transparency, and authorship accountability. The chapter argues that while AI holds great potential to augment scholarly inquiry, its integration must be guided by rigorous ethical standards and human oversight to preserve the integrity, equity, and creativity central to academic work.

This chapter explores the integration of Artificial Intelligence (AI) in education for formative and summative assessment. The educational shift from teacher-based assessment to AI-powered assessment tools have evolved to increase the learning outcomes for the students and helped teachers to implement best assessment practices. The relevance of AI in assessment has created a balanced approach to improve assessment in education. Moreover, AI-powered tools have created new landscapes

Foreword

In an era defined by exponential technological advancement, few topics are as pressing and transformative as the integration of artificial intelligence into educational practice. Dr. Viktor Wang's latest work, is a timely and forward-looking contribution to this emerging discourse. With the insight of a scholar, the experience of a practitioner, and the clarity of a visionary, Dr. Wang invites us to consider how AI is not simply a set of tools, but a catalyst for reimagining learning itself.

The promise of AI in education has often been misunderstood or oversimplified. Too frequently, discussions revolve around automation, efficiency, or novelty. What Dr. Wang accomplishes in this volume is a reframing—he asks not merely how we can use AI to enhance what we already do, but how we might transform our understanding of teaching, learning, and leadership in the digital age. The book challenges us to go beyond surface-level integration and consider deeper pedagogical, andragogical/adult educational, ethical, and humanistic implications.

Drawing from decades of leadership in adult and career education, and supported by a rich foundation of global collaboration, Dr. Wang provides a framework that is both pragmatic and aspirational. He does not present AI as a panacea, but rather as a toolset that, when applied thoughtfully, can foster equity, creativity, and lifelong learning. The transformative aspect lies not in the technology itself, but in how we choose to engage with it.

This book arrives at a moment when educational leaders across the globe are asking fundamental questions: How do we prepare students for an unpredictable future? How can we use emerging technologies to close equity gaps rather than widen them? And how do we uphold the values of critical thinking, ethical reasoning, and human connection in an increasingly digital world? Dr. Wang's work offers not only tools, but a compass—a way to navigate the profound shifts that AI will inevitably bring to education systems, institutions, and individuals.

Educators, policymakers, and scholars alike will find this book both illuminating and provocative. It is a call to action, a guide for thoughtful implementation, and a blueprint for transformation. I am confident that this volume will become a foundational text for those who not only study AI in education, but who seek to lead change in a world that demands both innovation and wisdom.

As you turn the pages ahead, I encourage you to engage with the ideas not just as possibilities, but as imperatives. Let this book inspire you to think boldly, lead ethically, and educate with a vision that is as compassionate as it is forward-thinking. The future of learning is not written yet—but with works like this, we are beginning to sketch its outlines.

John A. Henschke
University of Missouri, USA & Lindenwood University, USA

Preface

INTRODUCTION

The idea for this book, *Foundations and Frameworks for AI in Education*, emerged from the convergence of two lifelong passions: my dedication to advancing adult, career, and higher education, and my deep curiosity about the potential of artificial intelligence to reshape the ways we teach, learn, and lead. As an educator, researcher, and mentor with more than two decades of global academic engagement, I have had the privilege of witnessing—and contributing to—many waves of educational reform. Yet none has been as rapid, as disruptive, or as full of possibility as the current era of AI innovation.

My academic foundation is rooted in one of the most influential departments in the history of adult education—the Department of Vocational and Adult Education at the University of Arkansas, where I earned both my doctoral degree in education and a master's degree in educational technology. This is the same department where the late Dr. Malcolm Knowles, the father of andragogy, taught until his passing in 1997. It is a profound honor to have graduated from a department so deeply connected to the origins of adult learning theory. I have proudly carried Dr. Knowles' torch of andragogical leadership forward, guiding research across disciplines and continents, and advancing his legacy through my own teaching, writing, and mentorship.

To date, I have published over 240 refereed works, including approximately 80 volumes of scholarly books. My publications are held in the libraries of leading universities such as Stanford, New York University, and Princeton, a testament to their relevance and scholarly impact. I have had the privilege of publishing articles and book chapters authored by some of the most respected figures in the field of education, including Dr. Stephen Brookfield. Furthermore, my *Encyclopedia of Strategic Leadership and Management* drew contributions from over 300 scholars worldwide, reflecting a truly global conversation around leadership and learning in a changing world.

I also take great pride in my long-standing relationship with Dr. John A. Henschke, one of Malcolm Knowles' own doctoral students and a towering figure in his own right. Dr. Henschke has been both a mentor and a friend, and it is with deep gratitude that I acknowledge his contribution of a foreword to this volume. His lifelong dedication to andragogical principles and international education has deeply shaped my thinking and my work.

The inspiration for this work also draws from a career in teaching that spans continents. I have had the distinct honor of teaching in both China and across many states in the United States, including California, Florida, Arizona, and Montana. My classrooms have included doctoral candidates, educational leaders, adult learners, and pre-service teachers—all eager to make sense of the complexities of learning in the 21st century. Across all these settings, a common thread emerged: the desire to understand how technology, when guided by values and vision, can support deeper, more inclusive learning experiences.

This book is the result of ongoing conversations with colleagues, students, institutional leaders, and policymakers from around the world. It is built upon decades of work in instructional leadership, curriculum development, and the integration of andragogical principles in both physical and virtual learning environments. Over time, I began to realize that while AI was gaining traction in the fields of industry, healthcare, and business, its application in education was often misunderstood, oversimplified, or siloed. There was—and still is—a need for thoughtful, ethical, and strategically guided exploration of what AI can actually do to support and uplift teaching and learning.

My intent with this book is not to celebrate technology for its own sake. Rather, it is to invite educators, leaders, and learners into a dialogue about how AI can be used to advance the values we hold most dear: access, inclusion, equity, adaptability, and lifelong learning. I firmly believe that AI tools, when integrated intentionally and reflectively, can serve as catalysts for educational transformation—not only enhancing instructional efficiency, but also deepening human connection and creativity in ways that support the full spectrum of learning.

ORGANIZATION OF THE BOOK

The book is organized into several volumes, each focused on a specific aspect of AI in education—from practical tools and case studies to theoretical frameworks and future-facing models of leadership. The contributors to this work represent a wide range of disciplines and global perspectives. Together, we aim to highlight both the promise and the limitations of AI, always with the understanding that technology must serve human development—not replace it.

Chapter 1: AI and the Future of Education A Transformative Vision

Chapter 1 explores the profound impact of Artificial Intelligence on education, highlighting its potential to revolutionize teaching, learning, and administration. The chapter examines AI's role in personalizing education, enhancing teacher effectiveness, and streamlining administrative processes, while also addressing ethical challenges such as data privacy, algorithmic bias, and equitable access. By envisioning a future where AI complements human ingenuity, this chapter underscores the transformative power of AI to create a more inclusive, innovative, and effective educational landscape, preparing learners for the demands of a rapidly evolving global workforce.

Chapter 2: Navigating Ethical AI: Ensuring Fairness in Educational Technologies

As artificial intelligence (AI) rapidly transforms educational spaces, this chapter comprehensively explores ethical considerations surrounding its use in teaching, learning, and school administration. Navigating Ethical AI brings together frameworks, case studies, and pedagogical practices to address how AI systems may reinforce bias, marginalize learners, or erode trust when designed or deployed without sufficient care. The chapters examine fairness metrics, human-in-the-loop strategies, regulatory approaches, and classroom-level interventions. Central to the book is a call for inclusive co-creation between students, educators, developers, and policymakers to ensure AI serves as a tool for justice rather than control. By combining technical insight with ethical reflection, this volume lays the foundation for a more transparent, equitable, and human-centered AI future in education.

Chapter 3: AI and the Ethics of Student Data Privacy

As artificial intelligence (AI) becomes increasingly integrated into education, concerns about student data privacy and ethical AI use are growing. AI-driven learning platforms and predictive analytics rely on vast amounts of student data to personalize education, but this raises ethical challenges related to data security, informed consent, algorithmic bias, and potential misuse. This chapter explores the implications of AI on student data privacy, examining current legal frameworks such as FERPA and GDPR, best practices for ensuring transparency and accountability, and strategies for equitable and secure AI implementation in education. By addressing these concerns, institutions and policymakers can create AI-driven learning environments that protect student privacy while maximizing innovation and educational benefits.

Chapter 4: Addressing the Digital Divide: Ensuring Equal Access to AI Tools

This chapter explores the persistent inequalities in access to artificial intelligence technologies across socioeconomic, geographic, and educational contexts. It examines how disparities in digital infrastructure, device availability, and digital literacy can limit equitable participation in the AI-driven future. Through analysis of current policies, case studies, and equity-focused frameworks, the chapter highlights strategies for bridging the divide—particularly in underserved communities. It calls on educators, policymakers, and technology developers to prioritize inclusive design and investment to ensure that the benefits of AI are accessible to all.

Chapter 5: Co-Creating with AI: Augmenting, Enhancing, and Elevating Instructional Design

This chapter explores the integration of generative artificial intelligence (genAI) into instructional design in higher education, addressing both its potential and its challenges. It introduces the SCALE Framework (Substitution, Co-Construction, Automation, Learning, Evolution), a progressive model for faculty AI literacy that builds on established educational theories like Bloom's Revised Taxonomy, UDL, and TPACK, as well as emergent AI-specific and sociocultural perspectives. The framework positions AI as a collaborative partner, guiding educators through stages from automating routine tasks (Substitution, Automation) to fostering more complex collaboration (Co-Construction), personalized learning (Learning), and transformative instructional redesign (Evolution). This chapter emphasizes the importance of iterative, practice-based approaches to AI integration, ensuring that technology augments rather than replaces human expertise, ultimately enhancing cognitive performance and supporting more personalized, impactful learning experiences.

Chapter 6: AI and Curriculum: Designing for the Future

The integration of artificial intelligence (AI) in curriculum development is transforming education by enabling personalized learning, adaptive assessments, and data-driven decision-making. This paper explores how AI-driven technologies enhance curriculum design, ensuring that educational programs remain relevant, future-oriented, and responsive to evolving workforce demands. Key advancements such as machine learning algorithms, AI-powered learning analytics, and automated content generation are examined for their impact on curriculum planning, instructional strategies, and learner engagement. Additionally, the authors discuss ethical considerations, challenges in AI adoption, and the role of educators in guiding AI-enhanced curriculum development. By properly embracing AI, providing the needed infrastructure and professional development alongside addressing ethical dimensions of AI in education institutions can foster innovation, inclusivity, and lifelong learning, preparing students for a rapidly changing digital landscape.

Chapter 7: AI in Higher Education: Opportunities and Challenges

Artificial Intelligence (AI) is transforming higher education by enhancing teaching, learning, and administrative processes. AI-driven technologies, such as intelligent tutoring systems, personalized learning platforms, and automated grading, provide educators with new tools to improve student engagement and learning outcomes. Additionally, AI streamlines administrative tasks, increases accessibility for diverse learners, and supports data-driven decision-making. However, integrating AI into higher education also presents challenges, including ethical concerns, data privacy risks, faculty adaptation, and the potential displacement of human roles. Institutions must address these issues through responsible AI governance, professional development programs, and policies that ensure AI serves as a complement to, rather than a replacement for, human educators. This paper explores the evolving role of AI in higher education, examining both its transformative potential and the critical considerations that must be navigated to ensure equitable and effective implementation.

Chapter 8: The Role of AI in Lifelong Learning

By enabling individualized and flexible educational experiences, artificial intelligence (AI) is revolutionizing lifelong learning. AI can help identify learning gaps and provide access to tools and resources for skill improvement in real time, which is crucial in the ever-changing job market. This chapter reviews how AI can support lifelong learning through recommendation systems, adaptive learning platforms, and intelligent tutoring systems—all of which help to increase access to education. Emphasizing personalized learning and skill development, the application of AI in corporate training and micro-credentialing is also covered. However, integrating AI into educational settings still presents ethical questions regarding algorithmic biases and data privacy. Stakeholders must engage in ongoing conversations about future educational systems that merge technology with human understanding to establish ethical and inclusive strategies that promote empowerment and equal access to lifelong learning through AI.

Chapter 9: Artificial Intelligence in Special Education: Supporting Diverse Learners

Students with disabilities make up a notable portion of today's classrooms. To address their varied educational, social, and life skill needs, schools utilize high leverage practices. One of these strategies is the use of technology and assistive technology. Artificial intelligence technology may meet the definition of assistive technology in increasing the functioning capabilities of individuals with disabilities. Research finds support for the use of extended reality, robot assisted, smart eyewear, health monitoring wearables, captioning, text creation, speech-to-text, and text-to-speech. This artificial intelligence can personalize the learning experience, increase motivation and engagement, and improve academic knowledge. Challenges of implementing artificial intelligence among students with disabilities include the lack of teacher knowledge, access, and costs. Additional concerns noted in the research are ethics, privacy, data, and security. Nonetheless, the use of artificial intelligence by students with disabilities holds promise to meet the diverse needs of students.

Chapter 10: The Use of AI in Teaching and Learning: The Power of Feedback

This chapter explores the transformative potential of artificial intelligence (AI) in delivering timely, personalized, and scalable feedback across educational contexts. Grounded in foundational learning theories—including behaviorism, constructivism, and cognitive load theory—it examines how AI-powered tools enhance self-regulated learning, motivation, and equity. Technologies such as natural language processing, intelligent tutoring systems, and affective computing are analyzed for their role in fostering responsive and dialogic feedback. The chapter also critically addresses ethical concerns, including bias, data privacy, and automation bias. Through practical examples and design principles, it advocates for human-centered AI feedback systems that align with pedagogical goals, empower educators, and promote learner agency. Ultimately, it argues that feedback must remain relational and ethically grounded to truly enrich teaching and learning in the digital age.

Chapter 11: Co-Designing with AI: Human-Centered Approaches for Future-Ready Course Design

As AI technologies continue to evolve, they are reshaping the educational landscape and opening new possibilities for curriculum innovation and course design. While AI has traditionally supported task automation—such as grading, content generation, and revision—this chapter repositions AI as a collaborative partner in instructional design. Rather than viewing AI as a tool that mimics human functions, we propose embracing it as a co-designer that enhances the expertise of educators and instructional designers. We advocate a human-centered, intentional application of AI through meaningful prompts, adaptive workflows, and sound pedagogical strategies. Grounded in foundational instructional design models—Backward Design, ADDIE, and Gagné's Nine Events—and aligned with frameworks such as Bloom's Taxonomy, QM, QLT, and UDL, this chapter offers a learner-centered approach. Through case studies and practical examples, we show how AI can help create inclusive, engaging, and innovative courses while maintaining pedagogical integrity and instructional excellence.

Chapter 12: Transforming Student Support with AI-Powered Tutoring

This article explores how AI-powered tutoring systems are transforming student support across K–12, higher education, corporate training, and lifelong learning. Leveraging machine learning, natural language processing, and data analytics, these systems offer personalized, scalable, and interactive alternatives to traditional tutoring. The shift from human-led to AI-enabled tutoring is examined, along with benefits such as adaptive learning paths, immediate feedback, accessibility, and engagement. Challenges like data privacy, bias, and the role of human mentors are addressed. The article identifies trends such as predictive analytics in global tutoring networks and smart corporate systems. Ethical concerns—transparency, fairness, and access—are discussed as essential to responsible AI use. Recommendations emphasize a hybrid model that integrates AI tools with human-centered pedagogy, ensuring meaningful learning and future workforce readiness.

Chapter 13: Integrating Artificial Intelligence in Education: Insights from a Teacher Training Workshop

This chapter explores the impact of an in-person AI training workshop on Chilean in-service teachers across a network of four schools. Through a mixed-methods approach—including pre- and post-surveys with qualitative and quantitative data—the study examines shifts in teacher attitudes, knowledge, and intentions to use AI in educational practice. Results show increased confidence, pedagogical alignment, and ethical awareness, particularly regarding inclusion and differentiated instruction. The chapter also highlights the importance of contextualized training, gender representation, and long-term support to ensure equitable and meaningful AI integration in Latin American classrooms

Chapter 14: Effortless Game Creation: A Teacher's Guide to Using Generative AI in Social Science Education

This chapter pursues two primary objectives. First, it aims to guide teachers new to AI game design, from the essentials to their initial steps in exploring deeper prompting. Second, it evaluates the effectiveness of AI-generated games based on three factors: their artistic merit (analyzed via Aristotelian drama structure), adherence to the provided sociological theory, and students' quiz performance and lesson engagement. For the sake of demonstration, two AI-generated game demos are explored: a Role-Playing Game (RPG) and a branching narrative game, whose plots are developed based on Strain Theory and Max Weber's concepts.

Chapter 15: Artificial Intelligence in Academic Research: Applications, Challenges, and Future Directions

Artificial Intelligence (AI) is rapidly transforming academic research by streamlining literature reviews, data collection, statistical analysis, and academic writing. This chapter traces the evolution of AI in research, from early rule-based systems to current machine learning and deep learning applications. It explores key areas where AI enhances research productivity and insight, while also addressing pressing ethical and methodological concerns such as algorithmic bias, data privacy, transparency, and authorship accountability. The chapter argues that while AI holds great potential to augment scholarly inquiry, its integration must be guided by rigorous ethical standards and human oversight to preserve the integrity, equity, and creativity central to academic work.

Chapter 16: Relevance of Artificial Intelligence in Assessment: A Balanced Approach

This chapter explores the integration of Artificial Intelligence (AI) in education for formative and summative assessment. The educational shift from teacher-based assessment to AI-powered assessment tools have evolved to increase the learning outcomes for the students and helped teachers to implement best assessment practices. The relevance of AI in assessment has created a balanced approach to improve assessment in education. Moreover, AI-powered tools have created new landscapes for students' assessment for both formative as well as summative assessments. The chapter discusses the role of AI in student assessment such as formative and summative assessment with AI, personalized learning paths, adaptive learning, instant feedback, tracking progress, Integration of AI in Pedagogy, and Behavioral and Engagement Analytics to improve students learning outcomes. Additionally, it addresses the challenges in implementing AI-powered assessment for efficient resources allocation, and fairness, bias, and ethical consideration in AI algorithms.

Chapter 17: AI in Education Past, Present, and Future

This chapter explores the evolution of Artificial Intelligence (AI) in educational technology, tracing its journey from early computational models like computer-assisted instruction (CAI) and intelligent tutoring systems (ITS) in the 1960s and 1970s, which laid the groundwork for AI's current transformative role in classrooms and beyond. Today, AI-powered tools are reshaping personalized learning, automating administrative tasks, and creating immersive learning experiences through virtual and augmented reality. Looking ahead, AI is expected to foster lifelong learning, improve assessment methods, and address equity and accessibility challenges, while also raising ethical concerns around data privacy and algorithmic bias. The chapter emphasizes AI's potential to revolutionize education by making it more inclusive, accessible, and tailored to individual learning needs, ultimately reshaping the way we teach, learn, and engage with knowledge.

CONCLUSION

It is no coincidence that this work includes contributions from educators and thought leaders across continents. We are in a moment of global transformation, and our responses must be equally global. AI is not a trend—it is an inflection point. And the choices we make now, as educators and institutions, will determine whether we amplify opportunity or exacerbate inequality. This book is a humble offering in service of the former.

I would like to express my deepest gratitude to my co-authors, contributors, reviewers, and institutional partners who have supported this project. Your insights and commitment have shaped every chapter. I also want to thank the students and doctoral candidates I've mentored over the years—you continue to inspire me with your questions, your resilience, and your determination to make education more inclusive and more effective for future generations.

I also wish to extend my heartfelt appreciation to IGI Global, the publisher of this volume, for their enduring commitment to scholarly excellence and their support in bringing this multi-volume work to fruition. Their dedication to disseminating transformative research in education and leadership has been instrumental throughout this process.

Special thanks are also due to the many reviewers whose critical feedback helped refine the clarity, depth, and coherence of the chapters included. Your thoughtful engagement enriched the work in ways too numerous to count.

To the global network of contributors who lent their voices, perspectives, and expertise—thank you. Your diverse insights and dedication to educational advancement have shaped this book into a truly international and collaborative effort.

Finally, I wish to express deep gratitude to the university libraries around the world—including Stanford University, New York University, and Princeton University—that continue to catalog and share my work. Your support ensures that knowledge remains accessible, visible, and impactful for future generations of learners and researchers.

To the readers: whether you are a faculty member rethinking your curriculum, a dean or provost leading systemic change, a policymaker designing new frameworks, or a student exploring the frontiers of digital learning—I hope you find in these pages not only knowledge, but encouragement. This is your invitation to engage, to question, and to lead. The future of education is not just about digital tools or predictive algorithms—it's about the people who wield them with wisdom and care.

In closing, I offer this book as both a scholarly resource and a starting point for transformation. May it spark ideas, challenge assumptions, and serve as a guide for all who believe in the power of education to shape a better, more equitable world—one learner, one classroom, one innovation at a time.

This book, *Foundations and Frameworks for AI in Education*, is the first in the *Transformative AI Tools for Use in Education and Learning* series. It focuses on foundational theories, ethical frameworks, and structural approaches to integrating AI into education. It sets the stage for the books that follow by offering conceptual clarity and thematic grounding, ideal for educators, researchers, and policy leaders seeking a broad understanding of AI's role in shaping the future of learning.

Viktor Wang
California State University, San Bernardino, USA

Chapter 1
AI and the Future of Education: A Transformative Vision

Viktor Wang
https://orcid.org/0000-0001-9557-0054
California State University, San Bernardino, USA

Geraldine Torrisi-Steele
https://orcid.org/0000-0002-6045-4114
Griffith University, Australia

ABSTRACT

Chapter 1, AI and the Future of Education: A Transformative Vision, explores the profound impact of Artificial Intelligence on education, highlighting its potential to revolutionize teaching, learning, and administration. The chapter examines AI's role in personalizing education, enhancing teacher effectiveness, and streamlining administrative processes, while also addressing ethical challenges such as data privacy, algorithmic bias, and equitable access. By envisioning a future where AI complements human ingenuity, this chapter underscores the transformative power of AI to create a more inclusive, innovative, and effective educational landscape, preparing learners for the demands of a rapidly evolving global workforce.

INTRODUCTION

Artificial Intelligence (AI) is no longer confined to the realms of science fiction; it is a present-day reality. Rapidly advancing, AI is reshaping the way we live, work, and interact. AI is transforming industries, economies, and societies on a global scale, and the field of education is no exception (Rahiman & Kodikal, 2024) (Farooq,

DOI: 10.4018/979-8-3373-2397-8.ch001

Malik, & Syed, 2024). AI is already playing an increasingly pivotal role in the educational sector, offering unprecedented opportunities to enhance teaching, learning, and administrative processes. The integration of AI technologies into education is not just about automation or efficiency; it is about reimagining the very nature of education itself and creating a future where personalized, adaptive, and intelligent learning environments can thrive. The aim of this chapter is to explore the ways in which AI is transforming the educational landscape, offering a transformative vision that redefines traditional models of teaching, learning, and administration in the 21st century.

Traditional classroom settings are usually characterized by a one-size-fits-all approach. The reality is that classrooms are filled with a diversity of students. In any one classroom, knowing, and meeting, the needs of students with varying learning styles, paces, and abilities is challenging. One of the greatest promises of AI is to enable personalized learning experiences tailored to the unique needs of individual students (Cinar, Rafferty, Cutting, & Wang, 2024). The algorithms in the AI suite of technologies can analyze vast amounts of data to identify patterns in student performance, preferences, and behaviors, helping us to understand the learning profiles of students (Sarker, 2021). Founded on student profiles, and assisted by AI technologies, learning resources that can adapt to each student's strengths, weaknesses, and interests can be developed. . This data-driven approach to teaching allows educators to make informed decisions about how best to support their students, ensuring that each learner receives the attention and guidance they need to succeed (Kumar, Haque, Mishra, Islam, & Ahmad, 2023). By providing tailored recommendations, resources, and assessments, AI can help students progress at their own pace, ensuring that no one is left behind. This personalized approach not only enhances learning outcomes but also fosters a deeper engagement with the material, as students feel more empowered and supported in their educational journey (Towfek, Khodadadi, Abualigah, & Rizk, 2024). (Tafazoli, 2024) (Ozsevim & Ng, 2023) (Kumar, Haque, Mishra, Islam, & Ahmad, 2023).In addition to personalized learning, AI has the potential to transform teaching methods by providing educators with powerful tools to enhance their instructional practices. Teachers can leverage AI to automate administrative tasks, such as grading assignments, tracking attendance, managing schedules, generating slide designs and so on, freeing up valuable time to focus on more meaningful interactions with students (Lee, et al., 2024). AI-powered teaching assistants can support teachers in real-time by providing instant feedback on student performance, suggesting instructional strategies, and even identifying students who may require additional attention. Moreover, AI can play a critical role in improving student outcomes by identifying at-risk students early on and providing targeted interventions to help them stay on track.

At levels beyond the classroom, the integration of AI into education also has the potential to enhance the administrative functions of educational institutions, making them more efficient, data-driven, and responsive to the needs of students, faculty, and staff (Sposato, 2025). AI can streamline administrative processes by automating routine tasks, such as scheduling, resource allocation, and student enrollment, reducing the administrative burden on staff and allowing them to focus on higher-level decision-making. AI-powered analytics can provide valuable insights into student performance, retention rates, and engagement, enabling administrators to make data-informed decisions about curriculum design, resource allocation, and student support services (Sposato, 2025) (Ifenthaler, et al., 2024)By leveraging AI to optimize administrative processes, educational institutions can create more efficient, responsive, and student-centered environments that foster academic success.

Without doubt, AI is an impressive suite of technologies with great potential to transform education. But there is a caveat. AI can enable positive transformation and enormous benefit but it can also cause harm (Pangrazio, 2024, p. 1049). While the potential benefits of AI in education are vast, the integration of AI technologies also raises important questions about equity, ethics, and the future of work. As AI becomes more prevalent in education, it is essential to ensure that all students have access to the tools and resources necessary to benefit from these advancements. This includes addressing issues of digital literacy, access to technology, and the potential for AI to exacerbate existing inequalities (Pangrazio, 2024)(Khan, Umer, & Faruge, 2024). For example, students in underserved communities may not have the same access to AI-powered learning tools as their peers in more affluent areas, potentially widening the digital divide. To mitigate these risks, it is crucial for policymakers, educators, and technology developers to work together to ensure that AI is implemented in ways that promote equity and inclusion, rather than perpetuating existing disparities.

Ethical considerations surrounding the use of AI in education are of paramount importance. AI systems rely on vast amounts of data, which raises concerns about privacy, security, and the potential for bias in decision-making. For example, AI algorithms used to assess student performance or predict academic outcomes may inadvertently perpetuate biases related to race, gender, socioeconomic status, or other factors, leading to unfair or discriminatory outcomes. It is essential to ensure that AI systems are transparent, accountable, and designed with ethical principles in mind to prevent harm and promote fairness. Additionally, as AI continues to advance, there are concerns about its impact on the future of work and the role of human educators. While AI has the potential to augment and enhance teaching practices, it is unlikely to replace human teachers entirely (Felix, 2021). The role of the educator will remain central to the learning process as guiding and facilitating learning (Al-Zahrani & Alasmari, 2024), but AI can serve as a valuable tool to support and enhance their work, allowing them to focus on more meaningful aspects of teaching, such as fostering critical thinking, creativity, and emotional intelligence.

Looking ahead, the future of AI in education is both exciting and uncertain. As AI technologies continue to evolve, they will undoubtedly play an increasingly prominent role in shaping the educational landscape. However, the successful integration of AI into education will require careful planning, collaboration, and a commitment to ensuring that AI is used in ways that benefit all students, educators, and institutions. This will involve addressing the challenges of equity, ethics, and accessibility, as well as developing new pedagogical models that leverage AI to create more personalized, engaging, and effective learning experiences. AI as a tool for transformation, rather than a replacement for human interaction, is the starting point for unlocking its full potential to create a more inclusive, equitable, and innovative educational system.

That AI will "trigger transformative change is undeniable" (Bozkurt, 2023, p. 199) The integration of AI into education is not just about technology; it is about reimagining the possibilities of what education can be and how it can better serve the diverse needs of students in a rapidly changing world. By harnessing the power of AI while remaining mindful of its potential risks and challenges, we can create an educational landscape that is more inclusive, engaging, and effective for all learners AI is poised to reshape the future of education in profound and transformative ways, but only, and only if, we design, and work with the tools in ethical, transparent and just ways. With this theme at the center, the present chapter is an overarching discussion of the transformative view of AI for education.

PERSONALIZED LEARNING: EDUCATION FOR THE INDIVIDUAL

AI's integration into education has catalyzed the development of a range of transformative technologies that are reshaping the way teaching and learning occur. Adaptive learning systems, intelligent tutoring, and personalized learning experiences are just a few of the innovations that have emerged because of AI's increasing presence in educational settings. These technologies are not tools for efficiencies in education. It is imperative to explore how these tools can also be used to provide more effective learning experiences to diverse cohorts of students. This exploration necessarily requires a fundamental shift in how educators approach the process of teaching and how students experience and engage with learning. The advent of AI technologies in education inevitably leads to re-examine what it means to teach and what it means to learn (Lee, et al., 2024; Seo, Tang, Roll, Fels, & Yoon, 2021) Perhaps the biggest excitement about AI in education is about personalization of learning

(Walter, 2024) (Febriantl, Tari, Ariska, & Reni, 2025) (Merino-Campos, 2024). At the heart of AI's ability to personalize education is the use of machine learning algorithms. These algorithms analyze vast amounts of data generated by students as they interact with learning materials, complete assignments, and participate in various activities. This data can include test scores, quiz results, time spent on tasks, patterns of interaction with educational content, and even behavioral indicators such as engagement levels and attention span. By processing this data, AI systems can identify patterns and trends that reveal a student's learning needs, preferences, and potential areas for improvement. This data-driven approach allows AI to provide real-time insights into how a student is progressing, enabling the system to adapt and recommend personalized learning paths that best suit the individual learner.

Fuelling adaptive learning systemsare algorithms to analyze data on student performance, including responses to assessments, learning activities, and interactions with educational content. Based on this data, the system adjusts the difficulty, pacing, and content of lessons to match the learner's individual progress. For example, if a student is struggling with a particular concept, the system might present additional practice problems or offer supplementary resources to help the student master the material. Conversely, if a student demonstrates proficiency in each area, the system can accelerate the learning process by presenting more advanced content. This dynamic approach to learning ensures that students are consistently challenged at an appropriate level, neither being bored by material that is too easy nor overwhelmed by content that is too difficult. For example, if a student struggles with a particular concept in mathematics, an AI-powered system can identify this challenge based on the student's performance and engagement with the material. In response, the system may recommend additional practice problems, alternative explanations, or even interactive simulations to help the student better understand the concept. Conversely, if a student excels in a certain area, AI can accelerate their learning by providing more advanced content or introducing more complex problems to challenge them further. This dynamic and adaptive approach ensures that each student receives the appropriate level of challenge and support, helping them stay engaged and motivated throughout their learning journey. The impact of adaptive learning on student engagement is profound (Swiecki, et al., 2022) and evidence is mounting that students tend to do better in adaptive learning environments (Kumar, Haque, Mishra, Islam, & Ahmad, 2023) (Matz, et al., 2023).. Traditional classroom instruction often requires teachers to divide their attention among many students, each with their own learning needs. This can result in some students feeling disengaged or left behind, as they may not receive the individualized attention they require. Adaptive learning systems, however, provide a solution to this problem by offering personalized experiences for each student, ensuring that every learner is engaged at their own level. By continuously adjusting to the student's needs, these systems help maintain a sense of challenge and achievement, keeping students motivated and focused on their learning goals, thereby increasing performance and satisfaction (Contarino, Ryeyes_Millán, Vázquez-Villegas, & Membrillo-Hernández, 2024).

Intelligent tutoring systems (ITS) represent another key development in the use of AI in education (Kumar, Haque, Mishra, Islam, & Ahmad, 2023). These systems are designed to mimic the role of a human tutor, providing students with personalized guidance and support as they work through learning tasks. ITSs can deliver instruction, assess student responses, and provide immediate feedback, all while adapting to the individual needs of the learner. For example, if a student answers a question incorrectly, the ITS might provide hints or explanations to help the student understand the correct answer. In addition, ITSs can identify patterns in student behavior and performance, allowing them to predict where students are likely to struggle in the future and offer proactive support (Guo, et al., 2021).

Personalization through AI also extends to the pacing of learning. In a traditional classroom, students are often required to move through lessons at the same pace as their peers, regardless of whether they have mastered the material or are struggling to keep up. This can lead to frustration and disengagement for students who find the material too difficult or too easy. AI systems, however, allow students to learn at their own pace. If a student is struggling with a particular topic, they can take more time to review and practice it until they feel confident. On the other hand, students who grasp the material quickly can move ahead without being held back by the pace of the class. This flexibility in pacing ensures that students are not rushed through the learning process or left behind, promoting a deeper understanding of the content and a more positive learning experience overall.

In addition to pacing, AI also plays a crucial role in addressing different learning styles. Not all students learn in the same way, and traditional teaching methods often fail to accommodate this diversity. Some students are visual learners, benefiting from diagrams, charts, and videos, while others are auditory learners who thrive on listening to explanations or discussions. Still, others may learn best through hands-on experiences or by engaging in interactive activities. AI-powered learning platforms can cater to these diverse learning styles by offering a variety of content formats and delivery methods (El-Sabagh, 2021). For instance, if a student struggles with a text-heavy explanation, the AI system might offer a video or interactive simulation that presents the same concept in a different format. This ability to tailor content to individual learning preferences helps ensure that every student receives the most effective instruction for their unique needs.

The benefits of intelligent tutoring extend beyond simply providing immediate feedback. One of the most significant advantages of ITS is their ability to support students in a way that is not always possible in traditional classroom settings. In a typical classroom, a teacher may not have the time or resources to provide one-on-one support to every student who needs it. Intelligent tutoring systems, on the other hand, can provide continuous, personalized guidance to students, even outside of class time. This allows students to work at their own pace, receiving support whenever they need it, without the pressure of keeping up with the rest of the class. Additionally, ITSs can offer a more tailored approach to instruction, adapting to each student's learning style and preferences. Some students may benefit from visual aids or interactive simulations, while others may prefer textual explanations or verbal prompts. ITSs can adjust their delivery to accommodate these different learning styles, ensuring that each student receives the type of instruction that is most effective for them (Contarino, Ryeyes_Millán, Vázquez-Villegas, & Membrillo-Hernández, 2024). These platforms use data from assessments, student interactions, and learning history to develop a customized learning path for each student, which is designed to optimize their learning experience. This approach not only helps students learn more effectively, but it also allows them to take ownership of their education by enabling them to set their own learning goals and track their progress.

The potential of personalized learning to improve student outcomes is enormous. Research has shown that when students are given the opportunity to learn in a way that suits their individual needs, they are more likely to stay engaged, retain information, and perform better on assessments (Contarino, Ryeyes_Millán, Vázquez-Villegas, & Membrillo-Hernández, 2024). By providing a learning experience that is tailored to each student's pace and level of understanding, AI can help students make steady progress and achieve their full potential. This personalized approach also fosters a sense of autonomy and self-direction, which are critical skills for lifelong learning. As students become more accustomed to managing their own learning, they develop the skills necessary to navigate an increasingly complex and dynamic world.

One of the most powerful aspects of AI in education is its ability to provide real-time feedback to both students and educators (Venter, Coetzee, & Schmulian, 2024). AI-driven analytics can analyze data from a wide range of sources, including assessments, assignments, and classroom interactions, to generate insights into student performance. This data-driven approach allows educators to identify learning gaps and areas where students may be struggling, often before the student even realizes it. By providing timely feedback, AI enables educators to intervene early and offer targeted support to students who need it. For example, if a student is consistently performing poorly in a particular subject area, AI can flag this issue and recommend additional resources or interventions to help the student improve. This proactive approach to intervention can prevent small problems from becoming larger issues, helping students stay on track and succeed in their studies.

Real-time feedback also benefits students by providing them with immediate insights into their performance. In traditional education settings, students may have to wait for days or even weeks to receive feedback on assignments or exams. This delay can make it difficult for students to understand where they went wrong and how they can improve. With AI-powered feedback systems, students can receive instant feedback on their work, allowing them to identify mistakes and correct them in real-time (Escalante, Pack, & Barrett, 2023). This immediate feedback loop helps students learn more efficiently, as they can quickly adjust their approach and continue making progress.

AI-driven analytics can predict student performance with remarkable accuracy (Rodrigues, dos Santos, Costa, & Lillis Moreira, 2022) (Yağcı, 2022) (Ren & Yu, 2024). By analyzing patterns in student data, AI systems can identify students who are at risk of falling behind or failing to meet academic standards. These predictive models are based on a wide range of factors, including past performance, engagement levels, and even behavioral indicators. By identifying at-risk students early on, AI enables educators to intervene before the student's performance deteriorates further. This predictive capability is especially valuable in large classrooms or online learning environments, where it may be difficult for educators to monitor every student's progress in real-time. With AI, educators can receive alerts about students who may need additional support, allowing them to provide targeted interventions and resources to help those students succeed.

The ability to predict student performance also has implications for curriculum design and resource allocation. By analyzing data on student outcomes, AI can help educators and administrators identify which areas of the curriculum are most challenging for students and which teaching strategies are most effective. This data-driven approach to curriculum design allows educators to make evidence-based decisions about how to improve their teaching practices and optimize learning outcomes. Additionally, AI can help schools and universities allocate resources more efficiently by identifying areas where additional support or materials are needed. For example, if AI data shows that a particular subject area is consistently challenging for students, the institution may decide to invest in additional resources, such as tutoring services or supplementary learning materials, to support students in that area.

The potential for AI to personalize education extends beyond individual students to the entire classroom. By analyzing data from multiple students, AI can help educators identify trends and patterns in class-wide performance, enabling them to adjust their teaching strategies and content delivery accordingly. For example, if many students in a class are struggling with a particular concept, the AI system can recommend alternative teaching methods or resources to help address the issue. This data-driven approach to teaching allows educators to make evidence-based decisions that are more likely to improve student outcomes.

ENHANCING TEACHER EFFECTIVENESS

AI is not a replacement for teachers but rather a powerful tool designed to support and enhance their effectiveness and enable them to focus on (Seo, Yoo, Dodson, & Jin, 2024) (Terwiesch, 2023) Interactions with students for meaningful learning. In the ever-evolving landscape of education, teachers have become more than just knowledge dispensers; they are facilitators of learning, guides for personal and academic growth, and mentors who support students through both academic and emotional challenges. However, the demands placed on teachers have grown exponentially in recent years, with increasing class sizes, administrative responsibilities, and the need to stay current with rapidly changing technologies and pedagogical trends. This is where AI comes in, offering a range of solutions to automate repetitive and time-consuming tasks, thereby freeing up educators to focus on the more human aspects of teaching.

One of the most significant ways in which AI enhances the role of teachers is by automating administrative tasks that traditionally consume a considerable amount of time (Kumar, R., 2023) (Awidi, 2024). Grading, for instance, is a task that can take up a large portion of an educator's time, especially in subjects that require extensive written assessments or assignments. AI-powered grading systems, equipped with natural language processing (NLP) algorithms, can efficiently evaluate written responses, essays, and even open-ended questions. These systems can analyze text for grammar, coherence, and content accuracy, providing instant feedback to students. This not only reduces the time teachers spend on grading but also ensures that feedback is delivered promptly, allowing students to learn from their mistakes and improve their understanding of the material in real-time. Moreover, AI systems can grade at scale, making them especially valuable in large classrooms or online courses where teachers might otherwise struggle to provide timely feedback to all students.

Attendance tracking is another administrative task that can be automated using AI (Chiang, et al., 2022). Traditionally, teachers must take attendance manually, which can be time-consuming and prone to errors. AI-powered systems can automatically track student attendance using facial recognition technology, biometric scanning, or even through engagement analytics in online learning platforms. This automation reduces the burden on teachers, allowing them to focus on their core responsibilities of instruction and student engagement. In addition, AI systems can flag patterns of absenteeism or disengagement, enabling teachers to identify students who may need additional support or intervention before issues escalate.

Lesson planning, too, can be significantly enhanced by AI (Clark, 2024). AI-powered platforms can analyze curriculum standards, student performance data, and available resources to assist teachers in creating personalized lesson plans that align with both educational goals and individual student needs. These platforms can recommend teaching strategies, activities, and resources that are best suited to the class's specific learning objectives and the individual strengths and weaknesses of the students. For example, if a teacher notices that many students are struggling with a particular concept, the AI system might suggest alternative teaching methods, additional resources, or even specific interventions to help address the issue. By automating the more time-consuming aspects of lesson planning, AI enables teachers to focus on crafting more dynamic and engaging lessons that foster deeper learning.

Beyond administrative tasks, AI also supports teachers in delivering high-quality instruction and staying updated with the latest pedagogical trends. In today's rapidly changing educational environment, teachers are often required to stay current with new teaching methods, technologies, and research on effective pedagogy. However, keeping up with these developments can be overwhelming, especially for educators who already have a full teaching load. AI-powered virtual assistants can help teachers stay informed by curating relevant articles, research papers, and resources based on their teaching subjects and interests. These virtual assistants can also suggest professional development opportunities, webinars, and conferences that align with the teacher's goals for growth and improvement. By offering personalized recommendations, AI ensures that educators have access to the latest trends and best practices, empowering them to continuously improve their teaching and enhance student outcomes.

AI can also assist teachers in identifying the most effective teaching methods for their students. Through the analysis of student performance data, AI systems can provide insights into which instructional strategies are working well and which may need adjustment. For instance, if a particular teaching method leads to improved outcomes for a subset of students, AI can recommend that the teacher use that method more broadly. Conversely, if certain strategies are not yielding the desired results, AI can suggest alternative approaches or resources. This data-driven approach to teaching allows educators to make informed decisions about how to best meet the needs of their students, ensuring that instruction is both effective and engaging.

AI can also foster a more collaborative and interactive learning environment. Through AI-powered tools, students can work together on projects, engage in discussions, and collaborate on problem-solving tasks, all while receiving real-time feedback and guidance. These tools can also facilitate communication between students and teachers, allowing for more efficient sharing of resources, assignments, and feedback. For instance, AI-powered platforms can enable teachers to track student progress in real-time, allowing them to identify areas where students are excelling or struggling and adjust their teaching strategies accordingly. This level of real-time insight helps teachers provide more targeted support and ensure that students are on track to meet learning objectives.

While AI offers numerous benefits for teachers, it is important to recognize that it is not a replacement for human educators but it can augment teachers (Hemachandran et al., 2022). Teachers bring a unique set of skills, experiences, and emotional intelligence to the classroom that AI cannot replicate. The role of the teacher goes beyond delivering content; teachers are mentors, motivators, and guides who provide emotional support, encouragement, and inspiration to their students. AI, while powerful, cannot replace the human connection that is so vital to the learning process. Rather, AI should be viewed as a tool that complements and enhances the work of teachers, allowing them to focus on the aspects of teaching that require human empathy, creativity, and critical thinking.

Despite the potential of AI to enhance education, there are also challenges and ethical considerations that must be addressed. One concern is the potential for AI to perpetuate biases if the data it is trained on is not diverse or representative. If AI systems are trained on biased data, they may inadvertently reinforce stereotypes or make unfair recommendations, particularly for marginalized groups of students. To mitigate this risk, it is essential to ensure that AI systems are designed with fairness, transparency, and inclusivity in mind. Additionally, data privacy and security are major concerns, as AI systems rely on the collection and analysis of large amounts of student data. Protecting this data and ensuring that it is used ethically is crucial to maintaining trust in AI-powered educational tools.

It is important to note that despite its potential, AI is not a replacement for teachers but a powerful tool that can enhance their effectiveness and enable them to focus on the most important aspects of education. By automating administrative tasks such as grading, attendance, and lesson planning, AI frees up educators to devote more time to teaching, mentoring, and fostering relationships with students. AI-powered resources also help teachers stay updated with the latest pedagogical trends and provide personalized support to students. While AI offers significant benefits, it is important to recognize that it should be used to complement, not replace, the human elements of teaching. As AI continues to evolve, its potential to transform education will only grow, offering exciting possibilities for both educators and students alike. However, it is essential to address ethical considerations and ensure that AI is used responsibly and equitably to maximize its impact.

AI IN EDUCATIONAL ADMINISTRATION

Beyond the classroom, AI is revolutionizing educational administration by transforming how institutions manage and optimize their operations. Traditionally, educational administration has been a complex and time-consuming process, requiring significant human effort and resources to handle tasks such as admissions, resource allocation, budgeting, and long-term planning. However, with the advent of AI technologies, these processes have become more streamlined, efficient, and data-driven, leading to improved decision-making and better outcomes for students, faculty, and staff alike. AI is enabling educational institutions to operate more effectively, manage resources more efficiently, and make informed decisions that shape the future of education.

One of the key areas where AI is making a significant impact is in the admissions process. Admissions departments at educational institutions often face a high volume of applications, each requiring careful review and consideration. This process can be overwhelming, especially for large universities or schools with thousands of applicants each year. AI-powered systems can automate much of the admissions process, from sorting and categorizing applications to analyzing student data and making initial recommendations. By leveraging machine learning algorithms, AI can analyze a wide range of factors, such as academic performance, extracurricular activities, standardized test scores, and personal statements, to assess the suitability of applicants for specific programs or institutions.

AI systems can also help identify patterns and trends in the applicant pool, allowing admissions officers to make more informed decisions. For example, AI can analyze past admissions data to predict which types of students are more likely to succeed in a particular program or institution, based on factors such as academic background, career interests, and socioeconomic status. This predictive capability can help institutions better align their admissions strategies with the types of students who are most likely to thrive, ensuring that they admit students who are a good fit for the institution's academic environment and culture.

In addition to streamlining the admissions process, AI is also transforming how educational institutions manage their resources. Resource allocation has always been a critical aspect of educational administration, as institutions must ensure that they have the necessary personnel, facilities, and materials to support the needs of students and faculty. AI-powered systems can optimize resource allocation by analyzing data on student enrollment, faculty workloads, and facility usage to ensure that resources are distributed effectively. For example, AI can help administrators identify patterns in course enrollment, enabling them to adjust class sizes or offer additional sections of popular courses. Similarly, AI can analyze faculty workloads to ensure that teaching assignments are distributed fairly and that faculty members are not overburdened.

AI can also help institutions optimize their physical resources, such as classrooms, laboratories, and other facilities. By analyzing data on facility usage, AI can identify times when certain spaces are underutilized and recommend scheduling changes to maximize their use. For instance, if a particular classroom is rarely used during certain hours, AI could suggest that it be made available for other purposes, such as student study groups or faculty meetings. By improving the utilization of physical resources, AI can help institutions reduce costs and make more efficient use of their available infrastructure.

In addition to optimizing resource allocation, AI is playing a key role in helping educational institutions manage their budgets and finances. Budgeting and financial planning are essential aspects of educational administration, as institutions must balance competing priorities and ensure that they are making the most effective use of their financial resources. AI-powered predictive analytics can help institutions anticipate future financial needs and make more informed budgeting decisions. By analyzing historical financial data, AI can identify trends and patterns that can inform future budget projections. For example, AI can analyze enrollment data to predict future tuition revenue, helping institutions plan for fluctuations in enrollment and adjust their budgets accordingly.

AI can also assist in managing operational costs by identifying areas where efficiencies can be gained. For instance, AI-powered systems can analyze data on energy usage, staffing levels, and other operational factors to identify opportunities for cost savings. AI can recommend strategies for reducing energy consumption, optimizing staffing schedules, or streamlining administrative processes to lower costs and improve financial sustainability. By providing administrators with real-time insights into financial performance, AI enables institutions to make data-driven decisions that support their long-term financial health.

One of the most transformative aspects of AI in educational administration is its ability to support predictive analytics, which enables institutions to anticipate future trends and make proactive decisions. Predictive analytics uses machine learning algorithms to analyze historical data and identify patterns that can inform future outcomes. In the context of education, predictive analytics can be used to forecast enrollment trends, student performance, and even the financial health of the institution.

For example, AI can analyze past enrollment data to predict future trends in student admissions. By examining factors such as demographic shifts, geographic trends, and economic conditions, AI can provide institutions with insights into how enrollment patterns may change in the coming years. This information allows administrators to plan for future enrollment fluctuations and make data-driven decisions about staffing, facility usage, and resource allocation. Predictive analytics can also help institutions identify potential challenges, such as a decline in enrollment from certain regions or a decrease in the number of students pursuing particular programs. By anticipating these challenges in advance, institutions can take proactive measures to address them, such as adjusting marketing strategies or offering new programs to attract students.

In addition to enrollment forecasting, predictive analytics can also be used to predict student performance and retention rates. By analyzing data on student behavior, academic performance, and engagement, AI can identify students who may be at risk of falling behind or dropping out. For example, if a student is consistently absent from class, performing poorly on assignments, or exhibiting signs of disengagement, AI can flag these behaviors and alert administrators or faculty members to intervene before the student's performance declines further. This proactive approach to student support can help institutions improve retention rates and ensure that students receive the assistance they need to succeed.

Another area where AI is transforming educational administration is in the management of faculty and staff. AI-powered systems can help institutions optimize faculty recruitment, professional development, and performance evaluation. By analyzing data on faculty qualifications, teaching effectiveness, and research output, AI can assist in identifying faculty members who are excelling in their roles and those who may need additional support or training. AI can also help institutions identify gaps in faculty expertise and recommend strategies for recruiting new faculty members with the necessary skills and qualifications.

AI can also support professional development by recommending personalized learning opportunities for faculty and staff. For instance, AI can analyze faculty performance data and suggest relevant training programs, workshops, or conferences that align with their teaching goals and areas for growth. By providing targeted professional development opportunities, AI can help institutions foster a culture of continuous improvement and ensure that faculty members have the skills and knowledge they need to succeed in an ever-changing educational landscape.

Furthermore, AI is improving the way institutions manage student services and support. AI-powered chatbots and virtual assistants are increasingly being used to provide students with real-time assistance and information. These AI-driven systems can answer common questions about admissions, financial aid, course offerings, and campus resources, freeing up staff members to focus on more complex inquiries. AI can also help students navigate administrative processes, such as registering for courses, applying for financial aid, and accessing academic advising services. By providing students with instant access to information and support, AI improves the overall student experience and enhances the efficiency of student services.

AI's ability to enhance efficiency and decision-making in educational administration extends beyond the immediate tasks of admissions, resource allocation, and budgeting. It also enables institutions to make more informed, data-driven decisions that shape their long-term strategies and goals. By harnessing the power of AI, educational institutions can not only optimize their operations but also improve student outcomes, enhance faculty effectiveness, and ensure financial sustainability.

AI is revolutionizing educational administration by automating routine tasks, optimizing resource allocation, and supporting data-driven decision-making. From streamlining the admissions process to predicting enrollment trends and managing budgets, AI is helping institutions operate more efficiently and effectively. Predictive analytics is enabling institutions to anticipate future needs and proactively address challenges, leading to improved outcomes for students, faculty, and staff. As AI continues to evolve, its impact on educational administration will only grow, offering new opportunities for institutions to enhance their operations, improve student experiences, and achieve their long-term goals. However, it is essential that AI is implemented thoughtfully and responsibly, with careful attention to ethical considerations and the potential for bias, to ensure that its benefits are realized in an equitable and inclusive manner

ETHICAL CONSIDERATIONS AND CHALLENGES

Without doubt AI has tremendous potential to transform education. But,.. positive impact of the transformation is not implicit. Amid the excitement of AI's potential, there is one crucial question that must be addressed: How do we ensure positive transformation, that is, how do we ensure transformation that benefits humanity, transformations that are inclusive, human-centered and reduces inequalities? While Artificial Intelligence (AI) offers tremendous potential to transform education, it also raises significant ethical concerns that by necessity, must be addressed to ensure its equitable and responsible implementation. As AI becomes increasingly integrated into educational systems, it brings with it a host of challenges related to data privacy, algorithmic bias, and the digital divide. These issues have the potential to exacerbate existing inequalities, undermine trust in educational systems, and lead to unintended consequences for students, educators, and institutions alike. This chapter delves into these ethical challenges and emphasizes the importance of establishing robust ethical frameworks for the deployment of AI in education, ensuring that its benefits are distributed fairly and that its risks are mitigated.

Data Privacy Concerns

One of the most pressing ethical concerns surrounding AI in education is data privacy. AI systems rely heavily on vast amounts of data to function effectively, and in the context of education, this data often includes sensitive personal information about students, teachers, and institutions. This can include academic records, attendance data, behavioral patterns, and even personal identifiers such as names, addresses, and contact details. As AI systems collect, analyze, and store this data, there is a risk that it could be misused, hacked, or inadvertently exposed, leading to breaches of privacy and potential harm to individuals.

The collection of student data is essential for the personalization and optimization of learning experiences, but it also raises important questions about consent, transparency, and control. Who owns the data, and who has access to it? Are students and parents fully informed about how their data will be used, and are they given the option to opt out of data collection? In many cases, students may not fully understand the extent to which their data is being collected and analyzed, and they may not have the ability to control how that data is shared or used. This lack of transparency can lead to a sense of mistrust and anxiety among students and parents, particularly when sensitive information is involved.

To address these concerns, educational institutions must prioritize data privacy and ensure that AI systems are designed with robust safeguards to protect personal information. This includes implementing strong encryption protocols, ensuring compliance with data protection regulations such as the General Data Protection Regulation (GDPR) in Europe, and providing clear, accessible information to students and parents about how their data will be used. Additionally, institutions should give individuals control over their data, allowing them to access, update, or delete their information as needed. By prioritizing data privacy, educational institutions can foster trust and ensure that AI is used responsibly and ethically.

Algorithmic Bias and Fairness

Another significant ethical concern in the deployment of AI in education is algorithmic bias. AI systems are only as good as the data they are trained on, and if that data reflects existing biases or inequalities, the AI algorithms can perpetuate and even amplify those biases. In education, this could manifest in a variety of ways. For example, AI systems used for admissions or recruitment could unintentionally favor certain demographic groups over others, based on historical patterns in the data. Similarly, AI-powered grading systems could be biased against certain groups of students, leading to unfair assessments of their performance.

Bias in AI algorithms is often the result of biased data, which can stem from a variety of sources. Historical inequalities in education, such as disparities in access to resources or opportunities for different racial, ethnic, or socioeconomic groups, can be reflected in the data used to train AI systems. For instance, if an AI system is trained on historical data from standardized tests that have been criticized for cultural bias, it may perpetuate that bias in its assessments of students' abilities. Similarly, if an AI system is trained on data from previous admissions decisions that reflect systemic discrimination, it may replicate those biases in future admissions processes.

The consequences of algorithmic bias in education can be far-reaching. Students who are unfairly disadvantaged by biased AI systems may experience lower academic achievement, reduced opportunities for advancement, and diminished self-esteem. Moreover, biased algorithms can exacerbate existing inequalities in education, further marginalizing vulnerable groups and reinforcing social and economic disparities. This is particularly concerning in the context of AI, as these systems are often perceived as objective and impartial, which can make it difficult for individuals to recognize and challenge bias when it occurs.

To address algorithmic bias, it is essential that AI systems in education are designed and tested with fairness in mind. This involves ensuring that the data used to train AI algorithms is representative and free from discriminatory patterns. It also requires ongoing monitoring and evaluation of AI systems to identify and correct any biases that may emerge over time. Additionally, educators, administrators, and AI developers must be trained to recognize the potential for bias in AI systems and to take proactive steps to mitigate it. By prioritizing fairness and inclusivity in the design and implementation of AI, educational institutions can help ensure that AI systems promote equity and do not inadvertently reinforce existing inequalities.

The Digital Divide

A third major ethical concern in the use of AI in education is the digital divide. The digital divide refers to the gap between those who have access to technology and the internet and those who do not. While AI has the potential to improve education for students around the world, its benefits are not equally accessible to all. In many parts of the world, students and schools lack the necessary infrastructure, devices, and internet connectivity to fully participate in AI-driven learning experiences. This disparity is particularly pronounced in low-income communities, rural areas, and developing countries, where access to technology is limited and digital literacy is often low.

The digital divide has significant implications for the equitable distribution of educational opportunities. Students who lack access to AI-powered tools and resources may be left behind in terms of academic achievement and skill development. Moreover, the rapid integration of AI into education could exacerbate existing inequalities, as students with access to advanced technology will have a distinct advantage over those who do not. This could lead to a widening achievement gap, with certain groups of students being disproportionately affected by the digital divide.

To address the digital divide, it is essential that policymakers, educators, and technology developers work together to ensure that all students have access to the tools and resources they need to succeed in an AI-driven educational environment. This may involve providing subsidized or free access to devices and internet connectivity for students in underserved communities, as well as offering training and support to help students develop the digital literacy skills necessary to navigate AI-powered systems. Additionally, educational institutions should prioritize the development of inclusive AI tools that are accessible to students with diverse needs, including those with disabilities or limited technological proficiency.

The Role of Ethical Frameworks

Given the ethical concerns outlined above, it is crucial that AI in education is deployed within the context of clear and robust ethical frameworks. These frameworks should provide guidance on how to address issues such as data privacy, algorithmic bias, and the digital divide, ensuring that AI is used in ways that are fair, transparent, and inclusive. Ethical frameworks for AI in education should be developed collaboratively, involving input from educators, policymakers, technology developers, and other stakeholders, and should be regularly updated to reflect new developments in AI technology and emerging ethical challenges.

One key component of an ethical framework for AI in education is the principle of transparency. AI systems should be designed in a way that makes their decision-making processes understandable and accessible to all stakeholders, including students, teachers, and administrators. This includes providing clear explanations of how AI algorithms work, how data is collected and used, and how decisions are made. Transparency is essential for building trust in AI systems and ensuring that they are used responsibly.

Another important principle is accountability. Educational institutions and AI developers must be held accountable for the decisions made by AI systems, particularly when those decisions impact students' lives and futures. This includes establishing mechanisms for monitoring AI systems, addressing complaints or concerns, and providing avenues for redress when harm occurs. Accountability ensures that AI systems are not used in ways that violate ethical standards or cause harm to individuals or communities.

Finally, ethical frameworks for AI in education should prioritize equity and inclusivity. AI systems should be designed to promote fairness and ensure that all students, regardless of their background or circumstances, have access to the same opportunities for learning and success. This involves addressing issues such as algorithmic bias, the digital divide, and data privacy in ways that ensure that AI benefits all students, not just a select few.

In conclusion, while AI holds tremendous promise for transforming education, it also raises important ethical concerns that must be carefully addressed. Issues such as data privacy, algorithmic bias, and the digital divide have the potential to undermine the fairness and effectiveness of AI in education. To ensure that AI is deployed responsibly and ethically, it is essential that educational institutions and technology developers work together to establish clear ethical frameworks that prioritize transparency, accountability, and equity. By addressing these ethical challenges, we can ensure that AI is used in ways that promote positive outcomes for all students and contribute to a more just and inclusive educational system.

A VISION FOR THE FUTURE

The future of education lies in a harmonious blend of Artificial Intelligence (AI) and human ingenuity. This partnership promises to redefine the way we teach, learn, and engage with knowledge, offering new opportunities to enhance the educational experience for both students and educators. As AI continues to evolve, it holds the potential to amplify the strengths of educators, foster lifelong learning, and prepare students for a workforce that is increasingly driven by technological advancements. By embracing AI responsibly and thoughtfully, education can become more inclusive, innovative, and impactful, ensuring that no student is left behind and that all learners are equipped with the skills and knowledge they need to thrive in a rapidly changing world.

The integration of AI into education is not just about introducing new technologies into classrooms; it is about reimagining the entire educational ecosystem. From personalized learning experiences to data-driven insights that inform teaching strategies, AI offers a wealth of possibilities to improve the quality and accessibility of education. However, realizing the full potential of AI in education requires a deep understanding of its capabilities, limitations, and ethical considerations. It requires a commitment to ensuring that AI is used in ways that benefit all students, foster collaboration between humans and machines, and prepare learners for the challenges and opportunities of the future.

At the heart of this transformation is the recognition that AI is not a replacement for human educators but a powerful tool that can enhance their effectiveness and support their work. Teachers are the cornerstone of the educational system, and their expertise, empathy, and creativity are irreplaceable. AI can help alleviate some of the administrative burdens that teachers face, such as grading, lesson planning, and student assessments, allowing them to focus more on the aspects of teaching that require human insight, such as mentoring, coaching, and fostering critical thinking. By automating repetitive tasks and providing real-time data on student performance, AI can give educators more time and resources to engage with students on a deeper level, fostering more personalized and meaningful learning experiences.

AI's ability to analyze vast amounts of data can also provide valuable insights into student performance and learning patterns. By tracking individual progress, identifying areas of improvement, and offering targeted recommendations, AI can help educators tailor their instruction to meet the unique needs of each student. This level of personalization is particularly important in a world where learners have diverse backgrounds, learning styles, and needs. AI-powered systems can adapt to each student's pace, offering customized learning paths that allow students to progress at their own speed, reinforcing concepts they struggle with, and challenging them with more advanced material when they are ready. This approach moves away from the traditional one-size-fits-all model of education and fosters a more inclusive and equitable learning environment.

Furthermore, AI can support the development of lifelong learning. In a rapidly changing world, the need for continuous learning has never been greater. The workforce of tomorrow will require individuals who are adaptable, creative, and capable of learning new skills throughout their careers. AI can play a pivotal role in facilitating lifelong learning by providing learners with access to personalized learning resources, adaptive learning platforms, and opportunities for skill development at every stage of life. By offering on-demand learning opportunities, AI enables individuals to acquire new skills and knowledge whenever they need it, empowering them to stay competitive in an ever-evolving job market.

The future of education is also closely tied to the changing nature of work. As automation, artificial intelligence, and other technological advancements reshape industries and economies, the skills required to succeed in the workforce are evolving. Many jobs that exist today may not be relevant in the future, while new jobs and careers will emerge, demanding a different set of skills. AI can help bridge the gap between education and employment by equipping students with the knowledge and competencies needed for the jobs of tomorrow. Through AI-powered platforms, students can gain hands-on experience, participate in simulations, and engage with real-world scenarios that reflect the challenges and opportunities of the modern workforce. This experiential learning can help students develop the critical thinking, problem-solving, and technical skills that will be essential in the future job market.

Moreover, AI has the potential to foster greater equity and inclusion in education. One of the key challenges in education today is ensuring that all students, regardless of their background or circumstances, have access to high-quality learning opportunities. AI can help address this challenge by providing personalized learning experiences that are tailored to the needs of individual students, including those with disabilities, language barriers, or other learning challenges. AI-powered tools, such as speech recognition, text-to-speech software, and real-time translation, can make learning more accessible to students with diverse needs, ensuring that they have the support they need to succeed. Additionally, AI can help identify and address disparities in educational outcomes, enabling educators and policymakers to make data-driven decisions that promote equity and inclusivity.

However, while the opportunities presented by AI in education are vast, it is important to recognize the challenges and risks associated with its widespread adoption. The rapid pace of technological change means that educators, students, and institutions must be prepared to navigate a complex and evolving landscape. There are concerns about the ethical implications of AI, including issues related to data privacy, algorithmic bias, and the digital divide. As AI systems collect and analyze vast amounts of data, there is a need for clear guidelines and regulations to ensure that students' personal information is protected and that AI algorithms are fair, transparent, and accountable. Additionally, the digital divide, which refers to the gap between those who have access to technology and those who do not, poses a significant challenge in ensuring that AI benefits all students equally. Without addressing these issues, the potential for AI to exacerbate existing inequalities in education and society could become a reality.

To ensure that AI is used responsibly and ethically in education, it is essential that educators, policymakers, and technology developers work together to establish clear frameworks for its implementation. These frameworks should prioritize transparency, accountability, and fairness, ensuring that AI systems are designed with the best interests of students in mind. Educators must be involved in the development and deployment of AI technologies, ensuring that these tools align with pedagogical goals and are used to enhance, rather than replace, human teaching. Furthermore, there must be a commitment to ongoing professional development for educators, helping them to understand and navigate the complexities of AI and its potential impact on teaching and learning.

The vision for the future of education is one where AI and human ingenuity work in tandem to create more personalized, inclusive, and impactful learning experiences. AI has the potential to revolutionize education by enabling teachers to focus on what they do best—engaging with students, fostering critical thinking, and inspiring a love of learning. At the same time, AI can help students develop the skills and knowledge they need to succeed in a rapidly changing world, providing them with the tools to thrive in the workforce of tomorrow. By embracing AI responsibly, education can become more dynamic, flexible, and responsive to the needs of learners, preparing them for the challenges and opportunities of the future.

As we embark on this transformative journey, it is essential to navigate the opportunities and challenges with a clear vision and a commitment to equity and excellence. The future of education is not a distant dream; it is a reality that is unfolding before our eyes. By embracing the potential of AI and integrating it into the fabric of education, we can create a more inclusive, innovative, and impactful educational system that empowers learners and educators alike. This chapter sets the stage for exploring AI's multifaceted role in shaping the future of education and society, highlighting the transformative potential of AI while also acknowledging the challenges that must be overcome to ensure its responsible and equitable implementation. The journey ahead is one of collaboration, innovation, and dedication to the goal of providing every student with the opportunity to succeed in a rapidly evolving world.

CONCLUSION

The integration of Artificial Intelligence (AI) into education presents a transformative opportunity to reshape the learning landscape. AI's potential to personalize education, enhance teaching effectiveness, and improve administrative efficiency is already becoming evident across educational institutions. By leveraging machine learning, data analytics, and adaptive technologies, AI enables educators to provide customized learning experiences that cater to the unique needs, interests, and abilities of each student. This personalized approach not only improves engagement but also fosters a deeper, more meaningful connection to the learning process, empowering students to take control of their educational journeys.

Furthermore, AI's role in automating administrative tasks and providing real-time insights into student performance allows teachers to focus more on their core responsibilities—teaching, mentoring, and guiding students through complex concepts. The ability to offload time-consuming tasks such as grading, attendance, and lesson planning allows educators to devote more attention to building relationships with students, addressing their individual challenges, and fostering critical thinking skills. AI's support for teachers also extends to professional development, where AI-powered tools can help educators stay informed about the latest pedagogical trends and best practices, ensuring that they remain effective and adaptable in an ever-evolving educational environment.

AI's influence extends beyond the classroom, revolutionizing educational administration by streamlining processes like admissions, resource allocation, and budgeting. Predictive analytics enable institutions to anticipate trends, optimize their operations, and plan for future needs. These efficiencies not only improve the management of educational institutions but also create a more responsive and adaptive system that can better serve students and faculty alike.

However, while AI offers immense promise, it also raises important ethical considerations. Issues such as data privacy, algorithmic bias, and the digital divide must be addressed to ensure that AI is deployed in ways that are equitable, transparent, and fair. Ensuring that AI technologies are accessible to all students, regardless of their background or resources, is crucial for preventing further inequalities in education.

Looking to the future, AI has the potential to create a more inclusive, innovative, and impactful educational system that prepares students for the challenges and opportunities of a rapidly changing world. By embracing AI responsibly and thoughtfully, we can enhance the effectiveness of educators, empower learners, and create a more dynamic and responsive educational ecosystem. The journey toward integrating AI in education is just beginning, and it is an exciting path forward that promises to shape the future of learning for generations to come.

REFERENCES

Al-Zahrani, A., & Alasmari, T. (2024). Exploring the impact of artificial intelligence on higher education: The dynamics of ethical, social, and educational implications. *Humanities & Social Sciences Communications, 11*, 912. Advance online publication. DOI: 10.1057/s41599-024-03432-4

Bozkurt, A. (2023). Generative artificial intelligence (AI) powered conversational educational agents: The inevitable paradigm shift. *Asian Journal of Distance Education, 1*, 198–204.

Cinar, O., Rafferty, K., Cutting, D., & Wang, H. (2024). AI-powered VR for enhanced learning compared to tradtional methods. *Electronics (Basel), 13*(23). https://www.mdpi.com/2079-9292/13/23/4787

Contarino, M., Ryeyes_Millán, M., Vázquez-Villegas, P., & Membrillo-Hernández, J. (2024). Using an adaptive learning tool to improve student performance and satisfaction in online and face-to-face education for a more personalized approach. *Smart Learning Environments, 11*(6). Advance online publication. DOI: 10.1186/s40561-024-00292-y

El-Sabagh, H. (2021). Adaptive e-learning environment based on learning styles and its impact on development students' engagement. *International Journal of Educational Technology in Higher Education, 18*, 53. DOI: 10.1186/s41239-021-00289-4

Escalante, J., Pack, A., & Barrett, A. (2023). AI-generated feedback on writing: Insights into efficacy and ENL student preference. *International Journal of Educational Technology in Higher Education, 20*, 57. DOI: 10.1186/s41239-023-00425-2

Farooq, U., Malik, S., & Syed, A. (2024, March). Revolutionizing higher education: The transformative impact of artificial intelligence on teaching, learning and career preparation. *ShodhKosh:Journal of Visual and Performing Arts, 5*(3), 789–794.

Febriantl, C., Tari, K., Ariska, Y., & Reni, L. (2025). The Use of Artificial Intelligence in Personalizing Learning.Experiences at Schools. *PPSDP International Journal of Education, 4*, 1–16.

Felix, C. (2021). The Role of the Teacher and AI in Education. *International Perspectives on the Role of Technology in Humanizing Higher Education - Innovations in Higher Education Teaching and Learning., 33*, 33-48.

Guo, L., Wang, D., Bu, F., Li, Y., Wang, Y., & Zhou, R. (2021). Evolution and trends in intelligent tutoring systems research: A multidisciplinary and scientometric view. *Asia Pacific Education Review, 22*, 441–461.

Ifenthaler, D., Majumdar, R., Gorissen, P., Judge, M., Mishra, S., Raffaghelli, J., & Shimada, A. (2024). Artificial Intelligence in Education: Implications for Policymakers, Researchers, and Practitioners. *Tech Know Learn*, *29*, 1693–1710.

Kumar, D., Haque, A., Mishra, K., Islam, F., & Ahmad, S. (2023). Exploring the transformative role of artificial intelligence and metaverse in education: A comprehensive review. *Metaverse Basic and Applied Research*, *2*(55), 1–12.

Lee, D., Arnold, M., Srivastava, A., Plastow, K., Strelan, P., Ploeckl, F., & Palmer, E. (2024). The impact of generative AI on higher education learning and teaching: A study of educators' perspectives. *Computers and Education: Artificial Intelligence*, *100221*. Advance online publication. DOI: 10.1016/j.caeai.2024.100221

Matz, S., Bukow, C., Peters, H., Deacons, C., Dinu, A., & Stachl, C. (2023). Using machine learning to predict student retention from socio-demographic characteristics and app-based engagement metrics. *Scientific Reports*, *13*, 5705. DOI: 10.1038/s41598-023-32484-w PMID: 37029155

Merino-Campos, C. (2024). The Impact of Artificial Intelligence on Personalized Learning in Higher Education: A Systematic Review. *Trends in Higher Education*, *4*(2). Advance online publication. DOI: 10.3390/higheredu4020017

Ozsevim, I., & Ng, A. (2023). *Deepening and democratising learning*. Retrieved from AI Magazine: https://aimagazine.com/articles/andrew-ng-deepening-and-democratising-learning

Pangrazio, L. (2024). Data Harms: The Evidence Against Education Data. *Postdigital Science and Education*, *6*, 1049–1054.

Rahiman, H., & Kodikal, R. (2024). Revolutionizing education: Artificial intelligence empowered learning in higher education. *Cogent Education*, *11*, 1–24.

Ren, Y., & Yu, X. (2024). Long-term student performance prediction using learning ability self-adaptive algorithm. *Complex & Intelligent Systems*, *10*, 6379–6408.

Rodrigues, L., dos Santos, M., Costa, I., & Lillis Moreira, M. (2022). Student Performance Prediction on Primary and Secondary Schools-A Systematic Literature Review. *Procedia Computer Science*, *214*, 680–687.

Sarker, I. (2021). Data Science and Analytics: An Overview from Data-Driven Smart Computing, Decision-Making and Applications Perspective. *Springer Nature Computer Science*, *2*(5), 377. PMID: 34278328

Seo, K., Tang, J., Roll, I., Fels, S., & Yoon, D. (2021). The impact of artificial intelligence on learner–instructor interaction in online learning. *International Journal of Educational Technology in Higher Education, 18*(54). Advance online publication. DOI: 10.1186/s41239-021-00292-9 PMID: 34778540

Sposato, M. (2025). Artificial intelligence in educational leadership: a comprehensive taxonomy and future directions. *ernational Journal of Educational Technology in Higher Education, 22*(20), 1-18.

Tafazoli, D. (2024, December). Exploring the potential of generative AI in democratizing English language education. *Computers and Education: Artificial Intelligence, 7.*

Towfek, S., Khodadadi, N., Abualigah, L., & Rizk, F. (2024). AI in Higher Education: Insights from Student Surveys and Predictive Analytics using PSO-Guided WOA and Linear Regression. *JAIEP*(https://jaiep.journals.ekb.eg/article_354003_19fe159da1d32d8628a13261bd5d9309.pdf)

Venter, J., Coetzee, S., & Schmulian, A. (2024). Exploring the use of artificial intelligence (AI) in the delivery of effective feedback. *Assessment & Evaluation in Higher Education, 21*(1). https://doi-org.libraryproxy.griffith.edu.au/10.1080/02602938.2024.2415649

Walter, Y. (2024). Embracing the future of Artificial Intelligence in the classroom: The relevance of AI literacy, prompt engineering, and critical thinking in modern education. *International Journal of Educational Technology in Higher Education, 21*(15). Advance online publication. DOI: 10.1186/s41239-024-00448-3

Yağcı, M. (2022). Educational data mining: Prediction of students' academic performance using machine learning algorithms. *Smart Learn. Environ, 9*(11). Advance online publication. DOI: 10.1186/s40561-022-00192-z

Chapter 2
Navigating Ethical AI:
Ensuring Fairness in Educational Technologies

Andi Asrifan
https://orcid.org/0000-0002-9934-6129
Universitas Negeri Makassar, India

Rismawati Sudirman
https://orcid.org/0000-0001-8046-6764
Universitas Muhammadiyah Palopo, Indonesia

Vivit Rosmayanti
https://orcid.org/0000-0002-3648-9878
Universitas Negeri Makassar, Indonesia

Andi Annisa Sulolipu
https://orcid.org/0009-0007-8212-577X
Universitas Negeri Makassar, Indonesia

ABSTRACT

As artificial intelligence (AI) rapidly transforms educational spaces, this chapter comprehensively explores ethical considerations surrounding its use in teaching, learning, and school administration. Navigating Ethical AI brings together frameworks, case studies, and pedagogical practices to address how AI systems may reinforce bias, marginalize learners, or erode trust when designed or deployed without sufficient care. The chapters examine fairness metrics, human-in-the-loop strategies, regulatory approaches, and classroom-level interventions. Central to the book is a call for inclusive co-creation between students, educators, developers, and policymakers to ensure AI serves as a tool for justice rather than control. By combining technical insight with ethical reflection, this volume lays the foundation

DOI: 10.4018/979-8-3373-2397-8.ch002

for a more transparent, equitable, and human-centered AI future in education.

INTRODUCTION

Understanding Ethics in Artificial Intelligence

Artificial Intelligence (AI) is rapidly transforming the educational landscape, offering unprecedented tools for personalization, assessment, and student engagement. However, as AI becomes more embedded in classrooms and administrative decision-making, questions surrounding its ethical use grow increasingly urgent. Understanding ethics in AI is not a supplementary concern—it is a foundational requirement for building systems that are just, inclusive, and aligned with educational values (Adams et al., 2023; Gouseti et al., 2024; KARAKUŞ et al., 2025).

Ethics in AI refers to the principles and guidelines that shape how intelligent systems are developed, deployed, and evaluated. In educational settings, these principles help ensure that technologies serve the best interests of all learners, especially those from historically marginalized backgrounds. Key ethical values include **fairness**, **transparency**, **accountability**, **privacy**, and **autonomy** (Adams et al., 2023; Boulay, 2023; Lin & Su, 2024; Nguyen et al., 2022). These values are not abstract ideals—they directly influence how students experience learning and how educators make decisions.

Fairness is at the heart of ethical AI in education. It demands that AI systems avoid reinforcing existing inequalities or introducing new forms of discrimination. For instance, an AI-driven grading tool should not penalize students based on linguistic patterns associated with cultural or regional diversity. Transparency complements fairness by ensuring that stakeholders understand how algorithms make decisions (Gnanaprakasam & Lourdusamy, 2024; Liang et al., 2023; Roshanaei et al., 2023). Teachers, students, and parents should have access to information about what data is used, how it is analyzed, and what outcomes it produces.

Accountability is another critical pillar. Developers, policymakers, and school leaders must take responsibility for the impacts of AI tools, intended or otherwise. This includes creating pathways for redress when systems cause harm and ensuring that ethical standards are baked into the development process. Privacy, particularly in educational contexts, must be respected through careful data governance and consent practices (Adams et al., 2023; Al-Zahrani, 2024; Boulay, 2023).

Ultimately, ethics in AI is about centering humanity in technological progress. In schools, this means putting student well-being above efficiency, safeguarding democratic values, and treating learners not as data points but as individuals with agency and dignity. As this book will explore, building a culture of ethical AI in education requires shared understanding, thoughtful design, and an unwavering commitment to fairness in every layer of technology use.

Historical Evolution of Bias in Educational Technologies

Bias in educational technology is not a new phenomenon. Long before artificial intelligence entered the classroom, tools and systems intended to support learning often reflected the assumptions and limitations of their designers. Understanding the historical evolution of bias in educational technologies helps us recognize that ethical concerns with AI are part of a much longer story—one shaped by systemic inequality, cultural exclusion, and uneven access to opportunity (Al-Zahrani, 2024; Boulay, 2023).

In the early decades of educational computing, software and assessment tools were primarily developed by and for dominant cultural groups, often neglecting the linguistic, cognitive, and social diversity of learners. Multiple-choice tests designed for standardized measurement, for example, frequently embedded cultural assumptions that disadvantaged students from underrepresented backgrounds. Similarly, early reading and math software often relied on examples or language patterns unfamiliar to non-native speakers or students from low-income communities.

As digital learning platforms became more sophisticated, new layers of bias emerged. Algorithms used to sort students by ability or predict academic performance were often trained on historical data—data that reflected existing disparities in access, achievement, and discipline. These algorithms could, unintentionally, perpetuate and amplify those disparities. For instance, predictive systems might flag students for intervention based on patterns that correlate more closely with socioeconomic status than actual learning needs (Baker & Hawn, 2021; Kizilcec & Lee, 2022).

The rise of adaptive learning systems, facial recognition in classrooms, and automated essay scoring tools brought ethical concerns to the forefront. Questions arose about whose knowledge was being prioritized, whose experiences were being ignored, and whether the pursuit of efficiency was overshadowing the need for equity and inclusion.

Importantly, these historical patterns of bias have not been accidental—they result from decisions made without full awareness of their consequences. Recognizing this history challenges educators, developers, and policymakers to approach AI not as a neutral tool, but as a product of human design and cultural influence.

We can build a more just technological future by learning from past missteps. Acknowledging the legacy of bias in educational tools allows us to develop AI systems that actively resist inequity, honor diversity, and empower all learners, especially those historically left out of the digital conversation.

The Moral Responsibility of AI Designers and Educators

In an era where algorithms are shaping learning experiences, grading practices, and even access to educational resources, the people behind these technologies—AI designers and educators—carry immense moral responsibility. Their technical and pedagogical choices determine whether AI reinforces existing inequalities or opens pathways to greater fairness and inclusion (Adams et al., 2023; Al-Zahrani, 2024; Dieterle et al., 2022).

For AI designers, the responsibility begins at the design stage. Every line of code, every data source selected, and every model trained reflects a series of human decisions. These decisions are not neutral. Worldviews, assumptions, and implicit biases influence them. When educational tools are designed without diverse perspectives or an awareness of systemic inequities, they risk replicating the very barriers they aim to solve (Estrellado, 2024; Gaskins, 2022; Omodan, 2023). Designers have a duty to ask difficult questions: Whose data is being used? Who benefits from this system? Who might be harmed?

Transparency and accountability must become core design principles. Documenting model decisions, explaining how systems work in plain language, and creating avenues for feedback are all ethical practices that build trust and prevent harm. Designers should also actively seek partnerships with educators, students, and marginalized communities to ensure the tools they create serve real needs rather than assumed ones.

Educators, too, have a critical role to play. While they may not build AI systems, they decide how these tools are used in classrooms. Choosing which technologies to adopt, how to interpret AI-generated insights, and how to protect student data all require ethical discernment. Educators must remain vigilant, questioning whether a tool aligns with their values of care, equity, and human dignity. They must also help students develop their own critical perspectives on AI—teaching them to engage not just with how systems function, but with what they mean (Adams et al., 2023; Dieterle et al., 2022).

Importantly, the moral responsibility of both designers and educators does not lie in perfection but in reflection. It requires a willingness to listen, to learn from mistakes, and to center the well-being of students above convenience or innovation. By embracing this shared responsibility, AI designers and educators can co-create educational technologies that reflect compassion, fairness, and a deep respect for the diverse humanity they serve.

SOURCES AND IMPLICATIONS OF ALGORITHMIC BIAS

How Bias Enters AI Systems: Data, Design, and Deployment

AI systems are not immune to human bias despite being mathematical at their core. They often reflect and amplify the very inequalities they aim to address. Understanding how bias enters AI systems—through data, design, and deployment—is essential for anyone seeking to create or implement ethical technologies in education (Dieterle et al., 2022).

Bias often begins with data. Machine learning models rely on historical data to learn patterns and make predictions. However, if the data reflects existing societal disparities, such as unequal access to education, economic privilege, or racial profiling, then the AI system may reproduce those patterns in its outputs (Peña et al., 2023). For instance, a student success prediction model trained on data from predominantly affluent schools may misjudge students' potential from under-resourced communities, not because they lack ability, but because the system has never seen them succeed.

Next, bias can be introduced through design choices. How developers frame a problem, select input variables, and define success criteria can embed subjective assumptions into the system. If a tool is designed to measure "engagement" using only keyboard activity or screen time, it may undervalue students who learn best through reflection or discussion (Rusko et al., 2023; Xu et al., 2023). These design decisions, often made unconsciously, shape how the system perceives learners and what behaviors it rewards or penalizes.

Finally, deployment adds another layer of complexity. Even well-designed systems can behave unfairly if used in inappropriate contexts or without adequate oversight. An AI-powered writing assistant might support student learning in one setting but contribute to surveillance and discipline in another. How educators interpret, trust, or act upon algorithmic recommendations plays a significant role in how bias manifests in practice (Darvishi et al., 2023; Gaskins, 2022; Hutson, 2024).

Fixing the code is not enough to mitigate bias. We must interrogate the full lifecycle of AI—who defines the problem, who builds the model, what data is used, and how decisions are applied. Ethical AI begins with an awareness that technology is never separate from the people and values that shape it.

Impact of Bias on Learner Equity and Opportunity

When artificial intelligence is integrated into education without careful ethical scrutiny, its hidden biases can lead to real-world harm—particularly for students who already face structural barriers. Algorithmic bias does not just skew predictions or mislabel students; it can shape educational pathways, limit access to resources, and subtly influence learners' perceptions and support. The stakes are high: bias in AI can widen, rather than narrow, existing gaps in learner equity and opportunity (Al-Zahrani, 2024; Baker & Hawn, 2021; Dieterle et al., 2022; Gaskins, 2022; Roshanaei et al., 2023).

One significant area of concern is student profiling. AI systems used to predict academic performance, behavior risks, or learning styles can unintentionally reinforce stereotypes. For example, if an algorithm consistently rates students from certain socioeconomic or ethnic backgrounds as "at risk," it may lead educators to lower their expectations or allocate resources inequitably. Such profiling often masks potential and reduces learners to data points, stripping away context and individuality.

Bias can also emerge in adaptive learning technologies. These tools adjust content based on student responses, but if the underlying algorithms have not been trained on diverse learning patterns, they may misinterpret a student's pace or style. A student who processes information more slowly or uses non-standard language might be directed toward remedial material even if they possess deep conceptual understanding. Over time, this misalignment can hinder progress and erode confidence.

Opportunity gaps are further widened when AI tools are used to allocate scholarships, interventions, or placement in advanced programs. If these systems rely on biased data or narrow success criteria, they may consistently overlook capable students who do not conform to dominant norms. The result is a feedback loop where those with privilege continue to benefit, while others are further marginalized—not due to lack of ability, but due to flawed assumptions coded into the system (Bounds & Posey, 2022; Kashikar et al., 2023; Kizilcec & Lee, 2022).

Ultimately, algorithmic bias in education is not just a technical error—it is a social justice issue. Ensuring fairness in AI means recognizing its power to shape lives and futures. Educators, developers, and policymakers must work collaboratively to audit, question, and redesign systems with equity at their core, ensuring that no learner is left behind simply because the algorithm failed to see them clearly.

Unpacking Case Studies of Biased EdTech Systems

To fully grasp the dangers of algorithmic bias in education, we must move beyond theory and examine what has already happened. Several case studies have emerged in recent years revealing how educational technologies, despite good intentions, have produced unfair outcomes for students—especially those from marginalized backgrounds. These examples underscore the importance of transparency, diverse data representation, and continuous ethical evaluation (Dieterle et al., 2022; Gaskins, 2022; Roshanaei et al., 2023).

A widely cited case comes from the UK's 2020 exam grading crisis, where an algorithm was used to predict student A-level scores after exams were canceled due to the COVID-19 pandemic. The system heavily relied on historical data from schools, which led to systematic downgrading of students from underperforming schools—typically those in low-income areas—while students from elite schools saw minimal impact. The backlash was swift and intense. The algorithm, though technically defensible, failed to account for individual student growth and potential, ultimately reinforcing social inequities instead of mitigating them (Kizilcec & Lee, 2022; Roshanaei et al., 2023; Swist & Gulson, 2022).

Another example is found in automated essay scoring platforms used in various school systems across the United States. Some of these tools have been shown to reward longer essays regardless of coherence or critical thinking, and to misinterpret non-standard grammar or dialects as indicators of lower ability. Students who speak in vernacular English or who use culturally distinct expressions may be unfairly penalized, reducing their confidence and narrowing their academic opportunities (Hassan et al., 2021; Kim, 2020).

In yet another case, predictive policing-style algorithms adapted for school safety were used to identify students "at risk" of behavioral issues. These systems relied on historical disciplinary data—data often influenced by subjective teacher perceptions, racial bias, or inconsistent reporting. As a result, students of color were disproportionately flagged, leading to increased surveillance and discipline without addressing root causes or providing meaningful support.

These cases share a troubling pattern: biased inputs, opaque decision-making, and disproportionate consequences for already vulnerable groups. They remind us that technology in education must be approached with humility, vigilance, and inclusive design. Ethical EdTech requires more than innovation; it requires courage to confront uncomfortable truths and a commitment to centering students' dignity at every step of technological development.

FRAMEWORKS AND STANDARDS FOR FAIR AI USE

International Guidelines and Regulatory Approaches

As artificial intelligence becomes increasingly central to education systems worldwide, the call for global ethical standards and regulatory frameworks has grown louder. No longer is AI development the sole domain of engineers and private enterprises; educators, policymakers, and international bodies are stepping forward to ensure these technologies uphold fairness, equity, and human dignity. Several landmark initiatives and regulatory models are now shaping how AI is governed in educational contexts (Adams et al., 2023; Saheb & Saheb, 2024; Samuel et al., 2023).

One of the most influential efforts comes from UNESCO, which published its Recommendation on the Ethics of Artificial Intelligence in 2021. This document outlines core principles such as inclusiveness, accountability, data privacy, and human oversight. Notably, it emphasizes the need for AI systems in education to promote inclusive learning environments and to be designed with cultural and linguistic diversity in mind. It also encourages public awareness campaigns and teacher training to support informed use of AI in schools (Adams et al., 2023; Al-Zahrani, 2024; Lin & Su, 2024).

In the European Union, the proposed AI Act introduces a risk-based approach to regulation. Educational AI systems—particularly those used in assessment, behavior monitoring, or predictive profiling—are classified as "high risk," requiring transparency, robustness, and strict oversight. This approach seeks to balance innovation with ethical safeguards, compelling developers to provide documentation, explainability, and bias mitigation strategies.

The IEEE Global Initiative on Ethics of Autonomous and Intelligent Systems has also produced a detailed framework: Ethically Aligned Design. This initiative invites interdisciplinary collaboration and centers human well-being in the design of intelligent technologies. It stresses the importance of value-sensitive design, especially when technologies interact with vulnerable populations such as students(Ethically Aligned Design, 2023; The IEEE Global Initiative 2.0 on Ethics of Autonomous and Intelligent Systems, 2023).

Beyond these major players, countries like Canada, Singapore, and South Korea have begun integrating AI ethics into national education strategies, focusing on inclusion, digital equity, and responsible data use.

Together, these frameworks offer a collective foundation for action. While their specifics may differ, they all point toward a shared vision: AI systems that are transparent, accountable, inclusive, and human-centered. For educators and institutions, aligning with these guidelines means committing to a higher standard—where fairness is not assumed, but actively built into every layer of educational technology.

Fairness Metrics and Auditing Practices for Educational AIs

Ensuring fairness in educational AI systems requires more than ethical intentions—it demands concrete methods for measuring, monitoring, and correcting bias. Fairness metrics and auditing practices are essential tools for developers, educators, and policymakers seeking to hold intelligent systems accountable for their impacts on diverse learners. These tools translate abstract principles into actionable safeguards, turning ethical aspirations into operational standards (Adams et al., 2023; Corrêa et al., 2023; Kılınç, 2024; Nguyen et al., 2022).

Fairness metrics aim to detect and quantify how equitably an AI system performs across different groups. In education, this often involves evaluating whether an algorithm's outcomes vary based on protected characteristics such as race, gender, socioeconomic status, language background, or disability. Commonly used metrics include demographic parity, which checks whether outcomes are equally distributed; equalized odds, which compares error rates across subgroups; and predictive parity, which examines whether predictions are equally accurate regardless of group identity (Carey & Wu, 2022; Khalil et al., 2021; Kizilcec & Lee, 2022; Ravindranath et al., 2024).

However, fairness is context-dependent. A metric that appears just in one setting may introduce distortion in another. For instance, demographic parity might be inappropriate in certain educational interventions if underlying needs differ across student groups. Thus, choosing the right metric requires collaboration between technical experts and domain stakeholders—teachers, students, and community leaders—who understand the lived realities of learners.

Auditing practices complement fairness metrics by offering a systematic review of AI systems over time. These audits may be internal (conducted by the organization that developed or deployed the system) or external (led by independent reviewers). Educational AI audits typically assess data sources, model performance, decision pathways, and downstream effects. They also examine whether the system supports transparency, allows recourse for errors, and includes diverse perspectives in its evaluation (Corrêa et al., 2023; Kokina et al., 2025; Mökander, 2023).

To be truly effective, audits must be recurring, not one-time checks. Technology evolves, and so do educational needs. Continuous auditing ensures that fairness is not a fixed state but an ongoing commitment. Moreover, findings from audits should be communicated in accessible language and shared with all stakeholders—especially students and educators who experience the system firsthand.

In sum, fairness metrics and audits are not technical luxuries—they are ethical necessities. By embedding these practices into the lifecycle of educational AI, institutions can build systems that are not only smart, but also just, inclusive, and worthy of the trust we place in them.

Human-in-the-Loop and Transparent Design Strategies

One of the most effective ways to ensure fairness and accountability in AI systems—especially those deployed in education—is to keep humans meaningfully involved in the loop. The "human-in-the-loop" (HITL) approach acknowledges that while machines can process data and identify patterns at scale, they should not operate in isolation when making decisions that impact people's lives, particularly learners. Combining algorithmic efficiency with human judgment allows for nuance, empathy, and context—all of which are critical in educational environments (Akgün & Greenhow, 2021; Dieterle et al., 2022; Paolucci et al., 2024; Topali et al., 2024).

In practice, HITL means that educators, administrators, or designated experts remain actively engaged in interpreting and overseeing AI recommendations. For example, if an AI system suggests a student is falling behind, it is not the system alone that determines intervention. Instead, a teacher reviews the data, considers contextual factors, and makes a final decision. This model respects the complexity of human learning and recognizes the limitations of purely data-driven conclusions.

Transparency is a natural partner to HITL. AI systems must be designed in ways that make their processes understandable—not just to developers, but to teachers, students, and parents. This includes clear documentation, explainable interfaces, and feedback mechanisms that allow users to question or challenge outcomes. When people understand how a system works, they are more likely to trust it, engage with it critically, and use it responsibly (Bhat & Long, 2024; Corrêa et al., 2023; Evans et al., 2024; Haque et al., 2022).

Transparent design also involves being upfront about data sources, model limitations, and areas of uncertainty. No AI is perfect, and pretending otherwise can lead to misplaced confidence or harm. Developers and institutions are responsible for communicating what the system can and cannot do and ensuring that users are not required to accept decisions passively.

Furthermore, involving diverse stakeholders, especially those historically underrepresented in technology design, enhances both HITL and transparency. Students, teachers, and community members can provide insights that improve system relevance, reduce bias, and build cultural responsiveness.

Ultimately, human-in-the-loop and transparent design strategies shift AI from a tool of control to a partner in empowerment. When technology serves people, not replaces them, it becomes an ally in the broader mission of equitable and ethical education.

PEDAGOGICAL PRACTICES TO FOSTER AI ETHICS AWARENESS

Integrating AI Ethics into the Classroom

As artificial intelligence becomes increasingly present in students' lives—through recommendation algorithms, learning analytics, and virtual tutors—classrooms must evolve to not only teach what AI is, but also how it affects society and why ethics matter. Integrating AI ethics into everyday instruction is not about adding a new subject; it is about reimagining how we prepare students to think critically, act responsibly, and shape technology that serves the public good (Akgün & Greenhow, 2021; Kajiwara & Kawabata, 2024; Williams et al., 2022).

To begin with, ethics should be treated as an essential dimension of AI learning, not an afterthought. Lessons that explore how algorithms make decisions, what data they use, and who gets to design them provide powerful opportunities for inquiry. Even at the primary level, teachers can ask questions like: "Is it fair if a robot decides who gets extra help?" or "What would you do if an AI said you were wrong, but you knew you were right?" These questions prompt students to reflect on power, fairness, and voice (Adams et al., 2023; Holmes et al., 2021; McKay & Macomber, 2021; Williams et al., 2022).

In middle and high school settings, project-based learning is an effective method for integrating AI ethics. Students might explore real-world dilemmas—such as algorithmic bias in grading systems or privacy concerns in educational apps—and propose solutions through debates, presentations, or digital storytelling. These projects invite them to become not only consumers of technology, but also creators of ethical change.

Cross-curricular integration is also vital. Ethics discussions don't belong solely in computer science. Language arts classes can analyze dystopian fiction to explore AI futures. Social studies can unpack surveillance and justice. Science courses can discuss data ownership and environmental impacts of large AI models. This approach reinforces the idea that ethical thinking is a shared, interdisciplinary responsibility.

For ethics integration to succeed, teachers must be supported. Professional development should offer strategies, case studies, and space for reflective dialogue. Educators don't need to be AI experts—they need to feel confident facilitating ethical conversations and empowering student voice (Çelik, 2022; Cukurova et al., 2023; KARAKUŞ et al., 2025; Williams et al., 2022).

Ultimately, integrating AI ethics into the classroom builds more than technical literacy. It fosters moral imagination, empathy, and civic awareness. These are the traits that will enable today's learners to become tomorrow's responsible innovators—individuals who not only understand AI, but care about the world it shapes.

Engaging Students in Critical AI Literacy and Ethical Dialogue

In a world where algorithms influence everything from what students read to how they are assessed, it is essential that learners are not only aware of artificial intelligence but also equipped to question it. Critical AI literacy goes beyond understanding how AI works—it empowers students to examine who designs it, whose values it reflects, and what consequences it creates. When paired with structured ethical dialogue, this literacy becomes a tool for civic engagement, social justice, and digital empowerment (Kajiwara & Kawabata, 2024; Tzirides et al., 2024).

Engaging students in critical AI literacy begins with asking the right questions. Who benefits from this AI system? Who might be excluded or harmed? What assumptions is the algorithm making? These questions help students uncover the hidden layers of AI tools they interact with every day—whether it's a recommendation algorithm on a video platform or an automated score in a writing app. By teaching them to look beyond surface functionality, educators cultivate habits of inquiry and ethical sensitivity (Akgün & Greenhow, 2021; Williams et al., 2022).

Ethical dialogue provides the platform for students to express, challenge, and refine their thinking in a shared space. Teachers can facilitate classroom discussions, Socratic seminars, or fishbowl conversations where students debate the fairness of real-world AI scenarios—such as facial recognition in schools, predictive analytics in grading, or the use of chatbots in counseling. These conversations develop not only critical thinking, but also empathy and the capacity to see issues from multiple perspectives (Al-Zahrani, 2024; Aure & Cuenca, 2024; Williams et al., 2022).

Project-based learning can also serve as a vehicle for critical AI literacy. Students might research cases of algorithmic discrimination and present ethical redesign proposals. Others may conduct community interviews or design awareness campaigns about digital rights and AI transparency. These activities link AI ethics to real-life issues students care about, making learning more relevant and action-oriented.

Finally, student voice must be central. Creating opportunities for students to co-create classroom norms around ethical technology use, reflect on their digital experiences, or critique emerging AI tools empowers them as ethical agents in their own right.

Engaging students in critical AI literacy is not about instilling fear of technology—it's about nurturing wisdom, curiosity, and the confidence to shape a future where technology supports, rather than defines, humanity.

Teacher Training and Ethical AI Professional Development

Teachers are at the frontline of shaping how artificial intelligence is understood, used, and questioned in educational settings. Yet many educators report feeling unprepared to navigate the ethical dimensions of AI, often due to a lack of training, resources, or time. To build ethical AI awareness in the classroom, we must begin by investing in the people who guide students every day. Thoughtful, inclusive, and ongoing professional development is key to empowering educators as both ethical leaders and critical users of AI (Borenstein & Howard, 2020; Williams et al., 2022).

Effective teacher training in this area should start by demystifying AI. Educators do not need to become data scientists to teach AI ethics. What they need is a foundational understanding of how algorithms work, how data influences outcomes, and where bias can arise. Workshops and training sessions should present real-life examples—such as algorithmic grading, facial recognition in schools, or AI-driven tutoring platforms—and create space for educators to reflect on both opportunities and risks (Alqahtani et al., 2023; Al-Zahrani, 2024; Dieterle et al., 2022).

Equally important is providing tools for ethical facilitation. Teachers must be equipped to guide student conversations about fairness, privacy, surveillance, and social impact. This includes access to discussion frameworks, case studies, ethical dilemmas, and culturally relevant teaching materials. Training should emphasize strategies for inclusive dialogue, where diverse perspectives are not only welcomed but centered (Lin & Su, 2024; Stahl & Eke, 2023).

Collaborative learning models are especially effective. Professional learning communities, interdisciplinary cohorts, and peer-led workshops can help educators share practices, explore questions, and build confidence. These models foster mutual support and highlight the value of collective ethical reasoning in complex technological contexts (Winiecki et al., 2020; Yu & Chao, 2022).

Importantly, teacher training must address emotional and relational aspects. Many educators fear using new technologies incorrectly or unintentionally harming students. A supportive development environment acknowledges these concerns, promotes reflection over perfection, and encourages a growth mindset in navigating AI ethically.

Ultimately, empowering teachers with ethical AI knowledge is not a luxury—it is a necessity. When educators feel prepared and supported, they become catalysts for transformation: helping students not only understand intelligent systems, but also challenge them, question them, and use them to create a more just and inclusive world.

Creating a fair and ethical future for AI in education requires more than top-down policies or technical fixes—it demands the active participation of those most affected by educational technologies: students, families, educators, and local communities. Co-creation is the practice of involving diverse stakeholders in the design, implementation, and evaluation of AI tools. When done with authenticity and care, it transforms AI development (Adams et al., 2023; Dieterle et al., 2022; Swist et al., 2024) from a process of imposition into one of collaboration and shared ownership.

Students, in particular, bring critical insights into how AI systems shape their learning experiences, agency, and sense of fairness. Too often, they are positioned as passive recipients of technological decisions. In a co-creation model, they become active partners—engaged in identifying needs, generating ideas, testing tools, and even shaping policy. Whether through youth advisory boards, participatory design workshops, or classroom-based design challenges, student voice becomes central to the ethical development of educational AI.

Communities, too, hold deep knowledge about the social, cultural, and historical contexts in which AI operates. Parents, local leaders, and grassroots organizations can help identify blind spots in design, especially regarding equity, language inclusion, and cultural relevance. By inviting these voices into the process, developers and institutions can avoid common pitfalls—like building systems that overlook linguistic diversity or reinforce systemic disparities.

Successful co-creation requires intentional structures. This might include community listening sessions, co-design labs, or open calls for student innovation. It also involves redistributing power—ensuring that contributions from students and communities are not symbolic, but truly shape decisions (Blithe & Fidelibus, 2021; Deserti et al., 2024; Könings et al., 2020).

Importantly, co-creation is not just about improving AI products; it's about cultivating trust, transparency, and relational accountability. When learners and communities see that their insights are valued and their realities reflected, they are more likely to engage with technology critically, ethically, and creatively.

In building a future where AI enhances, rather than limits, educational justice, co-creation is not optional—it is foundational. It reminds us that ethical AI is not a product we build for students, but a process we build with them.

Building Ethical Ecosystems: Schools, Developers, and Policymakers

A fair and sustainable future for AI in education cannot be built in silos. It requires the creation of ethical ecosystems—networks of schools, developers, and policymakers working in concert to design, implement, and regulate technologies that prioritize equity, transparency, and human dignity. Each stakeholder brings a unique perspective and set of responsibilities, but only through intentional collaboration can we create systems that serve all learners fairly (Akgün & Greenhow, 2021; Kühn et al., 2023; Roshanaei et al., 2023).

Schools are the testing ground where AI technologies interact most directly with students and teachers. Educators need support not only in understanding how AI works, but in identifying ethical red flags and advocating for responsible use. School leaders must foster cultures where teachers feel empowered to question tools, raise concerns, and involve students in ethical dialogue. Procurement decisions should be guided by ethical rubrics—not just efficiency or novelty—and should consider long-term impacts on student agency and equity (Holmes et al., 2021; Pleasants et al., 2023; Striking a Balance: Navigating the Ethical Dilemmas of AI in Higher Education, 2024).

Developers, meanwhile, must go beyond technical performance to embed fairness, inclusivity, and explainability into their design processes. This means collaborating with educators and students early in the development cycle, using diverse datasets, and building transparent and user-centered interfaces. Developers should publish clear documentation on model limitations, involve ethicists in design teams, and establish mechanisms for user feedback and redress when harm occurs (Borenstein & Howard, 2020; Gurevich et al., 2022; Rossi & Lenzini, 2020).

Policymakers play a vital role in setting the standards and incentives that shape how AI is deployed in schools. Regulatory frameworks should include mandatory impact assessments for educational AI tools, protections for student data and privacy, and mechanisms for algorithmic accountability. Funding should prioritize ethical innovation, interdisciplinary research, and inclusive technology adoption across all school types and regions (Al-Zahrani, 2024).

Building an ethical AI ecosystem is not about placing blame—it is about building bridges. It means creating shared language, shared goals, and shared responsibility. When schools, developers, and policymakers work as partners rather than isolated actors, the result is a system where fairness is not an afterthought but an embedded value.

In this interconnected future, ethical ecosystems will not only shape better technology—they will shape better societies.

Future Trends and Challenges in Ethical AI for Learning

As artificial intelligence continues to evolve at a rapid pace, the future of ethical AI in education will be shaped not only by technological innovation, but by the values, choices, and collaborations that guide its development. While emerging trends promise new possibilities for personalized, efficient, and engaging learning, they also raise critical ethical challenges that must be addressed with foresight and care (Adams et al., 2023; Shonfeld et al., 2021; Zain, 2020).

One significant trend is the rise of generative AI—tools capable of creating text, images, and even lesson plans. While these technologies can support teacher creativity and reduce administrative burden, they also introduce new risks: from plagiarism and misinformation to the homogenization of student thought. Ensuring that these tools support, rather than replace, authentic learning experiences will be a central ethical task in years to come.

Another growing trend is the integration of emotion-detection and biometric data into AI systems. These tools aim to assess student engagement or mental states through facial recognition, voice analysis, or wearable sensors. While intended to enhance support for learners, such technologies raise urgent questions about consent, surveillance, and psychological safety (Dakakni & Safa, 2023; Ho et al., 2023). Balancing data-driven insights with respect for student autonomy will be a persistent tension.

Algorithmic transparency and explainability will remain central challenges. As AI models grow more complex—especially with the adoption of deep learning architectures—explaining how a system arrived at a particular recommendation becomes harder, yet more essential. Without clear explanations, trust erodes, and biases go unchallenged. Developing "explainable AI" that is both technically sound and pedagogically accessible will be a critical research and design priority (Haque et al., 2022; Weber et al., 2020).

Finally, the global inequality in AI access and governance must not be ignored. Many schools in low-income or rural communities remain excluded from AI-enhanced learning due to infrastructure gaps, language barriers, or lack of training. Ethical AI for education cannot be confined to well-resourced settings. Future efforts must prioritize inclusion, cultural relevance, and equitable participation in shaping AI policies and tools (Dieterle et al., 2022; Gayed, 2025; Holmes et al., 2021; Lin & Su, 2024).

The future of AI in education is not predetermined—it is being written now. By anticipating ethical risks, fostering inclusive dialogue, and designing for dignity, we can shape technologies that do more than teach—they reflect the values of a just and compassionate society.

CONCLUSION

The promise of artificial intelligence in education lies not only in its computational power but in our collective ability to direct that power ethically, inclusively, and transparently. Throughout this volume, we have examined how AI intersects with fairness, equity, and human dignity in school environments—from predictive analytics and automated grading to surveillance technologies and adaptive platforms.

What becomes clear is that no AI system is neutral. Its values, assumptions, and blind spots reflect the choices of its creators and implementers. As such, the future of ethical AI in education cannot be outsourced to engineers alone. It must be shaped by collaborative ecosystems of educators, students, developers, communities, and policymakers who share responsibility and vision.

We have argued for a fundamental reorientation: from technology-centered solutions to human-centered design. From convenience and efficiency to deliberate care and inclusion. This involves co-creation with learners, continuous auditing, culturally responsive curriculum integration, and strong governance rooted in global and local contexts.

Looking forward, we face growing challenges: the rise of generative AI, increased datafication of student behavior, and the risk of deepening global digital divides. But we also see opportunity—an invitation to build a generation of learners who not only understand AI, but are equipped to question, shape, and redefine it for the better.

Ethical AI in education is not a destination but a commitment—a continuous practice of reflection, participation, and justice. In honoring this commitment, we do more than design better tools; we nurture more just and compassionate learning environments, worthy of the students they serve.

REFERENCES

Adams, C., Pente, P., Lemermeyer, G., & Rockwell, G. (2023). Ethical principles for artificial intelligence in K-12 education. *Computers and Education Artificial Intelligence*, *4*, 100131. DOI: 10.1016/j.caeai.2023.100131

Akgün, S., & Greenhow, C. (2021). Artificial intelligence in education: Addressing ethical challenges in K-12 settings [Review of Artificial intelligence in education: Addressing ethical challenges in K-12 settings]. AI and Ethics, 2(3), 431. Springer Nature. https://doi.org/DOI: 10.1007/s43681-021-00096-7

Al-Zahrani, A. M. (2024). Unveiling the shadows: Beyond the hype of AI in education. *Heliyon*, *10*(9). Advance online publication. DOI: 10.1016/j.heliyon.2024.e30696 PMID: 38737255

Alqahtani, T., Badreldin, H. A., Alrashed, M., Alshaya, A., Alghamdi, S. S., Saleh, K. B., Alowais, S. A., Alshaya, O. A., Rahman, I., Yami, M. S. A., & Albekairy, A. (2023). The emergent role of artificial intelligence, natural learning processing, and large language models in higher education and research [Review of The emergent role of artificial intelligence, natural learning processing, and large language models in higher education and research]. Research in Social and Administrative Pharmacy, 19(8), 1236. Elsevier BV. https://doi.org/DOI: 10.1016/j.sapharm.2023.05.016

Aure, P. A. H., & Cuenca, O. (2024). Fostering social-emotional learning through human-centered use of generative AI in business research education: An insider case study. *Journal of Research in Innovative Teaching & Learning*, *17*(2), 168. DOI: 10.1108/jrit-03-2024-0076

Baker, R. S., & Hawn, A. (2021). Algorithmic Bias in Education. *International Journal of Artificial Intelligence in Education*, *32*(4), 1052. DOI: 10.1007/s40593-021-00285-9

Bhat, M., & Long, D. (2024). Designing Interactive Explainable AI Tools for Algorithmic Literacy and Transparency. *Designing Interactive Systems Conference*, 939. https://doi.org/DOI: 10.1145/3643834.3660722

Blithe, S. J., & Fidelibus, B. (2021). Faculty-Undergraduate Course Curriculum Collaboration. *College Teaching*, *70*(2), 237. DOI: 10.1080/87567555.2021.1920879

Borenstein, J., & Howard, A. (2020). Emerging challenges in AI and the need for AI ethics education. *AI and Ethics*, *1*(1), 61. DOI: 10.1007/s43681-020-00002-7 PMID: 38624388

Bounds, D. T., & Posey, P. (2022). A Resistance Framework for Racially Minoritized Youth Behaviors During the Transition to Adulthood. *Journal of Research on Adolescence, 32*(3), 959. DOI: 10.1111/jora.12792 PMID: 35980807

Carey, A. N., & Wu, X. (2022). The statistical fairness field guide: Perspectives from social and formal sciences. *AI and Ethics, 3*(1), 1. DOI: 10.1007/s43681-022-00183-3

Çelik, İ. (2022). Towards Intelligent-TPACK: An empirical study on teachers' professional knowledge to ethically integrate artificial intelligence (AI)-based tools into education. *Computers in Human Behavior, 138*, 107468. DOI: 10.1016/j.chb.2022.107468

Corrêa, N. K., Galvão, C., Santos, J. W., Pino, C. D., Pinto, E. P., Barbosa, C., Massmann, D., Mambrini, R., Galvão, L., Terem, E., & Oliveira, N. de. (2023). Worldwide AI ethics: A review of 200 guidelines and recommendations for AI governance [Review of Worldwide AI ethics: A review of 200 guidelines and recommendations for AI governance]. Patterns, 4(10), 100857. Elsevier BV. https://doi.org/DOI: 10.1016/j.patter.2023.100857

Cukurova, M., Miao, X., & Brooker, R. A. (2023). Adoption of Artificial Intelligence in Schools: Unveiling Factors Influencing Teachers' Engagement. In Lecture notes in computer science (p. 151). Springer Science+Business Media. https://doi.org/DOI: 10.1007/978-3-031-36272-9_13

Dakakni, D., & Safa, N. (2023). Artificial intelligence in the L2 classroom: Implications and challenges on ethics and equity in higher education: A 21st century Pandora's box. *Computers and Education Artificial Intelligence, 5*, 100179. DOI: 10.1016/j.caeai.2023.100179

Darvishi, A., Khosravi, H., Sadiq, S., Gašević, D., & Siemens, G. (2023). Impact of AI assistance on student agency. *Computers & Education, 210*, 104967. DOI: 10.1016/j.compedu.2023.104967

Deserti, A., Eckhardt, J., Kaletka, C., Krüger, D., Rizzo, F., & Schmittinger, F. (2024). Siscode. In *Routledge eBooks* (p. 144). Informa., DOI: 10.4324/9781003319481-18

Dieterle, E., Dede, C., & Walker, M. E. (2022). The cyclical ethical effects of using artificial intelligence in education. *AI & Society, 39*(2), 633. DOI: 10.1007/s00146-022-01497-w PMID: 36185064

du Boulay, B. (2023). Artificial Intelligence in Education and Ethics. In Handbook of Open, Distance and Digital Education (p. 93). https://doi.org/DOI: 10.1007/978-981-19-2080-6_6

Estrellado, C. J. P. (2024). MATATAG Curriculum: Why Curriculum [must] Change? *Journal of Interdisciplinary Perspectives*, *2*(1). Advance online publication. DOI: 10.69569/jip.2024.0001

Ethically Aligned Design. (2023). https://standards.ieee.org/industry-connections/ec/ead1e-infographic/

Evans, R., Bryant, L., Russell, G., & Absolom, K. (2024). Trust and acceptability of data-driven clinical recommendations in everyday practice: A scoping review [Review of Trust and acceptability of data-driven clinical recommendations in everyday practice: A scoping review]. International Journal of Medical Informatics, 183, 105342. Elsevier BV. https://doi.org/DOI: 10.1016/j.ijmedinf.2024.105342

Gaskins, N. R. (2022). Interrogating Algorithmic Bias: From Speculative Fiction to Liberatory Design. *TechTrends*, *67*(3), 417. DOI: 10.1007/s11528-022-00783-0 PMID: 36160677

Gayed, J. M. (2025). Educators' perspective on artificial intelligence: Equity, preparedness, and development. *Cogent Education*, *12*(1). Advance online publication. DOI: 10.1080/2331186x.2024.2447169

Gnanaprakasam, J., & Lourdusamy, R. (2024). The Role of AI in Automating Grading: Enhancing Feedback and Efficiency. In *Artificial intelligence*. IntechOpen., DOI: 10.5772/intechopen.1005025

Gouseti, A., James, F., Fallin, L., & Burden, K. (2024). The ethics of using AI in K-12 education: A systematic literature review. *Technology, Pedagogy and Education*, *1*. Advance online publication. DOI: 10.1080/1475939x.2024.2428601

Gurevich, E., Hassan, B. E., & Morr, C. E. (2022). Equity within AI systems: What can health leaders expect? *Healthcare Management Forum*, *36*(2), 119. DOI: 10.1177/08404704221125368 PMID: 36226507

Haque, A. B., Islam, A. K. M. N., & Mikalef, P. (2022). Explainable Artificial Intelligence (XAI) from a user perspective: A synthesis of prior literature and problematizing avenues for future research. *Technological Forecasting and Social Change*, *186*, 122120. DOI: 10.1016/j.techfore.2022.122120

Hassan, W. N. F. W., Awang, S., & Abdullah, N. (2021). Fillers as Communication Strategies Among English Second Language Speakers in Job Interviews. *International Journal of English Linguistics*, *12*(1), 30. DOI: 10.5539/ijel.v12n1p30

Ho, M. T., Mantello, P., & Ho, M. T. (2023). An analytical framework for studying attitude towards emotional AI: The three-pronged approach. *MethodsX*, *10*, 102149.

Holmes, W., Porayska-Pomsta, K., Holstein, K., Sutherland, E., Baker, T. T., Shum, S. B., Santos, O. C., & Rodrigo, Ma. M. T., Cukurova, M., Bittencourt, I. I., & Koedinger, K. R. (2021). Ethics of AI in Education: Towards a Community-Wide Framework. *International Journal of Artificial Intelligence in Education, 32*(3), 504. DOI: 10.1007/s40593-021-00239-1

Hutson, J. (2024). Rethinking Plagiarism in the Era of Generative AI. *Journal of International Communication, 4*(1). Advance online publication. DOI: 10.54963/jic.v4i1.220

Kajiwara, Y., & Kawabata, K. (2024). AI literacy for ethical use of chatbot: Will students accept AI ethics? *Computers and Education Artificial Intelligence, 6*, 100251. DOI: 10.1016/j.caeai.2024.100251

KARAKUŞ, N., Gedik, K., & Kazazoğlu, S. (2025). Ethical Decision-Making in Education: A Comparative Study of Teachers and Artificial Intelligence in Ethical Dilemmas. *Behavioral Sciences (Basel, Switzerland), 15*(4), 469. DOI: 10.3390/bs15040469 PMID: 40282090

Kashikar, L., Soemers, L., Lüke, T., & Grosche, M. (2023). Does the 'Learning Disability' label lower teachers' performance expectations? *Social Psychology of Education, 26*(4), 971. DOI: 10.1007/s11218-023-09775-1

Khalil, H., Ameen, D., & Zarnegar, A. (2021). Tools to support the automation of systematic reviews: a scoping review [Review of Tools to support the automation of systematic reviews: a scoping review]. Journal of Clinical Epidemiology, 144, 22. Elsevier BV. https://doi.org/DOI: 10.1016/j.jclinepi.2021.12.005

Kılınç, S. (2024). Comprehensive AI Assessment Framework: Enhancing Educational Evaluation with Ethical AI Integration. Journal of Educational Technology and Online Learning. https://doi.org/DOI: 10.31681/jetol.1492695

Kim, A. I. (2020). (De)legitimation of monolingual ideologies in a US teachers' online forum. *International Journal of Bilingual Education and Bilingualism, 25*(3), 1021. DOI: 10.1080/13670050.2020.1740163

Kizilcec, R. F., & Lee, H. (2022). Algorithmic fairness in education. In *Routledge eBooks* (p. 174). Informa., DOI: 10.4324/9780429329067-10

Kokina, J., Blanchette, S., Davenport, T. H., & Pachamanova, D. A. (2025). Challenges and opportunities for artificial intelligence in auditing: Evidence from the field. *International Journal of Accounting Information Systems, 56*, 100734. DOI: 10.1016/j.accinf.2025.100734

Könings, K. D., Mordang, S. B. R., Smeenk, F. W. J. M., Stassen, L. P. S., & Ramani, S. (2020). Learner involvement in the co-creation of teaching and learning: AMEE Guide No. 138. *Medical Teacher, 43*(8), 924. DOI: 10.1080/0142159x.2020.1838464 PMID: 33153367

Kühn, C., Khoo, S., Czerniewicz, L., Lilley, W., Bute, S. J. R., Crean, A., Abegglen, S., Burns, T., Sinfield, S., Jandrić, P., Knox, J., & MacKenzie, A. (2023). Understanding Digital Inequality: A Theoretical Kaleidoscope. *Postdigital Science and Education, 5*(3), 894. DOI: 10.1007/s42438-023-00395-8 PMID: 40479087

Liang, W., Yüksekgönül, M., Mao, Y., Wu, E. Q., & Zou, J. (2023). GPT detectors are biased against non-native English writers. *Patterns (New York, N.Y.), 4*(7), 100779. DOI: 10.1016/j.patter.2023.100779 PMID: 37521038

Lin, T., & Su, Y.-S. (2024). Ethical Implications and Principles of Using Artificial Intelligence Models in the Classroom: A Systematic Literature Review. *International Journal of Interactive Multimedia and Artificial Intelligence, 8*(5), 25. DOI: 10.9781/ijimai.2024.02.010

McKay, C., & Macomber, G. (2021). The Importance of Relationships in Education: Reflections of Current Educators. *Journal of Education, 203*(4), 751. DOI: 10.1177/00220574211057044

Mökander, J. (2023). Auditing of AI: Legal, Ethical and Technical Approaches. *Deleted Journal, 2*(3). Advance online publication. DOI: 10.1007/s44206-023-00074-y

Nguyen, A., Ngo, H. N., Hong, Y., Dang, B., & Nguyen, B.-P. T. (2022). Ethical principles for artificial intelligence in education. *Education and Information Technologies, 28*(4), 4221. DOI: 10.1007/s10639-022-11316-w PMID: 36254344

Omodan, B. I. (2023). Unveiling Epistemic Injustice in Education: A critical analysis of alternative approaches. *Social Sciences & Humanities Open, 8*(1), 100699. DOI: 10.1016/j.ssaho.2023.100699

Paolucci, C., Vancini, S., Bex, R. T., Cavanaugh, T., Salama, C., & Araujo, Z. de. (2024). A review of learning analytics opportunities and challenges for K-12 education [Review of A review of learning analytics opportunities and challenges for K-12 education]. Heliyon, 10(4). Elsevier BV. https://doi.org/DOI: 10.1016/j.heliyon.2024.e25767

Peña, A., Serna, I., Morales, A., Fiérrez, J., Ortega, A., Sánchez, A. H., Saéz, M. A., & Ortega-García, J. (2023). Human-Centric Multimodal Machine Learning: Recent Advances and Testbed on AI-Based Recruitment. *SN Computer Science, 4*(5). Advance online publication. DOI: 10.1007/s42979-023-01733-0

Pleasants, J., Krutka, D. G., & Nichols, T. P. (2023). What Relationships Do We Want with Technology? Toward Technoskepticism in Schools. *Harvard Educational Review*, *93*(4), 486. DOI: 10.17763/1943-5045-93.4.486

Ravindranath, R., Stein, J. D., Hernandez-Boussard, T., Fisher, A., Wang, S. Y., Amin, S., Edwards, P. A., Srikumaran, D., Woreta, F. A., Schultz, J. S., Shrivastava, A., Ahmad, B., Bryar, P. J., French, D. D., VanderBeek, B. L., Pershing, S., Lynch, A. M., Patnaik, J. L., Munir, S., & Ramachandran, R. (2024). The Impact of Race, Ethnicity, and Sex on Fairness in Artificial Intelligence for Glaucoma Prediction Models. *Ophthalmology Science*, *5*(1), 100596. DOI: 10.1016/j.xops.2024.100596 PMID: 39386055

Roshanaei, M., Olivares, H., & Lopez, R. R. (2023). Harnessing AI to Foster Equity in Education: Opportunities, Challenges, and Emerging Strategies. *Journal of Intelligent Learning Systems and Applications*, *15*(4), 123. DOI: 10.4236/jilsa.2023.154009

Rossi, A., & Lenzini, G. (2020). Transparency by design in data-informed research: A collection of information design patterns. *Computer Law & Security Review*, *37*, 105402. DOI: 10.1016/j.clsr.2020.105402

Rusko, R., Koivisto, S.-A., & Jestilä, S. (2023). *Algorithms as Decision-Makers*., DOI: 10.1007/978-981-19-9658-0_2

Saheb, T., & Saheb, T. (2024). Mapping Ethical Artificial Intelligence Policy Landscape: A Mixed Method Analysis. *Science and Engineering Ethics*, *30*(2). Advance online publication. DOI: 10.1007/s11948-024-00472-6 PMID: 38451328

Samuel, Y., Brennan-Tonetta, M., Samuel, J., Kashyap, R., Kumar, V., Kaashyap, S. K., Chidipothu, N., Anand, I., & Jain, P. (2023). Cultivation of human centered artificial intelligence: Culturally adaptive thinking in education (CATE) for AI. *Frontiers in Artificial Intelligence*, *6*. Advance online publication. DOI: 10.3389/frai.2023.1198180 PMID: 38106981

Shonfeld, M., Cotnam-Kappel, M., Judge, M., Ng, C. Y., Ntebutse, J. G., Williamson-Leadley, S., & Yildiz, M. N. (2021). Learning in digital environments: A model for cross-cultural alignment. *Educational Technology Research and Development*, •••, 1–20.

Stahl, B. C., & Eke, D. (2023). The ethics of ChatGPT – Exploring the ethical issues of an emerging technology. *International Journal of Information Management*, *74*, 102700. DOI: 10.1016/j.ijinfomgt.2023.102700

Striking a Balance: Navigating the Ethical Dilemmas of AI in Higher Education. (2024). https://er.educause.edu/articles/2024/12/striking-a-balance-navigating-the-ethical-dilemmas-of-ai-in-higher-education

Swist, T., & Gulson, K. N. (2022). School Choice Algorithms: Data Infrastructures, Automation, and Inequality. *Postdigital Science and Education*, *5*(1), 152. DOI: 10.1007/s42438-022-00334-z

Swist, T., Shum, S. B., & Gulson, K. N. (2024). Co-producing AIED Ethics Under Lockdown: An Empirical Study of Deliberative Democracy in Action. *International Journal of Artificial Intelligence in Education*, *34*(3), 670. DOI: 10.1007/s40593-023-00380-z

The IEEE Global Initiative 2.0 on Ethics of Autonomous and Intelligent Systems. (2023). https://standards.ieee.org/industry-connections/ec/ead-v1/

Topali, P., Ortega-Arranz, A., Rodríguez-Triana, M. J., Er, E., Khalil, M., & Akçapınar, G. (2024). Designing human-centered learning analytics and artificial intelligence in education solutions: A systematic literature review. *Behaviour & Information Technology*, *1*. Advance online publication. DOI: 10.1080/0144929x.2024.2345295

Tzirides, A. O., Zapata, G. C., Kastania, N. P., Saini, A. K., Castro, V., Ismael, S. A., You, Y., dos Santos, T. A., Searsmith, D., O'Brien, C., Cope, B., & Kalantzis, M. (2024). Combining human and artificial intelligence for enhanced AI literacy in higher education. *Computers and Education Open*, *6*, 100184. DOI: 10.1016/j.caeo.2024.100184

Weber, K., Tinnes, L., Huber, T., Heimerl, A., Reinecker, M.-L., Pohlen, E., & André, E. (2020). Towards Demystifying Subliminal Persuasiveness: Using XAI-Techniques to Highlight Persuasive Markers of Public Speeches. In Lecture notes in computer science (p. 113). Springer Science+Business Media. https://doi.org/DOI: 10.1007/978-3-030-51924-7_7

Williams, R., Ali, S., Devasia, N., DiPaola, D., Hong, J., Kaputsos, S. P., Jordan, B. T., & Breazeal, C. (2022). AI + Ethics Curricula for Middle School Youth: Lessons Learned from Three Project-Based Curricula. *International Journal of Artificial Intelligence in Education*, *33*(2), 325. DOI: 10.1007/s40593-022-00298-y PMID: 35935456

Winiecki, D. J., Catlin, L., & Ackler, H. (2020, September 8). Developing and Applying Knowledge and Skills in Ethics and Professional Morality: An Evidence-based Practice Paper. *2020 ASEE Virtual Annual Conference Content Access Proceedings*. https://doi.org/DOI: 10.18260/1-2--34423

Xu, X., Shi, Z., Bos, N. A., & Wu, H. (2023). Student engagement and learning outcomes: An empirical study applying a four-dimensional framework. *Medical Education Online*, *28*(1). Advance online publication. DOI: 10.1080/10872981.2023.2268347 PMID: 37807698

Yu, T., & Chao, C. (2022). Encouraging teacher participation in Professional Learning Communities: Exploring the Facilitating or restricting factors that Influence collaborative activities. *Education and Information Technologies*, *28*(5), 5779. DOI: 10.1007/s10639-022-11376-y PMID: 36373046

Zain, S. (2020). Digital transformation trends in education. In *Elsevier eBooks* (p. 223). Elsevier BV., DOI: 10.1016/b978-0-12-822144-0.00036-7

Chapter 3
AI and the Ethics of Student Data Privacy

Geraldine Torrisi-Steele
https://orcid.org/0000-0002-6045-4114
Griffith University, Autralia

ABSTRACT

As artificial intelligence (AI) becomes increasingly integrated into education, concerns about student data privacy and ethical AI use are growing. AI-driven learning platforms and predictive analytics rely on vast amounts of student data to personalize education, but this raises ethical challenges related to data security, informed consent, algorithmic bias, and potential misuse. This chapter explores the implications of AI on student data privacy, examining current legal frameworks such as FERPA and GDPR, best practices for ensuring transparency and accountability, and strategies for equitable and secure AI implementation in education. By addressing these concerns, institutions and policymakers can create AI-driven learning environments that protect student privacy while maximizing innovation and educational benefits.

INTRODUCTION

The fallout from the digitization of education is an enormous volume of data. The use of artificial intelligence (AI) in education exacerbates the production of data. 'Big data' in education, as in other domains, is touted as having significant potential benefits. The collection and analysis of big data is facilitated by machine learning and other algorithms developed in the field of AI. In education, the integration of AI technologies into classrooms has spawned a growing movement towards personalized education. It seems that the vision of providing highly student-centered, individualized

DOI: 10.4018/979-8-3373-2397-8.ch003

education, tailored to the needs of individual students in mass education systems, is a real possibility. Embedded in the excitement about the possibilities enabled by AI and big data is a significant (and well-justified) concern.

With the increasing reliance on AI-based educational technologies, institutions must carefully navigate the social, ethical and legal challenges associated with student data collection, storage, and use. AI-powered learning management systems, predictive analytics, and automated assessments generate massive datasets that contain sensitive personal information, including academic performance, behavioral patterns, and even biometric data in some cases. Without proper safeguards, this data can be susceptible to breaches, unauthorized access, or misuse by third parties. Moreover, AI algorithms, if not properly designed and monitored, can perpetuate biases, inaccuracies, and privacy violations, further complicating the ethical landscape of AI in education (Baker & Hawn, 2021) (Idowu, Koshiyama, & Treleaven, 2024).

The aim of the present chapter is to add voice to the necessity of addressing the ethical and legal challenges associated with the collection, analysis and use of student data in an increasingly AI rich education system.

THE COLLECTION AND USE OF STUDENT DATA

Artificial intelligence (AI) is revolutionizing education by enabling new methods of instruction, assessment, and student engagement. AI-driven technologies are transforming traditional learning environments, making education more personalized, efficient, and data-driven (Peng, Ma, & Spector, 2019) (Rahiman & Kodikal, 2024).

AI applications in education are designed to improve learning outcomes by leveraging vast amounts of student data to create personalized learning experiences. Personalized learning platforms use AI algorithms to analyze students' strengths, weaknesses, and learning preferences, tailoring instructional content to their specific needs. AI-powered tutoring systems, such as Carnegie Learning's MATHia (https://www.carnegielearning.com/solutions/math/mathia/) and IBM Watson Tutor, provide real-time feedback and individualized lesson plans, ensuring that students receive targeted support in areas where they struggle (Georgia Tech, 2016). These technologies enable a more student-centered approach to education, enhancing engagement and retention by delivering content at the right difficulty level for each learner.

In addition to personalized learning, adaptive assessments have gained traction in AI-powered education (Khine, 2024). Traditional standardized tests often fail to capture students' true abilities, as they do not account for individual learning progress and contextual factors. AI-driven adaptive assessments adjust in real time based on student responses, ensuring that each question matches their skill level. This method provides a more accurate measurement of student proficiency, reducing test anxiety and enhancing motivation. AI-powered grading systems, such as Gradescope, automate assessment processes, allowing educators to focus on instruction and mentoring rather than administrative tasks.

Another ready source of data from the application of AI in education is learning analytics. The function of learning analytics is to data-driven insights to help educators monitor student progress and identify potential learning gaps (Joshi, Desai, & Tewari, 2020). AI algorithms analyze patterns in student behavior, engagement levels, and performance, allowing educators to intervene before students fall behind. For example, predictive analytics tools can flag at-risk students based on attendance records, assignment completion rates, and participation levels, enabling institutions to provide targeted support. AI-powered dashboards present this data in an intuitive format, making it easier for teachers to make informed decisions about curriculum adjustments and personalized interventions (Joshi, Desai, & Tewari, 2020) (Lee, Cheung, & Kwok, 2020)

AI systems in education increasingly rely on student data to enable personalization and adaptation of learning, facilitate student profiling and enable decision making in the classroom and within the institution (Papamitsiou & Economides, 2014). Subsequently, concerns regarding data privacy, security, and ethical considerations in education contexts are growing (Huang, 2023; Liu & Khalil, 2023). Safeguarding student data is not only crucial for protecting individuals' rights but also essential for maintaining trust in educational institutions and AI-powered learning tools (Raza, Fatima, Arif, & Muhammad, 2024).

Data in education is collected in and out of the classroom. Data at classroom level data includes assessment performance, student experience surveys, learning behaviors and interaction with learning management systems. At administrative level data may include enrolments, progress in programs of study, financial and other personal data. Data may also be collected and stored in national student databases (Veldkamp, Schildkamp, Keijsers, Visscher, & de Jong, 2021). The volume and great diversity in location and use of data raises concerns of growing a "surveillance culture" in schools (Cope & Kalantzis, 2016).

The types of student data collected by AI systems loosely (Hernandez-de-Menendez, Morales-Menendez, Escobar, & Arinez, 2021)fall into four categories: academic records, behavioral and engagement data, health information, and biometric data (Innovare, 2023) (Baig, Shuib, & Yadegaridehkordi, 2020) (Howard, et al., 2022)

Academic Records: AI-powered learning management systems (LMS), intelligent tutoring systems, and adaptive learning platforms track student progress, grades, assignments, and course completion rates. These platforms use data analytics to identify learning gaps, recommend personalized content, and predict student performance (Yousufi, Naidu, Jesrani, & Dattana, 2022).

Behavioral and Engagement Data: AI-driven educational tools monitor student engagement, interaction patterns, and online activities to determine learning preferences and identify students who may need additional support (Gomes, et al., 2023). For example, AI can analyze how long students spend on different tasks, their participation in online discussions, and their response patterns to assessments. This information helps educators personalize instruction but also raises concerns about surveillance and data ethics. If not properly regulated, behavioral data could be used to create student profiles that influence academic opportunities in unintended ways.

Health Information: Some AI applications in education collect mental health and wellness data, (Luo & Nie, 2025), detecting signs of stress or depression, and provide mental health support. While these tools can be beneficial in identifying at-risk students and offering early interventions, they also pose risks related to data sensitivity and confidentiality. Unauthorized access to student health data could lead to stigmatization or discrimination, particularly if such information is shared without proper consent.

Biometric Data: AI systems are increasingly incorporating biometric data, such as facial recognition, fingerprint scans, voice recognition, and eye-tracking technology, to authenticate student identities, monitor attendance, and improve security (Hernandez-de-Menendez, Morales-Menendez, Escobar, & Arinez, 2021; Necochea-Chamorro, Asalde, Nuñez, & del Rosario Vasquez Valencia, 2024). While biometric authentication enhances security, it also introduces concerns about privacy invasion, potential misuse, and the long-term storage of sensitive personal identifiers. If compromised, biometric data cannot be reset like passwords, making it especially vulnerable to identity theft and fraud.

The personal nature of the data necessarily raises concerns about biases, security, and privacy. Unfortunately, although concerns are well-recognized in literature, in practice, the role of data in schools and other educational institutions is insufficiently questioned (Pangrazio, 2024). "Data gathering became crucial to new regimes of 'accountability' and 'new public management' that emerged in the late 1990s, and aligns with neoliberal approaches to education that rely on performance measures and top-down surveillance of teachers and students" (Pangrazio, 2024, p. 1049). The great value placed on data for education obscures the reality that "education data can cause harm" including student alienation, bias, increased teacher labor and the erosion of learners' digital privacy (Pangrazio, 2024, p. 1049)

PRIVACY AND CONSENT

"Data privacy, also called "information privacy," is the principle that a person should have control over their personal data, including the ability to decide how organizations collect, store and use their data" (Kosinski & Forrest, 2023, p. para 1)."Information privacy is about promoting the protection of information that says who we are, what we do and what we believe in" (Australian Government - Office of the Australian Information Commissioner, n.d., p. para 4).

Estimates are that 402.74 million terabytes of data are created every single day (Beamer, 2025, p. para 1) and the volume is surging rapidly! In our digital world, for most people, many aspects of their lives (who they are, what they do, what they think, what activities they engage in, their state of health and so on) is continuously digitized, and their data is present across multiple locations on the planet. No wonder that data privacy is an overarching concern across all social domains. In the domain of education, as in other social domains, the situation is no different. The proliferation of digital learning platforms and now artificial intelligence throughout the educational domain significantly adds to data generated. The concern is not that there are vast volumes of data being generated. Rather the concern is what is being done with the data? What decisions are being made, based on which data? Who is accessing the data, for what purposes? Who is sharing the data and with whom and why? These are pivotal questions that must be asked throughout the conversation of how big data and artificial intelligence are revolutionizing learning and teaching.

There are two key related themes relevant to the discussion of issues in data in education: Consent and, privacy and protection.

Consent

Consent is about whether students (and particularly in school settings, parents) are aware of what data is being collected and how it is used. Consent refers to individual's permission to collect and use data about them. The elements of consent include giving consent voluntarily, informing the individual adequately, how specific consent is, currency of consent, and whether the individual can understand and communicate consent (Information and Privacy Commission New South Wales, 2023). Consent is a multi-faceted, complicated issue, and especially so in school settings where students are under the legal age. Consent issue is further complicated when data is being collected by third- party digital services being used in educational settings:

"it was asking her to consent to her daughter's personal details being used on more than 20 "third party online service providers [that] are external to the school… The school was asking for permission to disclose details including her daughter's full name, date of birth, school, classroom and other identifying and personal details to all these third parties. But there was little guidance about the risks or benefits of using each of these services and only generic descriptions of what they were or how they would be used, along with a directive that parents should read the terms of service and privacy policies for all 20 platforms" (Elvery & Tan, 2025, pp. para 4-7)

Informed consent is a mainstay of data ethics, but do individuals really understand (or are even data literate enough to have interest in) what they are consenting to in digital environments? The question remains open to debate (Hayes, 2020).

Additionally, in education settings, there is the issue of consent when minors are involved. There is debate, which is "inflected differently in different countries and cultures, regarding the parent's rights over their child, including the parent's right to manage (or invade) their child's privacy (Livingstone, Stoilova, & Nandagiri, 2019, p. 13).

Data Privacy and Protection

"Education, Big Data, and student privacy are a combustible mix" (Reidenberg & Schaub, 2018, p. 263)

Inextricable from the issue of digital consent is the privacy and protection. In these discussions, questions about data ownership, control, security, and the ethical and transparent use of data must simultaneously arise. Student data privacy in the context of AI applications refers to the responsible collection, storage, and use of student information while ensuring compliance with legal and ethical standards. It involves safeguarding sensitive information from unauthorized access, preventing data misuse, and maintaining transparency in how AI-driven educational tools handle student records.

Transparency is particularly problematic when data is being analysed or collected via AI technologies. A key strategy impacting is ensuring ethical AI development by promoting transparency, accountability, and fairness in AI-driven decision-making. Educational institutions and technology developers should provide clear explanations of how AI algorithms work, allowing students, parents, and educators to understand the factors influencing AI-generated recommendations. Transparency reports, ethical AI audits, and bias-detection tools can help ensure that AI applications are designed and implemented responsibly. Another major concern is the misuse of student data, particularly when AI systems are designed without clear governance policies. If AI-powered educational tools are not transparent about how they collect, process, and store data, student information could be used for unintended purposes, such as targeted advertising, profiling, or algorithmic decision-making that disadvantages certain students. For instance, AI-based predictive analytics may unintentionally reinforce biases, making assumptions about a student's future performance based on historical data rather than actual potential.

Data security is paramount in the protection of privacy. The term 'security' implies "a state or condition in which the integrity of an entity is not biased;[where] the entity should remain immune against threats, risks and damages" (Moghaddasi, Sajjadi, & Kamkarhaghighi, 2016).

There are multiple models in the field of cybersecurity which aim to define characteristics or attributes of data that must be considered for managing effective protection of data. The foundational model, which effectively encapsulates key dimensions is the CIA definition of security which defines three inter-related properties of secure data, It sets out three fundamental goals for cybersecurity as being confidentiality, integrity and availability.

"Confidentiality: 'property that information is not made available or disclosed to unauthorized individuals, entities, or processes' (Lundgren & Möller, 2019, p. 420). Confidentiality of data in education raises questions about who can access to which data, and by extension, what might those seeing the data do with it. The 'wrong people' having the ability to see data obviously has serious implications (Nweke, 2017).

Integrity: 'property of accuracy and completeness' (Lundgren & Möller, 2019, pp. 420-421). Integrity is really about the accuracy and completeness of data that is being stored. It's about ensuring that the data being stored is unchanged from its original (Nweke, 2017). Data that has lost integrity is not only inaccurate but can also lead to issues in interpretation and use. For example, a snippet of a message taken out of context can be wrongly interpreted or portray incorrect information that is different from what was intended originally (Nweke, 2017)

Availability: 'property of being accessible and usable upon demand by an authorized entity'" (Lundgren & Möller, 2019, p. 421). Availability is about authorized users being able to do what they need to do and have the resources required to do so (Nweke, 2017).

At the core of cybersecurity is data ownership and control. Data ownership and control, because they are so complex, are often ambiguous in policies. Adding to ambiguity and complexity is use of third-party technology vendors (where data is often stored in the cloud) which is very common in education settings,

User control of data ties in with the lack of clear consent and control over data usage. Students and parents often have limited awareness of how AI systems handle personal data, leading to concerns about whether they have the right to opt out of data collection or request data deletion. Schools and educational institutions must implement clear data privacy policies and ensure that students and families have a say in how their information is used. There is a lack of legal clarity around data ownership and control in education (and other) settings (Corrin, et al., 2019).

Transparency and student autonomy are also critical elements of ethical AI implementation in education. Students and their families should have a clear understanding of how AI technologies impact their learning experiences, and they should be given the right to opt out of AI-based decision-making processes when possible. Institutions should develop AI ethics policies that outline their commitments to student data protection, fairness, and accountability, ensuring that students' rights remain at the center of AI deployment in education.

There is a growing and urgent need for "comprehensive education data governance – the regulation of who collects what data, how it is used and why… Technologically data can be collected by third parties, rendering schools unable to control their use" (Hillman, 2022, p. 1)Institutions must implement strong data governance frameworks that establish clear policies on data access, storage, and sharing. These policies should define who has permission to use student data, how long data is retained, and under what circumstances it can be shared with third parties. Schools and universities should also provide training for educators and administrators on the ethical implications of AI in education, ensuring that decision-makers understand the risks associated with AI-driven data collection and analysis.

The security of student data is a growing concern, particularly as cyberattacks targeting educational institutions become more frequent. Unfortunately, despite the growing number of cyberattacks on educational institutions, cyberthreats on educational institutions tend to be overshadowed by high profile attacks on other large organizations such as government, financial or business organizations (Fouad, 2021). AI systems store large amounts of personal and academic data, making them attractive targets for hackers. Data breaches can lead to identity theft, financial fraud, and reputational damage for both students and institutions. To mitigate these risks, schools and ed-tech companies must implement robust cybersecurity measures, including encryption, secure authentication, and regular audits to prevent unauthorized access to sensitive information.

LEGAL FRAMEWORKS

Legal frameworks and regulations play a critical role in protecting student data privacy in AI-driven education. Laws such as the General Data Protection Regulation (GDPR) and the Family Educational Rights and Privacy Act (FERPA) in the United States and) in Europe set guidelines for how student data should be collected, processed, and shared.

Article 5 in GDPR contains seven principles related to processing of personal data and what those controlling the data need to be aware of and comply with (An Coimisiún um Chosant Sonrai - Data Protection Commission, 2019). The principles are lawfulness, fairness, and transparency; purpose limitation, data minimization; accuracy; storage limitation; and accountability (An Coimisiún um Chosant Sonrai - Data Protection Commission, 2019). One of the key features of GDPR is the requirement for explicit and informed consent before collecting and processing personal data. AI-powered educational platforms must clearly state how student data will be used, ensuring that students (or their guardians) have control over their information. GDPR also enforces the right to be forgotten, allowing students to request the deletion of their data from AI-driven systems. This provision is particularly important in education, where students may not want their academic records to be stored indefinitely in AI databases.

Additionally, GDPR introduces strict security requirements for data storage and processing, requiring organizations to implement data encryption, access controls, and regular risk assessments. AI developers working with educational institutions must ensure that AI algorithms comply with GDPR principles of fairness, transparency, and accountability. Failure to adhere to GDPR regulations can result in severe penalties, including hefty fines and legal action. FERPA "affords parents the right to have access to their children's education records to see to have the records amended, and the right to have some control over the disclosure of personally identifiable information from the education records" (U.S. Department of Education, n.d., p. para 1). FERPA, enacted in 1974, is the primary U.S. federal law that protects the privacy of student education records. Under FERPA, schools and educational institutions receiving federal funding must obtain parental or student consent before disclosing personally identifiable information (PII) from student records. The law also grants students the right to access and amend their records. In the context of AI-powered education, FERPA requires that AI systems handling student data comply with its regulations, ensuring that institutions do not share student information with third parties without proper authorization.

FERPA also has provisions for data security, requiring schools to implement safeguards that prevent unauthorized access to student records. However, as AI-driven educational tools become more widespread, FERPA faces challenges in keeping pace with emerging technologies. Many AI-based learning platforms operate on cloud-based infrastructures, storing vast amounts of student data across multiple locations, which raises questions about jurisdiction, data ownership, and security measures.

These regulations emphasize the importance of obtaining informed consent, ensuring data minimization, and granting students and parents the right to access and correct their data. However, compliance with these regulations can be challenging, particularly as AI technologies evolve at a rapid pace.

Although legal frameworks are useful, the concerns about digital data protection, privacy and ethical use are far from resolved. The dynamic nature of technologies and the accompanying rapid pace of social, political and economic change means that policy makers are struggling to keep up. In the background, there is an almost silent "creep of data collected with and without permission" and this 'creep' is "greater than most people realize" (Robertson & Mulrhead, 2022). The policy gaps surrounding digital privacy and education must be acknowledged and deliberate efforts must be made to narrow these gaps. Educational institutions and AI developers must work together to ensure that AI-driven systems align with existing legal frameworks while adapting to emerging privacy concerns.

PRIVACY BY DESIGN

The concept of 'privacy by design' developed by Ann Cavoukian, in the 1990s "refers to the philosophy and approach of embedding privacy into the design specifications of various technologies…[it is achieved by building the principles of Fair Information Practices (FIPs) into the design, operation and management of information processing technologies and systems" (Cavoukian, n.d.). Essentially, privacy by design is the concept that privacy and its protection are not an afterthought and considered at implementation of technologies, but that privacy considerations must permeate the whole process from conceptualization of the technology right through to implementation. It is about truly embedding privacy into technologies.

Balancing the benefits of AI with the need to protect student privacy requires the implementation of best practices and ethical guidelines. One key strategy is the adoption of privacy-by-design principles, which involve integrating privacy safeguards into AI systems from the outset. This approach ensures that data protection measures are embedded into the design and functionality of AI tools, rather than being added as an afterthought. Privacy-by-design principles also promote data anonymization, reducing the risk of personally identifiable information being misused or compromised. One of the primary concerns regarding AI-driven student data collection is informed consent and transparency. Many educational institutions and technology providers collect data without fully explaining how it will be used, who has access, and how long it will be stored. Without clear guidelines, students and parents may unintentionally agree to data-sharing practices that expose personal information to third parties, including advertisers, researchers, or corporate entities. This lack of transparency undermines trust (Polonetsky & Jerome, 2014). and raises ethical questions about the commercialization of student data.

Case Studies of AI and Student Data Privacy

As artificial intelligence (AI) continues to reshape education, its applications in personalized learning, predictive analytics, and administrative automation have raised significant concerns about student data privacy. AI-driven tools in education collect vast amounts of data, ranging from academic performance records to behavioral insights, prompting educators, institutions, and policymakers to address ethical and security risks. While AI has enabled adaptive learning, intelligent tutoring systems, and automated grading, it has also introduced new vulnerabilities regarding data security, consent, and transparency. Examining real-world examples of AI applications in education, as well as case studies of data breaches, provides insight into both the potential benefits and risks of AI-powered education technologies. Furthermore, institutions that have proactively addressed ethical concerns regarding AI and data privacy can serve as models for best practices in safeguarding student data.

One notable example of AI in education is Carnegie Learning's MATHia, an adaptive learning platform that analyzes student performance in mathematics and provides personalized instruction. MATHia collects and processes real-time student data, using AI to predict learning gaps and suggest tailored exercises. While this technology has improved student engagement and learning outcomes, it also raises questions about data ownership and whether students and parents fully understand how their data is used. Transparency in AI decision-making and informed consent remain key concerns as educational institutions integrate such platforms.

Another widely adopted AI-powered tool is Turnitin's AI-driven plagiarism detection system, which scans student submissions to detect potential instances of plagiarism. While Turnitin plays a crucial role in maintaining academic integrity, concerns have been raised about data storage policies—particularly the indefinite retention of student work in proprietary databases. Turnitin's lack of explicit opt-in mechanisms, highlights the need for greater autonomy in data usage.

Additionally, AI-powered chatbots and virtual teaching assistants, such as IBM Watson Tutor, have been implemented in universities to automate student support, answer administrative questions, and guide learners through coursework. These AI-driven assistants collect data on student inquiries, learning patterns, and behavioral trends, raising concerns about data protection and third-party access. While these systems offer efficiency and accessibility, institutions must ensure that they comply with data privacy laws such as FERPA and GDPR to prevent misuse.

Despite the promise of AI in education, there have been multiple high-profile data breaches and cases of student data misuse, underscoring the risks associated with weak cybersecurity measures. One of the most alarming examples is the 2019 Pearson data breach, in which the educational publishing giant suffered a security breach that exposed the records of over 13,000 school and university accounts. The compromised data included student names, email addresses, and some academic records. This breach highlighted the vulnerabilities in AI-powered cloud-based learning systems and the need for stronger encryption, data anonymization, and access control measures to protect student information.

Another major case occurred in 2020 when ProctorU (Patty, 2020), an AI-based remote exam monitoring platform, suffered a data breach, exposing the personal information of nearly 444,000 students worldwide. ProctorU's AI-driven surveillance system uses facial recognition, keystroke tracking, and video monitoring to prevent cheating, but the breach revealed how large-scale AI-powered surveillance tools can become privacy liabilities. Students and privacy advocates raised concerns about the ethical implications of AI-based exam proctoring, citing excessive data collection, algorithmic bias, and the psychological stress caused by AI surveillance.

In another controversial case, the Los Angeles Unified School District (LAUSD) faced criticism over the use of an AI-driven predictive analytics system to assess student risk factors. The system, designed to identify at-risk students, collected behavioral data, attendance records, and academic performance metrics to predict potential dropouts. While the initiative aimed to provide early intervention for struggling students, it also faced backlash for lacking transparency in its decision-making process and failing to address concerns about algorithmic bias. Critics argued that AI-driven risk assessments could reinforce socioeconomic and racial disparities, particularly if historical biases were embedded in training data.

"Some edtech experts contacted by EdSurge say that the implosion of the cutting-edge AI tool offers lessons for other schools and colleges working to make use of generative AI. Most of those lessons, they say, center on a factor that is more difficult than many people realize: the challenges of corralling and safeguarding data." (Young, 2024).

In response to growing concerns about AI and student data privacy, many educational institutions have implemented proactive measures to address ethical challenges and strengthen compliance with data protection laws. For example, the University of California system has established AI governance committees to oversee how AI tools are implemented across campuses, ensuring that they align with ethical standards, transparency, and student privacy rights.

"While AI has the potential to streamline administrative workflows; enhance classroom experiences; and enable more efficient, data-driven decision-making across UC, we must remain vigilant about potential risks such as accidental disclosure of proprietary, confidential, or personal data, and the inadvertent violation of University policy and/or state and federal laws" (University of California, n.d., p. para 1)

By creating institutional policies that prioritize data security and fairness, universities can better regulate the deployment of AI in education.

Similarly, the United Kingdom's Office for Students (OfS) has issued guidance on responsible AI usage, emphasizing the importance of data minimization, informed consent, and fairness in algorithmic decision-making (Hough, 2023). The OfS has encouraged regular audits of AI-driven learning platforms and has called for greater student involvement in decisions regarding data privacy policies.

Some institutions have gone further by developing privacy-first AI models that rely on federated learning, a technique that enables AI systems to learn from decentralized data sources without centralizing sensitive student information. For example, some European universities are testing privacy-preserving AI models that anonymize student data before analysis, reducing the risk of breaches and unauthorized access.

Another emerging practice is the implementation of AI ethics training programs for educators and administrators. Recognizing that many educators may not fully understand the implications of AI on student privacy, institutions such as Stanford University and MIT have integrated AI ethics courses into teacher training programs. These courses help educators navigate the ethical dilemmas associated with AI in education, including data consent, algorithmic bias, and cybersecurity best practices. Stanford university encourages teachers to analyze "the implications of AI" in courses (Standford University, n.d.) pointing to the benefits as well as potential risks of using AI in teaching.

Additionally, organizations like the International Society for Technology in Education (ISTE) have developed guidelines for AI implementation in schools, promoting responsible AI governance, student data protection policies, and transparency in AI-driven learning tools. ISTE recommends that educational institutions adopt AI ethics frameworks, ensure that students and parents have control over their data, and require ed-tech companies to provide clear explanations of AI decision-making processes. ISTE promotes the GenerationAI movement as a "groundbreaking educational movement designed to empower K-12 educators with the knowledge, tools, and confidence to safely and responsibly capture the power of Artificial Intelligence (AI) in the classroom" (ISTE, n.d.).Ultimately, the growing presence of AI in education requires a balanced approach that maximizes the benefits of AI-powered learning while ensuring robust data privacy protections. Institutions must be vigilant in enforcing data security protocols, fostering transparency, and upholding ethical AI practices. The lessons learned from past AI-related data breaches and controversies highlight the urgent need for stricter regulations, improved institutional oversight, and greater collaboration between policymakers, educators, and AI developers.

As AI continues to evolve, ensuring student data privacy must remain a top priority. By integrating privacy-first AI models, enhancing digital literacy among educators, and holding ed-tech providers accountable, institutions can create a safer, more ethical AI-driven learning environment that prioritizes student rights, data protection, and educational equity.

THE FUTURE OF AI AND STUDENT DATA PRIVACY

The centrality of data for AI in education, brings issues of data privacy and protection to the forefront of the future of education in the digital age. Some maintain that "privacy and data protection are a major stumbling blocks (sic) for a data-driven educational future" (Hoel & Chen, 2018, p. para 1).

As artificial intelligence (AI) continues to evolve, emerging technologies are reshaping education and raising new concerns about student data privacy. AI-driven innovations such as machine learning algorithms, natural language processing (NLP), facial recognition, and predictive analytics are becoming integral to personalized learning, automated assessments, and student performance tracking. While these advancements offer opportunities for more effective and inclusive education, they also present significant privacy risks that must be addressed through strong legal frameworks, ethical guidelines, and institutional safeguards. It seems that as technologies develop, they impinge on more deeply personal data. The emerging use of facial recognition technologies in education are a prime example. Beyond facial recognition for campus security, it can also be applied to attendance monitoring, tracking student activities and behaviors or perhaps as indicators of student engagement and learning (Andrejevic & Selwyn, 2020).The potential benefits of these emerging and very personal technologies must be acknowledged and explored, but it is important that the benefits are explored together with the potential risks and harms

Emerging AI technologies have the potential to enhance learning experiences, administrative efficiency, and student engagement, but their increasing reliance on student data demands greater scrutiny and oversight. Predictive analytics, for example, can assess student behavior, academic performance, and risk factors to provide early intervention strategies. However, these models rely on large-scale data collection, making students vulnerable to data breaches, unauthorized access, and profiling biases. Similarly, AI-powered proctoring tools, which use facial recognition and behavioral monitoring to prevent cheating during online exams, raise concerns about constant surveillance, data security, and potential misuse of biometric information.

Another major concern is the rise of voice recognition and AI-driven chatbots in education. These technologies, powered by NLP and machine learning, offer real-time student assistance and adaptive tutoring. However, they also require continuous data collection, including voice recordings and text interactions, creating potential privacy risks. Without clear data retention policies and encryption protocols, student interactions with AI-driven systems may be stored indefinitely, exposing them to data misuse and security vulnerabilities.

As AI capabilities expand, the legal and ethical landscape surrounding student data privacy is evolving to keep pace with technological advancements. Existing regulations such as the Family Educational Rights and Privacy Act (FERPA) in the U.S. and the General Data Protection Regulation (GDPR) in Europe provide important protections for student data, but they were not designed to address the unique challenges posed by AI-driven education technologies. Newer regulations, such as the Artificial Intelligence Act proposed by the European Union, aim to classify and regulate AI applications based on their risk levels, ensuring that high-risk AI systems, including those used in education, meet stringent transparency and fairness requirements.

Despite these efforts, regulatory gaps remain. Many AI-powered education platforms operate across multiple jurisdictions, leading to conflicts in data protection standards and enforcement mechanisms. For example, while GDPR grants students the right to be forgotten, requiring companies to delete personal data upon request, FERPA does not offer the same level of protection. This inconsistency creates challenges for multinational institutions and technology providers that must navigate varying legal frameworks while ensuring compliance with student data privacy regulations.

Beyond legal compliance, ethical guidelines for AI in education are gaining traction. Organizations such as the Institute of Electrical and Electronics Engineers (IEEE) and the World Economic Forum have developed frameworks for trustworthy AI, emphasizing transparency, fairness, and accountability. These guidelines encourage AI developers and educational institutions to prioritize privacy-by-design principles, ensuring that AI systems are developed with built-in safeguards to protect student data from misuse.

Looking ahead, the future of AI in education will be shaped by ongoing advancements in data security, ethical AI governance, and privacy-preserving technologies. AI will likely become even more embedded in classrooms, with smart classrooms, AI-driven assessment tools, and real-time student engagement analytics becoming standard components of modern education systems. However, these innovations will also necessitate greater investment in cybersecurity measures, such as decentralized data storage, zero-trust security frameworks, and AI-driven threat detection systems to prevent data breaches and unauthorized access.

As AI continues to evolve, the challenge of maintaining student data privacy will require proactive collaboration between governments, technology companies, educational institutions, and advocacy groups. The development of internationally recognized privacy standards, interoperable data protection policies, and transparent AI deployment practices will be essential in ensuring that AI-driven education remains both effective and ethical. Without robust privacy safeguards, the increasing reliance on AI in education risks eroding student trust, institutional credibility, and legal compliance.

Ultimately, while AI presents unprecedented opportunities to transform education, it must be implemented responsibly, transparently, and ethically. The balance between technological innovation and student data privacy will define the future of AI in education, making it crucial for stakeholders to continuously assess risks, adapt policies, and uphold ethical AI standards to protect students in an increasingly digital learning environment.

POLICY RECOMMENDATIONS FOR PROTECTING STUDENT DATA PRIVACY IN AI

Ensuring student data privacy in AI-driven education requires a collaborative effort among educational institutions, policymakers, and AI developers. As AI-powered learning tools become more widespread, these stakeholders must implement comprehensive strategies to safeguard student information while maintaining the benefits of AI-driven innovation. Strong data governance frameworks, transparent privacy policies, and continuous monitoring of AI systems are essential to achieving ethical AI use in education. By adopting best practices and proactive measures, institutions can create an environment where AI enhances learning without compromising student privacy.

Educational institutions play a critical role in upholding student data privacy by establishing clear policies and best practices for AI implementation. Schools and universities should adopt privacy-by-design principles, ensuring that AI systems are designed with built-in safeguards to protect student data from misuse. This includes limiting data collection, anonymizing personally identifiable information (PII), and securing data storage through encryption and access controls.

Institutions should also implement student and parent consent mechanisms, allowing individuals to understand how their data is used and giving them the option to opt out of data collection when appropriate. Regular privacy audits should be conducted to assess the security of AI-driven platforms and identify potential vulnerabilities. Additionally, digital literacy programs can help students and educators develop an understanding of AI technologies, data privacy rights, and ethical considerations, empowering them to make informed decisions about their data.

Policymakers must establish robust legal frameworks that govern the use of AI in education. While regulations like FERPA and GDPR provide a foundation for student data protection, policymakers should work to update these frameworks in response to emerging AI challenges. Governments should also develop standardized AI governance policies that ensure AI-driven educational tools comply with privacy regulations, ethical guidelines, and data security standards.

To further protect student data, policymakers should mandate third-party accountability measures, requiring AI vendors to demonstrate compliance with privacy laws and ethical AI development practices. This can be achieved through certification programs, independent audits, and regulatory oversight. Governments can also invest in AI research and education programs, ensuring that institutions have the necessary resources to implement AI responsibly and train educators in data protection best practices.

AI developers must take responsibility for designing ethical AI systems that prioritize privacy, transparency, and fairness. Developers should incorporate privacy-by-design principles, ensuring that AI-driven educational platforms collect only the minimum necessary data and provide users with clear explanations of how AI decisions are made. AI models should undergo bias detection and fairness testing, preventing discriminatory outcomes that disproportionately affect certain student groups.

Developers should also work closely with educators and policymakers to establish ethical AI guidelines and data governance frameworks. By collaborating with schools, universities, and regulatory bodies, AI companies can align their technologies with privacy standards and ensure that AI-powered tools meet ethical and educational objectives.

Data governance frameworks play a crucial role in promoting responsible AI use in education. These frameworks establish rules and guidelines for data collection, storage, sharing, and security, ensuring that student information is handled ethically. Institutions should implement comprehensive data governance policies that outline who has access to student data, how long it is retained, and under what circumstances it can be shared.

Data governance frameworks should also include protocols for AI system audits, ensuring that AI-driven educational platforms operate within legal and ethical boundaries. Transparency reports, outlining how AI processes student data and makes decisions, can help institutions build trust with students, parents, and educators.

Continuous monitoring and adaptation of privacy practices is essential as AI technologies evolve. AI-driven educational tools are constantly updated with new algorithms, data processing techniques, and learning models, which may introduce new privacy risks. Institutions, policymakers, and developers must implement ongoing risk assessments to identify emerging threats and update privacy measures accordingly.

Educational institutions should establish dedicated AI ethics committees that review AI-driven learning tools, assess privacy risks, and recommend policy adjustments. Additionally, schools and universities should engage in regular cybersecurity training, ensuring that educators and administrators stay informed about best practices for data protection.

Policymakers should also establish adaptive legal frameworks that evolve alongside AI advancements. Regulations should include mechanisms for updating privacy laws, incorporating feedback from education stakeholders, AI researchers, and privacy advocates. Additionally, governments should facilitate cross-sector collaborations, encouraging partnerships between technology companies, educational institutions, and privacy organizations to develop comprehensive AI data protection strategies.

AI developers must commit to long-term AI accountability measures, ensuring that their platforms remain compliant with evolving privacy laws. This includes real-time monitoring of AI systems, addressing algorithmic biases, and integrating user feedback into system updates. AI companies should also promote open-source AI initiatives, allowing researchers and policymakers to evaluate AI models for transparency, fairness, and security.

In conclusion, ensuring student data privacy in AI-powered education requires a multi-layered approach involving educational institutions, policymakers, and AI developers. By implementing strong data governance frameworks, privacy-conscious AI design, and continuous monitoring of AI systems, stakeholders can create an ethical and secure learning environment. The future of AI in education depends on our ability to balance technological innovation with robust privacy protections, ensuring that students' rights remain at the center of AI-driven education.

CONCLUSION

As artificial intelligence (AI) continues to shape the future of education, ensuring the ethical use of student data is a pressing concern for educators, policymakers, and AI developers. AI-driven learning platforms, predictive analytics, and adaptive assessments rely on vast amounts of student data to personalize learning experiences and improve educational outcomes. However, this increased reliance on data collection presents significant privacy risks, including unauthorized access, data breaches, algorithmic bias, and potential misuse of sensitive information. Without proper safeguards, the use of AI in education can erode student trust, institutional credibility, and compliance with legal frameworks.

The chapter serves to keep to the fore that while the potential benefits of AI in education are many, those benefits can only be realized when the ethical issues and concerns related to AI technologies and their integration into education. Questions about how AI systems collect, process, and analyze student information were posed and some best practices for ethical AI implementation specifically related to data privacy and protection were discussed. Key topics included transparency, informed consent, data minimization, encryption, and regulatory compliance to ensure that

AI-driven education tools align with privacy laws such as FERPA, GDPR, and emerging international standards.

By addressing concerns and issues raised in the chapter, educational institutions can better harness the transformative potential of AI while maintaining student privacy, ethical accountability, and regulatory compliance. Ultimately, responsible AI implementation in education is needed to create secure, equitable, and transparent learning environment that benefits students, educators, and all human society.

REFERENCES

An Coimisiún um Chosant Sonrai - Data Protection Commission. (2019, October). Retrieved May 2025, from Quick Guide to the Principles of Data Protection: https://www.dataprotection.ie/sites/default/files/uploads/2019-11/Guidance%20on%20the%20Principles%20of%20Data%20Protection_Oct19.pdf

Andrejevic, M., & Selwyn, N. (2020). Facial recognition technology in schools: Critical questions and concerns. *Learning, Media and Technology*, *45*(2), 115–128.

Australian Government - Office of the Australian Information Commissioner. (n.d.). *What is Privacy?* Retrieved May 2025, from Australian Governement - Privacy: https://www.oaic.gov.au/privacy/your-privacy-rights/your-personal-information/what-is-privacy

Baig, M., Shuib, L., & Yadegaridehkordi, E. (2020). Big data in education: A state of the art, limitations, and future research directions. *International Journal of Educational Technology in Higher Education, 17*. Advance online publication. DOI: 10.1186/s41239-020-00223-0

Baker, R., & Hawn, A. (2021). Algorithmic bias in education. *International Journal of Artificial Intelligence in Education, 32*, 1052–1092.

Beamer, T. (2025, April 19). *402.74 Million terrabytes of Data is Created Every Day.* Retrieved April 2025, from Tech News: https://www.techbusinessnews.com.au/blog/402-74-million-terrabytes-of-data-is-created-every-day/

Cavoukian, A. (n.d.). *Privacy by Design.* Retrieved May 2025, from Information and Privacy Commissioner of Ontario: https://www.ipc.on.ca/en/media/1826/download?attachment

Cope, B., & Kalantzis, M. (2016). Big Data Comes to School: Implications for Learning, Assessment, and Research. *AERA Open, 2*(2), Big Data Comes to School: Implications for Learning, Assessment, and Research.

Corrin, L., Kennedy, G., French, S., Shum, S., Kitto, K., Pardo, A., . . . Colvin, C. (2019). *The ethics of learning analytics in Australian Higher Education - Discussion Paper.*

Elvery, S., & Tan, T. (2025, February 27). *You read the terms and conditions, right?* Retrieved April 2025, from ABC News - Australian Broadcasting Commission: https://www.abc.net.au/news/2025-02-27/classroom-apps-technology-kids-data-terms-conditions/104966952

Fouad, N. (2021). Securing higher education against cyberthreats: From an institutional risk to a national policy challenge. *Journal of Cyber Policy*, *6*(2), 137–154.

Georgia Tech. (2016, November 10). *Meet Jill Watson: Georgia Tech's first AI teaching assistant.* Retrieved April 2025, from Professional Education College of Lifetime Learning: https://pe.gatech.edu/blog/meet-jill-watson-georgia-techs-first-ai-teaching-assistant

Gomes, S., Costa, L., Martinho, C., Dias, J., Xexéo, G., & Santos, A. (2023). Modeling students' behavioral engagement through different in-class behavior styles. *International Journal of STEM Education*, *10*, 21. DOI: 10.1186/s40594-023-00407-w

Hayes, S. (2020). Informed Consent and Data Literacy Education are Crucial to Ethics. In *B. Franks, 97 Things About Ethics Everyone in Data Science Should Know* (pp. 42–44). O'Reilly Media.

Hernandez-de-Menendez, M., Morales-Menendez, R., Escobar, C., & Arinez, J. (2021). Biometric applications in education. [IJIDeM]. *International Journal on Interactive Design and Manufacturing*, *15*(2-3), 365–380. PMID: 40477322

Hillman, V. (2022). Bringing in the technological, ethical, educational and social-structural for a new education data governance. *Learning, Media and Technology*, *48*, 1–16.

Hoel, T., & Chen, W. (2018). Privacy and data protection in learning analytics should be motivated by an educational maxim—Towards a proposal. *Research and Practice in Technology Enhanced Learning*, *13*(1), 20. DOI: 10.1186/s41039-018-0086-8 PMID: 30595748

Hough, D. (2023, October 10). *Student Guidance for the Responsible Use of AI - blog post.* Retrieved May 2025, from #ALTC Blog - News & Views from the ALT Community: https://altc.alt.ac.uk/blog/2023/10/student-guidance-for-the-responsible-use-of-ai/#gref

Howard, S., Swist, T., Gasevic, D., Bartimote, K., Knight, S., Gulson, K., & Selwyn, N. (2022). Educational data journeys: Where are we going, what are we taking and making for AI? *Computers and Education: Artificial Intelligence*, *3*, 100073. DOI: 10.1016/j.caeai.2022.100073

Huang, L. (2023). Ethics of artificial intelligence in education: Student privacy and data protection. *SIEF*, *16*(2), 2578–2587.

Idowu, J., Koshiyama, A., & Treleaven, P. (2024). Investigating algorithmic bias in student progress monitoring. *Computers and Education: Artificial Intelligence*, *7*, 100267. DOI: 10.1016/j.caeai.2024.100267

Information and Privacy Commission New South Wales. (2023, June). *Fact Sheet - Consent.* Retrieved April 2025, from Fact Sheet - Consent: https://www.ipc.nsw.gov.au/fact-sheet-consent

Innovare. (2023, May 10). *The Different Types of Data in Education: A Complete Guide.* Retrieved May 2025, from Innovare - Data in K-12 Schools: https://innovaresip.com/blog/types-of-data-in-education/

ISTE. (n.d.). *GenerationAI - Educators Reimagining Learning for a Connected World.* Retrieved April 2025, from GenerationAI - Educators Reimagining Learning for a Connected World: https://iste.org/generationai

Joshi, A., Desai, P., & Tewari, P. (2020). Learning Analytics framework for measuring students' performance and teachers' involvement through problem based learning in engineering educatio. *Procedia Computer Science, 172*, 954–959.

Khine, M. (2024). Using AI for Adaptive Learning and Adaptive Assessment. In Khine, M. (Ed.), *Artificial Intelligence in Education* (pp. 341–466). Springer.

Kosinski, M., & Forrest, A. (2023, December 19). *What is data privacy?* Retrieved April 2025, from IBM: https://www.ibm.com/think/topics/data-privacy

Lee, L., Cheung, S., & Kwok, L. (2020). Learning analytics: Current trends and innovative practices. *Journal of Computers in Education, 7*, 1–6.

Liu, Q., & Khalil, M. (2023). Understanding privacy and data protection issues in learning analytics using a systematic review. *British Journal of Educational Technology, 54*(6), 1715–1747.

Livingstone, S., Stoilova, M., & Nandagiri, R. (2019). *Children's data and privacy online growing up in a digital age. An evidence review.* London School of Economics and Political Science.

Lundgren, B., & Möller, N. (2019). Data information security. *Science and Engineering Ethics*, •••, 419–441. PMID: 29143269

Luo, Y., & Nie, Z. (2025). A Model for Building Student Physical Health Information Management in a Big Data Environment. *Systems and Soft Computing, 200262.* Advance online publication. DOI: 10.1016/j.sasc.2025.200262

Moghaddasi, H., Sajjadi, S., & Kamkarhaghighi, M. (2016). Reasons in Support of Data Security and Data Security Management as Two Independent Concepts: A New Model. *The Open Medical Informatics Journal, 10*, 4–10. PMID: 27857823

Necochea-Chamorro, J., Asalde, C., Nuñez, M., & del Rosario Vasquez Valencia, Y. (2024). Systematic Literature Review: Biometric Technology Applied to Educational Institutions. *TEM Journal*, *13*(1), 570–580.

Nweke, L. (2017). Using the CIA and AAA Models to Explain Cybersecurity Activities. *PM World Journal, VI*(XII), https://pmworldlibrary.net/wp-content/uploads/2017/05/171126-Nweke-Using-CIA-and-AAA-Models-to-explain-Cybersecurity.pdf

Pangrazio, L. (2024). Data Harms: The Evidence Against Education Data. *Postdigital Science and Education*, *6*, 1049–1054.

Papamitsiou, Z., & Economides, A. (2014). Learning analytics and educational data mining in practice: A systematic literature review of empirical evidence. *Journal of Educational Technology & Society*, *17*(4), 49–64.

Patty, A. (2020, August 6). *Hackers hit university online exam tool*. Retrieved May 2025, from The Sydney Morning Herald: https://www.smh.com.au/national/hackers-hit-university-online-exam-tool-20200806-p55j6h.html

Peng, H., Ma, S., & Spector, J. (2019). Personalized adaptive learning: An emerging pedagogical approach enabled by a smart learning environment. *Smart Learning Environments*, *6*(9), 1–14.

Polonetsky, J., & Jerome, J. (2014, October). *Student data: trust, transparency and the role of consent*. Retrieved March 2025, from Data quality campaign: https://dataqualitycampaign.org/wp-content/uploads/2016/03/FPF_Education_Consent_StudentData_Oct2014.pdf

Rahiman, H., & Kodikal, R. (2024). Revolutionizing education: Artificial intelligence empowered learning in higher education. *Cogent Education*, *11*, 1–24.

Raza, S., Fatima, I., Arif, S., & Muhammad, S. (2024). The Future of Learning: Building Trust and Transparency in AI Education. *Journal of Management Practices Humanities and Social Sciences*, *8*(3), 62–74.

Reidenberg, J., & Schaub, F. (2018). Achieving big data privacy in education. *Theory and Research in Education*, *16*(3), 263–279.

Robertson, L., & Mulrhead, B. (2022). Developing privacy in mainstream of education. *The Open Cybernetics & Systemics Journal*, *18*(7), 118–125.

Standford University. (n.d.). *Stanford Teaching commons*. Retrieved April 2025, from Analyzing the implications of AI for your course: https://teachingcommons.stanford.edu/teaching-guides/artificial-intelligence-teaching-guide/analyzing-implications-ai-your-course

University of California. (n.d.). *AI Governance and Transparency*. Retrieved May 2025, from AI Governance and Transparency: https://ai.universityofcalifornia.edu/governance-transparency/

U.S. Department of Education. (n.d.). *PRogecting Student Privacy*. Retrieved May 2025, from What is FERPRA?: https://studentprivacy.ed.gov/faq/what-ferpa

Veldkamp, B., Schildkamp, K., Keijsers, M., Visscher, A., & de Jong, T. (2021). Big Data Analytics in Education: Big Challenges and Big Opportunities. In Wilmers, A., & Jornitz, S. (Eds.), *International Perspectives on School Settings, Education Policy and Digital Strategies: A Transatlantic Discourse in Education Research* (pp. 266–282). Verlag Barbara Budrich.

Young, J. (2024, July 15). *An Education Chatbot Company Collapsed. Where Did the Student Data Go?* Retrieved May 2025, from EdSurge: https://www.edsurge.com/news/2024-07-15-an-education-chatbot-company-collapsed-where-did-the-student-data-go

Yousufi, A., Naidu, V., Jesrani, K., & Dattana, V. (2022). Tracking Students' Progress using Big Data Analytics to enhance student's Employability: A Review. *SHS Web of Conferences-ICTL 2022*, (p. https://doi.org/). Muscat, Oman.DOI: 10.1051/shsconf/202315607001

Chapter 4
Addressing the Digital Divide:
Ensuring Equal Access to AI Tools

Geraldine Torrisi-Steele
https://orcid.org/0000-0002-6045-4114
Griffith University, Australia

ABSTRACT

This chapter, Addressing the Digital Divide: Ensuring Equal Access to AI Tools, explores the persistent inequalities in access to artificial intelligence technologies across socioeconomic, geographic, and educational contexts. It examines how disparities in digital infrastructure, device availability, and digital literacy can limit equitable participation in the AI-driven future. Through analysis of current policies, case studies, and equity-focused frameworks, the chapter highlights strategies for bridging the divide—particularly in underserved communities. It calls on educators, policymakers, and technology developers to prioritize inclusive design and investment to ensure that the benefits of AI are accessible to all.

INTRODUCTION

The digital divide is a significant barrier to technological progress and equal opportunity in today's digital age. In simplest terms, the digital divide is about 'missing out' on technological tools . The digital divide manifests in different ways, from socio-economic factors to disparities in internet connectivity and device availability through to varying levels of digital literacy (Kitsara, 2022). Socio-economic factors at country, social or individual level mean that technologies or access to them cannot be afforded (Kitsara, 2022). The digital divide exists for those who do not have

DOI: 10.4018/979-8-3373-2397-8.ch004

access to infrastructure and/or technologies. Lack of access to infrastructure can be due to geographic location (urban versus rural). The difference in infrastructure access is commonly due to geographic reasons, particularly with respect to rural and urban areas. The digital divide arising because of living in a rural vs an urban area is so prominent, that it is sometimes referred to as the Rural-Urban divide (Weeks, Spelhaug, Weinstein, & Ferres, 2024). Typically, in highly developed urban centers, individuals often have access to high-speed internet, advanced AI-driven applications, and digital learning platforms. However, in rural and low-income communities, limited broadband infrastructure and a lack of affordable devices restrict access to these technologies. Cities often serve as technology hubs, where universities, research institutions, and businesses drive AI innovation and adoption. In contrast, rural communities frequently lack the infrastructure needed to support AI-based learning, telemedicine, and workforce development programs (Weeks, Spelhaug, Weinstein, & Ferres, 2024). For example, in health domains, AI-powered diagnostic tools, telemedicine, and predictive analytics have improved patient care in urban hospitals and medical centers (Adewole, Akingbola, Adegbesan, Ndu-Esekea, & Olalemi, 2025). However, rural healthcare facilities often lack the necessary broadband connectivity and digital infrastructure to support these advancements. As a result, patients in rural areas may not receive the same level of AI-enhanced medical care as those in urban centers, exacerbating health inequalities.

One of the most significant factors influencing access to AI technologies is socio-economic status. Income disparities determine whether individuals, families (exacerbated in low income countries) can afford the necessary devices, internet services, and software subscriptions required to engage with AI tools (Thomas, et al., 2023) (Khan, Umer, & Faruge, 2024). High-income households typically have access to state-of-the-art technology, including high-speed internet, AI-powered learning platforms, and digital assistants that can enhance educational and professional opportunities. In contrast, low-income families may struggle to afford even basic internet access, let alone AI-enhanced learning tools or workforce training programs that require digital literacy.

In education, socio-economic disparities play a crucial role in determining which students have access to AI-powered learning platforms (Capraro, et al., 2024). Students from well-funded schools often benefit from AI-driven personalized learning systems, automated tutoring programs, and advanced computational tools that enhance their academic experiences. Meanwhile, students in underfunded schools may rely on outdated technology or have limited internet access, preventing them from fully engaging with AI-based educational resources. This discrepancy perpetuates existing inequalities, as students from wealthier backgrounds are better prepared for AI-integrated workplaces and higher education opportunities.

The impact of socio-economic status of individuals or countries on AI access extends beyond education. In employment, high-income professionals often work in industries that integrate AI technologies, providing them with tools for data analysis, automation, and decision-making support. Conversely, low-income workers are more likely to be employed in sectors that are at risk of automation, where AI replaces rather than enhances human labor. Without access to AI-driven upskilling programs, these workers face challenges in transitioning to AI-related job opportunities, widening the socio-economic divide.

Unfortunately, while the discourse around AI centers on how AI could revolutionize human undertakings, it is important to remember, that yet, this isn't quite a global phenomenon. Many regions around the world, particularly in developing countries and remote areas, lack the broadband infrastructure and the reliable high-speed internet that is needed to support many AI technologies, and furthermore, across the globe in socio-economic disparities among individuals and groups of individuals are an enduring issue.

However, having access to infrastructure or having the finances to afford technologies does not mean that the digital divide isn't present.

People may lack the knowledge and skills (literacy) to access or use the technology in an empowering way (Kitsara, 2022) (Wang, Boerman, Kroon, Möller, & de Vreese, 2024) The digital divide has existed for as long as digital technologies have. The significance of the digital divide for individuals or groups of individuals becomes more pronounced as the permeation of technologies into everyday life increases. Often, the digital divide means that certain individuals or groups are not able to effectively carry out necessary daily activities that are required in society. For example, there is an increasing number of business organizations that no longer take cash and require the ability to effectively use internet applications for digital payments. A companion concept to the digital divide is digital equity. "Digital equity denotes that all individuals and communities have equitable access to the information technology required to participate in digital life and can fully capitalize on this technology for their individual and community gain and benefits" (Turin, et al., 2022, p. 1). As AI becomes increasingly integrated into various aspects of society, the disparities caused by the digital divide can either be addressed through inclusive AI policies or exacerbated if access to AI tools remains limited to privileged groups or even if the physical access to AI tools is present, a lack of digital literacy inhibits the use of the tools and excludes people full participation in society (Lyons, Kass-Hanna, Zuchetti, & Cobo, 2020). With AI-powered systems, many individuals, especially in underserved populations, lack the training and skills necessary to navigate these systems, limiting their ability to benefit from emerging technological advancements.

In the present chapter, the author's explore the critically important concept of the digital divide in the context of AI. They highlight the significance of the digital divide in pivotal domains of education and healthcare and provide guidance on fruitful directions for addressing the digital divide.

AI AND THE DIGITAL DIVIDE

The rapid permeation of AI into most dimensions of human activity has brought renewed emphasis to the issue of the digital divide. Interestingly, researchers recognize AI as the proverbial 'double edged sword'. That is, AI technologies have the potential to narrow the digital divide, but AI technologies also have the potential to significantly deepen the digital divide (Božić, 2023). The emphasis on AI and the digital divide arises because compared with other digital technologies, AI is one of the most sophisticated and it is potentially one of the most disruptive and transformative technologies to date. Hence, the impact of 'missing out' on AI technologies and their benefits, is greater than ever.

The growing array of AI technologies enable the integration of AI into a myriad of other technologies in a cross-section of industries. Because of this AI is a "textbook case in industry [and social] disruption" (Luttrell, Wallace, McCollough, & Lee, 2020, p. 470). AI plays a transformative role in various sectors, offering solutions that can improve efficiency, decision-making, and problem-solving. AI is transforming medical practice and is having impact on the healthcare system (Bajwa, Munir, Nori, & Williams, 2021; Silcox, et al., 2024). For example, AI-powered diagnostic tools help detect diseases earlier and recommend personalized treatment plans

business operations, automating administrative tasks, optimizing supply chains, and enhancing customer interactions (Bruno, 2024). Additionally, in government and social services (Kulal, Rahiman, Suvama, Abhishek, & Dinesh, 2024), AI has the potential to improve resource allocation, detect fraud, and streamline public service delivery.

AI and the Digital Divide in Education

In education, AI-driven adaptive learning platforms tailor content to individual students' needs, ensuring that learners receive personalized instruction, as most agree, AI is revolutionizing learning and teaching, paving the way for truly student-centered education (Farooq, Malik, & Syed, 2024; Al-Zahrani & Alasmari, 2024; Wang, et al., 2024).

Despite these benefits, AI's increasing influence presents a paradox: while it has the potential to bridge gaps in access to education, healthcare, and economic opportunities, it can also deepen existing inequalities if access to AI tools is not equitably distributed. The digital divide means that those without access to AI-powered technologies may miss out on educational advancements, economic opportunities, and improved healthcare outcomes. If AI-based services become standard in these fields but remain inaccessible to marginalized communities, the gap between privileged and underserved populations will widen.

In education, the intersection of AI and the digital divide is pronounced. Digital classrooms, which leverage AI to facilitate remote learning and interactive instruction, have become an essential part of modern education, especially in the wake of the COVID-19 pandemic. AI-powered tools enable teachers to create virtual learning environments, automate administrative tasks, and provide students with data-driven insights into their progress. However, the shift to digital classrooms has also highlighted the disparities in technology access. While students in well-equipped schools can participate in AI-enhanced online learning, those in underprivileged areas often lack access to reliable internet, appropriate devices, and digital literacy skills. This inequality prevents them from fully engaging in remote learning, further widening the educational divide.

AI-driven learning platforms, such as intelligent tutoring systems and adaptive learning tools, provide students with customized educational experiences based on their performance and needs. These tools have the potential to revolutionize learning by offering personalized feedback, identifying areas of difficulty, and adapting content to each student's pace (Rahiman & Kodikal, Cogent Education). AI-powered systems not only enhance efficiency but also promote student engagement and self-directed learning. However, the benefits of AI-enhanced education are not universally accessible. The lack of reliable internet access, insufficient funding for AI-powered resources, and limited teacher training in digital tools further exacerbate these disparities.

Additionally, AI-based assessments and learning analytics, which provide educators with data-driven insights into student progress, are predominantly used in technologically advanced institutions. Without equal access to these tools, students in underserved communities may continue to rely on outdated educational models that do not fully leverage AI's potential to improve learning outcomes. Addressing these disparities requires systemic efforts to provide schools with the necessary technology, training, and infrastructure to ensure equitable access to AI-enhanced education.

Furthermore, students are more likely to attend schools equipped with AI-enhanced learning platforms, smart classrooms, and STEM-focused curricula that incorporate AI applications. Rural schools, on the other hand, may struggle with outdated textbooks, limited internet connectivity, and a lack of trained educators who can integrate AI into teaching. This disparity puts rural students at a disadvantage, reducing their exposure to AI tools and limiting their ability to develop digital skills that are crucial for future employment.

In educational institutions, limited internet access prevents students from engaging with AI-powered learning tools that require cloud-based processing and real-time data analysis. Schools with inadequate bandwidth may experience slow or unreliable connections, making it difficult for students and teachers to access AI-driven resources. Similarly, AI-powered virtual labs, coding platforms, and online simulations are inaccessible to students without high-speed internet, restricting their ability to gain hands-on experience with emerging technologies.

Furthermore, elite universities with strong funding often invest in AI research, offer specialized courses in machine learning and artificial intelligence, and provide students with access to cutting-edge AI tools. In contrast, students at smaller or underfunded colleges may have fewer opportunities to engage with AI technologies, limiting their exposure to critical AI-related skills. This gap extends to research opportunities, where students at well-funded institutions are more likely to participate in AI-driven projects and collaborations with industry leaders.

Schools and universities play a key role in preparing students for an AI-driven future, but not all educational institutions have the resources to integrate AI into their curricula. The divide between well-funded and underfunded schools is stark, with students in wealthier institutions having access to AI-powered learning platforms, coding courses, and advanced STEM programs, while those in lower-income schools face limited exposure to these opportunities.

Teacher preparedness is another critical factor related to AI access (Fundi, Sanusi, Oyelere, & Ayere, 2024; Ayanwale, Sanusi, Adelana, Aruleba, & Oyelere, 2022). Educators in resource-rich schools often receive professional development training on how to incorporate AI into their teaching methods, allowing them to use AI-driven assessments, adaptive learning systems, and data analytics to enhance instruction. In contrast, teachers in underfunded schools may lack access to AI training programs, making it difficult for them to effectively integrate AI into their curriculum. Without adequate training, educators may struggle to introduce students to AI concepts, leaving them unprepared for the increasing role of AI in higher education and the workforce.

As AI becomes an integral part of education and the workforce, students from marginalized backgrounds may find themselves at a disadvantage when competing for jobs that require digital proficiency and AI literacy (Thomson, Pickard-Jones,

Baines, & Otermans, 2024). The lack of exposure to AI technologies limits their ability to develop critical 21st-century skills, further perpetuating educational and economic inequalities (Thomson, Pickard-Jones, Baines, & Otermans, 2024).

In addition to academic consequences, unequal access to AI tools can contribute to lower confidence and motivation among students in underfunded schools. When students see their peers in wealthier districts benefiting from AI-enhanced learning experiences, they may feel left behind or less capable. This disparity can lead to disengagement, higher dropout rates, and reduced aspirations for higher education. Addressing these issues requires targeted efforts to ensure that all students, regardless of their socio-economic status, have access to AI-driven educational opportunities.

Case studies of schools and communities affected by the digital divide provide insight into the real-world impact of unequal AI access in education. In the United States, many rural schools face significant challenges in integrating AI-driven learning platforms due to limited broadband infrastructure. For example, in Mississippi, a study found that students in rural districts often struggle with inadequate internet access (Mader, 2014), making it difficult to use AI-enhanced digital learning tools. Teachers in these areas report that slow or unreliable connectivity prevents students from participating in online assessments, accessing interactive lessons, or utilizing AI-powered tutoring systems. As a result, students in rural schools miss out on the advantages of AI-driven personalized learning, widening the achievement gap between them and their urban counterparts.

Similarly, in low-income urban areas, the lack of funding for AI technology has hindered its adoption in classrooms. The disparity in AI access not only affects academic performance but also reduces students' exposure to STEM-related careers, limiting their future job prospects in AI-driven industries (Thomson, Pickard-Jones, Baines, & Otermans, 2024).

Globally, the digital divide in AI access is even more pronounced. In developing countries, limited infrastructure, high costs, and inadequate teacher training prevent the widespread adoption of AI-driven educational tools. A case study in rural India found that while AI-powered language learning platforms could significantly improve literacy rates, access to these technologies remains out of reach for many students due to the lack of affordable internet and digital devices. Similarly, in parts of Africa, AI-enhanced educational initiatives have shown promise, but challenges related to electricity shortages, network connectivity, and a shortage of trained educators continue to hinder progress.

AI and the Digital Divide in Healthcare

Healthcare is another critical area where AI and the digital divide intersect. AI-powered medical applications, including predictive analytics, diagnostic tools, and telemedicine platforms, are transforming healthcare delivery by improving patient outcomes and streamlining medical procedures. AI can detect patterns in medical data, helping doctors diagnose conditions earlier and develop personalized treatment plans. Telemedicine, which has gained popularity in recent years, allows patients to consult with healthcare providers remotely, reducing the burden on hospitals and making healthcare more accessible.

However, access to AI-driven healthcare solutions is not equally distributed (Badr, Motulsky, & Denis, 2024; Bhoyar, Vagha, Mishra, Agrawal, & Kambala, 2024). In rural and underserved areas, inadequate healthcare infrastructure and limited internet connectivity prevent residents from benefiting from telemedicine and AI-powered diagnostics. Additionally, many patients in these regions lack the digital literacy required to use AI-driven healthcare applications effectively. If AI-powered healthcare tools become the norm in urban centers while remaining unavailable to marginalized populations, health disparities will continue to grow, leading to unequal healthcare outcomes. To bridge this gap, governments and healthcare providers must invest in expanding broadband access, training healthcare professionals in AI applications, and ensuring that AI-driven healthcare solutions are designed with inclusivity in mind.

Beyond education and healthcare, the digital divide also affects economic and workforce opportunities. AI is driving automation and reshaping industries, creating new job roles that require digital proficiency and particularly AI literacy (Celik, 2023). Companies are increasingly using AI-powered tools for recruitment, workforce management, and training. While these advancements offer opportunities for workers to gain new skills and improve productivity, individuals without access to AI tools or digital literacy training may struggle to compete in the evolving job market. If underserved communities are not provided with the resources to develop AI-related skills, they risk being left behind in an economy that increasingly values technological proficiency.

The digital divide in AI access also has implications for governance and civic engagement. Governments worldwide are leveraging AI for various functions, including automating administrative processes, predicting public policy outcomes, and enhancing cybersecurity. AI is also being used to combat misinformation, monitor environmental changes, and manage public resources more effectively. However, if AI-driven governance tools are only accessible to digitally connected populations, certain communities may be excluded from important decision-making processes.

The healthcare sector is subject to the geographic divide (Delamater, Messina, Shortridge, & Grady, 2012) and subsequently subject to disparities in AI access across different geographical locations, predominantly urban and rural areas. AI-powered diagnostic tools, telemedicine, and predictive analytics have improved patient care in urban hospitals and medical centers. However, rural healthcare facilities often lack the necessary broadband connectivity and digital infrastructure to support these advancements. As a result, patients in rural areas may not receive the same level of AI-enhanced medical care as those in urban centers, exacerbating health inequalities., AI-powered diagnostic tools rely on large datasets and cloud computing, requiring strong internet connectivity to function effectively. Medical facilities in regions with poor infrastructure may not be able to utilize AI for early disease detection, treatment recommendations, or patient monitoring, leading to disparities in healthcare outcomes. Additionally, businesses in underdeveloped areas may struggle to implement AI-driven automation and data analysis, limiting economic growth and innovation.

ADDRESSING THE DISPARITIES

Addressing these disparities requires a multi-pronged approach that includes policy reforms (Keskin & Vermeulen, 2024), infrastructure investment (Adams, 2024), educational initiatives, and corporate responsibility (Elliott, et al., 2021). Governments must prioritize expanding digital infrastructure in underserved areas, ensuring that all communities have access to high-speed internet and AI-driven learning tools (Elliott, et al., 2021).

Public-private partnerships can also play a significant role in closing the digital divide (Prasad, et al., 2024) (Sharma, 2024) (Younus & Zaenurl, 2024) Technology companies can invest in initiatives that provide free or low-cost AI education resources, donate AI-enabled devices to schools, and support digital literacy programs in underserved communities. AI developers must also prioritize designing inclusive technologies that are accessible to diverse populations, ensuring that AI tools do not reinforce existing inequalities.

Ultimately, bridging the AI digital divide requires a collaborative effort between governments, educators, businesses, and communities. By addressing socio-economic, geographic, infrastructure, and educational barriers, society can ensure that AI technologies benefit everyone, rather than exacerbating existing inequalities. As AI continues to shape the future, ensuring equitable access to AI tools will be critical in creating a more inclusive and technologically empowered world.

Efforts to bridge the AI digital divide in education require a multi-pronged approach (Shams, Zowghi, & Bano, 2025). As Zowghi and Bano (2024) inclusion in AI is based on 5 pillars, "humans, data, process, system, and governance". Hence inclusion in AI and bridging the digital divide is a collaborative and holistic approach. Governments and policymakers must prioritize investment in digital infrastructure to ensure that all students have access to reliable internet and modern devices. Schools should implement AI literacy programs that train teachers and students to effectively use AI-driven learning platforms. Public-private partnerships can play a crucial role in providing funding, technological support, and affordable AI-powered educational tools to underserved communities.

Additionally, AI scientists, developers and designers must prioritize inclusivity (Hond, van Buchem, & Hernandez-Boussard, 2022) when designing educational technologies (as well as technologies in other domains). AI-driven platforms should be optimized for low-bandwidth environments, ensuring that students in regions with limited internet access can still benefit from personalized learning experiences. Open-source AI educational tools and initiatives that provide free or subsidized access to AI-powered learning resources can help level the playing field for students from disadvantaged backgrounds.

Community-based initiatives can also contribute to reducing AI access disparities. The Good Things Foundation (https://goodthingsaustralia.org/) initiative in Australia is an excellent example of people, across different sectors, working together to close the digital divide. The Good Things Foundation focuses on four priority areas to close the digital divide: "1. Essential digital skills programs for priority groups including women re-entering the workforce, people with disability, CALD communities and First Nations people. 2. Adoption of telehealth and digital health initiatives through extending nationally coordinated community-based education programs 3. Digital media literacy for vulnerable adults to reduce online harms and assist communities to find reliable information. 4. Affordable internet access and devices for all Australians to maximize participation in the digital economy." (Good Things Foundation Australia, 2022). Public libraries, non-profit organizations, and local community centers can serve as hubs for AI learning, providing students with access to AI-powered educational tools, workshops, and training programs. By creating spaces where students can engage with AI technologies, these initiatives can help bridge the gap between privileged and underserved learners.

Ultimately, ensuring equitable access to AI-powered learning platforms, personalized education tools, and digital classrooms is essential for creating a more inclusive and fair education system. The need for policy and action in this domain cannot be understated, as Stephens and Loble (Loble & Stephens, 2024) strongly point out in the University of Sydney's (Australia) report entitled "Securing Digital Equity in Australian Education" . AI has the potential to revolutionize learning, but its benefits must be accessible to all students, regardless of their socio-economic background or geographic location. By addressing the digital divide through policy reforms, infrastructure investments, and community-driven efforts, we can work towards an educational system where AI enhances learning opportunities for every student. As AI continues to shape the future of education, bridging the gap in AI access will be crucial in ensuring that all learners have the tools they need to succeed in an increasingly AI-driven world.

ENSURING EQUAL ACCESS TO AI TOOLS IN EDUCATION

Ensuring equitable access to artificial intelligence (AI) tools in education requires a collaborative effort among governments, non-profit organizations, and the private sector. As AI continues to reshape education by providing personalized learning experiences, adaptive assessments, and intelligent tutoring systems, it is crucial that all students, regardless of their socio-economic background or geographic location, have access to these transformative technologies. Policies are imperative as are initiatives aimed at bridging the digital divide (chan, 2023). Policies and initiatives must focus on expanding digital infrastructure, funding AI-powered learning tools, and providing training for educators to integrate AI effectively into classrooms. By developing targeted strategies, stakeholders can ensure that AI-enhanced education reaches students in low-income and rural communities, empowering them with the skills needed to thrive in an AI-driven world.

One of the most effective ways to address disparities in AI access is through policies and initiatives that prioritize digital inclusion. Governments play a critical role in setting regulations and allocating resources to expand access to AI-powered learning tools. National and regional policies aimed at improving internet connectivity, providing affordable digital devices, and integrating AI into school curricula can help bridge the digital divide. For instance, initiatives such as the U.S. Federal Communications Commission's (FCC) E-Rate Program (https://www.fcc.gov/general/e-rate-schools-libraries-usf-program) have been instrumental in expanding broadband access to schools and libraries in underserved areas. Similarly, programs like the European Union's Digital Education Action Plan (https://education.ec.europa.eu/focus-topics/digital-education/action-plan) aim to enhance digital literacy (including responsible use of AI) and promote the use of digital learning technologies in schools across member states.

Governments can also implement funding programs that subsidize AI-powered educational tools for low-income schools. Providing grants to schools to purchase AI-driven learning platforms, adaptive learning software, and intelligent tutoring systems ensures that students in disadvantaged communities have access to the same technological resources as their peers in wealthier districts. Additionally, government-backed research initiatives can focus on developing open-source AI education tools, reducing the financial burden on schools while promoting inclusive learning.

Non-profit organizations play a vital role in addressing the digital divide by advocating for equitable technology access and developing community-driven solutions. Many non-profits partner with schools, governments, and technology companies to provide students in low-income and rural areas with access to AI-enhanced education. Organizations such as One Laptop per Child (OLPC) (https://laptop.org/) and Code.org (https://code.org/) have launched initiatives to equip students with digital devices and AI literacy skills. By focusing on early exposure to AI concepts and programming, these initiatives help bridge the technological gap and prepare students for future careers in AI-driven industries.

Non-profits also provide training programs for educators, ensuring that they are equipped to integrate AI tools into their teaching methods. Organizations such as ISTE (International Society for Technology in Education) (https://iste.org/aia) offer professional development programs that teach educators how to use AI-powered assessments, adaptive learning platforms, and data-driven insights to enhance instruction. By empowering teachers with the necessary skills, these initiatives help maximize the impact of AI technologies in the classroom:

"ISTE+ASCD empowers educators worldwide to safely and responsibly use AI in learning. As the largest provider of AI professional development, ISTE+ASCD brings educators together to enhance learning and prepare students to become the next generation of AI designers and problem-solvers. Join us in exploring the ways AI tools can support Transformational Learning Experiences while addressing the ethical considerations of using this powerful new technology for learning." (ISTE, n.d., p. para 1)

The private sector also plays a significant role in expanding AI access in education. Technology companies and ed-tech startups have the resources and expertise to develop AI-driven learning tools that cater to diverse student populations. Many corporations, such as Google, Microsoft, and IBM, have launched initiatives focused on AI education and digital inclusion. For example, Google's AI for Education program provides free AI-powered learning resources, while Microsoft's AI for Accessibility initiative aims to develop inclusive AI tools for students with disabilities.

Public-private partnerships have been particularly effective in addressing AI access disparities. By collaborating with governments and non-profits, technology companies can distribute AI-powered learning platforms to underserved schools, offer teacher training workshops, and develop infrastructure solutions for communities with limited internet access. Corporate social responsibility (CSR) programs further support AI education by funding research on ethical AI implementation in schools and promoting diversity in AI-related fields.

Ensuring that AI tools are integrated into classrooms in a way that benefits all students requires thoughtful implementation strategies. One approach is to prioritize AI-driven learning platforms that are optimized for low-bandwidth environments, ensuring that students in rural and low-income areas can access digital resources despite internet limitations. Developers should focus on creating lightweight AI applications that can function offline or with minimal connectivity, allowing students with limited access to broadband to engage with AI-powered learning experiences.

Another strategy is to develop scalable AI solutions that are cost-effective and adaptable to different educational contexts. Schools with limited budgets should prioritize open-source AI educational tools, which provide free or low-cost alternatives to proprietary AI platforms. Governments and non-profits can support these efforts by funding the development of AI-driven learning resources that are tailored to the needs of disadvantaged communities.

In addition to infrastructure and affordability, equity in AI education requires targeted outreach programs to ensure that students from all backgrounds can participate in AI-driven learning. Schools should implement AI literacy programs that introduce students to the fundamentals of AI, including machine learning, data ethics, and algorithmic decision-making. These programs should be designed with inclusivity in mind, incorporating diverse perspectives and examples that resonate with students from various socio-economic backgrounds.

Training and supporting educators is essential for successfully integrating AI tools into diverse educational settings. Many teachers may be unfamiliar with AI technologies and require professional development to effectively use AI-powered tools in their instruction. Schools and districts should invest in AI training programs that provide hands-on experience with AI-driven learning platforms, adaptive assessments, and intelligent tutoring systems.

Teacher training programs should also focus on ethical considerations in AI education, helping educators understand the implications of algorithmic bias, data privacy, and responsible AI usage. Ensuring that teachers are aware of the ethical dimensions of AI allows them to guide students in critical discussions about the role of AI in society, fostering digital literacy and ethical awareness.

Furthermore, teacher support networks can enhance the effectiveness of AI integration in schools. Peer mentoring programs, professional learning communities, and online forums provide educators with opportunities to share best practices, troubleshoot challenges, and collaborate on AI-enhanced lesson plans. By fostering a culture of continuous learning and innovation, these networks help educators stay informed about emerging AI trends and their applications in education.

As AI continues to shape the future of education, it is imperative that policies, initiatives, and training programs are designed to promote inclusivity and accessibility (Fu, Y.; Weng, Z., 2024). By leveraging the collective efforts of governments, non-profits, and the private sector, stakeholders can ensure that AI-driven learning tools are available to all students, regardless of their socio-economic background. Strategies such as expanding digital infrastructure, funding AI education programs, and providing teacher training will be key to closing the digital divide and ensuring that AI's benefits reach the students who need them most.

Ultimately, equitable access to AI tools in education is not just about technology; it is about ensuring that all students can learn and succeed in an AI-driven world (Knox, Wang, & Gallagher, 2019). By addressing barriers to AI access and fostering inclusive educational environments, policymakers, educators, and technology leaders can create a future where AI serves as a tool for empowerment, bridging gaps rather than widening them. As AI becomes increasingly integrated into classrooms, ensuring that no student is left behind will be essential in shaping a more equitable and technologically advanced education system.

AI in Healthcare: Bridging the Divide in Medical Access

Artificial intelligence (AI) is transforming the healthcare industry, offering innovative solutions that improve patient care, enhance diagnostic accuracy, and optimize treatment plans (Olawade, et al., 2024). AI-powered tools are being increasingly adopted in areas such as telemedicine, medical diagnostics, and personalized treatment, enabling healthcare providers to deliver faster, more precise, and efficient care (Kuziemsky, et al., 2019). However, while AI-driven healthcare solutions have the potential to revolutionize medicine, their benefits are not equally accessible to all populations. The digital divide—characterized by disparities in access to technology and digital literacy—prevents many individuals, particularly those in underserved and rural areas, from benefiting from these advancements. Addressing these disparities requires targeted strategies to promote equitable access to AI-driven healthcare solutions, ensuring that all patients, regardless of their socio-economic status or geographic location, can receive high-quality medical care.

AI plays a crucial role in telemedicine, which has become an essential component of modern healthcare, particularly in the wake of the COVID-19 pandemic. Telemedicine platforms leverage AI to facilitate virtual consultations, monitor patient symptoms, and provide remote diagnoses. AI-powered chatbots and virtual assistants help triage patient concerns, guiding them to appropriate healthcare services based on their symptoms. These tools enhance accessibility by allowing patients to consult with healthcare providers without the need for in-person visits, reducing barriers related to distance, mobility, and availability of medical professionals.

Despite its advantages, the effectiveness of AI-driven telemedicine is significantly impacted by the digital divide. Many patients in rural or low-income communities lack the necessary technology—such as high-speed internet, smartphones, or computers—to engage with telemedicine services. Limited digital literacy can also prevent individuals from navigating telehealth platforms effectively, further restricting their access to AI-assisted medical care (Campanozzi, et al., 2023). Additionally, language barriers and the lack of culturally competent AI healthcare applications can make telemedicine less effective for non-English speaking populations, exacerbating healthcare disparities.

Beyond telemedicine, AI-powered diagnostic tools are transforming the way medical conditions are detected and analyzed. Machine learning algorithms can process vast amounts of medical data, identifying patterns and anomalies that may be overlooked by human physicians. AI-driven imaging tools, such as those used in radiology and pathology, assist in detecting diseases such as cancer, cardiovascular conditions, and neurological disorders at earlier stages, improving the chances of successful treatment. Moreover, wearable devices equipped with AI-powered sensors can continuously monitor vital signs, alerting healthcare providers to potential health risks before symptoms become severe. It is important to note here that the nature of the algorithms themselves play a role in ensuring access and inclusivity. Machine learning algorithms draw on vast data sets, but the data sets they draw on can introduce unintended biases towards certain populations. Ensuring participatory and community involvement in the design and development of algorithms is imperative (Chan, Neves, Majeed, & Faisal, 2024).

However, access to these AI diagnostic tools remains uneven. Advanced imaging technologies and AI-powered screening tools are often concentrated in well-funded hospitals and urban healthcare facilities, leaving rural and low-income communities at a disadvantage. Patients in these underserved areas may have to travel long distances to receive AI-assisted diagnostic services, leading to delays in diagnosis and treatment. Additionally, the cost of implementing AI-driven diagnostic tools can be prohibitive for small clinics and community health centers, further limiting access to these life-saving technologies.

Another transformative application of AI in healthcare is personalized treatment planning, where AI algorithms analyze a patient's medical history, genetic information, and lifestyle factors to recommend individualized treatment approaches. Precision medicine, which tailors treatment plans based on a patient's unique characteristics, has the potential to improve patient outcomes and reduce adverse reactions to medications. AI also plays a role in optimizing medication management by predicting how patients will respond to different treatments, ensuring that they receive the most effective therapies.

Despite these advancements, disparities in access to AI-driven personalized medicine persist. Patients from low-income backgrounds may not have the financial resources to undergo genetic testing or access AI-powered predictive analytics that inform personalized treatment plans. Additionally, limited awareness of AI-assisted treatment options among healthcare providers in underserved areas can prevent patients from benefiting from these innovations. Ensuring equitable access to personalized medicine requires policies that support subsidized healthcare programs and initiatives that promote AI literacy among both patients and providers.

Addressing the digital divide in AI-driven healthcare requires comprehensive strategies that focus on expanding access to technology, improving healthcare infrastructure, and increasing digital literacy among marginalized populations. One of the primary challenges in ensuring equitable healthcare access is the lack of reliable internet and digital infrastructure in rural and underserved areas. Many AI-driven healthcare applications rely on high-speed internet to process data, conduct virtual consultations, and provide real-time patient monitoring. Expanding broadband infrastructure in these regions is essential to enabling widespread access to AI-powered medical care.

In addition to improving infrastructure, targeted initiatives must focus on affordability and accessibility. Governments and healthcare organizations can implement programs that provide subsidized or free access to AI-driven healthcare tools for low-income populations. For example, community health centers can be equipped with AI-powered diagnostic tools and telemedicine kiosks, ensuring that patients who lack personal digital devices can still access high-quality medical services. Additionally, offering free or low-cost wearable health monitoring devices to at-risk populations can help detect health issues early, reducing long-term medical costs and improving health outcomes.

Another crucial aspect of bridging the digital divide in AI healthcare is enhancing digital literacy. Many individuals in underserved communities may be unfamiliar with how to use AI-powered healthcare applications or may distrust AI-driven medical decisions. Educational programs designed to improve health technology literacy can help patients and caregivers better understand and utilize AI tools. Community outreach programs, public health campaigns, and digital health workshops can educate individuals about the benefits of AI-driven healthcare while addressing concerns related to data privacy, algorithmic bias, and medical ethics.

Healthcare providers also need training and support to effectively implement AI-driven solutions. Physicians, nurses, and medical staff in community clinics and rural hospitals may not have experience using AI-powered diagnostic tools or telemedicine platforms. Investing in professional development programs that provide healthcare workers with hands-on training in AI applications can ensure that these technologies are used effectively. Additionally, integrating AI literacy into medical education curricula can prepare future healthcare professionals to work with AI-driven tools from the outset of their careers.

Public-private partnerships can play a vital role in expanding access to AI-driven healthcare solutions. Technology companies, healthcare institutions, and non-profit organizations can collaborate to develop inclusive AI applications that prioritize accessibility for diverse populations. For example, AI healthcare tools should be designed with multilingual support, voice recognition capabilities, and culturally sensitive recommendations to accommodate patients from different backgrounds. Additionally, open-source AI healthcare platforms can reduce costs and make innovative medical technologies available to a broader range of healthcare providers.

Government policies and regulatory frameworks must also prioritize ethical AI implementation to prevent biases and ensure equitable healthcare access. AI algorithms used in medical diagnostics and treatment planning should be regularly audited for biases that could disproportionately impact marginalized communities (Chan, Neves, Majeed, & Faisal, 2024). Transparency in AI decision-making processes, combined with strict data privacy protections, is necessary to build trust in AI-driven healthcare solutions. Policymakers must also establish guidelines that require AI healthcare tools to be tested across diverse patient populations to ensure fairness and effectiveness.

Ultimately, the potential of AI in healthcare can only be fully realized if its benefits are accessible to all individuals, regardless of their socio-economic background or geographic location. By addressing the digital divide, investing in infrastructure improvements, affordability initiatives, digital literacy programs, and healthcare provider training, stakeholders can work towards a more inclusive healthcare system. The integration of AI-driven healthcare solutions has the potential to reduce health disparities, improve patient outcomes, and create a more equitable healthcare landscape for future generations.

CORPORATE AND COMMUNITY-BASED SOLUTIONS TO ADDRESS THE DIGITAL DIVIDE

As artificial intelligence (AI) continues to shape industries and redefine the way we interact with technology, ensuring equitable access to AI tools has become a critical issue. Many underserved communities lack the resources, infrastructure, and training necessary to benefit from AI-driven innovations. Addressing this challenge requires a multi-faceted approach that involves corporate social responsibility (CSR) initiatives, community-based efforts, and collaborative partnerships. These efforts aim to bridge the digital divide by providing internet access, digital literacy programs, and AI training opportunities to disadvantaged populations. Several successful case studies demonstrate how these initiatives have positively impacted communities by fostering technological inclusion and empowering individuals with the skills needed to thrive in an AI-driven world.

Corporate social responsibility (CSR) initiatives play a pivotal role in expanding access to AI tools in underserved communities. Many technology companies have recognized the importance of promoting digital equity and have launched programs designed to provide AI education, internet access, and digital training to marginalized populations. Tech giants such as Google, Microsoft, IBM, and Amazon have implemented CSR programs that focus on increasing AI accessibility and fostering technological literacy.

One notable initiative is Google's AI for Social Good (https://ai.google/advancing-ai/social-impact/), which funds projects that leverage AI to address global challenges, including education and healthcare access for underserved populations. Google has partnered with non-profits, academic institutions, and community organizations to develop AI-powered solutions that improve access to essential services. For example, Google.org has provided grants to organizations that create AI-driven tools for personalized learning, enabling students in low-income areas to receive tailored educational support.

Similarly, Microsoft's AI for Accessibility (https://www.microsoft.com/en-us/accessibility/innovation) program is dedicated to designing AI-driven technologies that support individuals with disabilities. This initiative funds projects that develop AI-powered assistive tools, such as speech-to-text applications, real-time captioning services, and predictive text solutions, ensuring that individuals with disabilities can fully engage with digital technologies. Microsoft has also collaborated with schools and community centers to provide digital literacy training for students and educators in underprivileged communities.

IBM has contributed to bridging the AI accessibility gap through its IBM SkillsBuild (https://skillsbuild.org/) program, which offers free AI and technology training courses to students, job seekers, and professionals looking to expand their digital skills. The initiative focuses on equipping learners with AI literacy and technical skills, preparing them for careers in AI and related fields. By partnering with non-profits, IBM has ensured that disadvantaged groups, including women, minorities, and refugees, have access to high-quality AI education and training resources.

One approach to bridging the digital divide is expanding broadband access to remote and underserved areas. Community-led initiatives such as Detroit's Equitable Internet Initiative (EII) (https://detroitcommunitytech.org/eii) have successfully provided affordable high-speed internet to residents who previously lacked connectivity. The EII trains local "digital stewards" to install and maintain broadband networks in low-income neighborhoods, ensuring that community members have reliable internet access to engage with AI-driven learning platforms and online job opportunities.

In addition to internet access, community organizations have launched digital literacy programs that equip individuals with the skills needed to navigate AI technologies. The National Digital Inclusion Alliance (NDIA) (https://www.digitalinclusion.org/) has spearheaded efforts to promote digital equity through training workshops, resource distribution, and advocacy programs. NDIA collaborates with libraries, schools, and community centers to provide hands-on training in AI fundamentals, coding, and data analytics, empowering individuals to participate in the AI-driven workforce.

Another example of a successful community-led initiative is AI4ALL (https://ai-4-all.org/), a non-profit organization dedicated to increasing diversity in AI education. AI4ALL partners with universities to offer free AI training programs to high school students from underrepresented backgrounds. These programs provide students with mentorship, hands-on AI project experience, and exposure to career opportunities in technology fields. By targeting students from low-income communities, AI4ALL aims to create a more inclusive AI workforce and reduce barriers to entry in the field.

Case studies of successful community-driven initiatives highlight the transformative impact of bridging the AI digital divide. One notable success story is Kenya's Digital Learning Program (Ndaka & D'Agostino, 2024), Through a collaboration between the Kenyan government, private sector partners, and international non-profits, this initiative has distributed tablets to schools with limited digital resources. By enabling students to access adaptive learning content, the program has improved literacy rates and math proficiency among children in remote regions.

Another example is Raspberry Pi Foundation's AI Education Outreach (https://www.raspberrypi.org/teach/ai-education), which provides low-cost computing devices and AI education kits to schools and community centers worldwide. This initiative enables students in developing countries to experiment with AI technology, build machine learning models, and gain hands-on experience with AI-driven applications. Through workshops and training sessions, students learn how AI can be used for problem-solving and innovation, preparing them for future careers in technology.

In the United States, Chicago's Smart Communities Program (https://www.smartchicagocollaborative.org/work/broadband-technology-opportunities-program/smart-communities/) has successfully implemented digital training and workforce development initiatives for low-income residents. This program, funded through public-private partnerships, offers AI certification courses, digital literacy workshops, and mentorship programs for job seekers interested in AI-related careers. By collaborating with local businesses, the program has connected graduates with employment opportunities in AI-driven industries, helping to break cycles of poverty and unemployment.

Ensuring equitable access to AI tools requires continued investment in infrastructure, education, and workforce development. Governments, businesses, and community organizations must work together to expand digital inclusion efforts and create pathways for individuals to benefit from AI technologies. Policies that promote affordable broadband, subsidized AI training programs, and school-based AI education curricula are essential in fostering technological equity.

AI has the potential to empower individuals and communities, but only if access to AI tools is equitably distributed. Corporate social responsibility initiatives, community-led digital inclusion programs, and targeted AI education efforts have demonstrated success in reducing barriers to AI access. However, sustained efforts are needed to continue expanding these initiatives and ensuring that marginalized populations are not left behind in the AI revolution. By fostering inclusive AI policies and programs, society can harness the power of AI to drive innovation, improve education and employment opportunities, and create a more equitable technological future.

THE FUTURE OF AI AND THE DIGITAL DIVIDE

Even a brief search of literature, both academic and grey literature shows that the discussion around AI and the digital divide is robust. Additionally, as is highlighted in the preceding sections, there are some promising actions been taken at government and community level to make positive inroads into addressing the digital divide. The digital divide is a complex, multi-layered problem with no obvious simple solution. However, as artificial intelligence (AI) continues to evolve, its impact on society will become increasingly profound, shaping industries, economies, and daily life and it is imperative to seek to remediate existing inequalities as well as to plan and design for a digital future that brings positive benefits for all . AI has the potential to bridge gaps in education, healthcare, and economic opportunities, offering innovative solutions that empower individuals and communities. However, without deliberate and inclusive policies, AI could also exacerbate existing inequalities, widening the digital divide between those who have access to cutting-edge technologies and those who do not. This section explores predictions for the future of AI and its role in addressing—or deepening—the digital divide, the impact of emerging technologies like 5G in improving AI accessibility, and the ethical implications of AI-driven solutions in a world where access to technology remains uneven.

In the coming years, AI is expected to play an even greater role in everyday life, influencing everything from personalized education and precision medicine to automated decision-making in businesses and governance. As AI-powered solutions become more sophisticated and widespread, there is potential for these tools to democratize access to knowledge, healthcare, and economic resources. AI-driven translation tools, for example, could make educational content available to non-English speakers, breaking down language barriers. Similarly, AI-enhanced telemedicine can bring expert healthcare advice to remote and underserved areas, reducing disparities in medical care.

However, the risk of AI widening the digital divide is also significant. If access to AI-driven technologies is limited to wealthier individuals, urban centers, or well-funded institutions, those who are already disadvantaged may fall even further behind. AI-powered hiring platforms, for instance, could inadvertently favor applicants from privileged backgrounds if training datasets are not diverse and inclusive. Additionally, as AI automates more jobs, individuals without access to digital upskilling programs may struggle to compete in the evolving labor market, further entrenching socio-economic disparities.

Despite advancements, technological infrastructures such as those provided by 5G connectivity alone will not be sufficient to close the digital divide. Ethical considerations must be addressed to ensure that AI-driven solutions promote inclusivity rather than deepen existing disparities. One of the primary ethical concerns is algorithmic bias, where AI systems trained on incomplete or unrepresentative data may produce biased outcomes that disadvantage marginalized groups. If AI tools are not carefully designed with inclusivity in mind, they could reinforce systemic inequalities in areas such as hiring, credit scoring, and law enforcement.

Data privacy and security is an ever-present issue which is exacerbated as the sophistication of technologies grows and technologies penetrate more deeply into nearly all aspects of human activity. AI-powered platforms rely on vast amounts of personal data to deliver personalized experiences, raising concerns about how this information is collected, stored, and used. In underserved communities where digital literacy may be lower, individuals might not fully understand the implications of data sharing or lack the ability to opt out of intrusive data collection practices. Ensuring strong data protection regulations and transparent AI governance is essential to safeguarding user rights and building trust in AI technologies.

The commercialization of AI raises concerns about the affordability of AI-driven services. If access to AI-powered education, healthcare, and job training is restricted to paid platforms, economically disadvantaged individuals may be left behind. Governments, technology companies, and international organizations must work together to develop open-source AI tools, subsidized programs, and public-private partnerships that prioritize accessibility for all, rather than just those who can afford premium services.

To prevent AI from exacerbating the digital divide, stakeholders must adopt a multi-faceted approach that includes policy interventions, infrastructure investment, ethical AI development, and public awareness initiatives. Governments can implement regulations that require AI systems to be transparent, fair, and inclusive, ensuring that marginalized communities are not disproportionately affected by AI-driven decision-making. Education and workforce development programs must integrate AI literacy training to equip individuals with the skills needed to navigate an AI-driven world.

Ultimately, AI's impact on the digital divide will depend on how it is designed, deployed, and governed. If AI technologies are developed with inclusivity at their core, they have the potential to empower individuals, bridge socio-economic gaps, and create more equitable opportunities for all. However, without proactive measures, AI could further entrench inequalities, reinforcing barriers that prevent underserved populations from accessing the benefits of technological progress. The challenge ahead is to ensure that AI serves as a tool for inclusion and empowerment, rather than a force that deepens existing divides.

The preceding discussions highlight issues and show the complex nature of the issue of the digital divide in the age of AI. The preceding discussion also brings to the fore some important aspects of policy and action for bridging the digital divide. In summary, policy recommendations key points made include:

Need for AI Equity in Society

- *AI integration in sectors like education and healthcare risks widening the digital divide.*
- *Policymakers must ensure equitable access to AI tools for marginalized communities.*

Policy Frameworks for Inclusive AI Deployment

- *Develop national AI strategies focused on accessibility and inclusivity.*
- *Design AI solutions with diverse socio-economic, linguistic, and ability backgrounds in mind.*
- *Mandate bias audits to prevent reinforcing inequalities in AI systems.*

Improving Digital Infrastructure

- *Expand broadband infrastructure and affordable internet access, especially in rural and low-income areas.*
- *Offer subsidies and community internet access programs.*
- *Encourage ISPs to provide affordable connectivity plans.*

Role of Public-Private Partnerships

- *Collaborate with tech companies, non-profits, and academia for scalable solutions.*
- *Support infrastructure projects, AI education tools, and digital literacy programs.*
- *Examples include Google's AI for Social Good and Microsoft's AI for Accessibility.*

Non-Profit Contributions

- *Organizations like NDIA and AI4ALL advocate for inclusive AI policies and diverse education opportunities.*

Education and Workforce Development

- *Integrate AI literacy in school curricula and provide teacher training.*
- *Establish workforce upskilling programs and AI training centers.*
- *Offer tax incentives for companies investing in employee AI training.*

Ethical AI Development

- *Require fairness, transparency, and accountability in AI systems.*
- *Implement bias detection and ensure explainable AI.*
- *Support open-source AI tools and data privacy protections.* (OpenAI, 2025)

CONCLUSION

The authors' have, in the present chapter, provided comprehensive exploration of the digital divide, outlining the systemic barriers that contribute to unequal access to AI-driven solutions. By examining disparities in internet connectivity, digital literacy, and technology affordability, the chapter will highlight the real-world consequences of AI inaccessibility, including limited educational opportunities, poorer healthcare outcomes, and reduced workforce competitiveness.

The digital divide has existed for as long as digital technologies have been present in human society. It remains significant challenge. Let's not forget that underpinning the digital divide is the much older dimension of the human condition – a long history of exclusion of certain groups and of disparities in opportunities among populations.

The rapid pace of technological development and accelerated rate of technological permeation in society brings growing urgency to issue of the digital divide. AI is perhaps the most powerful and transformative technology humans have developed to date. But, to use the adage ‘with great power comes great responsibility’, the responsibility for ensuring positive transformation of society, for the benefit of all, through AI technologies belongs to all stakeholders of the AI endeavor. The lynchpin in the discussion around the potential of AI is inclusivity, transparency, and ethics - and this can only happen through genuinely collective, collaborative and participatory approaches in the decision making that occurs throughout the design, development, implementation of AI, in any domain of application.

Ultimately, by addressing the digital divide, we can build a more inclusive and equitable future where AI technologies serve as a tool for empowerment rather than exclusion. Ensuring that AI’s benefits reach all communities will not only enhance innovation but also contribute to a more just and globally connected society.

REFERENCES

Adams, Y. (2024, September 1). *The Digital Divide in the Age of AI: Addressing the Growing Gap in Access and Education.* Retrieved from The Creative Collective: https://thecreativecollective.com.au/the-digital-divide-in-the-age-of-ai/

Adewole, O., Akingbola, A., Adegbesan, A., Ndu-Esekea, T., & Olalemi, S. (2025). Leveraging artificial intelligence to improve health insurance access and address disparities in rural Africa. *Journal of Medicine, Surgery, and Public Health, 5*, 100172. DOI: 10.1016/j.glmedi.2024.100172

Al-Zahrani, A., & Alasmari, T. (2024). Exploring the impact of artificial intelligence on higher education: The dynamics of ethical, social, and educational implications. *Humanities & Social Sciences Communications, 11*(912), 1–12.

Ayanwale, M., Sanusi, I., Adelana, O., Aruleba, K., & Oyelere, S. (2022). Teachers' readiness and intention to teach artificial intelligence in schools. *Computers and Education: Artificial Intelligence, 3*, 100099. DOI: 10.1016/j.caeai.2022.100099

Badr, J., Motulsky, A., & Denis, J. (2024). Digital health technologies and inequalities: A scoping review of potential impacts and policy recommendations. *Health Policy (Amsterdam), 146*, 105122. DOI: 10.1016/j.healthpol.2024.105122 PMID: 38986333

Bajwa, J., Munir, U., Nori, A., & Williams, B. (2021). Artificial intelligence in healthcare: Transforming the practice of medicine. *Future Healthcare Journal, 8*(2), e188–e194. PMID: 34286183

Bhoyar, A., Vagha, S., Mishra, V., Agrawal, M., & Kambala, S. (2024). Addressing the Digital Divide in Health Education: A Systematic Review. *Cureus, 16*(9), e70048. DOI: 10.7759/cureus.70048 PMID: 39449933

Božić, V. (2023). Artificial Intelligence as the Reason and the Solution of Digital Divide. *Language and Education Technology.*, *3*(2), 96–109.

Bruno, Z. (2024). The Impact of Artificial Intelligence on Business Operations. *Global Journal of Management and Business Research: D Accounting and Auditing, 24*(1), 1-8.

Campanozzi, L., Gibelli, F., Bailo, P., Nittari, G., Sirignano, A., & Ricci, G. (2023). The role of digital literacy in achieving health equity in the third millennium society: A literature review. *Frontiers in Public Health, 11*(1109323). Advance online publication. DOI: 10.3389/fpubh.2023.1109323 PMID: 36891330

Capraro, V., Lentsch, A., Acemoglu, D., Akgun, S., Akhmedova, A., & Bilancini, E. Longoni. (2024). The impact of generative artificial intelligence on socioeconomic inequalities and policy making. *PNAS Nexus*, *3*(6), 1–18. PMID: 38864006

Celik, I. (2023). Exploring the Determinants of Artificial Intelligence (AI) Literacy: Digital Divide, Computational Thinking, Cognitive Absorption. *Telematics and Informatics*, *83*, 102026. DOI: 10.1016/j.tele.2023.102026

Chan, S., Neves, A., Majeed, A., & Faisal, A. (2024). Bridging the equity gap towards inclusive artificial intelligence in healthcare diagnostics. *BMJ*(384:q490), doi: .DOI: 10.1136/bmj.q490

chan, C. (2023). A comprehensive AI policy education framework for university teaching and learning. *International Journal of Educational Technology in Higher Education, 38*(20), https://doi.org/.DOI: 10.1186/s41239-023-00408-3

Delamater, P., Messina, J., Shortridge, A., & Grady, S. (2012). Measuring geographic access to health care: Raster and network-based methods. *International Journal of Health Geographics*, *11*(15). Advance online publication. DOI: 10.1186/1476-072X-11-15 PMID: 22587023

Elliott, K., & Price, R. shaw, P., Spiliotopoulos, T., Ng, M., Coopamootoo, K., & van Moorsel, A. (2021). Towards an Equitable Digital Society: Artificial Intelligence (AI) and Corporate Digital Responsibility (CDR). *Society, 58*, 79–188. https://doi-org.libraryproxy.griffith.edu.au/10.1007/s12115-021-00594-8

Farooq, U., Malik, S., & Syed, A. (2024, March). Revolutionizing higher education: The transformative impact of artificial intelligence on teaching, learning and career preparation. *ShodhKosh:Journal of Visual and Performing Arts*, *5*(3), 789–794.

Fu, Y., & Weng, Z. (2024). Navigating the ethical terrain of AI in education: A systematic review on framing responsible human-centered AI practices. *Computers and Education: Artificial Intelligence*, *7*, 100306. DOI: 10.1016/j.caeai.2024.100306

Fundi, M., Sanusi, I., Oyelere, S., & Ayere, M. (2024). Advancing AI education: Assessing Kenyan in-service teachers' preparedness for integrating artificial intelligence in competence-based curriculum. *Computers in Human Behavior Reports*, *14*, 100412. DOI: 10.1016/j.chbr.2024.100412

Good Things Foundation Australia. (2022, January). *Good Things Foundation Australia Pre-Budget Submission 2022/23.* Retrieved April 2025, from Australian Government Treasury: https://treasury.gov.au/sites/default/files/2022-03/258735_good_things_foundation_australia.pdf

Hond, A., van Buchem, M., & Hernandez-Boussard, T. (2022). Picture a data scientist: A call to action for increasing diversity, equity, and inclusion in the age of AI. *Journal of the American Medical Informatics Association : JAMIA*, *29*(12), 2178–2181. PMID: 36048021

ISTE. (n.d.). *Artificial Intelligence in Education*. Retrieved March 2025, from ISTE: https://iste.org/ai

Keskin, T., & Vermeulen, F. (2024). *Overcoming the Digital Divide in the Era of Artificial Intelligence. Proceedings of the 57th Hawaii International Conference on System Sciences | 2024*. University of Hawaii., https://aisel.aisnet.org/hicss-57/

Khan, M., Umer, H., & Faruge, F. (2024). Artificial intelligence for low income countries. *Humanities & Social Sciences Communications*, *1422*. Advance online publication. DOI: 10.1057/s41599-024-03947-w

Kitsara, I. (2022). Artificial Intelligence and the digital divide: From an innovation perspective. In A. Bounfour, *Platforms and Artificial Intelligence The Next Generation of Competences* (pp. 245–265). Springer.

Knox, J., Wang, Y., & Gallagher, M. (2019). AI, inclusion, and 'everyone learning everything. *Artificial Intelligence and Inclusive Education*, https://www.pure.ed.ac.uk/ws/portalfiles/portal/80705572/KnoxJ_2019_AIIE_Introduction_AI_Inclusion_and_Everyone_Learning_Everything.pdf

Kulal, A., Rahiman, H., Suvama, H., Abhishek, N., & Dinesh, S. (2024). Enhancing public service delivery efficiency: Exploring the impact of AI. *Journal of Open Innovation*, *10*(3), 100329. DOI: 10.1016/j.joitmc.2024.100329

Kuziemsky, C., Maeder, A., John, O., Gogia, S., Basu, A., Meher, S., & Ito, M. (2019). Role of Artificial Intelligence within the Telehealth Domain. *Yearbook of Medical Informatics*, *28*(1), 35–40. PMID: 31022750

Loble, L., & Stephens, K. (2024). Retrieved April 2025, from Securing digital equity in Australian education: https://apo.org.au/node/329196

Luttrell, R., Wallace, A., McCollough, C., & Lee, J. (2020). The Digital Divide: Addressing Artificial Intelligence in Communication Education. *Journalism & Mass Communication Educator*, *75*(4), 470–482.

Lyons, A., Kass-Hanna, J., Zuchetti, A., & Cobo, C. (2020). *Leaving No One Behind: Measuring the Multidimensionality of Digital Literacy in the Age of AI and other Transformative Technologies*. Retrieved April 2025, from Global Solutions - The world Policy Forum: https://www.global-solutions-initiative.org/wp-content/uploads/2025/03/GS19_PolicyBrief_7.5.pdf

Mader, J. (2014, July 14). *In Mississippi Schools, Access to Technology Lacking, Uneven*. Retrieved April 2025, from Washington Monthly: https://washingtonmonthly.com/2014/07/14/in-mississippi-schools-access-to-technology-lacking-uneven/

Ndaka, C., & D'Agostino, T. (2024). *Digital Learning in Kenya: Towards equitable and inclusive digital learning*. University of Notre Dame, Pulte Insitute for Global Development -. *Policy Brief*.

Olawade, D., David-Olawade, A., Wada, O., Asaolu, A., Adereni, T., & Ling, J. (2024). Artificial intelligence in healthcare delivery: Prospects and pitfalls. *Journal of Medicine, Surgery, and Public Health*, *3*, 100108. DOI: 10.1016/j.glmedi.2024.100108

Open, A. I. (2025, April 22). *Response generated by ChatGPT to a request for a summary of a user-written text*. Retrieved from https://chat.openai.com/

Prasad, K., Karanam, S., Gamesh, D., Liyakat, K., Talasila, V., & Purushotham, P. (2024). AI in public-private partnership for IT infrastructure development. *The Journal of High Technology Management Research*, *35*(1), 100496. DOI: 10.1016/j.hitech.2024.100496

Rahiman, H., & Kodikal, R. (Cogent Education). Revolutionizing education: Artificial intelligence empowered learning in higher education. *11*, 1-24.

Shams, R., Zowghi, D., & Bano, M. (2025). AI and the quest for diversity and inclusion: A systematic literature review. *AI and Ethics*, *5*, 411–438.

Sharma, R. (2024, November 19). *How public-private partnerships can ensure ethical, sustainable and inclusive AI development*. Retrieved April 2025, from World Economic Forum: https://www.weforum.org/stories/2024/11/public-private-partnerships-ensure-ethical-sustainable-inclusive-ai-development/

Silcox, C., Zimlichmann, E., Huber, K., Rowen, N., Saunders, R., McClellan, M., & Bates, D. (2024). The potential for artificial intelligence to transform healthcare: Perspectives from international health leaders. *npj. Digital Medicine*, *7*(88), 1–3. PMID: 38594477

Thomas, J., McCosker, A., Parkinson, S., Hegarty, K., Featherstone, D., Kennedy, J., . . . Ganley, L. (2023). Measuring Australia's Digital Divide: Australian Digital Inclusion Index: 2023. Melbourne: ARC Centre of Excellence for Automated Decision-Making and Society: RMIT.

Thomson, S., Pickard-Jones, B., Baines, S., & Otermans, P. (2024). The impact of AI on education and careers: What do students think? *Frontiers in Artificial Intelligence*, *7*. Advance online publication. DOI: 10.3389/frai.2024.1457299 PMID: 39610850

Turin, T., Subroto, S., Raihan, M., Kock, K., Wiles, R., Ruttan, E., & Chowdhury, N. (2022). Identifying Challenges, Enabling Practices, and Reviewing Existing Policies Regarding Digital Equity and Digital Divide Toward Smart and Healthy Cities: Protocol for an Integrative Review. *JMIR Research Protocols*, *11*(12), 1–12. PMID: 36480264

Wang, C., Boerman, S., Kroon, A., Möller, J., & de Vreese, C. (2024). The artificial intelligence divide: Who is the most vulnerable? *New Media & Society*, *00*(0), 1–23.

Wang, S., Wang, F., Zhu, Z., Wang, J., Tran, T., & Zhao, D. (2024). Artificial intelligence in education: A systematic literature review. *Expert Systems with Applications*, *252*, 1–19.

Weeks, W., Spelhaug, J., Weinstein, J., & Ferres, J. (2024). Bridging the rural-urban divide: An implementation plan for leveraging technology and artificial intelligence to improve health and economic outcomes in rural America. *The Journal of Rural Health*, *40*(4), 762–765. PMID: 38520683

Younus, M., & Zaenurl, M. (2024). Public-Private Collaboration to Overcome the Digital Divide in Digital Transformation of Government. *Digital Zone Information & Communication Technology Journal*, *15*(1), 28–40.

Zowghi, D., & Bano, M. (2024). AI for all: Diversity and Inclusion in AI. *AI and Ethics*, *4*, 873–876.

Chapter 5
Co-Creating With AI: Augmenting, Enhancing, and Elevating Instructional Design

Angela Elkordy
https://orcid.org/0000-0001-5154-9368
National Louis University, USA

Michael McVey
https://orcid.org/0000-0002-7290-4944
Eastern Michigan University, USA

ABSTRACT

This chapter explores the integration of generative artificial intelligence (genAI) into instructional design in higher education, addressing both its potential and its challenges. It introduces the SCALE Framework (Substitution, Co-Construction, Automation, Learning, Evolution), a progressive model for faculty AI literacy that builds on established educational theories like Bloom's Revised Taxonomy, UDL, and TPACK, as well as emergent AI-specific and sociocultural perspectives. The framework positions AI as a collaborative partner, guiding educators through stages from automating routine tasks (Substitution, Automation) to fostering more complex collaboration (Co-Construction), personalized learning (Learning), and transformative instructional redesign (Evolution). This chapter emphasizes the importance of iterative, practice-based approaches to AI integration, ensuring that technology augments rather than replaces human expertise, ultimately enhancing cognitive performance and supporting more personalized, impactful learning experiences.

DOI: 10.4018/979-8-3373-2397-8.ch005

INTRODUCTION

Instructional design is the process of planning experiences for learners to gain new knowledge (Briggs et al., 1991). Designing impactful instruction involves the intersection of several knowledge sets and skills, including domain or content knowledge (what), teaching and instructional strategies (how), and both formative and summative assessment strategies to determine next instructional steps as well as the extent of learning. In higher education contexts, the role of faculty members has typically been subject matter experts or SMEs ("smees") - in other words, sharing expertise in the content or subject matter. Instructional designers' work requires expertise in learning design, instructional technologies such as learning management and authoring systems, and project management. While the skill sets complement one another, there's not always a great deal of overlap.

Accelerated by the need for primarily online learning environments in the COVID-19 pandemic, the role of instructional designers has shifted to primarily create online and hybrid courses, in addition to asynchronous experiences. The shift to online learning in higher education has resulted in corresponding shifts in skill sets and responsibilities in learning design. Although faculty members have always maintained an essential role as SMEs, faculty are increasingly called upon to design classes for online delivery or to convert course content and practices to a hybrid or fully online context. Despite faculty playing a pivotal yet often informal role in instructional design, they often lack formal training in curriculum development, course modification, and instructional (re)design (Khalil & Elkhider, 2016). Many faculty members independently navigate these responsibilities without dedicated instructional support or access to professional training in learning sciences, technology integration, or instructional design best practices. Also, faculty often collaborate with institutional instructional designers with expertise in learning design.

Collaborations of professionals with different priorities, knowledge sets, expectations, and schedules can be challenging, particularly without clear guidelines or understanding about roles (Rubin, 2009). "Many faculty members have not been exposed to instructional design practices and theories; therefore, collaborating with an instructional designer (ID) in the creation of an online course can be a daunting prospect" (Halupa, 2019, p. 55). Some of the unique skills of an instructional designer include possessing an understanding both intuitively and conceptually of how people learn, understanding innovative instructional strategies, and writing effective instructions (Halupa, 2019).

As higher education institutions increasingly expect faculty to actively develop new courses, revise existing curricula, and integrate emerging technologies, new advances in generative AI present unique opportunities to augment, enhance, and elevate these instructional design processes. The COVID-19 pandemic necessitated a widespread adoption of many digital tools by faculty, but according to Crompton and Burke (2023), the rapid adoption of technology left "little time to explore the possibilities of AI to transform learning, and AI may have been used to replicate past teaching practices, without considering new strategies previously inconceivable with the affordances of AI" (p. 9).

Figure 1. Motivations for faculty engagement in course design

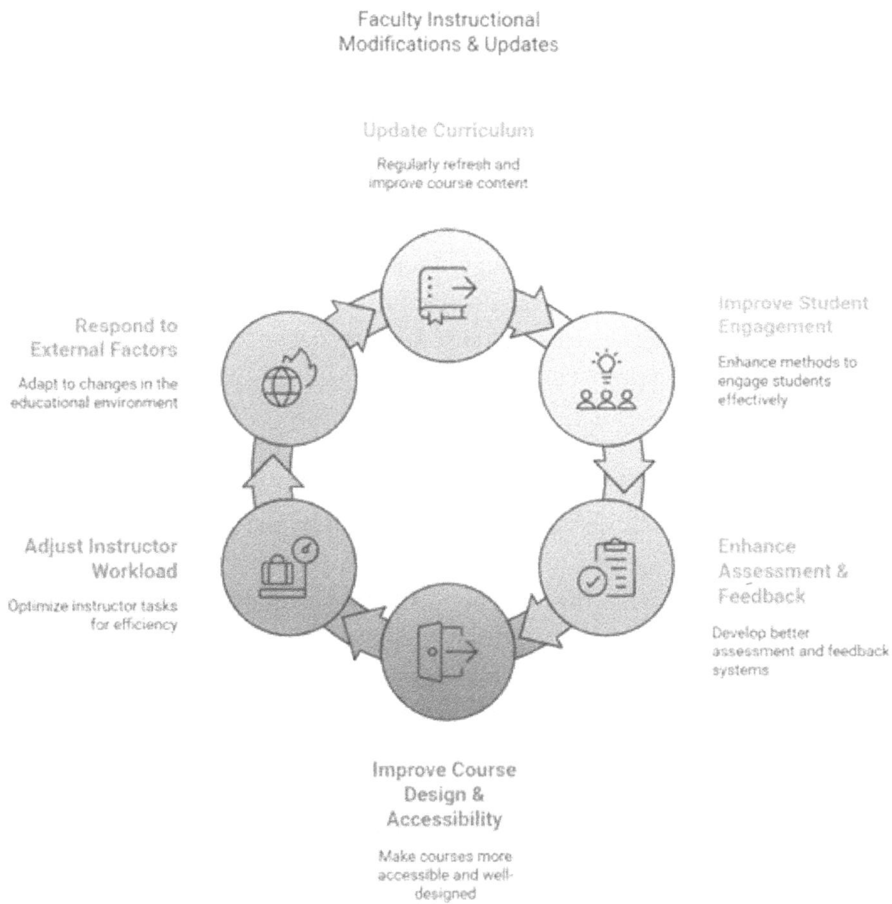

Figure 1 illustrates the primary motivations for driving faculty engagement in course design for online and blended learning. Factors that obligate or motivate faculty decisions to invest time and effort in developing and enhancing curricula and course materials may be intrinsic to the course design or external, such as program or standards alignment. These motivations often include updating curricula, improving student learning outcomes, aligning course content with emerging digital tools, addressing diverse learner needs, increasing efficiency, responding to external demands for integration of standards or pedagogies or improving aspects of the course such as student engagement or accessibility and ease of use. In light of increased use of AI in educational contexts, there is an urgent need for faculty to engage in ongoing learning and adaptation.

The affordances of AI can be leveraged to augment, enhance, and elevate instructional design in higher education, but are unlikely to replace instructional faculty or designers due to the highly personalized and humanistic nature of designing learning experiences (Gibson, 2023).

This chapter introduces the SCALE Framework (Substitution, Co-Construction, Automation, Learner, Evolution), which provides faculty with a clear roadmap for AI integration in instructional design. By aligning the SCALE Framework with existing instructional design models such as SAMR, this chapter offers practical strategies for faculty to enhance their teaching effectiveness, streamline course development, and improve student engagement through AI-driven tools and methodologies. Additionally, this chapter will examine the evolving role of AI in faculty-led instructional design, demonstrating the need for structured AI literacy and integration frameworks through examples and a practical case study.

INTEGRATING AI INTO INSTRUCTIONAL DESIGN: FRAMEWORKS AND FACULTY-LED COURSE DEVELOPMENT

Artificial intelligence has been integrated into education for decades. The recent surge of interest and use may stem from the emergence of generative AI technologies. Artificial intelligence is revolutionizing modern education through advanced algorithms and are now perceived as integral to learning management and training systems with the potential for delivering such features as tutoring applications which use the power of Large Language Models (LLMs) to deliver personalized learning support and intelligent feedback across a wide range of subject areas such as mathematics, programming, and language learning (Wang et al., 2024).

Instructional design relies on established frameworks that guide the development, modification, and refinement of curriculum and learning experiences. Despite the widespread use of instructional design models in faculty-instructional designer collaborations (Halupa, 2019), as noted earlier most faculty members are not formally trained in these frameworks and must navigate course design independently. AI presents an opportunity to support and augment instructional design efforts by streamlining key tasks such as generating learning objectives aligned with competency-based learning models, developing assessment strategies that measure student learning progress and outcomes, or aligning content with accreditation standards and discipline-specific frameworks. It can also enhance the instructional process by creating learning activities that promote engagement and active learning, for example, by curating open educational resources (OER), and by developing supplemental materials that enrich course content and introduce innovative instructional methods. Faculty can also use AI to elevate their instructional design and strategies by leveraging the unique affordances that will be discussed in depth later in this chapter.

Figure 2. Ways GenAI can enhance course design

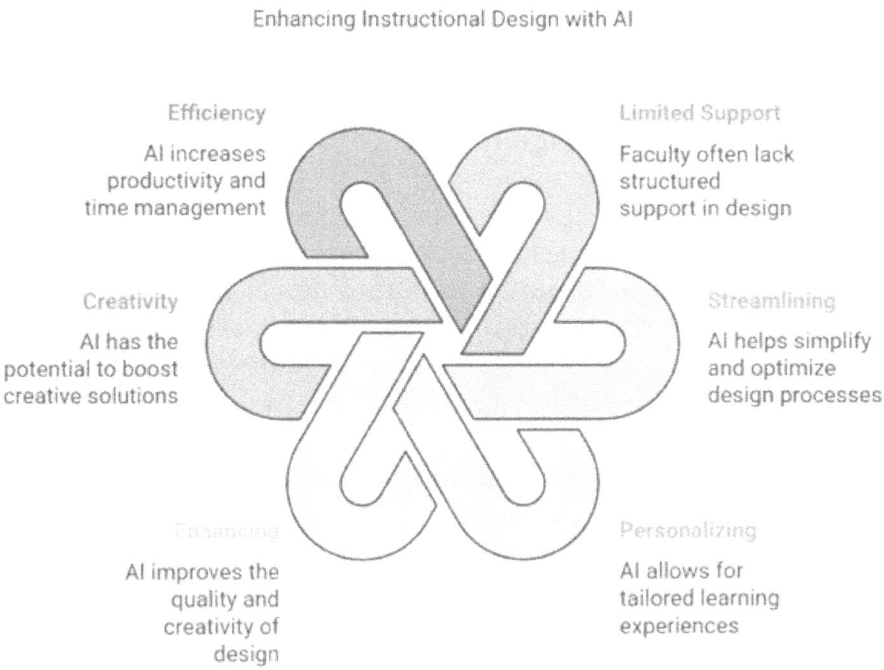

Generative AI can be leveraged to enhance various aspects of course design providing essential support to faculty. AI tools can be used to streamline course preparation, personalize learning experiences, optimize content delivery and learning experiences, and support innovative instructional strategies (Figure 2). Furthermore, this representation serves as a guide for faculty seeking to incorporate AI into their teaching practices, aligning with the SCALE framework's emphasis on innovation and co-construction.

Examples of this partnership abound through AI-driven applications that will help designers and instructors organize research, summarizing and analyzing large numbers of scholarly article, leveling lexical levels if needed, translating digital materials, designing graphics, creating slide presentations, finding trends in anecdotal materials, and even generating images from natural language prompts. These listed affordances are by no means an exhaustive list.

By integrating AI into these processes, faculty can reduce the time spent on administrative instructional design tasks and focus on pedagogy, student engagement, and meaningful learning experiences. As a Co-Constructor guided by human-led review and domain expertise, AI tools can assist with curriculum development at multiple stages, from course planning to ongoing adaptation based on learner progress. As we continue our discussion, we focus on the design of impactful learning experiences through Learner Experience Design.

Learner Experience Design (LXD)

This chapter focuses on skills related to Learner Experience Design (LXD), which prioritizes creating engaging and memorable learning experiences by addressing the learner's needs and preferences. A thematic review of book chapters on LXD (Schmidt & Huang, 2022) identified four key design principles: human-centric, theoretically grounded, informed by User Experience Design (UXD), and socio-culturally sensitive. Understanding these principles is essential:

Human-Centric: LXD emphasizes the importance of focusing on *learners* rather than general users, highlighting the human and learner-centric approach to designing learning experiences.

Theoretically-Grounded: Scholarly literature often adopts a theoretical lens to describe LXD, with learning theory dominating many studies and guiding practical applications, alongside frameworks from various fields.

Informed by UXD Methods: Design thinking processes and techniques are recurring themes in LXD literature, transcending basic usability. One researcher suggested viewing design thinking and usability in LXD as a 'mindset' (Stefaniak and Sentz, 2020).

Socio-culturally Sensitive: LXD inherently focuses on learners across diverse settings, recognizing that learners have unique characteristics and experiences, thus valuing subjective and differentiating learner qualities.

Throughout this chapter, we will focus on the ways AI can be used to augment, enhance, and elevate the basic elements of Learner Experience Design through the development of partnership of sorts between the instructional designer and the selected generative AI tools.

Supporting Evidence and Theoretical Frameworks

The integration of AI into instructional design is supported by established educational theories and models that guide faculty in structuring effective learning experiences. As this chapter examines the development of a progressive framework for AI in instructional design, the underlying elements are built upon several frameworks that support how AI can enhance the instructional design process. These established frameworks are outlined briefly below, with a brief examination of some contemporary research that demonstrates their relevance to the development of this model. These theoretical frameworks as well as sociocultural theories and their relationship to AI are outlined in Table 1.

Figure 3. Theoretical and conceptual frameworks of the SCALE framework

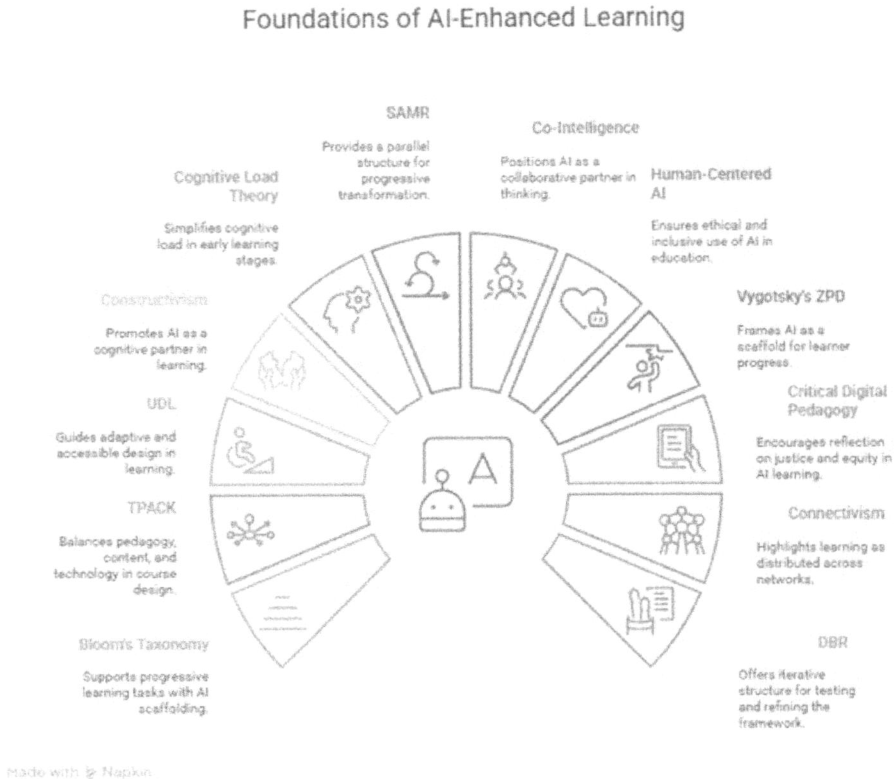

The SCALE framework incorporates foundational theories and frameworks that provide support for integrating AI into instructional design. It includes well-established educational models such as Bloom's Revised Taxonomy, TPACK, UDL, Constructivism, Cognitive Load Theory, and the SAMR model, as well as emerging frameworks like Co-Intelligence and Human-Centered AI. These frameworks provide a theoretical foundation for understanding how AI can enhance teaching and learning by aligning technology, pedagogy, and content knowledge (Figure 3).

Revised Bloom's Taxonomy (Krathwohl, 2002). AI can generate learning objectives, scaffold assessments, and provide adaptive learning experiences that align with cognitive skill development. Applications of this model when learners are engaged with AI-related activities have shown a potential to enhance their critical thinking and metacognitive skills, and potentially acquire a deeper understanding of subject matter (Hui, 2024). This model has proven helpful to many scholars, especially those concerned that redesigns of pedagogical thinking should prioritize critical thinking (Mogavi et al., 2024). Other scholars have even suggested further elaboration of this model by suggesting additional phases such as familiarizing, conceptualizing, inquiring, evaluating, and synthesizing with a goal of improving critical thinking (Yusuf et al., 2024).

TPACK (Technological Pedagogical Content Knowledge) Framework (Koehler et al., 2013). AI enhances the integration of technology with pedagogical strategies, helping faculty effectively align instructional content with AI-driven learning tools. Recent research suggests that instructors may have a better understanding of the pedagogical contributions of AI when they have a deeper technological knowledge, which could allow instructors to better assess the output of AI. Such knowledge is even more valuable to instructors when combined with pedagogical knowledge (Celik, 2023).

Universal Design for Learning (UDL) (CAST, 2017). The UDL framework aims to make learning more inclusive for all learners by proactively planning for diversity, including the range of backgrounds and abilities (Hyatt & Owenz, 2024). AI contributes to inclusive education by offering adaptive pathways, personalized content delivery, and multimodal engagement for diverse learners. One goal of these adaptive pathways is to incorporate flexible and responsive AI tools into the implementation of UDL principles in educational settings. A recent systematic review of AI education found that AI can be grounded in the three core UDL principles (i.e., engagement ("why"), representation ("what"), and action & expression ("how") (Song et al., 2024).

Constructivist Learning Theory (Liu & Matthews, 2005). AI-facilitated peer learning, automated discussion prompts, and adaptive tutoring systems can provide real-time scaffolding. One exploration into current literature on AI in education found that thoughtfully designed and ethically vigilant use of AI in constructivist pedagogy has the potential for more engaging, personalized, and transformative learning (Grubaugh et al., 2023).

Cognitive Load Theory (Sweller, 1994). In brief, cognitive load describes the degree of effort on working memory. AI can assist in the reduction of extraneous cognitive load by automating repetitive instructional tasks and personalizing content delivery. Recent research has found that simplifying complex problems with AI can reduce the distractions of cognitive load (Patac & Patac, 2025). Enhancing the presentation of content in this way can be of great value to the instructional design process.

SAMR Model (Puentedura, 2006). The SAMR model can describe good technology integration, and in the same way, it can demonstrate how AI has the potential to move instructional design thinking beyond substitution and automation toward transformative instructional redesign, modifying and redefining learning experiences. A recent study of secondary teachers demonstrated that the use of AI in their lesson development enabled them to move up to the redefinition of SAMR with ease (Shamir-Inbal et al., 2024).

Table 1. Theoretical foundations and integration with the SCALE framework

Framework / Theory	Role in the SCALE Framework
Bloom's Revised Taxonomy	Supports progressive learning tasks; aligns with AI-assisted scaffolding across all levels.
TPACK	Informs balance of pedagogy, content, and technology in AI-supported course design.
UDL (Universal Design for Learning)	Guides adaptive and accessible design in later stages of the model.
Constructivism	Promotes AI as a cognitive partner in co-constructing understanding and meaning.
Cognitive Load Theory	Supports chunking and simplifying cognitive load in early stages of the model, and cognitive off-loading as a
SAMR	Provides parallel structure to the SCALE Framework's progressive transformation.
Co-Intelligence (Mollick)	Positions AI as a collaborative partner in thinking and creation at the advanced levels of the model.
Human-Centered AI	Ensures AI is used ethically and inclusively especially in personalization and innovation.
Vygotsky's Zone of Proximal Development	Frames AI as a scaffold to support learner progress in their ZPD.
Critical Digital Pedagogy	Encourages reflection on justice, equity, and cultural relevance in AI-enhanced learning.
Connectivism	Highlights learning as distributed across human and AI networks; aligns with autonomy and agency.
Design-Based Research (DBR)	Offers iterative, practice-based structure for testing and refining the SCALE Framework in faculty Professional Development.

AI-Specific and Sociocultural Theories

As noted earlier, the SCALE Framework is grounded in contemporary and foundational learning theories, but it also draws upon emergent perspectives that recognize the complexities of teaching and learning with artificial intelligence. This includes AI-specific theories that reframe AI as a partner in learning, as well as sociocultural and critical frameworks that ensure equity, ethics, and learner agency are preserved in digitally mediated environments.

Co-Intelligence (Mollick, 2024). Co-Intelligence emphasizes AI as a collaborative intelligence that is best used when human users engage with it during reflective, purposeful, and iterative stages in instructional design. AI is thus positioned as a thinking partner, extending human creativity and insight. This theory undergirds the *Co-Construct, Automate & Optimize*, and *Innovate & Evolve* phases of SCALE, where AI is deployed not only for content or task generation, but as a co-creative force in instructional design.

Human-Centered AI (Auernhammer, 2020). Human-Centered AI prioritizes ethical design, transparency, and inclusivity, especially in educational contexts. In SCALE, this theory aligns closely with the *Learn & Adapt* stage, ensuring that the personalization of learning the AI supports does not come at the cost of student privacy, accessibility, or human dignity. It also reinforces the need for faculty to critically evaluate AI tools for bias, equity, and ethical alignment.

Zone of Proximal Development (ZPD) (Vygotsky & Cole, 1978). The ZPD frames learning as most effective when students are supported within a zone that extends just beyond their current independent capabilities. In AI-enhanced learning environments, AI can act as a scaffold, offering hints, resources, and adaptive feedback. The *Learn & Adapt* and *Co-Construct* levels of SCALE reflect this theory by positioning AI as a flexible, just-in-time guide aligned with learner needs.

Critical Digital Pedagogy (Stommel, 2014). Critical digital pedagogy reminds us that AI is not neutral and challenges educators to ask who is empowered or marginalized by technology, and to design instruction that foregrounds equity, justice, and learner voice. This lens supports ongoing reflection at all stages of SCALE, but especially at the *Innovate & Evolve* level, where AI may be used to design culturally responsive assessments, co-author narratives, or bring in underrepresented perspectives.

Connectivism (Siemens, 2005). Connectivism redefines learning in a networked age by recognizing that knowledge is distributed across systems, platforms, and people, including AI agents. Learners must develop the ability to navigate and synthesize across the nodes of these systems. This theory is embedded in all levels of SCALE, but especially the upper levels, where agency, autonomy, and networked reasoning are emphasized.

Design-Based Research (DBR) (Brown, 1992). DBR provides a methodological foundation for SCALE by framing instructional design as iterative, context-responsive, and co-developed with practitioners. The use of SCALE in faculty professional development can follow DBR cycles—testing, evaluating, and improving instructional design tasks involving AI.

By integrating AI with these frameworks, faculty can create more effective, engaging, and personalized learning experiences for students. The SCALE Framework builds on these theoretical foundations to offer a structured approach for faculty to seamlessly incorporate AI into instructional design, ensuring alignment with evidence-based pedagogical strategies.

THE SCALE FRAMEWORK: A PROGRESSIVE MODEL FOR AI IN LEARNING DESIGN

The Infusion of AI into Instructional Design

AI can be used to substitute routine or mundane instructional design tasks, freeing up faculty to focus on more creative aspects of instructional design that require specialized skills and experience. AI has the potential to augment, enhance, or even elevate into a redefinition of some of these tasks and roles. This section of chapter will review the various roles of instructional designers and apply the SCALE Framework through research-grounded examples and as a guide to categorizing the increasingly complex relationship of co-creation with artificial intelligence to illustrate its role in the instructional design processes.

Substitution

At the substitution level, the "S" of the SCALE Framework, straightforward tasks typically performed by an instructional designer can largely be replaced by AI, effectively reducing the more mundane work done by humans and delegating it to an intelligent agent.

Course Syllabi (Substitution). Among the many tasks higher education faculty must perform, often mandated by their department or university, is the production of a course syllabus. Frequently, these syllabi are copied from semester to semester with minor tweaks, such as textbook updates, room allocations, and other similar elements. AI can be highly beneficial in refining a syllabus each year, especially when prompted to include key university requirements or to ensure that nothing essential has been missed or overlooked (Kim & Koo, 2024).

Co-construction with the Instructional Designer. A designer can collaborate with AI as a co-designer to review a list of course references, identifying potential gaps or weaknesses, such as an overabundance of articles over 10 years old. AI can recommend additional articles for the reference list, but the human designer must review and evaluate each recommendation for inclusion.

Discussion Prompts (Substitution). AI can analyze relevant course data and generate discussion prompts, which can be particularly useful for incorporating new articles into a course (Nazari & Saadi, 2024). This capability allows faculty to facilitate engaging and insightful discussions based on the latest research and developments.

***Co-Construction with the Instructional Designer*.** Using AI as a co-designer can be highly valuable, as it allows the designer to refine discussion prompts based on the natural flow of the conversation and insights gathered from previous discussions that may have gone off-topic or required clearer wording. Classroom instructors rely on their accumulated observations to generate discussion prompts that are relevant and seamlessly integrate with naturally occurring classroom discussions.

Research Summaries (Substitution). AI can not only summarize complex research articles but also compare multiple articles to identify consistent commonalities or touchpoints (Glickman & Zhang, 2024). Designers can train AI to highlight central or core concepts from research studies that might be glossed over or overlooked entirely in a summary.

Co-construction with the Instructional Designer. Sometimes, the most important part of an article, as it relates to the course, can be found in the final section, "Areas for future investigation." These areas may serve as hinge points or catalysts for subsequent lessons that the instructor wishes to explore. While AI can effectively summarize an article, the human designer must ensure that the essential heart of the article is being studied.

Co-Construction

At the Co-Construction level, the "C" of the SCALE Framework, the many digital materials that are generated or gathered can be managed effectively by AI. These materials can also include the curation of strategies from traditional multiple-choice test banks and sets of potential message questions to alternative assessment strategies tailored to revised instructional goals.

Course Materials (Co-Construction). There are several excellent tools available for instructors at almost every grade level to maintain a robust and current set of course resources. For example, many instructors use storage systems like Google Drive to develop their repository of digital resources, which often need to be sorted and categorized. AI can effectively handle the storage and sorting aspects of these tasks, making it easier for instructors to manage their resources.

***Co-Construction with the Instructional Designer*.** Curating these resources is a nuanced task that requires a deep understanding of the learners, the scope and sequence of the course, the training of the learner, and the potential for digital overload (Ahmad et al., 2025). It also demands the experience to assess the relative value of each resource. Such higher-order reasoning skills, involving a comprehensive understanding of the entire body of resources, are skills that most instructors are not willing to relinquish at this moment.

Evaluating Student Learning (Co-Construction). AI can effortlessly generate numerous quiz questions (Rezigalla, 2024) and suggest essay response questions tailored to course readings. Additionally, AI can propose alternative assessment methods or inspire new ones (Meehan et al., 2024). Many instructors prefer not to use quizzes, and AI can be utilized to create alternative ways to assess student understanding (Zheng et al., 2024). This multitude of assessment options can be managed by AI.

Co-Construction with the Instructional Designer. Whether teaching online or in a face-to-face classroom, instructors have numerous digital approaches to assessment available to them, requiring careful consideration of which strategies to employ (Barkatsas & McLaughlin, 2021). While AI can generate instructional assessments, it does not possess the nuanced understanding needed to determine which assessments will truly facilitate deeper student understanding.

Automation

At the Automation level, the "A" of the SCALE Framework, many digital tasks can be effectively managed by AI. These tasks include those in which an instructional designer must diligently check for the accuracy of course elements that vary from semester to semester, such as dates and reading lists.

Course Structure and Timeline (Automation). Certain aspects of course planning involve relatively mundane tasks. The instructor has a set number of weeks during the course, along with a set number of class meetings, examinations, assignments, readings, labs, and experiences that need to be accomplished within those parameters. AI can conveniently and quickly provide a rough draft, serving as a time-saver for the instructor.

Co-Construction with the Instructional Designer. An AI-constructed course structure should be considered a rough draft because the instructor needs to account for the development of a set of skills that scaffold one on top of the other throughout the course (Malik et al., 2024). The instructor also needs to be aware of the potential for cognitive overload. If students are given too little time to develop a deep understanding of a concept, it may require additional class time to resolve misunderstandings or reteach key concepts.

Reading Lists (Automation). Although not considered AI tools (Hosseini et al., 2024), powerful search tools like EndNote, Mendeley, and Zotero are capable of conducting systematic literature searches. These tools can adhere to extremely narrow search parameters based on sets of keywords, key phrases, dates of publication, languages of publication, and types of resources. While not necessarily AI, they are precursors to tools in development that might soon provide personalized reading lists based on educators' goals. Beyond searches of strictly scholarly and peer-reviewed research sources, AI can easily tailor a list of bibliographic references based on factors such as readability, date of publication, word length, or genre, and can do so in a variety of languages.

Co-Construction with the Instructional Designer. While we acknowledge that existing AI applications can generate extensive lists of readings on a subject, it is also important to recognize that AIs can sometimes produce hallucinatory responses. These responses can range from simple errors, such as incorrect rendering of a researcher's name or publication dates, to complete fabrication of readings. Without double-checking by the instructional designer, these inaccuracies can lead to a significant waste of time for students attempting to locate the references.

Formative Quizzes (Automation). AI can be utilized to generate formative quizzes that adapt to student responses. Given a learning objective in the course, AI can review student answers to a question and develop quizzes to assess the current state of student understanding of a topic (Diwan et al., 2023). Additionally, AI can generate private notes for the instructor, highlighting trends in student errors that may indicate an unclear understanding of key concepts.

Co-construction With the Instructional Designer. Rather than using AI-generated quizzes solely as formative assessment tools, a best practice would be to inquire about the rationale behind the creation of those questions. This allows the instructional designer to evaluate whether the formative assessment is suitable for the students.

Rubric Creation (Automation). AI can assist in creating grading rubrics to ensure alignment with learning outcomes. Rubric development tools have been commonplace in classrooms for at least two decades and are highly modifiable (Hasselquist & Bertolini, 2018). Despite their modifiability, rubrics are sometimes based on generic submission types such as essays, presentations, and other standard classroom assessment features. Uploading an entire lesson and inviting AI to generate a rubric based on the task is simple. The complicating factors arise when modifying the rubric to determine how many points are assigned for each element and how many elements are evaluated.

Co-Construction with the Instructional Designer. It is up to the instructional designer to determine if the points assigned by AI for each element are reasonable and aligned with the overarching goals of the task. For example, 50 points for a self-introductory paragraph might be excessive compared to the overall point allocation for other assignments throughout the course.

Research Organization (Automation). AI can organize qualitative data for educator research projects. Qualitative data comes in many forms and has the potential to inform and clarify. However, the wide variety of its forms can be enormously challenging. For example, a survey of community members on a particular issue might result in very brief, almost cryptic comments or 500-word opinion pieces. AI can quickly summarize and categorize these data to provide a sense of trends that might inform further research (Jafari, 2024).

Co-Construction with the Instructional Designer. Although AI can summarize large blocks of comments of varying sizes, categorize them, and suggest patterns, it is ultimately the responsibility of the instructional designer to determine if those patterns make sense at a human level (Auernhammer, 2020). Additionally, the designer must decide how to use those patterns in future research.

Learner

At the Learner level, the "L" of the SCALE Framework, you will begin to see AI being put to use to manage many instructional tasks that require an understanding of the unique needs of individual learners. Changing the reading level (lexical set) and complexity of a required reading may not degrade the content but may increase its accessibility to an English Language Learner or a student with specific learning disabilities.

Inclusive Materials (Learner). As AI has become more sophisticated, it can provide detailed accessibility assessments of online and digital materials and even develop those same materials entirely (Palmer & Oswal, 2025). Additionally, many Learning Management Systems have embedded accessibility checkers. However, it is more challenging for AI to detect evidence of bias, which could undermine content quality (Wavre et al., 2024).

Co-Construction with the Instructional Designer. Sometimes, digital resources may harbor unconscious bias from the instructor who designed them. One clear example is when seeking images to illustrate web pages or course pages. There may be a lack of images featuring females or people of color, or the images may be presented in broad caricatures. A sensitive or trained instructional designer can help check for potential bias in digital resources.

Adaptive Feedback (Learner). AI can suggest adaptive feedback on lesson plans created by in-service teachers. Although lesson plans are falling out of favor, many tools, especially those advertised as driven by AI, still help teachers generate lesson plans (Romaniuk & Łukasiewicz-Wieleba, 2024). AI-generated feedback can be tailored to suit an in-service teacher's career stage or if the instructor is creating a lesson plan for a newly constructed course. AI algorithms can enhance the learning process by providing more accurate feedback to students (Rouhiainen, 2019).

Co-Construction with the Instructional Designer. It remains the task of the instructional designer to identify learning gaps and determine the urgency or necessity of modifying the curriculum. The instructional designer must address the needs of the instructor in real time. When using an AI-generated lesson planning tool, the designer should review the lesson based on the principles of sound lesson design.

Instructional Strategies (Learner) AI can recommend alternative instructional strategies based on data trends within the course and program (Chiu, 2024). For example, if students are writing an assignment based on acknowledged standards from an organization such as the International Society for Technology in Education (ISTE), AI could suggest instructional strategies based on standards that previous assignments have insufficiently addressed or were identified as areas of weakness. AI can suggest activities to support strategies such as collaborative learning, increasing opportunities for social engagement, enhancing student retention, interaction and critical thinking (Brooks & Grady, 2022).

Co-Construction with the Instructional Designer. The instructional designer's role is to evaluate AI-generated recommendations and determine if the resulting instructional strategies add value to the course. This evaluation should be based on how the course has been structured up to that point and the designer's experience with the students.

Curriculum Design (Learner). AI can assist in creating tailored curriculum plans with feedback. In K-12 classrooms, many educators aim to differentiate instruction by modifying strategies based on learners' needs. In higher education, differentiation is less common, but AI has the potential to adapt the curriculum based on learners' needs (Karataş et al., 2024). Examples of this adaptation include modifying reading lists or seeking differentiated examples based on students' backgrounds. In a professional development setting, it makes sense to modify the curriculum to be more relevant to the subject area being taught. Relevant examples for a high school English teacher would differ from those for a math or science teacher.

Co-Construction with the Instructional Designer. A deep understanding of the backgrounds and professional development needs of the learners would enable a more nuanced AI prompt. This type of curriculum adaptation is based on the idea that educators engage learners' interests and needs and contextualize the curricular content with the diversity of students (Fernandes et al., 2013). The instructional designer would rely on a deep understanding of the learners' context to make adaptations to the curriculum, such as omitting, extending, replacing, or revising content to create an effective curriculum (Meidl & Meidl, 2011).

Role-Playing Exercises (Learner). AI can generate scenarios for classroom management practice. While it is relatively straightforward to create a role-playing exercise ahead of a class meeting, AI can generate role-playing exercises with specifically tailored prompts based on various parameters, including student age, gender, and language (Hwang et al., 2024). These exercises can be built around timely, culturally responsive issues and tuned to the neighborhood in which the class is located.

Co-Construction with the Instructional Designer. The instructional designer should determine which factors to include based on input from the instructor. Classroom management is a challenging concept for new teachers to master. The designer can modify the experience and collaborate with AI to generate realistic scenarios for students, as well as adjust the types of responses.

Lesson Restructuring (Learner). AI can help modify lesson plans to meet Universal Design for Learning (UDL) standards. Many Learning Management Systems, including major ones like Canvas, can incorporate tools from organizations such as CAST (Center for Applied Special Technology), which perform rigorous reviews of accessibility. AI can also review digital resources to determine whether modifications are needed to adhere to UDL standards (Saborío-Taylor & Rojas-Ramírez, 2024).

Co-Construction with the Instructional Designer. The instructional designer's role is to determine how the end product should look and feel for the learner. For example, deciding if an image is essential to convey meaning in the text or is merely decorative. Working in conjunction with AI, the designer can quickly review digital resources to ensure that alt tags, heading levels, and other features are included to ensure accessibility to the coursework.

Evolution

At the Evolution level, the "E" of the SCALE Framework, AI in tandem with instructional designers can elevate course design to a new level that would not be possible without either AI or the human in the loop. In Puentedura's SAMR framework (2006), the redefinition of learning tasks using technology is at the apex. However, total redefinition of learning assignments should not always be the main goal of co-construction with AI. Instead, AI and instructional designers can collaborate to develop something profoundly impactful in the act of teaching.

Decision Making (Evolution). AI can produce scenarios that challenge and test learners in a fluid and dynamic way. Imagine a textbook chapter that responds to you as a learner, assesses your readiness for the next part of the lesson, modifies the presentation of concepts based on your previous responses, and leads you at a pace suited to your level and instructional goals. For example, AI can simulate real-time school leadership decision-making using dynamic case studies and provide numerous scenarios a school administrator might reasonably need to react to. In a pre-computer exercise for students training to become school administrators, an engaging challenge called "The Superintendent's Inbox" involved students opening and responding to increasingly challenging memos and mail from various district stakeholders. These challenges, usually strung together on a single theme, included cost analysis for a new piece of equipment that had broken down in a school, a complaint from a community member, an expression of concern from a group of teachers forwarded through their union representative, a relevant research article, a not-so-subtle letter of inquiry from a school board member, and a request for a comment from a local news agency. Similarly, an AI chatbot can interact in a conversational style with a human, creating a back-and-forth to train future school administrators (Adams & Thompson, 2025).

Co-Construction with the Instructional Designer. Rather than overwhelm a student with too many unrelated scenarios that might be disconnected from the realities of their local community, a designer could build a customized GPT consisting of documents related to one school district. This customization is important since school districts vary by population size, relative wealth and discretionary spending ability, curriculum, and even facility needs based on unique weather patterns. For example, a district in the North may need to reconsider purchasing snow removal equipment, while a district in the South may need to consider new water pumps in case of flooding. The human designer would be able to stack up those relatable and relevant cases and data sets into the training of the GPT.

Design Thinking Workshops (Evolution). AI can facilitate design thinking workshops with AI-generated personas and scenarios. With precise prompts in a customized GPT, AI can generate realistic scenarios and personas for participants to interact with in a workshop setting (Salminen et al., 2024). In classroom settings, AI can be configured to take an opposing point of view in a debate or, in a design thinking workshop, point out errors and inconsistencies that require students to rethink their approach to a problem.

Co-Construction with the Instructional Designer. With a firm understanding of the course structure, the skill sets of the students, and the demands of the student learning objectives, a designer can be inspired by AI to generate scenarios and find ways to infuse AI into the design thinking process.

Interactive Coaching (Evolution). AI can power real-time interactive coaching by responding to educators' classroom challenges. In the classroom, lessons sometimes fall flat, and instructors are not always sure what caused the lesson to flop. Something that worked perfectly the year before might come apart at the seams the next year. Many studies have demonstrated that reviewing teaching videos can encourage teacher self-reflection toward improvement (Hamel & Viau-Guay, 2019). Similarly, engaging with AI might generate conversations that bring to light some of the root causes of the breakdown in the lesson, which may be a series of factors beyond the instructor's control.

Co-Construction with the Instructional Designer. It is straightforward for AI to generate a series of potential reasons for a lesson's failure, but the human designer is the one who will make the judgment call to determine which scenario is most relevant and needs to be focused on.

Virtual Mentorship (Evolution). AI can create a virtual mentor for in-service teachers, offering guidance and feedback (Bondie, 2024). The induction phase of a teacher's career, the first few years of actual day-to-day classroom experience, can be extraordinarily challenging. This is the period where many teachers give up their ambitions of being educators and move on to something less overwhelming, confusing, frustrating, and exhausting. By customizing a GPT, a teacher or instructional designer can outline their work frustrations, share them with a sympathetic ear, and ask for reasonable suggestions they may have overlooked (Bondie et al., 2023).

Co-construction with the Instructional Designer. Teaching is a very human activity, despite the vast amounts of data it can generate for third-party review. The designer, in collaboration with AI, can work through difficulties in the classes they are helping to co-design and provide grounded feedback to the instructors. In this context, "grounded" refers to feedback that is realistic, common sense, and functional.

ENHANCING AND ELEVATING INSTRUCTIONAL DESIGN BY CO-CONSTRUCTION WITH AN AI PARTNER

Since the rise of multimedia interactivity through classroom computer technology, many interactive curriculum -driven lessons have been created using episodic storytelling. These have taken the form of Adventure Games, or Educational Adventure Games, video games in which the player assumes the role of the protagonist in stories driven by exploration and puzzle-solving. The player, in reality the learner, guides the main character or avatar through scenarios and interacts with people and objects to advance the plot. These games are characterized by a strong focus on storytelling. One early example of this approach to teaching basic neuroscience and microbiology to middle school students used a scenario of a great plague that would affect humankind set 200 years in the future (Miller et al., 2004).

In designing lessons around storytelling, key elements of instructional design come into play at the most basic level requiring a designer to create several key elements: a) the story to narrate, b) the world the protagonist explores, c) the puzzles the player has to solve, d) the learning contents to convey and effective ways to convey them, and e) strategies to assess the player/student performance (D'Apice et al., 2015). These are elements that AI can generate to assist in the development of learning games.

Case Study: Odeum

A US-based educational software company, Odeum, has developed a tool for teaching a variety of curricula in which learners interact with virtual characters in three-dimensional settings and progress through an episodic story structure as they advance through learning objectives.

Odeum is an AI-powered platform for designing immersive, role-playing educational games. Engaging quests, branching dialogues, and interactive assessments provide educators with tools to edit experiences and enhance context-rich learning environments.

The process of developing the lesson structure results from an interaction between instructional designers and sophisticated AI tools on the back end. The structure for building an educational game is outlined below.

Define Learning Objectives

The instructional designer begins by outlining the desired overarching learning objectives, vocabulary, skills, scope and sequence, and key concepts. These learning objectives, regardless of their source, serve as the foundation for the story elements and assessments within the game.

Generation of Story Spines

Odeum's system generates three story-based spines, or core narrative outlines, that interweave the lesson objectives into what is hoped will be an engaging plot for the episodic story. The goal for each storyline is to immerse students in a meaningful context to enhance relevance and motivation.

Creation of Quests and Characters

After the instructional designer selects a storyline, Odeum automatically develops quests, and interactive non-player characters (NPCs), and then places them within a themed environment. At this stage, the instructional designer can customize how the lesson is differentiated. This framework ensures that students learn by doing and practicing skills within an authentic, story-rich setting.

Mapping of Skills and Assessments

Odeum identifies, using artificial intelligence, the key skills and in-game assessments needed for each objective. The platform differentiates quests to offer additional support for students who, based on their responses, might need help meeting the objectives.

Game Creation and Editing

Once the quests and characters are generated, the instructor can preview and edit the game as needed. This editing task can be as simple as checking which dialogue appears for the player or as complex as modifying specific questions in a task. Dialogue can be customized at this point, and difficulty levels can be adjusted to fit the needs of an individual student or an entire class.

Assessments and Tracking

Odeum automatically generates an assessment page, allowing educators to monitor student progress and skill mastery in real time. These data help instructional designers adapt instruction, improve the lesson experience, and ensure that each learner reaches the defined objectives.

This process exemplifies an AI-infused, dynamic, adaptive assessment system where the human instructional designer retains significant control over the AI output. The overall learner experience design (LXD) follows a framework that adheres to user-centric approaches, personalization, differentiation, adaptive pathways, and engagement. According to a lead programmer from Odeum, a sense of flow is maintained by ensuring that the challenge level closely matches the learner's capability (I. Natzmer, personal communication, March 12, 2025).

Figure 4. An advertising image and caption for "Hua Mulan" from Odeum

Travel back in time to help defend Hua Mulan against evil time bandits all while learning Chinese in this story-driven, role-playing, open 3D world episodic adventure.

SELF-ASSESSMENT TOOL: EVALUATING FACULTY AI LITERACY

As with all emerging technologies, it sometimes takes a while for even the most interested faculty to adopt the technology. An added issue with artificial intelligence as a tool for instructional design is that there are multiple starting points. One might know how to generate a prompt for AI but may not know how to refine that prompt for better accuracy. Additionally, without guidance in the form of professional development, new users may feel frustrated at the lack of accuracy or completeness of AI output. For that reason, a strategic training program should be provided to all faculty who intend to use artificial intelligence as a co-constructor in the pursuit of instructional design.

This chapter recommends that the sequence of skills, as evidenced by competence with the activity, should follow the SCALE Framework and consider its progression from basic competence to developing expertise. Doing tasks at the Substitution level might be considered the work of new users at best. Tasks completed at the Evolution level should involve multiple steps, a keen review of the output, and multiple revisions before moving the evolution tasks to the classroom. Even then, the best practitioners of instructional design will use whatever final output of the AI as a stepping stone toward future revision. Good AI use is always iterative and intentional.

This chapter also recommends that faculty training be evaluated against the SCALE Framework and consider setting a goal or competency at each level. Table 2 reflects the overarching goals for each level. The institution responsible for professional development in this area may consider awarding badges for each level.

Table 2. Overarching goal of each level of the SCALE framework

SCALE Level	Goal
Substitution	Practitioner is able to use AI to replace tasks usually done manually
Co-Construction	Practitioner is able to use AI to either generate a digital resource or maintain a set of resources
Automation	Practitioner is able to train AI to do a specific task of value to the instructional design process
Learning	Practitioner is able AI to modify the output based on the differentiated needs of the learners in their classroom
Evolution	Practitioner is able to use AI in an iterative way to accomplish a complicated task under the oversight of an instructional designer

An actionable step would be to have an experienced instructional designer create this five-level training program and evaluate participants' success in achieving each level.

IMPLICATIONS FOR PRACTICE

Figure 5. GenAI integration for course design

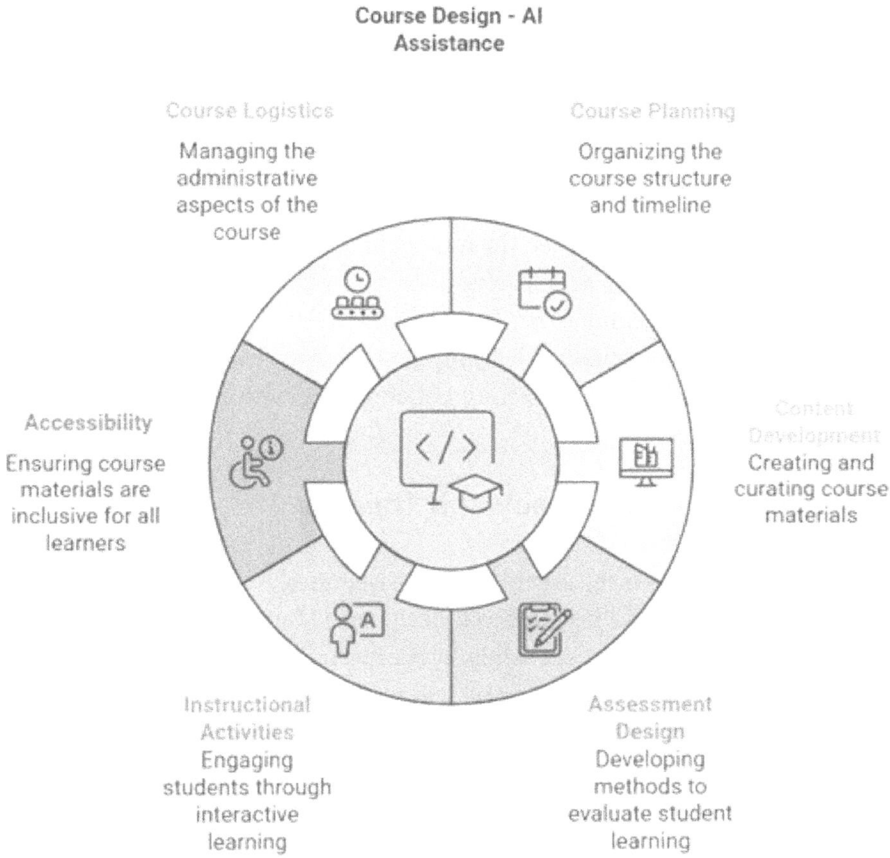

This chapter has outlined a skill-based set of competencies with a focus on instructional design and AI literacy. As Ethan Mollik noted in his book *Co-Intelligence* (2024), a human should always be in the loop when working with artificial intelligence. Considering that a mistake or inappropriate use of AI on the part of an instructional designer will affect tuition-paying students and learners of all ages, it becomes imperative not to let AI do any work unsupervised.

When used appropriately, AI can be a powerful tool for course planning, organizing and creating course content, designing assessments and instructional materials as well as managing administrative aspects of the course and ensuring accessibility (Figure 5). The integration of generative artificial intelligence into instructional design presents significant opportunities and implications for the future of teaching and learning in higher education. Far from simply automating existing tasks, AI could reshape the roles of faculty and instructional designers, necessitating new approaches to professional development, ethical considerations, and pedagogical innovation.

Evolving Roles and Collaboration

The landscape of instructional design, already modified by the demand for online and hybrid courses, will continue to evolve. AI is unlikely to replace human instructional faculty or designers due to the inherently personalized and humanistic nature of learning design. However, the future points towards a model of co-creation and collaboration where AI acts as a partner and intelligence augmentation tool. This partnership model emphasizes humans and AI working together to enhance cognitive performance, including learning and decision-making. The future will likely see increased instances of faculty collaborating with AI as a "co-designer" or thought partner.

The Imperative of AI Literacy and Training

A critical implication is the urgent need for structured AI literacy and integration frameworks for faculty and instructional designers. Many educators are currently unsure how to effectively or responsibly integrate AI. Future professional development programs must move beyond basic automation tools to explore AI's potential for creative, transformative pedagogy. The SCALE Framework, introduced in this chapter, offers a potential roadmap for such training, outlining a progressive path from basic substitution to advanced evolution in AI use. Evaluating faculty competency against such a framework and offering structured training programs will be a crucial next step.

Frameworks as Guides for Integration

Established instructional design frameworks (such as Revised Bloom's Taxonomy, TPACK, UDL, Constructivism, Cognitive Load Theory, and SAMR) will remain foundational, but their application will be enhanced and modified by AI. AI-specific and sociocultural theories like Co-Intelligence, Human-Centered AI, ZPD, Critical Digital Pedagogy, and Connectivism will become increasingly important lenses through which to understand and guide ethical and effective AI integration. The future use of AI in instructional design must be grounded in these theoretical perspectives to ensure progressive learning tasks, balanced technology integration, adaptive design, co-construction of understanding, reduced cognitive load, and transformative learning experiences.

Transformative Pedagogical Possibilities

AI's affordances extend far beyond mere automation. The future holds the potential for AI to enable transformative instructional redesign and examples of this include:

- Creating dynamic case studies and scenarios for real-time decision-making practice
- Facilitating design thinking workshops with AI-generated personas and challenges
- Providing real-time interactive coaching and feedback for educators
- Developing virtual mentors for teachers, especially those in their induction phase
- Assisting in the creation of immersive, story-driven educational games that adapt to learner needs, as exemplified by the Odeum case study.

These examples highlight the potential for AI to help create more engaging, personalized, and impactful learning experiences, aligning with the principles of Learner Experience Design.

Navigating Ethical Challenges

As AI becomes more integrated, addressing ethical considerations will remain paramount. Issues of bias in digital resources and AI outputs, student privacy, accessibility, and ensuring human dignity must be proactively managed. The future of AI in instructional design requires faculty and designers to critically evaluate AI tools and their outputs for ethical alignment.

Iterative Design and Research

The nature of AI integration suggests an iterative future. Like Design-Based Research, the use of AI in instructional design will involve continuous testing, evaluation, and refinement. This iterative process will inform best practices and the development of new activities at each level of the SCALE Framework.

TOWARD A SELF-ASSESSMENT STRUCTURE

Similar to how digital technologies have allowed student self-assessment tasks to be adaptive, scalable, and multimodal (Nieminen et al., 2025), we believe self-assessment tools can be created for instructional designers and faculty who are attempting to integrate or infuse artificial intelligence into their tasks following the SCALE framework. The authors have provided an initial list of potential activities for each of the following areas aligned with the SCALE framework (Appendix One).

We are proposing a self-assessment structure that places digital technologies as a key element of the self-assessment and not merely the mode by which they are conducted. Since faculty and instructional designers interact with digital technologies in many ways that require a range of digital skills, knowledge, and attitudes, we are recommending a combination to form a sense of digital competence when it comes to incorporating AI in the development of lessons and educational pedagogies.

Substitution

At the substitution level of the SCALE framework, an instructional designer would have to use generative AI to complete basic teaching tasks without significant changes. For example, using AI for lesson planning, for generating accurate images for slides or illustrations, and the creation of texts such as worksheets or modifications of text using text leveling tools.

Co-Construction

At the co-construction level of the SCALE framework, instructional designers will assess their abilities to incorporate generative AI into lessons in ways that will help students to complete tasks. For example, they should be able to use course-centric agents to help answer basic student questions, to use AI to co-create content and digital materials in conjunction with students, and to offer enhancements of student work with AI feedback.

Automation

At the automation level of the SCALE framework, instructional designers should be able to provide students with opportunities to apply generative AI in meaningful ways. For example, they should be able to model or teach prompt engineering or curation of materials, assign projects that make use of AI tools, and facilitate peer feedback of AI output.

Learner

At the learner level of the SCALE framework, instructional designers should be able to demonstrate that they can promote deeper learning by transforming and reimagining activities that serve to differentiate for varying learner skill levels, foster critical-thinking about AI output, and even facilitate an AI-generated dialogue or simulation, as well as analyzing media generated by an AI.

Evolution

At the evolution level of the SCALE framework, instructional designers should be able to exhibit ways that encourage learners to explore the ethical use and wider impacts of generative AI. For example, they should be able to discuss rights and responsibilities regarding the ethical use of AI, guide inquiry into the implications of AI tools, and use AI as a topic for debate or civic dialogue.

GenAI tools have the potential to significantly disrupt educational practices and pedagogy, but this potential can only be realized if educators fully embrace and leverage these technologies while carefully mitigating their risks. As Dr. Philippa Hardman highlighted in her 2023 TEDx talk, "The AI Education Revolution is Coming – Or Is It?", the transformative power of AI in education depends largely on our collective willingness to adapt to change (Hardman, 2023). However, without intentional and thoughtful integration, AI risks reinforcing existing educational models rather than truly transforming them. Educators need on-going professional development and reflection to effectively collaborate with genAI tools for teaching, learning and assessment. The proposed SCALE framework provides a model to scaffold and support faculty reflection and progressive learning for innovative instructional design.

REFERENCES

Adams, D., & Thompson, P. (2025). Transforming School Leadership with Artificial Intelligence: Applications, Implications, and Future Directions. *Leadership and Policy in Schools*, *24*(1), 77–89.

Ahmad, M., Imran, M., Iqbal, M., & Khan, A. M. (2025). Digital Information Overload and Its Impact on Library Users: Assessing User Experience and Service Adaptations in Female Higher Education Students. *Research Journal for Social Affairs*, *3*(2), 89–96.

Auernhammer, J. (2020). Human-centered AI: The role of Human-centered Design Research in the development of AI, in Boess, S., Cheung, M. and Cain, R. (eds.), *Synergy - DRS International Conference 2020*

Barkatsas, T., & McLaughlin, P. (2021). *Authentic Assessment and Evaluation Approaches and Practices in a Digital Era*. Brill.

Bondie, R. (2024). AI-powered simulation drives teacher learning. *The Learning Professional*, *45*(2), 48–51.

Bondie, R., Zusho, A., Wiseman, E., Dede, C., & Rich, D. (2023). Can differentiated and personalized mixed-reality simulations transform teacher learning? *Technology, Mind, and Behavior,* T(l). tmb.apaopen.org/ pub/4gk68mil

Briggs, L. J., Gustafson, K. L., & Tillman, M. (1991). *Instructional Design: Principles and Applications*. Educational Technology Publications.

Brooks, R., & Grady, S. D. (2022). Course design considerations for inclusion and representation. A quality matters white paper.

Brown, A. L. (1992). Design experiments: Theoretical and methodological challenges in creating complex interventions in classroom settings. *Journal of the Learning Sciences*, *2*(2), 141–178.

Celik, I. (2023). Towards Intelligent-TPACK: An empirical study on teachers' professional knowledge to ethically integrate artificial intelligence (AI)-based tools into education. *Computers in Human Behavior*, *138*, 107468.

Chiu, T. K. (2024). *Empowering K-12 Education with AI: Preparing for the Future of Education and Work*. Taylor & Francis.

Crompton, H., & Burke, D. (2023). Artificial intelligence in higher education: The state of the field. *International Journal of Educational Technology in Higher Education*, *20*(1), 22. DOI: 10.1186/s41239-023-00392-8

D'Apice, C., Grieco, C., Piscopo, R., & Liscio, L. (2015). Dms2015short-2: Advanced learning technologies for elearning in the enterprise: Design of an educational adventure game to teach computer security. *Journal of Visual Languages and Computing*, *31*, 260–266.

Diwan, C., Srinivasa, S., Suri, G., Agarwal, S., & Ram, P. (2023). AI-based learning content generation and learning pathway augmentation to increase learner engagement. *Computers and Education: Artificial Intelligence*, *4*, 100110.

Fernandes, P., Leite, C., Mouraz, A., & Figueiredo, C. (2013). Curricular contextualization: Tracking the meanings of a concept. *The Asia-Pacific Education Researcher*, *22*(4), 417–425. DOI: 10.1007/s4029 9-012-0041-1

Gibson, R. (2023). 10 ways artificial intelligence is transforming instructional design. *EDUCAUSE Review*, •••, 14.

Glickman, M., & Zhang, Y. (2024). AI and Generative AI for Research Discovery and Summarization. *Harvard Data Science Review*, *6*(2). Advance online publication. DOI: 10.1162/99608f92.7f9220ff

Grubaugh, S., Levitt, G., & Deever, D. (2023). Harnessing AI to Power Constructivist Learning: An Evolution in Educational Methodologies. *EIKI Journal of Effective Teaching Methods*, *1*(3). Advance online publication. DOI: 10.59652/jetm.v1i3.43

Halupa, C. (2019). Differentiation of roles: Instructional designers and faculty in the creation of online courses. *International Journal of Higher Education*, *8*(1), 55–68.

Hamel, C., & Viau-Guay, A. (2019). Using video to support teachers' reflective practice : A literature review. *Cogent Education*, *6*(1). Advance online publication. DOI: 10.1080/2331186X.2019.1673689

Hardman, P. (2023, May 4). The AI Education Revolution is Coming – Or Is It? [Video]. TEDx Talks. https://www.ted.com/talks/dr_philippa_hardman_the_ai_education_revolution_is_coming_or_is_it

Hasselquist, L., & Bertolini, K. (2018). Developing effective rubrics. *NACTA Journal*, *62*(4), 379–380.

Hosseini, M., Rasmussen, L. M., & Resnik, D. B. (2024). Using AI to write scholarly publications. *Accountability in Research*, *31*(7), 715–723. PMID: 36697395

Hua Mulan. (2024, February). Steam Community. Retrieved March 1, 2025, from https://steamcommunity.com/app/1251360

Hui, E. S. Y. E. (2024). Incorporating Bloom's taxonomy into promoting cognitive thinking mechanism in artificial intelligence-supported learning environments. *Interactive Learning Environments*, •••, 1–14.

Hwang, Y., Lee, S., & Jeon, J. (2024). Integrating AI chatbots into the metaverse: Pre-service English teachers' design works and perceptions. *Education and Information Technologies*, •••, 1–32.

Hyatt, S. E., & Owenz, M. B. (2024). Using Universal Design for Learning and artificial intelligence to support students with disabilities. *College Teaching*, •••, 1–8.

Jafari, E. (2024). Artificial intelligence and learning environment: Human considerations. *Journal of Computer Assisted Learning*, *40*(5), 2135–2149.

Karataş, F., Eriçok, B., & Tanrikulu, L. (2024). Reshaping curriculum adaptation in the age of artificial intelligence: Mapping teachers' AI-driven curriculum adaptation patterns. *British Educational Research Journal*.

Khalil, M. K., & Elkhider, I. A. (2016). Applying learning theories and instructional design models for effective instruction. *Advances in Physiology Education*. PMID: 27068989

Kim, H., & Koo, T. K. (2024). The Impact of Generative AI on Syllabus Design and Learning. *Journal of Marketing Education*, •••, 02734753241299024.

Koehler, M. J., Mishra, P., & Cain, W. (2013). What is technological pedagogical content knowledge (TPACK)? *Journal of Education*, *193*(3), 13–19.

Krathwohl, D. R. (2002). A revision of Bloom's taxonomy: An overview. *Theory into Practice*, *41*(4), 212–218.

Liu, C. H., & Matthews, R. (2005). Vygotsky's Philosophy: Constructivism and Its Criticisms Examined. *International Education Journal*, *6*(3), 386–399.

Malik, R., Abdi, D., Wang, R., & Demszky, D. (2024). Scaffolding middle school mathematics curricula with large language models. *British Journal of Educational Technology*.

Meehan, K., Wilson, S., & Farrelly, W. (2024). Evaluating alternatives to essay-based assessment in a world where generative AI is pervasive. In *ICERI2024 Proceedings* (pp. 1152-1159). IATED.

Meidl, T., & Meidl, C. (2011). Curriculum integration and adaptation: Individualizing pedagogy for linguistically and culturally diverse students. *Current Issues in Education (Tempe, Ariz.)*, *14*(1), 1–30.

Miller, L. M., Moreno, J., Estrera, V., & Lane, D. (2004). Efficacy of MedMyst: An internet teaching tool for middle school microbiology. *Microbiology Education*, *5*(1), 13–20. PMID: 23653553

Mogavi, R. H., Deng, C., Kim, J. J., Zhou, P., Kwon, Y. D., Metwally, A. H. S., Tlili, A., Bassanelli, S., Bucchiarone, A., & Gujar, S. (2024). ChatGPT in education: A blessing or a curse? A qualitative study exploring early adopters' utilization and perceptions. *Computers in Human Behavior: Artificial Humans*, *2*(1), 100027. DOI: 10.1016/j.chbah.2023.100027

Mollick, E. (2024). *Co-intelligence: Living and working with AI.* Penguin.

Nazari, M., & Saadi, G. (2024). Developing effective prompts to improve communication with ChatGPT: A formula for higher education stakeholders. *Discover Education*, *3*(1), 45.

Nieminen, J. H., Yan, Z., & Boud, D. (2025). Self-assessment design in a digital world: Centring student agency. *Assessment & Evaluation in Higher Education*, •••, 1–15.

Palmer, Z. B., & Oswal, S. K. (2025). Constructing websites with generative AI tools: The accessibility of their workflows and products for users with disabilities. *Journal of Business and Technical Communication*, *39*(1), 93–114.

Patac, L. P., & Patac, A. V.Jr. (2025). Using ChatGPT for academic support: Managing cognitive load and enhancing learning efficiency–A phenomenological approach. *Social Sciences & Humanities Open*, *11*, 101301.

Puentedura, R. (2006). Transformation, Technology, and Education. Presentation given August 18, 2006, as part of the *Strengthening Your District Through Technology workshops*, Maine, US. Retrieved from https://hippasus.com/resources/tte/part1.html

Rezigalla, A. A. (2024). AI in medical education: Uses of AI in construction type A MCQs. *BMC Medical Education*, *24*(1), 247. PMID: 38448870

Romaniuk, M. W., & Łukasiewicz-Wieleba, J. (2024). Generative Artificial Intelligence in the teaching activities of academic teachers and students. *International Journal of Electronics and Telecommunications*, 1043-1048.

Rouhiainen, L. (2019). How AI and data could personalize higher education. *Harvard Business Review*, *14*, 2–6.

Rubin, H. (2009). *Collaborative leadership: Developing effective partnerships for communities and schools.* Corwin Press.

Saborío-Taylor, S., & Rojas-Ramírez, F. (2024). Universal Design for Learning and artificial intelligence in the digital era: Fostering inclusion and autonomous learning. *International Journal of Professional Development, Learners and Learning, 6*(2).

Salminen, J., Liu, C., Pian, W., Chi, J., Häyhänen, E., & Jansen, B. J. (2024, May). Deus ex machina and personas from large language models: investigating the composition of AI-generated persona descriptions. In *Proceedings of the 2024 CHI Conference on Human Factors in Computing Systems* (pp. 1-20).

Schmidt, M., & Huang, R. (2022). Defining learning experience design: Voices from the field of learning design & technology. *TechTrends*, *66*(2), 141–158.

Shamir-Inbal, T., Levi, L., & Blau, I. (2024). The Use of Artificial Intelligence to Promote Changes in Teaching and Learning Processes. In *EDULEARN24 Proceedings* (pp. 142-145). IATED.

Siemens, G. (2005). Connectivism: Learning as network-creation. *ASTD Learning News*, *10*(1), 1–28.

Song, Y., Weisberg, L. R., Zhang, S., Tian, X., Boyer, K. E., & Israel, M. (2024). A framework for inclusive AI learning design for diverse learners. *Computers and Education: Artificial Intelligence*, 100212.

Stefaniak, J., & Sentz, J. (2020). The role of needs assessment to validate contextual factors related to user experience design practices. Learner and user experience research: An introduction for the field of learning design & technology. EdTech Books. https://edtechbooks. org/ux/role_of_needs_assessment

Stommel, J. (2014). *Critical digital pedagogy: A definition.* Hybrid Pedagogy.

Sweller, J. (1994). Cognitive load theory, learning difficulty, and instructional design. *Learning and Instruction*, *4*(4), 295–312.

Vygotsky, L. S., & Cole, M. (1978). *Mind in society: Development of higher psychological processes*. Harvard university press.

Wang, S., Wang, F., Zhu, Z., Wang, J., Tran, T., & Du, Z. (2024). Artificial intelligence in education: A systematic literature review. *Expert Systems with Applications*, *252*, 124167.

Wavre, S. P., Kuknor, S., Dhaktod, P., & Khokale, S. (2024, May). Spot Unconscious Biases by Using Digital Tool. In *2024 9th International Conference on Business and Industrial Research (ICBIR)* (pp. 0257-0262). IEEE.

Yusuf, A., Bello, S., Pervin, N., & Tukur, A. K. (2024). Implementing a proposed framework for enhancing critical thinking skills in synthesizing AI-generated texts. *Thinking Skills and Creativity, 53*, 101619. DOI: 10.1016/j.tsc.2024.101619

Zheng, C., Yuan, K., Guo, B., Hadi Mogavi, R., Peng, Z., Ma, S., & Ma, X. (2024, May). Charting the future of AI in project-based learning: a Co-design exploration with students. In *Proceedings of the 2024 CHI Conference on Human Factors in Computing Systems* (pp. 1-19).

APPENDIX I

SCALE-AI Literacy Tool – Reflective Self-Assessment Guide (All Levels)

This reflective tool supports educators in exploring how they use generative AI tools in instructional design. Organized by the five progressive levels of the SCALE framework—Substitute, Co-Construct, Automate & Optimize, Learn & Adapt, and Evolve & Innovate —each level features practice examples, realistic applications, and reflective questions. This guide emphasizes growth, thoughtful design, and framework-aligned instructional practices.

Table 3. Level: Substitute

Practice Example	What This Looks Like	Reflective Prompt
Generate course syllabi using AI prompts	Use ChatGPT or similar tool to auto-fill standard syllabus components like schedule, policies, objectives.	How does this save you time? What parts still require your human judgment?
Create lecture notes and summaries	Use AI to generate summaries of textbooks or lecture slides.	Are these summaries accurate and aligned with your intended learning outcomes?
Develop discussion questions from readings	Ask AI to generate 3–5 open-ended questions based on chapter excerpts.	Do these questions prompt critical thinking or recall? What would make them more meaningful?
Generate quiz questions from content	Use AI to create multiple-choice or true/false questions based on lesson materials.	Are the questions valid, fair and unbiased? What kinds of errors does AI tend to make?
Create course announcements and templates	Generate weekly check-in messages or reminders using AI.	Does this improve communication? How do you personalize these messages for your students?
Summarize research articles for course use	Paste article into a summarization tool to extract key points.	Do you verify accuracy? What is lost when the AI summarizes scholarly work?
Develop basic rubrics for assignments	Prompt AI to generate criteria for standard assignments (e.g., discussion board participation).	Are these rubrics useful? What modifications do you need to make to meet your context?
Draft standard feedback comments	Use AI to create reusable comments for student work (e.g., grammar, structure).	Does this make your grading and feedback processes more efficient? How do students respond to AI-generated feedback?
Organize course materials into LMS-ready text	Use AI to format and chunk information for module pages or LMS descriptions.	What formatting tasks are best suited for AI? Which tasks require human judgment?
Translate simple instructions for multilingual learners	Use AI to translate assignment instructions into students' home languages.	How do you verify translation accuracy? How can this support inclusion?

Table 4. Level: Co-construct

Practice Example	What This Looks Like	Reflective Prompt
Co-develop assignments or assessments with AI	Work with AI to scaffold a writing prompt or design multiple versions of an assignment.	What aspects of this task benefited from collaboration? How did you shape the AI output?
Generate examples and non-examples for teaching concepts	Use AI to quickly provide multiple scenarios for comparison.	How does this support conceptual understanding? Are examples inclusive and accessible?
Co-create case studies from prompts or scenarios	Prompt AI to generate case study outlines or student dilemmas.	What role does your judgment play in reviewing and revising these cases?
Develop simulations or role-plays with AI assistance	Generate role-specific dialogue or scenarios for learners to engage in.	How realistic and engaging are these simulations? How do they align with your learning objectives and student outcomes?
Collaborate with AI to revise text for tone or clarity	Use AI to revise materials to better match student reading levels or engagement.	What do you notice when comparing your original and AI-revised versions?
Use AI to develop multimedia presentation content	Generate slide outlines or suggested images from a lesson objective.	How does this influence your visual storytelling or design thinking?
Refine AI output collaboratively with students	Students prompt and critique AI outputs together with the teacher.	How does this shift student ownership or meta-cognitive awareness?
Prompt AI for student writing supports	Provide examples of thesis statements or topic outlines with AI assistance.	Are students gaining independence or over-relying?
Use AI in co-authoring protocols or templates	Generate formats for team-based assignments or peer reviews.	How do you ensure these are clear, fair, and aligned with your learning goals?
Personalize examples collaboratively using AI	Create contextualized examples based on student input.	Does personalization improve relevance and motivation?

Table 5. Level: Automation

Practice Example	What This Looks Like	Reflective Prompt
Set up auto-grading for quizzes or formative checks	Use AI or LMS-integrated tools to evaluate background or content-aligned questions.	How does automation impact your time and feedback quality?
Use AI to streamline LMS communications	Generate weekly reminders or responses to FAQs.	How do you maintain a human voice in automated messages?
Design rubrics that auto-fill comments with AI support	Develop structured feedback comment banks for reuse.	Do students perceive the feedback as personalized?
Analyze student submissions for trends with AI tools	Use AI to review common errors or patterns in discussion posts.	How do you verify AI's interpretation of patterns?

continued on following page

Table 5. Continued

Practice Example	What This Looks Like	Reflective Prompt
Use chatbots for general course FAQ responses	Deploy an AI chatbot for standard questions or office hours.	What role does the chatbot play in your teaching presence, if any?
Automate feedback on writing mechanics	AI checks grammar, clarity, and mechanics.	How do you help students interpret and apply AI feedback?
Organize and tag uploaded resources using AI	Use AI to generate metadata or categories.	Does this make access and navigation easier for learners?
Use AI to generate pacing guides based on calendars	Plan term schedules using AI input from content and events.	What decisions still need to be made manually? How does your knowledge of student learning progressions inform the schedule?
Create a dashboard to visualize student engagement	Use AI data tools to flag disengaged or struggling students.	What are the underlying assumptions, perhaps unintentionally incorporated into your tools? How do you act on this data responsibly and equitably?
Optimize discussion threads using AI moderation tools	Use AI to analyze responses or flag issues in forums.	What risks and benefits are involved summarizing and organizing student discussions?

Table 6. Level: Learner

Practice Example	What This Looks Like	Reflective Prompt
Develop adaptive learning paths informed by student needs	Use AI to suggest different content sequences based on performance.	How do you monitor and adjust AI-driven recommendations? Are they helpful?
Create personalized feedback using AI prompts	Tailor AI-generated comments to each student's work.	What increases student engagement with this feedback? How are you managing confidentiality in using AI for analysis?
Incorporate aspects of learner variability in instructional materials and practices	Use AI to understand where learners may differ in their understanding and prior knowledge; use AI to surface and assess for common misconceptions	How do these practices enhance your knowledge of learning progressions or to anticipate frequent misconceptions?
Design differentiated instruction modules with AI support	Use AI to create leveled versions of assignments or texts.	How do you maintain rigor across variations? How do you measure outcomes?
Use AI to support language learners or accessibility	Translate content or adjust readability.	How do you ensure linguistic and cultural accuracy?
Provide UDL-aligned resources using multimodal AI tools	Offer visual/ audio/ interactive resources generated by AI.	Do these resources enhance access and learning outcomes?

continued on following page

Table 6. Continued

Practice Example	What This Looks Like	Reflective Prompt
Match AI supports to student learning profiles	Customize tools and tasks for different learning needs.	How do students respond to this personalization?
Prompt AI to create scaffolded versions of a text	Simplify language or insert guiding questions into a passage.	How does this impact comprehension or engagement?
Develop personalized quizzes for remediation	AI generates questions targeting known gaps.	What patterns emerge in students' learning gaps?
Implement student-led AI exploration for metacognition	Invite students to design their own AI learning supports.	How do students reflect on their process and tool use?
Analyze learning gaps and generate micro-interventions	Use AI tools to identify needs and recommend strategies.	What data do you need to verify and have confidence in these suggestions?

Table 7. Level: Evolve

Practice Example	What This Looks Like	Reflective Prompt
Design AI-enhanced project-based learning units	Integrate AI tools in research, synthesis, or storytelling.	What changes in student thinking or creativity do you observe?
Use AI to create immersive simulations for critical thinking	Build branching scenarios using AI-generated characters and choices.	How do students respond to simulated complexity? How do you integrate and leverage the format from a pedagogical perspective?
Build AI-infused learning communities or peer feedback loops	Students use AI to give or refine peer feedback.	What new dynamics emerge in collaborative learning?
Implement co-intelligent student research projects	Students use AI as a thinking partner in inquiry.	What supports are needed for critical evaluation of AI? Are learning outcomes enhanced?
Develop curriculum with iterative AI-supported design	Rapid prototype lessons with AI-enhanced cycles.	What role does human judgment play in iteration?
Lead faculty professional learning on AI integration	Share strategies and tools with colleagues.	What successes or challenges shape your leadership?
Pilot experimental uses of AI aligned with research	Test new AI tools and strategies in instructional settings.	How do you document impact or outcomes? How does experimentation inform & impact your teaching practice?
Co-design learning analytics dashboards with stakeholders	Collaborate with students, faculty, and IT to track meaningful metrics.	How do you protect privacy and promote equity in data use?

continued on following page

Table 7. Continued

Practice Example	What This Looks Like	Reflective Prompt
Explore ethical dilemmas through AI-assisted debate formats	Generate prompts and counterpoints to stimulate ethical reasoning.	What values do these debates surface? Are they shared values? Equitable?
Develop new models of instruction blending human + AI roles	Experiment with flipped AI-tutor models, or AI peer reviewers.	How are roles and responsibilities shifting in your classroom? How do these practices augment, elevate or extend your practice?

Chapter 6
AI and Curriculum:
Designing for the Future

Geraldine Torrisi-Steele
https://orcid.org/0000-0002-6045-4114
Griffith University, Australia

ABSTRACT

The integration of artificial intelligence (AI) in curriculum development is transforming education by enabling personalized learning, adaptive assessments, and data-driven decision-making. This paper explores how AI-driven technologies enhance curriculum design, ensuring that educational programs remain relevant, future-oriented, and responsive to evolving workforce demands. Key advancements such as machine learning algorithms, AI-powered learning analytics, and automated content generation are examined for their impact on curriculum planning, instructional strategies, and learner engagement. Additionally, the authors discuss ethical considerations, challenges in AI adoption, and the role of educators in guiding AI-enhanced curriculum development. By properly embracing AI, providing the needed infrastructure and professional development alongside addressing ethical dimensions of AI in education institutions can foster innovation, inclusivity, and lifelong learning, preparing students for a rapidly changing digital landscape.

INTRODUCTION

The three core capabilities of artificial intelligence (AI) are analytics, personalization, and automation. Applying these AI capabilities to the design and development of curriculums is gaining popularity among educators. The rapid evolution of AI technologies is reshaping the way educators design and implement curricula, fostering more personalized, adaptive, and future-oriented learning experiences (Rahiman &

DOI: 10.4018/979-8-3373-2397-8.ch006

Kodikal, Cogent Education). AI-driven curriculum development has the potential to revolutionize traditional educational frameworks by offering data-driven insights, automating content creation, and optimizing instructional strategies to better align with the needs of diverse learners (Swiecki, et al., 2022). As institutions worldwide strive to equip students with the necessary skills to navigate an increasingly digital landscape, AI's integration into curriculum development represents both a transformative opportunity and a complex challenge.

The use of AI in curriculum design and development can enhance personalization, allowing for tailored learning experiences that cater to individual student needs, learning styles, and pace (Peng, Ma, & Spector, 2019). By leveraging machine learning algorithms and predictive analytics, AI can analyze vast amounts of student data to recommend customized learning pathways, ensuring that students receive instruction that aligns with their strengths and areas for growth. Adaptive learning technologies, powered by AI, can modify course content in real-time, adjusting to each student's progress and providing targeted support where needed. This level of personalization has potential to improve student engagement and comprehension and to help bridge learning gaps, making education more inclusive and equitable (Peng, Ma, & Spector, 2019) (Tafazoli, 2024) (Ozsevim & Ng, 2023) (Ahmed, 2024).

AI can streamline the curriculum design process by automating administrative tasks such as syllabus creation, resource allocation, and assessment design. AI-powered tools can analyze educational standards, industry trends, and pedagogical research to generate curriculum frameworks that align with both academic requirements and workforce demands. By reducing the time educators spend on these tasks, AI allows teachers to focus more on instruction, mentorship, and student interaction, fostering a more dynamic and engaging learning environment. Additionally, AI-driven analytics can provide continuous feedback on curriculum effectiveness, enabling educators to make data-informed decisions that enhance student learning outcomes (Towfek, Khodadadi, Abualigah, & Rizk, 2024).

Despite its potential benefits, the application of AI for curriculum development raises several ethical considerations that must be carefully addressed. One primary concern is data privacy and security, as AI systems often rely on collecting and analyzing large amounts of student data to function effectively. Ensuring that information remains secure and is used responsibly is critical in maintaining trust and safeguarding individuals' rights, both students and educators. Additionally, the risk of algorithmic bias in AI-driven curriculum design poses a significant challenge. If AI systems are trained on biased data sets, they may inadvertently reinforce existing inequalities, leading to disparities in educational opportunities and outcomes. Addressing these ethical concerns requires a commitment to transparency, inclusivity, and accountability in the development and deployment of AI technologies in education.

Another crucial consideration is the balance between AI-driven automation and human creativity in curriculum design. While AI can process vast amounts of information and optimize instructional strategies, it cannot fully replicate the intuition, empathy, and contextual understanding that educators bring to the teaching process. Curriculum development is not solely a technical endeavor; it requires a deep understanding of student needs, societal values, and cultural contexts. Therefore, educators must approach AI integration with a critical perspective, leveraging its capabilities to enhance their work rather than replace their expertise. The most effective approach to AI in curriculum development is one that combines the efficiency of AI with the pedagogical wisdom of human educators, ensuring that curricula remain dynamic, relevant, and responsive to the needs of learners.

AI's role in curriculum development is also closely tied to preparing students for future careers in an increasingly digital and automated world. As industries continue to evolve, the skills required in the workforce are shifting, necessitating curricula that emphasize digital literacy, critical thinking, problem-solving, and adaptability. AI can play a pivotal role in shaping competency-based curricula that focus on real-world applications and experiential learning. By analyzing job market trends and industry demands, AI can help educators design courses that equip students with the skills needed for emerging careers. Moreover, AI-powered simulations and virtual learning environments can provide hands-on experiences that bridge the gap between theoretical knowledge and practical application.

However, implementing AI-driven curriculum design and development requires institutional support, investment in technology infrastructure, and professional development for educators. Schools and universities must ensure that faculty members are equipped with the necessary skills to effectively integrate AI tools into their curriculum planning and instructional practices. Professional development programs should focus on training educators to use AI responsibly, interpret AI-generated insights critically, and adapt their teaching methods to align with AI-enhanced learning experiences. Additionally, institutions must foster a culture of innovation and collaboration, encouraging interdisciplinary partnerships that bring together educators, technologists, and policymakers to shape the future of AI in education.

Ultimately, the integration of AI into curriculum development holds immense promise for creating more personalized, adaptive, and future-focused educational experiences. However, realizing this potential requires a thoughtful and ethical approach that prioritizes student well-being, educational equity, and pedagogical integrity. By addressing the challenges and leveraging the opportunities presented by AI, educators and institutions can harness its power to enhance curriculum design and better prepare students for the complexities of the digital age. As AI continues to evolve, ongoing research and dialogue will be essential in shaping its role in education, ensuring that it serves as a tool for empowerment and progress rather than a mechanism for reinforcing existing disparities. This chapter aims to provide an exploration of AI's impact on curriculum development, offering insights and recommendations for educators, policymakers, and institutions seeking to navigate this transformative landscape.

This chapter will serve as a roadmap for successfully implementing AI in curriculum development, offering practical strategies and recommendations for educators and institutions. Topics will include best practices for AI integration, strategies for ensuring ethical AI usage, approaches for addressing digital accessibility, and methods for empowering educators to make informed decisions about AI-enhanced learning experiences. By adopting a balanced approach that leverages AI's potential while maintaining educational integrity, institutions can create dynamic, inclusive, and future-ready curricula that prepare students for the challenges of the digital age.

AI AND CURRICULUM DESIGN: OPPORTUNITIES

"Artificial intelligence is a technology that enables computers and machines to simulate human learning, comprehension, problem solving, decision making, creativity and autonomy " (IBM, n.d.)

"The word curriculum refers to the planned activities and experiences that education systems organize for students to help them achieve learning goals that are usually specified at national, school, and classroom levels "(Wyse & Manyukhina, 2024, p. para 1).

"The curriculum represents the expression of educational ideas in practice... [it] includes all the planned learning experiences of a school or educational institution... It is underpinned by a set of values and beliefs about what students should know and how they come to know it... A curriculum has at least four important elements: content; teaching and learning strategies; assessment processes; and evaluation processes. The process of defining and organising these elements into a logical pattern is known as curriculum design." (Prideaux, 2003, p. 268).

Curriculum design is inevitably complicated because the learning process and experience of learning facilitated by the implemented curriculum are also highly complex (Mulpeter, McCormack, & O'Flaherty, 2023). Learning is a deeply contextual and individualized. This means that the implementation of the planned curriculum is experienced very differently among individual learners in their various situations. For this reason, the actual outcome of an implemented curriculum design is, despite best efforts and best practices, uncertain. Subsequently, curriculum design is really a problem-solving process. Typically, educators draw on their knowledge of educational theories and best practices, their philosophy of learning and teaching, and their understanding of discipline and their students to design and implement curricula to the best of their ability. Educators at school and classroom level need to make many decisions as they seek to define and organize content, identify strategies and design assessment as part of their curriculum plan. Frequently, educators will need to seek out resources and materials to incorporate into their curriculum designs. Furthermore, once the curriculum is implemented, it must be evaluated carefully, and the outcome of the evaluation will feed into the next iteration of the curriculum plan. Conceivably, all of this takes a great deal of time and effort. It is no wonder then, that educators are turning to artificial intelligence technologies, keen to explore artificial intelligence technologies for both efficiency and effectiveness in curriculum design.

AI, Machine Learning and Big Data for Adaptability and Personalization

Adaptability and personalization of the curriculum requires intimate knowledge of the attributes of learners as well as of their learning contexts (and this will change over time!). For human curriculum designers such detailed knowledge of learner cohorts is near-impossible. However, one of the attributes of AI technologies is the ability to analyze vast volumes of data. These vast volumes of data are difficult if not impossible for humans to analyze and are known as big data (Baig, Shuib, & Yadegaridehkordi, 2020). The analysis of big data is largely dependent on machine learning (Sarker, 2021). Machine learning, a subset of AI, enables computers to 'learn' from vast volumes of data and make predictions or decisions without being explicitly programmed to do so.

The analysis of big data can show learner behaviors and patterns in their learning activities which enables modelling and prediction of a range of parameters pertinent to student learning, engagement and retention (Papamitsiou & Economides, 2014) (Luan, et al., 2020). AI in education leverages computational intelligence to process large volumes of educational data, extract meaningful patterns, and optimize curriculum structures. Unlike conventional static curricula, which often follow a predetermined sequence of topics and assessments, AI-enhanced curriculum design dynamically adapts based on student interactions, performance metrics, and emerging trends in education and the job market. Traditional educational curriculum design models often struggle to accommodate diverse learning styles, paces, and student backgrounds. AI-powered systems, however, can analyze individual student data to create tailored learning pathways. Additionally, predictive analytics can forecast student learning outcomes, enabling institutions to implement proactive interventions that support student success.

By incorporating AI into curriculum development, educators can ensure that learning materials are continuously updated, personalized to individual students, and aligned with industry demands. As education continues to evolve in response to technological advancements, AI-driven curriculum design offers opportunities to make learning more effective. Every student learns at a different pace and in unique ways. Through adaptive learning platforms, AI can identify areas where a student excels and where they may need additional support, adjusting the curriculum accordingly. This personalized approach not only enhances student engagement but also improves knowledge retention and skill development. Machine learning algorithms in the adaptive systems can track students' progress over time and provide customized recommendations on supplementary materials, assignments, and assessments that best suit their learning needs (Kumar, Haque, Mishra, Islam, & Ahmad, 2023). Furthermore, algorithms can analyze historical student performance data, identify common learning obstacles, and suggest modifications to instructional content. These insights empower educators to refine curricula in ways that enhance student comprehension and learning efficiency. With proper consideration of the algorithms behind data analytics and with proper consideration of the data sets being used for analysis and prediction, big data analysis can also facilitate a more inclusive and empowering curriculum for a wider range of learners in a wider range of contexts (Tafazoli, 2024) (Ozsevim & Ng, 2023).

One of the most promising applications of AI in curriculum development is for intelligent tutoring systems (ITS). These AI-powered platforms provide real-time, personalized instruction to students, simulating one-on-one tutoring experiences AI-driven adaptive learning platforms like those found in ITS can enhance personalization of a course curriculum by providing individualized lesson plans, assignments, and assessments. These platforms use predictive analytics to assess how a student interacts with learning materials and recommend specific resources that align with their learning trajectory. For example, if a student demonstrates proficiency in a particular subject, the AI system can introduce more advanced topics to challenge them, whereas if a student struggles, the system can provide supplementary materials, additional practice exercises, or alternative explanations. This level of personalization not only improves academic performance but also enhances student motivation by making learning more relevant and engaging (Kumar, Haque, Mishra, Islam, & Ahmad, 2023).By continuously assessing student performance and adjusting instructional content accordingly, ITS can ensure that students receive targeted support tailored to their unique learning needs (Kumar, Haque, Mishra, Islam, & Ahmad, 2023). With the functionality of adaptive learning, adopting an ITS can also help educators structure course materials in a way that maximizes engagement and comprehension. As AI continues to advance, its role in education will extend beyond curriculum development to include predictive analytics that anticipate student needs and challenges. AI-driven predictive modeling can identify students at risk of falling behind and recommend targeted interventions to support their academic success (Kumar, Haque, Mishra, Islam, & Ahmad, 2023). By analyzing historical performance data, engagement levels, and behavioral patterns, AI can help educators proactively address learning difficulties before they escalate. This proactive approach has the potential to significantly reduce dropout rates and improve overall student achievement (Matz, et al., 2023).The application of AI in curriculum design extends beyond the classroom to include workforce alignment and career preparation. As job markets evolve due to technological advancements, educational institutions must ensure that curricula remain relevant to industry needs. AI can analyze labor market trends, job postings, and employer requirements to identify emerging skill demands. By integrating this data into curriculum development, educators can design programs that equip students with the skills and competencies required for future careers. Further, by building these analytic capabilities into curriculum design systems, AI technologies can identify any 'misalignment' between curriculum and the workforce and suggest updates to the curriculum (Webb, 2024). Because the job market is so rapidly changing (mostly social change is in pace with the rate of change in technologies), curriculum need to be much more responsive, if not proactive to ensure that students are well-prepared for the job market. Curriculum design supported by data analytics fosters a more dynamic connection between education and the workforce, reducing skill gaps and enhancing employability (Webb, 2024).

AI has potential to shape the future of education is through the increased emphasis on lifelong learning (Palenski, Hills, Unnikrishnan, & Eynon, 2024). As the job market continues to evolve, individuals will need to acquire new skills and adapt to changing industry demands throughout their careers. AI-driven learning platforms will play a crucial role in facilitating continuous education by offering personalized recommendations for skill development and career advancement. AI-powered upskilling and reskilling programs will allow professionals to acquire new competencies in a flexible, efficient and on-demand format (Schiff, 2021), ensuring they remain competitive in an increasingly digital economy. This shift toward lifelong learning will require educational institutions to rethink traditional curriculum structures and develop programs that support continuous professional development.

In addition to aligning curricula with workforce demands, AI can facilitate experiential learning opportunities (Goldberg & Robson, 2023) that prepare students for real-world challenges. Virtual and augmented reality platforms powered by AI can simulate workplace scenarios, allowing students to gain hands-on experience in fields such as healthcare (Anthamatten & Holt, 2024), engineering, and finance. AI-driven mentorship programs can also connect students with industry professionals, providing guidance on career pathways and skill development (Bhattacharya, Bhattacharya, & Bhattacharya, 2024) (Chang, Hui, Justus-Smith, & Wang, 2024).

By integrating these elements into curriculum design, AI ensures that students are not only academically prepared but also equipped with practical knowledge that enhances their employability. AI-driven virtual tutors, chatbots, and augmented reality experiences will provide students with interactive and immersive learning opportunities beyond the traditional classroom setting. These tools will enhance student engagement by offering real-world applications of academic concepts, making learning more meaningful and applicable to everyday life. Additionally, AI-powered social learning platforms facilitate collaboration among students, educators, and industry professionals, creating a global learning network that fosters knowledge-sharing and innovation. All these tools can support curriculum design processes at classroom level that have the potential to increase effectiveness of learning.

ITS platforms are particularly beneficial in STEM education, where students often require iterative practice and concept reinforcement. For instance, an ITS for mathematics can assess a student's problem-solving approach and provide step-by-step guidance tailored to their learning style. In language learning, AI-powered tutoring systems, such as Duolingo's AI-driven adaptive learning engine, customize vocabulary and grammar exercises based on individual proficiency levels. The ability of ITS platforms to deliver targeted instruction enhances student engagement and promotes mastery of complex subjects. There exist a growing number of AI powered platforms which enable educators to construct personalized and more accessible learning for their students (the proviso is of course, that the educators have the necessary literacy and knowledge to use these platforms effectively). The evidence is mounting that AI can significantly add functionality to curriculum tools for more effective and engaging learning. Some examples of AI powered platforms and their uses is given below.

AI-driven curriculum initiatives in K-12 education have focused on creating personalized learning experiences that adapt to students' unique learning styles and paces. One of the most widely recognized AI-driven platforms in K-12 education is DreamBox Learning (https://www.dreambox.com/). DreamBox is an adaptive math learning platform that uses AI algorithms to assess student performance in real-time and adjust lesson content accordingly. By analyzing students' problem-solving approaches, DreamBox identifies areas where they need additional support and offers personalized instruction. This AI-driven approach ensures that students receive targeted learning interventions, making math education more effective and engaging. Studies have shown that students using DreamBox experience higher proficiency gains compared to traditional instruction methods.

Another notable AI initiative in K-12 education is Century Tech (https://www.century.tech/), a UK-based learning platform that combines AI, neuroscience, and learning science to personalize student learning. Century Tech provides individualized learning pathways based on real-time data analytics, identifying each student's strengths and weaknesses. Teachers receive AI-generated insights that help them adjust lesson plans and allocate resources more effectively. This AI-driven approach enhances curriculum delivery by ensuring that students receive the right level of challenge and support, leading to improved learning outcomes.

Higher education institutions have also embraced AI to enhance curriculum design and student engagement. One of the most successful applications of AI in higher education is the Georgia Institute of Technology's use of AI-powered teaching assistants. Georgia Tech's AI teaching assistant, Jill Watson, was developed using IBM's Watson platform to support students in an online course (Georgia Tech, 2016). Jill Watson was programmed to answer students' frequently asked questions and provide guidance on course-related topics. The AI teaching assistant significantly reduced the workload of human instructors while improving student engagement. This initiative demonstrated how AI could be integrated into curriculum support systems to enhance student learning experiences without compromising instructional quality (Georgia Tech, 2016).

In addition to AI-powered teaching assistants, many universities have adopted AI-driven course recommendation systems to support student learning pathways. For example, Arizona State University (ASU) implemented an AI-driven platform known as eAdvisor (https://eadvisor.asu.edu/institutions), which uses predictive analytics to recommend courses and guide students toward timely degree completion. By analyzing student performance data, course enrollments, and academic goals, eAdvisor provides personalized course recommendations, helping students make informed decisions about their academic journey. This AI-driven approach has been credited with increasing student retention and graduation rates, demonstrating the effectiveness of AI in curriculum planning (Gustavo, 2024).

AI-powered adaptive learning environments are another area where AI has been successfully integrated into curriculum design. One prominent example is Carnegie Learning's MATHia (https://www.carnegielearning.com/solutions/math/mathia/), an AI-driven platform used in both K-12 and higher education settings. MATHia provides students with a personalized math learning experience, continuously assessing their progress and adapting instructional content in real-time. The platform's AI algorithms identify gaps in students' understanding and provide targeted support to reinforce concepts. This adaptive learning model ensures that students receive instruction tailored to their individual needs, reducing frustration and improving overall learning outcomes.

Another successful AI-driven adaptive learning initiative is the University of Central Florida's (UCF) use of AI-powered learning analytics to enhance online course delivery. UCF implemented an AI-driven system that analyzes student engagement patterns, identifies at-risk students, and provides instructors with data-driven insights to optimize curriculum delivery. By using AI-generated recommendations, instructors can adjust course materials, modify assessments, and offer personalized feedback to students. This data-driven approach has led to increased student success rates and more effective curriculum implementation in online learning environments (University of Central Florida, n.d.).

AI-driven curriculum design is also being applied in medical and professional education. The Mayo Clinic has incorporated AI-powered simulations and virtual learning platforms to train medical students and healthcare professionals (Mayo Clinic, n.d.). AI-driven simulations use natural language processing and machine learning algorithms to create realistic clinical scenarios, allowing students to practice medical decision-making in a risk-free environment. These AI-powered curriculum enhancements provide learners with hands-on experience, reinforcing theoretical knowledge through practical application. The success of AI-driven simulations in medical education highlights the potential for AI to revolutionize curriculum design in highly specialized fields (Mayo Clinic, n.d.).

AI-based assessment tools are also transforming curriculum development by automating evaluation processes and providing data-driven insights. Traditional assessments, such as multiple-choice exams and written assignments, often require significant time and effort for grading. AI-powered assessment tools, such as Gradescope (https://www.gradescope.com/) and Turnitin's AI-based feedback system (https://www.turnitin.com.au/), streamline the grading process by using machine learning algorithms to evaluate student submissions. These tools can identify patterns in student responses, detect plagiarism, and provide instant feedback, reducing the workload for educators while ensuring consistency in grading (Oliveira & Barba, 2021) (Lin, Huang, & Lu, 2023) (Wang, Huang, & Martin, 2024).Beyond grading automation, AI-based assessment tools enhance formative assessment practices by offering real-time feedback. Formative assessments, which focus on monitoring student learning during instruction, are critical for identifying knowledge gaps and adjusting curriculum content accordingly. AI-powered platforms, such as Packback (https://www.packback.co/) and Knewton https://www.knewton.com)use natural language processing to analyze student-written responses, generating personalized feedback that helps students refine their understanding of course material. By integrating AI into assessments, educators can create more interactive and responsive learning environments that promote continuous improvement.

The above discussed examples of AI tools and approaches for supporting curriculum development that is engaging and personalized reinforce the view that AI has great potential for innovative curriculum. Not only does AI as a foundational tool for curriculum development enable customization and innovation, but it also plays an important role in fostering interdisciplinary learning (Southworth, et al., 2023) . Traditional curricula often compartmentalize subjects, limiting opportunities for students to see connections between different fields. AI can help break down these barriers by integrating content across disciplines, creating a more holistic learning experience. For example, AI-driven platforms can analyze a student's progress in science and suggest related concepts in mathematics, engineering, or environmental studies. This approach encourages students to develop critical thinking skills and apply their knowledge across multiple domains, better preparing them for complex, real-world challenges.

One of the most widely used AI tools in education is in the Learning Management System (LMS). LMS platforms, such as Blackboard, Moodle, and Canvas, serve as centralized digital environments where educators can create, manage, and deliver curriculum content. AI-powered LMS platforms enhance traditional course management by offering automated grading, personalized learning pathways, and real-time analytics. For example, AI algorithms within an LMS can analyze student engagement patterns and recommend customized resources based on individual learning needs. Additionally, LMS platforms equipped with AI chatbots can provide students with instant responses to course-related inquiries, reducing administrative burdens on educators. LMS are one of the enabling vehicles for implementing AI capabilities in education (Wang, et al., 2024)

In addition to LMS, ITS, and AI-based assessment tools (Georgouli, 2002) (Swiecki, et al., 2022) (Gnanaprakasam & Lourdusamy, 2024), AI-driven content generation platforms are playing an increasingly important role in curriculum development. AI-powered tools, such as OpenAI's GPT-4 and Google's BERT, can generate educational content, summarize complex concepts, and create personalized learning materials. These AI models enable educators to develop customized lesson plans, quizzes, and reading assignments that align with specific learning objectives. By leveraging AI-generated content, instructors can expand their teaching resources while ensuring that curriculum materials remain current and relevant.

Moreover, AI-powered tools support collaborative curriculum development by enabling educators to co-create and share resources in real-time. Cloud-based platforms, such as Google Classroom and Microsoft Teams, incorporate AI-driven features that facilitate teamwork among educators, allowing them to collectively design and refine curriculum materials. AI-driven collaboration tools streamline communication, automate document organization, and provide data-driven recommendations for curriculum enhancements. This collaborative approach fosters innovation in curriculum design, ensuring that educators have access to diverse perspectives and best practices.

Looking ahead, AI is poised to shape the future of learning by enabling new educational models that emphasize flexibility, adaptability, and student-centered instruction. One emerging trend is the rise of competency-based education, which moves away from traditional time-based learning structures in favor of mastery-based progression. In this model, students advance through a curriculum based on their ability to demonstrate proficiency in specific skills rather than adhering to a fixed schedule. AI-driven assessments and learning analytics can support this approach by continuously monitoring student progress and providing real-time feedback. By enabling students to learn at their own pace, AI-powered competency-based education has the potential to create a more inclusive and effective learning environment (Tafazoli, 2024).

One key recommendation for successful AI integration is fostering a culture of collaboration between educators, administrators, and technology specialists. AI-driven curriculum development should not be implemented in isolation but rather as a collaborative effort involving multiple stakeholders. Faculty members should work closely with instructional designers, IT teams, and AI developers to create curricula that incorporate AI in meaningful and pedagogically sound ways. Additionally, engaging students in the conversation about AI integration can provide valuable insights into their learning preferences and help shape AI-driven instructional strategies.

To maximize the benefits of AI in curriculum development, educators must adopt best practices that align AI-driven curriculum design with educational goals and institutional values. One of the most critical best practices is maintaining a balance between AI-driven automation and human oversight. While AI can streamline administrative tasks and generate data-driven insights, educators must remain actively involved in the decision-making process. AI should be viewed as a tool to enhance or augment human teaching, not as a replacement for educator expertise.

Automating Content Generation

Big data analytics facilitated by machine learning and designing adaptable and personalized curriculum resources is just one way that AI technologies are impacting curriculum design and development. Another branch of AI, generative AI is making significant impact on curriculum design. "Generative artificial intelligence (AI) is a form of AI that can autonomously generate new content, such as text, images, audio, and video" (Lv, 2023, p. 208). The backbone of generative AI technology is Natural language processing (NLP) ((Samant, Bachute, Gite, & Kotecha, 2022). NLP allows humans to interact with computers by using human language to write prompts. There are many types of generative AI tools, some for generating text, others for generating images and sound, or for doing an increasing array of routine tasks. Probably the most well-known generative AI tool is Chat GPT Initially, generative AI tools such as Chat GPT in education were greeted with concern about what that might mean for maintaining academic integrity, but perspectives have since evolved to how generative AI can be integrated into the curriculum to support student learning as well as to develop AI literacy in students.

Generative AI tools like ChatGPT and others can help to streamline curriculum design, automate routine tasks and catalyze innovation (Conrad & Hall, 2024). AI-powered platforms can create lesson plans, quizzes, and assessments tailored to specific learning objectives. These tools enable educators to streamline the curriculum development process, saving time and allowing them to focus on more meaningful instructional interactions (Conrad & Hall, 2024). Additionally, AI-driven content generation ensures that curricula remain up to date with the latest developments in various fields, providing students with relevant and timely information. As AI continues to advance, its ability to generate high-quality, customized educational materials will become even more sophisticated, further enhancing curriculum design.

Within learning systems, AI-powered chatbots and virtual assistants utilize natural language processing to provide instant feedback, answer student queries, and facilitate interactive learning experiences. In curriculum design, NLP can be used to analyze vast repositories of educational content, extract relevant information, and generate structured learning materials based on predefined educational objectives (Pereira, Reis, Barroso, Sousa, & Pinto, 2022). This capability allows educators to streamline curriculum development by leveraging AI-generated insights and recommendations.

CHALLENGES

Incorporating AI into curriculum development is not without its challenges. While AI-driven initiatives have demonstrated significant benefits, educators and institutions must address potential barriers to implementation. One major challenge is ensuring that AI-driven curricula remain accessible to all students, regardless of their socioeconomic background (Ali, Murray, Momin, Dwivedi, & Malik, 2024). The digital divide continues to be a concern, with some students lacking access to the necessary technology and internet connectivity to benefit from AI-enhanced learning platforms (Vesna, 2025; Bentley, Naughtin, McGrath, Irons, & Cooper, 2024) (Vesna, 2025) To address this issue, institutions must invest in infrastructure improvements and provide resources to students in need, ensuring that AI-driven curriculum innovations do not exacerbate existing educational inequities.

Another challenge is maintaining ethical AI practices in curriculum design. AI-driven platforms rely on data collection and analysis to personalize learning experiences, raising concerns about data privacy and security (Huang, 2023) (Al-Zahrani, 2024). As AI relies on vast amounts of student data to personalize learning experiences, it is crucial to establish robust safeguards that protect sensitive information (Liu & Khalil, 2023) (Karan & Angadi, 2024). Educational institutions must implement strict data governance policies to ensure transparency, accountability, and compliance with privacy regulations. Educational institutions must implement strict data protection policies to safeguard student information and ensure compliance with privacy regulations.

Transparency in AI decision-making is also crucial to prevent algorithmic biases that could disadvantage certain student groups (Memarian & Doleck, 2023). By adopting ethical AI guidelines and involving educators in AI-driven curriculum decisions, institutions can mitigate these challenges and promote responsible AI integration.

The role of educators in an AI-driven curriculum landscape must be carefully considered (Gentile, Citta, Perna, & Allegra, 2023). While AI can automate administrative tasks and provide data-driven insights, human teachers remain essential in fostering critical thinking, creativity, and emotional intelligence. AI should be viewed as a tool that supports educators rather than replacing them. Professional development programs must be implemented to equip teachers with the skills and knowledge necessary to effectively integrate AI into their instructional practices. By combining AI's analytical capabilities with human expertise, educators can create more engaging and effective learning experiences.

The positive impact of AI in curriculum partly rests with ensuring that AI-driven curriculum development remains accessible to all students, regardless of their socioeconomic background. The digital divide remains a significant barrier to equitable education, with some students lacking access to the necessary technology and internet connectivity required for AI-enhanced learning. To address this issue, policymakers, educators, and technology companies must collaborate to develop inclusive AI solutions that provide equal learning opportunities for all students. This includes investing in infrastructure, expanding access to affordable devices, and creating AI-driven educational tools that accommodate diverse learning needs.

Another best practice is ensuring that AI-driven curriculum development aligns with the principles of inclusivity and equity. AI algorithms must be carefully evaluated for potential biases that could disproportionately impact certain student groups. Institutions should implement bias detection measures and regularly audit AI-driven learning platforms to ensure fairness. Additionally, AI-powered curricula should be accessible to all students, including those with disabilities or limited access to technology. Institutions can achieve this by offering AI-driven learning experiences that accommodate various accessibility needs, such as speech-to-text features, multilingual support, and alternative assessment formats.

Transparency and ethical considerations must also be central to AI-driven curriculum development. Educators and institutions should clearly communicate how AI is being used in the curriculum, including how student data is collected, analyzed, and applied. Providing students and parents with information about AI-driven learning processes fosters trust and encourages responsible AI usage. Moreover, institutions should develop policies to safeguard student data privacy and establish guidelines on ethical AI implementation to prevent misuse or exploitation of student information

To successfully integrate AI into curriculum development, educators must receive adequate professional development and training (Selçuk, Nalbantoglu, Celik, & Dogan, 2024). Many educators may feel uncertain about how to use AI tools effectively, making it essential for institutions to provide ongoing support and professional learning opportunities. Training programs should focus on helping educators understand AI's capabilities, interpret AI-generated insights, and apply AI-driven strategies in their teaching practices.

One effective approach to professional development is offering hands-on workshops and AI literacy courses (Dilek, Baran, & Aleman, 2025) . These programs can introduce educators to AI tools such as intelligent tutoring systems (ITS), AI-based assessment platforms, and adaptive learning technologies. By engaging in practical applications, educators can build confidence in using AI to enhance curriculum design. Additionally, institutions can provide mentorship opportunities where experienced educators collaborate with peers to share best practices for AI integration.

Institutions should also establish AI learning communities where educators can exchange ideas, discuss challenges, and explore emerging AI trends (Ratzmer, 2023). These communities create a support network that encourages continuous professional growth and innovation in AI-driven curriculum development. Furthermore, institutions can partner with AI developers and industry leaders to provide educators with insights into the latest advancements in AI education technologies.

Another crucial aspect of professional development is ensuring that educators understand the ethical and pedagogical implications of AI. While AI can improve efficiency and student outcomes, it must be used responsibly. (Brazil, Yang, & van der Kleij, 2025) . Educators should be trained to critically evaluate AI-generated recommendations, assess the reliability of AI-driven analytics, and make informed decisions that align with educational objectives. Ethical AI training programs can help educators recognize potential biases in AI algorithms, understand the importance of data privacy, and implement AI in ways that promote equity and inclusion. (Brazil, Yang, & van der Kleij, 2025).

In addition to training educators, institutions must provide the necessary infrastructure and resources to support AI-driven curriculum development. Schools and universities should invest in AI-compatible learning platforms, ensure high-speed internet access, and provide access to AI-powered tools that enhance teaching and learning. Institutions must also allocate funding for AI research and development initiatives that explore innovative applications of AI in curriculum design.

As AI continues to evolve, educators and institutions must remain adaptable and open to continuous improvement. AI-driven curriculum development is not a static process but an ongoing journey that requires regular assessment and refinement. Institutions should establish feedback loops where educators, students, and administrators can evaluate the effectiveness of AI-driven learning experiences and suggest improvements. By actively engaging in reflective practice, institutions can ensure that AI remains a valuable and relevant tool for enhancing curriculum design.

CONCLUSION

Despite these challenges, the future of AI-driven curriculum development is promising. As AI technologies continue to advance, their applications in education will become more sophisticated and widespread. Emerging AI-driven initiatives, such as intelligent tutoring systems, automated grading platforms, and virtual reality-enhanced learning experiences, are poised to further transform curriculum design. Institutions that embrace AI as a tool for enhancing curriculum development will be better positioned to provide students with personalized, data-driven, and future-ready educational experiences.

AI-driven curriculum initiatives in K-12 and higher education are reshaping traditional instructional methods by introducing personalized learning, adaptive environments, and data-driven decision-making. Case studies from institutions such as Georgia Tech, Arizona State University, and the Mayo Clinic demonstrate the successful integration of AI in curriculum design, leading to improved student engagement, retention, and learning outcomes. While challenges such as accessibility, ethical considerations, and data privacy must be addressed, the potential of AI in education remains vast. By leveraging AI responsibly and strategically, educational institutions can create curricula that enhance student learning experiences, prepare learners for the future, and drive innovation in education.

Artificial Intelligence (AI) has the potential to revolutionize curriculum development by providing educators with tools that create personalized, data-driven, and adaptable learning experiences. By leveraging AI technologies, educational institutions can design curricula that are more responsive to student needs, align with workforce demands, and incorporate emerging trends in digital learning. However, the successful integration of AI into curriculum development requires a thoughtful approach that addresses ethical concerns, ensures equitable access, and preserves the essential role of educators in shaping the learning process.

One of the key advantages of AI in curriculum development is its ability to personalize learning experiences. Traditional curricula often follow a standardized model, which may not accommodate the diverse learning styles, paces, and needs of students. AI-powered adaptive learning platforms can analyze student data to identify strengths and weaknesses, allowing for tailored instruction that meets individual learning needs. These platforms can adjust lesson content in real time, ensuring that students receive targeted support and enrichment opportunities. This level of personalization fosters engagement, improves retention, and helps students develop a deeper understanding of the material.

Data-driven decision-making is another transformative aspect of AI in curriculum development. AI can process vast amounts of student performance data, providing educators with insights into learning patterns, comprehension levels, and potential gaps in instruction. By analyzing these data points, AI can help educators refine curriculum content, adjust teaching methodologies, and implement evidence-based strategies to enhance student learning outcomes. Additionally, predictive analytics can anticipate future learning challenges, allowing institutions to proactively address them before they impact student success.

Despite its benefits, AI integration in curriculum design must be approached with caution to address ethical concerns. One major issue is algorithmic bias (Xlimi & Carballido, 2023), where AI systems may inadvertently reinforce existing inequalities in education. If AI models are trained on biased datasets, they may produce recommendations that favor certain student demographics over others. To mitigate this risk, institutions must ensure that AI-driven curriculum tools are designed with fairness and inclusivity in mind. Regular audits, transparent decision-making processes, and diverse representation in AI training data are essential steps in preventing bias and promoting equitable learning opportunities.

Ensuring equitable access to AI-driven education is another critical challenge (Kitsara, 2022). While AI has the potential to enhance learning experiences, students from underprivileged backgrounds may lack access to the necessary technology and internet connectivity required to benefit from these innovations. Educational institutions must work toward closing the digital divide by providing resources such as subsidized devices, internet access programs, and AI-enhanced learning materials that cater to diverse student populations. Policymakers, educators, and technology providers must collaborate to create AI-driven curricula that are accessible to all learners, regardless of socioeconomic status.

Preserving the role of educators is fundamental to the successful integration of AI in curriculum development. While AI can automate certain aspects of curriculum design, such as grading and content recommendations, it cannot replace the human elements of teaching, such as mentorship, creativity, and emotional intelligence. Educators play a vital role in interpreting AI-generated insights, adapting curriculum content, and fostering meaningful interactions with students. AI should be viewed as a supportive tool that enhances, rather than replaces, the expertise of teachers.

Institutions must invest in professional development programs to equip educators with the skills needed to effectively integrate AI into their teaching practices.

Looking to the future, the potential of AI in curriculum development is boundless. As AI technologies continue to evolve, they will enable even greater levels of personalization, adaptability, and efficiency in education. The development of AI-powered learning assistants, virtual reality-enhanced lessons, and real-time language translation tools will further transform the way students engage with curriculum content. AI will also facilitate the creation of dynamic, evolving curricula that respond to societal changes, industry needs, and scientific advancements.

In conclusion, AI is set to play an increasingly transformative role in curriculum development, shaping the future of education in profound ways. From personalized learning and interdisciplinary integration to lifelong education and predictive analytics, AI offers numerous opportunities to enhance teaching and learning. However, its successful implementation will require careful planning, ethical considerations, and a commitment to ensuring accessibility for all students. By embracing AI as a tool for innovation and collaboration, educators and institutions can create more effective, inclusive, and future-ready curricula that prepare students for success in an ever-changing world.

REFERENCES

Ahmed, F. (2024). The digital divide and AI in education: Addressing equity and accessibility. *Journal of AI in Education: Innovations, Opportunities, Challenges, and Future Directions*, *1*(2), 12–23.

Al-Zahrani, A. (2024). Unveiling the shadows: Beyond the hype of AI in education. *Heliyon*, *10*(9), e30696. DOI: 10.1016/j.heliyon.2024.e30696 PMID: 38737255

Ali, O., Murray, P., Momin, J., Dwivedi, Y., & Malik, T. (2024). The effects of artificial intelligence applications in educational settings: Challenges and strategies. *Technological Forecasting and Social Change*, *199*(123076). Advance online publication. DOI: 10.1016/j.techfore.2023.123076

Anthamatten, A., & Holt, J. (2024). Integrating Artificial Intelligence Into Virtual Simulations to Develop Entrustable Professional Activities. *The Journal for Nurse Practitioners*, *20*(9), 105192. DOI: 10.1016/j.nurpra.2024.105192

Baig, M., Shuib, L., & Yadegaridehkordi, E. (2020). Big data in education: A state of the art, limitations, and future research directions. *International Journal of Educational Technology in Higher Education*, *17*(44), 1–23.

Bentley, S., Naughtin, C., McGrath, M., Irons, J., & Cooper, P. (2024). The digital divide in action: How experiences of digital technology shape future relationships with artificial intelligence. *AI and Ethics*, *4*, 901–915.

Bhattacharya, S., Bhattacharya, K., & Bhattacharya, N. (2024). Surgical Mentorship in the Era of Artificial Intelligence. *Indian J Surg*, https://doi-org.libraryproxy.griffith.edu.au/10.1007/s12262-024-04252-1

Brazil, J., Yang, S., & van der Kleij, F. (2025). *AI systems in teaching and learning: principles and practical examples.* Retrieved March 2025, from ACER: https://research.acer.edu.au/cgi/viewcontent.cgi?article=1021&context=digital_learning

Chang, C., Hui, J., Justus-Smith, C., & Wang, T. (2024). Navigating STEM careers with AI mentors: A new IDP journey. *Frontiers in Artificial Intelligence*, *7*. Advance online publication. DOI: 10.3389/frai.2024.1461137 PMID: 39439844

Conrad, E., & Hall, K. (2024). Leveraging Generative AI to Elevate Curriculum Design and Pedagogy in Public Health and Health Promotion. *Pedagogy in Health Promotion*, *10*(3), 178–186.

Dilek, M., Baran, E., & Aleman, E. (2025). AI Literacy in Teacher Education: Empowering Educators Through Critical Co-Discovery. *Journal of Teacher Education, 0*(0). https://doi-org.libraryproxy.griffith.edu.au/10.1177/00224871251325

Gentile, M., Citta, G., Perna, S., & Allegra, M. (2023). Do we still need teachers? Navigating the paradigm shift of the teacher's role in the AI era. *Frontiers in Education, 8.* Advance online publication. DOI: 10.3389/feduc.2023.1161777

Georgia Tech. (2016, November 10). *Meet Jill Watson: Georgia Tech's first AI teaching assistant.* Retrieved April 2025, from Professional Education College of Lifetime Learning: https://pe.gatech.edu/blog/meet-jill-watson-georgia-techs-first-ai-teaching-assistant

Georgouli, K. (2002). The design of a motivating intelligent assessment system. (pp. 811-820). San Sebastian, Spain and Biarritz France: Lecture Notes in computer Science.

Gnanaprakasam, J., & Lourdusamy, R. (2024). *The Role of AI in automating grading: Enhancing feedback and efficiency.* Retrieved from https://www.intechopen.com/chapters/1181936

Goldberg, B., & Robson, R. (2023). *AI to Support Guided Experiential Learning. Artificial Intelligence in Education. Posters and Late Breaking Results, Workshops and Tutorials, Industry and Innovation Tracks, Practitioners, Doctoral Consortium and Blue Sky. AIED 2023.Communications in Computer and Information Science, 1831, pp.* Springer., https://doi-org.libraryproxy.griffith.edu.au/10.1007/978-3-031-36336-8_16

Gustavo, D. (2024, September 03). *How Arizona State University is Leading the Way in AI-Driven Personalized Learning: Insights from ChatGPT and Claude.* Retrieved April 2025, from LinkedIn: https://www.linkedin.com/pulse/how-arizona-state-university-leading-way-ai-driven-learning-demoner-yhu7c

Huang, L. (2023). Ethics of artificial intelligence in education: Student privacy and data protection. *SIEF, 16*(2), 2578–2587.

IBM. (n.d.). *What is generative AI?* Retrieved from IBM Blog - Explainer: https://research.ibm.com/blog/what-is-generative-AI

Karan, B., & Angadi, G. (2024). Potential Risks of Artificial Intelligence Integration into School Education: A Systematic Review. *Bulletin of Science, Technology & Society, 43*(3-4), 67–85.

Kitsara, I. (2022). Artificial Intelligence and the digital divide: From an innovation perspective. In A. Bounfour, *Platforms and Artificial Intelligence The Next Generation of Competences* (pp. 245–265). Springer.

Kumar, D., Haque, A., Mishra, K., Islam, F., & Ahmad, S. (2023). Exploring the transformative role of artificial intelligence and metaverse in education: A comprehensive review. *Metaverse Basic and Applied Research*, *2*(55), 1–12.

Lin, C., Huang, A., & Lu, O. (2023). Artificial intelligence in intelligent tutoring systems toward sustainable education: A systematic review. *Smart Learning Environments*, *10*(41). Advance online publication. DOI: 10.1186/s40561-023-00260-y

Liu, Q., & Khalil, M. (2023). Understanding privacy and data protection issues in learning analytics using a systematic review. *British Journal of Educational Technology*, *54*, 1715–1747.

Luan, H., Geczy, P., Lai, H., Gobert, J., Yang, S., Ogata, H., & Tsai, C. (2020). Challenges and future directions of big data and artificial intelligence in education. *Frontiers in Psychology*, *11*, 1–10. PMID: 33192896

Lv, Z. (2023). Generative artificial intelligence in the metaverse era. *Cognitive Robotics*, *3*, 208–217.

Matz, S., Bukow, C., Peters, H., Deacons, C., Dinu, A., & Stachl, C. (2023). Using machine learning to predict student retention from socio-demographic characteristics and app-based engagement metrics. *Scientific Reports*, *13*, 5705. DOI: 10.1038/s41598-023-32484-w PMID: 37029155

Mayo Clinic. (n.d.). *Mayo Clinic Harper Family Foundation Artificial Intelligence Education in Medicine Program*. Retrieved March 2025, from Mayo Clinic Harper Family Foundation Artificial Intelligence Education in Medicine Program: https://education.mayo.edu/mayo-clinic-harper-family-foundation-artificial-intelligence-education-in-medicine-program/

Memarian, B., & Doleck, T. (2023). Fairness, Accountability, Transparency, and Ethics (FATE) in Artificial Intelligence (AI) and higher education: A systematic review. *Computers and Education: Artificial Intelligence*, *5*, 100152. DOI: 10.1016/j.caeai.2023.100152

Mulpeter, N., McCormack, O., & O'Flaherty, J. (2023). Purpose, focus and voice? Lessons from a curriculum development advisory committee. *Irish Educational Studies*, (4), 1025–1042.

Oliveira, E., & Barba, P. (2021). Enabling adaptive, personalised and context-aware interaction in a smart learning environment: Piloting the iCollab system. *Australasian Journal of Educational Technology*, *37*(2), 1–23.

Ozsevim, I., & Ng, A. (2023). *Deepening and democratising learning.* Retrieved from AI Magazine: https://aimagazine.com/articles/andrew-ng-deepening-and-democratising-learning

Palenski, T., Hills, L., Unnikrishnan, S., & Eynon, R. (2024). How AI Works: Reconfiguring Lifelong Learning. *Postdigital Science and Education*, *6*, 1216–1239.

Papamitsiou, Z., & Economides, A. (2014). Learning analytics and educational data mining in practice: A systematic literature review of empirical evidence. *Journal of Educational Technology & Society*, *17*(4), 49–64.

Peng, H., Ma, S., & Spector, J. (2019). Personalized adaptive learning: An emerging pedagogical approach enabled by a smart learning environment. *Smart Learning Environments*, *6*(9), 1–14.

Pereira, R., Reis, A., Barroso, J., Sousa, J., & Pinto, T. (2022). *Virtual Assistants Applications in Education. Technology and Innovation in Learning, Teaching and Education. TECH-EDU 2022. 1720.* Springer., https://doi-org.libraryproxy.griffith.edu.au/10.1007/978-3-031-22918-3_38

Prideaux, D. (2003). ABC of learning and teachng in medicine.Curriculum design. *BMJ (Clinical Research Ed.)*, *326*(7383), 268–270. DOI: 10.1136/bmj.326.7383.268 PMID: 12560283

Rahiman, H., & Kodikal, R. (Cogent Education). Revolutionizing education: Artificial intelligence empowered learning in higher education. *11*, 1-24.

Ratzmer, M. (2023, March 29). *Artificial Intelligence Communities of Practice.* Retrieved April 2025, from The University of Adelaide - Learning and Teaching: https://www.adelaide.edu.au/learning/news/list/2023/03/29/artificial-intelligence-communities-of-practice

Samant, R., Bachute, M., Gite, S., & Kotecha, K. (2022). Framework for deep learning-based language models using multi-task learning in natural language understanding: A systematic literature review and future directions. *IEEE Access : Practical Innovations, Open Solutions*, *10*, 17078–17097.

Sarker, I. (2021). Data Science and Analytics: An Overview from Data-Driven Smart Computing, Decision-Making and Applications Perspective. *Springer Nature Computer Science*, *2*(5), 377. PMID: 34278328

Schiff, D. (2021). Education for AI, not AI for Education: The Role of Education and Ethics in National AI Policy Strategies. *International Journal of Artificial Intelligence in Education*, https://doi-org.libraryproxy.griffith.edu.au/10.1007/s40593-021-00270-2

Selçuk, D., Nalbantoglu, U., Celik, I., & Dogan, N. (2024). Artificial intelligence professional development: A systematic review of TPACK, designs, and effects for teacher learning. *Professional Development in Education, 1*. Advance online publication. DOI: 10.1080/19415257.2025.2454457

Southworth, J., Migliaccio, K., Glover, J., Glover, J., Reed, D., McCarty, C., & Thomas, A. (2023). Developing a model for AI Across the curriculum: Transforming the higher education landscape via innovation in AI literacy. *Computers and education. Artificial Intelligence*, *4*, 100127. DOI: 10.1016/j.caeai.2023.100127

Swiecki, Z., Khosravi, H., Chen, G., Martinez-Maldonado, R., Lodge, J., Millifan, S., & Gasevic, D. (2022). Assessment in the age of artificial intelligence. *omputers and Education. Artificial Intelligence*, *3*, 1–10.

Tafazoli, D. (2024, December). Exploring the potential of generative AI in democratizing English language education. *Computers and Education: Artificial Intelligence, 7*.

Towfek, S., Khodadadi, N., Abualigah, L., & Rizk, F. (2024). AI in Higher Education: Insights from Student Surveys and Predictive Analytics using PSO-Guided WOA and Linear Regression. *JAIEP*(https://jaiep.journals.ekb.eg/article_354003_19fe159da1d32d8628a13261bd5d9309.pdf)

University of Central Florida. (n.d.). *AI research at UCF*. Retrieved April 2025, from Unlocking the Future of Artificial Intelligence: https://www.ucf.edu/artificial-intelligence/

Vesna, L. (2025). Digital Divide in AI-Powered Education: Challenges and Solutions for Equitable Learning. *Journal of Information Systems Engineering & Management*, *10*(21), 300–308.

Wang, S., Wang, F., Zhu, Z., Wang, J., Tran, T., & Du, Z. (2024). Artificial intelligence in education: A systematic literature review. *Expert Systems with Applications, 252 Part A*, 124167. https://doi.org/.DOI: 10.1016/j.eswa.2024.124167

Wang, X., Huang, R., & Martin, F. (2024). The Efficacy of Artificial Intelligence-Enabled Adaptive Learning Systems From 2010 to 2022 on Learner Outcomes: A Meta-Analysis. *Journal of Educational Computing Research*, *62*(6), 1568–1603.

Webb, B. (2024, September 19). *AI-Driven Curriculum Adaptation: Navigating the Future of Education and Work.* Retrieved from LinkedIn: https://www.linkedin.com/pulse/ai-driven-curriculum-adaptation-navigating-future-education-webb-rl33e

Wyse, D., & Manyukhina, Y. (2024, April 17). *Curriculum development.* Retrieved 05 April 2025, from https://oxfordre.com/education/view/10.1093/acrefore/9780190264093.001.0001/acrefore-9780190264093-e-1860

Xlimi, Z., & Carballido, B. (2023). Navitating the ethical challenges of artificial intelligence in higher education: An analysis of seven global AI ethics policies. *TEM Journal, 12*(2), 590–602.

Chapter 7
AI in Higher Education: Opportunities and Challenges

Geraldine Torrisi-Steele
https://orcid.org/0000-0002-6045-4114
Griffith University, Australia

ABSTRACT

Artificial Intelligence (AI) is transforming higher education by enhancing teaching, learning, and administrative processes. AI-driven technologies, such as intelligent tutoring systems, personalized learning platforms, and automated grading, provide educators with new tools to improve student engagement and learning outcomes. Additionally, AI streamlines administrative tasks, increases accessibility for diverse learners, and supports data-driven decision-making. However, integrating AI into higher education also presents challenges, including ethical concerns, data privacy risks, faculty adaptation, and the potential displacement of human roles. Institutions must address these issues through responsible AI governance, professional development programs, and policies that ensure AI serves as a complement to, rather than a replacement for, human educators. This paper explores the evolving role of AI in higher education, examining both its transformative potential and the critical considerations that must be navigated to ensure equitable and effective implementation.

INTRODUCTION

Artificial Intelligence (AI) is reshaping the landscape of higher education in profound ways. With advancements in machine learning, natural language processing, and data analytics, AI is being integrated into universities and colleges worldwide to enhance teaching, learning, research, and administration. AI-powered technologies, such as intelligent tutoring systems, automated grading, and adaptive learning

DOI: 10.4018/979-8-3373-2397-8.ch007

platforms, are revolutionizing the way students interact with educational content. Additionally, AI has the potential to personalize education, making learning more accessible and inclusive for students of diverse backgrounds, abilities, and learning styles. However, while AI brings immense opportunities, it also presents significant challenges, including ethical concerns, data privacy risks, job displacement fears, and issues surrounding equity and accessibility. This paper explores the multifaceted role of AI in higher education, discussing both the transformative benefits and the critical challenges that institutions must address to maximize AI's potential in a responsible and sustainable manner.

Higher education institutions are increasingly turning to AI-driven solutions to improve educational delivery and institutional efficiency. AI applications in higher education can be broadly categorized into four key areas: personalized learning, administrative automation, research enhancement, and student engagement. These applications are designed to make learning more student-centric, reduce administrative burdens on faculty and staff, and create data-driven strategies for institutional growth.

One of AI's most promising applications in higher education is personalized learning. AI-powered learning platforms analyze student data, including academic performance, learning habits, and engagement levels, to create customized learning pathways. Adaptive learning systems adjust the difficulty of assignments, recommend tailored study materials, and provide instant feedback to enhance the student learning experience. Intelligent tutoring systems (ITS) use AI algorithms to mimic human tutors, offering students real-time assistance and personalized support outside the classroom.

For example, AI-based tools like Carnegie Learning's MATHia and IBM's Watson Tutor assist students in mastering complex subjects by providing step-by-step explanations and adaptive problem-solving exercises. These systems help bridge gaps in understanding, particularly for students who may struggle with traditional learning methods. By offering continuous assessment and feedback, AI enhances student retention and academic success rates.

Beyond the classroom, AI plays a crucial role in streamlining administrative processes within higher education institutions. AI-powered chatbots, virtual assistants, and automated systems help universities manage student inquiries, enrollment procedures, and scheduling. AI-driven analytics also aid in decision-making, allowing institutions to forecast student enrollment trends, optimize course offerings, and allocate resources more effectively.

Universities are leveraging AI-powered chatbots, such as Georgia State University's Pounce chatbot, to handle student inquiries regarding admissions, financial aid, and campus services. By automating repetitive administrative tasks, AI enables faculty and staff to focus on more complex and high-value responsibilities. Additionally, AI-driven predictive analytics help institutions identify at-risk students by analyzing behavioral and academic data, allowing early intervention strategies to improve retention and graduation rates.

AI is also transforming academic research by accelerating data analysis, automating literature reviews, and identifying emerging trends in various disciplines. AI-powered tools, such as Elsevier's Scopus AI and Google Scholar's machine learning algorithms, assist researchers in retrieving relevant academic papers, summarizing key findings, and detecting patterns within vast datasets. AI's ability to process large volumes of information quickly enhances the efficiency and accuracy of research endeavors.

Furthermore, AI is driving innovation in fields such as medicine, engineering, and social sciences by enabling advanced simulations, predictive modeling, and automated data classification. For instance, AI-powered image recognition technology is revolutionizing medical research by assisting in disease diagnosis and drug discovery. AI's computational capabilities allow researchers to analyze complex biological, environmental, and behavioral data, opening new frontiers in scientific discovery.

AI-driven tools are enhancing student engagement by providing interactive learning experiences and fostering collaboration. Virtual reality (VR) and augmented reality (AR), powered by AI, are being integrated into coursework to create immersive learning environments. AI-powered recommendation systems also help students discover relevant resources, including academic articles, online courses, and professional development opportunities tailored to their interests and career aspirations.

Moreover, AI is improving student support services by offering mental health and career counseling through virtual assistants. AI-driven career guidance platforms analyze student profiles, skills, and industry trends to provide personalized career recommendations. For example, platforms like LinkedIn Learning use AI algorithms to suggest courses and certifications based on students' career goals and industry demands.

While AI presents numerous opportunities in higher education, its implementation also raises ethical, social, and technical challenges that institutions must navigate carefully.

One of the primary concerns surrounding AI in higher education is data privacy and security. AI-driven systems collect and analyze vast amounts of student data, raising

Chapter Overview

The integration of Artificial Intelligence (AI) in higher education is transforming the landscape of teaching, learning, and administration. AI-powered tools and systems are increasingly being used to personalize education, automate administrative processes, enhance research capabilities, and improve student engagement. This transformation is driven by advancements in machine learning, natural language processing, and data analytics, which enable AI to analyze vast amounts of data and provide insights that enhance decision-making at all levels of academia.

One of the most significant opportunities AI presents in higher education is the ability to create personalized learning experiences. Adaptive learning platforms use AI algorithms to assess students' strengths and weaknesses, tailoring instructional materials and assessments to meet their individual needs. This technology can provide real-time feedback, identify learning gaps, and recommend resources that help students master complex subjects. Intelligent tutoring systems further enhance this personalized approach by offering targeted assistance and interactive learning experiences outside the traditional classroom setting. These AI-driven solutions improve student outcomes by making education more accessible and responsive to individual learning styles.

AI is also playing a crucial role in streamlining administrative tasks, allowing institutions to operate more efficiently. Universities are deploying AI-powered chatbots to assist with student inquiries regarding admissions, financial aid, and course registration. These virtual assistants provide instant responses, reducing the workload on administrative staff and improving the overall student experience. Additionally, AI-driven predictive analytics help institutions forecast enrollment trends, optimize course scheduling, and allocate resources effectively. By leveraging AI for these tasks, universities can enhance operational efficiency while freeing up human resources for more complex and strategic initiatives.

In the realm of research, AI is revolutionizing the way scholars conduct studies and analyze data. AI-powered tools can process vast datasets, identify patterns, and generate insights that would take humans significantly longer to uncover. For example, AI is being used in medical research to detect diseases through image recognition, in social sciences to analyze behavioral trends, and in engineering to optimize design processes. Furthermore, AI-driven literature review tools assist researchers in finding relevant academic papers, summarizing key findings, and identifying emerging areas of study. These applications not only accelerate the research process but also improve the quality and depth of scholarly work.

Despite its many advantages, the integration of AI in higher education also presents several challenges that institutions must navigate carefully. Ethical considerations are among the most pressing concerns, particularly regarding data privacy and security. AI systems rely on large volumes of student data to function effectively, raising questions about how this data is collected, stored, and used. Universities must establish robust data governance policies to protect sensitive information and ensure compliance with regulations such as the General Data Protection Regulation (GDPR) and the Family Educational Rights and Privacy Act (FERPA).

Equity is another critical issue associated with AI adoption in higher education. While AI has the potential to enhance accessibility for students with disabilities through features like speech-to-text and real-time translation, disparities in digital access can create new barriers for underprivileged students. Not all students have equal access to AI-powered educational tools, particularly those from low-income backgrounds or rural areas with limited technological infrastructure. To address this challenge, institutions must implement inclusive AI policies and invest in initiatives that promote digital equity.

Another significant concern is the potential for job displacement among faculty and staff. As AI takes over routine tasks such as grading assignments, providing feedback, and managing administrative workflows, some fear that academic and support roles may be reduced. However, AI should be viewed as a tool that complements rather than replaces human educators. By automating repetitive tasks, AI allows faculty to focus on more meaningful aspects of teaching, such as mentoring students, fostering critical thinking, and facilitating discussions. Universities should invest in professional development programs to equip educators with the skills needed to integrate AI into their teaching methodologies effectively.

Through a comprehensive analysis, this chapter aims to provide a balanced view of AI's impact on higher education. While AI offers transformative potential to enhance educational practices, increase efficiency, and support research, it also introduces challenges that require careful consideration. By developing policies that promote ethical AI use, ensuring equitable access to technology, and fostering collaboration between AI and human educators, institutions can maximize the benefits of AI while mitigating its risks. The responsible integration of AI in higher education will not only improve student learning outcomes but also shape the future of academia in a way that is innovative, inclusive, and sustainable.

Introduction to AI in Higher Education

The suite of emergent technologies that are generically referred to as artificial intelligence or AI hold the potential to positively impact on the landscape of higher education. The deluge of extreme reactions and the accompanying volumes of literature following the release of ChatGPT in November 2022 makes it feel like AI in education is something completely new. AI in education has a long history, spanning several decades. If one considers that AI has a lot to do with automation, then it the history of AI in education goes as far back as the mid-20th century when during the 1950's and 1960's, researchers began exploring the potential of computers in education, leading to the development of the first computer-based learning programs. to the time in the 1960's when computers were introduced as tools for teaching problem solving. Way back in the 1970's and 1980's Intelligent tutoring systems made an appearance. These systems adapted to students' progress and could provide feedback. Although the systems were very limited in what they could do, the aim was to somehow replicate the one-on-one tutoring experience. By the early 2000's adaptive learning environments were developed. These learning environments made use of machine learning algorithms which enabled adjustment to individual learning paths and the personalization of learning environments. However, the time and technology were not yet ripe for these tools to be implemented on a larger scale. Nonetheless, AI in education bubbled away at a steady pace. Some headway was made into using AI for automating learning and automating administrative tasks as well personalizing learning. Despite this, AI didn't really "take off". It was perhaps the conversational capabilities popularized by the public release of ChatGPT that really drew attention to AI. ChatGPT did more than just rapidly popularize AI in education. Its advent created a sense of urgency for dealing with and bringing AI into Education. The urgency translates into AI in learning and teaching as a priority for many educational institutions. The increased emphasis on AI in education, advancement of technologies, and growing accessibility to AI technologies position AI as a truly transformative force in education.

OPPORTUNITIES: APPLICATIONS OF AI IN HIGHER EDUCATION

Artificial Intelligence (AI) is revolutionizing various aspects of higher education, offering innovative solutions that enhance both teaching and learning experiences (Rahiman & Kodikal, Cogent Education) (Al-Zahrani & Alasmari, 2024). (Farooq, Malik, & Syed, 2024). The application of AI technologies in the higher education sector covers is wide-ranging but can be loosely categorized into three domains of application: administrative, supporting learning, prediction and modelling student behaviors Among its most significant contributions are personalized learning, enhanced teaching tools, intelligent tutoring systems, data-driven decision-making, and administrative efficiency. These AI-driven advancements help institutions optimize student outcomes, improve instructional methods, and streamline institutional operations. By integrating AI into education, universities can create a more efficient, inclusive, and student-centered learning environment. Wang et. al. (2024) in their comprehensive systematic literature review of AI in education provides an excellent snapshot of the applications of AI technologies to education. These include Intelligent tutoring systems, adaptive hypermedia learning systems, Intelligent assessment systems, learning management systems, various profiling and prediction tools, and the integration of AI into other emerging technologies including educational robotics, AR and VR.

Among the most widely used AI-powered tools are intelligent tutoring systems and adaptive hypermedia systems. Intelligent tutoring systems can be defined as "computer programs that use AI techniques to provide intelligent tutors that know what they teach, whom they teach, and how to teach" (Alkhatlan & Kalita) . Adaptive learning systems, sometimes referred to as personalized adaptive learning are defined as "a technology-empowered effective pedagogy which can adaptively adjust teaching strategies timely based on real-time monitored (enabled by smart technology) learners' differences and changes in individual characteristics, performance, and personal development" (Peng, Ma, & Spector, 2019).These systems leverage natural language processing and machine learning algorithms to adapt to each student's unique learning pace, ensuring a customized educational experience. AI-driven chatbots and virtual assistants have also become increasingly popular, assisting students with administrative queries, course selections, and even mental health support. These AI tools help reduce faculty and staff workload while ensuring that students receive timely responses to their concerns. . Examples of widely used ITS include Carnegie Learning's MATHia, IBM Watson Tutor, and Socratic by Google. These systems enable students to receive personalized tutoring whenever they need assistance, enhancing learning retention and comprehension. ITS can also adapt to different learning styles by presenting information in multiple formats, such as text, audio, or visual demonstrations, making education more accessible and engaging.

Intelligent tutoring systems can be traced back to the early days of computer-based training. It was a study published by Bloom (1984) which propelled the application of AI to intelligent tutoring forward. In the study, Bloom refers to 2 Sigma problem which is the finding that students exposed to one-one tutoring will tend to perform two standard deviations above those that are not. But of course, one-one tutoring is time consuming and the required individualization of instruction is challenging. Hence, developing 'automated' intelligent tutoring systems which mimic the human tutor is an attractive proposition and has led to concerted efforts in the design and develop such systems. The maturation and accessibility of computing technologies and developments in AI technologies is facilitating the proliferation of intelligent tutoring systems in education. Additional impetus for the development of intelligent tutoring systems is gained from the contemporary higher education environment where institutions are battling with globalized competition, difficult economic times and increased pressures to cater for (engage and retain) diverse student cohorts, the development of intelligent tutoring systems. Increasingly, with the power of AI, adaptive systems are integrating with intelligent tutoring systems to provide personalized pathways and learning support to students (Peng, Ma, &

Spector, 2019).The distinction between adaptive learning systems and intelligent tutoring systems is blurring.

Some research is showing that students using intelligent tutoring systems are more engaged, do better academically and there a positive effect on retention (Kumar, Haque, Mishra, Islam, & Ahmad, 2023). It must be noted at this point, that the design of the intelligent tutoring system has bearing on how effective it is. There is substantial research focusing on how to design intelligent systems to facilitate learning and is often founded in psychology and pedagogical research (Guo, et al., 2021).

Personalized learning is one of AI's most transformative contributions to education. AI-driven platforms analyze individual student data, including learning habits, strengths, weaknesses, and engagement patterns, to create customized learning pathways. These adaptive learning systems adjust the difficulty of assignments, recommend tailored study materials, and provide targeted feedback to ensure that students grasp concepts at their own pace. By offering a more individualized approach to education, AI helps bridge learning gaps and supports students with diverse academic backgrounds and abilities. Platforms such as Coursera, edX, and Khan Academy use AI algorithms to recommend courses and content based on a learner's progress and preferences. Done properly, the individualization offered by AI can help to democratize education (Tafazoli, 2024) (Ozsevim & Ng, 2023).

Pivotal to effective student learning is assessment. Hence, attention is also directed to how AI can be used to deliver individualized. There are significant efforts to design intelligent and adaptive learning systems which improve student outcomes by facilitating learning through guided practice and presenting facilitative pathways suited to the individual needs of students are being extended to the domain of assessment. AI based assessment learning systems are "educational systems that should be able to identify as quickly as possible the gaps in the student's knowledge of the subject domain and to check for reasons for that. Like an expert human tutor does, should be mainly able a) to decide about how to present the assessing material and what to assess next, following the curriculum sequencing and b) to take under consideration the motivational state of the student" (Georgouli, 2002, p. 813). Some of the work on assessment learning systems is focused on formative (assessment for learning) (Memarian & Doleck, 2024) or diagnostic assessment. For example, Wang, et al., (2022) "develop an intelligent assessment and strategy implementation system for mathematics learning strategies by integrating AI technology and intelligently evaluating and diagnosing mathematics learning strategies of students from different schools and different regions, at any time anywhere. This system can also intelligently prescribe "prescriptions" based on the "cause of the disease" so that researchers can conduct targeted intervention studies "(p.1). These systems can analyze written responses, detect patterns, and provide constructive feedback, enabling students to understand their mistakes and improve performance.

It is well understood that assessment is a critical element for learning and in the learning experience itself. However, for educators designing, marking and providing feedback for a class assessment is extremely time-consuming. Designing and dealing with individualized assessments even more time-consuming, if not infeasible. AI tools can help alleviate these difficulties to make individual assessments feasible (Swiecki, et al., 2022).

While formative assessments are designed primarily for learning and diagnostic purposes, summative assessments are directed at evaluating student learning for the purpose of assigning grades (although the principle of assessment for learning is still present). The design of summative assessments has long been challenged by the effectiveness of assessment to evaluate more than simply rote learning, and by the issue of academic integrity. Scholarly researchers such as Owoseni, Kolade and Egbetokun (2024) explore the role of generative AI tools to help design "fair, unbiased, scalable" assessments.AI assisted assessment design aside, AI-assisted grading systems help educators evaluate assignments and exams quickly and efficiently, reducing workload while ensuring consistency in grading (Gnanaprakasam & Lourdusamy, 2024) (Dimari, Tyagi, Davanageri, & Kukret, 2024). AI-powered plagiarism detection and grading software have also gained widespread adoption, helping educators assess student work more efficiently while maintaining academic integrity (Elkhatat, Elsaid, & Almeer, 2023).

Generative AI technologies in higher education are also being explored for efficiencies by augmenting curriculum design and even automating the production of engaging media rich resources for e-learning (Fang & Broussard, 2024). (Blake, 2023) Additionally, AI is integrated into interactive and media rich tools such as virtual reality (VR) and augmented reality (AR), opening new scope for the creation of individualized immersive learning experiences (Cinar, Rafferty, Cutting, & Wang, 2024).

The fallout of the increased pervasiveness of digital learning systems is the large volume of data generated when users interact with these systems. These vast volumes of data are referred to as big data, and though difficult to process and analyze in traditional ways (Baig, Shuib, & Yadegaridehkordi, 2020), big data has the potential to provide insights into student learning patterns and behaviors. Properly analyzed, big data enables modelling and prediction of a range of learner behaviors that are useful for managing student learning, engagement and retention (Papamitsiou & Economides, 2014) (Luan, et al., 2020). Furthermore, this data can support administrative decision making at institutional level. AI algorithms provide the means for analysis of big data. Thus, another significant AI application in higher education is predictive analytics, which enables institutions to make data-driven decisions regarding student success and retention. By analyzing vast amounts of student data, AI algorithms can identify at-risk students and suggest targeted interventions to improve academic performance (Towfek, Khodadadi, Abualigah, & Rizk, 2024). Predictive analytics also assist in course scheduling, enrollment forecasting, and optimizing resource allocation (Agasisti & Bowers, 2017) .

AI is also playing a crucial role in improving institutional decision-making through data-driven analysis (Agasisti & Bowers, 2017). Universities collect vast amounts of data on student performance, enrollment trends, course effectiveness, and faculty workload. AI-powered analytics tools process this data to generate insights that help administrators make informed decisions about curriculum design, resource allocation, and student support services. Predictive analytics, for instance, can identify students at risk of dropping out by analyzing attendance records, grades, and engagement levels. Institutions can then implement early intervention strategies, such as academic counseling or financial assistance, to improve retention rates. AI-driven dashboards provide administrators with real-time visualizations of institutional performance, allowing for data-driven policymaking that enhances overall efficiency and student success (Agasisti & Bowers, 2017) (Wah, Suiying, & Shuangjie, 2019).

In addition to optimizing learning and teaching, AI is streamlining administrative operations in higher education (An, Yu, & James, 2025). Universities handle a multitude of routine administrative tasks, such as scheduling, admissions processing, and student support services. AI-powered chatbots and virtual assistants, like Georgia State University's Pounce (Burke & Fifield, n.d.), assist students with queries related to course registration, financial aid, and campus services, providing instant responses and reducing the workload on human staff. AI-driven scheduling systems help institutions manage course timetables, room assignments, and faculty workload distribution more effectively. Automating these processes not only increases operational efficiency but also improves the overall student experience by minimizing delays and ensuring seamless access to academic services (Agasisti & Bowers, 2017).

CHALLENGES IN AI ADOPTION

Despite the apparent usefulness of AI in higher education, no discussion of AI in higher education is complete (or accurate) without consideration of the challenges inherent to the adoption of AI in education. Like any other technology, AI is merely a tool. How the tool is designed and used determines not only its usefulness but also its impact, be it positive or negative, on individuals and society.

At the forefront of discussions on AI, are the ethical considerations (Fu & Weng, 2024). As artificial intelligence (AI) continues to reshape higher education, ethical considerations surrounding its implementation have become increasingly important. One of the primary concerns is addressing biases in AI algorithms and ensuring fairness in decision-making processes (Xlimi & Carballido, 2023; Al-Zahrani & Alasmari, 2024; Akgun & Greenhow, 2021). AI systems rely on large datasets to function, but if these datasets contain historical biases, the AI may reinforce or even exacerbate those biases. This issue is particularly critical in areas such as admissions, grading, and faculty evaluations, where biased AI algorithms could lead to unfair outcomes for certain demographic groups (Xlimi & Carballido, 2023). Institutions must take proactive measures to audit and refine AI algorithms to ensure they remain fair, transparent, and unbiased. Additionally, incorporating diverse datasets and perspectives in AI training models can help mitigate biases and promote equity in decision-making processes. As the rate of uptake of AI in higher education accelerates, dealing with biases in the AI algorithms is urgent and an imperative. Many uphold that AI has the potential to democratize higher education because of AI's capability for personalization in learning and support (Isayeva, 2024). Only when AI is ethically implemented, with human at the center can it be an enabler for the democratization of higher education, else it will only serve to widen (and even create new) inequities (Ahmed, 2024).

Equity and access are important conversations to be had in applying AI to education. As technologies such as AI emerge and are integrated into human activity such as education, there is always a risk of deepening the digital divide. The concept of the digital divide is multifaceted. At the base level, the digital divide is about access to infrastructure (e.g. the internet), access to devices (e.g. computers, mobile phones) or even access to software and applications. Access may be limited by location (e.g. no infrastructure) or by economics (e.g. can't afford to buy). At another level, the digital divide is due to the lack of literacy or digital skills (second level digital divide) or indeed they may lack the skills to take full advantage of technologies in a way that is empowering (third level) (Kitsara, 2022). This is a common situation among the many students from underprivileged backgrounds may lack access to the necessary technology, internet connectivity, and digital literacy skills required to fully benefit from AI-driven educational tools. Without targeted interventions, AI could exacerbate existing educational inequalities by providing advantages primarily to students with greater access to technological resources. Institutions must prioritize digital inclusion by ensuring that all students, regardless of socioeconomic status, have access to AI-powered learning platforms. This may include providing financial assistance for technology, expanding internet access in underserved communities, and implementing digital literacy programs to equip students with the skills needed to navigate AI-driven educational environments (Kitsara, 2022) (Khan, 2024)

Data privacy and security are also important concerns for the use of AI in higher education (Huang, 2023). AI systems in higher education collect vast amounts of sensitive student data, including academic performance records, behavioral analytics, and personal information. This data is often used to improve learning outcomes, personalize instruction, and optimize institutional decision-making. However, without strict data protection policies, there is a risk of data breaches, unauthorized access, and misuse of student information. Compliance with regulations such as the General Data Protection Regulation (GDPR) and the Family Educational Rights and Privacy Act (FERPA) (https://studentprivacy.ed.gov/faq/what-ferpa) is essential to safeguard student data. Institutions must implement robust cybersecurity measures, encrypt sensitive information, and establish clear policies regarding data collection, storage, and sharing. Additionally, students and faculty should be educated about data privacy rights and best practices for securing their personal information in AI-driven learning environments.

Another challenge in AI adoption in higher education is faculty resistance (Giray, 2024).. Many educators express skepticism about AI, fearing that it may undermine traditional teaching methods or diminish their role in the learning process (Giray, 2024). Some faculty members may be hesitant to adopt AI-driven tools due to concerns about losing autonomy over their curriculum or being forced to rely on technology for instructional decisions. Overcoming this resistance requires institutions to actively involve faculty in the AI integration process, providing them with opportunities to shape how AI is used in their courses. Professional development programs, workshops, and training sessions can help educators understand the benefits of AI, how it can enhance rather than replace their teaching methods, and how they can leverage AI to improve student engagement and learning outcomes (Nazaretsky, Ariely, Cukurova, & Alexandron, 2022). Encouraging faculty to experiment with AI tools and collaborate on AI-enhanced course designs can foster a sense of ownership and trust in AI technologies.

One of the most pressing concerns surrounding AI adoption in higher education is job displacement (Jose & Jose, 2024). As AI automates routine administrative tasks, such as grading assignments, responding to student inquiries, and managing course registrations, there is growing concern that certain faculty and staff positions may become redundant. Teaching assistants, administrative personnel, and support staff may face the greatest risk of job displacement as AI systems become more sophisticated. While AI can increase efficiency, institutions must carefully consider the human impact of automation and take measures to ensure that AI is used to augment rather than replace human roles. Instead of eliminating positions, universities can focus on reskilling and upskilling employees, enabling them to take on more strategic and high-value roles that require human insight, creativity, and critical thinking. Additionally, AI should be framed as a tool that supports educators rather than one that replaces them. AI can handle repetitive administrative tasks, allowing instructors to dedicate more time to mentoring students, facilitating discussions, and engaging in research.

As AI continues to evolve, institutions must strike a balance between harnessing its benefits and addressing its ethical challenges. Ethical AI governance frameworks should be developed to ensure fairness, transparency, and accountability in AI-driven decision-making. Additionally, higher education institutions should foster cross-disciplinary collaborations between AI researchers, educators, and policymakers to ensure that AI is implemented responsibly. By prioritizing equity and access, enhancing data privacy protections, addressing faculty concerns, and mitigating job displacement risks, institutions can create an AI-powered educational environment that is both inclusive and effective.

Ultimately, AI has the potential to revolutionize higher education by making learning more personalized, efficient, and accessible. However, its implementation must be guided by ethical principles that prioritize human dignity, fairness, and inclusivity. Institutions that proactively address these challenges will be better positioned to leverage AI as a force for good, ensuring that technology enhances rather than hinders the quality of education. The future of AI in higher education will depend on thoughtful policies, responsible innovation, and a commitment to maintaining the human-centered values that define academic excellence.

CASE STUDIES AND EXAMPLES

Artificial Intelligence (AI) is revolutionizing higher education worldwide, with universities and colleges increasingly leveraging AI-driven tools to enhance learning experiences, streamline administrative tasks, and improve student outcomes. The successful implementation of AI in educational institutions highlights its potential to transform traditional teaching and learning methods, making education more personalized, efficient, and accessible. From AI-powered chatbots to adaptive learning platforms and AI-based grading systems, institutions across the globe are integrating AI technologies to enhance both academic and administrative functions.

Several universities have pioneered AI adoption, demonstrating how AI can support faculty, students, and administrative staff. One of the most notable examples is Georgia State University in the United States, which implemented an AI-powered chatbot named Pounce (Georgia State University, 2022) to assist students with common inquiries related to admissions, financial aid, and enrollment. By providing instant responses to student queries, Pounce has significantly improved student engagement and reduced summer melt, a phenomenon where accepted students fail to enroll due to confusion or administrative barriers. The chatbot's success has encouraged other institutions to adopt similar AI-driven student support services, reducing the workload on administrative staff while improving response times and accuracy.

In the United Kingdom, the University of Essex has integrated AI into its teaching and research programs, using machine learning to analyze student performance data and provide personalized recommendations for improvement (Stream by Kortext, n.d.). By leveraging AI-driven analytics, the university can identify at-risk students early and implement targeted interventions to support their academic success. AI-based predictive analytics have also been used to optimize course offerings, ensuring that students receive guidance on selecting courses that align with their skills and career aspirations.

China has been at the forefront of AI implementation in higher education, with institutions such as Tsinghua University and Peking University incorporating AI-driven tools to enhance teaching methods. AI-powered facial recognition technology is being used to monitor student attendance, ensuring accurate tracking without manual record-keeping. Additionally, AI-driven platforms such as Squirrel AI have gained popularity in China's education sector (Knox, 2020), offering adaptive learning solutions that adjust content delivery based on individual student progress. These platforms provide customized learning experiences, helping students master complex subjects at their own pace.

Another successful implementation of AI in higher education is found at Arizona State University (ASU), where AI-based adaptive learning platforms are transforming how students engage with course materials(Vignare, Tesene, & Lorenzo, 2020). ASU has partnered with companies such as CogBooks and McGraw Hill to integrate AI-driven adaptive learning into its curriculum. These platforms analyze student interactions with coursework and provide personalized recommendations, ensuring that learners receive targeted content based on their strengths and weaknesses. The use of AI in adaptive learning has led to higher retention rates and improved academic performance among students.

AI-powered chatbots have become a valuable resource for universities, offering round-the-clock support to students. Institutions such as Stanford University (Peterrkin, 2024) and the University of California, Los Angeles (UCLA) have deployed AI-driven chatbots to assist students with academic advising, course registration, and general inquiries. These chatbots use natural language processing to understand and respond to student questions, providing instant assistance without the need for human intervention. By automating these routine interactions, universities can allocate human resources more effectively, allowing staff to focus on complex student concerns that require personalized attention.

AI-based grading systems have also gained traction in higher education, reducing the burden on faculty while ensuring consistent and objective assessments. One example is the implementation of automated grading software at the Massachusetts Institute of Technology (MIT) (MIT Sloan Teaching & Learning Technologies, 2024). AI-powered grading tools analyze student responses, detect patterns in written work, and provide feedback on assignments. These systems are particularly useful for grading large-scale online courses, where instructors may struggle to evaluate hundreds or even thousands of submissions manually. AI-driven grading solutions enhance efficiency while maintaining high standards of academic assessment.

AI is also playing a crucial role in research and development within universities. Institutions such as the University of Oxford and Harvard University are using AI to conduct advanced research in fields such as medicine, engineering, and social sciences. AI-driven algorithms analyze massive datasets, identify trends, and generate insights that contribute to groundbreaking discoveries. For example, AI is being used to model climate change scenarios, develop personalized healthcare treatments, and optimize urban planning strategies. The ability of AI to process and interpret vast amounts of data has accelerated the pace of research, enabling universities to address complex global challenges more effectively.

Another compelling example of AI in action is the use of AI-driven virtual reality (VR) and augmented reality (AR) in education. Institutions such as the University of Melbourne and Stanford University have incorporated AI-powered VR simulations into their curricula to enhance student learning (ADAPT, n.d.). These immersive experiences allow students to engage with course material in innovative ways, from exploring historical landmarks in virtual environments to conducting complex scientific experiments in simulated laboratories. AI-powered VR technology provides hands-on learning opportunities that would otherwise be challenging or costly to implement in traditional classroom settings.

As universities continue to explore AI's potential, they must also address the challenges associated with AI adoption. While AI-powered tools offer numerous benefits, institutions must ensure that these technologies are implemented ethically and equitably. Data privacy and security concerns must be carefully managed, particularly when handling sensitive student information. Additionally, faculty and staff must be provided with the necessary training and support to integrate AI into their teaching and administrative workflows effectively.

The successful implementation of AI in universities and colleges worldwide demonstrates the transformative potential of AI in education. From chatbots that assist students with administrative tasks to adaptive learning platforms that personalize instruction and AI-driven grading systems that enhance assessment processes, AI is reshaping the higher education landscape. By leveraging AI strategically and addressing the ethical considerations surrounding its use, institutions can create a more efficient, accessible, and student-centric educational experience. As AI continues to evolve, universities will need to remain agile and innovative, ensuring that they maximize the benefits of AI while mitigating potential risks.

STRATEGIES FOR SUCCESSFUL AI INTEGRATION

As artificial intelligence (AI) continues to shape the future of higher education, institutions must develop strategic approaches to integrate AI technologies effectively. AI has the potential to enhance learning experiences, streamline administrative processes, and improve institutional efficiency. However, to maximize its benefits while addressing potential risks, universities and colleges must adopt thoughtful implementation strategies that align with their goals, values, and educational missions.

A key recommendation for higher education institutions is to develop a comprehensive AI integration framework that outlines the objectives, benefits, and potential challenges associated with AI adoption. In Australia, the Tertiary Education Quality and Standards Agency has developed a good practice hub for AI (Australian Government Tertiary Education Quality and Standards Agency., n.d.). Government lead guides like this provide a platform for institutions to develop frameworks suited to their local context. Institutions should conduct thorough needs assessments to determine where AI can have the most meaningful impact, whether in personalized learning, faculty support, student services, or administrative operations. Establishing a clear roadmap for AI implementation ensures that investments in AI technologies are purposeful and aligned with institutional priorities.

Collaboration between faculty, administrators, IT specialists, and policymakers is crucial for ensuring the smooth integration of AI technologies. AI adoption should not be driven solely by technological advancements but should involve input from educators, students, and institutional leaders. Institutions should establish cross-functional committees or task forces that oversee AI implementation, evaluate its impact, and address any concerns that arise. Engaging faculty in decision-making processes fosters a sense of ownership and ensures that AI solutions are implemented in ways that enhance, rather than disrupt, the teaching and learning experience.

To ensure that AI solutions align with institutional goals and values, universities must prioritize ethical considerations, data privacy, and inclusivity. AI should be used to promote equitable access to education and avoid reinforcing biases in decision-making processes. Institutions must implement robust data governance policies to protect student information, comply with privacy regulations, and ensure transparency in AI-driven decision-making. Additionally, universities should adopt AI systems that are designed to be interpretable and accountable, providing clear explanations for how AI-generated insights and recommendations are made.

Another important aspect of AI integration is the careful selection of AI vendors and technology partners. Higher education institutions should work with reputable AI providers that align with their academic and ethical standards. Institutions should conduct thorough evaluations of AI solutions, assessing their accuracy, reliability, and potential biases. Open-source AI tools and university-led AI research projects can also provide alternative solutions that allow institutions to maintain greater control over AI-driven initiatives. Partnering with AI experts, industry leaders, and research institutions can further enhance AI adoption by bringing external expertise into the university environment.

AI implementation should also be accompanied by continuous monitoring and evaluation to measure its effectiveness and identify areas for improvement. Institutions should establish key performance indicators (KPIs) to assess the impact of AI on student success, faculty engagement, and institutional efficiency. Regular assessments and feedback loops will enable universities to refine AI applications, address challenges, and adapt to emerging trends in AI technology. Creating an AI ethics committee or advisory board can also help institutions navigate complex ethical dilemmas and ensure responsible AI use.

Another recommendation for universities is to promote AI literacy among students, equipping them with the skills needed to navigate an AI-driven world. AI literacy is imperative and "AI education [is] a cornerstone of opportunity for all students" (Southworth, et al., 2023, p. para 1)). AI is becoming increasingly integrated into various industries, and students should be prepared to understand, interact with, and leverage AI technologies in their future careers. Institutions can introduce AI-focused coursework, interdisciplinary AI programs, and experiential learning opportunities that allow students to engage with AI applications in real-world contexts. Encouraging critical discussions about AI ethics, biases, and societal implications will also foster a more informed and responsible generation of AI users.

Ensuring that AI solutions align with institutional goals requires a commitment to ongoing research, innovation, and adaptability. Institutions should remain proactive in exploring emerging AI trends and integrating new AI capabilities that enhance educational outcomes. Universities can create AI research labs, innovation hubs, and collaborative initiatives that explore AI's potential in education and beyond. Encouraging interdisciplinary research on AI can also lead to new discoveries and applications that benefit both academia and society.

Ultimately, the successful integration of AI in higher education depends on a balanced approach that prioritizes both technological innovation and human-centered education (Francis, Jones & Smith, 2025).

AI should be seen as a tool that enhances, rather than replaces, the human elements of teaching, mentorship, and critical thinking. By fostering collaboration, providing faculty support, addressing ethical concerns, and aligning AI initiatives with institutional values, universities can create a future where AI empowers educators, supports students, and advances the mission of higher education. As AI technology continues to evolve, institutions must remain flexible, forward-thinking, and committed to ensuring that AI serves as a force for positive transformation in higher education.

FUTURE DIRECTIONS AND IMPLICATIONS

Artificial Intelligence (AI) is continuously evolving, reshaping the landscape of higher education, and influencing the way students learn, educators teach, and institutions operate. The role of AI in academia is expanding beyond administrative automation and personalized learning, creating opportunities to enhance the overall academic experience. As AI technology advances, it has the potential to revolutionize traditional education models, foster lifelong learning, and equip students with essential 21st-century skills that are critical for success in the modern workforce.

The evolving role of AI in higher education can be observed in several key areas. AI-driven adaptive learning platforms are increasingly personalizing education by adjusting coursework and instructional strategies based on student performance and engagement. These systems provide real-time feedback, enabling students to progress at their own pace while receiving tailored support to reinforce their understanding of complex subjects. AI is also facilitating more immersive learning experiences through virtual and augmented reality, allowing students to engage with educational content in innovative ways. For example, AI-powered simulations enable medical students to practice surgeries in a virtual environment, while engineering students can conduct experiments in AI-driven digital laboratories.

AI is also transforming the way universities operate by enhancing institutional efficiency and decision-making. AI-powered analytics help universities predict student retention rates, optimize resource allocation, and improve course offerings based on real-time demand. By analyzing student data, institutions can identify at-risk students and implement early intervention strategies to improve academic success. Additionally, AI is streamlining faculty workload management, reducing administrative burdens, and allowing educators to focus more on mentoring and research.

The future of AI in higher education is likely to bring even more significant advancements. AI-driven intelligent tutoring systems are expected to become more sophisticated, offering students highly personalized learning experiences that mimic human tutoring. AI could also play a role in automating assessment and evaluation, reducing bias in grading while ensuring that students receive constructive feedback. Furthermore, AI may facilitate the creation of virtual academic advisors that can guide students through their academic journey, providing insights on career paths, skill development, and research opportunities.

As AI becomes more integrated into higher education, its impact extends beyond traditional academic structures to influence the development of 21st-century skills. The modern workforce requires individuals who possess critical thinking, problem-solving, adaptability, and digital literacy skills. AI-driven learning experiences can help students develop these competencies by promoting active learning, encouraging interdisciplinary approaches, and fostering collaboration through digital platforms.

One of the most valuable contributions of AI to 21st-century skill development is its ability to support lifelong learning. As industries continue to evolve and technological advancements reshape job markets, the need for continuous education and upskilling has never been greater. AI-powered learning platforms provide professionals with personalized learning pathways, enabling them to acquire new skills and stay competitive in their respective fields. AI-driven recommendations and analytics help learners identify relevant courses, certifications, and training programs tailored to their career aspirations and learning preferences.

AI also plays a significant role in bridging the gap between higher education and industry by aligning educational outcomes with workforce demands. Employers increasingly seek graduates who possess not only technical expertise but also soft skills such as communication, creativity, and collaboration. AI-powered career guidance tools help students navigate the job market, offering insights on emerging industry trends, skill requirements, and potential career paths. AI-driven mentorship programs connect students with industry professionals, providing networking opportunities and real-world insights that enhance employability.

Moreover, AI can enhance the inclusivity and accessibility of higher education by providing support for students with diverse learning needs. AI-driven tools such as speech-to-text and text-to-speech applications, language translation services, and personalized assistive technologies empower students with disabilities or language barriers to engage fully in academic programs. These AI-powered solutions promote equity in education, ensuring that all students have access to quality learning experiences regardless of their backgrounds or circumstances.

The integration of AI in higher education also encourages interdisciplinary learning, breaking down traditional academic silos and promoting collaboration across diverse fields. AI-powered research tools enable scholars to analyze vast datasets, identify patterns, and make data-driven discoveries in various disciplines, from healthcare to environmental science. AI-driven cross-disciplinary projects encourage students and faculty to work together on complex global challenges, fostering a culture of innovation and critical inquiry.

Despite its transformative potential, the integration of AI in higher education must be approached with careful consideration. Institutions must address ethical concerns related to data privacy, algorithmic bias, and the responsible use of AI in academic settings. Transparent AI policies, rigorous data protection measures, and faculty oversight are essential to ensuring that AI technologies are deployed in ways that align with institutional values and academic integrity.

As AI continues to evolve, it is crucial for higher education institutions to prepare for the future by investing in AI literacy programs for both students and faculty. Understanding how AI works, its capabilities, and its limitations will empower educators to integrate AI-driven tools effectively into their teaching methods and research practices. Additionally, fostering an ethical AI culture within academic institutions will help ensure that AI is used responsibly and equitably in education.

The future of AI in higher education holds immense potential to enhance learning experiences, foster lifelong education, and equip students with the skills needed to thrive in a rapidly changing world. By embracing AI as a tool for innovation, universities can create more personalized, inclusive, and efficient learning environments. As AI technology continues to advance, higher education institutions must remain adaptable, proactive, and committed to leveraging AI in ways that enhance academic excellence while upholding ethical and educational principles.

RESEARCH QUESTIONS

As artificial intelligence continues to shape higher education, several key questions emerge regarding its potential benefits, ethical considerations, and the balance between technology and human-centered learning.

How can AI enhance the personalized learning experience for students in higher education? AI-driven adaptive learning platforms can analyze student performance, learning preferences, and engagement patterns to tailor educational content accordingly. In what ways can institutions leverage AI to provide individualized learning experiences that accommodate diverse student needs? Additionally, how can universities ensure that AI-powered personalization remains inclusive and accessible to students from all backgrounds?

What are the ethical implications of using AI in higher education, and how can institutions address them? While AI offers numerous advantages, concerns regarding data privacy, algorithmic bias, and transparency remain significant challenges. How can universities develop ethical AI policies that protect student data while maintaining fairness and accountability? Moreover, what measures can be implemented to ensure that AI-driven decision-making does not reinforce existing inequalities or lead to unintended biases in admissions, grading, and student support services?

How can universities balance the benefits of AI with the need for human-centered teaching and learning? While AI can automate administrative tasks and enhance instructional methods, higher education remains fundamentally human-centered. What strategies can institutions adopt to integrate AI in ways that complement, rather than replace, human educators? Furthermore, how can faculty members be supported in adopting AI-driven tools while maintaining their roles as mentors, critical thinkers, and facilitators of meaningful discussions?

What role does AI play in improving institutional decision-making and administrative efficiency in higher education? Universities and colleges generate vast amounts of data related to student performance, resource allocation, and enrollment trends. How can AI-powered analytics help institutions make data-driven decisions that enhance operational efficiency and improve student outcomes? Additionally, what are the potential risks of over-relying on AI for decision-making, and how can universities strike a balance between automation and human oversight?

By exploring these questions, institutions can develop a deeper understanding of AI's role in shaping the future of higher education while ensuring that its implementation aligns with ethical standards, educational goals, and student success.

CONCLUSION

Artificial Intelligence (AI) holds significant potential to revolutionize higher education, offering transformative solutions that enhance personalized learning, streamline administrative functions, and enable data-driven decision-making. AI-powered tools and platforms can help institutions provide more adaptive and individualized learning experiences, improve student engagement, and optimize faculty and administrative workflows. However, while AI presents numerous opportunities, its integration into higher education must be approached with careful consideration of the ethical, social, and economic challenges it presents. Institutions must ensure that AI adoption aligns with their educational values, promotes inclusivity, and safeguards data privacy while fostering collaboration between technology and human-centered teaching.

One of the most significant ways AI is reshaping higher education is through personalized learning experiences. AI-driven adaptive learning platforms can analyze student performance, identify learning gaps, and customize course content to meet individual needs. These systems offer tailored recommendations, ensuring that students receive instruction at a pace that suits their learning style. By leveraging AI, institutions can improve student retention rates, facilitate engagement, and create a more effective learning environment that supports diverse student populations, including those with disabilities or non-traditional educational backgrounds.

In addition to enhancing student learning, AI can significantly improve teaching and faculty support. AI-powered tools assist educators in grading assignments, providing real-time feedback, and developing course materials. Automated grading systems, for example, reduce the burden of evaluating large volumes of student work, allowing faculty to focus on more complex aspects of teaching, such as mentorship and critical thinking development. AI-driven analytics can also help instructors identify struggling students early, enabling timely interventions that improve academic success. However, institutions must ensure that AI does not replace the role of educators but rather complements their efforts by providing valuable insights and automating time-consuming tasks.

Beyond the classroom, AI is streamlining administrative functions in higher education. Universities handle vast amounts of data related to student enrollment, course scheduling, financial aid distribution, and resource allocation. AI-powered administrative systems can process this data efficiently, reducing operational inefficiencies and enhancing decision-making. AI-driven chatbots, for instance, are being deployed in many universities to handle student inquiries, provide academic advising, and assist with campus services. These tools not only improve response times but also free up human staff to focus on complex, high-value tasks that require personal interaction.

AI's potential in higher education extends to research and innovation. AI-powered data analysis tools can help researchers process large datasets, detect patterns, and generate new insights across various disciplines. Universities are increasingly using AI to support scientific research, from medical advancements to social sciences and engineering. AI's computational power allows researchers to conduct experiments, model predictions, and automate tedious research tasks, accelerating the pace of discovery and expanding the boundaries of knowledge.

Despite these benefits, AI's integration into higher education presents several challenges that institutions must address. Ethical considerations are paramount, as AI-driven decision-making can inadvertently reinforce biases present in training data. If not carefully managed, AI algorithms may lead to unintended discrimination in areas such as admissions, grading, and student evaluations. Institutions must implement rigorous testing and oversight mechanisms to ensure that AI applications are fair, transparent, and aligned with ethical standards.

Another critical challenge is the issue of data privacy and security. AI systems rely on vast amounts of student and institutional data to function effectively. Ensuring that this data is securely stored and protected from breaches is a major concern for universities. Institutions must comply with privacy regulations such as the General Data Protection Regulation (GDPR) and the Family Educational Rights and Privacy Act (FERPA) while establishing strong cybersecurity measures to prevent unauthorized access to sensitive student information.

Economic and social implications also need to be considered. The implementation of AI requires substantial financial investment in infrastructure, software, and training. Not all institutions, particularly smaller colleges with limited budgets, may have the resources to fully integrate AI into their academic and administrative functions. Additionally, AI adoption raises concerns about job displacement, particularly among administrative staff whose roles may be automated. Universities must develop strategies to reskill and retrain employees to take on new roles that complement AI-driven processes, ensuring that technological advancements do not come at the cost of human employment.

Another important aspect of AI integration is faculty and student acceptance. Some educators may be resistant to adopting AI-driven tools due to concerns about their effectiveness, reliability, and potential impact on traditional teaching methods. Universities must provide comprehensive training programs that equip faculty with the necessary skills to use AI effectively in their courses. Encouraging faculty participation in AI research and decision-making processes can also help build trust and acceptance of AI technologies.

Looking ahead, institutions must develop a strategic roadmap for AI integration that prioritizes responsible innovation while maximizing its benefits. This includes setting clear objectives for AI implementation, establishing governance frameworks to ensure ethical AI use, and fostering interdisciplinary collaboration between educators, technologists, and policymakers. Universities should also continuously evaluate the impact of AI on student learning, faculty engagement, and institutional effectiveness, making necessary adjustments to optimize AI's role in higher education.

In conclusion, AI presents a transformative opportunity for higher education, offering significant improvements in personalized learning, teaching support, administrative efficiency, and research capabilities. However, its successful implementation requires careful planning, ethical oversight, and a commitment to inclusivity and transparency. By addressing the challenges associated with AI integration and ensuring that AI solutions align with institutional goals, universities can harness the power of AI to enhance educational outcomes and prepare students for an increasingly AI-driven world.

REFERENCES

ADAPT. (n.d.). *Adopting Augmented Reality for 3D Virtual Tours of The University of Melbourne*. Retrieved from ADAPT: https://adapt.com.au/resources/peer-insights/digital-transformation/adopting-augmented-reality-for-3d-virtual-tours-of-the-university-of-melbourne

Agasisti, T., & Bowers, A. (2017). Data Analytics and Decision-Making in Education: Towards the Educational Data Scientist as a Key Actor in Schools and Higher Education Institutions. In *G. Johnes, J. Johnes, T. Agasisti, & L. López-Torres, Handbook of Contemporary Education Economics* (pp. 184–210). Edward Elgar Publishing.

Ahmed, F. (2024). The digital divide and AI in education: Addressing equity and accessibility. *Journal of AI in Education: Innovations, Opportunities, Challenges, and Future Directions*, *1*(2), 12–23.

Akgun, S., & Greenhow, C. (2021). Artificial intelligence in education: Addressing ethical challenges in K-12 settings. *AI Ethics. Springer Nature*, *2*(3), 431–440. PMID: 34790956

Al-Zahrani, A., & Alasmari, T. (2024). Exploring the impact of artificial intelligence on higher education: The dynamics of ethical, social, and educational implications. *Humanities & Social Sciences Communications*, *11*(912), 1–12.

Alkhatlan, A., & Kalita, J. (n.d.). Intelligent Tutoring Systems: A Comprehensive Historical Survey with Recent Developments.

An, Y., Yu, J., & James, S. (2025). Investigating the higher education institutions' guidelines and policies regarding the use of generative AI in teaching, learning, research, and administration. *International Journal of Educational Technology in Higher Education*, *22*(10), 1–23.

Australian Government Tertiary Education Quality and Standards Agency. (n.d.). *Artificial intelligence*. Retrieved from TESQA Guides and Resources. Higher Education Good Practice.: https://www.teqsa.gov.au/guides-resources/higher-education-good-practice-hub/artificial-intelligence

Baig, M., Shuib, L., & Yadegaridehkordi, E. (2020). Big data in education: A state of the art, limitations, and future research directions. *International Journal of Educational Technology in Higher Education*, *17*(44), 1–23.

Blake, J. (2023). Unleashing the potential: Positive impacts of generative AI on learning and teaching. In S. Hai-Jew, *Generative AI in teaching and learning* (pp. 31–45). IGI Global.

Bloom, B. S. (1984). The 2 sigma problem: The search for methods of group instruction as effective as one-to-one tutoring. *Educational Researcher*, *13*(6), 4–16.

Burke, S., & Fifield, L. (n.d.). *Leveraging AI Chatbots for Student Success at Georgia State University.* Retrieved March 2025, from Georgia State University: https://completega.org/sites/default/files/meetings/MomentumIV/GSU_MSIV_Chatbots.pdf

Cinar, O., Rafferty, K., Cutting, D., & Wang, H. (2024). AI-powered VR for enhanced learning compared to tradtional methods. *Electronics (Basel)*, *13*(23). https://www.mdpi.com/2079-9292/13/23/4787

Dimari, A., Tyagi, N., Davanageri, M., & Kukret, R. (2024). "AI-Based Automated Grading Systems for open book examination system: Implications for Assessment in Higher Education,". *2024 International Conference on Knowledge Engineering and Communication Systems (ICKECS),* (pp. 1-7). Chikkaballapur, India

Elkhatat, A., Elsaid, K., & Almeer, S. (2023). Evaluating the efficacy of AI content detection tools in differentiating between human and AI-generated text. *International Journal for Educational Integrity*, *17*, •••.

Fang, B., & Broussard, K. (2024, August 7). *Augmented course design: Using AI to boost efficiency and expand capacity.* Retrieved from Educause Review: https://er.educause.edu/articles/2024/8/augmented-course-design-using-ai-to-boost-efficiency-and-expand-capacity

Farooq, U., Malik, S., & Syed, A. (2024, March). Revolutionizing higher education: The transformative impact of artificial intelligence on teaching, learning and career preparation. *ShodhKosh:Journal of Visual and Performing Arts*, *5*(3), 789–794.

Francis, N. J., Jones, S., & Smith, D. P. (2025). Generative AI in higher education: Balancing innovation and integrity. *British Journal of Biomedical Science*, *81*. Advance online publication. DOI: 10.3389/bjbs.2024.14048 PMID: 39850144

Fu, Y., & Weng, Z. (2024). Navigating the ethical terrain of AI in education: A systematic review on framing responsible human-centered AI practices. *Computers and Education: Artificial Intelligence*, *7*, 100306. Advance online publication. DOI: 10.1016/j.caeai.2024.100306

Georgia State University. (2022, March 21). *Georgia State University - Gerogia State News Hub*. Retrieved from Classroom Chatbot Improves Student Performance, Study Says Classroom Chatbot Improves Student Performance, Study Says.: https://news.gsu.edu/2022/03/21/classroom-chatbot-improves-student-performance-study-says/

Georgouli, K. (2002). The design of a motivating intelligent assessment system. (pp. 811-820). San Sebastian, Spain and Biarritz France: Lecture Notes in computer Science.

Giray, L. (2024). Educators Who Do Not Use AI Will Be Replaced by Those Who Do: Disadvantages of Not Embracing AI in Medical Education. *Journal of the Practice of Cardiovascular Sciences*, *10*(1), 43–47.

Gnanaprakasam, J., & Lourdusamy, R. (2024). *The Role of AI in automating grading: Enhancing feedback and efficiency.* Retrieved from https://www.intechopen.com/chapters/1181936

Guo, L., Wang, D., Bu, F., Li, Y., Wang, Y., & Zhou, R. (2021). Evolution and trends in intelligent tutoring systems research: A multidisciplinary and scientometric view. *Asia Pacific Education Review*, *22*, 441–461.

Huang, L. (2023). Ethics of artificial intelligence in education: Student privacy and data protection. *SIEF*, *16*(2), 2578–2587.

Isayeva, S. (2024). Democratizing Education AI and OpenAI Models for Global Access to Knowledge. In Demir, S., & Demir, M. (Eds.), *Enhancing Higher Education and Research With OpenAI Models. (pp.* (pp. 79–92). IGI Global.

Jose, J., & Jose, B. (2024, April). Educators' Academic Insights on Artificial Intelligence: Challenges and Opportunities. *Electronic Journal of e-Learning*, •••, 59–77.

Khan, W. (2024). Ethical challenges of AI in education: balancing innovation with data privacy. *AI in Education: Innovation, Challenges, and Future Perspectives.*, *1*(1), online. https://researchcorridor.org/index.php/jaieicfd/article/view/238/226

Kitsara, I. (2022). Artificial Intelligence and the digital divide: From an innovation perspective. In A. Bounfour, *Platforms and Artificial Intelligence The Next Generation of Competences* (pp. 245–265). Springer.

Knox, J. (2020). Artificial Intelligence and Education in China. *Learning, Media and Technology Special Issue - AI and Education: critical perspectives and alternative futures, 45*(3), 298-311.

Kumar, D., Haque, A., Mishra, K., Islam, F., & Ahmad, S. (2023). Exploring the transformative role of artificial intelligence and metaverse in education: A comprehensive review. *Metaverse Basic and Applied Research*, *2*(55), 1–12.

Luan, H., Geczy, P., Lai, H., Gobert, J., Yang, S., Ogata, H., & Tsai, C. (2020). Challenges and future directions of big data and artificial intelligence in education. *Frontiers in Psychology*, *11*, 1–10. PMID: 33192896

Memarian, B., & Doleck, T. (2024). A review of assessment for learning with artificial intelligence. *Computers in Human Behavior: Artificial Humans*, 1-11.

MIT Sloan Teaching & Learning Technologies. (2024, May 9). *AI-Assisted Grading: A Magic Wand or a Pandora's Box?* Retrieved from MIT Sloan Teaching & Learning Technologies: https://mitsloanedtech.mit.edu/2024/05/09/ai-assisted-grading-a-magic-wand-or-a-pandoras-box/

Nazaretsky, T., Ariely, M., Cukurova, M., & Alexandron, G. (2022). Journal of the Practice of Cardiovascular Sciences. *British Journal of Educational Technology*, *53*, 914–931.

Ozsevim, I., & Ng, A. (2023). *Deepening and democratising learning.* Retrieved from AI Magazine: https://aimagazine.com/articles/andrew-ng-deepening-and-democratising-learning

Papamitsiou, Z., & Economides, A. (2014). Learning analytics and educational data mining in practice: A systematic literature review of empirical evidence. *Journal of Educational Technology & Society*, *17*(4), 49–64.

Peng, H., Ma, S., & Spector, J. (2019). Personalized adaptive learning: An emerging pedagogical approach enabled by a smart learning environment. *Smart Learning Environments*, *6*(9), 1–14.

Peterrkin, O. (2024, November 7). *Chatting about chatbots: How AI tools can support teachers.* Retrieved from Stanford Graduate School of Education: https://ed.stanford.edu/news/chatting-about-chatbots-how-ai-tools-can-support-teachers

Rahiman, H., & Kodikal, R. (Cogent Education). Revolutionizing education: Artificial intelligence empowered learning in higher education. *11*, 1-24.

Southworth, J., Migliaccio, K., Glover, J., Glover, J., Reed, D., McCarty, C., & Thomas, A. (2023). Developing a model for AI Across the curriculum: Transforming the higher education landscape via innovation in AI literacy. *Computers and Education: Artificial Intelligence. Article, 100127.* Advance online publication. DOI: 10.1016/j.caeai.2023.100127

Stream by Kortext. (n.d.). *StREAM*. Retrieved from A strategic use of StREAM impacting student support, retention and data-informed decision making at University of Essex: https://kortext.com/stream/success-stories/university-of-essex/

Swiecki, Z., Khosravi, H., Chen, G., Martinez-Maldonado, R., Lodge, J., Millifan, S., & Gasevic, D. (2022). Assessment in the age of artificial intelligence. *omputers and Education. Artificial Intelligence*, *3*, 1–10.

Tafazoli, D. (2024, December). Exploring the potential of generative AI in democratizing English language education. *Computers and Education: Artificial Intelligence, 7.*

Towfek, S., Khodadadi, N., Abualigah, L., & Rizk, F. (2024). AI in Higher Education: Insights from Student Surveys and Predictive Analytics using PSO-Guided WOA and Linear Regression. *JAIEP*(https://jaiep.journals.ekb.eg/article_354003_19fe159da1d32d8628a13261bd5d9309.pdf)

Vignare, K., Tesene, M., & Lorenzo, G. (2020, July 13). *Case Study: Arizona State University [Case Study] Association of Public & Land-grant Universities and Every Learner Everywhere.* Retrieved from Case Study Arizona State University: https://www.everylearnereverywhere.org/resources/case-study-arizona-state-university-asu/

Wah, T., Suiying, T., & Shuangjie, A. (2019). Dashboards for decision making in higher education. *ASCILITE 2019* (pp. https://2019conference.ascilite.org/assets/papers/Paper-054.pdf). Singapore University of Social Sciences.

Wang, G., Chen, X., Zhang, D., Kang, Y., Wang, F., & Su, W. (2022). Development and applicaiton of an intelligent assessment system for mathematics learning strategy among high school students - take Jianzha Contry as an example. *Sustainability*, *14*(12265), 1–36.

Wang, S., Wang, F., Zhu, Z., Wang, J., Tran, T., & Zhao, D. (2024). Artificial intelligence in education: A systematic literature review. *Expert Systems with Applications*, *252*, 1–19.

Xlimi, Z., & Carballido, B. (2023). Navitating the ethical challenges of artificial intelligence in higher education: An analysis of seven global AI ethics policies. *TEM Journal*, *12*(2), 590–602.

Chapter 8
The Role of AI in Lifelong Learning

Kaye Shelton
https://orcid.org/0000-0001-5024-5629
Lamar University, USA

Ashley L. Dockens
https://orcid.org/0000-0002-9707-975X
Lamar University, USA

ABSTRACT

By enabling individualized and flexible educational experiences, artificial intelligence (AI) is revolutionizing lifelong learning. AI can help identify learning gaps and provide access to tools and resources for skill improvement in real time, which is crucial in the ever-changing job market. This chapter reviews how AI can support lifelong learning through recommendation systems, adaptive learning platforms, and intelligent tutoring systems—all of which help to increase access to education. Emphasizing personalized learning and skill development, the application of AI in corporate training and micro-credentialing is also covered. However, integrating AI into educational settings still presents ethical questions regarding algorithmic biases and data privacy. Stakeholders must engage in ongoing conversations about future educational systems that merge technology with human understanding to establish ethical and inclusive strategies that promote empowerment and equal access to lifelong learning through AI.

DOI: 10.4018/979-8-3373-2397-8.ch008

INTRODUCTION

By making learning more accessible, adaptive, and personalized, artificial intelligence (AI) has completely changed the way we approach education. This change is especially important in light of lifelong learning, which focuses on humans learning new things throughout their lives. Lifelong learning is crucial in the quickly changing world of today since people need to constantly adjust to new technologies, shifting employment markets, and profound societal shifts (Kaplan, 2016; Rial-Gonzalez et al., 2024). Because AI systems can influence human thought processes and social interactions, the speed of decision making and inherent biases can impact how people learn and work (Poquet & De Laat, 2021). In fact, studies show student engagement (often self-reported), self-motivation, and participation often increased with the use of adaptive learning systems (Edwards-Fapohunda & Adediji, 2024; Garcia-Martinez et al., 2023; Gligorea et al., 2023; Harry & Sayudin, 2023; Jares et al., 2019; Liu et al., 2022; Mishra, 2024; Standen et al,, 2020; Xiaoyu & Tobias, 2023). However, research is ongoing to determine if there is a true measurable impact in learning so we must be cautious asserting that AI increases student learning (Palenski et al., 2024).

By creating individualized educational experiences, developing adaptive learning pathways, and offering ongoing access to relevant educational resources, artificial intelligence (AI) has become a powerful tool that can improve lifelong learning (Mishra, 2024). At the forefront of this educational revolution are adaptive learning platforms and AI-driven tutoring. This chapter reviews how AI can support lifelong learning through recommendation systems, adaptive learning platforms, and intelligent tutoring systems—as well as the potential challenges.

BACKGROUND AND CONTEXT

Lifelong learning was first referred to in the academic literature as lifelong education in Eduard Lindeman's 1926 book, *The Meaning of Adult Education*. Yeaxlee (1925) followed with his book, *Lifelong Education*, focusing on adult education and recognizing learning as a continuous endeavor. The actual use of the phrase "lifelong learning" began in the 1970s, influenced by organization report such as UNESCO (Fauer et al., 1972) and the Organization for Economic Cooperation and Development (OECD) (Kallen & Bengtsson, 1973). Notably, the Delores Report for UNESCO (Delores, 1996) provided a global educational framework for lifelong learning and emphasizing its role in personal and societal development by identifying four pillars for a 21st-century learning society: Learning to Know, Learning to Do, Learning to Live Together, and Learning to Be.

In 1997, the Commission for a Nation of Lifelong Learners defined lifelong learning as "a continuously supportive process which stimulates and empowers individuals...to acquire all the knowledge, values, skills and understanding they will require throughout their lifetimes...and to apply them with confidence, creativity, and enjoyment in all roles, circumstances, and environments." Later, the Commission of the European Commission (2001) characterized lifelong learning as "All learning activity undertaken throughout life, with the aim of improving knowledge, skills and competencies within a personal, civic, social and/or employment-related perspective" (p. 9), which is one of the more common definitions used in the literature. Both definitions point to a process of lifetime learning (from birth to death) that supports personal growth, skill development, and competencies in both personal and professional areas of their lives. Some of the academic literature in lifelong learning refers to the following theories as frameworks: Self-Directed Learning Theory, Transformative Learning, and Experiential learning. Self-directed learning theory emphasizes the importance of self-directed learning, where individuals take initiative in identifying learning needs and seek out resources to fulfill them (Knowles, 1975). Transformative learning focuses on the changes in perspective that occur through critical reflection (Mezirow, 1991) and experiential learning highlights the role of experience in the learning process (Kolb, 1984). While all of these theories relate to adult learning, Steffans (2015) and Thwe and Kálmán (2023) assert a definitive lifelong learning theory has yet to formally exist in the literature.

Lifelong learning is more important than ever since individuals must now regularly acquire new skills to maintain competitiveness in the workforce, adapt to technological advancements, and contribute meaningfully to society. However, traditional educational systems, with structured timelines and established curricula, often fail to accommodate the evolving needs of learners throughout their lifespans and provide current, relevant, and necessary resources that are easily accessible. Bridgestock (2017) observed, "Universities are by and large walled gardens – closed ecosystems where learning and resources are kept secure from the outside world, including industry and community stakeholders." She points out the real learning occurs through networked and co-curricular experiences, often not facilitated by the institution and suggests universities should become distributed knowledge network hubs with constant connection to industry changes and requirements in order to support lifelong learning. Along with that, Lang (2023) recommends that higher education provide rapid micro-credentialing focused on lifelong learning to align with using AI in the quickly changing workplace.

AI offers significant potential to transform education through personalized, scalable, flexible, and ubiquitous learning experiences that can provide real-time feedback, all which support lifelong learning (Masrek et al., 2024; Mishra, 2024). Technologies such as machine learning, natural language processing, and intelligent tutoring systems create adaptive learning environments responsive to individual needs and learning preferences. By implementing ubiquitous AI-driven approaches, lifelong learning becomes more accessible, efficient, and customized to address the specific goals and challenges of each learner (Masrek et al., 2024).

THE ROLE OF AI IN PERSONALIZED LEARNING

Personalization can be key to effective lifelong learning by enabling individuals to progress at their own pace according to their specific requirements and interests at any point in their lives. AI contributes significantly to personalizing learning experiences by analyzing data on learners' behaviors, strengths and weaknesses, preferences, and performance to develop customized learning paths (Cooper, 2023; Hwang et al., 2020; Memarian & Doleck, 2023; Su & Yang, 2023). For example, AI teaching assistants offer personalized guidance, adapting to diverse learning styles through visual aids, auditory explanations, and continuous learning improvement (Zhao, 2024). Additionally, AI aids in analyzing students' learning status and progress, allowing for dynamic adjustments to enhance learning efficiency (Zhao, 2024). Adaptive Learning Systems, Intelligent Tutoring Systems, and Recommendation Systems are three examples of how artificial intelligence can support personalized lifelong learning.

Adaptive Learning Systems

AI-powered adaptive platforms adjust content and difficulty levels based on learner progress, using real time data to adapt the pace, content, and deliverability of instruction (Rane et al., 2024). These systems employ algorithms to assess the learner's individual strengths and weaknesses to create a learner profile, provide a specialized and tailored learning paths with preferred learning styles along with targeted interventions and resources to address knowledge gaps, while helping the learner move at their own pace in a more effective and inclusive educational environment (Rane et al., 2024; Strielkowski et al., 2024). In addition, real time feedback is quickly provided while student progress is monitored and analyzed in order to provide updated learning materials based upon the real time data analysis (Strielkowski et al., 2024).

Adaptive learning systems can also be used to help adult learners gain confidence in academic subjects they may have struggled with in the past. In addition, these systems support the development of 21st Century skills by delivering content in an interactive and experiential format such as the use of virtual reality and augmented reality (Rane et al., 2024; Strielkowski et al., 2024). In fact, according to Rane et al. (2024), "This not only enhances subject comprehension but also nurtures creativity, collaboration, and problem-solving abilities skills crucial for success in the contemporary global landscape" (p. 30).

Virtual Personal Assistants (VPAs) such as Google Assistant, or Alexa are examples of adaptive learning systems that utilize artificial intelligence to shape learning experiences, enhance productivity, and provide personalized support (Langston et al., 2025). These software applications are designed to perform tasks or services for an individual based on commands or queries, often utilizing natural language processing and machine learning techniques to understand and respond intelligently to user requests (Jacob et al., 2024). This capability allows them to manage schedules and to-do list, set reminders, create shopping list, and provide information on demand (Langston et al., 2025). As a result, VPAs not only streamline tasks but also encourage an environment conducive to continuous learning and skill development, making them assets in both educational and professional settings (Jacob et al., 2024). Langston et al. (2025) determined that VPAs, which Large Language Model based (ChatGpt4, Gemini), perform much better than those that are not (Google, Alexa). This suggests as the technology continues to improve, VPAs can further support personalized lifelong learning.

Intelligent Tutoring Systems (ITS)

AI-driven intelligent tutoring systems (ITS) have the ability to deliver individualized support by replicating the guidance of human tutors and are one of the most promising applications of AI in education (Harry & Sayudin, 2023; Wang et al., 2023). These systems provide personalized feedback, respond to inquiries, and guide learners through complex problem-solving processes (Rane et al. 2024; Singh et al., 2022). In fact, ITS can provide feedback when students are lacking instructor feedback and summative assessment (Harry & Sayudin, 2023). This kind of personalization offers learners the assistance and direction they need to reach their potential (Harry & Sayudin, 2023).

Intelligent Tutoring Systems prove particularly valuable for subjects that require mastery of foundational concepts before progressing to more sophisticated concepts. Strielkowski et al. (2024) suggest the use of ITS encourages independent learning with students having more control of their learning path. In addition, Lin et al. (2023) noted "AI-based tutoring systems help bridge the gap between educators and students by providing an innovative platform that makes education more accessible" (p. 18).

The following are selected benefits identified in the literature with using Intelligent Tutoring Systems:

- **Accessibility**: AI tutors can reach students in remote or underserved areas, providing better access to educational (Johnson & Davis 2024; Mishra, 2024; Zhang & Leong, 2024).
- **Cost-Effectiveness**: Once the initial cost of content development and platform are funded AI systems may reduce the cost of personalized education, making it more accessible and saving time for instructor (Ayers, 2024; Ozbey et al., 2023; Samala et al, 2024; Vujinović et al., 2024).
- **Non-native Language Support**: AI tutoring systems are integrating translation tools into course materials for real-time translation encouraging student engagement and participation along with practice tools for conversation (Baranwal, 2022; Dhananjaya, 2024; Memarian & Doleck, 2023; Mishra, 2024; Zhang & Leong, 2024).
- **Scalability**: Intelligent tutoring systems can simultaneously support thousands of students, making them a scalable solution for large educational institutions (Lui et al., 2025; Samala et al., 2024; Vujinović et al., 2024; Zhang et al., 2022).
- **Instructor Support**: The use of Intelligent Tutoring systems can offer additional time for educators to concentrate on teaching, remediation, and interacting with students. In addition, the data analysis performed allow ITS to identify student needs for intervention. (Mishra, 2024).

Recommendation Systems

Computerized Recommendation Systems have existed for decades (Goldberg et al., 1992) and were first in the e-commerce industry, but with the emergence of artificial intelligence, Recommendation Systems have improved significantly, incorporating advanced algorithms and machine learning techniques to provide increasingly personalized experiences for users (Jangda & Raazi, 2024). AI-based recommendation systems suggest relevant learning resources, courses, or specific content based on learners' interests, objectives, and previous educational experiences using real time data analysis (Dhananjaya, 2024). These systems assist learners in navigating educational resources, identifying materials most relevant to their specific requirements, and making informed choices (Mustafa et al., 2024; Zhang et al., 2021).

The literature describes three general types of Recommendation Systems:

- **Content-based filtering**: it recommends items by analyzing the attributes (content descriptions) of items a user has previously liked;
- **Collaborative filtering**: it relies on past user interactions and behaviors to suggest items based on similar preferences among users; and
- **Knowledge-based filtering**: it utilizes prior domain knowledge and user preferences to recommend items that meet specific criteria or requirements (Masciari et al., 2024; Zhang et al., 2021).

After the integration of artificial intelligence with the systems, four more types emerged:

- **Matrix Factorization:** Enhances recommendations by decomposing user-item interaction matrices into latent factors;
- **Deep Learning:** Employs neural networks to capture complex patterns in user behavior for more personalized recommendations;
- **Context-Aware Recommendation:** Considers contextual information like time, location, and device to provide more relevant suggestions; and
- **Reinforcement Learning:** Improves recommendations through an agent-based approach that learns from user feedback over time (Zhang et al., 2021).

As these systems continue to advance, they are becoming increasingly proficient at integrating real-time data and machine learning algorithms, allowing for better understanding of user behavior and preferences.

Recommendation systems can assist with lifelong learning by providing customized recommendations that can guide learners toward resources and opportunities that align with their interests, and needs for new skills and goals (Digel et al., 2023). As these systems continue to improve, they are incorporating advanced techniques such as deep learning and natural language processing, further enhancing their ability to predict user preferences with increased accuracy (Dhananjaya, 2024). While challenges such as data privacy, scalability, and equity must be addressed, lifelong learning will continue to benefit from improving AI Recommendation Systems that can offer even more accurate personalized learning, intelligent content delivery, and just-in-time professional development.

AI AND LIFELONG LEARNING IN THE WORKPLACE

The Internet, digitalization, and human-to-machine interactions have created significant changes including increased automation and a demand for new skills in the workplace as well as have blurred boundaries between work and personal life (Lang, 2023). This digital transformation is reshaping how individuals engage with information, learn, work, and make decisions (Poquet & De Laat, 2021; Rial-Gonzalez et al., 2024). As the workforce continues to change through technological advancement, lifelong learning is essential for career development and professional advancement (Fidalgo & Thormann. 2024; Rial-Gonzalez et al., 2024) in order to maintain employability in an environment characterized by profound changes, with lifelong learning being a strategic response to these emerging challenges (Rial- Gonzalez et al., 2024). AI can facilitate the effective administration of these transformations, cultivating an environment conducive to innovation and adaptability within the organization (Yusuf et al., 2024).

AI platforms such as intelligent tutoring systems can support workplace learning by delivering timely and personalized training for professional development opportunities with real time feedback, anytime, anywhere (Samala et al, 2024; Yusuf et al., 2024) with potential applications in areas such as efficient education management, personalized learning support, and automated assessment (Rial-Gonzalez et al., 2024). These tools can dynamically interact with human cognitive and social processes, influencing how individuals learn, work, and interact and have the potential to both enhance task performance and impact human cognition and social practices (Poquet & De Laat, 2021).

Poquet and De Laat (2021) suggested a "capability approach", a framework developed by Sen (1985) and later expanded by Nussbaum (2003). The researchers recommend this framework should be used as a guiding principle for supporting human development through lifelong learning. This approach focuses on individual agency, freedom, and equity in human development. By adopting the capability approach, individuals and organizations can enhance human development throughout the learning journey. This approach highlights the importance of personal goals, ownership in learning, and the role of technology in enabling value creation in lifelong learning processes. Poquet and De Laat (2021) suggest in order to maximize the benefits of AI in lifelong learning, a focus on capability development is essential as digital technologies and AI-driven analytics can provide insights into individual mastery, support self-regulation, and facilitate learner agency in career planning and skill development. By reframing lifelong learning through the lens of the capability approach, organizations can prioritize human development, agency, and equity in learning processes (Poquet & De Laat, 2021).

AI for Skill Development

The rapid pace of technological change is transforming the economy and creating a need for a diverse workforce with changing skill requirements (Siddiqi, 2024). AI systems identify skill gaps and recommend targeted learning opportunities by analyzing labor market trends and individual career trajectories. This approach helps professionals remain current with industry demands and develop capabilities required for future roles (Billiot, 2023). Organizations that delay adopting AI technologies and providing continuous training on AI risk losing relevance in the rapidly changing marketplace (Billiot, 2023). However, organizations adopting a skills-first approach should experience economic growth, enhanced equity, and foster greater inclusion by equipping individuals with the essential skills needed to thrive in a rapidly evolving job market (Siddiqi, 2024). Before establishing goals for skill development, organizations must assess employees' prior knowledge and attitudes toward AI to create personalized training programs as formative and summative evaluations are essential to measure learner progress, identify knowledge gaps, and assess employee performance.

As automation reshapes job landscapes, retaining talent through continuous upskilling becomes crucial, with human-centric skills like empathy and teamwork becoming more valuable and positioning AI as a supportive tool rather than a job replacement (Moehrle, 2024). The retirement of older workers intensifies the challenge of talent retention, emphasizing the societal implications of workforce transformation. Siddiqi (2024) observed that community colleges are key providers of skills training and should develop a variety of offerings for credentialing and lifelong learning using apprenticeship programs, continuing education, and short-term training. This includes preskilling, upskilling, and reskilling to ensure that employees can continuously adapt to evolving industry demands. to support lifelong learning (Siddiqi, 2024).

AI in Corporate Training

Artificial intelligence is changing how individuals engage with information as well as how they learn, work, and make decisions (Poquet & De Laat, 2021). Organizations are now implementing AI-powered platforms to deliver personalized training programs that can also assess employees' current competencies, recommend tailored learning modules, and monitor progress over time. According to Moehrle (2024), there are three primary areas for AI assistance in corporate training: AI enhancing learning practices efficiency and efficacy, leading to adaptations in learning and development (L&D) functions; significant automation creating a need for upskilling and reskilling within organizations, which corporate learning must proactively address; and enhancing AI literacy among employees to harness AI's potential for boosting productivity and user experience. Isensee et al. (2021) and

Moehrle (2024) suggest that ethical guidelines for how AI should be utilized must be clearly communicated to all employees and clarity provided.

Aoun and Kosslyn (2018) examined the quickly changing workforce landscape and the competencies that will be essential for human personnel to keep their positions within a technologically progressive economy. The authors contend that as artificial intelligence (AI) and automation advance in complexity, the most prized competencies will encompass contextual awareness, emotional intelligence, and distinctly "human" skills. The authors advocate that to ensure the continued relevance of humans, educational paradigms should prioritize the cultivation of skills and proficiencies related to contextual cognizance and emotional intelligence. Competencies anticipated to experience increased demand include the capacity to educate, mentor, and coordinate individuals, as well as creativity— all of which require an understanding of context and human-specific abilities.

Microlearning and AI

Artificial intelligence is also impacting micro-credentialing by enabling personalized learning paths and automated assessments (Ahsan et al., 2023; Shanmughan et al., 2024). Lang (2023) suggested the use of digital micro-credentials (small, assessed units of learning that can be stacked to build larger qualifications) as a key strategy to support lifelong learning and workforce upskilling and changing workforce needs. AI can facilitate microlearning and micro-credentialling through concise, focused learning segments that can be delivered using during brief intervals throughout their workday. AI powered micro-credentialing programs can provide flexible, modular competency based learning and targeted learning opportunities addressing immediate needs that allow learners to upskill and reskill throughout their careers without workflow disruption (Hunt et al., 2019; Lang, 2023).

Recent studies have emphasized the potential of micro-credentials to enhance accessibility, employability, and inclusivity in education (Msweli et al., 2022; Schutte, 2024). However, challenges remain, including ensuring academic rigor and addressing digital divide concerns (Rajabalee, 2023; Shanmughan et al., 2024). Some view micro-credentials as a potential replacement for traditional degrees, while others see them as the impetus to integrate vocational training within higher education (Ralston, 2021). This suggests a potential challenge in integrating with formal education systems and recognition of micro-credentials as transferable credits are ongoing issues (Rajabalee, 2023; Selvaratnam & Sankey, 2025). Despite these challenges, micro-credentials offer valuable opportunities for rapid skill updating and confidence-building, particularly for adult learners (Parsons et al., 2023) and are increasingly seen as a transformative force in education and career development.

AI AND LIFELONG LEARNING FOR DIVERSE POPULATIONS

Artificial intelligence offers considerable potential to address learning needs for diverse populations including those with disabilities, non-traditional learners, and individuals from underrepresented communities. AI can tailor content, provide instant feedback, and offer data-driven insights to support diverse learners (Masrek et al., 2024). By providing personalized learning experiences, AI helps reduce educational inequality and promotes inclusivity in lifelong learning. However, challenges remain in ensuring AI benefits all populations equitably (Zou & Schiebinger, 2021). To address this, the literature emphasizes the importance of AI literacy for the AI systems.

Disabled Learners

Adaptive educational platforms possess the capability to modify the level of difficulty, furnish alternative elucidations, or disseminate information in diverse modalities (visual, auditory, tactile) in order to accommodate the distinct learning preferences and challenges encountered by individual learners (Strielkowski et al., 2024). Furthermore, these technological advancements are capable of providing instantaneous feedback and reinforcement, which is especially helpful for students who require more frequent assistance (Strielkowski et al., 2024). Additionally, AI powered tools can support learners with disabilities through assistive technologies including speech-to-text, text-to-speech, and language translation tools, all of which support lifelong learning and increased inclusivity (Kumar et al., 2023). Adaptive algorithms and inclusive design principles are increasingly being adopted, ensuring that educational technologies are accessible to a broader spectrum of disabilities, including cognitive and neurodivergent conditions (Gibson, 2024). Recent advancements in artificial intelligence (AI) have demonstrated considerable potential in improving the everyday lives of those with disabilities through innovations such as decision-making support systems and navigation tools for those who are visually impaired (Smith & Smith, 2020). Almufareh et al. (2024) observed the convergence of support for disabilities and artificial intelligence suggests a more equitable and inclusive future, where technology empowers individuals to surmount obstacles and improve their quality of life.

The following are examples of how AI can help those with disabilities:

- **Speech-to-Text/Text-to-Speech**: Tools like Google Live Transcribe, Apple's VoiceOver, and AI dictation services enhance communication for those with hearing, speech, and visual impairments.
- **Image and Scene Recognition**: Apps like Seeing AI and Envision AI describe surroundings for the visually impaired.

- **Sign Language and Eye-Tracking**: AI-powered sign language translators such as Signapse and Sign-Speak and eye-tracking interfaces such has Tobi Dynsvox enable more inclusive communication.
- **Personalized Learning**: AI tutors like Cognii adapt to diverse learning styles, supporting students with dyslexia, ADHD, and cognitive disabilities.
- **Real-Time Captioning and Translation**: These technologies such as Google Transcribe Live, Ava, Otter.ai) foster greater participation in education and professional environments and are now included in virtual meeting spaces such as Zoom and Microsoft Teams.

While these technologies have enhanced accessibility for many, Smith and Smith (2020) assert important questions remain regarding their effectiveness, limitations, and the ethical considerations surrounding AI's role in decision-making processes. They propose that AI has the potential to act as a catalyst for inclusion and empowerment, provided it is developed with empathy and a comprehensive understanding of the diverse needs of disabled individuals.

Both Smith and Smith (2020) and Wald (2021) call for engaging individuals with disabilities as co-designers is essential for creating AI technologies that authentically address their needs and fulfill the potential benefits these systems promise for improving quality of life. Acosta-Vargas et al. (2024) and Lillywhite and Wolbring (2019) all urge for more collaboration among developers, accessibility specialists, and disabled users to bridge identified gaps, elevate inclusivity standards, and ensure that generative AI tools meet the diverse needs of all users and the ethical challenges they face. Ongoing innovation, ethical mindfulness, and active involvement from all stakeholders, including individuals with disabilities, will be essential in shaping an AI landscape that promotes empowerment, connectivity, and continuous progress in accessibility. Future research should investigate the ongoing evolution of accessibility guidelines and innovative methodologies that incorporate inclusive principles into generative AI, thereby promoting a more equitable and sustainable digital environment, which is a moral obligation critical for nurturing a just society (Acosta-Vargas et al., 2024).

AI for Underrepresented Learners

AI-powered platforms advocate for global access to educational resources, reducing geographical barriers and enabling students to engage with high-quality materials regardless of location (Abbas et al., 2023) while providing tailored learning experiences based on cultural contexts and educational backgrounds, making lifelong learning more accessible worldwide. For example, AI can facilitate improved learning internationally through language translation services, enabling individuals from different linguistic and cultural backgrounds to access educational content in their native languages. In addition, AI can serve underrepresented communities by addressing the digital divide and provide low-cost learning support using platforms such as Wikipedia and open educational resources (OERs) along with artificial intelligence for cross language translation in accessible formats (Bulathwela et al., 2024).

Bulathwela et al. (2024) suggest a unified knowledge base be developed, to facilitate interoperability among educational systems worldwide. They also noted that in order for AI to better serve this population, the amount of (OERs) would have to increase tremendously without the legal challenge of copyright and ownership barriers. In addition, Zhang and Leong (2024) point out the technological infrastructure may still be a barrier in some places. To overcome these challenges, concerted efforts must be made to enhance digital infrastructure while simultaneously advocating for policy changes that promote equitable access to technology and educational materials (Isontani et al., 2023). The academic literature calls for a balanced approach in utilizing AI for educational purposes, emphasizing the need to mitigate risks associated with the still existent digital divide while maximizing the benefits of AI in learning environments.

Such initiatives could involve partnerships between governments, educational institutions, and private sector organizations to ensure that resources are allocated efficiently and equitably across different regions (Isontani et al., 2023). This collaborative approach can help with gaps in technology and also promote an environment of innovation and inclusivity, ultimately enabling learners from diverse backgrounds to access AI-driven educational resources. By prioritizing investment in digital literacy programs, communities can equip individuals with the skills needed to navigate and effectively use the technologies. Investing in ongoing training and support for educators is equally crucial, as it ensures they are better able to integrate these technologies into their teaching practices and can guide students in maximizing their learning experiences. This strategy better prepares students for a rapidly evolving job market where digital skills are increasingly essential.

AI-DRIVEN ASSESSMENT AND FEEDBACK

Artificial Intelligence (AI) is also transforming assessment for lifelong learners by providing real-time, tailored feedback, enhancing student engagement and learning outcomes (Masrek et al., 2024; Oberdieck & Moch, 2024). These AI-powered assessment systems utilize machine learning, natural language processing, and learning analytics to analyze student data, predict performance, and generate personalized feedback (Bulut & Wongvorachan, 2022). Despite challenges with bias and privacy, AI has significant potential to transform educational assessment, offering more dynamic, efficient, and personalized evaluation methods that support diverse learner needs throughout their lifelong learning journey (Cheniti-Belcadhi, 2016). Overall, the findings suggest that generative AI tools can be leveraged to enhance self-directed learning, but educators must thoughtfully integrate these tools in a way that promotes authentic learning and preserves academic integrity (Marquardson, 2024).

Improved Assignment Activities for Assessment

AI powered tools for educators continue to improve and become more useful in the classroom with faculty slowly adopting and integrating its use for improving student assignment activities. For example, Marquardson's (2024) recent study using AI for a college-level capstone course suggested the student use of AI to create their learning activity did enhance self-directed learning. Marquardson points out clear guidelines and parameters must be used as well as a common AI tool for technology support questions. He reminds educators to thoughtfully integrate these tools in a way that promotes authentic learning and preserves academic integrity. While this study was focused the college level, the same self-directed activity could be used for adult learners. Johnson and Davis (2024) illustrate other assignment activities that incorporate AI, such as enhancing assessment case studies and formulating systematic instructional program plans by comparing AI-generated outputs with educational standards and individual student requirements. Assignments should promote the critical evaluation of AI-generated material and the application of pedagogical and assessment knowledge. However, Johnson and Davis also caution there recommend there be a balance and not an overreliance on AI for all assessment activities.

AI tools should be used to generate personalized assessments and evaluations for students, tailored to their individual abilities and learning needs (Zeb et al., 2024). In addition to more engaging learning activities, AI has the ability to automate evaluation processes for assignments, quizzes, and examinations, allowing learners to receive immediate feedback. This reduces response time and helps learners quickly identify areas requiring improvement.

Continuous Feedback

Feedback plays a critical role in the assessment process by enabling learners to monitor their progress and assisting instructors in personalizing content (Cheniti-Belcadhi, 2016). AI-powered platforms can provide ongoing feedback regarding learner progress, offering insights into strengths and areas for development. This continuous feedback mechanism helps learners remain engaged and motivated through real-time progress monitoring and adaptive learning strategy adjustment.

Abbas et al. (2023) noted that AI enhanced assessment tools present another significant benefit for both students and educators by delivering immediate feedback on assignments, quizzes, and exams. This prompt response mechanism allows students to recognize their errors in real-time, facilitating corrective measures that lead to faster improvement and a richer grasp of the subject (Abbas et al., 2023). In addition, these beneficial tools can streamline grading processes freeing up educators to interact more meaningfully with their students.

Data-Driven Insights for Educators

AI data platforms can provide educators with valuable performance data, enabling identification of trends, areas of concern, and opportunities for improvement. This data-driven approach helps educators improve teaching strategies and use targeted interventions to support learner success. AI can be instrumental in identifying areas where students may struggle. By employing predictive analytics, AI can analyze historical performance data to anticipate future student behavior, equipping educators to implement timely interventions for those at risk of lagging behind (Abbas, 2023). This proactive strategy not only supports comprehension but also helps avert substantial academic difficulties.

AI CHALLENGES and ETHICAL CONSIDERATIONS

Recent literature on lifelong learning and the challenges of using artificial intelligence (AI) reveals both obstacles and opportunities. Key challenges include technological integration issues and the need for organizational adaptability, ethical considerations and data privacy, and the impact on instructor student relationship in AI supported learning environments.

Technology Integration

Because the AI technology must be integrated into existing educational frameworks, this requires a shift in teaching methodologies and institutional practices (Milana, 2024). While AI has the potential to create dynamic learning environments, robust technological infrastructure and professional development of educators to use these technologies effectively in lifelong learning contexts are needed for effective AI integration (Asad & Ajaz, 2024; Masrek et al., 2024). However, despite advancements, limitations do exist with current AI technology platforms such as handling ambiguity, context-dependency, and complex cognitive tasks that require human-like reasoning and creativity (Mustafa et al., 2024; Sytnyk & Podlinyayevam, 2024). Furthermore, equity remains a significant challenge in the context of AI and lifelong learning. For example, Mutia et al. (2024) highlighted the potential of AI-powered tools to enhance learning experiences but remind us that unequal access to these technologies could perpetuate educational divides between different communities and regions.

Organizational Adaptability

The adaptability of educational organizations to AI technologies is key to overcoming the barriers to adopting the tools effectively. Comprehensive discussions regarding the policy and practice of artificial intelligence must occur in order to provide guidelines for responsible use that promotes equitable access and fosters inclusivity. Eynon and Young (2020) emphasize the importance of engaging a diverse array of stakeholders in discussions about AI and its role in lifelong education, arguing for a more democratic and inclusive approach to AI in learning to avoid narrow, personalized learning experiences that may overlook broader educational goals.

Rane et al. (2024) stress the importance of balancing technological innovation with ethical concerns for responsible integration. In addition, Fidalgo and Thormann (2024) suggest that lifelong learning should embrace technology at its core, advocating for a shift from fixed curricula to adaptive and personalized learning paths that reflect the continuous nature of learning. This adaptability is crucial for preparing learners for rapidly changing job markets and technological landscapes. As AI continues to reshape education and lifelong learning, there is a need for ongoing research, collaboration among stakeholders, and ethical considerations to ensure its responsible and equitable implementation (Aggarwal, 2023; Eynon & Young, 2020).

Ethics, Data Privacy, and Algorithmic Bias

Ethical implications associated with the implementation of artificial intelligence in educational contexts is mentioned in much of the recent literature. Some of the most significant challenges are ethical considerations and privacy concerns (Fildalgo & Thormann, 2024; Mustafa et al., 2024); Slimi, 2023; Zhao, 2024). AI systems rely on vast amounts of data, including personal information about students, which raises concerns about data privacy and security since personalized learning requires access to sensitive data, such as learning patterns, behavioral traits, and personal preferences, which can be vulnerable to misuse or unauthorized access (Fildalgo & Thormann, 2024, Xiao et al., 2025; Zhang et al., 2024).

However, the ethical implications extend beyond data privacy with issues such as algorithmic bias, transparency, and accountability. A notable concern is that AI algorithms can inadvertently perpetuate biases present in the data they are trained on, leading to unfair or discriminatory outcomes in areas such as grading, admissions, and resource allocation which could exacerbate existing inequalities in educational access (Abbas et al,, 2024; Asad & Ajaz,2024; Fildalgo & Thormann, 2024; George & Wooden, 2023; Mimoudi, 2024; Mustafa et al., 2024; Pandya, 2024; Sytnyk & Podlinyayevam, 2024).

Further ethical considerations center around the reliability and accuracy of the information provided by AI technologies, which can potentially mislead students and hinder their learning process (Ayers, 2024; Milana, 2024). Humble and Mozelieus (2022) noted the potential threats of AI in education, such as the fear of job replacement, privacy issues, and the need for an ethical framework to guide AI development and usage. And finally, the most cited concern is student cheating and plagiarism.

Instructor-Learner Relationship

While AI provides personalized support, it cannot substitute for the human connection between educators and learners. Purnama et al. (2023) notes, while AI may fulfill various functions, the inherent emotional intelligence and ethical decision-making of humans are irreplaceable aspects that contribute uniquely to society and the job market. In addition, instructors must shift to be guides, facilitators, and evaluators, providing personalized tutoring and guidance to meet students' learning needs effectively (Zhao, 2024). We must remember educators play crucial roles in cultivating motivation, empathy, and social interaction—fundamental aspects of the learning process. AI should complement rather than replace educators' roles.

THE FUTURE OF AI IN LIFELONG LEARNING

AI's capabilities offer tr learning experiences that are seamlessly integrated into daily life, reshaping education into a personalized, dynamic, and continuous journey (Masrek et al., 2024). As AI technologies continue to develop, their role in lifelong learning will expand, offering new opportunities for personalized, flexible, and inclusive education, with AI being anticipated to become a cornerstone in education (Southworth et al., 2023).

The literature suggests increased integration of AI with emerging technologies such as virtual reality (VR), augmented reality (AR), and the Internet of Things (IoT) that will create immersive and interactive learning environments that further enhance educational experiences (Dembe et al., 2024; Farahani et al., 2024). These integrated technologies offer new possibilities for experiential learning and skill development across multiple disciplines. In addition, AI application for lifelong learning will likely involve increasingly sophisticated systems adapting to learners' changing needs over time. The literature suggests the future of AI will include precision learning (Samala et al., 2024). These systems will anticipate learning objectives, provide timely guidance, and facilitate seamless transitions between different learning contexts—whether in formal educational settings, professional environments, or informal learning situations.

The role of AI in educational technologies for lifelong learning is transformative and as AI continues to improve, its integration into lifelong learning will shape educational futures and help individuals navigate an increasingly complex and changing world. By leveraging the incredible potential of AI while addressing its challenges, we can see a future where lifelong learning is both effective and accessible. Mishra (2024) asserted, "The future of AI in education lies not in replacing human educators but in creating a symbiotic relationship that leverages the strengths of both AI and human expertise" (p. 1189).

CONCLUSION

Artificial Intelligence (AI) is no longer a new technology but a central force reshaping lifelong learning into a personalized, dynamic, and continuous process (Masrek et al., 2024). As global economies shift and technologies evolve, the ability to continually learn, unlearn, and relearn has become essential. AI technologies now play a pivotal role in supporting this shift by enabling adaptive learning environments, intelligent tutoring systems, and context-aware recommendation platforms that respond to learners' unique needs and trajectories (Dhananjaya, 2024; Rane et al., 2024; Strielkowski et al., 2024).

The transformative potential of AI lies in its capacity to enhance both access and quality of learning across diverse contexts. AI empowers individuals with disabilities through assistive technologies like text-to-speech tools and personalized learning systems (Smith & Smith, 2020; Strielkowski et al., 2024). It also supports underrepresented and geographically isolated learners by removing language barriers and providing culturally contextualized content (Bulathwela et al., 2024; Zhang

& Leong, 2024). In the workplace, AI-driven training platforms deliver real-time feedback and individualized skill development pathways, allowing professionals to remain competitive in rapidly evolving industries (Siddiqi, 2024; Yusuf et al., 2024). Moreover, AI enables new forms of credentialing and assessment that are modular, responsive, and competency-based—good for today's fast-paced professional landscape (Lang, 2023; Shanmughan et al., 2024). These innovations allow for seamless integration of learning into daily life, fostering self-directed growth that is both immediate and sustained (Abbas et al., 2023; Marquardson, 2024).

However, the promise of AI must be tempered by thoughtful and ethical implementation. Key concerns include algorithmic bias, data privacy, unequal access to digital infrastructure, and the risk of reducing education to overly personalized or isolated experiences (Abbas et al., 2024; Fidalgo & Thormann, 2024; Mustafa et al., 2024). As Eynon and Young (2020) argue, the future of AI in education must involve broad stakeholder collaboration to ensure that technological innovation does not come at the expense of educational equity or learner agency.

Ultimately, the future of AI in lifelong learning hinges on creating a symbiotic relationship between human and machine intelligence. Rather than replacing educators, AI should amplify their impact—providing them with tools to personalize instruction, monitor progress, and focus on the social and emotional aspects of teaching (Mishra, 2024; Purnama et al., 2023). When guided by ethical frameworks and inclusive values, AI has the potential to make lifelong learning truly accessible, meaningful, and empowering for all. By implementing AI technologies thoughtfully, we can create more accessible, efficient, and inclusive learning experiences that enable individuals to continue learning throughout their lives (Aggarwal, 2023).

ACKNOWLEDGMENT

This research received no specific grant from any funding agency in the public, commercial, or not-for-profit sectors. Artificial intelligence was used to locate, compare and contrast relevant research studies and for editing purposes.

REFERENCES

Abbas, N., Ali, I., Manzoor, R., Hussain, T., Hussain, M., & Hussaini, A. (2023). Role of Artificial Intelligence tools in enhancing students' educational performance at higher levels. *Journal of Artificial Intelligence, Machine Learning, and Neural Network, 3*(5). Advance online publication. DOI: 10.55529/jaimlnn.35.36.49

Acosta-Vargas, P., Salvador-Acosta, B., Novillo-Villegas, S., Sarantis, D., & Salvador-Ullauri, L. (2024). Generative Artificial Intelligence and web accessibility: Towards an inclusive and sustainable future. *Emerging Science Journal, 8*(4). Advance online publication. DOI: 10.28991/esj-2024-08-04-021

Aggarwal, D. (2023). Exploring the scope of Artificial Intelligence (AI) for lifelong education through personalised & adaptive learning. *Journal of Artificial Intelligence. Machine Learning and Neural Network, 4*(1), 21–26. DOI: 10.55529/jaimlnn.41.21.26

Ahsan, K., Akbar, S., Kam, B., & Abdulrahman, M. D.-A. (2023). Implementation of micro-credentials in higher education: A systematic literature review. *Education and Information Technologies, 28*, 13505–13540. DOI: 10.1007/s10639-023-11739-z

Almufareh, M. F., Kausar, S., Humayun, M., & Tehsin, S. (2024). A conceptual model for inclusive technology: Advancing disability inclusion through Artificial Intelligence. *Journal of Disability Research, 3*(1). Advance online publication. DOI: 10.57197/JDR-2023-0060

Aoun, J. E., & Kosslyn, S. M. (2018). Outsmarting AI. *Liberal Education, 104*(4), 34–37.

Asad, M., & Ajaz, A. (2024). Impact of ChatGPT and generative AI on lifelong learning and upskilling learners in higher education: Unveiling the challenges and opportunities globally. *International Journal of Information and Learning Technology, 41*(5), 507–523. DOI: 10.1108/ijilt-06-2024-0103

Ayers, J. J. (2024). How can AI help transform CTE curricula? *Techniques, 2024*(September), 16–20.

Baranwal, D. (2022). A systematic review of exploring the potential of teachable agents in English Learning. *Pedagogical Research, 7*(1). Advance online publication. DOI: 10.29333/pr/11553

Billiot, T. (2023). Continuous learning and advancing technologies: A framework for professional development and training in artificial intelligence. *Development and Learning in Organizations, 37*(3), 28–31. DOI: 10.1108/dlo-04-2022-0064

Bulathwela, S., Pérez-Ortiz, M., Holloway, C., Cukurova, M., & Shawe-Taylor, J. (2024). Artificial intelligence alone will not democratize education: On educational inequality, techno-solutionism and inclusive tools. *Sustainability, 16*(2), 781. DOI: 10.3390/su16020781

Bulut, O., & Wongvorachan, T. (2022). Feedback generation through Artificial Intelligence. *The Open/Technology in Education, Society, and Scholarship Association Conference, 2*(1), Issue 1, 1–9. DOI: 10.18357/otessac.2022.2.1.125

Cheniti-Belcadhi, L. (2016). Personalized feedback for self-assessment in lifelong learning environments based on semantic web. *Computers in Human Behavior, 55a*, 562–570. DOI: 10.1016/j.chb.2015.07.042

Commission for a Nation of Lifelong Learning. (1997). *A nation learning: Vision for the 21st century.* Author.

Commission of the European Communities. (2001). *Making a European area of lifelong learning a reality.* Author. https://www.europarl.europa.eu/meetdocs/committees/cult/20020122/com(2001)678_en.pdf

Cooper, G. (2023). Examining science sducation in ChatGPT: An exploratory study of Generative Artificial Intelligence. *Journal of Science Education and Technology, 32*(3), 444–452. DOI: 10.1007/S10956-023-10039-Y

Delores, J. (1996). *Learning: The treasure within.* UNESCO Publishing.

Dembe, A. H. (2024). The integration of Virtual Reality (VR) and Augmented Reality (AR) in classroom settings. *Research Invention Journal of Engineering and Physical Sciences, 3*(1), 102-113. https://rijournals.com/the-integration-of-virtual-reality-vr-and-augmented-reality-ar-in-classroom-settings/

Dhananjaya, G. M., Goudar, R. H., Kulkarni, A. A., Rathod, V. N., & Hukkeri, G. S. (2024). A Digital Recommendation System for personalized learning to enhance online education: A review. *IEEE Access : Practical Innovations, Open Solutions, 12*, 34019. DOI: 10.1109/ACCESS.2024.3369901

Digel, S., Krause, T., & Biel, C. (2023). Enabling individualized and adaptive learning – the value of an AI-Based Recommender System for users of adult and continuing education platforms. In Wang, N., Rebolledo-Mendez, G., Dimitrova, V., Matsuda, N., & Santos, O. C. (Eds.), *Communications in computer and information science. Artificial intelligence in education: Posters and late breaking results, workshops and tutorials, industry and innovation tracks, practitioners, doctoral consortium and blue sky* (Vol. 1831, pp. 797–803). Springer., DOI: 10.1007/978-3-031-36336-8_121

Edwards-Fapohunda, M. O., & Adediji, M. A. (2024). Sustainable development of distance learning in continuing adult education: The impact of Artificial Intelligence. *Iconic Research and Engineering Journals*, *8*(1), 113–118. https://www.irejournals.com/paper-details/1706017

Eynon, R., & Young, E. (2020). Methodology, legend, and rhetoric: The constructions of AI by academia, industry, and policy groups for lifelong learning. *Science, Technology & Human Values*, *46*(1), 166–191. DOI: 10.1177/0162243920906475

Farahani, M. S., & Ghasmi, G. (2024). *Artificial Intelligence in education: A comprehensive study.*, *2*(3), 1379. DOI: 10.59400/fes.v2i3.1379

Fidalgo, P., & Thormann, J. (2024). The future of Lifelong Learning: The role of artificial intelligence and distance education. In Paloma, F. G. (Ed.), *Lifelong learning - education for the future world.*, DOI: 10.5772/intechopen.114120

García-Martínez, I., Fernández-Batanero, J. M., Fernández-Cerero, J., & León, S. P. (2023). Analysing the impact of artificial intelligence and computational sciences on student performance: Systematic review and meta-analysis. *Journal of New Approaches in Educational Research*, *12*(1), 171–197. DOI: 10.7821/naer.2023.1.1240

George, B., & Wooden, O. (2023). Managing the strategic transformation of higher education through artificial intelligence. *Administrative Sciences*, *13*(9), 196. DOI: 10.3390/admsci13090196

Gibson, R. (2024, September 10). The impact of AI in advancing accessibility for learners with disabilities. *EDUCAUSE Review*. https://er.educause.edu/articles/2024/9/the-impact-of-ai-in-advancing-accessibility-for-learners-with-disabilities

Gligorea, I., Cioca, M., Oancea, R., Gorski, A.-T., Gorski, H., & Tudorache, P. (2023). Adaptive Learning using Artificial Intelligence in e-Learning: A Literature Review. *Education Sciences*, *13*(12), 1216. DOI: 10.3390/educsci13121216

Goldberg, D., Nichols, D., Oki, B., & Terry, D. (1992). Using collaborative filtering to weave an information tapestry. *Communications of the ACM*, *35*(12), 61–70. DOI: 10.1145/138859.138867

Harry, A., & Sayudin. (2023). Role of AI in education. *Injurity: Interdisciplinary Journal and Humanity*, *2*(3), 260–268. DOI: 10.58631/injurity.v2i3.52

Humble, N., & Mozelius, P. (2022). The threat, hype, and promise of artificial intelligence in education. *Discover Artificial Intelligence*, *2*(1). Advance online publication. DOI: 10.1007/s44163-022-00039-z

Hunt, T., Carter, R., Zhang, L., & Yang, S. (2019). *Micro-credentials: the potential of personalized professional development*. Emerald., DOI: 10.1108/dlo-09-2019-0215

Hwang, G. J., Xie, H., Wah, B. W., & Gašević, D. (2020). Vision, challenges, roles and research issues of Artificial Intelligence in education. *Computers and Education: Artificial Intelligence*, *1*, 100001. DOI: 10.1016/J.CAEAI.2020.100001

Isensee, C., Griese, K., & Teuteberg, F. (2021). Sustainable Artificial Intelligence: A corporate culture perspective. *Sustainability Management Forum*, 29, 217-230. DOI: 10.1007/s00550-021-00524-6

Jacob, A. C., Reji, S. G., Manoj, H., Joseph, J., & Nikhil, M. (2024). AI based Virtual Personal Assistant. [IJISRT]. *International Journal of Innovative Science and Research Technology*, *9*(6), 2460–2466. DOI: 10.38124/ijisrt/ijisrt24jun1884

Jangda, S. I., & Raazi, S. M. K. (2024). *Recommender System F or Educational and Professional Growth*. 1–8. DOI: 10.1109/iconics64289.2024.10824485

Jares, T., Wilcox, W., Cahalan, R., & Dickey, G. (2019). An examination of the effectiveness of online adaptive learning technologies. *The Accounting Educators'. Journal*, *XXIX*, 61–80. https://aejournal.com/ojs/index.php/aej/article/view/489

Johnson, D. L., & Davis, C. G. (2024). Bridging the gap for underserved populations: Personalized AI solutions for college access and learning support. *New Directions for Higher Education*, *2024*(207), 47–62. DOI: 10.1002/he.20511

Kallen, D., & Bengtsson, J. (1973). *Recurrent education: A strategy for lifelong learning*. OECD. https://eric.ed.gov/?id=ED083365

Kaplan, A. (2016). Lifelong learning: Conclusions from a literature review. *International Online Journal of Primary Education, 5*(2), 43–50. https://files.eric.ed.gov/fulltext/EJ1243611.pdf

Knowles, M. S. (1975). *Self-directed learning: A guide for learners and teachers*. Follett.

Kolb, D. A. (1984). *Experiential learning: Experience as the source of learning and development*. Prentice Hall.

Kumar, V., Barik, S., Aggarwal, S., Kumar, D., & Raj, V. (2023). The use of artificial intelligence for persons with disability: A bright and promising future ahead. *Disability and Rehabilitation. Assistive Technology*, *19*(6), 2415–2417. DOI: 10.1080/17483107.2023.2288241 PMID: 38079540

Lang, J. (2023). Workforce upskilling: Can universities meet the challenges of lifelong learning? *International Journal of Information and Learning Technology*, *40*(5), 388–400. DOI: 10.1108/ijilt-01-2023-0001

Langston, E. M., Hattakitjamroen, V., Hernandez, M., Lee, H. S., Mason, H. C., Louis-Charles, W., Charness, N., Czaja, S. J., Rogers, W. A., Sharit, J., & Boot, W. R. (2025). Exploring Artificial Intelligence-Powered virtual assistants to understand their potential to support older adults' search needs. *Human Factors in Healthcare*, *100092*. Advance online publication. DOI: 10.1016/j.hfh.2025.100092

Lillywhite, A., & Wolbring, G. (2019). Coverage of ethics within the artificial intelligence and machine learning academic literature: The case of disabled people. *Assistive Technology*, *33*(3), 129–135. DOI: 10.1080/10400435.2019.1593259 PMID: 30995161

Lin, C., Huang, A. Y. Q., & Lu, O. H. T. (2023). Artificial intelligence in intelligent tutoring systems toward sustainable education: A systematic review. *Smart Learning Environments*, *10*(1). Advance online publication. DOI: 10.1186/s40561-023-00260-y

Lindeman, E. C. (1926). *The meaning of adult education*. New Republic.

Liu, H. L., Wang, T. H., Lin, H. K., Lai, C. F., & Huang, Y. M. (2022). The influence of affective feedback adaptive learning system on learning engagement and self-directed learning. *Frontiers in Psychology*, *13*, 858411. DOI: 10.3389/fpsyg.2022.858411 PMID: 35572271

Marquardson, J. (2024). Embracing Artificial Intelligence to improve self-directed learning: A cybersecurity classroom study. *Information Systems Education Journal*, *22*(1), 4–13. DOI: 10.62273/wzby3952

Masciari, E., Umair, A., & Ullah, M. H. (2024). A Systematic literature review on AI-Based recommendation systems and their ethical considerations. *IEEE Access : Practical Innovations, Open Solutions*, *12*, 121223. DOI: 10.1109/ACCESS.2024.3451054

Masrek, M. N., Susantari, T., Mutia, F., Yuwinanto, H. P., & Atmi, R. T. (2024). Enabling education everywhere: How artificial intelligence empowers ubiquitous and lifelong learning. *Environment-Behaviour Proceedings Journal*, *9*(SI18), 57–63. DOI: 10.21834/e-bpj.v9isi18.5462

Memarian, B., & Doleck, T. (2023). ChatGPT in education: Methods, potentials, and limitations. *Computers in Human Behavior: Artificial Humans*, *1*(2), 100022. DOI: 10.1016/j.chbah.2023.100022

Mezirow, J. (1991). *Transformative dimensions of adult learning*. Jossey-Bass.

Milana, M., Brandi, U., Hodge, S., & Hoggan-Kloubert, T. (2024). Artificial Intelligence (AI), conversational agents, and generative AI: Implications for adult education practice and research. *International Journal of Lifelong Education*, *43*(1), 1–7. DOI: 10.1080/02601370.2024.2310448

Mimoudi, A. (2024). AI, personalized education, and challenges. *Proceedings of the International Conference on AI Research, 4*(1), 271–280. DOI: 10.34190/icair.4.1.3133

Mishra, S. (2024). Transformative impact of AI on education: Personalizing learning and addressing challenges. *International Journal for Research in Applied Science and Engineering Technology*, *12*(8), 1183–1189. DOI: 10.22214/ijraset.2024.63891

Moehrle, M. (2024.). The role of AI in corporate learning. *EFMD Global Focus, 18*(1), 67–69. https://www.globalfocusmagazine.com/the-role-of-ai-in-corporate-learning/

Msweli, N. T., Twinomurinzi, H., & Ismail, M. (2022). The International case for micro-credentials for life-wide and life-long learning: A systematic literature review. *Interdisciplinary Journal of Information, Knowledge, and Management*, *17*, 151–190. DOI: 10.28945/4954

Mustafa, M. Y., Tlili, A., Lampropoulos, G., Huang, R., Jandrić, P., Zhao, J., Salha, S., Xu, L., Panda, S., Kinshuk, N., López-Pernas, S., & Saqr, M. (2024). A systematic review of literature reviews on artificial intelligence in education (AIED): A roadmap to a future research agenda. *Smart Learning Environments*, *11*(1). Advance online publication. DOI: 10.1186/s40561-024-00350-5

Mutia, F., Masrek, M., Baharuddin, M., Shuhidan, S., Soesantari, T., Yuwinanto, H., & Atmi, R. T. (2024). A comparative analysis of librarians' views on AI support for learning experiences, lifelong learning, and digital literacy in Malaysia and Indonesia. *Publications*, *12*(3), 21. DOI: 10.3390/publications12030021

Nussbaum, M. (2003). Capabilities as fundamental entitlements: Sen and social justice. *Feminist Economics*, *9*(2–3), 33–59. DOI: 10.1080/1354570022000077926

Oberdieck, T., & Moch, E. (2024). Lifelong learning with Artificial Intelligence: Potentials, challenges and future perspectives. *International Journal of Advanced Research*, *12*(6), 545–555. DOI: 10.21474/ijar01/18915

Ozbey, A. Y., Mubinova, S., Abdelgadir, M., & Gokgol, M. K. (2023). *Revolutionizing education: A study on Intelligent Tutoring Systems n U.S education*. London Journal of Social Sciences., DOI: 10.31039/ljss.2023.6.117

Palenski, T., Hills, L., Unnikrishnan, S., & Eynon, R. (2024). How AI works: Reconfiguring lifelong learning. *Postdigital Science and Education*, *6*, 1216–1239. DOI: 10.1007/s42438-024-00496-y

Pandya, K. S. (2024). *The role of artificial intelligence in education 5.0: Opportunities and challenges, 5*, e011. DOI: 10.37497/sdgs.v5igoals.11

Parsons, D., Sparks, H., Vo, D., & Singh, A. (2023). The student experience of technology-focused micro-credentials as part of a larger learning journey. *2023 IEEE International Conference on Teaching, Assessment and Learning for Engineering (TALE)*, Auckland, New Zealand. https://doi.org/DOI: 10.1109/TALE56641.2023.10398293

Poquet, O., & De Laat, M. (2021). Developing capabilities: Lifelong learning in the age of AI. *British Journal of Educational Technology*, *52*(4), 1695–1708. DOI: 10.1111/bjet.13123

Purnama, D. W., Rochman, C. B. A., Darmawan, R., Amaliyah, P., Baqi, A. D., & Zahidin, A. (2023). A Bibliometrics analysis for artificial intelligence implementation of employment in education institutions. *International Journal of Multidisciplinary Research and Analysis*, *7*(01). Advance online publication. DOI: 10.47191/ijmra/v7-i01-02

Rajabalee, Y. B. (2023). The implementation of micro-credentials in formal and informal learning: A systematic literature review. *International Journal of Learning and Teaching*, *9*(4). Advance online publication. DOI: 10.18178/ijlt.9.4.328-336

Ralston, S. J. (2021). Higher education's microcredentialing craze: A Postdigital-Deweyan critique. *Postdigital Science and Education*, *3*, 83–101. DOI: 10.1007/s42438-020-00121-8 PMID: 40476912

Rane, N. L., Choudhary, S. P., & Rane, J. (2024). Education 4.0 and 5.0: Integrating Artificial Intelligence (AI) for personalized and adaptive learning. *Journal of Artificial Intelligence and Robotics*, *1*(1), 29–43. DOI: 10.61577/jaiar.2024.100006

Rial-Gonzalez, P., Sarceda-Gorgoso, M. C., & Santamaría Queiruga, O. (2024). Lifelong learning as a response to the challenges of Industry 5.0 within the context of Horizon. *EDUCAR, 60*(2), 305–319). https://doi.org/DOI: 10.5565/rev/educar.2054

Samala, A. D., Rawas, S., Wang, T., Reed, J. M., Kim, J., Howard, N. J., & Ertz, M. (2024). Unveiling the landscape of generative artificial intelligence in education: A comprehensive taxonomy of applications, challenges, and future prospects. *Education and Information Technologies*, *29*(11). Advance online publication. DOI: 10.1007/s10639-024-12936-0

Schutte, F. (2024). Micro-Credentialing: The Janus of higher education. *International Review of Management and Marketing*, *14*(6), 389–399. DOI: 10.32479/irmm.17241

Selvaratnam, R. M., & Sankey, M. (2025). An integrative literature review of the implementation of micro-credentials in higher education: Implications for practice in Australasia. *Journal of Teaching and Learning for Graduate Employability*, *12*(1), 1–17. DOI: 10.21153/jtlge2021vol12no1art942

Sen, A. (1985). Well-being, agency and freedom: The Dewey lectures 1984. *The Journal of Philosophy*, *82*(4), 169–221. DOI: 10.2307/2026184

Shanmughan, P., & Joseph, J. (2024). S., B. N., S. M., A., C. S., A., & Jose, J. (2024). The AI revolution in micro-credentialing: Personalized learning paths. *Frontiers in Education*, *9*. Advance online publication. DOI: 10.3389/feduc.2024.1445654

Siddiqi, M. (2024). Navigating the skill-first economy: The evolving role of lifelong learning and career services at community colleges. *New Directions for Community Colleges*, *2024*(207), 159–168. DOI: 10.1002/cc.20645

Singh, N., Gunjan, V. K., Mishra, A. K., Mishra, R. K., & Nawaz, N. (2022). Seis-Tutor: A custom-tailored Intelligent Tutoring System and sustainable education. *Sustainability*, *14*, 4167. DOI: 10.3390/su14074167

Slimi, Z. (2023). The impact of Artificial Intelligence on higher education: An empirical study. *European Journal of Educational Sciences*, *10*(1). Advance online publication. DOI: 10.19044/ejes.v10no1a17

Smith, P., & Smith, L. (2020). Artificial Intelligence and disability: Too much promise, yet too little substance? *AI and Ethics*, *1*, 81–86. DOI: 10.1007/s43681-020-00004-5

Southworth, J., Migliaccio, K., Glover, J., Glover, J., Reed, D., McCarty, C., Brendemuhl, J., & Thomas, A. (2023). Developing a model for AI Across the curriculum: Transforming the higher education landscape via innovation in AI literacy. *Computers and Education: Artificial Intelligence*, *4*, 100127). DOI: 10.1016/j.caeai.2023.100127

Standen, P. J., Brown, D. J., Taheri, M., Trigo, M. J. G., Boulton, H., Burton, A., Hallewell, M. J., Lathe, J. G., Shopland, N., Gonzalez, M. B., Kwiatkowska, G. M., Milli, E., Cobello, S., Mazzucato, A., Traversi, M., & Hortal, E. (2020). An evaluation of an adaptive learning system based on multimodal affect recognition for learners with intellectual disabilities. *British Journal of Educational Technology, 51*(5), 1748–1765. DOI: 10.1111/bjet.13010

Strielkowski, W., Grebennikova, V., Lisovskiy, A., Rakhimova, G., & Vasileva, T. (2024). AI-driven adaptive learning for sustainable educational transformation. *Sustainable Development, 33*(2), 1921–1947. DOI: 10.1002/sd.3221

Su, J., & Yang, W. (2023). Unlocking the power of ChatGPT: A framework for applying Generative AI in education. *ECNU Review of Education, 6*(3), 355–366. DOI: 10.1177/20965311231168423

Sytnyk, L., & Podlinyayeva, O. (2024). AI in education: Main possibilities and challenges. *Scientific Collection, 45*(201), 569–570. DOI: 10.51582/interconf.19-20.05.2024.058

Thwe, W. P., & Kálmán, A. (2023). Lifelong learning in the educational Setting: A systematic literature review. *The Asia-Pacific Education Researcher, 33*(2), 407–417. DOI: 10.1007/s40299-023-00738-w

Vujinović, A., Luburić, N., Slivka, J., & Kovačević, A. (2024). Using ChatGPT to annotate a dataset: A case study in intelligent tutoring systems. *Machine Learning with Applications, 16,* 100557). DOI: 10.1016/j.mlwa.2024.100557

Wald, M. (2021). AI data-driven personalisation and disability inclusion. *Frontiers in Artificial Intelligence, 3.* Advance online publication. DOI: 10.3389/frai.2020.571955 PMID: 33733215

Wang, H., Tlili, A., Huang, R., Cai, Z., Li, M., Cheng, Z., Yang, D., Li, M., Zhu, X., & Fei, C. (2023). Examining the applications of intelligent tutoring systems in real educational contexts: A systematic literature review from the social experiment perspective. *Education and Information Technologies, 28*(7), 9113–9148. DOI: 10.1007/s10639-022-11555-x PMID: 36643383

Xiao, N., Pei, Y., Yuan, C., Bu, Y., & Cai, Z. (2025). *Transforming education with Artificial Intelligence: A comprehensive review of applications, challenges, and future directions, 2*(1), 337–356. DOI: 10.70693/itphss.v2i1.211

Xiaoyu, Z., & Tobias, T. C. R. (2023). Exploring the efficacy of adaptive learning technologies in online education: A longitudinal analysis of student engagement and performance. *International Journal of Science and Engineering Applications*, *12*(12), 28–31. DOI: 10.7753/IJSEA1212.1007

Yeaxlee, B. A. (1925). *Spiritual values in adult education*. Oxford University Press.

Yusuf, S. O., Abubakar, J. E., Durodola, R. L., Ocran, G., Paul-Adeleye, A. H., & Yusuf, P. O. (2024). Impact of AI on continuous learning and skill development in the workplace: A comparative study with traditional methods. *World Journal of Advanced Research and Reviews*, *23*(2), 1129–1140. DOI: 10.30574/wjarr.2024.23.2.2439

Zeb, A., Ullah, R., & Karim, R. (2024). Exploring the role of ChatGPT in higher education: Opportunities, challenges and ethical considerations. *International Journal of Information and Learning Technology*, *41*(1), 99–111. DOI: 10.1108/ijilt-04-2023-0046

Zhang, H., & Leong, W. Y. (2024). AI solutions for accessible education in underserved communities. *Journal of Innovation and Technology, 2024*(11). DOI: 10.32802/asmscj.2023.1895

Zhang, L., Hu, X., Andrasik, F., & Feng, S. (2022). Benefits and potential issues for Intelligent Tutoring Systems and pedagogical agents. In Hampton, A. J., & Defalco, J. A. (Eds.), *The frontlines of artificial intelligence ethics* (pp. 84–1010). Routledge., DOI: 10.4324/9781003030928-8

Zhang, Q., Lu, J., & Jin, Y. (2021). Artificial intelligence in recommender systems. *Complex & Intelligent Systems*, *7*, 439–457. DOI: 10.1007/S40747-020-00212-W

Zhang, X., Zhu, F., Wang, K., Cao, G., Xue, Y., & Liu, M. (2024). Bring the Intelligent Tutoring Robots to education: A systematic literature review. *IEEE Transactions on Learning Technologies*, (99), 1–21. DOI: 10.1109/TLT.2024.3428366

Zhao, C. (2024). Application and prospect of artificial intelligence in personalized learning. *Journal of Innovation and Development*, *8*(3), 24–27. DOI: 10.54097/nzxx6z36

Zou, J., & Schiebinger, L. (2021). Ensuring that biomedical AI benefits diverse populations. *EBioMedicine*, *67*, 103358. DOI: 10.1016/j.ebiom.2021.103358 PMID: 33962897

KEY TERMS AND DEFINITIONS

Adaptive Learning: An educational approach that uses AI algorithms to dynamically adjust learning content, pace, and assessments based on individual student performance and needs.

AI Literacy: The ability to understand, critically evaluate, and effectively interact with AI systems, including awareness of their capabilities, limitations, and societal implications.

Algorithmic Bias: The tendency of AI systems to produce unfair or discriminatory outcomes due to flaws in data, design, or implementation, often reflecting and amplifying existing societal biases.

Artificial Intelligence (AI): The field of creating computers that can carry out functions traditionally associated with human cognitive abilities. These include interpreting visual data, understanding spoken words, making complex decisions, and converting text between languages.

Chatbot: An AI-powered program designed to simulate human conversation through text or voice interactions, often used for customer service, information retrieval, or educational support.

Data Privacy: The protection of personal information collected, stored, and used by organizations, ensuring individuals' rights to control their data and maintain confidentiality.

Experiential Learning: An educational approach that emphasizes learning through direct experience and reflection, often involving hands-on activities, simulations, or real-world problem-solving; the process whereby knowledge is created through the transformation of experience (Kolb, 1984).

Intelligent Tutoring Systems (ITS):: AI-driven learning applications that have the ability to deliver individualized support by replicating the guidance of human by providing personalized feedback, respond to inquiries, and guide learners through problem solving.

Learning Analytics:: Learning analytics is the measurement, collection, analysis, and reporting of data about learners and their contexts, for the purpose of understanding and optimizing learning and the environments in which it occurs. Learning analytics become more powerful and sophisticated when assisted by AI.

Lifelong Learning: The ongoing, voluntary pursuit of knowledge and skill development throughout an individual's life, both for personal and professional growth.

Machine Learning: A subset of AI that focuses on developing algorithms and statistical models that enable computer systems to improve their performance on a specific task through experience.

Microlearning/Micro-credentialing: Microlearning provides the educational delivery method—small, focused learning experiences—while micro-credentials provide the verification/certification that learning has occurred and skills have been mastered.

Open Educational Resources (OERs): Teaching, learning, and research materials that are freely available for anyone to use, adapt, and redistribute without legal restrictions.

Personalized Learning: An educational approach with tailored instruction, content, and pacing to meet individual student needs, interests, and learning styles, often implementing technology to achieve customization at scale.

Recommendation Systems: AI-powered intelligent technologies that suggest relevant content, resources, or experiences to users based on their preferences, behavior patterns, and needs.

Self-Directed Learning: An approach to education where learners take initiative and responsibility for their own learning process, including setting goals, identifying resources, and evaluating outcomes (Knowles, 1975).

Transformative Learning:: Transformative Learning is a theory of adult education that describes how learners critically examine their beliefs, values, and assumptions to fundamentally change their perspective and approach to the world (Mezirow, 1991).

Virtual Personal Assistants (VPAs):: software agents that use artificial intelligence (AI) to perform tasks or services for an individual based on commands or questions.

Chapter 9
Artificial Intelligence in Special Education: Supporting Diverse Learners

Vicki J. Donne
https://orcid.org/0000-0002-3082-1649
Robert Morris University, USA

Mary A. Hansen
https://orcid.org/0000-0003-0051-4039
Robert Morris University, USA

ABSTRACT

Students with disabilities make up a notable portion of today's classrooms. To address their varied educational, social, and life skill needs, schools utilize high leverage practices. One of these strategies is the use of technology and assistive technology. Artificial intelligence technology may meet the definition of assistive technology in increasing the functioning capabilities of individuals with disabilities. Research finds support for the use of extended reality, robot assisted, smart eyewear, health monitoring wearables, captioning, text creation, speech-to-text, and text-to-speech. This artificial intelligence can personalize the learning experience, increase motivation and engagement, and improve academic knowledge. Challenges of implementing artificial intelligence among students with disabilities include the lack of teacher knowledge, access, and costs. Additional concerns noted in the research are ethics, privacy, data, and security. Nonetheless, the use of artificial intelligence by students with disabilities holds promise to meet the diverse needs of students.

DOI: 10.4018/979-8-3373-2397-8.ch009

INTRODUCTION

This chapter addresses the potential of artificial intelligence (AI) to enhance the educational experiences, access, and independence of students with various disabilities across all educational levels, from primary grades through postsecondary education. The potential of AI for personalized learning experiences is especially important due to the heterogeneous nature of the population of students with disabilities, but these same individualized needs of students present challenges for broad AI applications. This chapter addresses both the potential and the associated challenges for wide-spread implementation of AI.

The objectives of this chapter are for the reader to be able to:

1. Highlight statistics related to students with disabilities.
2. Describe the importance of technology and assistive technology for academic success for students with disabilities.
3. Describe artificial intelligence and its applicability as assistive technology for students with disabilities.
4. Summarize the proposed benefits identified in existing literature of AI for students with disabilities.
5. Compare the attributes of various AI across grade spans, from primary grades through higher education.
6. Discuss the attributes of various AI for students with specific disabilities.
7. Address challenges associated with accessing and using AI effectively and ethically.
8. Summarize future directions and potential of AI for students with disabilities.

BACKGROUND

Students with disabilities constitute approximately 7.5 million or 15% of students ages 3 through 21 in the United States (Irwin et al., 2024). The reported percentage of students with disabilities varies across individual states, accounting for between 12% and 21% of states' student population. Further, reported prevalence rates vary across disabilities, with the highest prevalence associated with specific learning disabilities (32%); and substantive percentages associated with speech or language impairments (19%); other health impairments (15%); and autism spectrum disorder (13%) (Irwin et al., 2024). Combined prevalence of individuals with any developmental disability including attention deficit/hyperactivity disorder (ADHD), learning disability, autism spectrum disorder (ASD), intellectual disability (ID), and other developmental delay are reported at 17% (Li et al., 2023). The most recent data indicated that 55% of students with disabilities went on to attend some type of postsecondary education program; however, only 22% of students with disabilities inform their postsecondary institution of their disability (NCES, 2022). These data show that students with disabilities make up a notable portion of today's classrooms. Disabilities can bring unique challenges that can impact students' learning, development, access to opportunities, and general outcomes.

Students with disabilities have lower short- and long-term educational, professional, and life outcomes (Cheng & Shaewitz, 2021; Li et al., 2023). These include lower high school graduation rates (McFarland et al., 2019; McKinley Yoder et al., 2024); lower likelihood of careers in science, technology, engineering, and mathematics (STEM) (Fisher et al., 2022); and increased challenges with social interactions (Dell'Anna et al., 2022). Students with disabilities also score lower on standardized tests (NCES, 2023), and parents and teachers have lower expectations for students with disabilities, contributing to their lower expectations of themselves (Shifrer, 2013).

Ward et al. (2023) highlight the struggles of educational systems to meet the needs of students with disabilities. These struggles stem from a lack of quality inclusive programs and systems for implementing high leverage practices, absence of resources, insufficient administrative support, unsuitable curriculum and assessment, and inadequate training (Alquraini & Gut, 2019; Bronwell et al., 2021-22; Lubin & Fernal, 2021; Miller et al., 2025).

Yet, fundamental to the educational system in the United States is the goal of ensuring students with disabilities have equal access to learning opportunities, and a free appropriate public education in the least restrictive environment possible (Individuals with Disabilities Education Act, 2004; Rehabilitation Act of 1973, 1973). Therefore, to combat gaps in academic, social, and behavioral outcomes that persist between students with and without disabilities, schools and teachers attempt to implement evidence-based practices to provide the best opportunities for students with disabilities to learn.

Ample research exists highlighting evidence-based practices that improve access and achievement for students with disabilities. For example, implementing Universal Design for Learning (UDL) principles, video modeling, and explicit instruction that reduces cognitive load are all strategies that improve access and/or achievement for students with disabilities (Cottrell et al., 2024; Dahlstrom-Hakki & Wallace, 2022; Goo et al., 2025; Stark et al., 2024). The Council for Exceptional Children and the CEEDAR Center categorized these evidence-based practices as 'high leverage practices' and the use of assistive and instructional technologies is one of the *Instruction in Behavior and Academics* high leverage practices (Brownell et al., 2020–2021; McLeskey et al., 2022).

ADDRESSING THE NEEDS OF STUDENTS WITH DISABILITIES

Technology Integration

Teachers use the technology available in their schools to provide instruction and engage students in the learning process. Effective educational technology use requires integration of technology tools and teaching methods, cohesively designed to enrich learning experiences (Raave et al., 2024). Successful technology integration can improve student engagement, increase achievement, and promote equitable learning opportunities. For students with disabilities to achieve these outcomes, technology integration should incorporate UDL and assistive technology (AT) (Hew & Brush, 2007). With continuous advancements in technology, much of the newer technological devices and applications utilize UDL thus have the same elements of AT – they are "symbiotic in nature." Israel et al (2014) note:

> *For example, speech recognition software, which is highly beneficial for students with dysgraphia or dyslexia, is routinely acknowledged as AT for students with disabilities. However, this same technology is ubiquitous on current smartphones and other mobile devices that people without disabilities use on a daily basis. (p. 7)*

Assistive Technology

Globally, AT has been defined as various products, systems, and services designed to "maintain or improve an individual's functioning related to cognition, communication, hearing, mobility, self-care and vision, thus enabling their health, well-being, inclusion and participation" (WHO, 2024, para. 2). In the United States, there are several pieces of legislation addressing various age groups and institutions that define AT and the obligations to provide AT. The first legislation to define AT was the Technology Assistance Act of 1988 (PL 100-407, 1988), now the Assistive Technology Act. This definition is also used in the Individuals with Disabilities Education Improvement Act (IDEIA) (2004). These laws define AT as "any item, piece of equipment, or product system, whether acquired commercially off the shelf, modified, or customized, that is used to increase, maintain, or improve the functional capabilities of a child with a disability" (C.F.R. §300.5). From early intervention to high school completion, IDEIA promotes the use of AT as integral to the provision of a free, appropriate, public education. The regulations also call for the provision of AT services such as evaluating, purchasing, training, and maintaining the selected devices (§300.6). AT devices and services should be considered for all students with disabilities. The Americans with Disabilities Act (ADA) (2010) mandates that government, public, and private facilities and programs, including postsecondary education institutions, provide accommodations and accessibility. AT is considered one of those accommodations. Postsecondary educational institutions must also follow regulations of Section 504 of the Rehabilitation Act (2024) which states that they must "furnish appropriate auxiliary aids and services where necessary to afford an individual with a disability an equal opportunity to participate in, and enjoy the benefits of, a service, program, or activity conducted by a public entity" (§84.77). AT falls under such auxiliary aids and services. One of the differences in the requirements under ADA and Section 504 from those in IDEIA is that postsecondary institutions do not have to provide personal AT devices (e.g., wheelchairs or personal assistants).

These definitions highlight the purpose of AT, which is to increase the functionality and capabilities of persons with a disability by using their abilities and technology to compensate for difficulties caused by a mismatch in the environment and their current skill level. AT encompasses a broad spectrum of equipment, software, and devices. There are different ways to categorize AT. One categorization groups AT by the area of compensation or area of use: positioning, mobility, AAC, computer access, assistive toys and games, adaptive environments, and instructional aids (Bowden Carpenter et al., 2015). Another categorization utilizes a technology continuum from no- or low-technology to high-technology devices. Finally, Pritchard et al. (2021) argue that AT can even be viewed for some individuals as extended cognition, in cases where the AT, such as a computer or mobile application, is utilized across environments and is fully integrated into a student's cognitive processes.

The use of technology and AT can improve student access and academic performance. For example, AT tools such as keyboards, spellcheck, technology-based graphic organizers, text-to-speech software, and word prediction software can provide support for various aspects of writing (Evmenova & Regan, 2019; Rowland et al., 2020). The use of math manipulatives and AT can increase student engagement and skill acquisition in math for some students with disabilities (Park et al., 2022). The use of multimedia hypertext, reading pens, and text-to-speech can improve reading comprehension for some students with disabilities (Perelmutter et al., 2017). Additionally, AT such as text-to-speech, voice recognition, screen readers, and built-in computer accessibility features enhance the accessibility for many students with disabilities (Gray et al., 2010).

One of the challenges with identifying and utilizing AT with students with disabilities relates to the heterogeneous population of students with disabilities. Assistive technology must be customized to the individual student's needs to be effective (Gray et al., 2010; Perelmutter et al., 2017), which poses a challenge to teachers. Students with disabilities have diverse strengths and needs, and teachers may face specific challenges when designing interventions and selecting AT to meet those needs (Johnston et al., 2018). Additionally, AT end users are often not involved in the design, selection, and training of devices, which in turn impacts the identification and utilization of appropriate AT (Abdi et al., 2021; Omiegbe, 2024).

Compounding those challenges to AT use in K-12 and higher education is the limited teacher or faculty knowledge of AT devices. Research has shown that throughout the years, coursework for pre-service teachers related to the use of AT has been limited (Bausch & Ault, 2012; Donne & Hansen, 2017; Judge & Simms, 2009). Once working in the field, teachers also report that they have limited training, knowledge, and skills in using AT (Abner & Lahm, 2002; Puckett, 2004). Furthermore, many teachers are not familiar with district AT policies and procedures making the process of identifying, purchasing, and maintaining AT difficult (Bausch et al., 2015). These challenges mark important considerations for teacher preparation programs and educational administrations (Abdi et al., 2021).

Artificial Intelligence as Assistive Technology

In the literature, many definitions of artificial intelligence (AI) may be found. For purposes of this chapter, the following definition of AI will be used:

Artificial intelligence (AI) systems are software (and possibly also hardware) systems designed by humans that, given a complex goal, act in the physical or digital dimension by perceiving their environment through data acquisition, interpreting the collected structured or unstructured data, reasoning on the knowledge, or processing the information, derived from this data and deciding the best action(s) to take to achieve the given goal. AI systems can either use symbolic rules or learn a numeric model, and they can also adapt their behaviour by analysing how the environment is affected by their previous actions (HLEG, 2018, p. 6; Samoili et al., 2020, p. 4)

AI has been integrated into technology in ways that improve the capabilities of students with disabilities, thus meeting the definition of AT (Gray et al., 2010). The most commonly used AI tools used in education are: machine learning, large language models, intelligent tutoring systems, chatbots, deep learning, augmented/virtual reality (AR/VR), robotics, adaptive systems, recommender system, and natural language processing (NLP) (Mustafa et al., 2024).

Research supports that these AI tools have the potential to increase, maintain, or improve the functional capabilities of an individual with a disability. For example, researchers report that VR can visually represent abstract concepts, making content easier for students with a disability to understand (Kellems et al., 2021). Chalkiadakis et al. (2024) reviewed studies in AI and VR technologies and found that "higher academic performance can be achieved, when AI and VR technologies are effectively incorporated in the educational process. This is either achieved through the increase in user-friendly, interactive platforms or through the increased development of students' education skills" (p. 14). In investigating other forms of AI, Tlili et al. (2020) reviewed robot-assisted instruction for students with disabilities, and found that students who engaged with the robot were motivated, engaged, and improved in their knowledge. Finally, Rice and Dunn (2023) conducted a review of various forms of AI and found research support for five areas: emotion, communication, social skills, reading, and language. Thus, AI as AT has the potential to increase access and capabilities of students with disabilities in various ways.

Potential for AI Integration to Improve Access and Success for Students with Disabilities

Integration of AI has the potential to improve access to instructional content. Some forms of AI have the ability to increase the accessibility of material. For example, text-to-speech has been used to improve the accessibility of text-based instructional materials for students who struggle with reading or have a vision loss. Speech-to-text capabilities may assist students with a physical disability to create text. At the same time, there are some concerns. For example, some voice recognition systems might not recognize the speech of some students with disabilities (i.e., some students with cerebral palsy, with an articulation communication disorder, or who are deaf/hard of hearing) (Omiegbe, 2024). Some AI has the ability to increase accessibility by providing audio support, font and size selection, and graphics. However, Nacheva and Czaplewski (2024) note that some AI have accessibility issues such as small font sizes, poor color contrast, lack of screen reader support, and inadequate audio options. Some AI provide for the creation and customization of readability levels for text. However, Nacheva and Czaplewski (2024) examined text readability using text generated with Open AI ChatGPT and Microsoft Copilot. Results revealed some spelling errors and text that was "too hard to read for the majority of readers" that may lack the background knowledge needed for comprehension (p. 115). How students with disabilities interact with AI "is shaped by their biological factors (e.g., vision, hearing, cognition) and technological affordances of AI tools (e.g., capturing information, acting upon received information)" (Zhang et al., 2024, p. 9).

Integration of AI also has the potential to improve progression in instructional content. Rather than students progressing through a curriculum based on a prescribed schedule, AI has the potential to personalize learning, where progression through a curriculum is based on mastery of content with students receiving real-time feedback. Based on student responses, the AI system can adjust the level of difficulty of the material, adapt the instructional content, and/or provide additional practice or enrichment activities (Hopcan et al., 2023). The learning experience can be personalized for the knowledge, interests, and abilities of the student and the instructional content can be adapted to meet the needs of individuals with disabilities. It is thought that this type of learning promotes inclusivity (Adeleye et al., 2024).

AI Studies Based on Area of Disability

The diversity of students presents some difficulty when researching the use of AI with students with disabilities. Additionally, many students with disabilities have concomitant disabilities adding another confounding variable in research. Because there may be small numbers of students who possess similar characteristics, research studies typically involve small sample sizes. Therefore, to examine the effectiveness of AI, several researchers have conducted research reviews and meta-analysis of existing small-scale studies. For example, Abdi et al. (2021) conducted a review of the literature on emerging technologies and reported their findings by common areas of disability. For example, they found emerging AT applications in the use of smart eyewear for navigation for individuals with vision loss, environmental controlling hearing aids for individuals with hearing loss, and health and emotional monitoring wearables for individuals with orthopedic impairments. They reported that most of the potential lies in the high technology AT solutions which often have associated high costs. The concern then is the perpetuation of inequitable AI use. Barau et al. (2022) reviewed the research on AI with students with autism, ADHD, and dyslexia and found that AI was effective for personalized learning. Pagliara et al. (2024) reviewed the research on various AI in education for students with disabilities and reported three main functions of AI in inclusive education: AI as a tool for personalized learning, AI as a moderator of educational processes, and AI as an environment such as an immersive and personalized environment.

Other researchers have focused their investigations specifically in one area of disability. Several studies examined AI use with students with sensory needs. Research suggests the potential for AI to generate automatic closed captions for accessibility for students who are deaf/hard of hearing (Omiegbe, 2024). Real time captioning or speech-to-text transcription for phone calls, videos, meetings and Dialogue Boost for Prime videos, are possible through AI, even analyzing speech to noise patterns to improve dialogue clarity (Kozma-Spytek, 2024). Ahmed et al. (2018) examined some research on AI systems to transfer sign language into speech or text and vice versa using glove-based or vision-based systems. After an extensive review of the literature, the researchers concluded that many problems need to be resolved before these systems have practical use in the field of education. Uluer and colleagues (2021) found use of AI robots during auditory tests improved children's experiences, motivation, and engagement during the tests. Several studies also investigated AI use for individuals with visual impairments. For example, Seeing AI uses deep learning and object recognition methods to instantly read text aloud from print, recognize faces, and identify paper currency, products, and signs (Demiral, 2023). These findings have current applications in education.

Other researchers examined AI for one of the largest incidence categories of disability, specific learning disabilities. Panjawani-Charani and Zhai (2025) identified seven types of AI applications to support students with specific learning disabilities, including adaptive learning, facial expression, chat robots, communication assistants, mastery learning, intelligent tutors, and interactive robots. Most of the studies in their review (63%) investigated AI to bypass difficulties in reading for students with dyslexia. For example, some studies reviewed the use of AI to change the readability level of text.

Many features of AI can assist students with orthopedic impairments (OI) or physical disabilities. Students with OI may be able to bypass physical barriers to participate in science experiments using VR (Chalkiadakis et al., 2024). AI accessibility features such as voice commands, eye tracking, and screen readers allow for alternative input methods to improve engagement for students with OI. These same features may assist students with intellectual disabilities. Additionally, AI can provide personalized learning content with real-time feedback. However, Standen et al. (2020) caution that many studies on personalized learning reviewed have short intervention periods (averaging 3 sessions), and engagement with AI may not be long enough to demonstrate significant differences in achievement.

Several published studies involve the use of AI with students with autism spectrum disorder (ASD). Kotsi et al. (2025) reviewed research on AI and ASD and found several studies using social robots, tablets and computers, and smart glasses. The studies concentrated on social, emotional, and cognitive activities focusing on facial expression recognition and maintaining eye contact in social situations. All studies reviewed demonstrated positive learning outcomes in communication, social skills, and emotional development. Mosher et al. (2022) reviewed existing research on the use of VR with students with ASD. Those studies focused on relationship skills (communication, social engagement, and relationship building), emotion recognition, social awareness, and executive functioning. The studies reviewed found high rates of generalization and maintenance of skills.

Research has also been conducted to examine the use of AI tools with students with intellectual disabilities. Pennington et al. (2014) found that robots could assist students with intellectual disabilities in generating text messages. Hong and Kim (2024) implemented an AI-based career education program and found improved career self-efficacy for students with intellectual disabilities. For younger children with intellectual disabilities, Griffin et al. (2024) utilized AI for a hand-washing task and found promising results. Collectively, research suggests that with the right safeguards in place, AI technologies can benefit students with a disability to learn and communicate.

AI Studies Based on Educational Level

Research involving the use of AI for students with disabilities has been conducted across educational levels. Some studies have focused on elementary and secondary students' use of AI (Mosher et al., 2022; Park et al., 2022; Rice & Dunn, 2023; Standen et al., 2020; Tlili et al., 2020). These studies examined various forms of AI (i.e., personalized learning, robot, virtual manipulatives, and VR) and a range of students with disabilities. Results indicated high levels of motivation and engagement (Park et al., 2022; Tlili et al., 2020), skill attainment (Park et al., 2022; Rice & Dunn, 2023; Standen et al., 2020; Tlili et al., 2020), and skill generalization and maintenance (Mosher et al., 2022) with the use of AI.

Other studies have looked at AI at the secondary and higher education levels (Ahmad et al., 2018; Perelmutter et al., 2017). These studies involved students with specific learning disabilities and AI AT for reading (Perelmutter et al., 2017) or hearing loss and the use of sensory systems and sign language (Ahmad et al., 2018). Results showed the promise of AI for increasing accessibility.

Reviews of AI focused specifically on higher education (Nacheva & Czaplewski, 2024; Omiegbe, 2024; Pierrès et al., 2023) examined students with disabilities across categories. The area of AI varied greatly from ethics (Pierrès et al., 2023), to any type of AI (Omiegbe, 2024), to test readability (Nacheva & Czaplewski, 2024), showing broad applications of AI.

The majority of studies looked at AI across educational levels (Chalkiadakis et al., 2024; Hopcan et al., 2023; Kotsi et al., 2025; Mustafa et al., 2024; Pagliara et al., 2024; Panjwani-Charani & Zhai, 2025). Most of these studies examined various types of AI with all students with disabilities (Chalkiadakis et al., 2024; Hopcan et al., 2023; Mustafa et al., 2024; Panjwani-Charani & Zhai, 2025). Pagliara et al. (2024) investigated personalized learning for students with disabilities and Kotsi et al. (2025) investigated various types of AI with students with ASD. Due to the wide-ranging nature of AI and broad scope of disabilities, drawing meaningful summaries is difficult.

Challenges of Widespread AI Implementation

Challenges exist related to the widespread implementation of AI to address the diverse needs of students with disabilities. Many users and teachers are neither aware of AI nor know how to use it (Demiral, 2023; Mishra et al., 2024). Without prior use of AI, teachers have little precedent to inform their work (So & Lee, 2023). In general, there has been a lack of training in AI and its impact on teaching methods (Mustafa et al., 2024). Therefore, teachers will need ongoing training on integrating technology, including AT and AI, into their teaching methods, as the technology is quickly advancing. The training should include adapting AI to meet the varied needs of students with disabilities (Chalkiadakis et al., 2024). Another factor in the need for training is the high turnover of staff or teachers and the need to retrain new team members (Mishra et al., 2024). In addition to lack of training on AI, teachers report that inadequate assessment processes, inability to integrate the AT into daily academic activities, and lack of funding are obstacles to AT and AI integration (Copley & Ziviani, 2004; Mishra et al., 2024).

Access to AI has been an issue for many students and schools. The high cost to gain access to some of the AI technology has been a deterrent for use (Chalkiadakis et al., 2024; Hopcan et al., 2023; Mishra et al., 2024; Mustafa et al., 2024). Involved costs relate to installing, maintaining, and repairing these technologies (Barau et al., 2022). Not all schools or students have the resources to acquire, maintain, or tailor AT to meet the needs of students (Kotsi et al., 2025).

Another challenge cited in the literature is technology abandonment. Researchers found that 30% of all devices are abandoned or not used (Phillips & Zhao, 1993; Scherer, 2005). There are a range of causes including change in user needs, poor fit of the device for the user; lack of training on the device; advanced technological level of the device; inability to maintain or repair the device; lack of motivation to use the device for particular tasks; and the lack of consideration of the family and child's preferences in the selection process (Judge, 2000; Phillips & Zhao, 1993; Scherer, 2005; Zaph et al., 2016). To date, no peer-reviewed published research on abandonment of specific AI technology as AT used with students with disabilities have been identified.

Ethical concerns associated with AI are also expressed in the research. In their review of AI in higher education, Pierrès et al. (2023) found that less than half of the research articles addressed ethical concerns. Another area of concern is that the perspectives and needs of the end users themselves are not taken into consideration. Pierrès et al. (2023) reported that only 5.5% of articles on AI reviewed mentioned students with disabilities and only 2.8% discussed accessibility. An important consideration is that while speech-to-text can be a great tool for some students with disabilities to facilitate the writing drafting process and text-to-speech may assist in the editing process, for other students with disabilities, the AI may be "unable to analyse or retrieve information from texts written by students with cognitive or intellectual disabilities who, for instance, may misspell words due to dyslexia" (Pierrès et al., 2023, p. 27822).

Additional ethical concerns involve the privacy and data security of information on students with disabilities (Kotsi et al., 2025). Ethical issues also surround informed consent for data use and algorithmic bias and discrimination. Rice and Dunn (2023) in their review of the literature on AI reported that "no methodologies or strategies used in any of the studies attempted to capture participants as co-designers" (p. 381).

Similar findings were reported in a review of AI in higher education (Pierrès et al., 2023). Excluding students with disabilities from algorithms that drive AI poses ethical and educational concerns, and violates principles of inclusion and UDL.

The growing use of AI has also raised ethical concerns related to academic integrity. Generative AI tools like ChatGPT have high potential for personalized learning, as these tools can create simplified text for students, rephrase student writing to improve grammar, and expand on student-generated responses. However, students may use AI to generate entire responses rather than as a complementary resource, raising concerns about academic integrity (Campia et al., 2023; Lo, 2023). Further, these tools can generate inaccurate information and non-existent references (Lo, 2023; Wilby & Essen, 2024; Zhou et al., 2023). Since students with disabilities do not have access to some activities that other students can readily access, responses from generative AI tools can be biased against these students (Pierrès et al., 2024).

Machine learning AI learns from massive data sets to identify rules and patterns and make predictions without explicit programming code. However, an identified lack of data diversity and inclusivity exists in training data sets; thus, training data sets may reflect bias or reflect limited current knowledge (Lo, 2023; Pierrès et al., 2023; Wibly & Essen, 2024). Exclusionary norms can result in situations when training data does not reflect the full population (Lo, 2023). Further, many research articles in higher education used log data and there is some question on the level of accessibility of the platforms and that accessibility can impact the data of students with disabilities, including the claim that AI personalized learning (Pierrès et al., 2023). Machine learning powers many AT used for students with disabilities, and shows great potential. However, concerns about data privacy, quality of training data, and the level of inclusiveness remain.

Future AI Use for Students with Disabilities

AI continues to evolve. Wearable technologies are one form of AI used for students with disabilities that can provide additional access, as they can address specific needs of students with disabilities. Existing wearable technologies have been used to promote mindfulness and self-regulation, reduce anxiety, improve mobility, and increase vision (Douglas et al., 2022; Evmenova et al., 2019; McMahon et al., 2021). These tools have the potential to monitor students' physiological signals, and can provide real-time feedback that can immediately be used to increase student access, learning, and motivation.

Robotic systems also show promise for students with disabilities, and they have been shown to support students with hearing loss during auditory tests, provide emotional support, support social communication, improve behavior, improve language and literacy skills, and increase achievement of students with varying disabilities (Lee & Hyun, 2015; Puglisi et al., 2022; Uluer et al., 2021; Zhang et al., 2023). Robots have been utilized for students from early childhood education through post-secondary education.

AI allows for more personalized learning opportunities that can benefit students with disabilities, as AI can allow their individualized needs to be met quickly and efficiently. With the incorporation of UDL principles into new AI-based technologies, AT coupled with AI can provide immediate access to students with disabilities. The integration of AI tools into learning management systems further increases accessibility for students with disabilities. With immediate access of text-to-speech and speech-to-text tools, coupled with generative AI and machine learning programs, educators can deliver personalized, adaptive instruction in real time that dynamically addresses each student's unique learning needs, reduces barriers to accessibility, and fosters greater engagement and independence for students with disabilities.

SOLUTIONS AND RECOMMENDATIONS

Implications of Current and Future Use of AI

Integration of AI-based tools into educational systems holds immense potential for improving access and achievement of students with disabilities. AI's capacity for personalization, along with its broad applicability across disciplines and students show its potential for advancing educational opportunities for students with disabilities. Yet, challenges related to student and teacher access and training, AI literacy, data privacy, bias, and academic integrity remain.

To mediate some of the challenges of AI implementation, teachers may need to assess if the selected AI is meeting the needs of the student. There are several instruments available to evaluate effective AT use, i.e. the Assistive Technology Implementation Plan (Bausch et al., 2006), the Matching Assistive Technology to Child & Augmentative Communication Evaluation Simplified (Zaph et al., 2016), and the Student Performance Profile (Fennema-Jensen, 2005). These tools can help educators evaluate the quality of specific AI for their students, expediting the choice of AI.

Implications for Policy

In their review of the literature on AI in education, Mustafa et al. (2024) found that "the most neglected stakeholders are found to be special education students and teachers" (p. 11). Of the 143 literature reviews on AI in education analyzed, only two discussed special education even though AI has the potential to support individuals with disabilities. These findings have important implications for policy makers in schools and postsecondary education. The educational institutions may wish to assess how well their teams are functioning in planning, implementing, and maintaining effective AT and AI. One existing instrument for this evaluation is the Quality Indicators for Evaluation of the Effectiveness of Assistive Technology rubric (QIAT Community, 2015). Additionally, district or school policies should include student involvement to reduce bias and device abandonment (Judge, 2000; Philips & Zhao, 1993). Establishing ethics committees within educational institutions may be another great way to address these issues (Chalkiadakis et al., 2024).

Companies are making some progress in developing AI for individuals with disabilities, with the development of new products that aim to provide more equity (Gibson, 2024). As developments and advances continue, policy development will gain importance. Policies surrounding the integration of AI into education systems are needed, and it is central that these policies reflect access and inclusion of students with disabilities (Aquino et al., 2024).

FUTURE RESEARCH DIRECTIONS

General research on AI ethics, standards, and training data sets, can lead to responsible use of AI for all individuals. With general advances, developers, teachers, and policy makers will need to work closely with individuals with disabilities to ensure that the emerging technologies address their diverse needs (Abdi et al., 2021; Omiegbe, 2024). Leadership teams need to be strategic in building capacity for various AI tools, and research surrounding the strategies used and their effectiveness will be needed (Ward et al., 2023). These teams have an opportunity to plan for building capacity while reducing over-reliance on often less effective, expensive AI tools (Ward et al., 2023).

Longitudinal research studies will be needed to examine the long-term effects of AI on students with disabilities (Mohamed et al., 2025). With much of the research on using AI for students with disabilities based on small data sets collected over short periods of time, larger scale quantitative studies as well as in-depth, structured reviews will continue to be needed to examine effectiveness of AI.

As robots and other AI become more accessible, teacher-to-peer and peer-to-peer relationships may suffer (Yi et al., 2024). Research that considers both positive and negative outcomes associated with robots and other AI in the classroom must be conducted.

Generative AI models provide access to students with disabilities as their teachers can develop tailored educational materials. Student use of such models to generate responses can be a beneficial accommodation. However, an understanding of the extent to which responses are student generated versus computer generated must be established to maintain academic integrity.

CONCLUSION

While the full potential of AI for improving the individualized educational experiences of students with disabilities is unknown due to rapid, continuous improvements in hardware and software, the incorporation of AI into education will continue to expand. In the changing landscape, educational practices and policies will need to change, and educators who stay current with these advances will be better able to create inclusive and equitable learning environments for the students they serve. As access to AI increases for software and hardware developers, teachers and students will continue to have improved educational resources.

REFERENCES

Abdi, S., Kitsara, I., Hawley, M. S., & De Witte, L. P. (2021). Emerging technologies and their potential for generating new assistive technologies. *Assistive Technology, 33*(sup1), 17-26. https://doi.org/DOI: 10.1080/10400435.2021.1945704

Abner, G. H., & Lahm, E. A. (2002). Implementation of assistive technology with students who are visually impaired: Teachers' readiness. *Journal of Visual Impairment & Blindness, 96*(2), 98–105.

Adeleye, O. O., Eden, C. A., & Adeniyi, I. S. (2024). Innovative teaching methodologies in the era of artificial intelligence: A review of inclusive educational practices. *World Journal of Advanced Engineering Technology and Sciences, 11*(02), 69–79. DOI: 10.30574/wjaets.2024.11.2.0091

Ahmed, M. A., Zaidan, B. B., Zaidan, A. A., Salih, M. M., & Lakulu, M. M. B. (2018). A review on systems-based sensory gloves for sign language recognition state of the art between 2007 and 2017. [Basel]. *Sensors (Basel), 18*(7), 2208. DOI: 10.3390/s18072208 PMID: 29987266

Alquraini, T., & Gut, D. (2019). Critical components of successful inclusion of students with severe disabilities: Literature review. *International Journal of Special Education, 34*(1), 36–54.

Americans with Disability Act (ADA). (2010). 42 U.S.C. § 12101. https://www.ada.gov/law-and-regs/ada/

Aquino, K. C., Lalor, A. R., & Parnther, C. (2024). Are institutions addressing accessibility in generative AI policy development? *Disability Compliance for Higher Education, 30*(2), 1–4. DOI: 10.1002/dhe.31804

Assistive Technology Act of 2004. (2004). https://www.govinfo.gov/content/pkg/PLAW-108publ364/pdf/PLAW-108publ364.pdf

Barau, P. D., Vicnesh, J., Gururajan, R., Oh, S. L., Pamer, E., Azizan, M. M., Kadri, N. A., & Acharya, U. R. (2022). Artificial intelligence enabled personalized assistive tools to enhance education of children with neurodevelopmental disorders – a review. *International Journal of Environmental Research and Public Health, 19*(3), 1192. DOI: 10.3390/ijerph19031192 PMID: 35162220

Bausch, M. E., & Ault, M. J. (2012). Status of assistive technology instruction in university personnel preparation programs. *Assistive Technology Outcomes and Benefits, 8*(1), 1–14.

Bausch, M. E., Ault, M. J., & Hasselbring, T. S. (2006). *Assistive technology planner: From IEP consideration to classroom implementation*. National Assistive Technology Research Institute.

Bausch, M. E., Ault, M. J., & Hasselbring, T. S. (2015). Assistive technology in schools: Lessons learned from the National Assistive Technology Research Institute. In Edyburn, D. (Ed.), *Efficacy of assistive technology interventions: Advances in special education technology* (Vol. 1, pp. 13–30).

Bowden Carpenter, L., Johnston, L. B., & Beard, L. A. (2015). *Assistive technology: Access for all students* (3rd ed.). Pearson.

Brownell, M. T., Ciullo, S., & Kennedy, M. J. (2020–2021). High-leverage practices: Teaching students with disabilities—and all students who need a learning boost. *American Educator, 44*(4), 12–19.

Chalkiadakis, A., Seremetaki, A., Kanellou, A., Kallishi, M., Morfopoulou, A., Moraitaki, M., & Mastrokoukou, S. (2024). Impact of artificial intelligence and virtual reality on educational inclusion: A systematic review of technologies supporting students with disabilities. *Education Sciences, 14*, 1223. DOI: 10.3390/educsci14111223

Cheng, L., & Shaewitz, D. (2021). *The 2021 youth transition report: Outcomes for youth and young adults with disabilities*. Institute for Educational Leadership.

Community, Q. I. A. T. (2015). Quality Indicators for Assistive Technology Services Self-Evaluation Matrices. Retrieved http://www.qiat.org

Copley, J., & Ziviani, J. (2004). Barriers to the use of assistive technology for children with multiple disabilities. *Occupational Therapy International, 11*(4), 229–243. PMID: 15771212

Dell'Anna, S., Pellegrini, M., Ianes, D., & Vivanet, G. (2022). Learning, social, and psychological outcomes of students with moderate, severe, and complex disabilities in inclusive education: A systematic review. *International Journal of Disability Development and Education, 69*(6), 2025–2041. DOI: 10.1080/1034912X.2020.1843143

Demiral, D. G. (2023). Emerging assistive technologies and challenges encountered. In Calp, M. H., & Butuner, R. (Eds.), *Current Studies in Technology, Innovation, and Entrepreneurship* (pp. 1–21). ISRES Publishing.

Donne, V., & Hansen, M. (2017). Opportunities for students with disabilities to learn technology. *Business Teacher Education Journal, 43*, 16–25.

Douglas, S. N., Shi, Y., Das, S., & Biswas, S. (2022). Validation of wearable sensor technology to measure social proximity of young children with autism spectrum disorders. *Focus on Autism and Other Developmental Disabilities*, *37*(1), 24–33. DOI: 10.1177/10883576211028223

Evmenova, A. S., Graff, H. J., Genaro Motti, V., Giwa-Lawal, K., & Zheng, H. (2019). Designing a wearable technology intervention to support young adults with intellectual and developmental disabilities in inclusive postsecondary academic environments. *Journal of Special Education Technology*, *34*(2), 92–105. DOI: 10.1177/0162643418795833

Evmenova, A. S., & Regan, K. (2019). Supporting the writing process with technology for students with disabilities. *Intervention in School and Clinic*, *55*(2), 78–85. DOI: 10.1177/1053451219837636

Fennema-Jensen, (2005). *An analysis of assistive technology outcomes in Ohio schools: Special education students' access to and participation in general education and isolating the contribution of assistive technology* [Doctoral dissertation, University of Wisconsin—Milwaukee].

Fisher, K. M., Shannon-Baker, P., Greer, K., & Serianni, B. (2022). Perspectives of students with disabilities and their parents on influences and barriers to joining and staying in extracurricular STEM activities. *The Journal of Special Education*, *56*(2), 110–120. DOI: 10.1177/00224669211054109

Gibson, R. (2024). *The impact of AI in advancing accessibility for learners with disabilities. EDUCAUSE Review*. https://er.educause.edu/articles/2024/9/the-impact-of-ai-in-advancing-accessibility-for-learners-with-disabilities

Goo, M., Nishida, M., Gonzalez, R., & Hines, B. (2025). Using video modeling in teaching augmentative and alternative communication for expressive language to children with autism spectrum disorders. *Journal of Special Education Technology*, *0*(0). Advance online publication. DOI: 10.1177/01626434251326320

Gray, T., Silver Pacuilla, H., Overton, C., & Brann, A. (2010). *Unleashing the power of innovation for assistive technology*. American Institutes for Research.

Griffen, B., Lorah, E. R., Caldwell, N., Hantula, D. A., Nosek, J., Tincani, M., & Lemley, S. (2024). The effects of artificial intelligence on implementors' fidelity of instructional strategies during handwashing acquisition in children with autism. *Journal of Developmental and Physical Disabilities*, *36*(5), 793–819. DOI: 10.1007/s10882-023-09937-1 PMID: 39280780

Hew, K. F., & Brush, T. (2007). Integrating technology into K-12 teaching and learning: Current knowledge gaps and recommendations for future research. *Educational Technology Research and Development, 55*, 223–252. DOI: 10.1007/s11423-006-9022-5

High Level Expert Group on Artificial Intelligence (HLEG). (2018). A definition of AI: Main capabilities and scientific disciplines. The European Commission. https://ec.europa.eu/futurium/en/system/files/ged/ai_hleg_definition_of_ai_18_december_1.pdf

Hong, H., & Kim, Y. (2024). Applying artificial intelligence in career education for students with intellectual disabilities: The effects on career self-efficacy and learning flow. *Education and Information Technologies, 29*(18), 25237–25256. DOI: 10.1007/s10639-024-12809-6

Hopcan, S., Polat, E., Ozturk, M. E., & Ozturk, L. (2023). Artificial intelligence in special education: A systematic review. *Interactive Learning Environments, 31*(10), 7335–7353. DOI: 10.1080/10494820.2022.2067186

Individuals with Disabilities Education Improvement Act of 2004 (IDEIA), 20 U.S.C. § 1400 (2004). https://sites.ed.gov/idea/about-idea/

Irwin, V., Wang, K., Jung, J., Kessler, E., Tezil, T., Alhassani, S., Filbey, A., Dilig, R., & Bullock Mann, F. (2024). Report on the Condition of Education 2024 (NCES 2024-144). U.S. Department of Education. National Center for Education Statistics. Retrieved 4/21/25 from https://nces.ed.gov/pubsearch/pubsinfo.asp?pubid=2024144

Israel, M., Marino, M., Delisio, L., & Serianni, B. (2014). Supporting content learning through technology for K-12 students with disabilities (Document No. IC-10). CEEDAR Center. http://ceedar.education.ufl.edu/tools/innovation-configurations/

Johnston, S. S., O'Keeffe, B. V., & Stokes, K. (2018). Early literacy support for students with physical disabilities and complex communication needs. *Teaching Exceptional Children, 51*(2), 91–99. DOI: 10.1177/0040059918802808

Judge, S., & Simms, K. (2009). Assistive technology training at the pre-service level: A national snapshot of teacher preparation programs. *Teacher Education and Special Education, 32*(1), 33–44. DOI: 10.1177/0888406408330868

Judge, S. L. (2000). Accessing and funding assistive technology for young children with disabilities. *Early Childhood Education Journal, 28*(2), 125-131. https://doi-org /DOI: 10.1023/A:1009507722653

Kellems, R., Yakubova, G., Morris, J., Wheatley, A., & Chen, B. B. (2021). Using augmented and virtual reality to improve social, vocational, and academic outcomes of students with autism and other developmental disabilities. In *Designing, deploying, and evaluating virtual and augmented reality in education* (pp. 164–182). IGI Global.

Kotsi, S., Handrinou, S., Iatraki, G., & Soulis, S. G. (2025). A review of artificial intelligence interventions for students with autism spectrum disorder. *Disabilities, 5*(7), 1–14. DOI: 10.3390/disabilities5010007

Kozma-Spytek, L. (2024). AI and other hearing technology advances. *Hearing Life,* (Spring 2024), 10-15.

Lee, H., & Hyun, E. (2015). The intelligent robot contents for children with speech-language disorder. *Journal of Educational Technology & Society, 18*(3), 100–113.

Li, Q., Li, Y., Zheng, J., Yan, X., Huang, J., Xu, Y., Zeng, X., Shen, T., Xing, X., Chen, Q., & Yang, W. (2023). Prevalence and trends of developmental disabilities among US children and adolescents aged 3 to 17 years, 2018–2021. [Nature Publisher Group]. *Scientific Reports, 13*(1), 17254. DOI: 10.1038/s41598-023-44472-1 PMID: 37828147

Lo, C. K. (2023) What is the impact of ChatGPT on education? A rapid review of the literature. *Education Sciences, 13,* 410. https://doi.org/ ci13040410DOI: 10.3390/educs

Lubin, J., & Fernal, F. S. (2021). Barriers to inclusion: Insights of special and general educators from the US and St. Lucia. *Journal of Research in Special Educational Needs, 22*(2), 116–125. DOI: 10.1111/1471-3802.12552

McKinley Yoder, C., Cantrell, M. A., & Hinkle, J. L. (2024). Disparities in high school graduation by identity and disability using intermediate and long-term educational outcomes. *The Journal of School Nursing: the Official Publication of the National Association of School Nurses, 40*(3), 266–274. DOI: 10.1177/10598405221078989 PMID: 35139668

McLeskey, J., Maheady, L., Billingsley, B., Brownell, M. T., & Lewis, T. J. (Eds.). (2022). *High leverage practices for inclusive classrooms.* Routledge.

McMahon, A. K., Cox, A. E., & Miller, D. E. (2021). Supporting mindfulness with technology in students With intellectual and developmental disabilities. *Journal of Special Education Technology, 36*(4), 284-296. https://doi-org/DOI: <ALIGNMENT.qj></ALIGNMENT>10.1177/0162643420924191

Mishra, S., Laplante-Levesqaue, A., Barbareschi, G., DeWitte, L., Abdi, S., Spann, A., Khasnabis, C., & Allen, M. (2024). Assistive technology needs, access, and coverage, and related barriers and facilitators in the WHO European region: A scoping review. *Disability and Rehabilitation. Assistive Technology*, *19*(2), 474–485. DOI: 10.1080/17483107.2022.2099021 PMID: 35906719

Mohamed, A. E., Youssif, E., & Omer Elsheikh, H. E., AbdAlgane, M., & Ali, R. (2025). Generative conversational AI: Active practices for fostering students with mild intellectual disabilities to improve english communication skills. *Contemporary Educational Technology*, *17*(1). Advance online publication. DOI: 10.30935/cedtech/15688 PMID: 34344946

Mosher, M. A., Carreon, A. C., Craig, S. L., & Ruhter, L. C. (2022). Immersive technology to teach social skills to students with autism spectrum disorder: A literature review. *Review Journal of Autism and Developmental Disorders*, *9*(3), 334–350. DOI: 10/1007/s40489-021-00259-6

Mustafa, M. Y., Tlili, A., Lampropoulos, G., Huang, R., Jandric, P., Zhao, J., Salha, S., Xu, L., & Panda, S., Kinshuk, Lopez-Pernas, S., & Saqr, M. (2024). A systematic review of literature reviews on artificial intelligence in education (AIED): A roadmap to a future research agenda. *Smart Learning Environments*, *11*(1), 1–33. DOI: 10.1186/s40561-024-0350-5

Nacheva, R., & Czaplewski, M. (2024). Artificial intelligence in helping people with disabilities: Opportunities and challenges. *HR & Technologies*, *1*, 102–124.

National Center for Education Statistics. (2023). Reading performance. *Condition of education*. U.S. Department of Education, Institute of Education Sciences. https://nces.ed.gov/programs/coe/indicator/cnb

National Center for Educational Statistics. (2022). Use of Supports among Students with Disabilities and Special Needs in College. https://nces.ed.gov/pubsearch/pubsinfo.asp?pubid=2022071

Omiegbe, O. (2024). Artificial intelligence in higher education: Bridging the gap for students with disabilities. *Brock Journal of Education*, *12*(12), 38–50. DOI: 10.37745/bje.2013/vol12n123850

Pagliara, S. M., Bonavolonta, G., Pia, M., Falchi, S., Zurru, A. L., Genu, G., & Mura, A. (2024). The integration of artificial intelligence in inclusive education: A scoping review. *Information (Basel)*, *15*(2), 774–793.

Panjwani-Charani, S., & Zhai, X. (2025). AI for Students with Learning Disabilities: A systematic review. In Zhai, X., & Krajcik, J. (Eds.), *Uses of artificial intelligence in STEM education*. Oxford University Press.

Park, J., Bryant, D. P., & Shin, M. (2022). Effects of interventions using virtual manipulatives for students with learning disabilities: A synthesis of single-case research. *Journal of Learning Disabilities, 55*(4), 325–337. DOI: 10.1177/00222194211006336 PMID: 33845673

Pennington, R., Welch, K. C., & Scott, R. (2014). Using robot-assisted instruction to teach students with intellectual disabilities to use personal narrative in text messages. *Journal of Special Education Technology, 29*(4), 49–58. DOI: 10.1177/016264341402900404

Perelmutter, B., McGregor, K. K., & Gordon, K. R. (2017). Assistive technology interventions for adolescents and adults with learning disabilities: An evidence-based systematic review and meta-analysis. *Computers & Education, 114*, 139–163. DOI: 10.1016/j.compedu.2017.06.005 PMID: 29276334

Phillips, B., & Zhao, H. (1993). Predictors of assistive technology abandonment. *Assistive Technology, 5*(1), 36–45. DOI: 10.1080/10400435.1993.10132205 PMID: 10171664

Pierrès, O., Christen, M., Schmitt-Koopmann, F. M., & Darvishy, A. (2024). Could the use of AI in higher education hinder students with disabilities? A scoping review. *IEEE Access : Practical Innovations, Open Solutions, 12*, 27810–27828. DOI: 10.1109/ACCESS.2024.3365368

Pierrès, O., Darvishy, A., & Christen, M. (2023). AI in higher education: Ethical concerns for students with disabilities. [). CEUR-WS.]. *CEUR Workshop Proceedings, 3442*, 7–9.

Pritchard, D., English, A. R., & Ravenscroft, J. (2021). Extended cognition, assistive technology and education. *Synthese (Dordrecht), 199*(3-4), 8355–8377. DOI: 10.1007/s11229-021-03166-9

Puckett, K. (2004). Project ACCESS: Field testing an assistive technology toolkit for students with mild disabilities. *Journal of Special Education Technology, 19*(2), 5–17.

Puglisi, A., Caprì, T., Pignolo, L., Gismondo, S., Chilà, P., Minutoli, R., Marino, F., Failla, C., Arnao, A. A., Tartarisco, G., Cerasa, A., & Pioggia, G. (2022). Social humanoid robots for children with Autism Spectrum Disorders: A review of modalities, indications, and pitfalls. *Children (Basel, Switzerland), 9*(7), 953. DOI: 10.3390/children9070953 PMID: 35883937

Raave, D. K., Saks, K., Pedaste, M., & Roa, E. R. (2024). How and why teachers use technology: Distinct integration practices in K-12 education. *Education Sciences*, *14*(12), 1301. DOI: 10.3390/educsci14121301

Rehabilitation Act of. 1973. (2024). Section 504. https://www.govinfo.gov/content/pkg/FR-2024-05-09/pdf/2024-09237.pdf

Rice, M. F., & Dunn, S. (2023). The use of artificial intelligence with students with identified disabilities: A systematic review with critique. *Computers in the Schools*, *40*(4), 370–390.

Rowland, A., Smith, S. J., Lowrey, K. A., & Abdulrahim, N. A. (2020). Underutilized technology solutions for student writing. *Intervention in School and Clinic*, *56*(2), 99–106. DOI: 10.1177/1053451220914893

Samoili, S., López Cobo, M., Gómez, E., DePrato, G., Martínez-Plumed, F., & Delipetrev, B. (2020). AI watch defining artificial intelligence towards an operational definition and taxonomy of artificial intelligence Joint Research Centre (JRC). https://www.sipotra.it/wp-content/uploads/2020/10/AI-Watch-Defining-Artificial-Intelligence-1.pdf

Scherer, M. J. (2005). Assessing the benefits of using assistive technologies and other supports for thinking, remembering and learning. *Disability and Rehabilitation*, *27*(13), 731–739. PMID: 16096225

Shifrer, D. (2013). Stigma of a label: Educational expectations for high school students labeled with learning disabilities. *Journal of Health and Social Behavior*, *54*(4), 462–480. DOI: 10.1177/0022146513503346 PMID: 24311756

So, S., & Lee, N. (2023). Pedagogical exploration and technological development of a humanoid robotic system for teaching to and learning in young children. *Cogent Education*, *10*(1), 2179181. DOI: 10.1080/2331186X.2023.2179181

Standen, P. J., Brown, D. J., Taheri, M., Galvez-Trigo, M. J., Boulton, H., Burton, A., Hallewell, M. J., Lathe, J. G., Shopland, N., Blanco-Gonzalez, M. A., Kwiatkowska, G. M., Milli, E., Cobello, S., Mazzucato, A., Traversi, M., & Hortal, E. (2020). An evaluation of an adaptive learning system based on multimodal affect recognition for learners with intellectual disabilities. *British Journal of Educational Technology*, *51*(5), 1748–1765.

Stark, K., Wexler, J., Shelton, A., Johnston, T. B., & Omohundro, K. (2024). Explicit and evidence-based literacy instruction in middle school: An observation study. *Reading and Writing*, *37*(9), 2253–2274. DOI: 10.1007/s11145-023-10470-y

Tlili, A., Lin, V., & Chen, N., S., Huang, R., & Kinshuk. (2020). A systematic review of robot-assisted special education from the Activity Theory perspective. *Journal of Educational Technology & Society*, *23*(3), 95–109.

Uluer, P., Kose, H., Gumuslu, E., & Barkana, D. E. (2021). Experience with an affective robot assistant for children with hearing disabilities. *International Journal of Social Robotics*, •••, 1–18. https://doI.org/10.1007/s12369-021-00830-5 PMID: 34804256

Ward, C., Ihlo, T., Ryan Jackson, K., & Farmer, S. (2023). Effective implementation capacity to impact change within state education systems to support students with disabilities. *Journal of Disability Policy Studies*, *34*(2), 104–114. DOI: 10.1177/10442073221096392

Wilby, R. L., & Esson, J. (2024). AI literacy in geographic education and research: Capabilities, caveats, and criticality. *The Geographical Journal*, *190*(1). DOI: 10.1111/geoj.12548

World Health Organization (WHO). (2024). Assistive technology. https://www.who.int/news-room/fact-sheets/detail/assistive-technology

Yi, H., Liu, T., & Lan, G. (2024). The key artificial intelligence technologies in early childhood education: A review. *Artificial Intelligence Review*, *57*(1), 12. DOI: 10.1007/s10462-023-10637-7

Zhang, L., Carter, R. A., Liu, Y., & Peng, P. (2024). Let's CHAT about artificial intelligence for students with disabilities: A systematic literature review and meta-analysis. *Review of Educational Research*, •••, 1–43.

Zhuo, T. Y., Huang, Y., Chen, C., & Xing, Z. (2023). Red teaming ChatGPT via jailbreaking: Bias, robustness, reliability and toxicity. Cornell University Library. https://arxiv.org/abs/2301.12867

Chapter 10
The Use of AI in Teaching and Learning: The Power of Feedback

Greg Kaiser
https://orcid.org/0009-0003-0954-5760
Azusa Pacific University, USA

Sue Kaiser
California State University, San Bernardino, USA

ABSTRACT

This chapter explores the transformative potential of artificial intelligence (AI) in delivering timely, personalized, and scalable feedback across educational contexts. Grounded in foundational learning theories—including behaviorism, constructivism, and cognitive load theory—it examines how AI-powered tools enhance self-regulated learning, motivation, and equity. Technologies such as natural language processing, intelligent tutoring systems, and affective computing are analyzed for their role in fostering responsive and dialogic feedback. The chapter also critically addresses ethical concerns, including bias, data privacy, and automation bias. Through practical examples and design principles, it advocates for human-centered AI feedback systems that align with pedagogical goals, empower educators, and promote learner agency. Ultimately, it argues that feedback must remain relational and ethically grounded to truly enrich teaching and learning in the digital age.

DOI: 10.4018/979-8-3373-2397-8.ch010

INTRODUCTION: WHY FEEDBACK MATTERS IN EDUCATION

Feedback is a cornerstone of effective teaching and learning, acting as a dynamic bridge between current performance and desired learning outcomes. Its core purpose is to help learners recognize the discrepancy between what they know and what they need to know, guiding them in closing this gap through actionable insights and reflection (Sadler, 1989). Decades of educational research underscore the potency of feedback as a high-impact instructional strategy. In fact, John Hattie's seminal meta-analyses (Hattie, 2009) consistently rank feedback among the most influential factors affecting student achievement, especially when it is timely, specific, and aligned with clearly defined learning goals (Hattie & Timperley, 2007).

Feedback not only supports academic growth but also promotes learner motivation, metacognition, and the development of self-regulated learning skills (Nicol & Macfarlane-Dick, 2006). High-quality feedback enables learners to make informed decisions about how to revise their work, adjust strategies, and deepen their understanding. In doing so, it transforms assessment into a continuous, dialogic process rather than a one-time judgment of proficiency.

Traditionally, educators have delivered feedback through handwritten comments, rubrics, one-on-one conferences, and peer evaluations. While these methods can be powerful, they face inherent scalability limitations. In large, asynchronous, or resource-constrained environments, the capacity to provide individualized, iterative feedback diminishes sharply. Teachers often struggle to balance the volume of student work with the time needed to deliver feedback that is both meaningful and actionable (Carless, 2006). As a result, many learners receive delayed or generic responses, missing key opportunities for growth, especially in domains that require frequent formative input such as academic writing, mathematics, science, and coding.

In this context, artificial intelligence (AI) has emerged as a transformative catalyst. Leveraging technologies such as machine learning, natural language processing (NLP), and adaptive algorithms, AI now offers the capability to deliver immediate, personalized feedback at scale. Intelligent tutoring systems (ITS), automated writing evaluation platforms, and AI-powered chatbots can simulate aspects of human tutoring by identifying misconceptions, suggesting targeted improvements, and encouraging reflective thinking (Graesser et al., 2005; Wang et al., 2022). These tools have the potential to reduce feedback latency, increase consistency, and free educators to focus on higher-order teaching tasks.

The urgency of these innovations became particularly evident during the COVID-19 pandemic. As institutions rapidly shifted to online and hybrid learning environments, disparities in feedback access became more pronounced. Students in under-resourced communities, who often depend on frequent teacher interaction, were disproportionately affected by the breakdown of traditional feedback mechanisms. AI-powered feedback systems, available across platforms and time zones, offer a promising solution to these equity challenges by ensuring that all learners receive timely and constructive input—regardless of classroom context (Holmes et al., 2019; Means et al., 2021).

Moreover, as the educational landscape evolves toward personalized, competency-based, and lifelong learning models, the demand for feedback that adapts to diverse learner pathways continues to grow. Effective feedback systems must now support not only academic achievement but also digital literacy, critical thinking, and transferable skills relevant to an AI-augmented workforce (Luckin et al., 2016; OECD, 2021). In this broader vision, feedback becomes a central mechanism for guiding learner agency and promoting just-in-time learning interventions across a lifespan of educational experiences.

However, the rise of AI-driven feedback systems also raises critical pedagogical, ethical, and philosophical questions. Can algorithms truly interpret student intent, emotion, and context? What are the implications of relying on data-driven feedback in spaces that traditionally prioritize human connection and judgment? How can we ensure that such systems are transparent, equitable, and aligned with educational values? Researchers caution that over-reliance on AI may dehumanize learning or inadvertently reinforce existing biases if not carefully designed and ethically governed (Selwyn, 2019; Williamson & Eynon, 2020).

This chapter aims to navigate these complex questions by exploring the evolving role of feedback in the age of AI. It begins by reviewing foundational theories of feedback and learning, then investigates how AI technologies are being applied to deliver feedback across diverse educational contexts. It further examines the benefits of AI-augmented feedback—such as immediacy, personalization, and scalability—while also addressing significant challenges, including issues of bias, privacy, and pedagogical misalignment.

THEORETICAL FOUNDATIONS OF FEEDBACK IN LEARNING

Understanding how feedback supports learning requires a grounding in its theoretical underpinnings. Over the decades, educational psychologists and instructional designers have developed diverse models that shape how feedback is conceptualized, delivered, and received. These theoretical perspectives—spanning behaviorism, constructivism, cognitive theories, and assessment-based frameworks—continue to influence both traditional feedback mechanisms and those powered by artificial intelligence (AI). In designing effective AI systems for education, it is imperative to align technological capabilities with these foundational pedagogical theories.

Behaviorist Perspectives

Behaviorist learning theories emphasize observable changes in behavior as the primary indicators of learning, asserting that knowledge is acquired through processes of reinforcement and conditioning. Rooted in the work of early psychologists like John Watson and further developed by B.F. Skinner (1954), behaviorism maintains that learning occurs when a stimulus-response connection is strengthened through repeated practice and timely feedback. Skinner's operant conditioning framework introduced the concept of reinforcement—positive or negative—as a mechanism to increase the likelihood of a desired behavior being repeated. In educational contexts, this translated into the use of immediate feedback as a central instructional strategy. When learners receive instant confirmation of correct responses or prompt correction of errors, they are more likely to internalize the correct behaviors and disengage from unproductive ones.

Skinner's ideas culminated in the development of programmed instruction, a highly structured pedagogical approach that presents learners with small units of content followed by questions or tasks, each paired with immediate feedback. This step-by-step progression ensured that learners could not advance without demonstrating mastery of each preceding concept, reinforcing learning through a predictable feedback loop. This model, while mechanistic, proved effective in certain domains such as rote memorization, language acquisition, and procedural skill training—areas where precision, repetition, and reinforcement are critical.

Modern AI-powered feedback systems retain echoes of this behaviorist lineage, particularly in tools that provide binary (right/wrong) responses or corrective cues during drills and practice exercises. Intelligent Tutoring Systems (ITS), for example, often mimic programmed instruction by guiding students through problem sets with structured hints and feedback loops designed to reinforce correct methods (VanLehn, 2006). While these systems are often criticized for promoting surface learning if used in isolation, their behaviorist foundations remain valuable in building fluency, automaticity, and foundational competencies—especially when integrated within broader, constructivist learning environments. As such, behaviorist principles continue to inform the design of AI-driven feedback tools, particularly when the goal is efficient skill acquisition, habit formation, or mastery of procedural tasks

AI applications such as Intelligent Tutoring Systems (ITS) are rooted in this tradition. ITS platforms provide real-time, rule-based feedback by verifying the accuracy of student inputs and offering corrective suggestions when errors occur (VanLehn, 2006). These systems are particularly effective in domains such as mathematics or science, where factual accuracy and procedural fluency are essential (Aleven et al., 2016). However, critics argue that an overreliance on verification-type feedback can promote rote learning rather than conceptual understanding (Nicol &

Macfarlane-Dick, 2006). Thus, while behaviorist-aligned feedback remains efficient and scalable, it should be augmented with deeper, elaborative feedback to support meaningful learning.

Constructivist and Socio-Constructivist Perspectives

Constructivist theories of learning, advanced by influential scholars such as Jean Piaget and Jerome Bruner, emphasize that learners are not passive recipients of information but active participants in the construction of knowledge. According to this perspective, learning occurs through the integration of new information with existing cognitive structures, often involving processes such as exploration, hypothesis testing, and reflection. Feedback within this framework serves a formative and developmental role—it is not simply corrective, but a tool for fostering cognitive dissonance, encouraging inquiry, and guiding learners toward deeper conceptual understanding. Rather than merely telling students what is right or wrong, constructivist feedback supports them in refining their mental models through meaningful engagement with tasks and ideas.

Socio-constructivist theories, particularly those articulated by Lev Vygotsky (1978), extend this view by underscoring the fundamentally social nature of learning. Vygotsky introduced the concept of the Zone of Proximal Development (ZPD)—the range between what a learner can do independently and what they can achieve with guidance. Feedback, in this context, is most effective when it functions as scaffolding, helping learners bridge this gap through supportive dialogue and collaboration. Here, feedback is situated within social interaction, where it serves to mediate understanding, co-construct meaning, and gradually transfer responsibility to the learner as competence increases.

Artificial Intelligence systems grounded in constructivist and socio-constructivist principles are designed to go beyond binary or evaluative feedback. Tools like AutoTutor exemplify this approach by using natural language dialogue to engage students in elaboration, explanation, and metacognitive reflection (Graesser et al., 2005). These systems simulate human tutor interactions and dynamically adjust questions and prompts based on student responses, thereby supporting individualized, interactive learning experiences. Rather than simply marking an answer as incorrect, AutoTutor may prompt a learner to reconsider an idea, explain their reasoning, or explore alternative perspectives—mirroring the strategies of expert human tutors.

In socio-constructivist learning environments, AI tools are increasingly leveraged to facilitate and improve collaborative learning. Technologies that employ Natural Language Processing (NLP) and discourse analytics are now capable of analyzing student contributions in online discussions and group projects. These systems assess the depth, coherence, equity, and diversity of contributions, offering both learners and instructors feedback on the quality of discourse (Rosé et al., 2008). For example, if a conversation becomes dominated by a single voice or lacks substantive engagement with key concepts, the system can flag these patterns and suggest strategies to encourage broader participation and deeper reflection. This type of AI-mediated feedback not only enhances the quality of group interaction but also supports inclusive and dialogic learning environments where all voices are heard and valued.

Cognitive Load Theory and Feedback Timing

Cognitive Load Theory (Sweller, 1988) highlights the importance of managing the finite capacity of working memory during learning. Feedback, according to this theory, must be designed to reduce extraneous cognitive load (unnecessary mental effort) while promoting germane cognitive load (mental effort directed toward learning). Improperly timed or overly complex feedback can overwhelm learners, particularly novices, and impede knowledge construction.

AI technologies excel at delivering adaptive feedback tailored to a learner's cognitive capacity, making them particularly effective in supporting differentiated instruction. Drawing from cognitive load theory, these systems recognize that novice and expert learners process information differently and require distinct types of support to optimize their mental effort and learning efficiency (Kalyuga, 2007). Adaptive learning platforms, such as ALEKS, Carnegie Learning, or Smart Sparrow, can assess a learner's proficiency and behavior in real time—monitoring patterns of response accuracy, speed, and engagement—to determine their current level of understanding. Based on this data, the AI system dynamically adjusts the complexity, specificity, and volume of feedback provided. For instance, beginners might receive more scaffolded, directive feedback focusing on foundational concepts, while more experienced learners may benefit from elaborative prompts that encourage abstraction, transfer of knowledge, or critical thinking.

This real-time adjustment not only enhances personalization but also prevents cognitive overload by aligning instructional support with the learner's zone of proximal development (Vygotsky, 1978). Moreover, adaptive feedback helps maintain motivation by ensuring that tasks remain appropriately challenging—not too easy to cause boredom, and not too difficult to induce frustration. By continually calibrating feedback in response to learner performance and needs, AI-powered systems promote more efficient and effective learning trajectories, fostering deeper engagement and long-term retention (Chen et al., 2016; VanLehn, 2011). This capability positions AI as a vital tool in creating inclusive, learner-centered environments that respond to diverse cognitive profiles and learning paces.

Delayed feedback, while less aligned with traditional behaviorist theories that emphasize immediate reinforcement, can serve as a powerful pedagogical tool in promoting deeper learning. When learners are given time to reflect on their performance before receiving external input, they engage in self-assessment, metacognitive processing, and hypothesis testing, all of which contribute to more meaningful learning experiences (Shute, 2008). This delay can encourage students to evaluate their reasoning, identify potential errors, and consider alternative strategies, thereby fostering a greater sense of ownership over their learning process. AI systems offer a unique opportunity to operationalize this principle by tailoring the timing of feedback delivery according to multiple contextual variables. For instance, in higher-order cognitive tasks such as problem-solving or essay writing, delayed feedback may support deeper comprehension and long-term retention. Conversely, for routine or procedural tasks, immediate feedback may be more appropriate to reinforce correct responses. By analyzing data such as learner history, task difficulty, and instructional goals, AI systems can be intelligently configured to strike an optimal balance between immediacy and reflectiveness—ensuring that feedback timing aligns with both cognitive theory and instructional intent.

Assessment and Feedback Loops

Formative assessment theory positions feedback as an essential process for monitoring student learning and informing ongoing instructional decisions. Unlike summative assessment, which evaluates learning outcomes at the end of an instructional period, formative assessment focuses on providing timely, actionable insights during the learning process to support improvement. Black and Wiliam's (1998) influential model of formative assessment centers on three foundational questions: *Where is the learner going? Where are they now? How can they close the gap?* These questions highlight the developmental nature of feedback, which should be used not merely to judge student performance but to guide and scaffold the learning journey. Effective formative feedback is iterative, meaning it builds upon previous learner responses, and it is responsive to learner needs—adapting over time to facilitate deeper understanding, skill acquisition, and performance improvement.

AI systems can effectively operationalize these principles by automating and enhancing the feedback loop through continuous monitoring and personalized interventions. Tools such as adaptive learning platforms and learning analytics dashboards provide instructors and students with real-time insights into learner progress. These systems analyze data from quizzes, activities, and user behavior to identify patterns, detect misconceptions, and recommend targeted resources or instructional adjustments. For instance, a learning analytics dashboard might highlight areas where a student consistently underperforms, enabling the system to adjust the difficulty level, provide scaffolding materials, or suggest review activities (Ifenthaler & Yau, 2020). From the student's perspective, this feedback becomes a resource for self-awareness and improvement. Visualizations of progress, such as heat maps or mastery trackers, allow students to reflect on their learning trajectory, set personalized goals, and make informed choices about their next steps. In this way, AI serves not only as a tool for teachers but also as a partner in fostering learner agency and ownership of the learning process.

Central to the effectiveness of formative feedback is its capacity to support self-regulated learning (SRL)—a metacognitive process wherein learners plan, monitor, and reflect on their learning strategies and progress. Zimmerman (2002) emphasized that self-regulated learners are active participants in their education, and they benefit most from feedback that enhances their ability to evaluate their understanding, adjust their approaches, and persist in the face of challenges. AI systems can play a critical role in cultivating these skills by embedding reflective prompts, guiding questions, and strategy suggestions into the feedback process. For example, when AI tools ask students, *"How confident are you in your answer?"* or *"What strategy did you use to solve this problem?"*, they promote metacognitive awareness and encourage students to think beyond correctness toward process and understanding (Panadero et al., 2017). These reflective interactions transform feedback from a static statement into a dialogic, learner-centered experience that supports autonomy, resilience, and lifelong learning skills. By embedding SRL-supportive features into AI systems, educators and developers can enhance not just student performance, but also the habits of mind that underpin deep and durable learning.

Summary

The theoretical foundations of feedback underscore its multidimensional role in learning. From behaviorist reinforcement to constructivist scaffolding, from cognitive efficiency to formative regulation, each perspective offers a lens through which to understand and design feedback. As AI continues to shape the educational landscape, aligning feedback systems with these rich theoretical traditions ensures that technology enhances—not diminishes—the pedagogical impact of feedback. AI-driven feedback must not only be accurate and timely but also meaningful, adaptive, and supportive of learner growth.

AI TECHNOLOGIES THAT POWER FEEDBACK

Artificial Intelligence offers an unprecedented ability to collect, analyze, and respond to learner data in real time. This capability hinges on a range of interrelated technologies—each contributing to the delivery of timely, personalized, and actionable feedback. These AI technologies not only scale formative and summative feedback processes but also promote differentiated instruction tailored to each learner's needs. In this section, we explore the foundational AI technologies driving feedback in education, from natural language processing to emerging multimodal learning analytics.

Natural Language Processing (NLP)

Natural Language Processing enables AI systems to understand, interpret, and generate human language. In educational contexts, NLP underpins many feedback systems by providing nuanced and context-aware interpretations of student language, whether written or spoken. Tools such as Grammarly, Turnitin's Revision Assistant, OpenAI's ChatGPT, and Ecree use NLP to deliver feedback on grammar, tone, clarity, coherence, and argumentation. These platforms go beyond rule-based spell checkers by offering suggestions on passive voice, word choice, and rhetorical structure, helping students revise in real time (Wilson et al., 2021).

More sophisticated applications such as AutoTutor utilize NLP to engage students in Socratic-style dialogue. These systems ask follow-up questions, probe student reasoning, and clarify misunderstandings through natural conversations (Graesser et al., 2005). NLP has also been instrumental in supporting peer review systems. Algorithms can assess the quality of student-generated feedback—scoring for specificity, constructiveness, and tone—to ensure that peer interactions are pedagogically valuable (Wambsganss et al., 2021).

Machine Learning and Adaptive Systems

Machine Learning (ML), a core subset of artificial intelligence, enables systems to improve performance over time by analyzing patterns in data. In the context of educational feedback, ML drives adaptive learning environments that dynamically adjust instructional materials and feedback based on individual student behaviors, interactions, and performance metrics. Platforms such as Knewton, DreamBox, Smart Sparrow, and ALEKS leverage ML algorithms to continuously assess student knowledge and modify the difficulty or sequencing of content to meet learners at their level. For instance, DreamBox analyzes more than 48,000 data points per student per hour to deliver personalized math instruction and feedback in real time, ensuring that each learner receives timely, relevant, and appropriately challenging support (Pane et al., 2015). In addition to content adaptation, ML underpins real-time learning analytics dashboards that provide instructors with actionable insights. These systems help identify at-risk students, flag common misconceptions, and generate predictive models to guide the timing and specificity of instructor interventions, ultimately enabling more precise and proactive feedback (Ifenthaler & Yau, 2020). Through these capabilities, ML significantly enhances the responsiveness, scalability, and effectiveness of feedback systems in both individual and classroom contexts.

Intelligent Tutoring Systems (ITS)

Intelligent Tutoring Systems (ITS) represent one of the most extensively researched and implemented forms of AI-driven feedback in education. These systems emulate expert human tutors by offering scaffolded, individualized instruction and feedback based on student interactions. Carnegie Learning's MATHia and ANDES physics tutor are examples of ITS that break down complex tasks into smaller cognitive steps and provide real-time guidance. Using Bayesian networks or constraint-based modeling, these systems adaptively respond to each learner's progress (VanLehn, 2011; Pane et al., 2017). Research shows that ITS can lead to significant learning gains, sometimes equaling or exceeding those achieved through one-on-one human tutoring in domains such as algebra, logic, and computer programming (Koedinger & Corbett, 2006; VanLehn, 2011).

Automated Essay Scoring and Feedback Systems

Automated Essay Scoring (AES) systems were originally developed for standardized assessments, but their role has expanded to include formative writing support. These tools analyze student writing for grammar, organization, coherence, and analytical depth, providing instant, revisable feedback. Examples include ETS's e-rater, Criterion, and Writing Mentor, which examine features such as syntactic variety, lexical richness, argument structure, and cohesion (Attali & Burstein, 2006). Some systems integrate plagiarism detection and APA formatting feedback, broadening their utility in higher education writing instruction.

Recent advances in neural networks and deep learning have enhanced these systems' ability to provide meaningful suggestions rather than just surface-level corrections (Zhang et al., 2020). This aligns AES tools more closely with writing pedagogy that values revision, reflection, and growth. By supporting writers through tailored, actionable feedback at various stages of composition, AI-powered writing tools help students develop as communicators, not just produce error-free texts. This capacity is particularly valuable in contexts where instructors face time constraints and cannot provide individualized comments on every draft. Furthermore, the real-time nature of these systems allows learners to engage in self-paced, autonomous improvement, helping them internalize key principles of effective writing and build confidence in their abilities. In sum, the integration of deep learning into AES tools marks a significant step toward a more nuanced, pedagogy-aligned approach to writing support in both K–12 and higher education settings.

Chatbots and Conversational Agents

AI-powered chatbots and conversational agents are increasingly being integrated into Learning Management Systems (LMS) and virtual learning environments, offering scalable and accessible support for students across diverse educational contexts. These tools provide 24/7 academic assistance, respond to frequently asked questions, and facilitate dynamic feedback exchanges that extend instructional support beyond traditional classroom hours. A widely cited example is Jill Watson, the AI teaching assistant developed at Georgia Tech, which successfully answered student queries in an online course with notable accuracy and efficiency, freeing up instructors to focus on deeper pedagogical engagement (Goel & Polepeddi, 2016). Beyond transactional support, chatbots can prompt learners to reflect on their progress, summarize key concepts, and revisit misunderstood topics—thereby modeling the feedback loop central to effective learning. Moreover, multilingual and culturally adaptive chatbots contribute to inclusion and equity by delivering feedback in a student's preferred language or dialect, which can enhance comprehension and reduce barriers for English language learners or linguistically diverse students (Følstad & Brandtzæg, 2017). As these systems continue to evolve, they are increasingly capable of simulating dialogic feedback conversations that support metacognitive development and foster self-regulated learning, helping students become more independent and reflective in their academic journeys.

Multimodal Learning Analytics

Multimodal Learning Analytics (MMLA) is an emerging field that leverages a wide range of data sources to generate comprehensive, real-time feedback that extends beyond traditional metrics like quiz scores or keystroke data. By capturing non-verbal and behavioral cues—including facial expressions, eye gaze, voice tone, and physical gestures—MMLA systems offer a more nuanced understanding of learner engagement and comprehension. Using technologies such as computer vision, affective computing, and sensor-based input, these platforms can assess critical learning dimensions such as cognitive load, emotional state, and attention levels. For instance, an MMLA-enabled environment might detect signs of confusion or frustration on a learner's face and respond by simplifying the content, offering encouragement, or adjusting the pacing of instruction (D'Mello & Graesser, 2012). In practice, MMLA is especially powerful in STEM simulations, language learning environments, and clinical skills labs, where it can monitor procedural accuracy, task timing, and collaboration dynamics. These insights allow educators and systems to provide rich, formative feedback that is both contextually responsive and instructionally meaningful, significantly enhancing the learning experience (Blikstein & Worsley, 2016).

Summary

AI technologies such as Natural Language Processing, Machine Learning, Intelligent Tutoring Systems, Automated Essay Scoring, Chatbots, and Multimodal Learning Analytics have revolutionized the way educators provide feedback. These tools support personalized, immediate, and data-driven feedback across multiple disciplines and modalities. While each technology plays a distinct role, their collective integration enables a more responsive and learner-centered feedback ecosystem. As educational institutions continue to adopt these technologies, attention must be paid to equity, transparency, and pedagogical integrity to ensure feedback remains meaningful and ethical.

APPLICATIONS ACROSS EDUCATIONAL CONTEXTS

AI-driven feedback is transforming teaching and learning across educational sectors, offering scalable, personalized, and data-rich forms of instructional support. From elementary classrooms to university lecture halls and continuing education platforms, these technologies are reshaping how feedback is designed, delivered, and used. While the core AI technologies may remain consistent, effective implementation demands context-specific adaptation based on learner characteristics, instructional goals, and technological infrastructure. This section explores the application of AI-powered feedback in three primary domains: K–12 education, higher education, and workforce/lifelong learning.

K–12 Education

In K–12 educational settings, AI-powered feedback systems are playing a critical role in shifting instruction away from one-size-fits-all models toward more personalized and responsive learning environments. These technologies are most commonly applied in subjects that benefit from iterative practice—such as mathematics, literacy, and writing—but their use is expanding into fields like science, social-emotional learning, and even the arts (One to One Plus, 2023). Several prominent platforms exemplify this transformation. Khan Academy employs AI algorithms to deliver real-time scaffolding and individualized learning pathways, enabling students to master skills at their own pace (Khan Academy, n.d.). DreamBox Learning, grounded in cognitive science principles, dynamically adapts its instructional content based on students' responses and interaction patterns, ensuring that feedback is both timely and contextually relevant (Shamir et al., 2021). Meanwhile, IXL provides skill-based exercises with immediate feedback and reinforcement, promoting mastery through guided repetition and adaptive practice (IXL Learning, 2021). Together, these tools illustrate how AI can enhance learning by tailoring instruction to meet the needs, pace, and preferences of each individual student.AI feedback in writing is particularly impactful in supporting early and sustained literacy development. Platforms like Writable and Scribo offer real-time feedback on writing mechanics, coherence, and argument structure. These platforms support recursive writing processes and allow teachers to allocate more time to higher-order concerns, such as content and voice (Roscoe et al., 2022).

Support for English learners (ELs) and students with special educational needs is another crucial domain where AI-powered feedback technologies are making a significant impact. These learners often face additional barriers in accessing and processing instructional content, particularly in linguistically and cognitively demanding environments (Fitas, 2025). AI-driven tools such as text-to-speech and speech recognition technologies help bridge these gaps by offering real-time, multimodal language support that enhances both accessibility and engagement. For example, platforms like Microsoft Immersive Reader, Google Read&Write, and SpeakIt! provide instant auditory feedback by reading digital text aloud, allowing students to hear correct pronunciation, internalize sentence structures, and better understand unfamiliar vocabulary (Viberg et al., 2018). These tools are particularly beneficial for reinforcing phonemic awareness, supporting bilingual transitions, and helping learners build listening comprehension skills through repeated exposure and adaptive pacing.

Teachers benefit significantly from AI-powered dashboard analytics that synthesize vast amounts of student data into actionable insights. These dashboards aggregate information on student performance, engagement patterns, time-on-task, and assessment results, presenting it through user-friendly visualizations that allow educators to identify learning gaps, monitor progress, and personalize instruction with greater precision (Khosravi et al., 2021). Instead of relying solely on intuition or limited observation, teachers can use these tools to make data-informed decisions about grouping, pacing, and differentiation (Teaching Times, 2024). This not only improves instructional efficiency but also supports a more equitable approach to intervention, as the system can help flag students who might otherwise be overlooked due to quiet disengagement or subtle misunderstandings (Pane, 2018).

Higher Education

In higher education, AI-powered feedback technologies are increasingly being adopted to address the complex demands of large-scale, asynchronous, and diverse learning environments. With the rapid growth of online programs, hybrid courses, and global student enrollments, traditional models of feedback—often reliant on one-on-one interaction—are no longer sufficient to meet student needs at scale. AI systems offer a promising solution by automating elements of feedback delivery, making it possible to provide timely, personalized, and consistent guidance across large student cohorts without sacrificing instructional quality.

These technologies are particularly effective in contexts where individualized input is difficult to scale, such as massive open online courses (MOOCs) and writing-intensive disciplines. In MOOCs, which may enroll tens of thousands of students from around the world, instructor-led feedback is often limited or absent. AI tools can fill this gap by providing immediate clarification, assessment, or guidance based on learner input. Similarly, in writing-intensive courses, where formative feedback on drafts and revisions is critical to student success, AI writing assistants and automated essay scoring tools offer scalable support by identifying areas for improvement in grammar, structure, coherence, and argumentation.

One of the most well-known and widely cited examples is Jill Watson, the AI teaching assistant developed at Georgia Institute of Technology. Built using IBM's Watson platform, Jill was integrated into an online graduate course in artificial intelligence and trained on thousands of prior discussion forum posts. She was able to respond to common student questions with near-human accuracy and efficiency—often without students realizing they were interacting with a machine (Goel & Polepeddi, 2016). This innovation not only enhanced students' access to timely and accurate feedback but also freed up instructional staff to focus on higher-order engagement, such as mentoring, grading complex submissions, and facilitating conceptual discussions.

Workforce and Lifelong Learning

AI-driven feedback is equally pivotal in adult learning contexts, where learners frequently balance their studies with full-time employment, caregiving responsibilities, and other personal commitments. To meet these unique needs, adult learners often seek flexible, self-paced, and competency-focused learning pathways that allow them to build relevant skills efficiently. Online platforms such as Coursera, edX, LinkedIn Learning, and Udacity utilize AI technologies to support these goals by providing instant assessment feedback, personalized learning trajectories, and skill-based content recommendations that align with job roles and career aspirations. These AI-enhanced features not only tailor learning experiences to individual needs but also foster greater autonomy and persistence by dynamically adjusting content difficulty and feedback in response to learner progress. As a result, adult learners are better equipped to remain engaged, motivated, and successful in pursuing their educational and professional goals (Popenici & Kerr, 2017).

Summary

Across K–12, higher education, and workforce training, AI-powered feedback systems are enhancing precision, scalability, and learner engagement. In primary and secondary education, they support differentiation and foundational skill-building. In higher education, they provide real-time feedback in writing, coding, and quantitative disciplines, while enabling deeper insight into learning behavior. In professional contexts, they foster lifelong learning through personalized, competency-based feedback that aligns with job performance and career pathways.

BENEFITS OF AI-DRIVEN FEEDBACK

Artificial Intelligence brings a powerful set of capabilities that enhance the quality, accessibility, and impact of feedback in educational environments. While traditional feedback mechanisms depend on human time and effort—often limited by large class sizes or lack of timely access—AI systems offer scalable, personalized, and responsive feedback at unprecedented levels. This section explores the key benefits of AI-driven feedback, including timeliness, personalization, support for self-regulated learning, motivation, and teacher empowerment.

Timeliness and Scalability

One of the most immediate and visible benefits of AI-powered feedback is its ability to deliver real-time or near-instant feedback, regardless of class size or location. Students no longer have to wait hours or days for instructors to review their work. Instead, AI systems can evaluate responses and provide feedback within seconds, enabling immediate correction of errors and reinforcement of learning. Tools like Gradescope can instantly grade math and short-answer questions, while platforms like Grammarly and Turnitin Feedback Studio can assess writing mechanics and offer improvement suggestions in real time. This reduces the cognitive lag between performance and reflection, which is critical for effective learning (Hattie & Timperley, 2007).

Scalability is equally important in the design and deployment of AI-powered feedback systems, particularly in large-enrollment courses and massive open online courses (MOOCs), where the sheer volume of learners makes individualized feedback from human instructors unfeasible. AI technologies provide a critical solution by ensuring that every student, regardless of class size or location, receives timely, consistent, and personalized feedback—a pedagogical element known to significantly influence student engagement and learning outcomes (Winkler & Hermann, 2019). Automated systems such as intelligent tutoring platforms, writing assessment tools, and AI chatbots can evaluate student work at scale and offer actionable suggestions almost instantly. Platforms like Gradescope and Turnitin Feedback Studio use AI to analyze written responses and provide immediate guidance on grammar, structure, and content coherence, even in courses with thousands of enrollees (Khosravi et al., 2021).

Scalability of AI feedback promotes educational equity, as students in under-resourced institutions or remote learning environments gain access to high-quality instructional support that might otherwise be unavailable (Holstein et al., 2020). By automating routine feedback tasks, AI also allows instructors to focus their time on higher-order pedagogical activities, such as mentoring, curriculum development, and individualized interventions for students who need additional support (Tubino, & Adachi, 2022).

Feedback can now extend beyond the traditional boundaries of classroom instruction and scheduled assessments, evolving into a continuous, integrated component of the learner's educational journey. Thanks to advancements in artificial intelligence and ubiquitous computing, intelligent learning platforms are increasingly embedding formative assessment and feedback into everyday digital learning environments—creating systems that provide *"always-on"* support regardless of when, where, or how learning occurs (Luckin et al., 2016). These platforms monitor student activity in real time, analyze performance patterns, and deliver immediate, personalized feedback embedded within the flow of learning tasks. This seamless integration transforms feedback from a periodic intervention into a persistent and responsive learning companion.

Personalization of Learning Feedback

Personalization of Learning Feedback enhances learner engagement by aligning instructional support with each student's unique needs, preferences, and pace of learning. When AI-powered systems tailor feedback, content, and pacing based on real-time learner data, they help ensure that students are neither overwhelmed by tasks that are too difficult nor disengaged by material that is too easy. This alignment supports differentiated instruction, a core principle of effective teaching that seeks to meet students where they are developmentally—often referred to as their Zone of Proximal Development (ZPD) (Luckin et al., 2016). By providing customized scaffolds and adaptive challenges, personalized AI systems can promote greater cognitive engagement, intrinsic motivation, and persistence, especially in complex or self-paced learning environments.

Beyond individual engagement, personalization also enables targeted educational interventions that address systemic inequities and reduce persistent achievement gaps. Students from historically underserved groups—such as English learners, students with disabilities, and those from low-income backgrounds—often face barriers to receiving timely and individualized feedback due to large class sizes or limited instructional resources. AI systems, when designed with equity-oriented frameworks, can help mitigate these disparities by delivering real-time, data-informed feedback and resources tailored to each learner's needs and context (Holmes et al., 2019). For example, intelligent tutoring systems can offer multilingual support, culturally relevant examples, or scaffolded explanations that align with students' prior knowledge and linguistic backgrounds.

When combined with educator oversight and ethical design, these tools become powerful allies in fostering inclusive learning environments where all students—regardless of background—can access high-quality, personalized support. Ultimately, the integration of AI-driven personalization in education holds the potential not just to improve academic performance, but also to promote educational equity and ensure that every learner has the opportunity to succeed.

Encouraging Self-Regulated Learning

AI-driven feedback plays a pivotal role in fostering self-regulated learning (SRL) by helping students take greater ownership of their cognitive, motivational, and behavioral processes throughout the learning cycle. Self-regulated learners actively engage in goal-setting, strategic planning, performance monitoring, and self-reflection, rather than relying solely on external instruction. Intelligent feedback systems—powered by artificial intelligence—can support these processes by delivering timely, personalized prompts that encourage learners to evaluate their understanding, identify obstacles, and adapt their learning strategies in real time.

According to Zimmerman (2002), SRL unfolds across three cyclical phases: forethought, performance, and self-reflection. AI tools can facilitate each phase by providing relevant and actionable feedback at the right moment. During the forethought phase, AI systems might prompt learners to set specific goals or choose learning paths based on prior performance. In the performance phase, AI can track learner engagement, detect off-task behavior, and provide hints or scaffolds that promote task persistence and strategic thinking. Finally, in the self-reflection phase, intelligent feedback systems can generate analytics dashboards or reflective prompts—such as "What did you find most challenging in this task?" or "How would you approach this problem differently next time?" to promote metacognitive evaluation and iterative improvement.

By embedding SRL-supportive feedback mechanisms into learning environments, AI empowers students to become more autonomous, strategic, and resilient learners. This is especially critical in online and blended settings, where the absence of immediate instructor guidance may leave students without the structure and feedback they need to stay motivated and on track. When AI systems are thoughtfully designed to promote SRL, they not only enhance academic outcomes but also help cultivate the lifelong learning skills essential for success in dynamic and complex environments.

Enhancing Student Motivation and Confidence

Research suggests that well-designed feedback can have significant motivational benefits. AI feedback tools can offer encouragement, praise, and motivational scaffolding when students succeed or persist after failure (Shute, 2008). Some systems include gamified feedback mechanisms such as badges, streaks, or leaderboards, which reinforce engagement. When feedback is framed positively and includes actionable steps, students are more likely to feel competent and maintain a growth mindset (Dweck, 2006). The immediacy and low-stakes nature of AI feedback can encourage risk-taking and reduce anxiety. Students can revise and improve their work in private before receiving formal evaluations, which is particularly empowering for learners with low academic confidence or those from non-dominant linguistic backgrounds (Wambsganss et al., 2021).

Supporting Teachers and Reducing Workload

Educators who integrate AI tools effectively into their instructional practice report a range of professional and pedagogical benefits, especially in hybrid and fully online teaching environments. One of the most commonly cited advantages is the reduction in grading fatigue, a challenge that often arises from managing large volumes of student work, particularly in writing-intensive or assessment-heavy courses. AI-powered tools such as automated grading systems, intelligent writing assistants, and formative assessment platforms can significantly streamline the evaluation process by handling routine, objective, or lower-level feedback tasks—such as grammar corrections, multiple-choice assessments, or rubric-based scoring. This automation allows educators to redirect their time and energy toward more strategic, human-centered aspects of teaching, such as lesson planning, curriculum development, and individualized student support (Holstein et al., 2019).

Beyond logistical efficiency, AI also enhances consistency and equity in student communication. In virtual and asynchronous learning environments, where students may reach out at varying times and from different locations, AI chatbots or virtual teaching assistants can provide reliable, 24/7 responses to frequently asked questions, assignment clarifications, or technical issues. This ensures that all students—regardless of schedule or time zone—receive timely and accurate information, which contributes to a more supportive and responsive learning environment.

In addition, AI can assist educators in conducting more granular and data-informed assessments. Through learning analytics, natural language processing, and pattern recognition, AI systems can identify subtle trends in student performance that may otherwise go unnoticed. For example, an AI-enhanced dashboard might reveal that a student consistently struggles with inferential reasoning in reading tasks or has difficulty applying mathematical concepts in real-world scenarios. These insights enable targeted interventions that are responsive to individual needs, allowing teachers to adapt instruction or provide supplemental resources at the right time. In this way, AI serves not just as a timesaving tool, but as a diagnostic partner that empowers educators to make more informed, proactive decisions that enhance student learning outcomes (Ifenthaler & Yau, 2020).

Summary

AI-driven feedback provides a host of pedagogical advantages, including speed, personalization, motivation, and support for learner autonomy. It also plays a crucial role in enabling teachers to manage workloads and maintain instructional quality at scale. These benefits, when aligned with educational goals and supported by thoughtful design, can significantly enhance teaching and learning experiences across all levels of education.

CHALLENGES AND ETHICAL CONSIDERATIONS

While AI-powered feedback systems offer considerable promise for improving learning, their deployment in educational settings is not without significant challenges. The effectiveness and fairness of AI feedback depend heavily on how these technologies are designed, implemented, and regulated. Without careful oversight, AI tools can unintentionally reinforce inequalities, infringe on privacy, reduce pedagogical nuance, and shift control away from educators and learners. This section explores the major ethical concerns associated with AI feedback systems—

emphasizing issues of bias, data privacy, automation bias, quality of feedback, and broader societal impacts.

Algorithmic Bias and Fairness

One of the most pressing challenges in the implementation of AI in education is the presence of algorithmic bias, which occurs when machine learning models trained on skewed or non-representative data sets reinforce existing societal inequalities. In educational feedback systems, this bias can manifest in several problematic ways. Language-based discrimination is a notable concern, as AI tools may undervalue or misinterpret responses written in non-standard dialects or by English language learners. For example, African American Vernacular English (AAVE) or regionally influenced expressions are often flagged as "incorrect" or "unclear" by writing feedback systems, despite being grammatically coherent within their linguistic context (Blodgett et al., 2020). Similarly, students with disabilities or neurodiverse learners may engage with digital platforms in atypical ways—such as using speech-to-text software, alternative pacing, or non-linear navigation—leading to misclassification or the provision of irrelevant, unhelpful feedback.

AI systems can reflect cultural biases by favoring dominant norms of writing style, argumentation, and voice. This can result in low ratings for essays or responses that draw from culturally grounded rhetorical traditions or present critical perspectives outside mainstream paradigms, even when the content demonstrates depth and originality (Benjamin, 2019). These disparities underscore the need for inclusive design, critical data practices, and human oversight to ensure AI tools in education support rather than marginalize diverse learners. The solution lies in adopting inclusive design principles—incorporating diverse training datasets, involving multicultural and multilingual educators in system development, and conducting regular bias audits. Developers must also make algorithms interpretable and allow users to report and contest unfair feedback (Holstein et al., 2020; Binns, 2018).

Data Privacy, Consent, and Surveillance

Key ethical concerns surrounding the use of AI in education center on data privacy, consent, and surveillance. One major issue is the lack of informed consent, as students are often unaware of what personal data is being collected, how long it will be stored, and who may access it. This lack of transparency undermines student autonomy and raises questions about digital rights in educational environments. A related concern involves third-party data sharing, where educational platforms may transmit student data to commercial entities—sometimes for advertising purposes or product development—without clearly disclosing these practices to users. Even more troubling is the rise of surveillance-based technologies, such as remote proctoring software that monitors eye movement, facial expressions, or background noise during assessments. While intended to uphold academic integrity, these tools often feel invasive and can trigger surveillance anxiety, particularly among students in unstable or crowded home environments. Furthermore, such technologies may misinterpret cultural behaviors—such as avoiding direct eye contact or moving frequently—as indicators of dishonesty or disengagement, disproportionately affecting students from marginalized or diverse backgrounds (Williamson & Piattoeva, 2020; Selwyn et al., 2021). These ethical dilemmas highlight the urgent need for transparent policies, student-centered data governance, and critical scrutiny of how AI is implemented in educational settings.To address these concerns, institutions must ensure transparency, data minimization, and student autonomy. Policies should require opt-in participation, clearly communicate data practices, and ensure compliance with legal standards like FERPA, GDPR, and COPPA (Slade & Prinsloo, 2013).

Automation Bias and Over-Reliance

Automation bias refers to the undue trust that individuals place in algorithmic outputs, often leading to over-reliance on AI systems at the expense of independent judgment and critical thinking. In educational contexts, this bias can have several detrimental effects. For instance, students may accept AI-generated feedback without question, even when it conflicts with their original intentions, voice, or creative choices. Similarly, teachers may defer to AI-generated scores or comments, diminishing their active role in the assessment process and reducing opportunities for pedagogical insight. At the institutional level, administrators may rely heavily on algorithmic data to make high-stakes decisions—such as student placement, performance evaluation, or curriculum adjustments—thereby fostering rigid, impersonal educational practices that overlook the nuanced needs of learners (Winkler & Söllner, 2018). A key strategy for mitigating automation bias is the development and adoption of explainable AI (XAI) systems that provide transparent reasoning or justifications alongside their outputs. This enables users to evaluate the basis of AI decisions rather than accepting them at face value. Equally important is equipping educators with the training necessary to engage critically and contextually with AI tools—using them as complementary resources rather than as substitutes for professional expertise and human judgment (Kraemer et al., 2011).

DESIGNING EFFECTIVE AI FEEDBACK SYSTEMS

The success of AI feedback in education hinges not only on technological sophistication but also on thoughtful pedagogical design, user experience, and ethical integration. Effective AI feedback systems must balance automation with human judgment, align with curricular objectives, and support diverse learners (U.S. Department of Education, Office of Educational Technology, 2023). This section outlines the key principles for designing effective AI feedback systems across four major domains: alignment with learning goals, user-centered design, iterative testing, and human-AI collaboration.

Aligning Feedback with Learning Objectives

For feedback to be effective in enhancing student learning, it must be explicitly aligned with well-defined learning objectives. When feedback is directly tied to the goals and criteria of a task, it provides learners with clear, actionable information about how to improve and what success looks like. This alignment helps ensure that feedback supports both formative assessment—guiding ongoing learning—and summative assessment, measuring final achievement (Hattie & Timperley, 2007). Misaligned feedback, in contrast, can confuse students, leading them to focus on irrelevant aspects of a task or misunderstand what is expected. AI-powered feedback systems must be carefully designed to reflect this alignment by referencing curricular standards, assessment rubrics, and cognitive skill levels, such as those outlined in Bloom's taxonomy (Shute, 2008). For example, in writing instruction, feedback should vary depending on whether the objective is to improve grammar, structure, argumentation, or creativity. When aligned with instructional goals, feedback not only supports academic achievement but also promotes self-regulated learning, as students gain insight into their progress and how to close the gap between current and desired performance (Sadler, 1989). Thus, aligning AI-generated feedback with learning objectives is essential for ensuring pedagogical relevance and optimizing student outcomes.

User-Centered and Inclusive Design

A foundational principle in the design of educational technology is user-centeredness—the practice of developing tools *with* and *for* the people who will use them. In the context of AI feedback systems, this principle emphasizes the importance of involving a broad range of stakeholders—including students, teachers, instructional designers, and accessibility experts—throughout the design and implementation process (Holstein et al., 2019; Luckin et al., 2016). Effective, user-centered AI feedback tools must prioritize accessibility, ensuring compatibility with screen readers, voice commands, and other assistive technologies, while also using clear and inclusive language free of unnecessary jargon (U.S. Department of Education, 2023). Additionally, systems should offer personalization options, allowing users to tailor the style, format, and frequency of feedback to their individual preferences. For instance, some students may benefit from concise, text-based prompts, whereas others might respond better to visual cues or spoken explanations (Følstad & Brandtzæg, 2017). Equally important is cultural responsiveness: AI systems must respect linguistic diversity, avoid penalizing non-standard dialects, and recognize the legitimacy of diverse cultural expressions in communication and writing (Benjamin, 2019; Blodgett et al., 2020). By centering user needs and contexts, AI feedback systems can become more inclusive, equitable, and effective in supporting meaningful learning experiences. Involving end-users in co-design workshops, beta testing, and feedback loops ensures that systems meet real-world needs and reduce barriers to equitable adoption (Holstein et al., 2019).

Human-AI Collaboration

The most effective educational feedback systems are not fully automated, but rather hybrid models that integrate the strengths of both human educators and AI technologies. This approach, commonly referred to as "AI-human complementarity," emphasizes that AI should support—not replace—the educator's role, enhancing feedback processes without diminishing human judgment or pedagogical relationships. In practical terms, this model can take several forms). For example, AI might generate initial feedback on a student's draft, identifying structural or grammatical issues, while the teacher adds deeper commentary that offers encouragement, clarifies content misunderstandings, or addresses conceptual nuances. In high-stakes assessments, teachers may review and approve AI-generated scores or annotations to ensure accuracy and fairness (Holstein & Aleven, 2021. Additionally, students might use AI tools for self-assessment—receiving immediate insights about their work—before discussing their interpretations with peers or instructors to deepen understanding. To facilitate meaningful human-AI collaboration, it is essential to design transparent interfaces that reveal how the AI reached its conclusions—such as referencing rubric criteria, linking to specific learning objectives, or explaining the rationale behind its suggestions. This transparency empowers both teachers and students to question, interpret, and learn from AI feedback, transforming it from a static judgment into an interactive learning resource (Weller et al., 2020).

Summary

Designing effective AI feedback systems requires a fusion of technological, pedagogical, and ethical expertise. Systems must align with learning goals, prioritize user needs, evolve through feedback, and complement rather than replace human instruction. When developed with care and intentionality, AI feedback systems can become powerful allies in fostering responsive, equitable, and learner-centered education.

THE FUTURE OF AI FEEDBACK

As artificial intelligence technologies advance, their role in delivering meaningful, personalized, and equitable feedback in education will become more sophisticated and impactful. AI feedback will increasingly serve not just as a corrective tool, but as a catalyst for student empowerment, cultural relevance, and pedagogical transformation. This section examines emerging trends in AI feedback systems—highlighting key innovations such as multimodal feedback, emotion-aware interactions, dialogic exchanges, and equity-centered design—and considers how these developments can reshape the future of teaching and learning.

Multimodal Feedback Systems

Multimodal AI feedback systems integrate various sensory inputs—such as speech, facial expressions, gestures, and gaze—to provide context-aware and embodied feedback. These systems transcend the limits of text-based feedback, allowing learners to interact with AI in ways that resemble human-to-human communication.

In language acquisition, tools like ELSA Speak evaluate pronunciation and intonation by analyzing acoustic signals and visual cues from mouth movements, offering real-time feedback that supports fluency and accent reduction. In STEM education, intelligent tutoring systems embedded in virtual laboratories use gesture tracking and motion sensors to detect procedural errors during simulated experiments, providing timely correction and scaffolding. Similarly, in performing arts and physical education, AI-powered systems like Kinetisense or Move.ai analyze posture, balance, and movement to provide formative feedback on technique and form.

Multimodal systems draw upon computer vision, audio signal processing, and sensor-based analytics to interpret complex learner behaviors and respond accordingly (Oviatt et al., 2018). As edge computing and cloud-based AI accelerate, the feasibility of real-time multimodal interaction in classroom and remote settings will expand—reinforcing active, hands-on learning aligned with experiential and constructivist paradigms.

Emotion-Aware AI and Affective Feedback

Affective computing—AI's capacity to detect and respond to emotional states—is another frontier in personalized learning feedback. These systems analyze paralinguistic signals such as tone, typing rhythm, eye movement, and facial expressions to identify emotional cues including frustration, boredom, or engagement (D'Mello & Graesser, 2012). Affective feedback enhances learner motivation and resilience by adjusting instructional strategies in response to perceived emotional states. For instance, an AI tutor might increase encouragement when a student appears disheartened or switch to a more challenging task when signs of boredom are detected. Moreover, it can modulate tone, simulate empathetic reactions (e.g., "You're doing great—let's try a new strategy"), and offer emotionally supportive scaffolds in moments of cognitive struggle (Calvo & D'Mello, 2010).

Feedback as Dialogic Interaction

One of the most transformative developments in AI-powered educational feedback is the shift from unidirectional correction to dialogic and conversational engagement. Rather than simply informing students whether their answers are right or wrong, advanced AI tools—particularly those powered by large language models (LLMs) such as GPT-4—now have the capacity to engage learners in reflective, back-and-forth discussions that closely resemble Socratic inquiry. This conversational mode of feedback encourages students to articulate their thought processes, thereby fostering metacognitive awareness. It also stimulates critical thinking by presenting alternative viewpoints, identifying contradictions, and prompting students to refine or reconsider their arguments. Moreover, by encouraging learners to apply knowledge across varied contexts, such feedback enhances transferable learning, helping students internalize concepts more deeply and flexibly (Chaudhri et al., 2023; Zhai, 2022). As a result, AI feedback is evolving from a corrective function into a collaborative learning partner, supporting cognitive development in more personalized and intellectually engaging ways.

Equity-Driven and Culturally Responsive Feedback

Designing AI feedback tools that are equitable and culturally responsive is a moral and pedagogical imperative (Grab, 2025). Historically, AI systems have reproduced societal biases embedded in training data, marginalizing students who do not conform to dominant cultural norms. As Benjamin (2019) powerfully argues, algorithmic systems are not neutral—they are shaped by the cultural, political, and historical forces embedded in the data and design choices behind them. In educational contexts, this means that without intentional intervention, AI tools can inadvertently reinforce systemic inequities, particularly for students from linguistically and culturally diverse backgrounds. The future of educational technology, therefore, demands a proactive reimagining of how AI can affirm—rather than suppress—learner diversity. This involves moving beyond surface-level inclusion to embedding cultural responsiveness, fairness, and accessibility at the core of AI design. Scholars such as Noble (2018) and Blodgett et al. (2020) emphasize the importance of addressing algorithmic bias in systems that shape how learners are assessed, supported, and categorized. For AI to serve as a force for educational justice, developers must involve marginalized communities in co-design processes, incorporate linguistically inclusive models, and implement transparency tools that reveal how decisions are made. Furthermore, frameworks like Universal Design for Learning (UDL) provide guidance for ensuring that AI systems support a broad spectrum of learning styles and abilities (CAST, 2018). Through these measures, AI can be transformed from a mechanism of exclusion into a catalyst for equity, voice, and cultural affirmation in the classroom.

Summary

The future of AI-driven feedback holds immense potential to transform learning experiences by making them more context-aware, empathetic, interactive, and equitable. As these technologies continue to evolve, the focus must shift from merely achieving technical efficiency to embracing human-centered design principles that prioritize the needs, values, and well-being of learners. Effective AI feedback should do more than correct errors—it should recognize and respond to learner emotions, foster motivation, and create opportunities for dialogic reflection that supports deeper understanding. Moreover, it should be sensitive to cultural identity and play a proactive role in challenging structural inequities rather than reinforcing them. This vision can only be realized if feedback systems are grounded in robust pedagogical theory, uphold ethical integrity, and are designed to empower learners as active agents in their educational journeys. When developed with these guiding principles, AI has the potential not just to enhance academic performance, but to humanize the feedback experience—transforming it into a medium of connection, affirmation, and growth.

CONCLUSION – HUMANIZING AI FEEDBACK IN EDUCATION

As artificial intelligence continues to reshape the educational landscape, feedback remains one of its most transformative and consequential domains. The capacity of AI systems to deliver timely, personalized, and scalable feedback represents a major evolution in instructional practice, particularly in an era defined by digital learning, global student populations, and the imperative for flexible, learner-centered pathways. Yet the ultimate value of AI feedback systems will not lie in their computational speed or analytic precision—but in their alignment with the human-centered values that make learning meaningful.

At its core, educational feedback is not merely transactional; it is relational, affective, and developmental. It involves not just identifying errors but cultivating insight, affirming learner identity, encouraging resilience, and sparking curiosity. Decades of research confirm that effective feedback fosters student motivation, enhances self-regulation, and deepens metacognitive awareness (Nicol & Macfarlane-Dick, 2006; Shute, 2008). These qualities require more than automation—they demand empathy, contextual awareness, and pedagogical intent.

Despite these gains, AI-driven feedback systems are not neutral. Their algorithms reflect the data on which they were trained and the assumptions of their designers. Without careful design, they can reproduce biases, misunderstand emotions, or reduce complex student responses to reductive scores. As Selwyn (2019) warns, educational technologies often advance under a logic of efficiency and surveillance rather than equity and care.

To ensure AI feedback systems truly enhance education, educational institutions and edtech developers must center three guiding imperatives: pedagogical soundness, ethical integrity, and human flourishing. First, pedagogical soundness requires that AI feedback be grounded in robust learning theory and adaptable to diverse instructional contexts. Effective systems should prioritize formative and descriptive feedback, rather than limiting themselves to summative judgments, and align closely with learning goals, rubrics, and student readiness levels (Wiliam, 2011). Moreover, they should support revision, reflection, and dialogue, allowing students to iteratively improve and actively engage with feedback. Second, ethical integrity is essential to prevent harm and preserve student agency. This entails protecting data privacy, minimizing invasive surveillance practices, and auditing systems for algorithmic bias, particularly across racial, linguistic, and neurodiverse identities (Binns et al., 2018). Clear opt-out mechanisms and human-in-the-loop protocols should be embedded to allow contestation of AI-generated feedback. Institutions must invest in AI literacy initiatives that empower faculty and students to understand, question, and make informed decisions about AI use in learning environments (Holmes et al., 2022). Finally, the imperative of human flourishing reminds us that feedback should nurture the whole learner—not just cognitive achievement but also emotional well-being and personal growth. Humanizing AI feedback means designing systems with affective sensitivity, especially in contexts involving identity, self-expression, or vulnerability.

FINAL REFLECTION: CENTERING HUMANITY IN A TECHNOLOGICAL AGE

As we integrate AI into educational systems, we must remain vigilant in asking: What values are encoded in these tools? Whose voices are shaping their design? And what kinds of learning relationships are we enabling or disrupting? Feedback is not merely a technical feature; it is an educational practice rooted in trust, care, and mutual growth. The most meaningful learning occurs when students feel seen, heard, and supported. AI can support these goals—but only if we treat it not as a replacement for human presence, but as a bridge to deeper, more responsive learning relationships. To that end, the future of AI feedback in education must be built not just on what is technologically possible, but on what is pedagogically sound, ethically responsible, and humanely attuned. The most powerful AI systems will not be those that dazzle with sophistication, but those that amplify the very best of what it means to teach and to learn.

REFERENCES

Aleven, V., McLaughlin, E. A., Glenn, R., & Koedinger, K. R. (2016). Instruction based on adaptive learning technologies. In Mayer, R. E., & Alexander, P. A. (Eds.), *Handbook of research on learning and instruction* (2nd ed., pp. 522–560). Routledge.

Attali, Y., & Burstein, J. (2006). Automated essay scoring with e-rater® V.2. *The Journal of Technology, Learning, and Assessment*, *4*(3), 1–30.

Benjamin, R. (2019). *Race after technology: Abolitionist tools for the new Jim code*. Polity Press.

Binns, R. (2018). Fairness in machine learning: Lessons from political philosophy. *Proceedings of the 2018 Conference on Fairness, Accountability, and Transparency*, 149–159.

Binns, R., Veale, M., Van Kleek, M., & Shadbolt, N. (2018). 'It's reducing a human being to a percentage': Perceptions of justice in algorithmic decisions. *Proceedings of the 2018 CHI Conference on Human Factors in Computing Systems*, 1–14. https://doi.org/DOI: 10.1145/3173574.3173951

Black, P., & Wiliam, D. (1998). Assessment and classroom learning. *Assessment in Education: Principles, Policy & Practice*, *5*(1), 7–74. DOI: 10.1080/0969595980050102

Blikstein, P., & Worsley, M. (2016). Multimodal learning analytics and education data mining: Using computational technologies to measure complex learning tasks. *Journal of Learning Analytics*, *3*(2), 220–238.

Blodgett, S. L., Barocas, S., Daumé, H.III, & Wallach, H. (2020). Language (technology) is power: A critical survey of "bias" in NLP. *Proceedings of the 58th Annual Meeting of the Association for Computational Linguistics*, 5454–5476. https://doi.org/DOI: 10.18653/v1/2020.acl-main.485

Bruner, J. S. (1966). *Toward a theory of instruction*. Harvard University Press.

Calvo, R. A., & D'Mello, S. K. (2010). Affect detection: An interdisciplinary review of models, methods, and their applications. *IEEE Transactions on Affective Computing*, *1*(1), 18–37. DOI: 10.1109/T-AFFC.2010.1

Carless, D. (2006). Differing perceptions in the feedback process. *Studies in Higher Education*, *31*(2), 219–233. DOI: 10.1080/03075070600572132

CAST. (2018). *Universal Design for Learning guidelines version 2.2*. http://udlguidelines.cast.org

Chaudhri, V. K., Reddy, S., & Stal, D. (2023). Large language models as Socratic tutors. *arXiv preprint arXiv:2303.07361*. https://doi.org//arXiv.2303.07361DOI: 10.48550

Chen, F., Lui, A. M., & Martin, P. (2016). Towards an integrated learner modeling framework using wearable, affective and physiological data. *Proceedings of the 21st International Conference on Intelligent User Interfaces*, 389–400. https://doi.org/ DOI: 10.1145/2856767.2856787

D'Mello, S. K., & Graesser, A. C. (2012). AutoTutor and affective autotutor: Learning by talking with cognitively and emotionally intelligent computers that talk back. *ACM Transactions on Interactive Intelligent Systems*, *2*(4), 1–39. DOI: 10.1145/2395123.2395128

Dweck, C. S. (2006). *Mindset: The new psychology of success*. Random House.

Ecree. (2021). *Ecree impact report: Improving writing performance at scale*. Internal publication.

Fitas, R. (2025). Inclusive education with AI: Supporting special needs and tackling language barriers. *arXiv*. https://arxiv.org/abs/2504.14120

Følstad, A., & Brandtzæg, P. B. (2017). Chatbots and the new world of HCI. *Interaction*, *24*(4), 38–42. DOI: 10.1145/3085558

Goel, A., & Polepeddi, L. (2016). Jill Watson: A virtual teaching assistant for online education. In *Proceedings of the 31st AAAI Conference on Artificial Intelligence*. https://research.cc.gatech.edu/aimosaic/sites/default/files/2017-08/Watson.pdf

Grab, M. Ö. (2025). Teaching for equity: An exploration of AI's role in culturally responsive teaching in higher education settings. *Journal of Educational Technology Research*, *38*(2), 123–145. DOI: 10.1007/s11423-025-1001-2

Graesser, A. C., Chipman, P., Haynes, B. C., & Olney, A. (2005). AutoTutor: An intelligent tutoring system with mixed-initiative dialogue. *IEEE Transactions on Education*, *48*(4), 612–618. DOI: 10.1109/TE.2005.856149

Hattie, J. (2009). *Visible learning: A synthesis of over 800 meta-analyses relating to achievement*. Routledge.

Hattie, J., & Timperley, H. (2007). The power of feedback. *Review of Educational Research*, *77*(1), 81–112. DOI: 10.3102/003465430298487

Holmes, W., Bialik, M., & Fadel, C. (2019). *Artificial intelligence in education: Promises and implications for teaching and learning*. Center for Curriculum Redesign.

Holmes, W., Bialik, M., & Fadel, C. (2022). *Artificial intelligence in education: Promises and implications for teaching and learning* (2nd ed.). Center for Curriculum Redesign.

Holstein, K., & Aleven, V. (2021). Designing for human–AI complementarity in K–12 education. *AI Magazine*, *42*(2), 23–35. DOI: 10.1002/aaai.12058

Holstein, K., McLaren, B. M., & Aleven, V. (2019). Designing for complementarity: Teacher and student needs for orchestration support in AI-enhanced classrooms. *Proceedings of the 2019 CHI Conference on Human Factors in Computing Systems*.

Holstein, K., McLaren, B. M., & Aleven, V. (2019). Co-designing a real-time classroom orchestration tool to support teacher–AI complementarity. *Journal of Learning Analytics*, *6*(2), 27–52. DOI: 10.18608/jla.2019.62.3

Holstein, K., McLaren, B. M., & Aleven, V. (2019). Designing for complementarity: Teacher and student needs for orchestration support in AI-enhanced classrooms. *Proceedings of the 2019 CHI Conference on Human Factors in Computing Systems*, 1–14. https://doi.org/DOI: 10.1145/3290605.3300831

Holstein, K., McLaren, B. M., & Aleven, V. (2020). Co-designing a real-time classroom orchestration tool to support teacher–AI complementarity. *Journal of Learning Analytics*, *7*(3), 27–47. DOI: 10.18608/jla.2020.73.3

Holstein, K., Wortman Vaughan, J., Daumé, H.III, Dudik, M., & Wallach, H. (2019). Improving fairness in machine learning systems: What do industry practitioners need? *Proceedings of the 2020 CHI Conference on Human Factors in Computing Systems*, 1–16.

Ifenthaler, D., & Yau, J. Y.-K. (2020). Utilising learning analytics for study success: Reflections on current empirical findings. *Research and Practice in Technology Enhanced Learning*, *15*(1), 1–15.

Kalyuga, S. (2007). Expertise reversal effect and its implications for learner-tailored instruction. *Educational Psychology Review*, *19*(4), 509–539. DOI: 10.1007/s10648-007-9054-3

Khan Academy. (n.d.). *AI for education*. https://www.khanacademy.org/college-careers-more/ai-for-education

Koedinger, K. R., & Corbett, A. T. (2006). Cognitive tutors: Technology bringing learning sciences to the classroom. *The Cambridge Handbook of the Learning Sciences*, 61–78.

Kraemer, F., van Overveld, C., & Peterson, M. (2011). Is there an ethics of algorithms? *Ethics and Information Technology, 13*(3), 251–260. DOI: 10.1007/s10676-010-9233-7

IXL Learning. (2021, October 21). *IXL's instructional resources: Tools to empower independent learning.*

Luckin, R., Holmes, W., Griffiths, M., & Forcier, L. B. (2016). *Intelligence unleashed: An argument for AI in education.* Pearson.

Means, B., Neisler, J., & Langer Research Associates. (2021). *Equity and online learning: Student access and success.* Digital Promise.

Nicol, D. J., & Macfarlane-Dick, D. (2006). Formative assessment and self-regulated learning: A model and seven principles of good feedback practice. *Studies in Higher Education, 31*(2), 199–218. DOI: 10.1080/03075070600572090

Noble, S. U. (2018). *Algorithms of oppression: How search engines reinforce racism.* NYU Press.

OECD. (2021). *Digital education outlook 2021: Pushing the frontiers with AI, blockchain and robots.* OECD Publishing., DOI: 10.1787/589b283f-

One to One Plus. (2023, October 3). *Personalized learning with AI: Revolutionizing K-12 education.* https://onetooneplus.com/personalized-learning-with-ai-revolutionizing-k12-education/

Oviatt, S., Graesser, A., & Cohen, P. R. (2018). *The Handbook of Multimodal-Multisensor Interfaces: Foundations, User Modeling, and Common Modality Combinations* (Vol. 2). ACM Books., DOI: 10.1145/3015783

Oviatt, S., Graesser, A., & Kapur, M. (2018). *Advances in multimodal learning analytics.* Springer.

Panadero, E., Jonsson, A., & Botella, J. (2017). Effects of self-assessment on self-regulated learning and self-efficacy: Four meta-analyses. *Educational Research Review, 22*, 74–98. DOI: 10.1016/j.edurev.2017.08.004

Pane, J. F. (2018). *Strategies for implementing personalized learning while evidence and resources are underdeveloped.* RAND Corporation., DOI: 10.7249/PE314

Pane, J. F., Griffin, B. A., McCaffrey, D. F., & Karam, R. (2017). *Effects of cognitive tutor algebra on student achievement in the Milwaukee public schools.* RAND Corporation.

Pane, J. F., Steiner, E. D., Baird, M. D., & Hamilton, L. S. (2015). *Continued progress: Promising evidence on personalized learning*. RAND Corporation.

Pane, J. F., Steiner, E. D., Baird, M. D., & Hamilton, L. S. (2017). *Continued progress: Promising evidence on personalized learning*. RAND Corporation., DOI: 10.7249/RR1365

Piaget, J. (1970). *Science of education and the psychology of the child*. Orion Press.

Popenici, S. A. D., & Kerr, S. (2017). Exploring the impact of artificial intelligence on teaching and learning in higher education. *Research and Practice in Technology Enhanced Learning*, *12*(1), 1–13. DOI: 10.1186/s41039-017-0062-8 PMID: 30595727

Roscoe, R. D., Snow, E. L., & McNamara, D. S. (2022). Intelligent writing feedback: A review and recommendations for teacher and student support. *Educational Psychologist*, *57*(1), 1–18.

Rosé, C. P., Wang, Y. C., Cui, Y., Arguello, J., Stegmann, K., Weinberger, A., & Fischer, F. (2008). Analyzing collaborative learning processes automatically: Exploiting the advances of computational linguistics in computer-supported collaborative learning. *International Journal of Computer-Supported Collaborative Learning*, *3*(3), 237–271. DOI: 10.1007/s11412-007-9034-0

Sadler, D. R. (1989). Formative assessment and the design of instructional systems. *Instructional Science*, *18*(2), 119–144. DOI: 10.1007/BF00117714

Selwyn, N. (2019). *Should robots replace teachers? AI and the future of education*. Polity Press.

Selwyn, N., Perrotta, C., Williamson, B., & Eynon, R. (2021). Surveillance in education: Mapping the landscape. *Oxford Review of Education*, *47*(3), 307–323.

Shamir, A., Mevarech, Z. R., & Gida, C. (2021). Digital adaptive learning systems in elementary math instruction. *Journal of Learning Analytics*, *8*(2), 56–74.

Shute, V. J. (2008). Focus on formative feedback. *Review of Educational Research*, *78*(1), 153–189. DOI: 10.3102/0034654307313795

Skinner, B. F. (1954). The science of learning and the art of teaching. *Harvard Educational Review*, *24*(2), 86–97.

Slade, S., & Prinsloo, P. (2013). Learning analytics: Ethical issues and dilemmas. *The American Behavioral Scientist*, *57*(10), 1510–1529. DOI: 10.1177/0002764213479366

Sweller, J. (1988). Cognitive load during problem solving: Effects on learning. *Cognitive Science*, *12*(2), 257–285. DOI: 10.1207/s15516709cog1202_4

Tubino, F., & Adachi, C. (2022). Developing feedback literacy capabilities through an AI-automated feedback tool. *ResearchGate*. https://www.researchgate.net/publication/365678797_Developing_feedback_literacy_capabilities_through_an_AI_automated_feedback_tool

U.S. Department of Education, Office of Educational Technology. (2023). Artificial intelligence and the future of teaching and learning: Insights and recommendations. https://tech.ed.gov/ai/

VanLehn, K. (2006). The behavior of tutoring systems. *International Journal of Artificial Intelligence in Education, 16*(3), 227–265.

VanLehn, K. (2011). The relative effectiveness of human tutoring, intelligent tutoring systems, and other tutoring systems. *Educational Psychologist, 46*(4), 197–221. DOI: 10.1080/00461520.2011.611369

Viberg, O., Hatakka, M., Bälter, O., & Mavroudi, A. (2018). The current landscape of learning analytics in higher education. *Computers in Human Behavior, 89*, 98–110. DOI: 10.1016/j.chb.2018.07.027

Vygotsky, L. S. (1978). *Mind in society: The development of higher psychological processes*. Harvard University Press.

Wambsganss, T., Niklaus, C., Cetto, M., & Bernstein, A. (2021). AL: An automated system for generating actionable feedback from peer reviews. *Proceedings of the ACM on Human-Computer Interaction*, 5(CSCW1), 1–29. https://doi.org/DOI: 10.1145/3449206

Wambsganss, T., Niklaus, C., Cetto, M., Söllner, M., & Weinhardt, C. (2021). Can AI-based feedback improve learning? Evidence from a field experiment. *Proceedings of the 54th Hawaii International Conference on System Sciences*, 15, 61–70. https://doi.org/DOI: 10.1080/17439884.2020.1798995

Wambsganss, T., Niklaus, C., Czerwinski, D., & Reichert, M. (2021). Towards automated feedback generation for open-ended questions in large-scale educational settings. *International Journal of Artificial Intelligence in Education, 31*(2), 323–351.

Wang, Y., Heffernan, N. T., & Heffernan, C. L. (2022). The evolving landscape of AI in education: Learning analytics, feedback, and personalized learning. *Educational Technology Research and Development, 70*(3), 911–933.

Watson, J. B. (1913). Psychology as the behaviorist views it. *Psychological Review, 20*(2), 158–177. DOI: 10.1037/h0074428

Weller, M., Jordan, K., & Farrow, R. (2020). Ethical dimensions of educational technology. In Spector, M., Ifenthaler, D., & Isaias, P. (Eds.), *Learning technology for education challenges* (pp. 25–36). Springer.

Wiliam, D. (2011). *Embedded formative assessment*. Solution Tree Press.

Williamson, B., & Eynon, R. (2020). Historical threads, missing links, and future directions in AI in education. *Learning, Media and Technology*, *45*(3), 223–235. DOI: 10.1080/17439884.2020.1798995

Williamson, B., & Eynon, R. (2020). Historical threads, missing links, and future directions in AI in education. *Learning, Media and Technology*, *45*(3), 223–235. DOI: 10.1080/17439884.2020.1798995

Williamson, B., & Piattoeva, N. (2020). Objectivity as standardization in data-scientific educational governance: Grasping the global through the local. *Research in Education*, *101*(1), 69–91.

Williamson, B., & Piattoeva, N. (2020). Objectivity as standardization in data-scientific education policy, technology and governance. *Learning, Media and Technology*, *45*(1), 64–76.

Wilson, C., Lan, A. S., & Baraniuk, R. G. (2021). Improving automated feedback for short-answer questions through adversarial example generation. *Proceedings of the AAAI Conference on Artificial Intelligence*, *35*(15), 13517–13525.

Winkler, R., & Hermann, T. (2019). Feedback technologies for learning. In Ifenthaler, D. (Ed.), *Digital transformation of learning organizations* (pp. 33–49). Springer.

Winkler, R., & Hermann, T. (2019). A systematic review of AI-based education support systems. *International Journal of Artificial Intelligence in Education*, *29*(2), 205–237. DOI: 10.1007/s40593-018-00175-4

Winkler, R., & Söllner, M. (2018). Unleashing the potential of chatbots in education: A state-of-the-art analysis. *Proceedings - Academy of Management*, *2018*(1), 10615.

Zhai, X. (2022). ChatGPT: A challenger or a facilitator? *AI and Ethics*, *3*, 219–221. DOI: 10.1007/s43681-022-00180-5

Zhang, H., Litman, D., & Heilman, M. (2020). Improving automated writing evaluation with discourse-aware neural models. *Transactions of the Association for Computational Linguistics*, *8*, 236–251.

Zimmerman, B. J. (2002). Becoming a self-regulated learner: An overview. *Theory into Practice*, *41*(2), 64–70. DOI: 10.1207/s15430421tip4102_2

Chapter 11
Co-Designing With AI: Human-Centered Approaches for Future-Ready Course Design

Eun-Ok Baek
https://orcid.org/0000-0002-0697-6763
California State University, San Bernardino, USA

Tracy Medrano
California State University, San Bernardino, USA

ABSTRACT

As AI technologies continue to evolve, they are reshaping the educational landscape and opening new possibilities for curriculum innovation and course design. While AI has traditionally supported task automation—such as grading, content generation, and revision—this chapter repositions AI as a collaborative partner in instructional design. Rather than viewing AI as a tool that mimics human functions, we propose embracing it as a co-designer that enhances the expertise of educators and instructional designers. We advocate a human-centered, intentional application of AI through meaningful prompts, adaptive workflows, and sound pedagogical strategies. Grounded in foundational instructional design models—Backward Design, ADDIE, and Gagné's Nine Events—and aligned with frameworks such as Bloom's Taxonomy, QM, QLT, and UDL, this chapter offers a learner-centered approach. Through case studies and practical examples, we show how AI can help create inclusive, engaging, and innovative courses while maintaining pedagogical integrity and instructional excellence.

DOI: 10.4018/979-8-3373-2397-8.ch011

INTRODUCTION

The rapid advancements in artificial intelligence (AI) are creating unprecedented opportunities for innovation in course design. AI isn't just a passing trend; it's actively reshaping the educational landscape and challenging us to rethink how courses are imagined and built. Yet simply plugging AI into existing workflows isn't enough. To truly unlock its potential, we need thoughtful strategies that integrate AI into the instructional design process while keeping human judgment, creativity, and pedagogical intent firmly at the center.

Traditionally, AI has been viewed as a tool for automation, streamlining processes, and administrative tasks. However, its transformative power extends far beyond efficiency, with emerging research highlighting AI's growing role in supporting more adaptive, creative, and learner-centered approaches to education (Ch'ng, 2023). Imagine AI not just as a tool, but as a creative partner, one that collaborates with educators and instructional designers to create meaningful learning experiences.

In this chapter, we'll explore how crafting meaningful prompts and developing adaptive workflows can turn AI from a passive tool into an active co-designer. By aligning AI capabilities with well-established instructional design models, such as Backward Design, ADDIE, and Gagné's Nine Events of Instruction, and anchoring our efforts in pedagogical best practices, we can create a synergy where AI augments, rather than replaces, human expertise. Throughout the chapter, contributions from instructional designers and AI experts showcase practical approaches for integrating AI in ways that are ethical, learner-centered, and aligned with established quality standards. These standards include Quality Matters (QM), a research-based rubric and global leader in online course design and quality assurance, and Quality Learning and Teaching (QLT), a research-based rubric and faculty development framework developed by the California State University (CSU) system. This chapter presents a methodological approach, supported by practical strategies and examples, to help educators and instructional designers harness AI's creative potential in building courses that are innovative, inclusive, and ready to meet the future of learning.

THE NEED FOR HUMANIZING AI IN COURSE DESIGN

As AI becomes an increasingly prevalent tool in education, its role in course design is rapidly evolving. AI has the potential to streamline content creation, enhance instructional effectiveness, and personalize learning experiences in ways that were once unimaginable (Luckin, Holmes, Griffiths, & Forcier, 2016; U.S. Department of Education, 2023). However, for learners to truly benefit, it is critical that AI serves as an extension of pedagogical intent rather than a replacement for human educators (Luckin et al., 2016; U.S. Department of Education, 2023).

Humanizing AI in course design means ensuring that technology amplifies human creativity, empathy, and intentional instructional planning (Lang-Raad, 2024). It requires more than efficient content production; it demands that educators thoughtfully guide AI to support student-centered learning, foster inclusivity, and uphold ethical practices. Without thoughtful human oversight, AI risks generating content that, while technically correct, may lack cultural awareness, relational depth, or meaningful alignment to learning goals. AI models are trained on vast datasets that do not inherently account for the diverse backgrounds, lived experiences, and emotional needs of learners (Wei, 2024). As a result, AI-generated content might unintentionally reinforce stereotypes, overlook inclusive perspectives, or fail to create the sense of connection and belonging that effective teaching requires.

Furthermore, AI lacks the ability to prioritize pedagogical strategies, such as scaffolding, critical thinking development, or formative feedback that are essential for deep, continuous learning. Without human educators and instructional designers actively reviewing, curating, and shaping AI outputs, there is a risk that course design becomes a surface-level exercise in efficiency, rather than a deliberate process of fostering engagement and helping learners build deep, meaningful understanding that they can apply beyond the classroom.

Understanding AI's impact on course design is essential to using it wisely and meaningfully. Human-centered approaches are needed to shape how AI is integrated, ensuring that the learning experience remains authentic and guided by educational and instructional design best practices (Lang-Raad, 2024). This chapter explores three critical areas for achieving this balance: the impact of AI on course design, the distinction between AI as a tool and AI as a co-designer, and the importance of guiding AI through meaningful prompts and adaptive workflows.

Impact of AI on Course Design

As we begin to thoughtfully integrate AI into course creation, it's important to first understand how AI is already influencing the design process itself. Course design has traditionally been understood as a human-centered endeavor, grounded in creativity (crafting engaging content and experiences), empathy (understanding learners' needs and challenges), and intentional planning (aligning objectives, assessments, activities, etc.) (Branch, 2009; Gagné et al., 2005; Wiggins & McTighe, 2005).

Today, however, AI is stepping into this space, not to replace the human element, but to expand what's possible. AI is now shaping how courses are imagined, developed, and delivered. From enhancing personalization to streamlining traditional workflows, its influence is opening new doors for innovation. When thoughtfully integrated, AI can support educators and instructional designers in both the design and delivery of instruction, helping to enhance efficiency, spark creativity, strengthen engagement, and provide stronger support for learners.

According to the ARCHED framework, a human-centered approach to AI-supported instructional design, these tools can assist with a wide range of tasks during the course design process (Li et al., 2025), including:

- Crafting clear and measurable learning objectives by suggesting action verbs tied to Bloom's Taxonomy and inferring the cognitive complexity or depth of knowledge intended.
- Analyzing and verifying alignment across learning objectives, instructional activities, and assessments to ensure a coherent, purposeful learning experience that promotes mastery.
- Recommending or generating instructional materials, such as videos, readings, simulations, and interactive media, that are directly linked to the desired learning outcomes and designed to engage diverse learners.
- Suggesting appropriate assessment types, including both formative and summative options, that align with course outcomes and encourage authentic demonstrations of learning rather than just memorization.
- Proposing active learning strategies (e.g., case-based learning, group projects, problem-solving exercises, scenarios-based activities) that are intentionally aligned to course content, learner characteristics, and support cognitive development and higher-order thinking skills.
- Advancing accessibility by generating transcripts, captions, alt text, simplified language summaries, and multilingual translations helping to break down barriers to learning and reinforce Universal Design for Learning (UDL) principles, while ensuring that diverse learner needs are anticipated and addressed through thoughtful course design.

In addition to design tasks, AI can play a transformative role in **personalizing instruction and scaffolding learning** through adaptive feedback systems, content differentiation, and real-time learner support (Sajja et al., 2024). These capabilities may include:

- Providing tiered support, such as step-by-step explanations, just-in-time hints, or guiding questions to help students tackle complex content at their own pace.
- Generating differentiated versions of content to meet learners at various readiness levels or with different learning preferences.

- Offering feedback loops by providing students with formative feedback on drafts, assignments, or quizzes before final submission, encouraging iterative improvement deeper self-reflection, and growth mindset development.
- Monitoring learner progress and identifying patterns of misunderstanding, enabling instructors to intervene early with targeted support rather than waiting for formal assessments.
- Recommending learning pathways, supplemental resources, or enrichment opportunities based on student performance or interest.

In the delivery of instruction, AI can enhance student learning through real-time feedback, personalization, and intelligent support tools (Jabbour et al., 2025). AI tools can be used to:

- Provide real-time feedback to students on low-stakes assessments, writing drafts, coding exercises, or practice problems, helping them revise and grow independently.
- Facilitate personalized learning experiences by adjusting the pace, content, or resources based on learner data or performance trends.
- Act as a virtual teaching assistant, answering frequently asked questions, explaining complex concepts in different ways, or guiding students through problem-solving processes.
- Support discussion and reflection by suggesting prompts, summarizing student responses, or even helping students expand on their ideas with probing questions.
- Automate routine communication, such as reminders, progress check-ins, or summaries of class announcements, to free up instructor time for meaningful interactions.
- Enhance student engagement with interactive tools like AI-powered chatbots, simulations, and adaptive quizzes that respond to student input.
- Support multilingual learners with instant translation, simplified language support, or culturally relevant examples that make content more relatable and accessible.
- Encourage metacognition by prompting students to reflect on what they've learned, what they still find challenging, and what strategies they might use next.

When AI is thoughtfully integrated into both course design and delivery, it can help educators create more inclusive, engaging, and adaptive learning environments. It can serve as a creative partner amplifying the strengths of human educators. While AI brings efficiency, scalability, and creative possibilities, its use must always be guided by clear instructional goals, ethical considerations, and a commitment to student success. When used purposefully, AI tools not only save time; they unlock new possibilities for reaching and supporting every learner, creating educational experiences that are not just efficient, but truly transformative.

AI as a Tool vs. AI as a Co-Designer

As we continue exploring the need for humanizing AI in course design, it becomes critical to distinguish how AI can be positioned within the educational process. AI can serve as a powerful partner, but its role depends entirely on how thoughtfully and intentionally it is integrated. Left unchecked, AI risks remaining a mere automation tool; guided by human creativity and pedagogical insight, however, it can evolve into a collaborative co-designer that supports deeper, more meaningful learning experiences.

At its most basic level, AI can assist instructional designers and educators with routine tasks, such as drafting course outlines, generating quiz questions, summarizing readings, producing visual aids, recommending instructional strategies, and suggesting accessibility enhancements. By streamlining these foundational activities, AI enables instructional designers to focus more deeply on crafting effective learning experiences and empowers educators to concentrate on high-impact practices, such as fostering deep student engagement, delivering personalized support, and building authentic relationships within the learning environment (Ch'ng, 2023).

However, the conversation around AI in education is rapidly evolving. Increasingly, AI is being viewed not merely as a support tool but as a potential creative co-designer that works alongside educators and instructional designers to shape, enhance, and personalize learning experiences (Moore et al., 2024). In this collaborative role, AI can assist by:

- Identify potential gaps in curriculum alignment;
- Suggest differentiated materials and pacing options for diverse learners;
- Adapt instructional strategies based on real-time learner data; and
- Offer recommendations for personalized learning pathways.

Understanding the distinction between these roles is essential for thoughtful AI integration:

- **AI as a tool:** Here, AI is used to automate or simplify routine. It is responsive to the input provided by educators and instructional designers but does not influence instructional direction, pedagogical decisions, or course design strategy. Think of it as an efficient assistant that saves time on operational tasks (Ch'ng, 2023).

- **AI as a co-designer:** Here, AI plays a more active and adaptive role in both course design and instructional delivery. It may suggest teaching strategies, recommend scaffolded resources, propose differentiated learning materials, or highlight areas for learner support. While AI can offer valuable insights and creative suggestions, it must be paired with the professional judgment of educators and instructional designers to ensure that all recommendations are pedagogically sound, ethically responsible, and aligned with learning goals (Ch'ng, 2023).

No matter how advanced AI becomes, the educator and instructional designer remain central to the teaching and learning process. It is the human professional who brings context, empathy, critical thinking, and ethical responsibility; qualities that AI is unable to replicate. Educators and designers set the goals, apply the pedagogical lens, and ultimately decide how, when, and why AI should be used to support student learning and success.

Humanizing AI Through Meaningful Prompts and Adaptive Workflows

To truly humanize AI in course design, educators and instructional designers must shape AI-generated content through deliberate, well-crafted prompts and structured adaptive workflows. AI outputs are only as meaningful and pedagogically sound as the quality and specificity of the input they receive. By developing intentional prompting strategies, educators and instructional designers can ensure that AI serves as a supportive tool, enhancing rather than overtaking the course design process, while maintaining the quality, relevance, and pedagogical integrity of outputs. Effective prompting practices include, but are not limited to, strategies supported by prompt engineering research (White et al., 2023), such as:

- Providing clear, specific, and context-rich instructions to avoid ambiguity and ensure that AI-generated materials align with course goals and learner needs (e.g., specifying the subject area, grade level, and instructional purpose).
- Incorporating examples or structured templates within prompts to model the desired format, style, or structure of AI outputs, leading to more organized and pedagogically sound materials.
- Using role-based prompts to guide AI to respond from a particular professional perspective (e.g., "Act as an instructional designer creating an online

module for adult learners on Universal Design for Learning"), which produces more targeted and relevant outputs.

- Setting explicit parameters and audience specifications, such as desired response length, tone, complexity, and intended student audience to tailor AI outputs for specific instructional contexts.
- Requesting step-by-step explanations or scaffolded responses for complex topics to promote clarity, logical sequencing, and instructional usability.
- Iterating and refining AI outputs through multiple prompt adjustments, using critical review to improve relevance, accuracy, inclusivity, and alignment with learning outcomes.
- Requesting multiple options when needed to encourage diverse approaches and creative possibilities in course design, allowing instructional designers and educators to select or adapt the best fit.

Ultimately, even well-constructed prompts cannot guarantee pedagogically perfect outputs. Educators and instructional designers must apply critical evaluation to AI responses, ensuring that generated materials uphold academic rigor, inclusivity, ethical standards, and alignment with learner needs and learning outcomes. AI can support creativity and efficiency, but human expertise remains essential for final review, adaptation, and meaningful instructional design.

While thoughtful prompting strategies help humanize AI during the course design phase, sustaining a human-centered approach requires more than just strong inputs. It calls for a broader, ongoing commitment to guiding AI's role throughout the entire instructional process. Successful integration depends on educators and instructional designers maintaining control over key pedagogical, ethical, and collaborative dimensions of course creation. The following section outlines essential themes that must remain at the forefront when working with AI to ensure that learning experiences remain purposeful, inclusive, and grounded in best practices.

Concluding Thoughts: Guiding Principles for Humanizing AI in Course Design

The successful integration of AI into course design requires maintaining a clear, human-centered foundation. Several key themes must remain central to guiding AI's role in educational environments:

- Pedagogical Best Practices: AI tools must be used in alignment with well-established instructional design models and evidence-based teaching strategies, ensuring that learning remains goal-oriented, structured, inclusive, and student-centered (Branch, 2009; Gagné et al., 2005; Wiggins & McTighe, 2005).

- Ethical Considerations: Educators and instructional designers must ensure transparency in the use of AI, proactively address potential biases in AI-generated materials, uphold academic integrity, and safeguard student data, privacy, and autonomy (Holmes et al., 2022; U.S. Department of Education, 2023).
- Human-AI Collaboration: Active human involvement remains essential. AI should function as a creative partner that supports instructional expertise, not a replacement for the nuanced judgment, relational insight, and ethical responsibility that educators and instructional designers bring to the learning experience (Luckin et al., 2016; Moore et al., 2024).

Understanding how AI interacts with and supports established instructional design frameworks is crucial to ensure that its integration strengthens, rather than weakens, course quality. Rather than viewing AI as a shortcut, educators and instructional designers must approach its use as an opportunity to reinforce foundational educational values while opening new avenues for creativity and personalization.

As we turn to the next section, we will explore key instructional design models and frameworks; Backward Design, ADDIE, Gagné's Nine Events of Instruction, Bloom's Taxonomy, Quality Matters (QM), and CSU Quality Learning and Teaching (QLT). We will consider how thoughtful integration of AI can enhance, rather than disrupt, the core principles that define effective teaching and learning.

THEORETICAL FOUNDATIONS FOR AI-INTEGRATED COURSE DESIGN

The successful integration of artificial intelligence (AI) into course design requires a solid grounding in established instructional design (ID) models. Instructional design models provide structured, research-based approaches for developing effective, purposeful learning experiences (Branch, 2009; Gagné et al., 2005). As AI continues to reshape educational environments, these frameworks offer essential guidance for leveraging AI tools in ways that enhance, rather than disrupt, pedagogical integrity.

According to Holmes et al. (2022), AI has the potential to streamline content creation, support differentiated instruction, and facilitate timely feedback processes. These possibilities are promising; however, the effective use of AI requires more than automation, it demands thoughtful alignment with instructional goals, learner needs, and quality assurance standards.

This section explores several key instructional design models and frameworks that can guide the meaningful integration of AI into educational environments. By grounding AI applications in models such as Backward Design, the ADDIE process, and Gagné's Nine Events of Instruction, as well as frameworks like Bloom's Taxonomy, Quality Matters (QM), and Quality Learning and Teaching (QLT), educators and instructional designers can ensure that AI-supported instruction remains learner-centered, ethically responsible, and pedagogically sound.

AI-Supported Backward Design: Starting with the End in Mind

Backward Design, developed by Wiggins and McTighe (2005), emphasizes starting with the end in mind: clearly defining learning outcomes before designing instruction and assessments. This approach ensures that every instructional decision remains anchored to what learners must ultimately know and be able to do.

Artificial intelligence (AI) tools can enhance the Backward Design process in several ways:

Identify Desired Results

- AI can assist in analyzing curriculum standards, past course data, or institutional goals to help educators articulate clear and measurable learning outcomes.
- AI language models can suggest refined wording for objectives, aligned with frameworks like Bloom's Taxonomy (Anderson & Krathwohl, 2001).

Determine Acceptable Evidence

- AI can support the creation of assessments (e.g., quizzes, performance tasks, rubrics) that align directly with the intended outcomes.
- AI can analyze learning objectives and suggest appropriate assessment formats based on cognitive complexity and learning goals.

Plan Learning Experiences and Instruction

- AI tools can recommend instructional activities, multimedia resources, or adaptive pathways that align with the desired outcomes and assessment criteria.
- AI can personalize learning sequences and support scaffolding by offering just-in-time content based on student readiness and performance data.

By applying AI thoughtfully within the Backward Design framework, educators and instructional designers can retain clarity of purpose while making use of AI's capacity to generate content, support assessment, and personalize instruction. This alignment is key to preserving pedagogical integrity while integrating new technologies (Wiggins & McTighe, 2005).

AI-Supported ADDIE: Enhancing Each Phase of the Instructional Design Process

The ADDIE process (Analysis, Design, Development, Implementation, and Evaluation) offers a flexible yet systematic approach to instructional design (Branch, 2009). AI can meaningfully support and enhance each phase of the ADDIE process:

1. **Analysis:** The goal of this phase is to **gather data** about the learners, content, goals, and context to inform design decisions. AI can support this phase by:
    - Synthesizing institutional or course data to identify learning gaps or performance trends.
    - Analyzing survey or discussion forum responses to identify learner preferences, motivations, and barriers.
    - Creating learner personas based on demographics, prior knowledge, or learning styles.
    - Conducting environmental scans or summarizing literature on best practices for similar audiences or course types.
    - Flagging potential misalignments between course goals and learner needs.
2. **Design:** This phase focuses on **planning the structure** of instruction, including learning objectives, assessments, instructional strategies, and sequencing. AI can support this phase by:
    - Recommending learning objectives aligned with Bloom's Taxonomy and course outcomes.
    - Proposing assessment types and rubrics tailored to each objective and cognitive level.
    - Suggesting instructional strategies that fit learner characteristics and course modality.
    - Assisting with mapping activities and assessments to ensure constructive alignment.
    - Generating high-level course outlines, lesson frameworks, or visual storyboards for review and refinement.
3. **Development:** The development phase involves **producing and assembling** content, media, and learning resources. AI can support this phase by:

- Drafting first versions of lectures, readings, quiz questions, or discussion prompts based on defined goals.
- Creating adaptive practice exercises or interactive media suggestions.
- Generating transcripts, alt text, and captioned media to support accessibility.
- Translating or simplifying content to support multilingual and neurodiverse learners.
- Recommending open educational resources (OER) and multimedia tools aligned with course topics.

4. **Implementation:** This phase involves the **rollout of instruction**, ensuring the learning experience is delivered effectively. AI can support this phase by:
    - Acting as a 24/7 virtual assistant or chatbot (e.g., course-specific GPTs) to address frequently asked questions, direct students to resources, or provide instant clarification on topics or assignments.
    - Monitoring learner interaction patterns and alerting instructors to disengagement or confusion.
    - Facilitating onboarding with AI-powered walkthroughs or interactive orientation modules.
    - Facilitate authentic simulations with custom GPTs where students can engage with AI-driven characters (e.g., a historical figure, a patient in a healthcare scenario, a corporate client) to practice applying course concepts in dynamic conversations. Custom GPTs can be designed to simulate real-world scenarios, act as role-playing partners, or provide personalized practice environments for students.
5. **Evaluation:** Evaluation includes both **formative** (during) and **summative** (after) assessment of course effectiveness and learner outcomes. AI can support this phase by:
    - Analyzing assessment data to identify patterns in student performance and misconceptions.
    - Collecting and summarizing student feedback from surveys or reflections.
    - Suggesting revisions to content or sequencing based on engagement metrics.
    - Generating comparison and visual reports for course improvement.
    - Supporting instructors in aligning post-course improvements with original objectives and learner outcomes.

By thoughtfully integrating AI at each phase of the ADDIE process, instructional designers and educators can streamline course development, enhance learner personalization, and strengthen alignment between objectives, activities, and assessments.

However, AI's role must remain carefully guided by pedagogical expertise to ensure that efficiency gains do not come at the expense of instructional quality or learner equity (Branch, 2009). Human creativity, critical thinking, and ethical responsibility continue to play a vital role in shaping how AI supports effective instructional design. Building on these foundations of process and structure, the next section turns to how cognitive frameworks, particularly Bloom's Taxonomy, can guide the thoughtful integration of AI in designing learning activities and assessments that promote deeper cognitive engagement.

AI-Supported Bloom's Taxonomy: Designing for Cognitive Growth and Higher-Order Thinking

Bloom's Taxonomy remains one of the most influential frameworks for categorizing cognitive skills, originally developed by Bloom and revised by Anderson and Krathwohl (2001). It organizes learning objectives into a hierarchy of increasing complexity: remember, understand, apply, analyze, evaluate, and create. Effective course design encourages learners not only to retain information but to critically analyze, synthesize, and apply their knowledge to new contexts.

AI can play a supportive role in applying Bloom's Taxonomy to both the creation of assessments and the design of learning activities. However, its use must be guided by careful instructional planning to ensure that higher-order thinking skills are authentically developed, not just superficially mimicked. Aligned with Bloom's hierarchy, AI can support educators and instructional designers in the following ways, starting with the lower-level to higher-order thinking:

Remember: Supporting Basic Recall of Knowledge

- Generating quizzes, flashcards, or knowledge checks that prompt students to recall factual information (e.g., key definitions, concepts, or dates).
- Creating review materials such as simple summaries, glossaries, or lists that reinforce foundational knowledge.

Understand: Facilitating Conceptual Comprehension

- Drafting concept maps, simplified explanations, or visual organizers that help students grasp relationships among ideas.
- Providing paraphrased versions of complex readings to promote understanding without altering core meaning.
- Suggesting comprehension questions that ask students to summarize, explain, or interpret course material in their own words.

Apply: Encouraging Use of Knowledge in New Situations

- Designing practice scenarios, case applications, or simulations where students apply theories or concepts to solve problems.
- Generating real-world examples or mini-cases for students to analyze and apply classroom concepts in different contexts.

Analyze: Promoting Critical Examination and Comparison

- Creating comparative case studies, classification tasks, or cause-effect analyses that require students to break information into parts and understand relationships.
- Suggesting guided questions that ask students to identify patterns, categorize ideas, or dissect arguments.

Evaluate: Supporting Critical Judgments and Decision-Making

- Drafting debate prompts, ethical dilemmas, or decision-making activities that encourage students to assess credibility, validity, or quality.
- Proposing rubrics or checklists that guide students in evaluating the strength of evidence or arguments.

Create: Fostering Innovation and Original Work

- Suggesting project-based assignments, design challenges, or solution proposals that ask students to synthesize information and produce original outputs.
- Generating prompts for students to develop new models, frameworks, or strategic plans based on their learning.

When used thoughtfully, AI can help educators design assessments and learning experiences that promote not just knowledge acquisition, but also critical thinking, creativity, and the ability to transfer learning across contexts (Anderson & Krathwohl, 2001). However, fostering deeper cognitive engagement requires more than aligning activities to thinking skills, it also demands careful attention to how learning is introduced, guided, practiced, and reinforced. Instructional sequencing plays a vital role in supporting learners' progression through increasingly complex cognitive tasks. The next section examines Gagné's Nine Events of Instruction, offering a guidance on how AI can be integrated to support effective learning sequences that maximize engagement, retention, and application.

AI-Supported Gagné's Nine Events of Instruction: Structuring Learning with Technology

Gagné's Nine Events of Instruction provide a structured and evidence-based sequence for designing effective learning experiences, grounded in cognitive learning theory (Gagné, Wager, Golas, & Keller, 2005). These events outline the essential steps needed to guide learners through the acquisition, application, and transfer of knowledge and skills. As artificial intelligence (AI) becomes more integrated into educational contexts, it offers new opportunities to support and enhance each instructional event while maintaining the integrity of Gagné's model.

When used thoughtfully, AI can assist educators and instructional designers in the following ways:

1. **Gain Attention:** Capture learners' curiosity and prepare them to engage cognitively.
    - **AI Support:** AI-generated multimedia, gamified activities, and adaptive simulations can create personalized attention hooks. Dynamic video introductions, AI-curated news articles, or interactive polls based on learner interests can help immediately connect content to relevance (Gagné et al., 2005).
2. **Inform Learners of Objectives:** Clarify what learners are expected to achieve.
    - **AI Support:** AI tools can help with the delivery of learning objectives by embedding objectives into course materials, video introductions, or module overviews. For example, AI can assist instructors by generating clear, learner-friendly rewordings of formal objectives or summarizing weekly learning targets in natural, conversational language. It can help highlight weekly learning objectives in natural language within module introductions, automatically linking objectives to key activities or assessments. This makes goals more accessible and easier for students to connect to their own learning journeys.
3. **Stimulate Recall of Prior Learning:** Activate existing knowledge to support new learning.
    - **AI Support:** AI can deliver spaced retrieval practice prompts, short diagnostic quizzes, or reflective questioning activities that encourage learners to recall and connect prior knowledge to the new topic.
4. **Present the Content:** Deliver instructional material clearly and engagingly.
    - **AI Support:** AI tools can help generate diversified instructional resources, such as custom videos, interactive simulations, case studies, or adaptive readings (Heir, 2023).

5. **Provide Learning Guidance:** Offer support and cues to assist learners during new tasks.
   - **AI Support:** Virtual mentors, intelligent tutoring systems, and chatbots can offer hints, guided questions, and personalized scaffolding when students struggle encouraging persistence without overwhelming them.
6. **Elicit Performance (Practice):** Allow learners to apply new knowledge and skills actively.
   - **AI Support:** AI can generate scaffolded practice exercises, simulations, or role-playing scenarios based on real-world applications. These tools can adapt in real-time, offering learners increasing challenges as their skills grow.
7. **Provide Feedback:** Deliver timely information on performance to guide improvement.
   - **AI Support:** AI-driven feedback systems can supply immediate, targeted, and personalized feedback, not just indicating correctness, but explaining why a response was correct or incorrect and suggesting next steps for growth (Holmes et al., 2022).
8. **Assess Performance:** Formally evaluate learner mastery of objectives.
   - **AI Support:** AI tools can analyze performance trends across assignments, exams, and interactions for common errors and identifying patterns in student work. This can guide instructors in providing targeted support or adjusting instruction as needed..
9. **Enhance Retention and Transfer:** Support the long-term application of knowledge beyond the course.
   - **AI Support:** AI recommends follow-up activities, generated review plans, and real-world application can help learners internalize and transfer their learning to new contexts, fostering lifelong learning skills.

Integrating AI thoughtfully within Gagné's framework can deepen learner engagement, personalize instruction, and optimize cognitive support throughout the learning journey. However, human oversight remains critical. Educators and instructional designers must continue to curate, adapt, and validate AI-supported experiences to ensure that learning events maintain their pedagogical rigor, ethical standards, and responsiveness to diverse learner needs.

AI-Supported Quality Matters (QM) and CSU Quality Learning and Teaching (QLT): Ensuring Instructional Quality in AI-Generated Content

As artificial intelligence (AI) becomes a more common support tool in course design, it is essential that educators and instructional designers remain committed to maintaining high-quality, student-centered learning experiences. Quality assurance frameworks such as Quality Matters (QM) rubric and the California State University (CSU) Quality Learning and Teaching (QLT) rubric provide critical standards that help ensure instructional effectiveness, accessibility, engagement, and academic integrity.

Although both frameworks emphasize alignment, engagement, accessibility, and continuous improvement, they differ in scope. QM, developed as a national standard, focuses exclusively on course design, the structure, clarity, and alignment of materials prepared before a course begins (Quality Matters, 2024). In contrast, QLT, developed within the California State University system, addresses both design and key elements of course delivery, including instructor presence, culturally responsive communication, and dynamic learner support (California State University, 2023).

Understanding these differences is critical for AI integration. While AI may assist with aspects of course design, effective course delivery and meaningful human interaction cannot be automated. Both QM and QLT stress that while AI may streamline aspects of course preparation, final decisions about instructional quality, ethics, and student support must remain firmly human-led.

AI tools, when used thoughtfully, can assist instructional designers and educators in supporting quality assurance standards across several critical areas:

Course Alignment

- **Human-Guided Standard:** Learning objectives, instructional materials, activities, and assessments must be clearly aligned to promote coherent learning pathways.
- **AI Support:** AI can assist by cross-referencing objectives with assessments, suggesting content revisions, and flagging potential misalignments to strengthen course coherence (Quality Matters, 2024).

Accessibility and Inclusivity

- **Human-Guided Standard:** Course content must be accessible to all learners and meet ADA and WCAG standards.

- **AI Support:** AI systems can assist by automatically generating alternative text for images, captioning videos, simplifying language for accessibility, translating content into multiple languages, and checking documents for compliance with Web Content Accessibility Guidelines (WCAG) standards (U.S. Department of Education, 2023).

Learner Engagement

- **Human-Guided Standard:** Courses must foster meaningful learner-content, learner-learner, and learner-instructor interaction.
- **AI Support:** AI can suggest interactive activities, generate personalized discussion prompts, or propose simulation-based learning tasks. Nonetheless, instructor presence and authentic engagement must be actively maintained by humans (Holmes et al., 2022; Quality Matters, 2024).

Assessment and Feedback

- **Human-Guided Standard:** Assessments must be varied, aligned with outcomes, and provide meaningful, actionable feedback.
- **AI Support:** AI can help generate diverse formative assessments (e.g., practice quizzes, self-check activities) and assist instructors in delivering personalized feedback through intelligent tutoring systems and automated feedback generators.

Transparency and Ethical AI Use

- **Human-Guided Standard:** Students must be informed when AI-generated or AI-assisted materials are incorporated into their learning environment. Transparent communication about AI's role fosters trust, supports academic integrity, and ensures students understand the origin and purpose of the resources provided (Quality Matters, 2024).
- **AI Support:** AI tools can assist instructors and instructional designers by generating content, feedback drafts, and activity ideas. However, educators remain responsible for clearly disclosing when AI tools have contributed to course materials, and for ensuring that such materials align with pedagogical goals, institutional policies, and ethical standards (Quality Matters, 2024).

Continuous Improvement

- **Human-Guided Standard:** Courses must undergo regular review and updates based on learner feedback, engagement analytics, and pedagogical best practices.
- **AI Support:** AI can provide data on learner behaviors, performance trends, and engagement patterns. These analytics can inform iterative design improvements, but human reflection and decision-making must guide final course adjustments.

Although AI can assist in operationalizing aspects of QM and QLT standards, it cannot replace the professional judgment, ethical decision-making, and relational expertise that educators and instructional designers bring to the learning environment. Final quality assurance reviews must be conducted by humans to ensure that AI-supported outputs demonstrate alignment, meet accessibility requirements, promote inclusive learning, foster critical engagement, and uphold academic integrity (Holmes et al., 2022; Quality Matters, 2024).

As AI becomes more embedded in educational practice, frameworks like QM and QLT serve as essential anchors ensuring that the human values at the heart of good teaching and learning continue to guide innovation, rather than being overshadowed by technological convenience.

AI-Supported Universal Design for Learning: Promoting Equitable Engagement through AI

Universal Design for Learning (UDL) is a research-based educational framework that guides educators in designing flexible learning environments to accommodate the inherent variability among learners (CAST, 2018). Rather than relying on a one-size-fits-all model, UDL emphasizes offering multiple means of engagement, representation, and action and expression to ensure that all students can access, participate in, and succeed within learning experiences.

As artificial intelligence (AI) tools become increasingly integrated into instructional design, they offer new opportunities when incorporating UDL principles. When thoughtfully applied, AI can expand options for how content is delivered, how learners interact with material, and how they demonstrate understanding. AI can support UDL Principles in the following ways:

Multiple Means of Representation (Presenting content in different ways)

AI tools can help diversify how information is presented by generating multiple content formats. In addition to producing audio versions or simplified text, AI can transform abstract or complex topics into visual formats, such as infographics, timelines, or scenario-based narratives.

Multiple Means of Engagement (Supporting diverse ways for students to demonstrate knowledge)

To foster sustained motivation, AI can assist in personalizing content based on student interests, lived experiences, or cultural context. It can generate discussion prompts aligned with learner profiles or offer scenario-based problem-solving activities that promote critical thinking and relevance. These capabilities help educators design learning environments that are not only responsive but also inclusive and emotionally engaging (CAST, 2018).

Multiple Means of Action and Expression (Increasing motivation and interaction)

AI can suggest a wide range of assessment and practice options to accommodate learner differences. For example, it can help generate alternate formats like case studies, interactive quizzes, or simulations that let students express their learning in diverse ways. Tools like speech-to-text, predictive writing aids, and AI-powered feedback systems can scaffold student expression and promote learning growth. Additionally, AI can recommend tiered activities tailored to different readiness levels, encouraging equity in performance expectations (Heir, 2023).

Despite its potential, AI cannot independently ensure that UDL principles are honored. Educators and instructional designers remain actively involved in reviewing, adapting, and critically assessing AI-generated resources to ensure that materials are inclusive, culturally responsive, and contextually appropriate for their specific learner populations. Ultimately, AI can be a powerful support for implementing UDL when it is viewed not as an autonomous designer, but as a tool shaped by human expertise, ethical responsibility, and a commitment to educational equity. Meaningful integration of AI into UDL-based course design requires an unwavering focus on the varied ways students learn, engage, and express themselves.

AI-Supported Accessibility: Designing Inclusive and Compliant Learning Content

Beyond pedagogical flexibility, AI integration must also meet legal and ethical standards of accessibility. Accessibility in instructional design refers to the practice of ensuring that all learners, including those with physical, sensory, cognitive, or neurological disabilities, can perceive, navigate, and interact meaningfully with digital content (Burgstahler, 2015; W3C, 2018). Accessible design is not only a matter of best practice; it is required by legal frameworks such as the Americans with Disabilities Act (ADA) and Section 508 of the Rehabilitation Act.

AI has the potential to assist educators and instructional designers in meeting accessibility standards by:

Auto-Generating Alternative Formats

AI can assist by automatically creating alt text for images, closed captions for videos, and transcripts for audio-based materials, helping meet basic accessibility standards.

Flagging Inaccessible Content

AI can detect and alert designers to issues such as low color contrast, missing section headings, improper use of tables, and non-descriptive hyperlinks, all of which are critical for screen reader users and visual learners.

Structuring Content for Assistive Technologies

AI can restructure and reformat course content, like creating proper heading hierarchies (H1, H2, etc.) and clear navigation menus to make it easier for screen readers and keyboard-only users to access.

Generating Multiple Language Versions

AI-powered translation tools can create content in multiple languages, supporting not only multilingual learners but also students with limited English proficiency, and offering alternative phrasing for clarity.

Simplifying Complex Language

AI tools can generate plain language summaries of dense academic content, helping students with cognitive disabilities, executive functioning challenges, or second-language learners better access and comprehend materials.

Supporting Alternative Assessments

AI can suggest or generate alternative assignment formats, like oral presentations, video submissions, or visual projects, that align better with the needs of students who may struggle with traditional text-based formats.

Auto-Detecting Inaccessible PDFs or Documents

Some AI tools can scan uploaded documents (e.g., syllabi, handouts) and flag missing text descriptions, improper reading order, or untagged images that need remediation to meet accessibility standards.

Personalizing Accessibility Supports

AI-driven tools can recommend specific accessibility features (like enlarged fonts, text-to-speech options, or background color adjustments) based on individual learner preferences or profiles, promoting more personalized inclusion.

It is critical to recognize that AI tools alone cannot guarantee accessibility compliance. While AI can streamline the detection and generation of accessible elements, human oversight is essential to ensure that content is not only technically compliant but also pedagogically meaningful and contextually appropriate. For example, AI-generated alt text might describe an image accurately, but miss its instructional significance within the learning activity.

Educators and instructional designers can use AI in combination with dedicated accessibility tools such as Microsoft's Accessibility Checker or UDOIT for Canvas. More importantly, ongoing professional development in digital accessibility is necessary in order for educators and instructional designers to make informed decisions that uphold both compliance requirements and the broader ethical commitment to inclusive education.

When guided by human expertise, AI can serve as a valuable ally in building learning environments that are accessible, equitable, and legally compliant; strengthening opportunities for all learners to succeed.

Concluding Thoughts: Foundational Frameworks for Responsible AI Integration

The effective use of artificial intelligence in course design begins with a strong foundation. Instructional design models such as Backward Design, ADDIE,, Gagné's Nine Events of Instruction, and frameworks like Bloom's Taxonomy, Universal Design for Learning (UDL), and accessibility standards offer structure and guidance. In parallel, quality assurance frameworks, including the Quality Matters (QM) rubric and the CSU Quality Learning and Teaching (QLT) rubric, ensure that AI-generated content upholds standards of clarity, alignment, and learner engagement across digital learning environments.

Together, these models and standards help educators and instructional designers maintain pedagogical integrity while thoughtfully integrating AI tools. When grounded in these frameworks, AI becomes a valuable extension of human expertise, enhancing rather than replacing the instructional design process.

However, realizing this potential is not just about choosing the right model or rubric, it also depends on how we engage with AI. Like any collaborative partner, AI responds to the quality of the direction it receives. That direction comes through prompts.

The next section explores how meaningful prompting transforms AI from a basic support tool into a responsive co-designer. Drawing on cognitive science and instructtional design principles, we'll look at how to structure prompts effectively and how educators and instructional designers can use this skill to collaborate with AI in ways that are purposeful, ethical, and creative.

AI AS A CO-DESIGNER: THE POWER OF MEANINGFUL PROMPTS

Earlier in this chapter, we emphasized the importance of humanizing AI through deliberate, structured guidance. Now, we move from theory to practice, exploring how instructional designers and educators can use prompt engineering as a powerful strategy for collaborating with AI not as a mere tool, but as a co-designer in the creative process. Effective prompting is foundational to ensuring that AI-generated outputs are pedagogically sound, inclusive, and aligned with instructional goals (Zawacki-Richter et al., 2019; Li et al., 2025).

When used intentionally, well-crafted prompts act as both cognitive and pedagogical scaffolds. They guide AI systems to generate materials that are not only relevant but also instructionally meaningful, making prompts a core skill for educators and instructional designers navigating AI integration in course design.

Defining and Structuring Effective AI Prompts

Prompts are not casual commands, they are carefully designed inputs that shape the AI's output. Research suggests that specificity of prompts significantly influences the clarity, depth, and usefulness of AI-generated responses (Brown et al., 2020). Effective prompts often include:

- **Clear Instructional Intent -** Rather than asking AI to "generate a quiz," a more effective prompt might read:
  > "Create a five-question multiple-choice quiz for an undergraduate instructional design course on Bloom's Taxonomy. Each question should target a different cognitive level."
- **Contextual Relevance -** Prompts should include background details to support instructional alignment:
  > "Design a scenario-based learning activity for a graduate-level course on constructivism that promotes peer interaction."
- **Iterative Refinement** - AI-generated content is rarely final in its first version. Educators must engage in an iterative process: reviewing, refining, and re-prompting to achieve instructional precision (Mollick & Mollick, 2023).
- **Structured Prompt Templates** - Including parameters such as audience, tone, length, format, and learning goal increases consistency and quality:
  > "Draft a 300-word reflective journal prompt for adult learners in an online professional development course on UDL. Use a warm, conversational tone and include a reference to the UDL guidelines."

Instructional Design and Cognitive Principles Behind Prompting

Effective prompting goes beyond technical formulation, it is deeply grounded in learning theory and instructional strategy. To use AI meaningfully in education, prompts must reflect the cognitive and pedagogical foundations that shape high-quality learning experiences.

Cognitive Learning Principles

Drawing from cognitive psychology, prompts can be used to guide AI in generating content that activates, supports, and deepens thinking. For example, prompts that ask AI to generate scenarios, dilemmas, or simulations tap into learners' ability to analyze, synthesize, and evaluate information, engaging higher-order cognitive processes described in Bloom's Taxonomy (Anderson & Krathwohl, 2001).

Prompts can also be designed to:

- **Activate prior knowledge** through retrieval-based question sets or reflective activities.
- **Foster metacognitive awareness** by asking AI to generate journal prompts or self-assessment rubrics.
- **Support cognitive load management** by prompting the creation of chunked explanations or visuals that scaffold complex ideas.

This strategic use of prompts supports constructivist learning approaches, where learners build meaning through guided inquiry, reflection, and problem-solving (Bransford et al., 2000).

Instructional Alignment

Well-designed prompts are not isolated actions, they must be anchored in broader instructional design frameworks that ensure coherence across learning objectives, activities, and assessments. When prompts are informed by models such as:

- **ADDIE**, they guide AI to produce outputs that align with each phase of the design process.
- **Bloom's Taxonomy**, they ensure cognitive diversity in tasks ranging from foundational knowledge checks to complex, evaluative challenges.
- **Universal Design for Learning (UDL)**, they foster inclusivity by prompting AI to generate content in multiple formats and with flexible engagement options.

This kind of constructive alignment (Biggs & Tang, 2011) ensures that AI-generated materials maintain the integrity of the learning environment by reinforcing instructional goals and supporting all learners.

Moreover, prompts that consider learner variability, such as cultural context, accessibility needs, or developmental level, can help AI produce content that is not only instructionally effective but also socially and ethically responsive (CAST, 2018; Holmes et al., 2022).

REAL-WORLD APPLICATIONS FROM INSTRUCTIONAL DESIGNERS

AI-supported instructional design is not a one-size-fits-all solution. It is a highly adaptable process shaped by human expertise, context, and goals. Across a range of settings, including K–12, higher education, adult learning programs, and professional development initiatives, instructional designers are applying meaningful prompting strategies to transform AI into a collaborative partner. These real-world examples illustrate how AI can enhance lesson planning, accessibility, differentiation, and feedback when guided by intentional design thinking. They also demonstrate that the effectiveness of AI depends not on the technology alone, but on how well educators and designers craft prompts that align with pedagogical principles, learner needs, and ethical standards. Whether designing a middle school science lesson, a graduate course module, or a faculty microlearning series, the examples that follow will show how AI can support innovation across diverse instructional contexts.

Real-World Applications

Course Planning Using Backward Design (Higher Ed)

At a mid-sized public university, an instructional designer applied the Backward Design model in collaboration with generative AI. Starting with clear learning outcomes, the designer prompted AI to generate aligned assessments and instructional strategies. Through multiple refinement cycles, the AI's output was shaped to ensure coherence with course goals, saving time during the planning process while maintaining academic rigor (Choi et al., 2024).

Enhancing Accessibility with Inclusive Prompts (Community College)

In a redesigned online psychology course, a community college instructional designer used AI to generate accessibility support, such as audio captions, simplified summaries, and alt text. Prompts were carefully crafted to align with UDL principles, and outputs were reviewed for cultural responsiveness and ADA/WCAG compliance (Li et al., 2025).

Supporting Differentiation in a Middle School Science Class (K–12)

In a 7th-grade science unit on ecosystems, a curriculum designer collaborated with a classroom teacher to use AI for differentiated content creation. AI was prompted to generate three versions of a reading passage; one simplified for English learners, one with embedded vocabulary supports, and one with extension questions for advanced students. The instructional designer reviewed all outputs for accuracy and pedagogical alignment before integrating them into the unit plan (Yadav, 2023).

Personalized Feedback in Writing Courses (Adult Learning)

Within an adult education writing program, AI was used to deliver formative feedback on drafts. Prompts were designed to target structure, grammar, and clarity. Instructors reviewed and adjusted the AI feedback to ensure alignment with course outcomes and tone before sharing with students, enhancing instructional reach while preserving human oversight (Ch'ng, 2023).

Prototyping Microlearning Modules (Faculty Development)

In a university faculty development center, instructional designers used AI to generate outlines for microlearning videos. Structured prompts specified topic, tone, duration, and learning objectives. AI-generated content provided a foundation that designers then refined to ensure alignment with institutional guidelines and learner needs (Choi et al., 2024).

Iterative Prompting in Design Sprints (Cross-Disciplinary Higher Ed)

During a multi-program course redesign sprint, instructional designers began with generic prompts that yielded underwhelming outputs. Over time, they adopted structured, role-based prompts incorporating learner demographics, course modality, and instructional goals. The AI-generated results became more aligned and useful, illustrating how design thinking and iterative prompting go hand in hand (Li et al., 2025).

Perspectives from AI Technicians

Professionals who develop and refine AI systems consistently emphasize the importance of prompt clarity, specificity, and ethical intent when using generative tools in educational settings. Their work informs educators and instructional designers about practical strategies for engaging AI in pedagogically sound and context-sensitive ways. These strategies include:

- **Prompt Iteration** - Rather than accepting the first AI-generated output, experts recommend prompting the system multiple times using slight variations or refinements. This process allows users to compare responses and adapt content to better match instructional goals.
- **Ethical Awareness** - Beyond accuracy and inclusivity, instructional designers must consider the ethical implications of using AI tools in educational environments. This includes being transparent with students about AI involvement, safeguarding learner data, and avoiding the replacement of authentic instructor presence with automated interactions. Ethical use of AI ensures that technology supports not diminishes human-centered pedagogy and trust in learning environments (Williamson & Eynon, 2020; Holmes et al., 2022).
- **Use of Role-Based Prompting** - A proven strategy involves instructing AI to "act as" a specific role. For example, an instructional designer, accessibility specialist, or subject-matter expert. This guides the AI's tone, structure, and content development in ways that are more consistent with user needs and professional context.
- **Contextual Embedding** - Technologists recommend embedding contextual cues within prompts, such as grade level, course modality, and specific learning goals so that AI-generated content is more accurately aligned with the intended audience and objectives (Holmes et al., 2022).
- **Scaffolded Prompt Sequences** - Instead of relying on a single prompt, users can sequence prompts to build on one another. First asking the AI to generate foundational content (like learning objectives), and then following up with related prompts (e.g., aligned assessments or case-based activities). This mirrors how human instructional designers typically think in phases and refines AI's contribution across steps.
- **Instructional Format and Output Control** - AI developers suggest using formatting directives, such as requesting lists, outlines, tables, or bullet points to improve the clarity, usability, and instructional effectiveness of AI outputs, particularly when designing course materials or assessment tools.
- **Collaborative Prompting in Teams** - In some instructional design teams, prompts are co-developed among team members (e.g., subject matter experts, technologists, and accessibility staff) to ensure that AI outputs reflect interdisciplinary priorities and meet both content and compliance requirements.
- **Flexible Output Formats for Diverse Learning Contexts -** AI systems can be prompted to generate or reformat content into various file types, such as HTML, accessible PDFs, Word documents, or LMS-compatible formats

(e.g., QTI files for quizzes). This flexibility supports seamless integration into different course platforms, accommodates varied institutional requirements, and improves access for learners using assistive technologies (W3C, 2018; Burgstahler, 2015).

- **Content Verification and Bias Checking -** While AI can generate instructional materials quickly, it may also produce information that is inaccurate, incomplete, or biased due to limitations in its training data (Bender et al., 2021). Educators and instructional designers must critically evaluate AI-generated content for factual correctness, representation, and cultural sensitivity to avoid misinformation or unintentional harm (Holmes et al., 2022). Human review is essential to ensure that AI outputs align with academic standards and institutional values.

Crafting effective prompts is not simply a technical exercise, it is a pedagogical skill grounded in learning theory, ethical responsibility, and intentional course design. By shaping how AI generates and refines instructional materials, educators and instructional designers maintain control over both the quality and relevance of AI-supported learning experiences. However, prompting is only the first step in a much broader collaboration. To fully harness AI's potential, it must be integrated into flexible, responsive workflows that allow for continuous feedback, personalization, and iterative refinement. The next section explores how adaptive workflows can extend the impact of meaningful prompting, offering dynamic strategies for optimizing course creation while keeping human insight at the center of the process.

ADAPTIVE WORKFLOWS: PERSONALIZING AND OPTIMIZING COURSE CREATION

Adaptive workflows refer to flexible, iterative design processes where instructional activities, assessments, and course materials are continuously refined based on new information, feedback, and performance data (Siemens, 2013). When paired with artificial intelligence (AI), adaptive workflows allow educators and instructional designers to collaborate with AI tools not as one-time assistants, but as ongoing partners in optimizing learning experiences.

Rather than designing a course in static phases, AI-supported adaptive workflows embed cycles of rapid prototyping, testing, feedback, and refinement into the instructional design process. This dynamic approach ensures that AI outputs remain aligned with instructional goals, responsive to learner needs, and anchored in pedagogical best practices (Branch, 2009).

AI tools can enhance adaptive workflows by:

- Assisting in the generation of multiple drafts and revisions of learning materials.
- Analyzing learner interaction and performance data to suggest adjustments.
- Supporting instructors in real-time responsiveness to evolving classroom needs.
- Helping instructional designers optimize alignment between objectives, content, and assessments over time.

When thoughtfully integrated, adaptive workflows can increase the personalization, accessibility, and effectiveness of course design while maintaining a clear commitment to human oversight, ethical responsibility, and learner equity (Holmes et al., 2022).

Examples of AI-Enhanced Adaptive Workflows Across Instructional Design Models

Instructional designers can embed AI-driven workflows into a variety of instructional models to support continuous course improvement:

Rapid Prototyping with ADDIE

In the traditional ADDIE, Analysis, Design, Development, Implementation, and Evaluation, AI tools can assist during rapid prototyping cycles by:

- **Analysis:** Using AI to synthesize learner needs analysis, flagging knowledge gaps or preferences (Branch, 2009).
- **Design/Development:** Drafting preliminary course materials, assessments, and outlines for review and refinement.
- **Implementation:** Deploying course pilots supported by AI chatbots or virtual assistants.
- **Evaluation:** Analyzing learner data to suggest immediate adjustments to content delivery or instructional strategies.

This adaptive approach shortens the timeline between design iterations while preserving instructional rigor.

Iterative Refinement in Backward Design

In Backward Design, where learning outcomes define the path of instruction (Wiggins & McTighe, 2005), AI supports adaptive workflows by:

- Continuously suggesting revisions to assessments as objectives are fine-tuned.
- Generating alternative instructional activities based on real-time learner performance analytics.
- Offering differentiated scaffolds or enrichment materials aligned with evolving mastery levels.

This ensures that instruction remains backward-aligned, but flexible to learner growth.

Agile Learning Design: Real-Time Adaptation

Agile Learning Design emphasizes quick cycles of design, testing, and refinement, an ideal model for AI integration (Bichelmeyer, 2005). In this context, AI can:

- Monitor student engagement and flag disengagement trends mid-course.
- Auto-generate alternate resources for underperforming students.
- Suggest course pacing adjustments or modular redesigns based on immediate learner needs.

AI thus supports a living, evolving curriculum that remains tightly coupled with learner realities.

Adding Course Mapping to Adaptive Workflows

Integrating AI into course mapping can significantly streamline the alignment process, ensuring that learning objectives, instructional activities, and assessments form a coherent learning experience (Wiggins & McTighe, 2005).

Within an adaptive AI workflow, course mapping typically involves:

- **AI-Generated Draft Map**: AI suggests initial mappings of course objectives to assessments, instructional materials, and learning activities.
- **Human Review for Alignment**: Instructional designers review and refine these suggestions to ensure pedagogical soundness, cognitive progression (e.g., using Bloom's Taxonomy), and inclusivity (e.g., following UDL principles).
- **Iterative Feedback Loops**: Mapping is updated based on feedback from subject matter experts, pilot testing, or learner analytics during the course implementation phase.

- **Living Document Model**: Adaptive workflows treat the course map as a dynamic, evolving document that AI and educators refine collaboratively as learner needs and instructional contexts change.

Example Workflow:

Input Learning Objectives → Output AI-Generated Alignment Suggestions → Human Review and Refine → Continuous Refinement

When AI supports course mapping within an adaptive workflow, instructional coherence can be maintained even across complex course builds, while still centering human pedagogical expertise and responsiveness (Biggs & Tang, 2011).

While AI can assist in drafting initial course maps by proposing alignments between objectives, content, and assessments, these outputs must be viewed as starting points rather than finalized designs. Educators and instructional designers play an essential role in validating the pedagogical soundness of these drafts. Human review ensures that the sequencing of activities supports cognitive scaffolding, that assessment strategies authentically measure intended learning outcomes, and that course materials are accessible and culturally responsive.

Furthermore, instructional designers refine AI-suggested course maps to maintain intentionality, correct for potential bias, and adapt content to the unique needs of their learner populations (Biggs & Tang, 2011; CAST, 2018; Holmes et al., 2022). Through this collaborative process, AI-generated suggestions are transformed into coherent, equitable, and instructionally rigorous learning experiences.

Examples of Custom AI Workflows for Course Design

Instructional designers are increasingly creating specialized workflows by combining generative AI tools like GPTs with traditional design frameworks:

- **Custom GPT Builders**: Instructional GPTs trained on ADDIE, Bloom's Taxonomy, or UDL principles to generate draft course outlines, objectives, and assessments. Further, to assist with course mapping; analyzing and refining course alignment with evidence-based models and provide tailored feedback.
- **AI-Powered Content Reviewers**: Systems that analyze courses for accessibility (using WCAG 2.1 standards), alignment with learning objectives, or potential cognitive overload risks.
- **Content Conversion Tools**: Automated conversion of lectures into e-learning modules or chunked summaries.

- **Discussion Prompt Generators**: AI tools that create high-quality, critical-thinking discussion questions linked to specific content areas.
- **Personalized Learning Pathway Creators**: Systems that design differentiated tracks based on diagnostic pre-assessments.
- **Assessment Diversity Engines**: AI workflows that produce a range of formative and summative assessments aligned to Bloom's levels.
- **Accessibility Enhancement Scanners**: AI checkers that evaluate documents, quizzes, and media against accessibility benchmarks.
- **Flexible Format Exporters**: Tools that reformat course content into accessible PDFs, LMS packages (e.g., QTI files), mobile-friendly versions, or visually enhanced HTML5 modules.

These examples illustrate how AI-driven workflows can make course development faster, more inclusive, and more sustainable when used thoughtfully alongside human instructional expertise.

Developing Effective Adaptive AI Workflows: A Step-by-Step Process

To implement adaptive workflows successfully, educators and instructional designers can follow these best practices:

1. **Define Goals**: Clearly articulate what aspects of course design AI will support (e.g., syllabus creation, assessment design).
2. **Choose Your AI Tool**: Decide whether to use a general-purpose AI model (e.g., ChatGPT) or build a custom GPT tailored to instructional design needs.
    - *Custom GPTs* trained on instructional models and frameworks (e.g., ADDIE process, Bloom's Taxonomy, UDL) can streamline workflows by embedding pedagogical principles directly into AI outputs.
    - *General AI models* can be equally effective but require carefully structured prompts and more rigorous human review to ensure outputs meet quality standards.
3. **Provide Structured Inputs**: Feed AI clear instructional objectives, learner profiles, and pedagogical priorities.
4. **Use AI for Initial Drafts**: Allow AI to generate early-stage drafts, outlines, or assessment ideas.
5. **Apply Human Refinement**: Review, revise, and align AI outputs with academic standards, accessibility guidelines, and institutional expectations.
6. **Pilot and Collect Feedback**: Test AI-assisted designs with learners or colleagues, capturing feedback on usability, clarity, and engagement.

7. **Iterate Continuously**: Use feedback and analytics to refine AI prompts and outputs, improving instructional materials over time.

Example Workflow:

Define Goal → Choose AI Tool → Input Clear Details → Output AI-Generated Draft → Human Review and Refine → Test and Gather Feedback → Continuous Improvement

Ethical Considerations in AI-Driven Adaptive Workflows

While adaptive workflows offer powerful opportunities, they also introduce important ethical considerations that must be addressed proactively:

- **Data Privacy and Consent**: Data used to personalize workflows must be collected and managed ethically, in compliance with FERPA and institutional policies (U.S. Department of Education, 2023).
- **Bias Detection and Mitigation**: AI-generated materials must be critically evaluated for bias, ensuring equitable representation across diverse learners (Bender et al., 2021).
- **Transparency**: Students should be informed when AI tools are used to generate instructional materials or feedback (Holmes et al., 2022).
- **Human Oversight**: AI outputs must be reviewed by qualified educators or instructional designers to ensure they meet academic, ethical, and accessibility standards.

Adaptive workflows should not replace human expertise, empathy, or responsibility. They should amplify it, ensuring that AI supports, but never defines, the educational experience.

PRACTICAL APPLICATIONS AND CASE STUDIES

To bridge theory and application, this section highlights real-world examples of AI use in instructional design across higher education, K–12 schools, and professional learning contexts. These case-based illustrations demonstrate how educators and instructional designers are using AI not only to enhance efficiency, but also to promote inclusivity, increase personalization, and support data-informed decision-making. This section serves as a practical reference point for those seeking adaptable strategies and inspiration for AI-integrated instructional design in diverse learning environments.

Case Example 1: Personalized Feedback in Writing-Intensive Courses (Higher Education)

At a large public university, faculty in an undergraduate writing program collaborated with instructional designers to implement AI-generated feedback loops. Students submitted drafts into an LMS-integrated AI tool that provided initial comments on structure, coherence, and clarity. Instructors then reviewed this feedback, personalizing it further before sharing with students. This process reduced feedback turnaround times while ensuring alignment with course rubrics and writing outcomes (Mollick & Mollick, 2023). Faculty reported increased student satisfaction and better revision quality.

Case Example 2: Microlearning for Faculty Development (Professional Learning)

A faculty development center used AI to design short, targeted learning modules for new instructors. Instructional designers created structured prompts asking AI to draft 10-minute microlearning lessons on topics like universal design, formative assessment, or inclusive discussion strategies. Designers refined the content for tone, clarity, and accessibility, embedding interactive components using AI-suggested quiz items and discussion starters. This approach supported faculty onboarding while modeling effective AI use in instructional workflows (Choi et al., 2024).

Case Example 3: Differentiated Instruction in Middle School Science (K–12)

In a 7th-grade classroom, a teacher partnered with a curriculum designer to use AI for creating tiered content on ecosystems. Prompts asked AI to generate:

- a simplified version for emerging readers,
- a version with embedded vocabulary supports,
- and a higher-level version with critical thinking questions.

All outputs were reviewed and adjusted for accuracy and pedagogical alignment. This practice improved student engagement and comprehension while supporting inclusive differentiation strategies (Yadav, 2023).

Case Example 4: Real-Time Engagement Insights in Online Courses (Higher Ed)

In an asynchronous graduate course, instructional designers integrated an AI-powered engagement dashboard to analyze clickstream and discussion board data. The tool flagged disengaged learners, prompting instructors to follow up with personalized outreach and adjustments to discussion pacing. Instructors also used the data to refine future modules. This approach allowed for proactive teaching interventions and ongoing course improvement (Holmes et al., 2022).

Case Example 5: Corporate Learning Pathways Using AI-Generated Recommendations

A corporate training department used AI to create adaptive learning paths for employees in leadership development programs. Pre-assessments informed the AI's content sequencing recommendations, suggesting modules based on knowledge gaps and job roles. Trainers reviewed and adjusted pathways before delivery, ensuring alignment with organizational competencies. Participants reported increased relevance of materials and greater autonomy in learning (Siemens, 2013).

Case Example 6: Accessibility Enhancements for Online Course Redesign (Community College)

In a system-wide redesign initiative, instructional designers used AI tools to identify accessibility issues in LMS-based content, such as missing alt text, low-contrast colors, and unreadable PDF files. Prompts helped AI generate alternative text, captions, and reformatted layouts. The team used UDOIT alongside AI suggestions, refining them for accuracy and compliance with WCAG and Section 508 standards. This initiative improved access for students with disabilities while also modeling inclusive design practices (CAST, 2018; W3C, 2018).

In addition, this next section presents a curated list of a few AI applications in instructional design across higher education, corporate training, and K–12 education. These examples illustrate innovative uses of AI that educators and instructional designers can adapt to enhance learning experiences.

Higher Education

- **Course Mapping:** GPT-based bots that can help analyze and refine course alignment with evidence-based models and provide tailored feedback to enhance learning effectiveness.

- **AI-Powered Personalized Learning Platforms**: Universities are leveraging AI to create adaptive learning environments that tailor content to individual student needs, improving engagement and outcomes.
- **Intelligent Tutoring Systems**: AI-driven tutoring systems offer personalized support, helping students grasp complex concepts through interactive learning.
- **24/7 AI Teaching Assistant**: AI-powered chatbot embedded in LMS to provide instant support on course logistics and content questions.
- **Personalized Study Guides Generator:** AI generates custom study guides based on individual learning goals and content mastery, aiding student review and test preparation.
- **Test Prep Bots for Midterms and Finals:** GPT-based bots simulate exam conditions with feedback loops to help students prepare more effectively and independently.

Corporate Training

- **Adaptive Learning Modules**: Companies are implementing AI to develop training programs that adapt to employee learning styles, enhancing skill acquisition.
- **AI-Driven Content Curation**: AI assists in curating relevant training materials, ensuring employees have access to up-to-date and pertinent information.
- **Predictive Analytics for Training Needs**: AI analyzes performance data to predict training needs, allowing for proactive skill development strategies.

K–12 Education

- **Course Mapping:** GPT-based bots that can help analyze and refine course alignment with evidence-based models and provide tailored feedback to enhance learning effectiveness.
- **Personalized Learning Paths**: AI creates customized learning experiences for students, addressing individual strengths and weaknesses.
- **Automated Administrative Tasks**: AI streamlines administrative duties such as scheduling and attendance tracking, freeing up educators to focus on teaching.
- **Early Intervention Systems**: AI identifies students at risk of falling behind, enabling timely interventions to support student success.
- **AI Homework Helper:** Interactive bot walks students through math problems, using inquiry-based support to encourage independent learning.

- **Multilingual Reading Comprehension Coach:** Adaptive reading tool adjusts questions and content difficulty based on real-time student responses, promoting literacy development.
- **Language Learning Coach:** An AI-powered assistant designed to support students enrolled in second or world language courses by providing personalized, on-demand language practice. It offers conversational prompts in the target language, delivers grammar corrections, vocabulary enrichment exercises, and pronunciation feedback. The tool can also generate instant translations, present culturally relevant examples to deepen contextual understanding, and recommend scaffolded activities tailored to learners' proficiency levels; whether beginner, intermediate, or advanced.

These applications demonstrate AI's effectiveness is beyond just content generation, and its versatility in enhancing instructional design across various educational settings. Whether it's personalizing learning in a K–12 setting, supporting busy professionals through microlearning, or scaling accessibility across courses, the key is that it should be thoughtful integration aligned with sound pedagogical frameworks.

FRAMEWORK FOR HUMAN-AI CO-DESIGN IN COURSE CREATION

Moving beyond individual applications, this section proposes a structured framework to guide the ethical and effective integration of AI into the instructional design process. Grounded in pedagogical principles and informed by real-world practice, this framework emphasizes the importance of maintaining human creativity, critical thinking, and ethical oversight in every phase of AI-supported course development.

Defining the Educator's and ID's Role in AI-Human Collaboration

Rather than seeing AI as a replacement for human expertise, educators and instructional designers should view AI as a collaborator; one that extends, but does not substitute, pedagogical decision-making and creativity. The educator's role includes:

- Setting clear instructional goals before engaging AI.
- Designing structured, context-specific prompts.
- Critically reviewing AI outputs for instructional validity and ethical compliance.

- Maintaining student-centered practices, including relational pedagogy and inclusivity.

Best Practices for Integrating AI into Course Development Workflows

Building on established instructional models and frameworks, like ADDIE, Backward Design, and UDL, the following best practices are recommended:

- **Integrate AI iteratively, not linearly.** Use AI to assist at multiple phases; analysis, design, development, implementation, and evaluation (Branch, 2009).
- **Maintain transparency.** Clearly disclose when and where AI tools are used in course creation and delivery.
- **Prioritize accessibility.** Ensure all AI-generated content meets accessibility standards (W3C, 2018).
- **Support learner agency.** Avoid over-automation that diminishes opportunities for critical thinking and creativity among students (CAST, 2018).

Suggested Workflow and Prompt Templates

A practical human-AI workflow might include:

1. Define Learning Outcomes → Human
2. Refine Learning Outcomes / Objectives → Human & AI
3. Generate Draft Materials (Lesson Plan, Quiz, Activity) → AI
4. Review for Alignment and Rigor → Human & AI
5. Refine for Inclusivity and Accessibility → Human & AI
6. Pilot and Collect Learner Feedback → Human & Analytics
7. Revise and Implement → Human

Prompt Template Example:

Structuring for clarity, purpose, and pedagogical alignment to guide AI tools in generating high-quality instructional materials. Prompts should specify the task, audience, tone, and instructional purpose.

- " Draft a 300-word discussion prompt for a graduate-level education course. The topic is the ethical implications of AI in educational settings. The tone should be academic yet conversational to encourage thoughtful peer dialogue.

Include a brief real-world example to ground the discussion and invite critical reflection."

Ensuring Ethical AI Use

Key ethical considerations include:

- Mitigating algorithmic bias in AI-generated examples and scenarios (Bender et al., 2021).
- Verifying the factual accuracy of AI content (Holmes et al., 2022).
- Respecting intellectual property rights when adapting or remixing AI-generated content (Williamson & Eynon, 2020).
- Prioritizing learner privacy and data protection in AI-supported platforms (U.S. Department of Education, 2023).

Looking ahead, emerging trends suggest that AI will become even more embedded in personalized learning systems, adaptive assessments, and student support services (Zawacki-Richter et al., 2019). However, ensuring that these technologies are human-centered and ethically grounded remains an ongoing responsibility for educators and instructional designers.

CONCLUSION: THE FUTURE OF AI AS A CREATIVE PARTNER IN EDUCATION

As artificial intelligence continues to evolve, its role in education is shifting from that of a passive tool to an active creative partner in instructional design and teaching. Far from replacing educators, AI's greatest potential lies in how it can support and extend human expertise; amplifying creativity, efficiency, personalization, and inclusivity in learning environments (Luckin et al., 2016; Holmes et al., 2022).

This chapter has explored how meaningful integration of AI requires grounding in established instructional design models, such as Backward Design (Wiggins & McTighe, 2005), the ADDIE process (Branch, 2009), and Gagné's Nine Events of Instruction (Gagné et al., 2005), and frameworks, such as Bloom's Taxonomy (Anderson & Krathwohl, 2001),Quality Matters (QM), and CSU Quality Learning and Teaching (QLT). Through deliberate prompting strategies, adaptive workflows, and continuous human oversight, educators and instructional designers can harness AI's capabilities while maintaining academic integrity, accessibility, and learner-centered practices.

One of the clearest takeaways from the current landscape is the need to balance AI's powerful capabilities with human judgment. While AI can suggest, generate, and even adapt content in response to data, it lacks the ethical reasoning, relational awareness, and contextual understanding that only human educators can provide (Zawacki-Richter et al., 2019; Bender et al., 2021). Instructional designers and educators must remain vigilant stewards of the design process; guiding, curating, and critically evaluating AI outputs to ensure that technology serves, rather than dictates, educational aims.

Ethical implementation of AI is not optional, it is foundational. Future applications must prioritize transparency, privacy, equity, and cultural responsiveness, recognizing that AI models carry biases rooted in their training data and can unintentionally reinforce inequities if left unchecked (Holmes et al., 2022; Bender et al., 2021). Building ethical AI integration practices is essential for ensuring that future innovations in education are both responsible and transformative.

Looking ahead, future research opportunities are increasing. Scholars and practitioners must continue to investigate how AI impacts learner outcomes, instructional design processes, and faculty development practices. Questions about long-term learner engagement, the role of AI in assessment, and the evolution of instructional design roles in AI-rich environments deserve ongoing exploration (Zawacki-Richter et al., 2019).

Ultimately, the future of AI in education is not about technological replacement, it is about creative partnership. When educators and instructional designers lead with pedagogical intent, ethical responsibility, and human-centered design principles, AI can become a force for expanding opportunity, creativity, and engagement that supports diverse learners helping us to reimagine what high-quality, inclusive, and meaningful education can look like.

REFERENCES

Anderson, L. W., & Krathwohl, D. R. (Eds.). (2001). *A taxonomy for learning, teaching, and assessing: A revision of Bloom's taxonomy of educational objectives.* Longman.

Bender, E. M., Gebru, T., McMillan-Major, A., & Shmitchell, S. (2021). On the dangers of stochastic parrots: Can language models be too big? *Proceedings of the 2021 ACM Conference on Fairness, Accountability, and Transparency*, 610–623. https://doi.org/DOI: 10.1145/3442188.3445922

Biggs, J., & Tang, C. (2011). *Teaching for quality learning at university: What the student does* (4th ed.). McGraw-Hill Education.

Branch, R. M. (2009). *Instructional design: The ADDIE approach.* Springer., DOI: 10.1007/978-0-387-09506-6

Bransford, J. D., Brown, A. L., & Cocking, R. R. (2000). *How people learn: Brain, mind, experience, and school.* National Academy Press.

Brown, T. B., Mann, B., Ryder, N., Subbiah, M., Kaplan, J., Dhariwal, P., & Amodei, D. (2020). Language models are few-shot learners. *Advances in Neural Information Processing Systems, 33*, 1877–1901.

Burgstahler, S. (2015). *Universal design in higher education: From principles to practice* (2nd ed.). Harvard Education Press.

California State University. (2023). *Quality Learning and Teaching (QLT) Rubric and Standards.* Retrieved from https://www2.calstate.edu/

CAST. (2018). *Universal Design for Learning Guidelines version 2.2.* Retrieved from https://udlguidelines.cast.org/

Ch'ng, L. K. (2023). How AI Makes its Mark on Instructional Design. *Asian Journal of Distance Education, 18*(1), 33–45. https://files.eric.ed.gov/fulltext/EJ1410083.pdf

Choi, G. W., Kim, S. H., Lee, D., & Moon, J. (2024). Utilizing Generative AI for Instructional Design: Exploring Strengths, Weaknesses, Opportunities, and Threats. *TechTrends, 68*(2), 123–134. DOI: 10.1007/s11528-024-00967-w

Gagné, R. M., Wager, W. W., Golas, K. C., & Keller, J. M. (2005). Principles of instructional design (5th ed.). Wadsworth/Thomson Learning.

Heir, M. (2023). Artificial intelligence and learner engagement in inclusive classrooms. *Journal of Digital Learning Research, 15*(2), 102–118.

Holmes, W., Bialik, M., & Fadel, C. (2022). *Artificial intelligence in education: Promises and implications for teaching and learning*. Center for Curriculum Redesign. https://curriculumredesign.org/wp-content/uploads/AIED-Book-Excerpt-CCR.pdf

Lang-Raad, N. (2024). *The AI Assist: Strategies for Integrating AI into the Very Human Act of Teaching*. ASCD.

Li, H., Fang, Y., Zhang, S., Lee, S. M., Wang, Y., Trexler, M., & Botelho, A. F. (2025). *ARCHED: A Human-Centered Framework for Transparent, Responsible, and Collaborative AI-Assisted Instructional Design*. arXiv preprint arXiv:2503.08931. https://arxiv.org/html/2503.08931v1

Luckin, R., Holmes, W., Griffiths, M., & Forcier, L. B. (2016). *Intelligence unleashed: An argument for AI in education*. Pearson. https://www.researchgate.net/publication/299561597_Intelligence_Unleashed_An_argument_for_AI_in_Education

Matters, Q. (2024, February). *AI implications in the QM Higher Education Rubric, Seventh Edition.* Presented at the QM Connect Conference. Retrieved from https://www.qualitymatters.org/sites/default/files/presentations/AI%20Implications%20in%20the%20QM%20Higher%20Education%20Rubric%2C%20Seventh%20Edition.pdf

Mollick, E., & Mollick, L. (2023). Assigning AI: Seven approaches for students with prompting guidelines. *Computers & Education*, *197*, 104760. DOI: 10.1016/j.compedu.2023.104760

Moore, A., Tillberg-Webb, H., & Stefaniak, J. (2024). *The use of generative AI to support inclusivity and design deliberation for online instruction*. Online Learning Journal, 28(3), 183–200. https://files.eric.ed.gov/fulltext/EJ1446883.pdf

Siemens, G. (2013). Learning analytics: The emergence of a discipline. *The American Behavioral Scientist*, *57*(10), 1380–1400. DOI: 10.1177/0002764213498851

U.S. Department of Education, Office of Educational Technology. (2023). *Artificial intelligence and the future of teaching and learning: Insights and recommendations*. https://www.ed.gov/sites/ed/files/documents/ai-report/ai-report.pdf

Wei, X. (2024). *Cultural sensitivity in AI language learning: Using NLP to enhance language understanding across cultural contexts*. ResearchGate. https://www.researchgate.net/publication/388059980_Cultural_Sensitivity_in_AI_Language_Learning_Using_NLP_to_Enhance_Language_Understanding_Across_Cultural_Contexts

Wiggins, G., & McTighe, J. (2005). *Understanding by design* (Expanded 2nd ed.). Association for Supervision and Curriculum Development.

Williamson, B., & Eynon, R. (2020). Historical threads, missing links, and future directions in AI in education. *Learning, Media and Technology*, *45*(3), 223–235. DOI: 10.1080/17439884.2020.1798995

World Wide Web Consortium. (W3C). (2018). *Web Content Accessibility Guidelines (WCAG) 2.1.* https://www.w3.org/TR/WCAG21/

Yadav, G. (2023). Scaling Evidence-based Instructional Design Expertise through Large Language Models. *arXiv preprint.* https://arxiv.org/abs/2306.01006

Zawacki-Richter, O., Marín, V. I., Bond, M., & Gouverneur, F. (2019). Systematic review of research on artificial intelligence applications in higher education – where are the educators? *International Journal of Educational Technology in Higher Education*, *16*(1), 1–27. DOI: 10.1186/s41239-019-0171-0

Chapter 12
Transforming Student Support With AI-Powered Tutoring

Eun-Ok Baek
https://orcid.org/0000-0002-0697-6763
California State University, San Bernardino, USA

Qi Guo
https://orcid.org/0000-0002-6674-8703
Brigham Young University, USA

Romina Wilson
University of Tennessee, USA

ABSTRACT

This article explores how AI-powered tutoring systems are transforming student support across K–12, higher education, corporate training, and lifelong learning. Leveraging machine learning, natural language processing, and data analytics, these systems offer personalized, scalable, and interactive alternatives to traditional tutoring. The shift from human-led to AI-enabled tutoring is examined, along with benefits such as adaptive learning paths, immediate feedback, accessibility, and engagement. Challenges like data privacy, bias, and the role of human mentors are addressed. The article identifies trends such as predictive analytics in global tutoring networks and smart corporate systems. Ethical concerns—transparency, fairness, and access—are discussed as essential to responsible AI use. Recommendations emphasize a hybrid model that integrates AI tools with human-centered pedagogy, ensuring meaningful learning and future workforce readiness.

DOI: 10.4018/979-8-3373-2397-8.ch012

INTRODUCTION TO AI-POWERED TUTORING SYSTEMS

Student support has been a recurring concern in education. Tutoring has been effective in providing personalized support, motivation and expertise as students resolve their education and career dilemmas. With the rapid growth of artificial intelligence (AI), we are now moving beyond a conversation between tutors and learners and entering the realm of AI-enabled tutorial systems. This chapter examines the ways in which AI-powered tutoring programs are revolutionizing student assistance in corporate, academic, and lifelong learning settings. The definition, development from traditional, human-centered coaching to AI-powered models, important technologies, benefits, difficulties, and ethical issues are all covered.

Defining AI-Powered Tutoring Systems

Artificial intelligence tutoring systems are game changers in the educational technology space that incorporate artificial intelligence to provide personalized, adaptive, and interactive educational experiences. AI tutoring systems use advanced technologies like machine learning, natural language processing (NLP), and data analytics to examine the unique needs of each student, provide immediate feedback, and direct students toward complex conceptual understanding (Ifenthaler et al., 2024; VanLehn, 2011). AI approaches provide a more scalable solution compared to traditional tutoring systems that are limited by the capacity and availability of human tutors, as artificial intelligence can learn to accommodate unique learning styles, paces, and levels of knowledge. For example, machine learning can analyze student behavior data to personalize content, while NLP offers conversational interfaces similar to human tutors to help engage learners in their learning and support comprehension (Crompton & Burke, 2023). AI tutoring systems are becoming more integrated into various digital platforms, such as smartphone applications and virtual classrooms, increasing access and ensuring equitable education in global contexts.

AI-powered tutoring systems may not just impact students but can also shape education systems. In many of such systems, AI-based tutoring has the potential to automate many low-level teaching activities, such as generating questions for practice or marking student responses, freeing up instructors' time to focus on deeper pedagogical missions, such as engaging students in critical thinking and creativity (Chiu et al., 2023). In addition, AI tutors can help students speaking different languages and situated in different cultural contexts, supporting multilingual learners, and closing global learning gaps in education. For example, Duolingo and Khan Academy employ AI to provide personalized lessons to millions of students across the globe, highlighting the flexibility and scalability of these types of systems (Al-Zahrani & Alasmari, 2024). As AI continues to develop, its newer iterations are added onto tutoring systems and other types of AI tutoring applications that can generate interactive, context-based content, so that the learning and education process is further individualized, ushering in a new perspective on education (Bojorquez & Vega, 2023).

The Evolution of Tutoring: From Traditional To AI-Driven Models

The history of tutoring represents a shift from resource-heavy, human-focused approaches to technologically advanced, AI-supported models. Tutoring, when performed individually or with small groups, has often been regarded as an effective method for improving student outcomes, as highlighted by Bloom's "2 Sigma Problem" (Bloom, 1984), which concluded that individualized tutoring is more effective than group learning. When tutoring is provided by a human, it becomes resource-heavy, a characteristic that makes it costly and inaccessible for many people. With the advent of digital technologies in the late 20th century came computer-based learning systems (early educational software) and other static content delivery systems that afforded limited personalization. AI-powered tutoring systems represent a disruptive leap in creating systems that can blend the scaled technology with human-like adaptivity and responsiveness to student needs (Al-Zahrani & Alasmari, 2024). These systems can use large data sets to dynamically, on the fly, adjust learning content, pace, and personalisation based on student responses, progress measures, and behavioural patterns.

This transformation has also benefited from the availability and improvement of AI. Since earlier systems relied upon known behavioral limitations from programming code, current-generation AI tutors are using cognitive models to illustrate how students learn and think. Cognitive models allow systems to adaptively intervene where students show signs of misconception and skill gaps (Graesser et al., 2018). The COVID-19 pandemic also accelerated the proliferation of AI tutoring across the globe. Many countries and educational systems now recognize and accept the need to scale up via distance learning with as much human essence as possible. Squirrel AI in China and Smart Tutors in India are examples of using AI technology to offer instruction without bounds and offer personalized learning to large populations of diverse students in diverse environments (Chiu et al., 2023). As AI tutoring systems continue to advance, incorporating multimodal elements such as sound recognition and gesture interpretation, they also create more seamless and immersive learning environments, thereby rendering the conventional classroom lecture model increasingly obsolete (Ifenthaler et al., 2024).

HOW AI-POWERED TUTORING SYSTEMS WORK

AI-powered tutoring systems represent an advancement in educational technology by providing highly personalized, adaptive, and responsive learning environments. They have radically evolved the tutor-student dynamic through real-time analysis of each student's performance, engagement, and learning needs. As they rely on advanced AI technologies like natural language processing, machine learning, and data analytics, these intelligent tutoring systems are moving away from the traditional, one-size-fits-all practice of instruction and towards flexible, student-centered learning environments.

Overview of AI Technologies Used in Tutoring Systems

Artificial intelligence is changing the way we educate by providing new technologies to improve teaching, user experiences, and administrative processes. Intelligent tutoring systems, conversational agents, predictive analytics, alarming/automatic assessment, and a number of innovations are essential to this advancement (Ifenthaler et al., 2024). AI-powered tutoring systems are built on a range of sophisticated technologies that work together to enable personalized learning. Natural language processing (NLP) allows systems to understand, process, and respond to human language, which means students and AI tutors can interact in meaningful ways. Products like AutoTutor, developed by researchers at the University of Memphis, use NLP to reproduce asking questions and providing responses that facilitate the development of critical thinking and comprehension skills (D'Mello & Graesser, 2012).

Machine learning (ML) enhances AI-powered tutoring systems to analyze massive amounts of data that are collected from student interactions to identify learning trajectories, identify students who display misconceptions, and create a plan to address those observations over time. Intelligent tutoring systems are perceived as examples of artificial intelligence that use machine learning to model student knowledge, adapt instruction in real-time, and ensure the most effective pathway of learning (Graesser et al., 2018). Conversational agents (powered by natural language processing) can initiate conversation, be responsive to learners' questions, clarify concepts, and provide support, reinforcing students' intrinsic motivation.

Data and analytics support the monitoring and assessment of how learners interact. AI systems will report metrics such as individual and overall response times, error patterns during activities, frequency of engaging with the tutoring system, and mastery of content. These metrics can be analyzed together to provide the educator and learner with actionable insights and allow for data-driven changes to learning plans. All effective AI tutoring systems rely on the continual collection and analysis of data on learners. Each student's interaction with an AI system is recorded, with all data being collected and used to generate a holistic learner profile. The continual collection of data points allows the AI system to engage in knowledge tracing and systematically map the evolution of a student's mastery of concepts over time.

Predictive analytics enhances instructional accuracy further by identifying students at risk of failure in a particular subject matter, and therefore creating value through predictive evaluations, which then leads to targeted intervention strategies. Feedback mechanisms can also be dynamically adjusted based on learner behaviour, which allows the system to effectively control (i.e., improve) the type, timing, and sophistication of the feedback it provides (Christensen, Horn, & Johnson, 2017). Data-fueled adaptability helps create a learner-centered environment in which the focus is mastery, rather than time, to measure the student's indicator of academic progress.

Substantial predictive analytics is also essential to use the analysis of past and real-time data to predict student performance, characterize risk, and develop recommendations for instruction (Chiu et al., 2023). AI tools support the tutor or teacher in streamlining administrative activities such as grading, scheduling, etc., affording them more time to concentrate on teaching. Ultimately, the interaction of natural language processing, machine learning, and data and analytics provides a powerful platform to support tutoring systems in delivering instruction that is not only responsive but predictive and preventive to support the many educational journeys of every learner (Graesser, Hu, Nye, & VanLehn, 2018).

Personalization Algorithms: Tailoring Tutoring Experiences To Individual Needs

One of the most significant contributions of AI-powered tutoring systems is their ability to deliver highly personalized learning experiences at scale. Through sophisticated personalization algorithms, these systems continuously assess students' behaviors, inputs, and learning trajectories to dynamically adapt instruction. By customizing the difficulty of tasks, suggesting alternative learning pathways, and adjusting feedback styles, AI-powered tutors ensure that each student receives support aligned with their cognitive profiles and evolving understanding.

Personalized learning paths, enabled by AI algorithms, play a central role in identifying knowledge gaps and delivering targeted interventions. These algorithms ensure that learners encounter appropriately challenging material while receiving the necessary support to succeed. The holistic application of AI in education also addresses diverse learning preferences, adapting both content delivery and assessment methods based on individual learner characteristics to foster higher levels of engagement and motivation (Mehendale, 2023).

Intelligent tutoring systems (ITS), such as Cognitive Tutors, demonstrate the possibilities that personalization presents for education. ITS models a student's mastery of particular skills in real time so as to provide customized, continually responsive instructional interventions (Aleven et al., 2016). All aspects of pedagogical techniques, including Socratic tutoring, modeling-scaffolding-fading, reciprocal teaching, and prior-knowledge building can also help students achieve deeper learning and fix deeply-rooted misconceptions (D'Mello & Graesser, 2012).

A particularly interesting component of AI tutoring is the potential for a teachable agent. In this approach, students learn actively by teaching a virtual character, who, in turn, engages in metacognitive skill development and deeper understanding (Biswas et al., 2005). Teaching requires students to sequence and articulate their knowledge explicitly, thus reinforcing their own learning in the process.

AI-powered tutoring systems are purposefully aimed at providing individual support across any subject. They can also initiate intelligent group work, so groups could create dynamically through AI algorithms that assess complementary skill bases and develop immersive experiences that allow students to be placed in real-world situations requiring problem-solving (Christensen et al., 2017). These can leverage advanced technologies such as natural language processing, machine learning, and data analytical capabilities not only as ideas and as intelligent processes, but as a responsive and inclusive educational ecosystem that empowers students as learners and fosters lifelong learning.

In the end, personalization algorithms in AI-powered tutoring systems can turn the static, one-world learning experience into a dynamic, personalized experience that supports each student where they are and takes them to their potential.

AI-Driven Communication Tools

AI-driven communication tools are one of the key aspects of contemporary tutoring systems, which offer interactive, timely, and personalized help that is similar to what a human tutor offers. AI communication tools such as chatbots, virtual assistants, and recommendation systems promote active exchange between the learner and the system toward a more dynamic, responsive, and engaging educational experience. AI-powered chatbots and virtual tutors can engage students through conversational interfaces and can answer questions and prompt for reflection and encouragement (D'Mello & Graesser, 2012). Chatbots, in particular, are used to simulate human conversation and give real-time feedback, allowing learners to participate in authentic contexts (AbuSahyon et al., 2023). In addition to dialogue, virtual teaching assistants use AI to help students navigate through complex course designs, assist with learning difficult concepts, and recommend specific resources to students based on real-time performance data analysis. Recommendation systems provide personalized content, such as additional videos, practice exercises, or readings based on the students' interaction with the material. These tools create a dynamic, supportive learning environment to encourage students to ask questions and learn new things more freely without the traditional barriers to learning support.

BENEFITS OF AI-POWERED TUTORING SYSTEMS

This section outlines the benefits of artificial intelligence (AI)-powered tutoring systems. Overall, AI-powered tutoring systems provide four facets of benefits to education: personalized learning paths, instant feedback and assessment, scalability and accessibility, and motivation and engagement.

Personalized Learning Paths: Adapting Instruction Based on Student Progress

Personalized learning emphasizes tailoring instruction to each learner's unique strengths and weaknesses. Reigeluth and Karnopp (2020) emphasize that personalized learning not only increases student engagement but also improves academic outcomes by aligning instruction closely with students' learning trajectory. According to the U.S. Department of Education's 2016 National Educational Technology Plan (NETP) and 2017 NETP Update, personalized learning refers to instruction tailored to each learner by adjusting the learning pace and teaching methods to best fit learners' needs. However, because of limitations in classroom size, instructor availability, and financial considerations, traditional classroom settings often have constraints and therefore frequently fail to meet individual student needs.

The most significant advantage of AI-powered tutoring systems is their personalization, offering adapted instruction based on individual student progress and ensuring that learners receive tailored support. For example, most traditional education settings adopt time-based learning, where teachers expect students to spend a certain amount of time on a particular learning outcome and allow student performance to vary when moving forward to the next level of learning (Graham et al., 2019). By utilizing AI tutoring systems, instructors are able to adopt mastery-based learning, where students must demonstrate mastery of skills or topics before advancing to the next level. Unlike time-based learning, mastery-based learning focuses on student performance rather than the amount of time spent to determine student progress through the curriculum.

Many researchers have discovered that AI-powered tutoring facilitates personalized learning. In their systematic literature review, Bayly-Castañeda et al. (2024) summarized that research on AI-driven personalized learning utilizes innovative tools and technologies such as AI chatbots, AI-aided LMS, and generative language models that redefine personalized learning and support continuous skill development. In their study, Zhang et al. (2023) integrated AI and Smart Classroom technology into English language and literature teaching. Teachers utilize AI and Smart Classroom to identify individual learners' preferences and proficiency levels and deliver personalized instruction. Results indicated AI and Smart Classroom enhanced student engagement, improved students' comprehension of English and literature, and strengthened their application skills.

Omar et al. (2024) propose a comprehensive framework—the Three Axes Learning Theory Design Space—that leverages AI to analyze learner data, preferences, and performance. This analysis enables the customization of training content, delivery methods, and assessment strategies aligned with individual learner needs and preferences. AI-driven personalized learning could also support students' skill development by tailoring education to personal strengths and weaknesses, fostering critical thinking, problem-solving, adaptability, and creativity to prepare students for real-world challenges (Ali et al., 2024). AI-powered tutoring systems allow more straightforward adaptation of individual learning goals, instructional strategies, and content and flow delivery. Through this, learners have access to activities that are relevant and aligned with their interests, often allowing for self-directed exploration.

Immediate Feedback and Assessment: AI's Role in Formative Assessment

Instructors utilize formative assessment throughout the learning process to guide student understanding, deliver continuous feedback, and refine teaching approaches to improve learning outcomes (Black & Wiliam, 1998). Unlike summative assessments, which evaluate learning at the end of a course or unit, formative assessments are embedded within daily or weekly instruction, providing immediate advice and timely instructional recommendations. AI plays a pivotal role in offering real-time feedback to learners through formative assessment. By offering formative assessment along with immediate feedback, AI helps students identify areas for improvement in real time, thereby promoting deeper understanding (Ejjami, 2024; Halkiopoulos & Gkintoni, 2024). Maghsudi et al. (2021) identified key obstacles to implementing personalized learning and examined how AI can support student assessment by analyzing performance on quizzes, assignments, and interactive activities while delivering immediate feedback to reinforce comprehension. This real-time feedback helps students quickly identify and correct misunderstandings, promoting continuous improvement and concept mastery. Take MATHia, developed by Carnegie Learning, as an example. It analyzes students' interactions in real time and adjusts its teaching methods accordingly. By providing customized hints, detailed explanations, and targeted practice problems, MATHia is able to address each learner's unique needs.

Instructors can also benefit from AI-generated learning analytics, highlighting common misunderstandings and difficulties and enabling targeted instructional interventions. Maghsudi et al. (2021) summarized three primary duties that instructors can assign to AI: (1) analyzing learner data to determine key areas for new content and refining assessment questions, (2) generating drafts of instructor responses and automatically verifying human-generated content, and (3) employing crowdsourcing to compile learning materials by collecting immediate feedback. For instance, the AutoTutor system engages students in interactive dialogues to assess their understanding and provide contextually relevant feedback on their responses.

Scalability And Accessibility: Expanding Educational Opportunities

Another significant benefit of AI-driven tutoring systems is their ability to expand access to quality education by reaching broader audiences from various locations with more available resources. According to Rehan (2023), scalability refers to the capability of adjusting resources in response to varying demands, enabling educational institutions to distribute resources more effectively and adapt to evolving requirements. O'Neill (2021) defines accessibility as "the means of enabling everyone to participate in society as independently as possible" (p. 1). It emphasizes removing barriers to ensure equal access for all individuals, including those with disabilities.

Traditional classroom settings often have constraints due to limitations in classroom size, instructor availability, and financial considerations (Chingos & Whitehurst, 2011; Cuseo, 2007). AI tutoring systems provide learning experiences at scale, ensuring that individual students receive tailored support regardless of their location or socioeconomic background and can also accommodate students with different health conditions (Jaliaawala & Khan, 2020; Panjwani-Charania & Zhai, 2023). These systems can operate 24/7, making high-quality learning resources accessible to individuals in remote or underserved areas who may lack access to expert instructors (Katiyar et al., 2024).

Furthermore, AI-powered tutoring enhances accessibility for learners with diverse needs. In their literature review, Panjwani-Charania and Zhai (2023) summarized seven types of AI applications supporting students with special needs, including adaptive learning, facial expression recognition, chat robots, communication assistants, mastery learning, intelligent tutors, and interactive robots. Assistive technologies through AI provide customized learning experiences that enable all students to succeed.

By integrating AI, educational institutions and organizations can expand learning accessibility, making quality education universally available rather than a selective privilege. As technology evolves, AI-powered tutoring will be instrumental in promoting lifelong learning, equipping individuals with essential skills in creating a more inclusive global education system.

Creativity, Engagement, and Motivation: AI-Driven Gamification and Interactivity

Beyond improving accessibility, AI-powered tutoring systems can incorporate gamified learning activities to foster creativity, boost motivation, and enhance engagement, creating a more dynamic and enjoyable learning experience. Creativity provides meaning, pleasure, and value (Sawyer, 2024). It is a mental combination that generates new ideas or products judged to be novel, appropriate, useful, or valuable (p. 9). Burop et al. (2020) describe engagement as the degree to which students are involved or interested in their learning and how connected they feel to their educational activities. They further define learner engagement as comprising three dimensions: affective, behavioral, and cognitive engagement. Meanwhile, motivation, as defined by Self-Determination Theory, is the drive to engage in activities influenced by the fulfillment of psychological needs for competence, autonomy, and relatedness (Ryan & Deci, 2000).

Previous studies have demonstrated the positive relationships between creativity, learner engagement, and motivation (Rich et al., 2015; Romero & Barbera, 2012). Tang et al., (2020) introduced Playful Design Jams, a series of learning activities incorporating playful elements and design thinking to promote problem-solving in interdisciplinary collaborations. During the learning process, participants reported increased motivation and engagement i, and that their creativity, communication, and collaboration skills have also improved. In their mixed-method research, Guo et al., (2024) discovered that students' lack of motivation significantly impeded their learning engagement, underscoring the critical role motivation plays in either fostering or limiting learner engagement

AI, as a technology-enhanced tool, can be utilized by instructors to design creative learning activities that make the learning process enjoyable and engaging, further increasing students' motivation to learn. McLaren and Nguyen (2023) reviewed AI integration in learning games and summarized four strategies: (a) offering personalized support during gameplay, such as hints, error messages, and appropriately leveled problems; (b) tailoring game difficulty and content to the individual learner's needs; (c) allowing learners to interact with AI characters to aid the learning process; and (d) leveraging AI for post-game analysis to better understand student interaction and iteratively improve the game. These adaptabilities allow learners to interact with content in unique ways, maintaining engagement and encouraging creativity.

Other researchers have developed AI-powered games incorporating elements like simulations and role-playing, allowing learners to explore complex concepts hands-on. For example, Xu et al. (2024), in their quasi-experimental research, developed a digital game-based AI chatbot system and compared the experimental group using the AI chatbot with a control group using a traditional chatbot. Results showed that the AI chatbot system effectively improved learners' motivation and engagement, though there was no significant difference in creativity. These dynamic environments foster creativity by enabling learners to experiment and engage with content in novel ways.

AI-enhanced games offer options based on learners' ongoing performance rather than making decisions for them (e.g., presenting the next problem or step). During gameplay, AI can track learners' progress in real time, offering feedback and adaptive support to help them improve, thus motivating learners by acknowledging progress and providing timely guidance. By making the learning process interactive, AI-driven games foster a more engaging and personalized environment, ultimately increasing both motivation and learning outcomes.

CHALLENGES AND ETHICAL CONSIDERATIONS

In the previous section, we explored the benefits of AI-powered tutoring systems, highlighting their ability to personalize learning, provide immediate feedback, enhance accessibility, and boost engagement. However, despite these advantages, the implementation of AI in education comes with its own set of challenges. In this section, we examine the obstacles educators and institutions face when utilizing AI-powered tutoring systems. First, we address data privacy issues and discuss strategies to ensure the security of learners' information. Next, we explore ways to mitigate potential biases in AI algorithms and promote fairness and transparency in designing AI-powered tutoring systems. We then highlight the importance of human support and adequate infrastructure. Lastly, we will address key ethical concerns and propose thoughtful approaches for the responsible use of AI-powered tutoring systems.

Data Privacy and Security: Protecting Student Information in AI Systems

The AI-powered tutoring system offers personalized learning experiences but also raises significant data privacy and security concerns. Key issues include the extensive collection of sensitive student data, such as academic performance, personal information, and behavioral patterns, which can lead to potential breaches if not properly safeguarded (Rehan, 2023; Katiyar et al., 2024). Protecting student information in AI-powered tutoring systems is crucial to ensuring privacy, security, and user trust and preventing misuse.

Researchers propose various strategies to strengthen data privacy and security in AI systems. Ali et al. (2024) propose three ways to technically safeguard data privacy: (a) training AI models with anonymized data to eliminate identifiable information such as names, addresses, and other personal information; (b) applying differential privacy techniques by adding noise to datasets to help protect individual identities while maintaining AI learning efficiency; and (c) utilizing local devices for AI model training instead of centralized servers to reduce data exposure and strengthen student privacy.

Katiyar et al. (2024) emphasize the importance of organizational strategies with a data governance process, which includes (a) obtaining informed consent from learners or their guardians, ensuring transparency about data collection and usage; (b) securely storing collected data using encryption, access controls, and monitoring to prevent unauthorized access or breaches; (c) regulating data sharing with educators, researchers, or third-party providers, ensuring it is used strictly for educational purposes and not for commercial exploitation; and (d) establishing clear policies for data retention periods and allowing learners to request the deletion of their personal data.

To effectively address data privacy and security issues, AI-powered tutoring systems should incorporate both technical safeguards, such as secure architectures and anonymization techniques; and organizational strategies, including data governance policies and educator training. Additionally, compliance with regulations such as the Family Educational Rights and Privacy Act (FERPA) and the General Data Protection Regulation (GDPR) is crucial to uphold data protection standards and maintain user trust. By integrating these safeguards and policies, AI-powered tutoring systems can create a secure environment that balances innovation with ethical data management.

Bias, Fairness, and Transparency in AI Tutoring Systems: Addressing Algorithmic Bias and Building Trust

AI-powered tutoring systems may result in biased and unfair outcomes. Students in a study conducted by Ali et al. (2024) reported that AI-driven personalized learning may produce biased evaluation outcomes and content recommendations. Another study by Warr (2024) demonstrated that several LLM models gave higher average scores to writing by a simulated student who preferred classical music compared to one who preferred rap music. AI algorithm biases can lead to unequal treatment of specific student groups, emphasizing the importance of ethical supervision and strong data protection measures (Katiyar et al., 2024; Rehan, 2023).

Educators can promote fairness by emphasizing content recommendations that are objective and unbiased in assessments (Ali et al., 2024). Reducing bias is essential for fostering an inclusive learning environment where all students, regardless of their personal characteristics or backgrounds, are given equal chances to succeed. Ali et al. (2024) proposed three procedures to mitigate bias and build fairness and transparency:

- Using Diverse Data Sources to Reduce Bias: Drawing from a wide range of data sources helps decrease bias in AI models, supporting fair and equitable learning experiences for all students.
- Ensuring AI Model Transparency: Making the decision-making processes of AI models visible allows biases to be detected and addressed more effectively, reinforcing accountability and fairness.
- Training on Balanced Datasets for Inclusive Representation: Building AI models with datasets that fairly represent students from diverse backgrounds helps prevent biased outcomes and supports a more inclusive educational environment.

As shown in Table 1, Katiyar et al. (2024) further proposed six techniques from AI training to designing and evaluating AI tutoring systems to enhance algorithmic fairness and trustworthiness.

Table 1. Six techniques for enhancing algorithmic fairness

Technique	Description
Identify bias	Conducting systematic reviews and corrective actions on training data to detect and reduce bias.
Fairness in AI training	Integrating fairness considerations directly into the AI models' training.
Diversity and inclusion in the development team	Prioritizing diverse and inclusive development teams for designing and developing personalized learning systems.
Communication transparency	Communicating the decision-making processes of personalized learning algorithms clearly.
Human review and intervention	Implementing human review and intervention to detect and address biased outcomes produced by AI systems.
Evaluation of AI systems	Ongoing assessment of AI systems to identify and mitigate disparate impacts and unintended biases.

As educators and instructional designers, three main steps are summarized to promote fairness and build trust in AI tutoring systems: maintaining transparency in AI decision-making, regularly auditing systems for biases, and involving a diverse group of stakeholders in the design and evaluation phases (Katiyar et al., 2024).

Balancing AI and Human Mentorship in Tutoring: Ethical Implications for Autonomy, Dependence, and Preserving the Human Touch

Autonomy and Dependence

As tutoring systems become more entrenched in AI, important ethical issues arise insofar as learner autonomy and dependence are concerned. Indeed, AI is a great support in terms of personalization and immediate feedback for students, but at the same time, it has introduced new dynamics that can empower as well as disempower student agency (Luckin et al., 2016; Holmes et al., 2019).

One of the most common concerns is that overdependence on AI systems may inhibit students' abilities to think independently and critically. Whenever students are guided continually by AI-recommended suggestions, prompts, and support, they tend to expect instant solutions or answers; thus, undermining their problem-solving tenacity and self-regulation skills (Williamson & Eynon, 2020). Learning itself forces students to struggle through the uncertainty, wrestle with abstractions, and engender meaning through effort and reflection. If it cushions students from these kinds of cognitive struggles, their development of independent intellectual skills would then be compromised (Selwyn, 2019).

Apart from this, even though adaptive towards the learning needs of the student, AI tutors operate based on patterns and probabilities, not on a student's internal goals, emotions, or ethical reasoning. True pedagogical autonomy goes beyond completing tasks; it requires students to exercise intelligent decision-making in terms of objectives, strategies, and values (Luckin et al., 2016). No matter how intelligent or well-programmed an AI system may be, it can never substitute for human guidance in constructing these higher-order elements of autonomy (Holmes et al., 2019). AI has been used for autonomy even in reflective ways. Personalized routes, timely comments, and pacing changes allow AI to grant learners more control over how they learn. Exploration, reflection, and self-assessment encourage adaptive structures in developing independent learning habits rather than dependence (Luckin et al., 2016; Holmes et al., 2019).

The ethical dilemma is balancing building and implementing AI-powered tutors with the kind of productive support without pre-empting it in the active, self-directed work that is the essence of authentic learning. It requires great care from educators and system designers to ensure that AI technologies do not substitute for critical, responsible activity with human co-facilitation (Williamson & Eynon, 2020).

At the end of the day, while AI indeed possesses the potential to facilitate more personalized education, there would still be a need for careful monitoring of its impacts on learner autonomy and dependency. Not only does academic success hinge on learners maintaining active agency in their own learning processes, but also lifelong intellectual and personal growth (Selwyn, 2019).

The Role of Human Mentors

AI has dramatically increased the efficiency of human mentors, and human mentors can utilize AI in many ways. As teachers, instructional designers, and educators, we can use AI to brainstorm engaging or innovative learning activities; generate scenarios to help learners connect what they learn to real-world issues; design assessment questions to evaluate learners; and grade learners' assignments more efficiently. However, AI-generated content may be based on inaccurate sources and, therefore, include incorrect information (Dwivedi et al., 2023). Human mentors must cautiously check the content and use it thoughtfully, as well as check AI-generated content before putting it into use, given its limitations and potential risk of undermining learner agency.

On the other hand, since AI is so convenient to use, human mentors may easily rely too heavily on AI without putting in the same level of effort as before the massive adoption of AI. AI is capable of generating information that looks real and professional. For example, when reviewing research papers, I have observed completely fabricated citations and references, likely resulting from human reliance on AI without closer examination. Human mentors must balance their relationship with AI-powered tutors, treating them as tools, resources, and even partners, but not as replacements for human mentors (Dwivedi et al., 2023; Katiyar et al., 2024).

Further, AI tutors can effectively detect students' cognitive engagement within specific learning tasks. However, students are human; they have diverse affective and behavioral needs that AI tutors often cannot adequately sense. Thus, there remains a crucial need for human mentors to observe, interact with, and care for students, ensuring that their voices are heard and their needs are addressed.

Advancing Equity Through AI: Expanding Access for Diverse Learners

Addressing the aforementioned fairness, bias, and transparency issues is crucial for ensuring quality education. Yet, balancing fairness and accuracy in AI systems is often difficult, as it involves navigating complex trade-offs (Chinta et al. 2024). Significant gaps in access remain, especially for marginalized and underserved students. Despite these challenges, tackling biases in AI remains essential in building educational environments that support all learners and advance equity. Emerging technologies such as AI also provide promising opportunities to bridge these gaps by expanding equitable access to education for diverse populations.

AI tutoring systems can be designed to accommodate diverse learning needs, including students with special needs and varying educational backgrounds. According to Gibson (2024), adaptive AI technologies can be used to support people with visual and auditory disabilities, such as automatically-generated descriptions for images and audio. AI technology can also be of help to t people with cognitive and physical disabilities, providing assistance with note-taking, mind mapping, and brainstorming. ZB, a social assistive AI robot developed by The University of Central Florida and United Cerebral Palsy of Central Florida, can help develop and improve social skills in students with disabilities. Teachers and instructional designers can utilize Ask Microsoft Accessibility to develop accessible course content, as advocated by s Gibson (2024), who also stated that "AI technology tools hold remarkable promise for providing more accessible, equitable, and inclusive learning experiences for students with disabilities." With this in mind, we as education practitioners need to balance the limitations and utilize AI thoughtfully.

AI TUTORING TOOLS AND REAL-WORLD IMPLEMENTATIONS

The use of Artificial Intelligence (AI) in education has made significant advancements across K–12 education, higher education, corporate training, and lifelong learning. This section presents AI tutoring tools organized by educational sectors and, where available, real-world implementations, illustrating how AI is applied in practice and its impact across various educational and training contexts.

AI Tutoring in K-12 Education

K–12 education is one of the most active contexts for adopting AI tutoring systems. Lots of schools are adopting AI systems to support personalized learning, engaging students, and addressing learning gaps. The following are a few noteworthy tools in this space and their real-world application when available.

- Khan Academy's Khanmigo: Khan Academy's Khanmigo is an AI-powered personal tutor and teaching assistant that promotes critical thinking by guiding students through problem-solving processes instead of giving them the answer. Early pilots in U.S. schools reported higher levels of student engagement and better understanding of content in both mathematics and the humanities (Khan Academy, 2023).
- MATHia: MATHia, Carnegie Learning's adaptive math learning software, is powered by AI for grades 6–12. MATHia serves as the student's own personalized one-on-one math coach that adapts to the student's individual problem-solving behavior and concepts learned. It examines the student's series of decisions leading to each answer. This enables MATHia to better adapt to the student's learning by providing stronger and more personalized learning experiences. MATHia has been implemented in various school settings according to their case studies. In Columbus City Schools, Ohio, MATHia was used in a blended learning model for middle and high school math, delivering personalized, AI-driven problem sets aligned with Common Core standards. LiveLab's real-time data helped teachers target instruction, boosting student confidence and engagement. However, the case study lacks specific test score data, focuses partly on ClearLanguages, and omits challenges like accessibility or training needs (Carnegie Learning, 2024).
- Squirrel AI Learning: Squirrel AI has a system of adaptive tutoring in China that diagnoses individual learning gaps and adjusts instruction dynamically. Pilot studies indicate students using Squirrel AI improved math performance, demonstrating a 32% advantage in math over those in traditional classrooms (Wang et al., 2023).

- DreamBox Learning: DreamBox has an AI-powered adaptive platform for K-8 students that modifies lessons on the fly based on learner responses. Research demonstrated that students who engaged with DreamBox for as little as 60 minutes a week obtained statistically significant gains in math achievement scores (Cruz et al., 2022).

Together, these platforms demonstrate how AI can help support differentiated instruction, promote independent learning, and support accelerated academic progress for young learners.

AI-Powered Learning Platforms in Higher Education

AI is changing the way higher education is personalized, creating predictive learning analytics, adaptive assessment, and real-time instructional support for students from institutions of higher education worldwide.

- ALEKS (Assessment and Learning in Knowledge Spaces): ALEKS, developed and launched by McGraw-Hill, is an adaptive online platform that offers both assessment and tutoring services. Initially specialized in Math and Science instruction, it now supports a wide range of K–12 and Higher Education courses (Harati et al., 2021). ALEKS assesses students' knowledge and skill sets in math and generates adaptive learning and instruction paths, giving real-time feedback and adaptive problems. Arizona State University (ASU) fully adopted the adaptive-learning platform, ALEKS, in three mathematics courses in the Fall of 2021 to help drive student success in mathematics courses. After implementing ALEKS, ASU Online saw an 11% increase in students earning a grade of C or better compared to the previous fall semester, with overall success rates increasing from 58% to 69%. Faculty use the analytics from ALEKS to identify students who might be at risk of failure early in the course and use identity analytics for appropriate intervention (ALEKS Math Outcomes, n.d.).
- Coursera's AI Coach: Coursera, an international online education platform, incorporates AI-driven features such as personalized learning pathways and automated grading in courses delivered by institutions like Imperial College London and the National University of Singapore. Coursera's AI Coach provides personalized study support and navigation through course content, increases learner engagement, and decreases dropout in online courses (Coursera, 2024). Coursera uses AI technology and tools like Coursera Coach to offer interactive and personalized learning experiences, as well as

demonstrative guides to acquiring new skills, help in course selection, and information on career planning (Coursera, 2024).

- MATHia: MATHia continues to support foundational math instruction in higher education, where students enrolled in remedial and entry-level college mathematics courses engage with key concepts through adaptive learning paths (MATHia, 2024).

These platforms demonstrate how AI allows institutions to shape more flexible, responsive, and student-centered learning experiences at scale. AI-powered learning platforms are actively utilized in higher education institutions around the world. For example, a study conducted at Ajman University in the UAE revealed that pre-service student teachers who engaged with AI-powered personalized learning tools demonstrated statistically significant improvements in academic performance, critical thinking, and motivation compared to peers using traditional instruction methods (Eltahir & Babiker, 2024). In South Africa, AI use in higher education encompasses automated assessment tools, intelligent tutoring systems, and adaptive learning platforms can enhance personalized learning experiences, increase student engagement and academic performance, as well as provide support in the management of educational resources (Funda & Mbangeleli, 2024).

In Kenya, a study was conducted to evaluate AI effectivity and accessibility in higher education institutions' use of Intelligent Tutoring Systems (ITS), Automated Grading Systems, and Learning Analytics Systems (LAS), employing a mixed-methods approach to gather data from faculty members, students, and administrators across 15 public and private universities and technical colleges throughout the country. Findings revealed that access to AI tools in higher education is significantly limited, with many respondents noting disparities in availability across departments. These platforms highlight how AI enables institutions to create more flexible, responsive, and student-centered educational experiences at scale.

AI Adoption in Corporate Training and Lifelong Learning

Professional education and training are no longer limited to traditional academic settings; AI tutoring systems are transforming professional development and lifelong learning across various industries. ChatGPT is being utilized in workplace learning environments. Companies use ChatGPT to streamline workflows, provide real-time assistance with employee inquiries, and support employee upskilling programs. Regardless, organizational impediments still exist, such as data privacy concerns, over-reliance on AI, and employee trust that need to be addressed through governance frameworks (Alhusban et al., 2024). Organizations are utilizing AI to drive upskilling, enhance onboarding, and facilitate personalized career progression pathways, examples of which are as follows:

- Shell Competence Management System: To enhance the global workforce, Shell implemented a comprehensive approach to building and maintaining technical and operational safety capabilities. As operational challenges evolved to involve more complex issues involving many stakeholders, Shell created a plan around capability and capacity development and management to ensure readiness over time. The overall approach focused on identifying critical competencies, developing scalable training plans, utilizing digital and AI-powered learning solutions to facilitate faster development, incorporating ongoing competency evaluations, embedding with operational excellence programs, and building a lasting culture of learning. Shell's framework was designed to satisfy both short-term business requirements and long-term talent development initiatives, while remaining adaptable to emerging risks, regulatory changes, and technology advancements (Gosselin et al., 2024).
- Career 4.0: An EU project involving partners from Bulgaria, Germany, Greece, Spain, Italy, and Hungary, it aims to enhance young people's employability through a digital mentoring concept focusing on developing personal development plans that help youth reflect on their employment opportunities and with mentors providing effective feedback in an open-ended process which also explores how AI tools can improve feedback efficiency for learners in the study. By leveraging IT and AI solutions such as adaptive learning systems, learning analytics, and intelligent CBR recommendation systems, the study aims to create a more effective and efficient feedback experience, and recommends transparent modelling of the feedback process in the implementation of these AI solutions (Kröll & Burova-Keßler, 2022).
- Duolingo's AI Tutors: Duolingo personalizes language learning for millions of adult learners globally through the use of AI-driven adaptive algorithms. In a study conducted using Duolingo with Chinese university students, the researchers found that users of Duolingo showed a greater willingness to communicate in English than those who did not use the app. The interactive and low-stakes environment that Duolingo used helped alleviate learners' anxiety and helped them develop confidence. Learners have a positive attitude about Duolingo being implemented in their English language learning, appreciating personalized learning pathways, adapting to learners' level of difficulty, and providing learning in an autonomous fashion (Ouyang et al., 2024).

These examples illustrate how AI is transforming the corporate learning ecosystem, creating relevant, scalable, and dynamic experiences to advance professional development. AI is also transforming corporate training and lifelong learning. AI-powered platforms offer adult learners opportunities for flexible, self-directed learning based on their pace, career pathways, and life circumstances. Increasingly, adult learners are using AI platforms to gain autonomy, gain confidence, and develop an educational pathway that suits their personal goals and previous experiences (Martinez & Ebardo, 2024). Across K–12, higher education, corporate training, and adult learning contexts, real-world implementations show that AI tutoring and learning platforms are reshaping educational experiences through personalization, accessibility, and adaptability. Through all these avenues, AI is increasing access to education and promoting digital inclusion while creating lifelong learning opportunities for diverse populations.

THE FUTURE OF AI-POWERED TUTORING SYSTEMS

Emerging Trends in AI-Powered Tutoring Technologies

AI-powered Adaptive Learning Systems are transforming rapidly, expanding to meet the various learning needs of students through innovative means, such as Cognitive Tutors, Constraint-Based Tutors, Dialog-Based Tutors, Adaptive Learning Systems, Game-Based Tutors, Collaborative ITS, and Affective Tutors. Each type of ITS is intended to adapt to the specific cognitive, affective, or social needs of the student, thus advancing personalized education (Avcı et al., 2025). In a way that meets the learning needs of diverse students and learners, they will eventually expand beyond K-12 and higher education to support lifelong learning and professional development from the time individuals move through different stages of their lives, facilitating skill development throughout life (Avcı et al., 2025). Additionally, emphasis will be placed on teaching soft skills, such as leadership and emotional intelligence, and facilitating this via AI-powered simulations and role-playing activities, considering the evolution of the workplace. We must recognize that AI also plays a vital role in student success and retention. By examining large data sets, researchers gain insight into how students learn and can adjust how teaching occurs, and provide timely learning and student support to students identified as potentially requiring them (Busu, 2024).

AI-powered tutoring is consistently developing, as increased AI advancement and integration into educational technology evolve educational contractors operating within the AI-powered ecosystem. A current trend is generative AI in educational systems and services. This innovative technology creates a tutoring system embedding the ability to generate content dynamically, foster student engagement, and provide a context-aware learning experience. An example of generative AI is the ability for a tutoring system to develop interactive simulations and digital content to create personalized study and training materials for the student based on their learning styles (Bojorquez & Vega, 2023). As an illustration, generative AI can create personalized math problems from an abstracted proficiency level or generate narrative history-based lessons based on personal interests, extra engagement, and student retention.

Another emerging technology is multimodal approaches utilizing AI. These combine text, speech, and visual inputs to create turbulent learning environments. Several authors (Chheang et al., 2023) provide an example of virtual reality (VR) tutoring environments that seamlessly bring together a series of activities to provide real-world problem-solving and modern learning situations. If a biology student is dissecting a frog in 3D and has an AI tutor coaching them about their technique, they can get real-time feedback and utilize the advantages of immersive technology on many things. On the other hand, the application of explainable AI (XAI) is establishing transparency in tutoring systems, with students/educators becoming aware of how AI informs its decisions or why the system is recommending certain content. In educational contexts, this transparency leads to trust and engagement (Mersha et al., 2024; Rachha & Seyam, 2023) within the AI tutoring system. Students who understand the rationale for AI-powered recommendations or prioritized suggestions will initiate the process of owning their learning. Moreover, the area of affective computing—AI that recognizes and analyzes student emotion, allowing it to listen to a student's tone or use facial recognition technology—is moving forward. A tutoring model that incorporates responsive intervention or stroke back presents the tutorial with the ability to react to a learner's emotional situation, providing encouragement when a learner indicates getting frustrated (D'Mello & Graesser, 2012). Together with other trends in education technology, the prospects for AI tutoring as adaptive, interactional, and empathetic are outstanding (educators need to screen their feedback systems) in providing learning solutions to diverse learners while reflecting the ever-changing landscape of its use in education.

The Evolving Role of AI in Student Success and Retention

AI is increasingly pivotal in helping students succeed and stay enrolled by proactively supporting them and utilizing data throughout their learning experience. AI tutoring systems moving from being reactive tools into predictive partners will help identify possible academic challenges and provide intervention before challenges arise to get students back on track (Chiu et al., 2023). For instance, AI can use data from course engagement by interpreting patterns, like time on task and number of interactions, which can allow platforms to provide suggestions that enhance motivation and persistence. One method to improve time on task is to recommend a break after an extensive period of focused work. Another example is recognizing a difficult concept and recommending working with a peer instead to create deeper understanding (Zawacki-Richter et al., 2024).

AI is also creating continuous feedback loops that make students feel fully responsible for their own learning, developing the self-regulated learning skills students will need to be successful long-term (Crompton & Burke, 2023). This applies more dynamically in higher education because self-directed learning is important, and AI tutors can assist students' goal-setting, progress-tracking, and reflection on learning strategies. AI also assists socio-emotional learning by identifying stress and disengagement signals, providing motivational suggestions, celebrating milestones, and providing encouragement while learning through difficult concepts (Ifenthaler et al., 2024). In K-12 contexts, AI tutors have also been introduced to support K-12 social-emotional learning curricula to support students in programmatically and systematically developing resilience and emotional intelligence along with academic learning (Indellicato, 2024). AI tutoring systems with socio-emotional learning capabilities address students' academic and social needs are key in assisting towards better retention rates for at-risk students in education to keep them engaged and leveled throughout their educational experience. Lastly, Henriksen et al. offer a thematic literature review on generative AI in relation to social emotional learning (SEL) and its implications on teacher education through generative AI, but also the potential to make a broader impact on education.

Predictive Analytics: Using AI To Forecast Student Outcomes and Intervene Early

Predictive analytics enables institutions to forecast student outcomes effectively, identifying retention concerns and designing specific efforts to reduce drop-out rates (Sihare, 2024). Moreover, AI supports cross-national academic partnerships and new learning materials, creating a global job of tutoring that crosses national borders (Adoui, 2024). Predictive analytics is an important technology in the future of AI tutoring, allowing the system to forecast student outcomes and intervene before students fall too far behind. AI has massive amounts of historical and real-time data at its disposal (i.e., grades, participation metrics, behaviour metrics) to predict which students will fall behind in the future and suggest personalized approaches for correcting the issue, such as with greater access to resources or more one-on-one support (Chiu et al., 2023). Georgia State University (2023), for example, reports a

60% increase in overall graduation rates over the last ten years through data-informed student success efforts.

In addition to individualized strategies, predictive analytics can inform institutional initiatives, allowing educators to construct a curriculum that manages common learning gaps. For example, educators may be able to adjust the pace of a math course that combines students who struggle with arithmetic with those who struggle with algebra (Zawacki-Richter et al., 2024, p. 165). Furthermore, predictive analytics has been described in relation to natural language processing when identifying students' discussions in online forums. Predictive algorithms can specify and analyze early signals of confusion or disengagement that are not captured in the numeric data (Paulchamy et al., 2024). Such a comprehensive understanding of pedagogy will allow for interventions that make sense in time and space, confronting the intellectual issues that arise. As predictive analytics develop, they can serve as more exact and immediate third-party interventions, reducing dropout rates and consequently increasing the ability of students to meet their maximum potential through AI and data-driven practices.

The Potential for AI to Foster Global Tutoring Networks

Artificial Intelligence-based tutoring solutions could create global tutoring networks that connect learners, educators, and resources, whenever and wherever, to develop a truly interconnected educational ecosystem. To begin with, AI connects a diverse group of thinkers, promoting cross-border global academic collaboration to come together and cultivate innovative learning content to form global tutoring networks (Adoui, 2024). AI, combined with cloud-based platforms for learning and AI-enhanced translation tools, can provide effective, personal instruction in multiple languages as it forges ahead, while eliminating any barriers and bridging isolated learning experiences (Al-Zahrani & Alasmari, 2024). Organizations such as the Global Education Coalition, organized by UNESCO, are exploring the role of AI in delivering tutoring for the disadvantaged in every corner of the globe, and for every program, which includes providing math tutoring to rural students in Africa, in their official languages (UNESCO, 2024).

Lifelong Tutoring: Supporting Students Beyond Graduation

Generative AI is continuing to impact lifelong learning and supports educators to plan curricula that enable responsible use of AI (Asad & Ajaz, 2024). To help students realize their potential in an AI-enabled future, curriculum development must focus on AI fundamentals, enhance quantitative skills, and provide competencies in disciplines such as data analysis and machine learning linked to job and career opportunities in the Data and AI Cluster (Rozman et al., 2023).

Learning systems guided by AI technology are getting ready to help people learn for life, supporting continuous education outside of the typical formal experience. In light of ongoing technological and economic changes, the demand for upskilling and reskilling is increasing and AI tutors can provide adult learners with personalized paths in learning, whether this is developing new skills or changing careers (Chheang et al., 2023). For instance, using AI to provide learners with course and micro-credential recommendations based on their career goals and prior knowledge profiles is being implemented on platforms such as Coursera and LinkedIn Learning, offering professional development for adult learners throughout their lifetimes. (Crompton & Burke, 2023). This change is relevant for adults in certain fields such as technology and healthcare, where professionals are expected to relearn the skills required in their profession, given new innovations such as their use of AI tools in diagnostic medicine or developing their skills using new programming languages (Zawacki-Richter et al., 2024). AI tutors also think specifically about adult learners, considering their unique characteristics, by providing flexible, self-paced learning that accounts for busy adult lifestyles, like providing a busy working parent with short pieces of instructional content or a busy professional wishing to get hands-on experience with online simulations (Bayly-Castaneda et al., 2024). Additionally, AI can facilitate lifelong learning by cultivating a growth mindset and empowering learners to engage with new subjects, like a retiree learning digital art or a mid-career employee learning about sustainability, through adaptive and engaging tutoring systems. Thus, by being able to tutor continuously, AI systems ensure that learning is carried on and available in an accessible way, enabling learners to confidently and capably navigate a world of unpredictable knowledge.\

Preparing Students for the AI-Driven Future of Work and Professional Development

AI tutoring systems are important both in helping students prepare for an AI-rich world of work and assisting students in developing hard and soft skills required for future success. These systems can impart new skills, including data literacy, a foundation in AI ethics, and computational thinking, to make sure students are prepared for today's workplace, where automation and AI technologies are ubiquitous (Chheang et al., 2023). For example, AI tutors can supervise students as they undergo coding when learning Python or teach students how to evaluate AI-generated outputs (skills seen as critical in the technology-driven industries) (Rachha & Seyam, 2023).

Similarly, AI systems could actually recreate a workplace scenario in which students learn how to develop teamwork strategies for managing virtual teams, working with a data set or making decisions about the ethical use of AI in their work (Paulchamy et al, 2024). While technical knowledge is important, many employers now require graduates to have soft skills such as adaptability, problem-solving, and teamwork and AI tutors have the unique ability to, for example, offer feedback on the quality of students' teamwork when they engage in teamwork-related activities or guide students as they build their unknowable projects such as think beyond the walls for creating a sustainable business model with in an imagined market (Ifenthaler et al., 2024). For example, an AI tutor may facilitate a group effort wherein students from multiple disciplines are collaborating to solve a global issue and provide real-time feedback about their communication and leadership abilities. More importantly, AI tutoring systems connect outcomes of education to the needs of the workforce, allowing students to be prepared to enter a future where AI is a tool for learning and a shift in professional development.

CONCLUSION

Summary

This article has examined the potentially transformational power of AI-powered tutoring systems to reshape student support in all types of educational situations. The introduction presented these systems as a sophisticated platform that uses machine learning, natural language processing, and data analytics to provide customized, scalable, and interactive learning experiences. It explored the progression of tutoring services through time, from the traditional human-led tutoring method to the point of AI-powered tutoring services; putting action to theories related to the role of artificial intelligence in education and opportunities that exist and challenges that result from the blending of both. The article elaborated on the mechanisms of AI tutoring systems, focusing on features that allow unique personalization, communication protocols, and tracking learning with data. It compared the advantages of AI tutoring, such as tailored learning paths, instantaneous feedback, scalable experiences, and improved learner engagement, along with its challenges, including data privacy concerns, possible algorithmic biases, and the importance of intervention throughout their experience with an AI tutoring system. Numerous cases of students learning through AI tutoring were presented in the K-12, higher education, corporate training, and lifelong learning contexts. Finally, the article looked ahead to the future of AI in education, including emerging trends such as predictive analytics, global networks of tutoring services, and the role of AI tutoring services to surface cognitive or non-cognitive skills needed to prepare learners for an AI-filled workforce.

AI-enabled tutoring systems provide immense potential for improving student success by making learning more personalized, accessible, and enjoyable. These systems aim to mitigate long-standing educational inequities by configuring instruction to individual variations, enabling real-time feedback, and expanding the scale of high-quality education to underrepresented communities, as noted by Bojorquez and Vega (2023). AI-driven systems have the potential to motivate students through gamified approaches and provide support for a range of students via personalized accommodations, which has been shown to lead to better retention and achievement (Chiu et al., 2023). Real-world applications of AI-enabled tutoring systems have shown meaningful impacts (e.g., Khan Academy, Squirrel AI) while emerging developments like predictive analytics and global tutoring systems indicate a future of AI-assisted learning that extends all the way from K-12 to lifelong learning. Realizing the potential of AI-enabled tutoring systems requires decision-makers to grapple with ethical challenges like ensuring equitable access to learning and retaining the human touch to develop a balanced, diverse educational ecosystem (Selwyn, 2019).

Recommendations

Incorporating AI-powered tutoring systems involves utilizing hybrid models that emphasize AI's speed and efficiency in completing tasks, while also using human mentorship to promote thoughtful decision-making, critical thought, and emotional support (Ifenthaler et al., 2024). Administrators must also make financial commitments towards professional development to let teachers develop the skills they need to use AI tools, with a preference for AI platforms that guarantee data privacy and enforce transparency (Karan & Angadi, 2024). Policymakers should produce regulations that enforce checks and balances on algorithm bias, equitable access to AI tools, and the ethical use of AI tools in education. Collaboration among stakeholders should prioritize testing programs, as has been the case in pilots conducted in K-12 and higher education systems in the US, to examine the effectiveness of AI-powered tutoring solutions before broad implementation, and to make adjustments in their programming according to their educational goals for students (Al-Zahrani & Alasmari, 2024).

The effective and ethical implementation of AI in tutoring is critical for its success. AI can create exceptional learning opportunities in ways that have never been seen before, but it must be used openly, responsibly, and equitably. Student data must be protected, biases eliminated, and equitable access to learning opportunities enhanced (Chinta et al., 2024). Moreover, the human factor—empathy, creativity, mentorship—that enables education to be so transformative must be maintained. If we can cultivate an environment where AI works collaboratively with human educators, we can envision a future of AI-enabled tutoring that helps students achieve educational outcomes and prepares them to thrive in a world driven by AI (Selwyn, 2019)—a world where students develop the skills, resilience, and ethical judgement to navigate an ever-changing global landscape.

REFERENCES

AbuSahyon, A. S. A. E., Alzyoud, A., Alshorman, O., & Al-Absi, B. (2023). AI-driven technology and Chatbots as tools for enhancing English language learning in the context of second language acquisition: A review study. *International Journal of Membrane Science and Technology*, *10*(1), 1209–1223.

Adoui, A. (2024). AI-driven empowerment of international higher education and international networking: A case study of Moroccan universities. *Simulacra*, *7*(1), 1–20.

Al-Zahrani, A. M., & Alasmari, T. M. (2024). Exploring the impact of artificial intelligence on higher education: The dynamics of ethical, social, and educational implications. *Humanities & Social Sciences Communications*, *11*, 912. DOI: 10.1057/s41599-024-03432-4

Aleven, V., Roll, I., McLaren, B. M., ... Help Helps, But Only So Much: Research on Help Seeking with Intelligent Tutoring Systems. *Internal Journal of Artificial Intelligence in Education* 26, 205–223 (2016). https://doi-org.libproxy.lib.csusb.edu/10.1007/s40593-015-0089-1

Alhusban, M. I., Alshurafat, H., & Khatatbeh, I. N. (2024). Exploring professional perspectives on integrating generative artificial intelligence into corporate learning and development: An organizational change perspective. *Development and Learning in Organizations*. Advance online publication. DOI: 10.1108/DLO-05-2024-0131

Ali, M., Siddique, A., Aftab, A., Abid, M. K., & Fuzail, M. (2024). AI-Powered customized learning paths: Transforming data administration for students on digital platforms. *Journal of Computing & Biomedical Informatics*, *6*(02), 195–204. DOI: 10.56979/602/2024

Asad, M. M., & Ajaz, A. (2024). Impact of ChatGPT and generative AI on lifelong learning and upskilling learners in higher education: Unveiling the challenges and opportunities globally. *The International Journal of Information and Learning Technology*, *41*(5), 507–523.

Avcı, G., Owusu-Boateng, O., Vampa, M., & Khalid, A. M. (2025). Intelligent tutoring systems. In Owusu-Boateng, O. (Ed.). (2025). *Unlocking the Potential: Artificial Intelligence in Education* (pp. 46–57). Deep Science Publishing. https://doi.org/DOI: 10.70593/978-93-49307-53-7_4

Bayly-Castaneda, K., Ramirez-Montoya, M. S., & Morita-Alexander, A. (2024). Crafting personalized learning paths with AI for lifelong learning: A systematic literature review. *Frontiers in Education*, *9*, 1424386. DOI: 10.3389/feduc.2024.1424386

Biswas, G., Leelawong, K., Schwartz, D., & Vye, N. (2005). Learning by teaching: A multiple case study of a teachable agent. *Journal of the Learning Sciences*, *14*(4), 487–526.

Black, P., & Wiliam, D. (1998). Assessment and classroom learning. *Assessment in Education: Principles, Policy & Practice*, *5*(1), 7–74. DOI: 10.1080/0969595980050102

Bloom, B. S. (1984). The 2 sigma problem: The search for methods of group instruction as effective as one-to-one tutoring. *Educational Researcher*, *13*(6), 4–16. DOI: 10.3102/0013189X013006004

Bojorquez, H., & Vega, A. (2023). The Importance of artificial intelligence in education for all students. IDRA Newsletter, 1(5). ED628667.

Carnegie Learning. (2024). Columbus City Schools Embrace ClearLanguages Solutions. Retrieved from https://cdn.carnegielearning.com/assets/research/2024-Columbus_City_Case_Study.pdf?_gl=1*ro3890*_gcl_au*MTUxMzU5MzY5Mi4xNzQwNDE4NTE3*_ga*OTYyMTk2MjU5LjE3NDA0MTg1MTc.*_ga_HT75DMPVPG*MTc0NTgwNTAwNy4zLjEuMTc0NTgwNTE5My42MC4wLjA

Chheang, V., Sharmin, S., Marquez-Hernandez, R., Patel, M., Rajasekaran, D., Caulfield, G., Kiafar, B., Li, J., Kullu, P., & Barmaki, R. L. (2023). Towards anatomy education with generative AI-based virtual assistants in immersive virtual reality environments. *arXiv preprint arXiv:2306.17278*. https://doi.org//arXiv.2306.17278DOI: 10.48550

Chingos, M. M., & Whitehurst, G. J. (2011). *Class size: What research says and what it means for state policy*. Brookings Institute., Retrieved from http://www.k12accountability.org/resources/Accountability-Committees/0511_class_size_whitehurst_chingos.pdf

Chinta, S. V., Wang, Z., Yin, Z., Hoang, N., Gonzalez, M., Le Quy, T., & Zhang, W. (2024). FairAIED: Navigating fairness, bias, and ethics in educational AI applications. *arXiv preprint arXiv:2407.18745*. https://arxiv.org/abs/2407.18745

Chiu, T. K. F., Xia, Q., Zhou, X., Chai, C. S., & Cheng, M. (2023). Systematic literature review on opportunities, challenges, and future research recommendations of artificial intelligence in education. *Computers and Education: Artificial Intelligence*, *4*, 100118. DOI: 10.1016/j.caeai.2022.100118

Christensen, C. M., Horn, M. B., & Caldera, C. (2017). *Is K-12 blended learning disruptive? An introduction to the theory of hybrids*. Clayton Christensen Institute.

Coursera. (2024). Announcing AI-powered capabilities enabling educators to use Coursera Coach to deliver interactive, personalized instruction. Retrieved from https://blog.coursera.org/announcing-ai-powered-capabilities-enabling-educators-to-use-coursera-coach-to-deliver-interactive-personalized-instruction/

Crompton, H., & Burke, D. (2023). Artificial intelligence in higher education: The state of the field. *International Journal of Educational Technology in Higher Education*, *20*(1), 22. DOI: 10.1186/s41239-023-00392-8

Cruz, X. M. M., Honrado, J. L. E., Libatique, N. J. C., Tangonan, G. L., Oppus, C. M., Cabacungan, P. M., Mamaradlo, J. P. A., Mercado, N. A. M., Dela Cruz, J. A., Dela Cruz, J. A., & Cruz, J. G. (2022). Design and demonstration of a resilient content distribution and remote asynchronous learning platform.In *Adjunct Proceedings of the 2021 International Conference on Distributed Computing and Networking* (pp. 98-103). https://doi.org/DOI: 10.1145/3427477.3428190

D'Mello, S., & Graesser, A. (2012). Do emotions matter during learning? A review of affective computing research in intelligent tutoring systems. *Computers & Education*, *58*(1), 18–29.

Ejjami, R. (2024). The Adaptive Personalization Theory of Learning: Revolutionizing Education with AI. *Journal of Next-Generation Research 5.0*. DOI: https://doi.org/DOI: 10.70792/jngr5.0.v1i1.8

Eltahir, M. E., & Babiker, F. M. E. (2024). The influence of artificial intelligence tools on student performance in e-Learning environments: Case study. *Electronic Journal of e-Learning*, *22*(9), 91–110. DOI: 10.34190/ejel.22.9.3639

Funda, V., & Mbangeleli, N. B. A. (2024). Artificial Intelligence (AI) as a Tool to Address Academic Challenges in South African Higher Education. *International Journal of Learning, Teaching, and Educational Research*, *23*(11), 520–537. DOI: 10.26803/ijlter.23.11.27

Georgia State University. (2023). *Student success: Georgia State University's national model*. https://success.gsu.edu/

Gibson, R. (2024). *The Impact of AI in Advancing Accessibility for Learners with Disabilities*. Educause Review. https://er.educause.edu/articles/2024/9/the-impact-of-ai-in-advancing-accessibility-for-learners-with-disabilities?utm_source=chatgpt.com

Gosselin, A., Abbasi, S., & Richards, A. (2024, September). *Shell's strategic competence development: Ensuring capability and capacity building across the global operational safety skill pool* [Conference paper]. SPE International Health, Safety, Environment and Sustainability Conference and Exhibition, Abu Dhabi, United Arab Emirates. https://doi.org/DOI: 10.2118/220340-MS

Graesser, A., Hu, X., & Sottilare, R. (2018). Intelligent tutoring systems. In Fischer, F., Hmelo-Silver, C. E., Goldman, S. R., & Reimann, P. (Eds.), *International Handbook of the Learning Sciences* (pp. 246–255). Routledge., DOI: 10.4324/9781315617572

Graham, C. R., Borup, J., Short, C. R., & Archambault, L. (2019). K-12 Blended Teaching: A Guide to Personalized Learning and Online Integration, 1. https://doi.org/DOI: 10.59668/2

Guo, Q., Graham, C. R., Borup, J., Sandberg, B., & West, R. E. (2024). Parental support challenges for K-12 student online engagement. *Distance Education*, *45*(4), 579–605. DOI: 10.1080/01587919.2024.2397481

Halkiopoulos, C., & Gkintoni, E. (2024). Leveraging AI in e-learning: Personalized learning and adaptive assessment through cognitive neuropsychology—A systematic analysis. *Electronics (Basel)*, *13*(18), 3762. DOI: 10.3390/electronics13183762

Harati, H., Sujo-Montes, L., Tu, C.-H., Armfield, S. J. W., & Yen, C.-J. (2021). Assessment and Learning in Knowledge Spaces (ALEKS) Adaptive System Impact on Students' Perception and Self-Regulated Learning Skills. *Education Sciences*, *11*(10), 603. DOI: 10.3390/educsci11100603

Henriksen, D., Creely, E., Gruber, N., & Leahy, S. (2025). Social-emotional learning and generative AI: A critical literature review and framework for teacher education. *Journal of Teacher Education*, *76*(3), 312–328. DOI: 10.1177/00224871251325058

Holmes, W., Bialik, M., & Fadel, C. (2019). *Artificial intelligence in education: Promises and implications for teaching and learning*. Center for Curriculum Redesign.

Ifenthaler, D., Majumdar, R., Gorissen, P., Judge, M., Mishra, S., Raffaghelli, J., & Shimada, A. (2024). Artificial intelligence in education: Implications for policymakers, researchers, and practitioners. *Technology. Knowledge and Learning*, *29*(4), 1693–1710. DOI: 10.1007/s10758-024-09747-0

Indellicato, R. (2024). Artificial intelligence and social-emotional learning: What relationship? *Journal of Modern Science*, *60*, 460–470. DOI: 10.13166/jms/196765

Jaliaawala, M. S., & Khan, R. A. (2020). Can autism be catered with artificial intelligence-assisted intervention technology? A comprehensive survey. *Artificial Intelligence Review*, *53*(2), 1039–1069. DOI: 10.48550/arXiv.1803.05181

Karan, B., & Angadi, G. R. (2024). Potential risks of artificial intelligence integration into school education: A systematic review. *Bulletin of Science, Technology & Society, 43*(3-4), 67-85. https://doi.org/ (Original work published 2023)DOI: 10.1177/02704676231224705

Kröll, M., & Burova-Keßler, K. (2022). Use of AI tools in learning platforms and the role of feedback for learning. In: Evangelos Markopoulos, Ravindra S. Goonetilleke and Yan Luximon (eds) Creativity, Innovation and Entrepreneurship. AHFE (2022) International Conference. AHFE Open Access, vol 31. AHFE International, USA. http://doi.org/DOI: 10.54941/ahfe1001504

Luckin, R., Holmes, W., Griffiths, M., & Forcier, L. B. (2016). *Intelligence unleashed: An argument for AI in education*. Pearson Education.

Maghsudi, S., Lan, A., Xu, J., & Van Der Schaar, M. (2021). Personalized education in the artificial intelligence era: What to expect next. *IEEE Signal Processing Magazine*, *38*, 37–50. https://ieeexplore.ieee.org/stamp/stamp.jsp?arnumber=9418572. DOI: 10.1109/MSP.2021.3055032

Martinez, M. R., & Ebardo, R. (2024). How AI supports returning adult learners in a developing economy: enhancing academic writing through self-determination theory. *International Conference on Computers in Education.* https://doi.org/DOI: 10.58459/icce.2024.4961

Math Outcomes, A. L. E. R. K. S. n.d. Retrieved from https://www.mheducation.ca/higher-education/learning-solutions/aleks/math-outcomes

McLaren, B. M., & Nguyen, H. A. (2023). Digital learning games in Artificial Intelligence in Education (AIED): A review. Handbook of Artificial Intelligence in Education, 440-484. https://doi.org/DOI: 10.4337/9781800375413.00032

Mehendale, P. (2023). Personalization in Education through AI. *European Journal of Advances in Engineering and Technology*, *10*(3), 60–65.

Mersha, M., Lam, K., Wood, J., AlShami, A., & Kalita, J. (2024). Explainable artificial intelligence: A survey of needs, techniques, applications, and future direction. *arXiv*. https://arxiv.org/abs/2409.00265

O'Neill, J. L. (2021). Accessibility for all abilities: How universal design, universal design for learning, and inclusive design combat inaccessibility and ableism. *Journal of Open Access to Law*, *9*, 1. https://ojs.law.cornell.edu/index.php/joal/article/view/107

Omar, Z. F., Mior Harun, M. H., Mohd Ishar, N. I., Mustapha, N. A., & Ismail, Z. (2024). Enhancing professional development and training through AI for personalized learning: A framework to engaging learners. International Journal of e-Learning and Higher Education (IJELHE), 19(3), 115-138. Retrieved from: https://ir.uitm .edu.my/id/eprint/97200

Ouyang, Z., Jiang, Y., & Liu, H. (2024). The effects of Duolingo, an AI-integrated technology, on EFL learners' willingness to communicate and engagement in online classes. *International Review of Research in Open and Distance Learning*, *25*(3), 97–115. DOI: 10.19173/irrodl.v25i3.7677

Panjwani-Charania, S., & Zhai, X. (2023). AI for students with learning disabilities: A systematic review. *In X. Zhai & J. Krajcik (Eds.), Uses of Artificial Intelligence in STEM Education (pp. xx-xx). Oxford, UK: Oxford University Press. Available at* SSRN*:* https://ssrn.com/abstract=4617715

Paulchamy, B., Selvaraj, V., Indumathi, N. M., Ananthi, K., & Teresa, V. V. (2024). Integrating sentiment analysis with learning analytics for improved student engagement. *International Journal of Computational and Experimental Science and Engineering, 10*(4). Advance online publication. DOI: 10.22399/ijcesen.781

Rachha, A., & Seyam, M. (2023). Explainable AI In Education: Current Trends, Challenges, And Opportunities. *SoutheastCon, Orlando, FL, USA, 2023*, 232–239. DOI: 10.1109/SoutheastCon51012.2023.10115140

Rehan, H. (2023). Shaping the future of education with cloud and AI technologies: Enhancing personalized learning and securing data integrity in the evolving EdTech landscape. *Australian Journal of Machine Learning Research & Applications*, *3*(1), 359–395. https://sydneyacademics.com/index.php/ajmlra/article/view/107/102

Reigeluth, C. M., & Karnopp, J. (2020). *Vision and action: Reinventing schools through personalized competency-based education*. Marzano Resources.

Rich, P. J., West, R. E., & Warr, M. (2015). Innovating how we teach collaborative design through studio-based pedagogy. In Orey, M. A., & Branch, R. M. (Eds.), *Educational media and technology yearbook* (Vol. 39, pp. 147–163). Springer International Publishing.

Romero, M., & Barberà, E. (2012). Computer-based creative collaboration in online learning. In *International conference on web-based learning* (pp. 330-336). Springer, Berlin, Heidelberg.

Ryan, R. M., & Deci, E. L. (2000). Self-determination theory and the facilitation of intrinsic motivation, social development, and well-being. *The American Psychologist*, *55*(1), 68. 10.1037110003-066X.55.1.68 PMID: 11392867

Sawyer, R. K., & Henriksen, D. (2024). *Explaining creativity: The science of human innovation*. Oxford university press.

Selwyn, N. (2019). *Should Robots Replace Teachers? AI and the Future of Education*. Polity Press.

Sihare, S. R. (2024). Student Dropout Analysis in Higher Education and Retention by Artificial Intelligence and Machine Learning. *SN Computer Science*, *5*(2), 202.

Tang, T., Vezzani, V., & Eriksson, V. (2020). Developing critical thinking, collective creativity skills and problem solving through playful design jams. *Thinking Skills and Creativity*, *37*, 100696.

The U.S. Department of Education's 2016 National Educational Technology Plan (NETP) and 2017 NETP Update. Retrieved from: https://www.ed.gov/

UNESCO. (2024). United for SDG4: the Global Education Coalition in action. https://unesdoc.unesco.org/ark:/48223/pf0000389072

VanLehn, K. (2011). The Relative Effectiveness of Human Tutoring, Intelligent Tutoring Systems, and Other Tutoring Systems. *Educational Psychologist*, *46*(4), 197–221. DOI: 10.1080/00461520.2011.611369

Wang, T., Lund, B. D., Marengo, A., Pagano, A., Mannuru, N. R., Teel, Z. A., & Page, J. (2023). Exploring the potential impact of Artificial Intelligence (AI) on international students in higher education: Generative AI chatbots, analytics, and international student success. *Applied Sciences (Basel, Switzerland)*, *13*(11), 6716. DOI: 10.3390/app13116716

Warr, M. (2024). Beat bias? Personalization, bias, and generative AI. In J. Cohen & G. Solano (Eds.), Proceedings of Society for Information Technology & Teacher Education International Conference (pp. 1481–1488). Association for the Advancement of Computing in Education (AACE). https://www.learntechlib.org/p/224163/

Williamson, B., & Eynon, R. (2020). Historical threads, missing links, and future directions in AI in education. *Learning, Media and Technology*, *45*(3), 223–235. DOI: 10.1080/17439884.2020.1798995

Zawacki-Richter, O., Bai, J. Y. H., Lee, K., van Tryon, P. J. S., & Prinsloo, P. (2024). New advances in artificial intelligence applications in higher education? *International Journal of Educational Technology in Higher Education*, *21*(32). Advance online publication. DOI: 10.1186/s41239-024-00464-3

Zhang, X., Sun, J., & Deng, Y. (2023). Design and application of intelligent classroom for English language and literature based on artificial intelligence technology. *Applied Artificial Intelligence*, *37*. Advance online publication. https://www.tandfonline.com/doi/pdf/10.1080/08839514.2023.2216051. DOI: 10.1080/08839514.2023.2216051

Chapter 13
Integrating Artificial Intelligence in Education:
Insights From a Teacher Training Workshop

María Carolina Ordenes Guzmán
https://orcid.org/0009-0001-6564-6465
Pontificia Universidad Católica de Chile, Chile

Camila Martínez Chacaltana
https://orcid.org/0009-0006-3486-2073
Academia de Biotecnología Agrícola, Chile

Aída Leyton Olguín
https://orcid.org/0009-0005-0055-9183
Academia de Biotecnología Agrícola, Chile

G. S. Prakasha
https://orcid.org/0000-0002-1287-7606
Christ University, India

ABSTRACT

This chapter explores the impact of an in-person AI training workshop on Chilean in-service teachers across a network of four schools. Through a mixed-methods approach—including pre- and post-surveys with qualitative and quantitative data—the study examines shifts in teacher attitudes, knowledge, and intentions to use AI in educational practice. Results show increased confidence, pedagogical alignment, and ethical awareness, particularly regarding inclusion and differentiated instruction. The chapter also highlights the importance of contextualized training, gender representation, and long-term support to ensure equitable and meaningful

DOI: 10.4018/979-8-3373-2397-8.ch013

INTRODUCTION

Artificial Intelligence (AI) is no longer a futuristic concept—it is actively transforming how we live, work, and learn. In the educational sector, AI applications such as adaptive learning systems, generative text tools, predictive analytics, and automated feedback mechanisms are increasingly being introduced in classrooms and school systems across the world. While these technologies offer opportunities for personalization, efficiency, and pedagogical innovation, they also raise critical questions regarding ethics, equity, access, and the evolving role of the teacher (Holmes et al., 2019; Luckin et al., 2016).

Recognizing the power and complexity of AI, international organizations such as UNESCO and the OECD have emphasized the need for human-centered and rights-based approaches to its integration in education. UNESCO's guidance for policymakers (2021) highlights the importance of digital inclusion, ethical governance, and professional development for educators. Similarly, the OECD (2021) has stressed the importance of ensuring that AI enhances—not replaces—human instruction, and that education systems invest in teachers' capacity to understand and shape AI in pedagogically meaningful ways.

However, these global aspirations contrast with highly unequal realities on the ground. While countries in the Global North are beginning to implement coordinated AI strategies in education, including investments in teacher training, many countries in the Global South remain at a disadvantage. In Latin America, the adoption of AI in education has been fragmented and limited by infrastructural inequalities, weak institutional capacity, and a lack of long-term vision. Few countries in the region have developed formal policies or curricula addressing AI literacy and even fewer have established sustained training programs for teachers (Zawacki-Richter et al., 2019).

While the global discourse on AI in education has accelerated, Latin America remains underrepresented in both research and policy development in this domain. A systematic review by Peñafiel-Jurado et al. (2024) highlights that most empirical studies on AI in education are concentrated in Europe, North America, and parts of Asia, with Latin America accounting for a minimal portion of global research output. Where studies do exist, they are often exploratory, fragmented, and seldom focus on teacher training or pedagogical integration.

Countries such as Brazil and Colombia have initiated national dialogues around digital innovation and AI. Brazil's *"Estratégia Brasileira de Inteligência Artificial"* (EBIA) includes education as a strategic area but lacks detailed planning regarding teacher development and pedagogical frameworks . Similarly, Colombia's National

AI Policy (CONPES 4144) outlines 106 actions to advance AI adoption but offers limited guidance on integrating AI into teacher training programs . Consequently, the responsibility of implementing AI tools often falls on individual schools or educators, who must navigate these emerging technologies with minimal institutional support.

In Chile, as in much of Latin America, teacher professional development related to AI remains scarce and disconnected from broader curricular or equity goals. Existing programs tend to focus narrowly on tool functionality without linking to critical pedagogy, national standards, or ethical considerations. As a result, teachers are often left to experiment individually or rely on informal networks, leading to uneven adoption and widening pedagogical gaps.

These trends underscore the urgent need for a Latin American approach to AI in education—one that is grounded in local realities, sensitive to structural inequalities, and committed to human rights and social justice. UNESCO's AI Competency Framework advocates for a human-centered approach to AI education, promoting critical thinking, ethical considerations, and responsible use of AI technologies. This framework emphasizes the co-construction of AI literacy initiatives with educators and communities, ensuring they are culturally relevant and not merely imported from global North contexts.

Chile presents a complex but revealing case. With one of the highest internet penetration rates in Latin America and a history of public investment in educational technology, the country has long been positioned as a regional leader in digital innovation. However, this reputation obscures persistent inequalities in access, capacity, and pedagogical integration. The COVID-19 pandemic made these disparities even more visible, particularly in public schools and rural areas, where limited access to devices, connectivity, and support led to significant disruptions in learning and teaching (Fundación País Digital, 2020).

Chile's trajectory in educational technology policy provides a crucial historical backdrop for understanding current challenges in AI integration. For over two decades, the *Enlaces* program—launched in the early 1990s—stood as the country's flagship initiative for ICT inclusion in schools. According to Claro and Jara (2020), *Enlaces* evolved from a hardware-distribution model to a broader strategy that emphasized pedagogical change, digital literacy, and teacher development. However, the program was ultimately phased out without institutional continuity, leaving a vacuum in public leadership for digital education. This discontinuity has had lasting effects on teacher preparedness. While *Enlaces* provided early infrastructure and training, its dismantling exposed a lack of systemic integration and long-term vision for digital transformation. These institutional fragilities directly inform the current need for coherent, future-oriented teacher training models—particularly in relation to emerging technologies like AI.

Although the Chilean Ministry of Science, Technology, Knowledge and Innovation updated its *National Artificial Intelligence Policy* in 2024 to align with international recommendations, the education sector remains underprepared. While the policy identifies teacher training as a priority, concrete mechanisms for capacity building remain underdeveloped. Teachers are expected to adopt and apply AI tools in their practice without adequate professional development, institutional support, or pedagogical guidance.

At the same time, the nature of AI presents unique challenges for educators. Unlike earlier waves of educational technology—often limited to hardware, productivity software, or digital content repositories—AI systems involve algorithmic decision-making, real-time data analysis, and probabilistic reasoning. Understanding these systems requires not only technical knowledge but also critical literacy: the ability to interrogate how AI tools work, whose knowledge they encode, and how they may affect students differently depending on language, gender, or socioeconomic status (UNESCO, 2021; Selwyn, 2019).

One of the most pressing concerns in the integration of AI in education relates to the ethical implications of surveillance and algorithmic bias. As AI systems increasingly rely on data from students' interactions, learning patterns, and behaviors, the boundary between pedagogical observation and personal surveillance becomes blurred. Scholars such as Williamson and Eynon (2020) argue that educational AI tools—while often presented as neutral or beneficial—embed specific logics of control and measurement that shape how learning is defined, valued, and assessed.

In Latin America, where data governance frameworks are often weak or underdeveloped, these concerns are magnified. AI tools developed in the Global North are frequently deployed without adequate adaptation to the linguistic, cultural, or pedagogical realities of the region. The use of predictive analytics for student performance, for instance, may reproduce existing biases by penalizing students from marginalized backgrounds or reinforcing deficit views of certain communities. Teachers are rarely trained to interrogate these systems, and institutional safeguards to protect students' data and agency are often absent.

Moreover, the automation of assessment and instructional decision-making can undermine teacher autonomy and pedagogical nuance. When decisions about what content to deliver, how to grade, or when to intervene are outsourced to algorithms, educators may find their roles diminished to that of supervisors of automated processes. This has significant implications for teacher identity and professional judgment, both of which are central to equitable, relational models of education. Thus, training programs must engage educators not only as users of tools, but as ethical stewards who critically evaluate the values and consequences embedded in AI systems.

While policy discourse often frames AI as an inevitable and universally welcomed innovation, teachers' reactions are far more complex. Across Chile and the wider Latin American region, educators express not only interest but also skepticism, fatigue, and even resistance toward the rapid introduction of new technologies. These responses are not necessarily technophobic; rather, they reflect a rational assessment of past experiences with innovation that overpromised and underdelivered—often without meaningful consultation or sustained support.

Teachers who work in under-resourced schools or in communities historically marginalized by education systems are particularly attuned to the risks of over-reliance on technology. Some view AI with suspicion, concerned that it may be used to justify budget cuts, reduce staffing, or introduce high-stakes monitoring. Others raise concerns about workload, noting that new technologies often create additional bureaucratic tasks rather than simplifying teaching. Still others critique the push toward AI as part of a broader neoliberal logic of educational reform—one that privileges metrics, standardization, and efficiency over care, creativity, and collective learning.

These forms of resistance and ambivalence should not be dismissed; rather, they offer valuable insights into the real conditions and priorities of teachers. Professional development programs that aim to build AI readiness must take these tensions seriously. They must create space for dissent, foster trust through transparency, and ensure that the conversation around AI remains grounded in the lived realities of the classroom. Only by acknowledging these complexities can we hope to co-construct AI futures that are not only innovative, but just.

Teachers are at the center of this transformation. They are not simply end-users of tools; they are professional decision-makers who shape the design, implementation, and ethical use of AI in the classroom. However, most teachers have not received systematic training in AI concepts or pedagogy. Surveys in Chile and other Latin American countries consistently show that teachers feel unprepared to integrate AI into their practice, even as they recognize its potential benefits.

In this context, the concept of AI readiness offers a valuable framework for thinking about teacher preparation. Wang et al. (2023) define AI readiness as a multidimensional construct that includes cognition, ability, vision and ethics dimensions. They argue that AI readiness is not a fixed trait but a dynamic capacity that can be developed through targeted interventions. Importantly, Wang's model also highlights the role of institutional factors—such as leadership support, peer networks, and access to tools—in shaping educators' ability to adopt AI effectively.

This chapter responds to these challenges by examining the case of a teacher training initiative designed to foster AI readiness in Chile. The study is situated within the context of a three-day pedagogical innovation workshop conducted in 2024, which brought together 260 in-service teachers from a network of four schools—two located in Santiago and two from regional areas who traveled to the capital to participate. The program was developed and delivered by the Agricultural Biotechnology Academy and was facilitated entirely by women educators, emphasizing gender equity in technological leadership. Participants represented a wide range of subject areas and levels, including both primary and secondary education. The initiative sought not only to introduce practical AI tools but to cultivate critical reflection, ethical engagement, and inclusive pedagogical planning. By documenting this intervention, the chapter aims to contribute to the growing field of AI in education by foregrounding the experiences and perspectives of teachers in the Global South—highlighting the conditions under which educational technologies can truly support equitable and human-centered innovation.

METHODS

Research Design

This study employed a mixed-methods exploratory design (Creswell & Plano Clark, 2018), combining quantitative and qualitative data to examine the impact of an artificial intelligence (AI) teacher training workshop in Chile. Mixed methods were selected to provide a more comprehensive understanding of the phenomenon than either quantitative or qualitative data alone could offer (Fetters et al., 2013). Specifically, the research was structured as a convergent parallel design, in which both qualitative and quantitative data were collected simultaneously, analyzed separately, and then interpreted together.

The research aimed to explore the following overarching questions:

- What was the level of AI knowledge, confidence, and pedagogical intention among teachers before and after the workshop?
- How did participants describe their learning experiences and perspectives on AI in the classroom?
- What patterns emerged in the correlation between attitudes, self-perceived readiness, and prior experience with educational technology?

Given the novelty of the intervention and the limited research on AI training for in-service teachers in the Chilean context, the exploratory nature of the study was crucial to uncovering unanticipated patterns, beliefs, and contextual insights (Creswell, 2014).

Participants and Setting

The training took place in Santiago, Chile, as part of a larger pedagogical innovation initiative conducted in 2024. A total of 260 in-service teachers from four K–12 schools participated. Two of the schools were based in Santiago, while the other two were located in regional areas of Chile. Teachers from the regional schools traveled to the capital to attend the sessions, which were held simultaneously over three full days.

The participating schools were part of a private educational network with a shared interest in pedagogical innovation and curricular transformation. Teachers spanned a wide range of subject areas, including: Language and Literature, Mathematics, Science, History and Social Studies, Technology and Informatics, Vocational Education, Physical Education, Arts, among others.

Educators also represented diverse levels of professional experience, from early-career teachers to senior educators with over 25 years in the profession. Data from the pre-workshop survey (n=147) show that approximately 78% of respondents were women, consistent with national trends in the Chilean teaching workforce. Participants taught across primary and secondary levels, and some reported leadership roles such as curriculum coordination or digital resource management.

Participation in the study was voluntary and informed by an introductory briefing before data collection. Only those who completed the pre- and/or post-workshop surveys and consented to participate were included in the analysis.

The Workshop: Structure and Pedagogical Design

The workshop, titled "Ai in the Classroom: Pedagogical Innovations for Teachers of the Future", was developed and delivered by the *Academia de Biotecnología Agrícola* and facilitated exclusively by a team of women experts in educational technology and AI. The program was simultaneous for all participants and designed as an interactive, applied training experience, combining exposition, live demonstration, group collaboration, and individual reflection.

The workshop was organized around three main thematic blocks, each building progressively toward classroom application:

1. Fundamentals of Artificial Intelligence and Ethics
    - Definitions and key concepts of AI, machine learning, and generative models
    - Ethical considerations, including data privacy, bias, and algorithmic responsibility
    - Reflective discussion on the teacher's role in an AI-mediated world

2. Hands-On Exploration of AI Tools for Education
   - o Demonstrations of AI-powered platforms such as ChatGPT, Eduaide.ai, Canva AI, MagicSchool
   - o Analysis of affordances and limitations for lesson planning, differentiation, and assessment
   - o Group tasks to simulate tool use in varied disciplinary contexts
3. Collaborative Planning and Integration into Teaching Practice
   - o Teachers co-designed short implementation proposals for their own classrooms
   - o Peer review of proposed uses, with a focus on alignment with learning outcomes
   - o Open discussion of challenges, institutional constraints, and support needs

Data Collection

Two researcher-made instruments were used: a pre-workshop survey and a post-workshop survey, both administered digitally via Microsoft Forms. The surveys were anonymous and designed to capture both quantitative and qualitative data. Although the numbers of participants was 260, only 147 consented to respond to the pre implementation of the workshop survey. In the case of the post implementation survey, a number of 134 consented to respond and participate in the study.

Each survey included:

- Demographic information (e.g., gender, years of experience, subject area)
- Likert-scale items (5-point scale) assessing:
  - o Familiarity with AI
  - o Confidence in using AI tools
  - o Perceived pedagogical usefulness of AI
  - o Ethical concerns or perceived risks
- Multiple-choice items on frequency and types of digital tools used
- Open-ended questions, such as:
  - o "What expectations do you have for this workshop?" (Pre implementation)
  - o "What challenges do you foresee in applying AI in your context?" (Pre implementation)
  - o "Describe your experience using any AI tool so far." (Pre implementation)
  - o "What part of the workshop did you find most useful or relevant to your teaching practice?" (Post implementation)
  - o "How do you plan to integrate any of the tools explored during the workshop into your lesson planning or instruction?"

Both instruments were reviewed for clarity and relevance by a small pilot group of teachers from outside the participant sample. Data collection was completed during the week of the workshop. The pre implementation survey was implemented at the beginning of the teacher training program and the post implementation survey was conducted right after the AI workshop.

DATA ANALYSIS

Quantitative Analysis

Quantitative data were analyzed using descriptive statistics to identify central tendencies and frequency distributions. Additionally, a correlational analysis was conducted to explore relationships between variables in the pre- and post-survey responses. For example, changes in confidence were examined in relation to prior experience with educational technology or self-reported subject area.

No inferential tests were conducted due to the exploratory nature of the study and the voluntary sample, which was not randomized. However, the analysis allowed for the identification of shifts in key variables, especially increases in familiarity and pedagogical intention.

Qualitative Analysis

Open-ended survey responses were analyzed using a hybrid thematic analysis approach. This process combined human-led coding conducted in Python (using *pandas* and *nltk* libraries) with AI-assisted categorization facilitated by ChatGPT. The analysis followed the inductive thematic analysis model described by Braun and Clarke (2006), which emphasizes the emergence of patterns from the data itself rather than applying predefined coding schemes.

The workflow involved several steps:

1. Initial data cleaning and anonymization
2. Tokenization and keyword extraction using Python
3. Grouping of responses into preliminary themes based on frequency and semantic similarity
4. Validation and refinement of thematic categories through comparison between human and AI-assisted coding

This hybrid approach allowed for both the efficiency of computational analysis and the interpretive depth of qualitative inquiry, enabling the research team to identify key areas of participant concern, enthusiasm, and transformation. Thematic categories that emerged included expectations of innovation, ethical concerns, perceived barriers to classroom use, and post-training confidence.

ETHICAL CONSIDERATIONS

The study adhered to ethical principles aligned with institutional research standards and Chilean national regulations. Participation was voluntary, and all data was collected anonymously. Respondents were informed of the purpose of the study and their right to withdraw at any time.

No identifying information was collected. The researchers ensured confidentiality during data handling and analysis. Since no minors or vulnerable populations were involved, and the activity was conducted as part of a teacher development program with institutional support, no formal IRB approval was required under current local norms. However, ethical review was conducted internally by the research team prior to data collection.

Trustworthiness and Limitations

Following Creswell and Plano Clark (2018), this study sought triangulation through the integration of multiple data sources and types (quantitative and qualitative), as well as methodological complementarity. The use of both structured Likert responses and open-ended reflections enabled a nuanced understanding of participant experience.

Nevertheless, several limitations must be noted:

- The sample was non-random and limited to a single school network.
- Surveys were self-reported, which may introduce social desirability bias.
- The post-survey was completed immediately after the workshop, limiting long-term insight into classroom application.
- While AI-assisted analysis added efficiency, it required human oversight to ensure interpretive accuracy.

Despite these limitations, the mixed-methods design offered valuable insights into how teachers engage with AI training, their perceived readiness, and the pedagogical and ethical frameworks they bring to technological innovation.

RESULTS

Pre-Workshop Survey Results

The pre-workshop survey was completed by 147 in-service teachers, representing a diverse range of teaching contexts across the four schools participating in the AI training initiative. This section outlines key descriptive findings concerning participants' professional profiles, familiarity with artificial intelligence (AI), prior experiences with AI tools, willingness to implement such tools in the classroom, and perceived needs for training.

Participant Profile

Respondents came from all four schools in the network. The sample reflected a wide distribution in terms of educational levels, subjects taught, and professional experience.

- Educational Levels: The majority of participants worked in secondary education followed by those teaching upper primary. A smaller proportion taught in the early primary grades.
- Subject Areas: The most commonly taught subjects were Mathematics, Language and Literature, Science, and History, followed by Vocational Education, Arts, and Physical Education.
- Experience: A significant portion of respondents had more than 10 years of teaching experience, while others reported having between 6–10 years, 3–5 years, or less than 3 years in the classroom.
- Gender: While gender identification was optional, among respondents who provided it, approximately 78% identified as women and 22% as men, aligning with national teaching workforce demographics in Chile.

This diversity provides a rich foundation for understanding how perceptions of AI vary across roles, experience levels, and disciplines.

Familiarity with Artificial Intelligence in Education

When asked whether they were familiar with the concept of AI in educational contexts, the vast majority (~90%) responded "yes". Many teachers had encountered the term in informal or professional development contexts but lacked structured training.

In open responses about how they would describe AI or what interests them about the field, teachers provided a mix of interpretations:

- Some highlighted technological curiosity ("how machines can learn like humans").
- Others emphasized practical classroom applications such as content generation, time-saving for planning, or differentiated instruction.
- A few demonstrated critical awareness, referring to ethical concerns, misinformation, or student dependence on AI.

This suggests that while there is broad awareness, understanding is still uneven and often based on informal experiences.

Use of AI Tools in the Classroom

In terms of direct experience using AI tools in their teaching practice:

- A majority of respondents (over 70%) reported not having used AI tools inside the classroom.
- Among those who had, most described limited or exploratory uses, such as using AI to generate quiz questions or improve grammar in student writing.

Among the few teachers who had experimented with AI tools prior to the workshop, examples of use were limited but pedagogically meaningful. One teacher shared, "AI helped me write differentiated instructions for students with special educational needs." Another noted, "I used ChatGPT to generate creative activities for my language class."

These responses suggest early-stage, yet purposeful, applications of AI in support of inclusion and curricular innovation. However, such uses were isolated and largely informal, reflecting the absence of structured training or institutional guidance. Interestingly, some teachers who had not used AI in class still expressed interest or intention, indicating an attitudinal openness to future use.

Use of AI Tools Outside the Classroom

More teachers reported using AI for personal or professional purposes outside the classroom than within it. These uses included:

- Content summarization
- Assistance with grading or rubrics
- Generating parent communications
- Planning support

Prior to the workshop, a notable number of teachers reported having used AI tools outside the classroom for personal or professional tasks. The most commonly mentioned platforms were ChatGPT, Canva AI, and Google Bard. These tools were primarily used to support planning and reduce the cognitive load associated with routine teaching responsibilities. As one participant stated, "AI helps me save time when planning".

Several teachers described using AI to assist with document editing, idea generation, and text summarization. One teacher commented, "I used ChatGPT to draft a letter to parents and to reword student feedback." Others highlighted the ability of AI to function as a personal assistant for managing content:

- "I asked it to help me create an evaluation rubric."
- "I use it to make summaries of articles I don't have time to read in full."

Some responses reflected creative or exploratory uses of AI. For example:

- "I use Canva AI to generate visual templates for my slides."
- "I've tried Bard for brainstorming questions for a debate."

While most uses remained at an informal level, the tone of these comments conveyed a sense of pragmatic enthusiasm. Teachers saw AI not as a radical transformation, but as a set of time-saving, low-stakes supports. As one participant summed up: "It helps me do the same things faster, not necessarily better—but it makes a difference when you're short on time."

These experiences, though limited in pedagogical depth, suggest that many teachers had already begun to engage with AI tools in ways that alleviate administrative burdens, even if not yet integrated into instruction or student-facing activities.

Willingness to Use AI with Students

Participants were asked to rate their willingness to use AI tools with students on a scale from 1 to 5, where 1 indicated no willingness and 5 indicated full openness. Despite some hesitation about classroom implementation, the overall disposition was highly positive:

- Most responses clustered around values 4 and 5.
- The average score was approximately 4.4.

Teachers who rated their willingness as 4 or 5 frequently mentioned potential benefits such as supporting differentiated instruction or helping students with limited literacy skills. However, some also noted the need for proper guidance and regulation.

Training Needs

When asked what kind of training they would need to effectively incorporate AI into their teaching practice, participants overwhelmingly emphasized the importance of practical, context-sensitive preparation. Responses revealed a strong desire for hands-on learning, as well as for content that aligns with their local curriculum, student needs, and ethical responsibilities as educators.

The most frequently requested types of training included:

- Practical, step-by-step demonstrations of AI tools in action
- Concrete examples aligned with the Chilean curriculum, especially in core subjects such as language, math, and science
- Strategies for using AI ethically and safely, particularly around student privacy, data protection, and responsible sourcing
- Guidelines for evaluating the accuracy and bias of AI-generated outputs, especially when using tools for grading or content generation

These preferences reflect teachers' recognition that AI must be integrated not only technically but pedagogically and ethically. Several participants specifically asked for short, targeted learning modules that could be applied immediately in their practice. For example: "We need short training capsules with concrete examples." Another participant emphasized differentiated instruction: "We need training that includes planning, assessment, and adaptation for diverse learning needs."

Some teachers also expressed a desire to explore AI for inclusive education, for example by using tools to support students with disabilities or language barriers. Others asked for guidance on institutional use, such as writing school communications or managing workflows.

Importantly, the demand for context-relevant training was consistent across subject areas and levels of experience—from early-career teachers to veteran educators. This suggests that while AI may still feel "new," the pedagogical questions it raises are deeply familiar: How do we adapt innovation to local needs? How do we ensure fairness, clarity, and quality in what we teach?

The emphasis on ethical discernment and classroom-level utility points to a critical takeaway: teachers are not simply asking how to use AI—they are asking how to use it well. This presents an opportunity to design future professional development programs that move beyond tool exposure and support critical, thoughtful, and culturally responsive integration.

Reasons for (Not) Using AI in Education

Participants' open-ended responses to the question "Why would you use or not use AI in the classroom?" revealed a complex and nuanced set of beliefs, reflecting both enthusiasm and critical concern. These responses clustered into several recurring themes, pointing to the pragmatic, ethical, and equity-related considerations shaping teachers' views.

Reasons for Using AI. Many respondents expressed interest in AI as a way to enhance efficiency, creativity, and adaptability in their teaching. Teachers noted that AI could help them:

- Save time during lesson planning and assessment
- Generate differentiated or personalized materials
- Support student engagement through novel activities

One teacher summarized this view as: "I would use it because it helps me be more efficient and focus on what matters most—teaching."

Others highlighted AI's potential to support students with diverse learning needs: "It could help me adapt reading tasks for students with different levels."

Reasons for Concern or Caution. Conversely, a substantial group of respondents voiced ethical, cognitive, and pedagogical concerns. Common worries included:

- Student overreliance on AI tools and a resulting loss of critical thinking
- Data privacy risks and the lack of clear guidelines for safe use
- The possibility that AI may oversimplify complex learning processes

One particularly reflective comment noted: “I worry that students will lose the ability to think for themselves if they get used to depending on an external tool.”

Others expressed concern about algorithmic bias, especially when using AI to grade or give feedback.

Equity and Access Considerations

Several teachers raised the issue of digital inequality. Even those open to using AI noted that it could deepen existing gaps if not all students had access to devices, stable internet, or digital literacy support. As one teacher explained: “I wouldn’t want to use something in class that only some students can access at home.”

This concern was especially present among educators working in under-resourced communities, where AI tools might exacerbate existing disparities in participation and learning outcomes.

Overall, these responses reveal that teachers are not uncritically embracing AI—they are reflecting, negotiating, and weighing its benefits against its potential harms. Their questions are less about whether AI is useful, and more about when, how, and for whom it should be used. These insights reinforce the need for professional development programs that respect teachers' pedagogical judgment and help them navigate the ethical and contextual complexities of innovation.

Tools Known or Used

Participants listed a wide variety of AI tools they were aware of or had experimented with. The most frequently mentioned were:

- ChatGPT
- Canva (AI-enhanced features)
- Eduaide.ai
- MagicSchool.ai
- Quillbot
- Google Translate (though not strictly an AI tool, often associated with automation)

Some listed tools they had only heard of but never used. A few responses reflected misconceptions about what qualifies as AI, demonstrating the need for clearer conceptual framing in training programs.

Post-Workshop Survey Results

The post-workshop survey was completed by 134 in-service teachers across the four participating schools. The purpose of this survey was to evaluate teachers' perceptions of the workshop's relevance, effectiveness, and applicability, as well as to gather feedback regarding specific AI tools explored, perceived risks and benefits, and their intentions to apply AI tools both inside and outside the classroom.

Participant Profile

Participants in the post-survey mirrored the demographic characteristics of the pre-survey sample:

- Gender: Approximately 60% identified as women, 32% as men, with some preferring not to disclose.
- Experience: The largest group reported having more than 10 years of teaching experience, followed by those with 6–10 years, 3–5 years, and less than 3 years.
- Subject Areas: Teachers from Mathematics, Language and Literature, Science, Physical Education, Religious Education, and Vocational Education responded.
- Educational Levels: The majority taught in secondary education, followed by upper and lower primary levels.

This diverse range of experience and discipline added depth to the perspectives gathered.

Usefulness and Relevance of the Workshop

The post-workshop survey revealed overwhelmingly positive perceptions of the training's usefulness. When asked whether the workshop had provided practical tools applicable to their teaching practice:

- 115 teachers (86%) responded "Yes"
- 9 teachers (7%) answered "Partially"
- Only a small number expressed uncertainty or did not respond

These results affirm that the workshop successfully addressed real classroom needs. Teachers highlighted the practical orientation of the sessions, praising the hands-on demonstrations, the accessibility of AI tools, and the clear links to everyday planning and instruction.

Several teachers specifically noted that the tools presented were directly usable in their subject areas, and that the workshop bridged the gap between theory and practice. As one participant shared: "The workshop gave me real tools I can start using right away. It wasn't just theory."

Others emphasized the value of having ready-to-use platforms, such as ChatGPT, Canva, and Eduaide, showcased in an applied context. One participant wrote: "What I liked the most was learning how to design lessons using ChatGPT." Another added: "I liked seeing all the AI programs that we explored."

And a third reflected: "What stood out to me was the ability to adapt content to my subject."

These responses suggest that teachers valued not only the content itself but also the pedagogical framing—seeing AI not as an external novelty but as something that could be relevant, personalized, and adaptable to their local realities and curricular frameworks.

The balance of practical exploration with opportunities for collaborative design was frequently mentioned as a key strength. Teachers appreciated working in groups to plan how to apply AI tools to their lessons, noting that the exchange of ideas across disciplines enriched their understanding.

Tools of Interest

Teachers were also asked which AI tools they would most like to explore further. Among the most frequently cited were:

- ChatGPT and ChatGPT Plus
- Slidesgo + AI-enhanced visual tools
- Eduaide.ai
- MagicSchool
- Canva AI

Some teachers mentioned free or open-access tools due to limited school budgets. Others included experimental platforms or plugins not covered in the session, suggesting that the workshop had piqued curiosity beyond the core tools introduced.

Intentions to Implement AI Tools in Teaching

One of the most telling outcomes of the post-workshop survey was the significant increase in teachers' stated intentions to apply AI tools in their practice. When asked whether they planned to implement AI in the classroom with students, the responses were overwhelmingly positive:

- Over 80% of participants responded affirmatively
- A small subset qualified their response, citing contextual limitations such as connectivity, licensing, or institutional policy gaps

Even among those who had expressed skepticism or uncertainty in the pre-workshop survey, many now indicated a tentative openness to experimentation. Their language often reflected a shift from resistance to cautious optimism. For example: "Yes, but my access would be limited by costs." Another participant stated: "Yes, I'd like to try using ChatGPT for guided writing activities."

These quotes illustrate a growing recognition of AI as a complementary tool, rather than a threat to their pedagogical role. Teachers no longer framed AI as distant or abstract, but rather as something worth testing, adapting, and learning from.

When asked about intentions to use AI tools outside the classroom, for purposes such as lesson planning, assessment design, or content generation, responses were nearly unanimous. Teachers identified AI as a valuable support in:

- Reducing time spent on routine administrative tasks
- Generating quizzes, rubrics, and summaries
- Adapting resources to different student needs

As one respondent shared: "Using AI to help with planning allows me to spend more time thinking about how to teach, not just what to teach." Another noted: "It's like having a virtual assistant—it gives me a starting point, especially when I'm stuck."

These reflections suggest that teachers see AI as a time-saving, creativity-boosting tool—particularly when used outside of direct instruction. For many, the appeal lies not in outsourcing their work, but in augmenting their capacity to focus on deeper pedagogical thinking and student interaction.

Together, these findings reflect a clear post-workshop transformation: from cautious awareness to purposeful intention. Teachers did not emerge as experts, but as informed professionals ready to explore, aware of risks, and motivated by potential.

Perceived Areas of Usefulness

In the post-workshop survey, teachers were asked to identify the domains of their practice where they believed AI tools could be most beneficial. Their responses revealed a broad but coherent vision of AI as a supportive force for key instructional processes, particularly those that demand adaptability and time efficiency.

The areas most frequently selected included:

- Lesson and class planning
- Creation of didactic materials
- Designing differentiated instruction
- Assessment creation and question design
- Developing strategies to increase student engagement

Among these, the generation and adaptation of content for diverse learners emerged as the most salient perceived benefit. Teachers emphasized AI's capacity to personalize learning experiences and address varying student needs more efficiently. As one teacher explained: “AI can help me renew my materials and connect more with my students’ current interests.” Another teacher highlighted the value of AI in preparing visual and written materials: “With tools like Canva or Eduaide, I can prepare resources that are more engaging and clear for different learning levels.” Several teachers noted that AI could also act as a scaffolding tool, helping them generate multiple versions of the same activity, or offering alternative explanations for complex topics: “I see AI being useful when I need to explain something in different ways for different students.”

The survey also revealed that teachers saw AI not only as a tool for student-facing materials but as a means of enhancing their own instructional decision-making. A few commented that AI could help them stay pedagogically current, serving as a prompt or companion for generating new ideas, updating content, or integrating interdisciplinary approaches. One participant noted: “I can use AI to brainstorm lesson openings or to check if my activities align with the curriculum.”

Taken together, these insights suggest that teachers perceive AI as a flexible, low-barrier tool that can assist with everything from content creation to personalization, planning, and engagement. Their responses reflect a balanced view—appreciating AI’s potential to support rather than replace human judgment, creativity, and adaptation.

Risks and Concerns

Although the majority of responses were positive, several teachers raised ethical and pedagogical concerns:

- Overreliance on AI by students
- Data privacy and algorithmic bias
- Loss of critical thinking
- Reinforcement of inequalities (e.g., differential access to tech)

These risks echoed concerns that had emerged in the pre-survey, but they were now articulated with greater clarity and specificity after the workshop experience. Rather than expressing general unease, teachers began to frame their critiques around pedagogical principles, ethical safeguards, and implementation strategies. A key theme that emerged was the non-negotiable role of teacher mediation in the responsible use of AI in the classroom. As one participant succinctly put it: “The tool is useful, but it must be used with clear educational objectives and sound teacher judgment.”

This comment reflects a common sentiment among workshop participants: that AI can enhance teaching, but should not override pedagogical intentionality or reduce teacher agency. AI, in their view, is a tool—not a method, and certainly not a replacement for professional expertise.

Suggestions for Improvement

Suggestions for future iterations of the workshop included:

- More time: Teachers felt the 3-day model was intense but too short for deeper exploration
- More individualized support or subject-specific examples
- Better sound/technical setup in some venues

Some participants offered constructive suggestions for enhancing future iterations of the workshop. One teacher proposed incorporating student simulation activities or “mock AI classrooms” to observe realistic implementation scenarios and better anticipate classroom dynamics when using AI. This points to a desire for training that not only introduces tools but also models their use in authentic pedagogical contexts. Others called for extended support and follow-up sessions to accompany initial training. As one participant remarked: “I would like a second part of the workshop, with real examples of implementation.”

These suggestions underscore participants’ recognition that professional learning is a process, not a one-time event. They reflect a commitment to ongoing reflection, refinement, and collaboration, and a belief that deeper transformation will come through continued engagement and the sharing of lived classroom experiences.

General Feedback

In the final open-ended section of the survey, participants expressed a strong sense of engagement, gratitude, and renewed motivation. Their comments reflected not only satisfaction with the workshop format and content, but also a deeper appreciation for the inclusive and empowering environment it fostered:

- "I'm very grateful for this experience. I leave feeling inspired."
- "I hope this training reaches more teachers in the network."
- "It was a very well-organized event, led by inspiring women."

Several participants specifically emphasized the significance of having an all-women team of facilitators leading an AI workshop—a field often perceived as male-dominated. These comments positioned the experience not just as instructional, but as a symbolic and practical intervention in gender equity, especially within the context of STEM education.

By centering women as knowledge leaders in a technology-oriented space, the workshop helped redefine who is seen as an innovator and expert. For many participants—particularly women educators—this visibility contributed to a greater sense of belonging, agency, and aspiration. It also aligned with the broader goals of inclusive educational transformation, demonstrating that equity must be embedded not only in AI implementation, but in who leads, designs, and teaches it.

Comparative Analysis: Impact of the Workshop

The final stage of the analysis focuses on evaluating the impact of the AI workshop by comparing teacher perceptions, familiarity, and willingness to use AI tools before and after the training. Drawing from the pre- and post-survey datasets, the contrast reveals a substantial shift in attitudes, readiness, and intentions regarding the integration of artificial intelligence into pedagogical practice.

Increased Disposition to Use AI Tools in the Classroom

Perhaps the most striking result of the comparison lies in the evolution of AI usage intentions. Prior to the workshop, only 25% of teachers reported having used AI tools in their classrooms. By contrast, post-workshop data show that 96% of respondents expressed a willingness to implement AI tools with their students, and 99.2% indicated intent to use them outside the classroom (e.g., for planning or administration).

This dramatic increase indicates that the workshop succeeded not only in raising awareness but in transforming attitudes into actionable pedagogical intentions. The shift is particularly meaningful in light of the exploratory nature of the study: teachers moved from tentative curiosity to concrete plans for integration. Even those who were initially skeptical voiced greater openness after engaging with practical examples and collaborative planning exercises.

Expanded Familiarity with AI Tools

The pre-workshop survey showed that while most participants had heard of AI, their practical experience was limited. Many teachers associated AI primarily with general productivity tools or held incomplete conceptions of what qualifies as artificial intelligence. This led to scattered or inconsistent uses, often confined to isolated tasks like proofreading or idea generation.

After the workshop, participants were able to:

- Name specific AI tools (e.g., ChatGPT, Eduaide, Canva AI)
- Identify relevant classroom applications
- Distinguish between ethical and unethical uses
- Develop lesson ideas grounded in their subject areas

This indicates not just increased awareness, but also a clearer and more pedagogically anchored understanding of what AI is and how it can be used.

Reinforcement of Pedagogical Intentions

Teachers' written reflections before and after the workshop suggest a clear shift in how they conceptualized the role of AI in education. In the pre-workshop phase, many responses expressed curiosity mixed with uncertainty, revealing a cautious interest without a clear pathway for implementation. As one teacher noted: "I'm not sure how to use it with students, but it sounds interesting."

In contrast, post-workshop reflections were markedly more grounded in pedagogical intentionality. Teachers articulated specific ways in which AI could support their instructional goals—particularly in differentiation and student-centered planning. One participant wrote: "I'd like to use AI to personalize writing exercises based on students' levels."

This evolution in framing indicates that the workshop successfully contextualized AI within real classroom practice. Rather than being perceived as an abstract or external innovation, AI was increasingly viewed as a flexible, adaptable tool that could be aligned with curricular objectives and responsive to student diversity.

Such a shift from general interest to purpose-driven application demonstrates the importance of professional development that goes beyond tool exposure. It highlights the value of pedagogical framing, ethical reflection, and subject-specific adaptation in preparing teachers to integrate AI meaningfully into their practice.

Ethical Awareness and Critical Reflection

Interestingly, while enthusiasm for AI increased, so too did ethical and critical awareness. Participants who had little to say about AI risks in the pre-survey voiced clear concerns post-workshop:

- Bias in content generation
- Dependence and cognitive passivity in students
- Privacy of student data

Rather than suppressing concerns, the workshop nurtured space for ethical deliberation, enabling teachers to develop a more nuanced understanding of both the potentials and limitations of AI.

Gender and Representation Impact

Although gender was not the explicit focus of the study, several comments suggest that the fact that the workshop was led by a woman carried symbolic and affective significance for participants—particularly for women teachers. As one participant shared: "Incredible session; the fact that it was led by a woman made it even more meaningful for me." This feedback underscores the importance of representation and identity in professional development—particularly within the context of AI and STEM education, where female leadership remains underrepresented. Beyond knowledge transmission, the workshop also modeled inclusive participation and equitable expertise, reaffirming that who delivers the message is as impactful as the message itself.

Reflections on Limitations and Long-Term Impact

Despite the overwhelmingly positive outcomes, some comparative reflections point to structural and institutional constraints that may hinder long-term implementation:

- Lack of devices or stable internet in some classrooms
- Unclear school policies on AI use
- Insufficient follow-up or support mechanisms

While the workshop succeeded in catalyzing interest and confidence, its impact will depend on whether schools provide sustained support, technical resources, and opportunities for continued experimentation and collaboration.

DISCUSSION

The results of this study offer compelling insight into how a carefully structured professional development program can meaningfully reshape teachers' understanding, attitudes, and intentions regarding the use of artificial intelligence (AI) in education. More than a simple training on digital tools, the workshop created a participatory space for reflection, experimentation, and collective sense-making. It encouraged teachers to position themselves not just as users of technology, but as pedagogical designers, ethical stewards, and agents of innovation. The substantial shifts observed—from limited experience with AI tools to nearly unanimous willingness to implement them—signal not only technical readiness, but a deeper process of professional reorientation. In what follows, we interpret these findings in light of broader educational, cultural, and ethical dynamics, particularly within the Latin American context.

AI Readiness as a Situated, Constructed Process

A multidimensional model of AI readiness offers a productive lens for understanding the transformation observed among participants. According to Wang et al. (2023) readiness involves the interplay of cognition, ability, vision and ethics. Prior to the workshop, many teachers in this study demonstrated a fragmented understanding of AI—recognizing its existence, but unsure how it applied to their classroom. Their confidence was low, and their intentions to implement were hesitant or conditional.

The workshop shifted this dynamic in a powerful way. By the end of the training, teachers had developed not only clearer conceptual understandings but also a renewed sense of self-efficacy. As one participant put it: "Now I feel that AI is not out of reach. It's not just for computer experts. I can use it to help my students." This shift from distance to proximity—from abstraction to action—is central to what it means to be "ready." Importantly, this readiness was not an individual trait, but a socially constructed state fostered through collaborative learning, contextual examples, and guided exploration.

This movement from potential to intention reflects a key insight from Desimone and Garet's (2015) work on professional development: effective learning occurs when training is sustained, collaborative, content-specific, and grounded in practice. The workshop was not a generic technology session but one that invited teachers to bring their own pedagogical challenges and curricular goals into the conversation. They explored how AI could support formative assessment, lesson design, content differentiation, and inclusive practices. The result was not merely technical competence, but a sense of ownership and purpose.

Such findings support Desimone and Garet's (2015) contention that effective professional development must be job-embedded, practice-oriented, and collaborative. The teachers in this study did not receive generic digital literacy training; they engaged in a pedagogical process where AI tools were interrogated, tested, critiqued, and tailored to real classroom needs. In doing so, they gained not only tools, but vision.

Pedagogical Innovation Rooted in Professional Identity

One of the most significant outcomes of the workshop was not the mere intention to use AI, but the way teachers spoke about their practice afterward. Rather than adopting a technocentric view of AI, participants emphasized how these tools could support differentiation, inclusion, creativity, and student engagement. One teacher explained: "With ChatGPT, I can create versions of the same activity for students at different levels. It helps me see my students more individually."

This pedagogically grounded perspective is especially important in a regional context where much of the digital innovation discourse is still dominated by platform providers or infrastructure-focused policies. By contrast, these teachers framed AI as a way to enhance, rather than displace, core teaching values. They retained their role as pedagogical decision-makers and emphasized human-centered use. As another participant noted: "It's not about replacing the teacher, it's about helping us be more effective with our time and creativity."

Structural Tensions and Ethical Ambivalence

While the workshop clearly increased enthusiasm and readiness, it also surfaced deeper concerns about the ethical and social risks of AI integration, particularly in under-resourced contexts. As participant feedback indicated, exposure to new tools raised not only interest but ambivalence and critical reflection. Teachers voiced worries about student overreliance, data privacy, surveillance, and the reproduction of social inequities.

One teacher stated: "What worries me is not the tool itself, but that students will stop thinking critically and start copying everything the machine says." Another added: "We still don't understand what happens with the information that these tools collect. I wouldn't want to put my students at risk."

These perspectives echo the concerns raised in the literature by Williamson and Eynon (2020), who warn that AI in education is often introduced through logics of efficiency and personalization, without sufficient attention to power, agency, and surveillance. Tools that promise to "optimize learning" may also normalize data extraction, algorithmic bias, and top-down control over curriculum and assessment. When teachers lack the training or institutional support to critically examine these dynamics, they are placed in a vulnerable position, expected to adopt innovations while absorbing the ethical consequences.

In Latin America, these risks are magnified by unequal infrastructure, limited digital rights legislation, and widespread disparities in school resources. As Fundación País Digital (2020) has documented, connectivity gaps and device access remain uneven, particularly between urban and rural areas, and between public and private schools. Even among the four schools in this study's network, there were substantial differences in terms of access to computer labs, bandwidth, and IT support. Some participants mentioned that their school could not provide the devices or Wi-Fi needed to use the tools demonstrated: "It's great, but back at school, we only have internet in the teacher's room."

These accounts reveal the structural fragility of innovation in systems shaped by inequity. AI tools may be compelling, but their adoption depends on layers of support—technical, institutional, and pedagogical—that are not evenly distributed. Without addressing these structural constraints, AI risks reinforcing existing divides rather than bridging them.

Teacher Agency and Resistance

Interestingly, teachers in this study did not respond to these tensions with rejection. Instead, many expressed a desire for more guidance, more conversation, and more time to explore. Their feedback was not technophobic, it was thoughtful, cautious, and grounded in professional experience.

As one teacher commented: "I'm open to trying it, but I want to be sure it aligns with my values as an educator." Another explained: "We need space to talk about how this changes our role. If AI is doing the writing or planning, what does that mean for what we teach?"

These responses highlight the reflective and ethical core of teaching, often overlooked in technology discourse. As Selwyn (2019) notes, educators are not passive recipients of innovation, they actively evaluate new tools based on pedagogical goals, classroom realities, and their relationships with students. What may be read by outsiders as "resistance" is often a form of professional discernment, rooted in concern for educational integrity.

This finding is particularly important in a region where technology adoption is often driven by external mandates, donor programs, or vendor interests, rather than bottom-up reflection. It underscores the need to involve teachers in the design, adaptation, and governance of AI in education, treating them not only as users but as co-authors of educational futures.

Gender, Inclusion, and Representational Equity

A distinctive feature of the workshop, and one that participants consistently emphasized, was the fact that it was designed and facilitated entirely by women. This was not incidental; it had a profound impact on participants' perceptions of expertise, representation, and empowerment within a technological field that is still heavily male-dominated.

These testimonials highlight that gender-inclusive facilitation was not only symbolically important—it directly contributed to participants' sense of belonging and agency in the AI learning space. In many Latin American contexts, women make up the majority of the teaching force but are underrepresented in tech leadership and innovation initiatives. This workshop, by centering women as facilitators and knowledge producers, challenged existing hierarchies and expanded the participants' understanding of who drives educational innovation.

This finding aligns with feminist scholarship on technology and pedagogy, which argues that inclusion is not just about who is in the room, but about who sets the agenda and how knowledge is constructed (Wajcman, 2004; Bonder, 2002). In this workshop, female facilitators modeled not only technical fluency, but pedagogical intentionality, ethical awareness, and relational leadership—qualities that resonated strongly with participants' own professional identities.

These gender dynamics should not be viewed as a side note—they are central to building just and inclusive AI futures. Equity in AI is not just about tools and access, but about voice, perspective, and power. Ensuring that women—and particularly women educators—play a leading role in shaping how AI is introduced, taught, and regulated in schools is essential for sustainable, human-centered transformation.

Toward a Pedagogy of Critical AI Literacy

Throughout the workshop and surveys, teachers repeatedly called for time and space to reflect on what AI means for education. They were not content to learn how to use tools, they wanted to ask why, when, and with what consequences. This desire points to the need for a more expansive and critical approach to AI literacy, one that includes but goes beyond technical skills.

In this view, AI is not just a tool—it is a cultural and epistemological phenomenon that reshapes how knowledge is produced, circulated, and evaluated. Educators must be equipped not only to navigate it, but to interrogate it. The workshop in this study created an entry point for that work; the next step is to institutionalize and expand this literacy in teacher training programs, school curricula, and educational policy.

Another critical dimension illuminated by the findings is the role of institutional culture in enabling or inhibiting innovation. While the workshop succeeded in raising awareness and building confidence, teachers also voiced concerns about implementation barriers: unclear school policies, lack of time, or competing priorities. These concerns are not merely logistical, they are expressions of structural constraint. As Ertmer and Ottenbreit-Leftwich (2010) remind us, teachers' beliefs interact with their institutional contexts. A supportive environment can reinforce motivation and experimentation, while a risk-averse or under-resourced setting can stifle it. Thus, the success of AI integration depends not only on teacher training but on the cultivation of organizational cultures that value innovation, risk-taking, and shared learning.

In this regard, the workshop's format also stands out: its simultaneous delivery to over 250 teachers from four different schools created a collective learning environment that fostered peer support, horizontal exchange, and cross-disciplinary dialogue. Teachers from different regions, disciplines, and career stages were able to see themselves reflected in the process of experimentation. This is critical because AI tools, while promising, are not one-size-fits-all solutions. Their value depends on adaptation, contextualization, and critical inquiry. The workshop created a space where these adaptations could begin, and where teachers could reflect not only on how AI might help them, but how it might change the way they understand teaching itself.

Implications for Transformation in the Global South

Finally, the study offers insights with broader relevance for the Global South. The Chilean case reflects many of the contradictions that define educational innovation in postcolonial and unequal societies: strong teacher engagement coexisting with weak institutional support; technological curiosity tempered by infrastructural fragility; pedagogical creativity in tension with policy inertia.

Rather than view these contradictions as obstacles, this study suggests they can be a source of insight and possibility. Teachers in this workshop did not ask for turnkey solutions, they asked for meaningful, dialogical spaces where they could learn, question, and build. They demonstrated that transformation is possible, but it must be pedagogically rooted, ethically grounded, and culturally situated.

In many ways, the most powerful outcome of the workshop was not a shift in tool usage, but a reframing of educational agency. Teachers emerged not only more prepared, but more curious, more cautious, and more confident. They began to see AI not as something being imposed from above, but as a resource they could appropriate, question, and transform according to their own values. As one participant said in closing: "AI doesn't replace what I do—it gives me new ways to do it. But I have to decide how, and that means learning, sharing, and thinking critically with others."

This vision of collaborative, reflective, and justice-oriented innovation is precisely what is needed if AI is to serve education—and not the other way around.

CONCLUSION

The integration of artificial intelligence (AI) in education is not simply a matter of introducing new technologies into the classroom, it is a process of cultural, pedagogical, and ethical transformation. This study, grounded in an exploratory mixed-methods approach, provides compelling evidence of how a carefully designed professional development experience can shift teachers' perceptions, confidence, and intentions regarding the use of AI. The workshop analyzed here catalyzed a significant transition: from general awareness and cautious curiosity to active pedagogical planning and a critical understanding of both the potential and the risks of AI.

At the outset of the intervention, most teachers had minimal direct experience with AI in education. Their knowledge was fragmentary, often based on isolated interactions with tools like ChatGPT or Canva, and they expressed uncertainty about how these tools could be integrated meaningfully into their practice. However, post-workshop data revealed a remarkable shift: nearly all participants reported a willingness to implement AI tools both inside and outside the classroom. Even more importantly, their open-ended reflections reflected an evolved understanding of AI's capabilities, limitations, and ethical considerations.

This transformation underscores a central conclusion of this chapter: AI readiness is not a fixed trait, nor is it reducible to technical proficiency. As Wang (2023) argues, readiness involves cognition, ability, vision and ethics dimensions that are shaped by context, culture, and support systems. The workshop's design, emphasizing participatory learning, subject-specific adaptation, and ethical reflection, activated all three dimensions. Teachers did not merely learn to use tools; they began to re-imagine their roles in AI-mediated educational futures.

Another key insight is the importance of contextualized professional development. Teachers consistently highlighted the value of concrete examples, collaborative planning, and critical dialogue. This aligns with well-established literature on effective professional learning (Desimone & Garet, 2015; Darling-Hammond et al., 2017), which emphasizes the need for training that is sustained, relevant, and anchored in classroom realities. The workshop did not offer a one-size-fits-all solution; it created a space for teachers to explore, adapt, and critique AI tools in ways that were responsive to their students, content areas, and institutional constraints.

Equally significant was the role of representation and identity. The fact that the workshop was designed and facilitated entirely by women was not merely symbolic; it actively challenged gendered assumptions about technological expertise. Many participants expressed feeling inspired by the facilitators, whose leadership expanded their sense of who can lead innovation in education. In a region where gender gaps in STEM persist and women educators are often marginalized in tech-related professional development, this model offers a powerful intervention. It affirms that equity must be both a goal and a method of educational transformation.

The study also brings to light the complex emotional landscape of innovation. Teachers expressed both enthusiasm and caution, excitement and skepticism. They saw AI as a tool that could support differentiation, creativity, and efficiency—but also worried about student dependence, ethical risks, and the erosion of critical thinking. This duality is not a contradiction; it is a marker of professional judgment. Effective professional development does not seek to eliminate doubt but to equip educators with the frameworks and communities needed to navigate it. In this regard, the workshop succeeded in building not only technical capacity but also ethical resilience.

That said, the findings must be interpreted in light of persistent structural challenges. Many teachers voiced concerns about connectivity, device availability, and the lack of clear institutional guidelines on AI use. These barriers are not new—they reflect longstanding inequalities in Chile's educational infrastructure, especially in public and rural schools. As noted by Fundación País Digital (2020) and CEPAL (2020), digital inequity remains a defining feature of Latin America's educational landscape. While workshops like this can empower teachers, their long-term impact depends on broader systemic support: investment in infrastructure, curricular alignment, and school-level leadership that fosters innovation.

From a research perspective, this study also demonstrates the value of teacher voice in AI scholarship. Much of the global literature on AI in education focuses on system-level policy or tool design, often neglecting the perspectives of those who implement these technologies on the ground (Zawacki-Richter et al., 2019; Selwyn, 2019). By foregrounding the reflections, doubts, and insights of practicing teachers, this chapter contributes to a more democratic and grounded understanding of AI's educational implications. It shows that meaningful integration requires listening—not only to data but to the lived experiences of educators navigating complex realities.

Looking ahead, several implications for policy, practice, and research emerge. First, professional development must be reimagined not as an auxiliary activity but as a central lever of digital transformation. This requires time, funding, and cultural change within institutions that still view innovation as external or optional. Second, equity must be embedded in every stage of AI integration—from tool selection to training to implementation. This includes addressing not only technological access but also epistemological diversity, ensuring that local knowledge, languages, and pedagogies are respected and uplifted. Third, future research should examine longitudinal impacts of AI training, exploring how teachers' intentions translate into classroom practices, and how students experience and respond to AI-mediated learning environments.

Finally, this chapter invites us to rethink what innovation means in education. Too often, innovation is equated with novelty or speed. But as the teachers in this study demonstrate, innovation can also mean reflection, dialogue, and ethical imagination. It can mean taking the time to ask not only what AI can do, but what it should do—and for whom. It can mean centering human relationships in technological change and insisting that educational futures be co-authored by those who live them every day.

In conclusion, artificial intelligence presents both an opportunity and a challenge for education in Latin America. This study shows that when teachers are trusted, supported, and inspired, they are more than ready to meet that challenge. They are not passive adopters of tools but active builders of more inclusive, thoughtful, and pedagogically grounded futures. It is now up to policymakers, institutions, and researchers to walk with them—and to learn from them—as we imagine what AI in education might truly become.

FUTURE DIRECTIONS

The findings presented in this chapter point to an urgent and promising path forward: one that calls for reimagining AI integration in education not as a technological project alone, but as a pedagogical, ethical, and social endeavor. If the workshop demonstrated anything, it is that teachers are ready to lead this transformation when given the space, tools, and support to do so.

A key priority for the future is the expansion of professional development grounded in local realities. The success of the workshop was not merely about exposing teachers to AI tools—it was about how those tools were introduced: through participatory, context-sensitive, and curriculum-aligned learning. Scaling this model means more than replicating its format; it requires adaptation to diverse school environments, subject areas, and institutional needs. Future programs should be co-constructed with teachers themselves, ensuring that AI training responds to actual classroom challenges rather than abstract policy goals.

Yet short-term workshops alone are not enough. To sustain meaningful change, educators need ongoing institutional support. This includes mentorship, communities of practice, and recognition of AI-related competencies in their professional development. Without structural backing—such as time, resources, and alignment with school innovation goals—teachers risk becoming isolated agents of change in systems that are not yet prepared to support them.

At the policy level, countries like Chile must move from aspirational visions to equitable and actionable frameworks for AI in education. National strategies should include ethical safeguards, clear usage guidelines, and commitments to infrastructure equity—particularly across rural and underserved areas. But policy must go further: it should also promote gender and cultural inclusion, and encourage collaborative leadership among ministries, universities, and school networks. AI integration cannot succeed if it is framed solely in technical terms; it must be situated within broader commitments to teacher agency, student rights, and educational justice.

One of the most powerful opportunities ahead lies in positioning teachers not just as users of technology, but as researchers and innovators. Their voices, experiences, and experiments with AI must inform how these tools evolve. Schools and universities can support this by investing in teacher-led inquiry, enabling local evaluation of AI's classroom impact, and building professional learning networks rooted in shared ethical frameworks.

Moreover, AI literacy should not stop at the classroom door. It must be extended to school leaders, who shape institutional culture and funding decisions and to students and families, who bring their own perspectives and values to the conversation. Building collective, critical engagement with AI is essential if the technology is to serve inclusive and democratic ends.

Finally, Chile's experience should be placed in dialogue with similar efforts across Latin America and the Global South. Regional collaboration can create shared resources, culturally relevant tools, and research partnerships that reflect the realities of the region. In doing so, Latin American educators can challenge the global narrative of AI as a one-size-fits-all solution and instead offer grounded, creative alternatives rooted in social justice, equity, and pedagogical imagination.

REFERENCES

Bonder, G. (2002). From access to appropriation: Women and ICT policies in Latin America and the Caribbean. *Women in Action (Rome, Italy)*, *1*, 94–103. https://www.un.org/womenwatch/daw/egm/ict2002/reports/Paper-GBonder.PDF

CEPAL. (2020). *La educación en tiempos de la pandemia de COVID-19*. Comisión Económica para América Latina y el Caribe (CEPAL). https://repositorio.cepal.org/handle/11362/45904

Claro, M., & Jara, I. (2020). The end of Enlaces: 25 years of an ICT education policy in Chile. *Education Policy Analysis Archives*, *28*(159). Advance online publication. DOI: 10.1344/der.2020.37.96-108

Creswell, J. W. (2014). *Research Design: Qualitative, Quantitative, and Mixed Methods Approaches* (4th ed.). SAGE Publications.

Creswell, J. W., & Plano Clark, V. L. (2018). *Designing and Conducting Mixed Methods Research* (3rd ed.). SAGE Publications.

Darling-Hammond, L., Hyler, M. E., & Gardner, M. (2017). *Effective Teacher Professional Development*. Learning Policy Institute., DOI: 10.54300/122.311

Desimone, L. M., & Garet, M. S. (2015). Best practices in teachers' professional development in the United States. *Psychology, Society, &. Education*, *7*(3), 252–263. DOI: 10.25115/psye.v7i3.515

Ertmer, P. A., & Ottenbreit-Leftwich, A. T. (2010). Teacher technology change: How knowledge, confidence, beliefs, and culture intersect. *Journal of Research on Technology in Education*, *42*(3), 255–284. DOI: 10.1080/15391523.2010.10782551

Fetters, M. D., Curry, L. A., & Creswell, J. W. (2013). Achieving integration in mixed methods designs—Principles and practices. *Health Services Research*, *48*(6pt2), 2134–2156. DOI: 10.1111/1475-6773.12117 PMID: 24279835

Fundación País Digital. (2020). *Brecha en el uso de internet, desigualdad digital en el 2020*. https://paisdigital.org/portfolio-item/brecha-en-el-uso-de-internet-2020/

Holmes, W., Bialik, M., & Fadel, C. (2019). *Artificial Intelligence in Education: Promises and Implications for Teaching and Learning*. Center for Curriculum Redesign.

Luckin, R., Holmes, W., Griffiths, M., & Forcier, L. B. (2016). *Intelligence Unleashed: An Argument for AI in Education*. Pearson Education.

OECD. (2021). *Artificial intelligence and education and skills.* https://www.oecd.org/en/topics/sub-issues/artificial-intelligence-and-education-and-skills.html

Peñafiel-Jurado, R., Márquez-Márquez, N., & Guamán-Villa, I. (2024). Artificial Intelligence in Education: Systematic Review of Perspectives, Benefits, and Challenges in Teaching Practice. *South American Research Journal, 4*(2), 5–15. DOI: 10.5281/zenodo.14509895

Selwyn, N. (2019). *Should robots replace teachers? AI and the future of education.* Polity Press.

UNESCO. (2021). *Artificial Intelligence and Education: Guidance for Policy-makers.* https://doi.org/DOI: 10.54675/PCSP7350

Wajcman, J. (2004). *TechnoFeminism.* Polity Press.

Wang, X., Linlin, L., Seng, C. T., Lu, Y., & Jun, L. (2023). Preparing for AI-enhanced education: Conceptualizing and empirically examining teachers' AI readiness. *Computers in Human Behavior, 146*(21), 107798. DOI: 10.1016/j.chb.2022.107798

Williamson, B., & Eynon, R. (2020). Historical threads, missing links, and future directions in AI in education. *Learning, Media and Technology, 45*(3), 223–235. DOI: 10.1080/17439884.2020.1798995

Zawacki-Richter, O., Marín, V. I., & Bond, M.. (2019). Systematic review of research on artificial intelligence applications in higher education – where are the educators? *International Journal of Educational Technology in Higher Education, 16*, 39. DOI: 10.1186/s41239-019-0171-0

Chapter 14
Effortless Game Creation:
A Teacher's Guide to Using Generative AI in Social Science Education

Lan Hoang Thanh Dang
https://orcid.org/0009-0004-5099-0388
University of Social Sciences and Humanities, Vietnam National University, Hanoi, Vietnam

ABSTRACT

This chapter pursues two primary objectives. First, it aims to guide teachers new to AI game design, from the essentials to their initial steps in exploring deeper prompting. Second, it evaluates the effectiveness of AI-generated games based on three factors: their artistic merit (analyzed via Aristotelian drama structure), adherence to the provided sociological theory, and students' quiz performance and lesson engagement. For the sake of demonstration, two AI-generated game demos are explored: a Role-Playing Game (RPG) and a branching narrative game, whose plots are developed based on Strain Theory and Max Weber's concepts.

INTRODUCTION

How can academic knowledge, often confined within the walls of institutions and scholarly communities, be made accessible to a broader public audience? This question serves as the starting point for this chapter. Integrating gamification into education offers a promising solution to simplify complex academic concepts and attract diverse groups to engage with them. According to a statistic, U.S. young people aged 15 to 24 years old spent an average of approximately 84.6 minutes daily

DOI: 10.4018/979-8-3373-2397-8.ch014

playing games and using computers for leisure in 2023 (Clement, 2024). If even a small fraction of that time could be combined with educational content, it would undoubtedly be time well spent. However, a significant challenge remains: serious games are scarce and often lack investment in design. A U.S. national survey of 694 K-8 teachers revealed that four out of five teachers found it difficult to locate curriculum-aligned games, and only two out of five believed a sufficient variety of such games even existed (Takeuchi & Vaala, 2014). Today, the era of generative AI has dawned, bringing about an incredible capability: to visualise abstract concepts vividly. In the past, an average teacher might have struggled to create fascinating images or videos, let alone program a functional game. Now, designing a game which tailors to their lesson is no longer a distant dream.

The first part of this chapter outlines a beginner-friendly process for creating educational games with AI assistance, tailored for educators, students, or anyone interested in integrating gamification into learning environments: From ideation and story plotting to generating images for environments and characters and finally navigating and getting acquainted with a game engine. It is important to note that the author, a sociology lecturer with zero prior experience in game design or programming, relied heavily on AI assistance throughout the entire process of creating the game demos. The chapter offers suggestions on prompting strategies for AI use. To demonstrate, prototypes from prompt experimentation involving two theoretical frameworks and two distinct game types are then presented. The first is a branching narrative game, which features static scenes and focuses on script management, scene transitions, and the crafting of meaningful player choices and consequences based on a theory (Strain Theory, specifically). The second is a Role-Playing Game (RPG), requiring character movement and programming, where AI was also tasked with constructing the plot around key concepts from Max Weber. Given these distinct characteristics, two implementation methods are introduced: using common presentation software and a game engine. The second objective of this chapter is to evaluate the effectiveness of these AI-generated games based on three factors: their artistic merit (analysed via Aristotelian drama structure), adherence to sociological theory, and quiz performance and learning experience of two student groups (the group exposed to the AI-generated game and the control group). Quantitative data from this small-scale research, combined with student reflections on using AI to create videos and games for learning, inform a brief discussion on the strengths and weaknesses of AI-driven gamification.

THE "TECHNE" IN SHORT

If you want to create an instant game, you can request an AI language model to help you with basic steps, which are as simple as those shown in the diagram below:

Figure 1. Basic workflow with AI to create a serious game

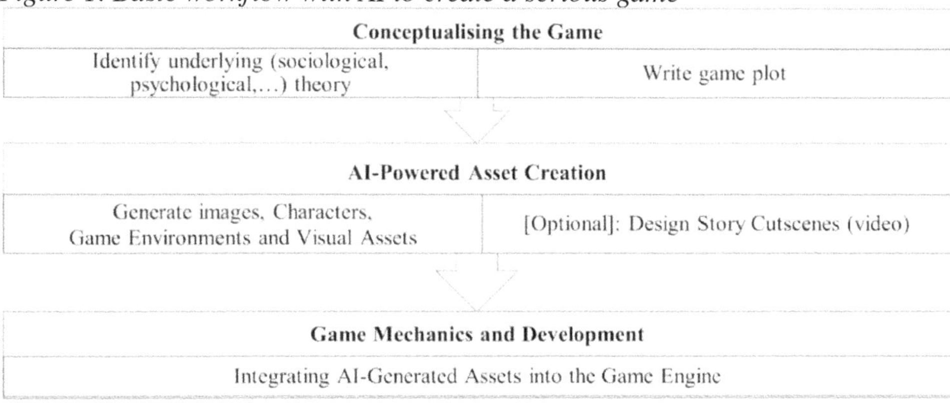

Note. Own work.

Key Elements of an Effective Prompt

- **Goal:** Think about what you want the prompt to achieve. What are you asking the AI to create? (For example, is it to draft a script, generate an image, compose a story, or write a poem/song?)
- **Context:** Consider the situation where the output will be used, or why you need it. Importantly, who is it for – who is your target audience? (For instance, is the output intended for first-year criminology students, or perhaps for international experts on drug prevention?)
- **Expected Outcome:** Try to specify what you imagine the final output will be like. What are its desired characteristics? (For example, the length or features of a game, its genre, the aesthetic style, colour pallet, etc.)
- **Source:** You might also want to include any reference files or source materials that should be used alongside the prompt.

Figure 2. Step 1 prompt example - Guiding the "AI friend" to read materials with the teacher

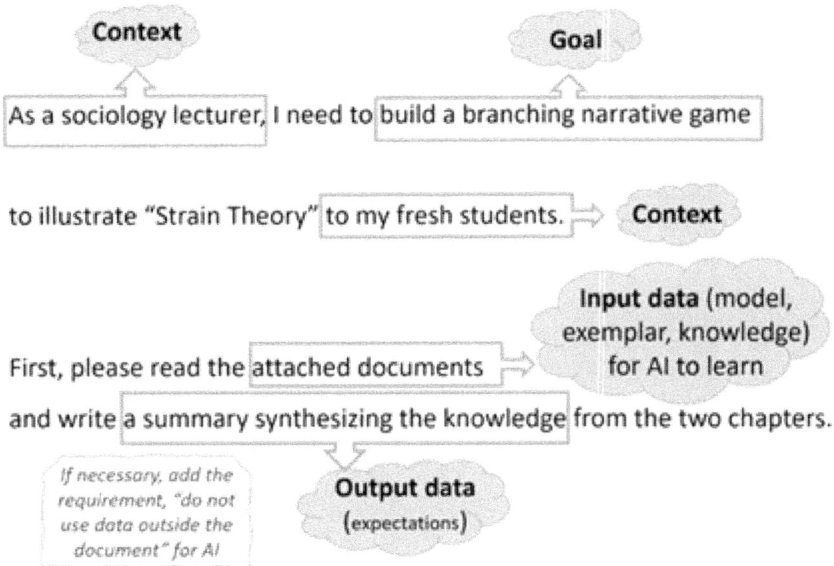

Note. Own work.

Step 1: Conceptualising the Game – AI to Study the Theory and Write a Game Plot

When writing prompts, try to make your request clear and to the point, but not too vague (avoid "blind prompts" where the AI does not quite know what you are aiming for), and make sure your terms are not conflicting. Generative AI prompt samples are also very good sources to inspire your prompting ideas. Some prompt banks are Copilot Prompt Gallery (Microsoft's), Vertex AI (Google's), PromptBase, etc.

Another good way to figure out what works best for you and your situation is to experiment with different prompting styles and the specific prompts themselves. Some cases fit best when the prompt is less specific, allowing more room for AI creativity (occasionally, video prompts). Some people work best with all-in-one prompts, which allow for more industrial, high-volume output quickly. Some others do not use high-volume output prompts, but one-step-at-a-time prompts, which give them finer control over the entire process. Here is a comparison example:

Table 1. Step 2 prompt example - Request AI to write a game plot, a comparative example

Prompting techniques	**Prompt examples**		
When using Step-by-Step / Iterative Prompting	[Prompt 1] As a sociology lecturer, I need to build a branching narrative game to illustrate "Strain Theory" to my first-year students. First, please read the attached documents and write a summary synthesising the knowledge from the two chapters.	[Prompt 2] Please try to develop a script for an animated film to illustrate the above knowledge about Strain Theory.	[Prompt 3] Could you write a branching narrative game plot, to help students summarise what they have learned about Strain Theory?
When not using Step-by-Step / Iterative Prompting	# CONTEXT: You are designing an educational game for college students. You teach "Introduction to Sociology". You want the game to help students become interested in the subject and understand the material more easily. # INSTRUCTION: - Create a plot for an indie game - The game's plot is based on Max Weber's concepts and theories, including: Authority, Social Action, Bureaucracy, Sociology of Religion (e.g. The Protestant Ethic and the Spirit of Capitalism), and Methodological Individualism (Ideal Types) # INPUT (SOURCE): Use Max Weber's theories (read the file attached) Character's name: Max Weber # OUTPUT REQUESTS: The game plot		

Note. A general request of writing "a story" will be very different from writing "a plot" or "a script". Own work.

In general, the effectiveness of a prompt is often manifested in: the accuracy of the response; its usefulness (improving efficiency in terms of time and resources, and increasing productivity); the user's positive experience; and its contribution to faster and more accurate decision-making (Yasar, 2023). You will hear about numerous prompting techniques (For example, Zero-shot prompting, Few-shot prompting, Persona pattern prompting, Conversational prompting, Recursive prompting (Banks, n.d.), Chain-of-Thought Prompting, Meta Prompting, Retrieval Augmented Generation (RAG), Multimodal CoT, etc. (DAIR.AI, n.d.; Greyling, 2023). If you, unfortunately, have a memory of a goldfish in tech and cannot call out the name of any of these, ask AI to be your Guru and help you create and improve your prompts! For example:

- Ask the AI language model to create prompts for you (you may also ask it to point out negative keywords for image prompts); help you outline a prompt creation plan; or break down complex tasks into a series of smaller, sequential prompts towards the final outcome

- Ask the AI to suggest refinements to your draft prompt, offer alternative phrasing
- Ask the AI if it needs any clarification before proceeding, to achieve the best possible outcome
- Ask the AI to explain its interpretation (why it responded that way) to identify what might have been unclear or misleading in the original prompt.

Case in point, for teachers with no experience designing games (like me!), AI will help by suggesting detailed steps for each stage.

Table 2. Conceptualizing the game: Some Notice

	Identifying Core Social Science Concepts	**Crafting a Relatable and Engaging Game Plot, Game Logic and Rules with AI Assistance**
What humans should provide to AI:	- The targeted topics or theories, terms, abstracts - Literary materials (books, articles, outlines,…)	- A specific game genre - A desired game (as an exemplar)
What humans can request (keywords that could be used in prompts for an AI to process the theories from provided texts):	**- Core Understanding & Extraction:** Analyse, extract key concepts, identify main arguments, define [specific term/theory], explain [specific theory], outline the structure of [argument/theory] **- Synthesising & Connecting:** Synthesise findings from [texts], compare and contrast [theory A] and [theory B], identify relationships between [concept X] and [concept Y], summarise [text/section], **- Applying & Generating Ideas (moving towards the game):** Apply [theory name] to [context, e.g., a small community, a power dynamic], generate examples illustrating [theory name], explore implications of [theory name] for [social system/interaction], brainstorm scenarios based on [theory name/synthesis] **- Structuring Output:** Provide a structured outline of..., create a table comparing..., explain for a game designer.	**Plot & Narrative:** Develop story (e.g. Plot points, character arcs, narrative hooks, conflict scenarios, dialogue options, backstory, lore snippets) **Game Logic & Rules Design:** Underlying systems and rules (e.g. Core mechanics, game rules/logic, win/loss conditions, ways to balance, variations of a rule or mechanic) **Connecting Plot & Mechanics:** How story and gameplay interact (e.g. How game mechanics reinforce the theme; Mechanics that reflect plot points or character traits; Puzzles or challenges based on narrative elements; How a specific rule impacts the player's experience of the story, Gameplay scenarios that illustrate a narrative conflict) **Ensuring Relatability & Engagement:** Refine elements to make the game more compelling for the player (e.g. Ways to make [character/situation] more relatable..., How player choice can enhance engagement; Potential player pain points in [mechanic/story section] and suggest solutions; Optional content that increases player immersion) **Refining & Iteration:** Revising the game designs (e.g. Refine [existing plot point/rule/dialogue], alternatives for [mechanic/narrative choice], potential inconsistencies in [plot/rules], simplify [complex rule/system])

Table 3. Chapter structure and Weberian concepts in "The Weberian Chronicles" game

Max Weber's Concepts	**Plot:**
	Overview: "The Weberian Chronicles" is an educational indie game that immerses players in the theories and concepts of Max Weber, offering a compelling narrative to understand complex sociological ideas. The game takes place in a fictional world where the player must navigate through various societal structures and understand their underlying principles to progress. **Prologue:** The player takes on the role of Max Weber, who awakens in Sociopolis with fragmented memories. Guided by a mysterious entity named "Spirit of Inquiry", Weber must restore balance to the land by understanding and applying his own sociological theories.
Power and Authority (Ninh, 2020): • **Power**: Ability to enforce one's will despite resistance. • **Legitimate Authority**: Power seen as just by those under it, divided into three types: o **Traditional Authority**: Rooted in customs, inherited or divinely granted (e.g., monarchs). Not based on qualifications. o **Rational-Legal Authority**: Based on laws and rules, resides in the office, not the individual (e.g., elected officials). Ensures smooth power transitions (e.g., U.S. presidency). o **Charismatic Authority**: Stems from an individual's extraordinary qualities (e.g., Gandhi, Hitler). Less stable, as it dies with the leader.	**Chapter 1: Authority Heights** • **Objective:** Navigate through the different realms of authority. • **Plot:** Weber encounters three leaders, each embodying a type of authority. The player must assist these leaders in resolving conflicts within their realms by understanding and leveraging their authority types. o *Traditional Authority*: Help a hereditary monarch secure their rule against a rebellious noble. o *Rational-Legal Authority*: Assist an elected official in enacting policies during a political crisis. o *Charismatic Authority*: Support a charismatic leader in uniting a fragmented community.

continued on following page

Table 3. Continued

Max Weber's Concepts	Plot:
Social Action (Nickerson, n.d.): • Examines motives behind behaviors, with Weber identifying four types: o **Instrumental Rational Action**: Efficient means to achieve goals (e.g., low wages for profit). o **Value Rational Action**: Pursuing a goal for its own sake (e.g., religious rituals for salvation). o **Traditional Action**: Habitual actions without reflection (e.g., attending college due to family tradition). o **Affectual Action**: Driven by emotions (e.g., grief or anger). • Weber noted modern societies prioritize instrumental action, sidelining ethics and tradition, leading to social issues.	**Chapter 2: Action Valley** • **Objective:** Understand and apply the four types of social action. • **Plot:** Weber meets individuals whose actions exemplify each type of social action. Through interactions and choices, the player learns how these actions shape societal outcomes. o *Instrumental-Rational*: Aid a merchant in optimizing trade routes. o *Value-Rational*: Support a scholar in preserving ancient knowledge. o *Traditional*: Assist villagers in maintaining cultural rituals. o *Affectual*: Help a poet express their emotions through art.
Bureaucracy[1]	**Chapter 3: Bureaucracy City** • **Objective:** Navigate and reform the bureaucratic structures. • **Plot:** Weber must work within a sprawling city governed by complex bureaucratic systems. The player learns about the pros and cons of bureaucracy and must streamline processes to solve a looming crisis. o Tasks include reorganizing departments, dealing with red tape, and ensuring efficiency while maintaining fairness.
Sociology of Religion (Todd et al., 2015): • In *The Protestant Ethic and the Spirit of Capitalism*, Weber argued Protestantism (especially Calvinism) fostered a work ethic that fueled capitalism in Holland and England. Success was seen as a sign of divine favor, with material success reflecting a "capitalist spirit." Other factors (e.g., government support) also contributed.	**Chapter 4: Protestant Plains** • **Objective:** Explore the relationship between religion and capitalism. • **Plot:** Weber investigates the impact of Protestant ethics on the local economy. The player interacts with various characters, from hardworking entrepreneurs to devout believers, uncovering how religious values drive economic success. o *Key Challenge*: Balancing ethical considerations with economic growth. **Epilogue:** After restoring balance to Sociopolis, Weber regains his memories and realizes the importance of his work in understanding and shaping societies. The Spirit of Inquiry reveals itself as the embodiment of knowledge and understanding, thanking Weber for his contributions to the world.

Experimenting with Outline Plot Development for Chapter 2 (Action Valley)

CHAPTER 2: VALLEY OF ACTION

- **Hook:**
  - o **Scene:** The serene Valley of Action unfolds before Max Weber. A colourful market bustles to his left, a solemn temple rises on a hill to his right, a quaint village nestles in the valley below, and a lone figure paints on a canvas near a sparkling river.
  - o **Dialogue:** Weber (to himself): "A fascinating tapestry of human activity. It seems the valley holds a key to understanding the very motivations that drive society."
- **Plot Point 1:** The Merchant's Dilemma (Instrumental-Rational)
  - o **Scene:** Weber approaches a frustrated merchant in the market, surrounded by maps and cargo.
  - o **Dialogue:** Merchant: "Professor Weber! A logistical nightmare! How can I get these spices to the farthest villages while minimizing costs?"
  - o **Mini-Game:** A map-based puzzle. Players help the merchant plot the most efficient trade routes using different modes of transport (caravans, ships) with varying costs and speeds. Success unlocks a "Trade Optimizer" badge for Weber.
- **Pinch 1:** The Scholar's Question (Value-Rational)
  - o **Scene:** At the temple, a scholar paces deep in thought.
  - o **Dialogue:** Scholar: "Professor Weber, the rituals here... are they merely traditions or do they hold a deeper meaning?"
  - o **Mini-Game:** A symbolic matching game. Players connect ritual objects (incense, offerings) with their underlying values (devotion, gratitude, purity) to uncover the temple's true purpose. Success earns Weber a "Symbol Interpreter" badge.
- **Midpoint:** The Village Tradition (Traditional)
  - o **Scene:** Weber enters the village, where preparations for a festival are underway.
  - o **Dialogue:** Villager: "Professor Weber, welcome! We're preparing for our annual celebration. Would you help us with some time-honoured traditions?"
  - o **Mini-Game:** A rhythm-based decorating game. Players follow musical cues to decorate a tree with ornaments, hang lights, and choose gifts for family members. Successfully completing the decorations earns Weber a "Tradition Keeper" badge.

- **Pinch 2:** The Poet's Anguish (Affectual)
    - o **Scene:** Weber finds the painter near the river, distraught and unable to finish his masterpiece.
    - o **Dialogue:** Poet: "Professor Weber, my muse has abandoned me. How can I convey the depths of my love through art?"
    - o **Mini-Game:** An emotional colour-mixing game. Players blend colours and brushstrokes to capture the poet's emotions (joy, sorrow, longing) on the canvas. A completed masterpiece earns Weber an "Emotion Weaver" badge.
- **Plot Point 2:** Weber's Revelation
    - o **Scene:** Weber reflects on his experiences in the valley.
    - o **Dialogue:** Weber (to himself): "I see now! Each action, whether driven by practicality, values, tradition, or emotion, shapes our social world."
- **Resolution:**
    - o **Scene:** Weber leaves the valley, a newfound understanding illuminating his path.
    - o **Dialogue:** Weber (to himself): "These actions, these motivations... they are the building blocks of society. I must share this knowledge!"
- **Lore:**
    - o The Valley of Action is a metaphorical representation of the diversity of human motivations.
    - o Each mini-game reinforces a specific type of social action, making the abstract concepts tangible and engaging for players.

Step 2: AI-Powered Asset Creation

Strategies to create game visuals

Strategy 1: Set up a prompt (with the basic elements mentioned in section 1.1).

Here is an example:

CONTEXT: You are designing a landscape for a strategy game. The purpose of the game is to introduce students to the work of the sociologist Max Weber.

#DATA: You can refer to the image of the game Dorfromantik.

#OUTCOME REQUESTS: Landscape image (Regions) for a game chapter, based on the setting of 19th century Germany. It should have some beautiful artwork, lovely little landscape tiles on the map. It's a world full of green trees, golden wheat fields, cosy cottages, chugging trains and lazy boats floating.

Figure 3. Landscape of "The Weberian Chronicles" Game, generated by AI

Note. These are the AI-generated images for the prompt above.

Strategy 2: Turn the AI's Script to AI Prompts

Above, we have asked the AI to create a game plot (or a script for cutscenes). With the script provided by the AI, you can turn the lines into image prompts for AI image-generation models. Below are some examples of images generated using these script lines.

Table 4. Examples of images generated using AI's script lines

Title of the lesson	Script excerpts generated by language AI models	Images generated by AI, based on the script lines
Robert K. Merton's Strain Theory	**Scene 2: The Divide** **[NARRATOR]** But what happens when the American dream feels out of reach? **[VISUAL]** The colours become muted. The scene splits into two: on one side, affluent neighbourhoods with manicured lawns; on the other, dilapidated buildings, graffiti, and boarded-up windows.	 
Introduction to Social Statistics	**[Narrator]:** ...we're constantly bombarded with information. But how much of it is reliable?" **[VISUAL], [Animation]:** The newspapers and magazines morph into question marks, swirling around the person's head. A news ticker scrolls across the bottom of the screen with contradictory headlines.	

Note. The images in this table are direct AI outputs illustrating Strategy 2, using the script lines from the adjacent column as prompts.

Strategy 3: Ask AI to Describe the Art Style You Want to Replicate.

You can leverage the AI's knowledge about art styles and illustration artists to learn about them and add specific details regarding art styles to your prompts. (e.g., illustration art genres, colour palettes, specific artists).

Table 5.

This image, selected from the Midjourney Explore Gallery, serves as the original picture for the style-replication shown below.

Prompt:	AI's response:
If I need a prompt for Midjourney to generate a picture that replicates as closely as possible to the original picture. What should I write for the prompt?	Minimalist illustration of anthropomorphic bears engaging in activities like carrying bags and holding fish, cosy and whimsical aesthetic, soft muted colour palette with beige, brown, and light green tones, flat graphic style, clean shapes and lines, subtle texture, simple background in solid beige, charming and playful composition, Scandinavian design influences, inspired by modern children's book art, Jon Klassen style, Aki Irie vibes, digital illustration.

Strategy 4: Ask the Language AI Model to Create an Image Prompt for a Specific Idea.

In case, you have no imagination about what should appear in your picture, give your AI tool the definition, and it may return to you surprising, brilliant idea options. Here is an example of when I got stuck for ideas:

Prompt: Please help me write a description for AI to generate a picture illustrating this definition:

"Nonresponse bias can occur when many people who are selected for the sample either do not respond at all or do not respond to some of the key survey questions. This may occur even when an appropriate random sample is selected and contacted. The survey is then based on a nonrepresentative sample, usually those who feel strongly about the issues. Some surveys don't even attempt to contact a random sample but instead, ask anyone who wishes to respond to

do so. Magazines, television stations, and Internet websites routinely conduct this kind of poll, and those who respond are called a self-selected sample or a volunteer sample. In most cases, this kind of sample tells you nothing about the larger population at all; it tells you only about those who responded" (Utts & Heckard, 2007).

Below is one of the responses of language AI (excerpt) and its result when being generated by another image AI model:

Image Description: A visual metaphor depicting the concept of nonresponse bias and self-selected sample in surveys and polls.

Core Elements:

- **Survey Distribution:** Show a diverse crowd of people, representing the general population. Survey invitations (envelopes, emails, or phone icons) are being distributed randomly among them.
- **Nonresponse:** A significant portion of the crowd ignores or discards the invitations, symbolizing nonresponse. These individuals should appear less engaged or interested.
- **Self-Selection:** In a separate section, depict a smaller, more passionate group actively seeking out a survey or poll. They could be reaching for a microphone, eagerly filling out an online form, or calling into a radio show.
- **Metaphorical Elements:** Consider using a megaphone or spotlight to highlight the self-selected group. The nonrespondents could be fading into the background or becoming translucent.
- **Conceptual and symbolic:** The image should prioritize conveying the abstract concepts rather than strict realism.

Figure 4. AI's illustration for the definition of "All-Self-Selected Sampling", a prompt written by AI

Note. This image was generated by a text-to-image AI model, based on a detailed prompt that was itself created by a generative language AI (see above).

Creating Characters

Generating Consistent Characters Across Multiple Images.

It will be a challenge for teachers as AI new learners to maintain character consistency. There are several effective techniques:

1. **Leverage specific AI model features:** Some platforms work by building upon underlying AI models (often Stable Diffusion) and integrating or providing access to specific features, workflows, or fine-tuned models (like LoRAs or checkpoints) that are designed to give users more control, including achieving better character consistency. In short, what you need to do is simply choose a model that is most eye-catching to you and instantly use it. Suggested platforms: Tensor.art, Piclumen.com, SeaArt.ai, Leonardo.ai, Creator.Nightcafe.studio, etc.
2. **Use consistent reference images:** Upload one or more reference images if your tool supports this feature.
   Suggested platforms: Midjourney.com; Automatic1111, ComfyUI; Fooocus. one; and other platforms built on Stable Diffusion (above)
3. **Develop a highly detailed & consistent text prompt:** Create a master description of your character that is as specific as possible. Use the exact same keywords and phrasing for the character's core description in every prompt you write for them. Copy-pasting is your friend here. Details may include:
   - **Art styles / Animation styles:** Low Poly Art, claymation, anime, cut-out, cartoony, chibi, pixel, doodle, flat art, cel shading, minimalist, isometric, voxel, geometric, monochromatic, vector art, magical realism, etc. It may be even better if you can call out the name of an exemplar for your desired style (although AI models, at least for now, do not seem to be well-updated with new artists' styles), such as Tim Burton, Ghibli, Tearaway game, etc.
   - **Physical Traits:** Age range, gender, skin (colour, moles, scars, freckles etc.), face shape (round, angular, etc.), eye (colour and shape), hairstyle (colour, length, texture, specific cut like mohawk, quiff, twin-tail, flipped-up ends etc.), build (slim, muscular, heavy), other distinct facial features (nose, lip, etc.)
   - **Clothing:** Outfit (eg, trench coat, gown, denim jacket, hoodies, shirt, etc.), accessories (glasses, jewellery, hat), and overall style (punk, formal, casual, geeky, fantasy armour, etc.).
4. **Maintain consistency in other prompt elements:** Other details may subtly influence how the characters appear. Include consistent style keywords, lighting terms (e.g., "studio lighting", "golden hour", "cinematic lighting"), camera

angles (e.g., “close-up”, “full body shot”), and even preferred expressions if possible.

5. **Create a character description template/sheet:** Managing the narrative elements, dialogue, visual descriptions, images, sound effects, and so on, for your game chapters and scenes in tables or sheets will make the process more systematic and convenient. This ensures you don't forget details between prompting sessions. You can also ask your AI model to help you create such management files.

Generating Various Poses for the Same Character.

When your character moves, you would likely want them to change poses to look more natural – perhaps looking straight ahead, to the side, or from behind. However, you will find that each time you generate an image, the AI will possibly create something new and different from previous attempts. A tip for keeping the same character consistent across these different poses is to instruct the AI, when generating, to divide the image into sections showing different postures. For example, one image could be divided into 3 or 4 frames, each showing a different pose or viewpoint.

Table 6. AI's generated different postures of the same characters

When you request AI to generate one image which is divided into multiple frames, each illustrating a different viewpoint, the character will maintain the same art style and appearance (clothes, hair, etc.) Let's try the prompt below to create images with a consistent character appearance, similar to the example on the right column: Background: I want to create a character game to teach students about Max Weber (Sociology) Character: A fictional version of Max Weber, wearing a suit, late 19th-century German clothing and holding an iron cage. Style: Simple or chibi. Soft colour tones. Expression: Cute and lively. Output: The image should have a completely white background, just the character without any ground or shadows. Divide the image into multiple frames, each frame showing a pose/view: Front, Back, Sitting, Running	
On the other hand, if you ask an AI to generate images multiple times, even with the exact prompt for the same character, likely, the character will not maintain a consistent appearance and art style. For example, an AI was asked to generate a game character twice in a row with the following prompts: A couple (2 game characters) holding hands, viewed from above. Style_ 2D cartoon game. The male character has red hair, and the girl has a hook on one of her hands. A couple (2 game characters) holding hands, viewed from above and from behind. Style_ 2D cartoon game. The male character has red hair, and the female character has a ponytail.	

Note. The images are direct AI outputs from the prompts provided in the left column.

Step 3: Game Mechanics and Development

For simple games like crosswords, anagrams, word searches, quizzes, etc., many tools already exist to generate them. However, this chapter has a greater ambition: to infuse games with an artistic atmosphere to enhance the learning experience and better engage learners. If this is your goal – to create your own serious game, perhaps alongside your students – we will need to explore some methods for building the game piece by piece.

Figure 5. Maze maps, generated by traditional tools and AI, which fulfil the requirements of having several towers

Note. Traditional tools are often limited to producing basic maze images (left), whereas generative AI creates far more vibrant ones (right). The one on the right was generated using the prompt: "Based on this basic maze, draw a hedge maze map in a fantasy 2D comic art style, with some towers or houses".

Creating Educational Games with Presentation Programs

Presentation programs like PowerPoint and Google Slides offer several advantages:

- Enable designers to manage layers (slides) visually, providing clarity for educators. Distinctly separated layers minimize errors from overlapping or confusing active layers during game design.
- Feature a user-friendly drag-and-drop interface with numerous attractive and functional effects.
- Allow embedding of videos, GIFs, and audio, enhancing game interactivity without requiring online uploads.

However, they have limitations, such as:

- Sharing challenges: Students without the app installed cannot view files on mobile devices.
- Embedding into websites may cause performance lag.
- Difficulty designing complex games, such as those with character movement in open-world environments.

Thus, PowerPoint and Google Slides are ideal for games with static or minimally moving characters and sprites, and for projects not requiring broad sharing. Use Hyperlinks to develop your game's narrative (Insert > Action > Hyperlink to > Slide…). When planning a design, you should note:

- Create a flowchart to visualise the narrative structure. Each node represents a story moment (slide), and arrows show how choices connect to other nodes.
- Label slides clearly in the slide sorter view (e.g., "Slide 1: Cat outside House", "Slide 2: Inside Cat House", "Slide 4: Broken Vase", etc.) to keep track of branches.
- Add a map slide with a button connected to it, and help players navigate the story.
- Plan multiple endings (e.g., success, failure, bittersweet) to reward player choices.

Figure 6. Example of a flowchart

Start: You saw a cat standing outside a house, and went to talk to the cat. The cat asked you to come inside.

├── Choice 1: Accept the invitation → Slide 2 (Come inside the house)

│ ├── Choice A: Click the flower vase → Slide 4 (a broken vase)

│ └── Choice B: Click the window → Slide 5 (a view, looked from the window)

└── Choice 2: Decline the invitation → Slide 3 (Life continues normally)

  └── Choice C: Go to school

Note. The images are direct AI outputs with the prompt: "The interior and exterior of a cute cat's cottage for a game, in pixel art style"

In Section 2.1, we will together examine a complete example of a branching narrative game, largely created by AI (scripted with various options). Finally, you can play the game offline with students in the classroom, or you can use the embed function to copy the code automatically generated by PowerPoint and paste it onto any website-building platform to share your PowerPoint file.

Generating Game Code with AI.

Teachers often feel anxious when starting to use a specialised programming platform. However, you can read the excerpt below from an AI-guided tutorial that helped me learn to use Godot (a free and open-source game engine) and feel reassured. With zero coding experience, I found AI to be the most patient IT teacher. There is no longer a fear of being judged for asking simple questions (like "Where is this button? I can't find it"). No worries about disturbing a teacher's time. AI will provide continuous guidance, available at any moment, with clear, detailed explanations for each command. This personalised learning experience vividly demonstrates AI's advances.

Step-by-step guide - Coding characters' movement in the maze game

Step 1: Add a Script to the Couple Node

To control the movement of the couple, you need to attach a script to the Couple node.

Select the Couple Node:
In the **Scene** tab (on the left), find the Couple node (which should be a CharacterBody2D).
Click on it to select it.
Attach a Script:
With the Couple node selected, go to the **Node** tab (next to the **Inspector** tab on the right).
Click the **Attach Script** button (a small script icon).
A dialog will appear. Ensure the language is set to **GDScript**.
Set the path to res://Couple.gd (this will save the script in the project's root directory).
Click **Create**.
Verify the Script:

After creating, the script editor will open with a basic template, and the Couple node in the **Scene** tab will show a small script icon next to it.

Step 2: Write the Code for Movement

You'll use CharacterBody2D's move_and_slide() function to handle movement and collision. The code will allow the couple to move using arrow keys or WASD, while stopping at the hedge (if Collision Layer and Collision Mask are set correctly, as discussed earlier).

Replace the default script content in Couple.gd with the following:

```
gdscript
extends CharacterBody2D
var speed = 200  # Movement speed in pixels per second
var direction = Vector2.ZERO  # Direction of movement
var initial_position = Vector2.ZERO  # Store the starting
position
func _ready():
    initial_position = position  # Save the initial position
at the center of the maze
    add_to_group("couple")  # Add to a group for resetting
position later
func _physics_process(delta):
    # Get input from the player
    direction.x = Input.get_axis("ui_left", "ui_right")  #
Left/Right movement
    direction.y = Input.get_axis("ui_up", "ui_down")     #
Up/Down movement
    # Normalize the direction to prevent faster diagonal
movement
    if direction.length() > 0:
        direction = direction.normalized()
        # Update velocity based on direction and speed
    velocity = direction * speed
        # Move the character and handle collisions
    move_and_slide()
func reset_position():
```

Troubleshooting Code Issues

AI does not just provide you with bug fixes, but also explains each issue (why the error occurred?), which helps you understand and avoid repeating similar mistakes in the future. After using the AI-provided code to make the character move on the screen, I discovered the character did not stop when hitting the Hedge sections, but moved freely across the map. I asked the AI to identify scenarios that could cause this error. However, reviewing based on the AI's predicted error scenarios did not fix the problem. (Actually, checking against common predicted errors felt similar to how we used to get general error lists before AI existed). Eventually, when I took a screenshot, the AI was able to immediately provide effective instructions that correctly fixed the specific game design error. Clearly, object recognition from screenshots is a significant advantage for AI. For example, when I provided the image "the illustration of maze map" (Figure 5), AI could recognize the approximate location of each tower in the image, from which it could provide code for events occurring when characters reach each tower.

Table 7.

<table>
<tr>
<td rowspan="3">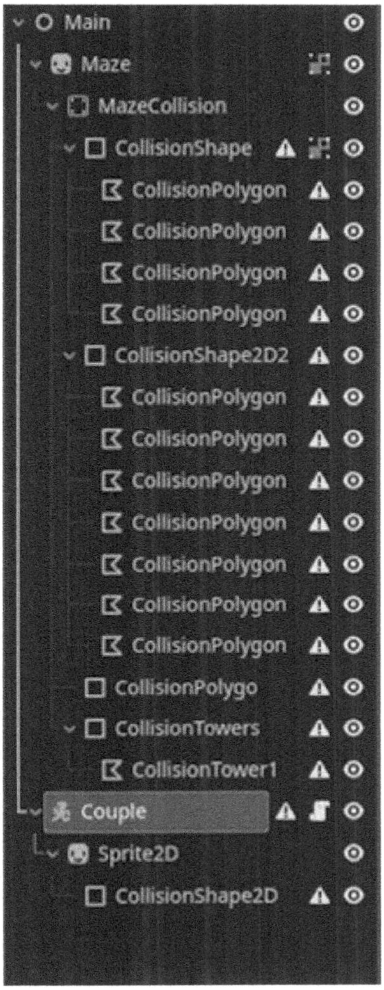
</td>
<td>Analysis of the Error
Cause of the Error
In your Scene Tree, the CollisionShape2D node is currently a child of Sprite2D (under “Couple”):
Couple (CharacterBody2D)
├── Sprite2D
│ └── CollisionShape2D # Incorrect position
Problem:
CollisionShape2D only works when it is a direct child of a node derived from CollisionObject2D (such as CharacterBody2D, StaticBody2D, RigidBody2D, etc.).
Sprite2D is not a type of CollisionObject2D, so when you place CollisionShape2D as a child of Sprite2D, Godot cannot use it to define a collision shape for “Couple” (CharacterBody2D). This results in the warning message.</td>
</tr>
<tr>
<td>Impact
Since CollisionShape2D is not in the correct position (it’s not a direct child of “Couple”), “Couple” currently does not have a valid collision shape. This can cause two issues:
“Couple” cannot collide with other objects (like “MazeCollision”), which may lead to it passing through the hedge.
If “Couple” still detects collisions (e.g., through move_and_slide()), it’s only because other objects (like “MazeCollision”) have collision shapes, but “Couple” won’t respond to collisions correctly.</td>
</tr>
<tr>
<td>Guidance for Fixing the Issue
To resolve the error, you need to move the CollisionShape2D out of Sprite2D and make it a direct child of “Couple” (CharacterBody2D). Here are the detailed steps:
1. Move CollisionShape2D in the Scene Tree
In the Scene Tree, select the CollisionShape2D node (currently a child of Sprite2D).
Drag the CollisionShape2D node out so that it becomes a direct child of “Couple” (CharacterBody2D).
After moving, the Scene Tree should look like this:
text
Copy
Couple (CharacterBody2D)
├── Sprite2D
└── CollisionShape2D # Correct position</td>
</tr>
</table>

ARTIFICIAL INTELLIGENCE: THE EMBODIMENT OF AN ARTISTIC CRAFTSMANSHIP?

Back in history, one of the earliest forms of narratives or storytelling was the Greek myths, which were often told as oral poetry and were and were imbued with almost magical powers: the Muses inspired them. The sacred realm was connected to it. Gods and Goddesses sent messages; And the divine knowledge was conveyed via the poets as the channel – These beliefs granted the storytellers the power known as charismatic authority, and they were revered. However, the understanding that these dramatic works stemmed from ecstatic and divine inspiration was, then, replaced by the reasoning that they were products of rational creation (Monami, 2017).

Aristotle, the famous ancient Greek philosopher, argued that poetry was a "mimetic art" that uses language, rhythm, and harmony to imitate real-life (Antony, 2005). Poets were active weavers of "techne" (crafts). This shift allowed Aristotle to approach poetry, in particular, and narratives, in general, with a scientific lens (Husain 2002: 17-34). He sought its constituent parts, principles, and rules. In this section, let us examine to what extent technology can breathe life into serious game designs.

Aesthetic and Narrative Design: The Case of AI-generated Plot for a Strain Theory Game

Figure 7. The three-act story structure reflected in the in-game movie

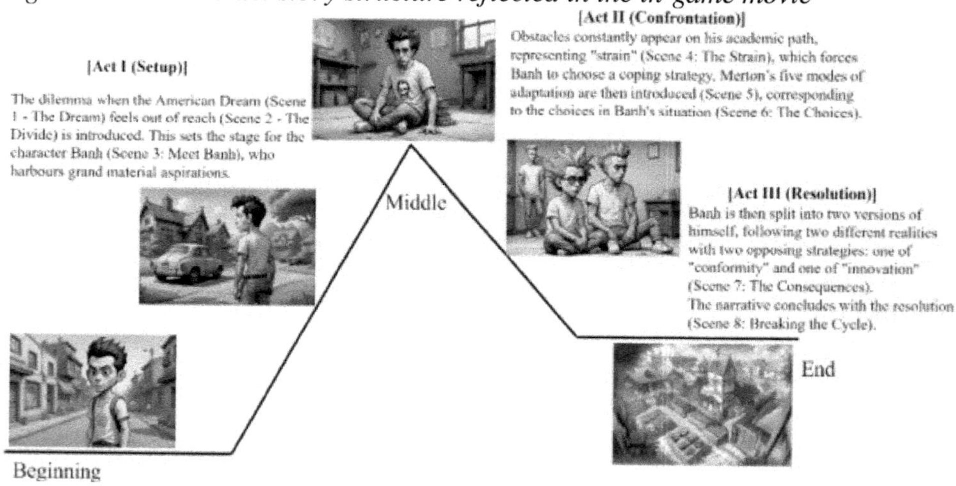

Note. The images are direct AI outputs from the prompts that are actually lines from a script (Table 6), which was also generated by a language AI.

"Is Frankenstein Capable of Creativity?"

Perhaps this question will be pondered now and for many years to come. For the time being, let's look at the surface evidence. We can observe that, even in a very short script, AI has seemingly developed certain elements of dramatic structure in its work:

Mimesis (Imitation): The Strain Theory script below imitates real-world sociological dynamics, portraying the tension between the American Dream and structural inequality. Through Banh's aspirations and struggles, it captures universal experiences of ambition thwarted by circumstance, resonating with audiences familiar with social disparities.

Plot (Mythos): A plot complete in itself has a clear beginning, middle, and end. In section 1.1, you were introduced to the prompt that requested a script for Strain Theory. The story generated by the AI has met this basic three-act story structure.

Character (Ethos): Banh is a "Tragic Hero", a relatable figure, aspiring to the American Dream but constrained by systemic barriers. His potential hamartia is the error of considering illegal "innovation" (e.g., drug dealing) over conformity (pursuing college). His friends in the gang are supporting characters here.

Thought (Dianoia): Thought encompasses the thematic or intellectual content conveyed through dialogue. The script's core theme - strain theory as an explanation for crime driven by inequality - is clearly articulated through the narrator's exposition and Banh's inner voice. This aligns well with Aristotle's view that thought should provoke deeper understanding.

Diction (Lexis): Aristotle values clear, poetic language appropriate to characters. Some narrator's lines (e.g., "Community gardens bloom, after-school programs thrive, job training centres open") or Banh's inner voice (e.g., "College? It's expensive, and what guarantees a good job after?"), I think sounds quite cinematic, and poetic a bit, compared to everyday language.

Melody and Spectacle: AI supports vivid visual spectacle, and it totally can generate sound effects for the game.

The Closeness of AI-Generated Video Scripts and the Strain Theory Document

Before the AI language model started writing a script for me, I provided it with an excerpt from the book "Criminology for Dummies" (Briggs & Friedman, 2009) as the guide source. Now, let's compare how close the AI's plot is to the theory:

Table 8. Alignment of AI's video script with Strain Theory

	Excerpts from the in-game-cinematic AI's Plot
The American Dream is presented as a universal goal ("work hard, play by the rules, and you can achieve anything"), but societal divides (affluent vs. dilapidated neighbourhoods) highlight unequal opportunities, aligning with Merton's anomie theory.	**[Act I (Setup)]: Introduces characters, setting, the foundations for the story, and the central conflict]:** **Scene 1 - The Dream** • **[VISUAL]** Upbeat, colourful animation. A montage of quintessential American imagery: gleaming skyscrapers, white picket fences, happy families, graduation ceremonies, people driving new cars. The colours become muted. The scene splits into two: on one side, affluent neighbourhoods with manicured lawns; on the other, dilapidated buildings, graffiti, and boarded-up windows. • **[NARRATOR]** The American Dream. A promise whispered in the ears of every citizen: work hard, play by the rules, and you can achieve anything. **Scene 2 - The Divide** • **[VISUAL]** The colours become muted. The scene splits into two: on one side, affluent neighbourhoods with manicured lawns; on the other, dilapidated buildings, graffiti, and boarded-up windows. • **[NARRATOR]** But what happens when the dream feels out of reach? When the path to success is blocked, not by lack of effort, but by circumstance?
Merton's Anomie Theory: Banh's aspiration for wealth ("I want that. The nice car, the big house") and recognition of barriers ("My school's falling apart. Jobs are scarce") reflect Merton's concept of anomie. Scene 5's depiction of Merton's adaptations (conformity, innovation, etc.) explicitly ties Banh's choices to the theory, with the criminal path (innovation) and educational path (conformity) as possible responses. **General Strain Theory (GST)**: Banh's frustrations (failing tests, job rejections) and exposure to negative influences (a friend in a gang) align with GST's broader strains, such as failure to meet expectations and delinquent peers. However, the script does not explore other GST strains, like loss of positive relationships (e.g., family separation). Therefore, the teacher added Banh's family's disadvantaged background (which still haunted him in the nightmares, of a drunk person coming back home, under flickering lights, behind old broken windows of neighbourhood): 	**Scene 3 - Meet Banh** • **[VISUAL]** Focus on a young man, Banh, walking through his rundown neighbourhood. He looks at a billboard showcasing a successful businessman. **[BANH'S INNER VOICE]** I want that. The nice car, the big house... But how? My school's falling apart. Jobs are scarce. **[Act II (Confrontation)]: The longest act, where the protagonist(s) face major obstacles]:** **Scene 4 - The Strain** • **[VISUAL]** A series of quick cuts: Banh failing a test, getting turned down for a job, seeing a friend get involved in a gang. The images distort, symbolizing his growing frustration. • **[NARRATOR]** This is strain. The gap between aspirations and reality. The pressure builds, seeking an outlet. **Scene 5 - Merton's Adaptations** • **[VISUAL]** A spinning wheel with five segments, each representing Merton's modes of adaptation: Conformity, Innovation, Ritualism, Retreatism, and Rebellion. **[NARRATOR]** Faced with strain, people adapt. Some conform, clinging to hope. Others innovate, finding new, often illegal, paths to success.

continued on following page

	Excerpts from the in-game-cinematic AI's Plot
Subculture Theories: The criminal path (Scene 6's "dark alley" with a drug-dealing friend) hints at subcultural influences, as in differential opportunity theory, where criminal role models offer alternative success paths. However, the script doesn't depict a developed subculture with values like violence or toughness, as in lower-class reaction theory, limiting alignment with these theories. The teacher added an option to express retreatism ("Or simply give up") and dialogue for ritualism ("Will I eventually become an old man with a salary only enough to walk on foot?)  	**Scene 6 - The Choices**    • **[VISUAL]** Banh at a crossroads. One path leads to a brightly lit college campus, the other to a dark alley where his friend is dealing drugs. • **[BANH'S INNER VOICE]** College? It's expensive, and what guarantees a good job after? Maybe quick money is the answer...

Table 8. Continued

	Excerpts from the in-game-cinematic AI's Plot
Institutional Anomie Theory: Banh's potential success through education (Scene 7) with community support (Scene 8) reflects the role of institutions in reducing strain, though the script doesn't explicitly mention family or church, key institutions in the theory. **Criminal Path (Innovation, Scene 7)**: Choosing the "dark alley" aligns with Merton's innovation, where individuals pursue societal goals (wealth) through illegal means due to blocked legitimate paths. The consequence (arrest) reflects strain theory's acknowledgement of crime's risks, supporting the document's (Briggs & Friedman 2009) note that innovation often leads to criminality (e.g., drug dealers seeking "bling"). **Educational Path (Conformity, Scene 7)**: Choosing college aligns with conformity, where individuals pursue goals through approved means despite challenges. The successful outcome (graduation, job) reflects strain theory's recognition that some overcome strain without crime, addressing the document's criticism that not all lower-class individuals turn to crime.	**[Act III (Resolution)]: The conflict is resolved, providing closure]:** **Scene 7 - The Consequences** • **[VISUAL]** Two possible futures flash: Banh graduating, successful; Banh in handcuffs, arrested.   • **[NARRATOR]** Strain doesn't guarantee crime, but it tilts the scales. The choices made in these moments shape lives, communities, and the very fabric of society. **Scene 8 - Breaking the Cycle** • **[VISUAL]** The scene brightens. Community gardens bloom, after-school programs thrive, job training centres open. • **[NARRATOR]** Strain theory isn't just about explaining crime; it's a call to action. By addressing inequality, providing opportunities, we can reduce strain and build a society where the dream is within reach for all.

Note. The images in this table are direct AI outputs, using the AI-generated script lines from the right column as prompts.

Table 9. The AI branching narrative game's plot and images generated from it

	Scene 1 - The Student [INTRODUCTION] Banh stands at a crossroads. The pressure of societal expectations bears down on him. Please choose a path for Banh: • Commit crime but quickly make money • Pursue a challenging academic career that requires effort, sacrifice, and discipline
Visual prompt: The alleyway beckons, its shadows concealing figures engaged in illicit activities 	[CHOICE 1] Banh chooses the path of crime. [NARRATION] The allure of quick money to swiftly satisfy society's aspirations is too strong. Banh falls into a life of crime, following the predicted trend of strain theory. But the consequences are harsh, and Banh soon realizes he is trapped. [REFLECTION] This path highlights the dangers of strain and the importance of providing legitimate opportunities to prevent individuals from turning to crime.
The university gates stand open, sunlight streaming through, illuminating a path lined with books and eager faces 	**[CHOICE 2]** Banh chooses the path of education. **[NARRATION]** Despite the challenges, Banh perseveres. He faces setbacks but, with support from friends, the community, and mentors, Banh graduates and finds a fulfilling job. He breaks the cycle of strain. **[REFLECTION]** This path demonstrates the power of resilience and the importance of social support in overcoming strain. It also shows that strain theory does not predict a fixed outcome; individuals can make positive choices even in difficult circumstances.
	**Scene 2 - The Policymaker** **[INTRODUCTION]** You are a newly elected official in a city struggling with high crime rates. You've studied strain theory and its impacts.
A montage of police sirens wailing, handcuffs snapping shut, and prison bars clanging. The city skyline looms in the background, its dark silhouette a reminder of pervasive fear and mistrust. 	**[CHOICE 1]** You focus on increasing law enforcement and penalties. **[NARRATION]** Crime rates initially dropped, but the underlying issues of poverty and inequality remain unaddressed. Strain continues to build, and crime eventually surges again. **[REFLECTION]** This path highlights the limitations of focusing solely on punishment. Strain theory suggests that addressing the root causes of strain is critical for long-term crime reduction.

continued on following page

Table 9. Continued

The community centre is bustling, filled with light and laughter. Children engage in after-school activities. Adults learn new skills, and a sense of hope and possibility permeates the air. 	**[CHOICE 2]** You invest in education, vocational training, and community programs. **[NARRATION]** It takes time, but gradually, the community begins to transform. More people find jobs, and crime rates steadily decline. **[REFLECTION]** This path demonstrates the potential of policies grounded in strain theory to create positive change. By addressing structural factors contributing to strain, communities can become safer and more prosperous.
	**Scene 3 - The Mentor** **[INTRODUCTION]** You are a volunteer mentor for at-risk youth. You notice signs of strain in one of your mentees.
A sterile classroom. The mentee's eyes glaze over, staring at the chalkboard, hearing warnings. The clock ticks. Time drags on slowly. The connection between them is missed. 	**[CHOICE 1]** You lecture them about the dangers of crime and the importance of staying in school. **[NARRATION]** The mentee feels unheard and misunderstood. Strain intensifies, and they become distant and disengaged. **[REFLECTION]** This path underscores the importance of empathy and understanding when working with individuals experiencing strain. Lecturing alone may not be effective.
In a cosy corner of the community centre, bathed in warm light, the mentor and mentee sit across from each other, engaged in heartfelt conversation. Books and resources are scattered on the table, representing possibilities and pathways ahead. 	**[CHOICE 2]** You listen to their concerns, offer support, and help them explore their options. **[NARRATION]** The mentee feels validated and empowered. They begin to see a way out of their challenges and make positive choices. **[REFLECTION]** This path demonstrates the power of positive relationships and mentorship in helping individuals cope with strain and avoid crime. It emphasizes the importance of addressing both the structural and emotional aspects of strain.

Comments on Societal Solutions

All resolutions align with:

Institutional Anomie Theory: The emphasis on community programs and opportunities reflects the theory's call for strengthening institutions to provide legitimate paths and reduce materialistic strain.

General Strain Theory: By addressing poverty and inequality, the resolution mitigates strains like failure to achieve goals, supporting GST's broader view.

Subculture Theories: The resolution implicitly counters subcultural crime by fostering positive community values, though it doesn't directly address subcultural values like instant gratification.

Strengths: The resolution directly applies strain theory's solutions, advocating for systemic change to reduce strain, aligning with the document's emphasis on addressing root causes.

Limitations: The resolution is somewhat idealistic, with less focus on challenges (e.g., funding, resistance) or the role of family and church, which institutional anomie theory highlights.

Note. The images in this table are direct AI outputs, using the AI-generated script lines from the left column as prompts.

Aesthetic & Experiences

There is an ancient memorisation technique named Loci (also known as the Memory Palace technique), where you associate information you need to remember with specific locations or objects within a familiar space, such as items on a desk, shops along a street, or rooms in your house. By imagining the information is "placed" or "stored" in these locations, you can easily recall it by mentally "walking through" that space. I wonder if electronic games can act as such "memory places" in the minds of students. Therefore, I hypothesised that serious games might impact students' retention of class lessons. The following presents the results of a small-scale research study I conducted over 3 weeks in May 2025, at the University of Social Sciences and Humanities-Vietnam National University (USSH-VNU), Hanoi.

Methods for Evaluating a Strain Theory Game

- Preparation:
    - A branching narrative game on Strain Theory (described above) was designed.
    - Three Google Forms were created for each class, including: one Pre-test form, one Post-test form (each with 10 quiz questions), and a feedback form.
    - A plan to divide classes into two groups: one group received the game before the lesson (group 1), while the other was unaware of it (group 0).
- Samples: Included over 100 students per class group. Voluntary participation (anonymous) led to varying response rates across forms.
- Data Analysis: Collected data were analysed using SPSS to compare the two groups' engagement with the lesson, perceptions of the instructor, interest in designing serious games, and quiz performance. Note: The second quiz was administered one week later to assess students' knowledge retention.

- Consistency: All lessons were taught by the same instructor (the author of this chapter) to minimise variations in content delivery across classes.

Figure 8. "Max Weber" characters generated by AI with features implying his notions of "iron cage" and "social action"

Note. AI-generated image. I try to relate my "Max Weber" characters to his theories by asking AI to generate features like a bearded, 19th-century, German man, who plays social "action" and holds an "iron cage". This aims to remind students of some of his works.

Overall Student Interest in General Games

(Only in classes where I presented my game were these questions asked)

Table 10.

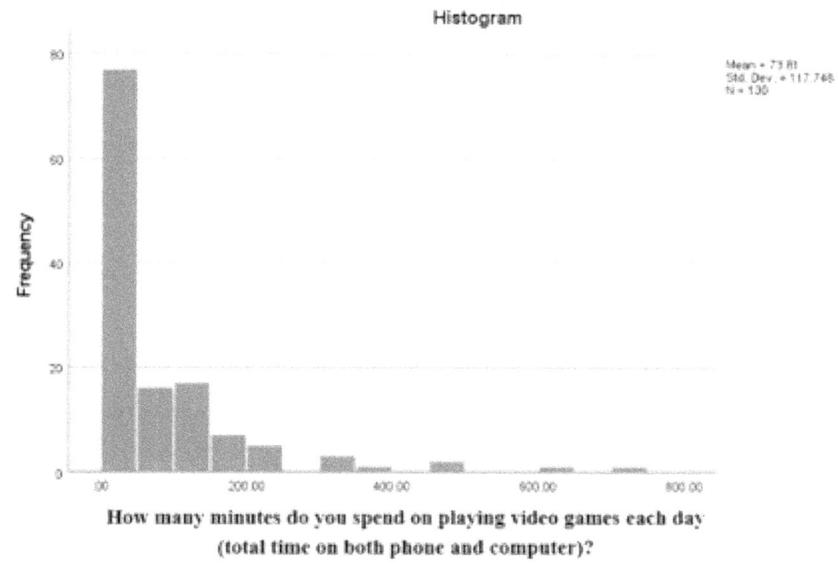

The majority of students either do not play electronic games or spend a moderate amount of time (a median of 30 minutes per day). However, a small subset of students engages in excessive gaming, with some spending up to 11.7 hours daily.	Sample Size: 130 responses Mean: 73.81 minutes per day. Median: 30.00 minutes per day. Standard Deviation: 117.75 minutes, indicating high variability. Percentiles: - 25th percentile: 0.00 minutes (25% of students spend no time gaming). - 50th percentile (median): 30.00 minutes. - 75th percentile: 120.00 minutes.

Figure 9. The distribution of students' liking for video games

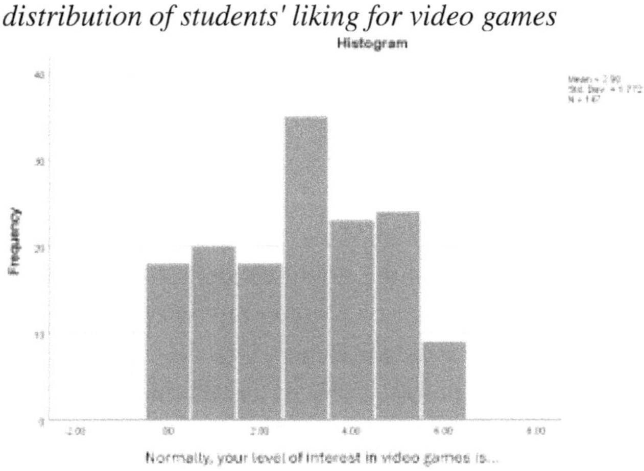

Note. Rated on a scale from 0 ("don't play, don't love") to 6 ("always fascinated, no matter how much I play, it doesn't feel like a waste of time")

Sample Size: 147 responses

Basically, the number of students who like video games quite a lot and do not like games at all is quite even. The majority feel "okay" or "kind of like" video games, not too much or too little

(around 35 to 40 of them fall somewhere between 3 and 4)

The Relationship Between My Teaching and the Branching Narrative Game

Impact of Game-Based Learning on Quiz Score Retention.

Figure 10. Comparison of quiz score retention between game and non-game groups

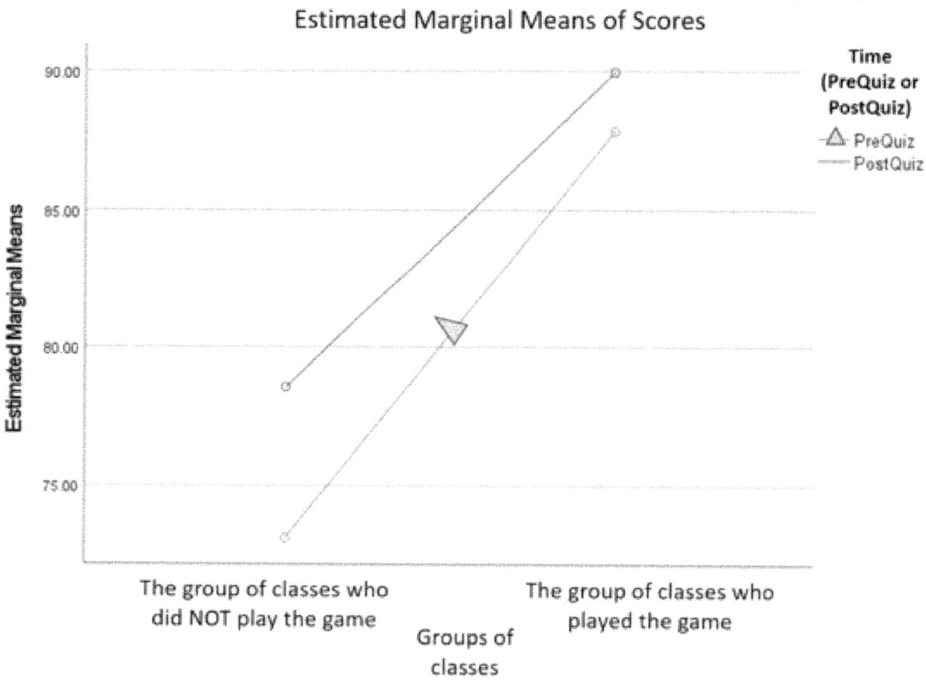

The current study investigates the effect of game-based learning on students' retention of the "Strain theory" lesson, comparing two groups: classes that played the branching narrative game about the theory, and classes that did not. Quiz scores were measured at two time points: PreQuiz (immediately after the lesson) and PostQuiz (one week later). The hypothesis (H1) posits that the game-playing group will exhibit better retention, reflected by a smaller decline in scores from PreQuiz to PostQuiz compared to the non-game-playing group.

The mean quiz scores for each group and time point are as follows:

- Non-game group:
  - PreQuiz: M = 73.1156, SD = 23.32991, N = 199
  - PostQuiz: M = 78.5616, SD = 22.42734, N = 146
- Game group:
  - PreQuiz: M = 87.6456, SD = 19.65466, N = 157
  - PostQuiz: M = 89.0758, SD = 17.93539, N = 185
- Total:
  - PreQuiz: M = 79.6067, SD = 22.95402, N = 356
  - PostQuiz: M = 84.6245, SD = 20.05093, N = 331

A Two-Way ANOVA was conducted using SPSS to analyse the effects of the two groups of classes (game vs. no game) and Time on quiz scores, including their interaction. The sample included 687 observations (345 from the non-game group and 342 from the game group). PreQuiz scores were collected immediately after the lesson, and PostQuiz scores were collected one week later to assess retention.

The game group (M = 88.34, SD = 18.79) outperformed the non-game group (M = 75.83, SD = 23.08), $F(1, 683) = 67.83$, $p < 0.001$, Partial $\eta^2 = 0.090$. The main effect of time was not significant, $F(1, 683) = 5.69$, $p = 0.017$, Partial $\eta^2 = 0.008$, with scores increasing slightly from PreQuiz (M = 79.61, SD = 22.95) to PostQuiz (M = 84.62, SD = 20.05). The interaction (Groups*Time) was not significant, $F(1, 683) = 1.11$, $p = 0.293$, Partial $\eta^2 = 0.002$, indicating no difference in score changes between groups over time. Thus, H1—that the game group would show better retention—was not supported. Levene's test revealed unequal variances, $F(3, 683) = 20.17$, $p < 0.001$, suggesting cautious interpretation.

In plain words, the game-playing group consistently outperformed the non-game group. Contrary to expectations, both groups showed an increase in scores from PreQuiz to PostQuiz (with the game group showing a smaller increase (ΔM^2 = 1.4302) compared to the non-game group (ΔM = 5.4460). This suggests external factors (e.g., additional study or familiarity with the quiz format*) may have influenced PostQuiz performance. Or simply, this could be because the PreQuiz scores of students in the game group had already been too high, and it will be harder to improve the scores on the PostQuiz to a perfect score.

*Observation: While working on the PostQuiz, one student suddenly blurted out to me, "Miss, can I look at the materials again? I totally got it when you explained it, I understood everything. But I haven't yet memorized the names of the categories. I can't recall which strategy this case falls under". (At that moment, I refused her to ensure fairness in scoring across classes, as they weren't allowed to do so during both quizzes).

Table 11. Descriptive statistics of students' ability to connect Strain Theory with the game

Score	Frequency	Percent
0	3	1.7
1	2	1.1
2	15	8.5
3	46	26.1
4	63	35.8
5	36	20.5
6	11	6.3
Total	176	

Note. The evaluation was rated on a scale from 0 to 6, where 0 indicates "Completely unaware, no connection or understanding of how the lecture content relates to the game", and 6 indicates "Fully understand and deeply connect the lecture content with the game, with detailed insights into the game's theoretical implications".

The majority of students who played the game rated their ability to connect the lecture on Role Strain Theory with the game between 3 and 5, with the most frequent score being 4 (35.8%, 63 students). This suggests that most students were able to make a good to very good connection between the lecture content and the game, indicating that the game was generally effective in helping them understand the theoretical concepts in a practical context. Over half of the students (56.3%, scores 4 and 5 combined) demonstrated a strong ability to link the lecture with the game, and 6.3% achieved the highest score of 6, showing a deep understanding of the underlying theoretical implications embedded in the game.

However, a small proportion of students struggled to make the connection: 1.7% scored 0 (completely unaware of the connection) and 1.1% scored 1 (minimal connection). Additionally, 8.5% scored 2, indicating a low level of connection. This suggests that while the game was effective for most students, a minority (11.3% with scores 0–2) found it challenging to link the lecture content with the game or to grasp the theoretical implications.

The distribution is slightly left-skewed, with more students rating their connection at the higher end (scores 4–6, totalling 62.6%) compared to the lower end (scores 0–2, totalling 11.3%). This indicates that the game generally facilitated a meaningful connection to Role Strain Theory for most students.

Comparisons of Two Groups' Perceptions.

The descriptive statistics reveal that the game introduction (Group 1) had a mixed impact on students' perceptions. It slightly increased interest in sociology (4.4 vs. 4.2) but also led to a minor increase in negativity toward the class (1.7 vs. 1.5). Focus and appreciation for the lecturer remained largely unchanged between the groups. While the game may have sparked greater curiosity about sociology, it also introduced a small degree of stress or fatigue for some students. These findings suggest that while the game has the potential to enhance engagement with the subject, its design or implementation may need adjustment to minimize any negative emotional impact on students.

Table 12. A descriptive comparison of the two groups' perceptions Group 0 (who were NOT introduced to the game):

		I was completely focused on the lecture about Merton's Role Strain theory[3]	I highly appreciated the lecturer[4]	I was excited to learn more about Sociology after the lecturer's session[5]	I felt NEGATIVE about the lecturer's class period[6]
N	Valid	142	142	142	139
	Missing	0	0	0	3
Mean		3.8944	5.1056	4.2113	1.5108
Median		4.0000	6.0000	4.0000	1.0000
Mode		4.00	6.00	4.00	1.00

Table 13. Group 1 (who were introduced to the game):

		I am completely focused on the lecture about Merton's Role Strain theory	I highly appreciate the lecturer	I am excited to learn more about Sociology after the lecturer's session	I feel NEGATIVE about the lecturer's class
N	Valid	147	147	148	147
	Missing	1	1	0	1
Mean		3.8776	5.0272	4.4189	1.7279
Median		4.0000	5.0000	5.0000	1.0000
Mode		4.00	6.00	5.00	1.00

Focus on the Lecture: Both groups reported nearly identical levels of focus (mean of 3.9 for both), suggesting that the game introduction did not significantly impact students' ability to concentrate on the lecture about Merton's Role Strain theory.

Appreciation for the Lecturer: Group 0 showed slightly higher appreciation (mean 5.1 vs. 5.0 in Group 1), indicating that the game introduction might have slightly distracted from the lecturer's perceived effort, though both groups still rated the lecturer highly overall.

Interest in Sociology: Group 1 displayed a slightly higher interest in learning more about sociology (mean 4.4 vs. 4.2 in Group 0), with a median/mode of 5 compared to 4 in Group 0. This aligns with the Mann-Whitney test result ($p = 0.086$) below, suggesting a potential trend where the game introduction may have increased curiosity about sociology, though not significantly.

Negativity about the Class: Group 1 reported slightly higher negativity (mean 1.7 vs. 1.5 in Group 0), which aligns with the Mann-Whitney test result ($p = 0.208$) showing a non-significant trend of increased negativity in the game-introduced group. However, both groups generally felt inspired (median/mode of 1), indicating that the game's impact on negativity was minimal.

Table 14. Mann-Whitney U Test comparison of the two groups' perceptions: Analysis results...

...on students' focus during the lecture across two groups	There is no evidence of a significant difference in focus during the lecture on Merton's Strain Theory between students who played the branching narrative game and those who did not ($U = 10{,}194.500$, $Z = -0.355$, $p = 0.723$). The intervention (playing the game) does not appear to have impacted students' focus levels in this context.
...on appreciation for the lecturer across two groups	There is no evidence of a significant difference in appreciation for the lecturer between students who played the branching narrative game and those who did not ($U = 9{,}625.000$, $Z = -1.232$, $p = 0.218$). The intervention (playing the game) does not appear to have impacted students' appreciation in this context.
...on the level of interest in learning more about sociology between two groups of students:	While the game introduction shows a promising trend in increasing students' interest in sociology, the evidence is not strong enough to confirm its effectiveness based on this test alone.
...on the level of negativity toward the lecturer's class between two groups of students	The introduction of a game before the lesson does not appear to have a statistically significant impact on students' negativity toward the lecturer's class ($p = 0.208$). While there is a slight trend suggesting that students in the game-introduced group felt more negative, this effect is not strong enough to draw a definitive conclusion.

Events:

The current small-scale study prompts a question for the researcher: Why did students in the game-based group achieve positive quiz results on the Role Strain lesson, yet report not very much difference in their overall experience? To understand this, I revisit the context of my teaching periods. Firstly, in terms of interaction and pedagogy from the instructor's perspective, during the lesson on Role Strain, I employed another technique, discourse analysis of music. A lot of students found engaging in the creative technique. Here is some feedback from students in the non-game group about the teacher:

"The lecturer is dedicated, weaving Gen Z trends into lessons, making them engaging. She chats cheerfully and shares music with us" (student feedback).

"Your energetic and creative teaching methods captivate us" (student feedback).

"Your practical approach counters students' distractions, sparking interest in the subject" (student feedback).

"Your humour fosters a relaxed, lively classroom, blending modern artistic elements with lessons to attract students" (student feedback).

A lesson's success depends not only on teaching techniques but also on the instructor's energy. When designing this study, I planned for the game to be played before the lecture, expecting it to capture students' attention for academic content. However, in practice, several issues arose, which risk reducing the positive experience of students on gamification. Notably, technical difficulties posed significant hurdles. When being run on a website, heavy video files of the game caused lag, missing slides, and video failures. Additionally, when I shared the game as a PowerPoint file, many students who relied on their phones and lacked the necessary app were unable to open it, further complicating the experience. In fact, my emotional state on that day was also unstable, as I had a minor traffic accident on my way to school—another potential factor that could have affected the students.

It was in contrast to my mood when I only presented the game for group 0 after the classes had completed both the lesson and all three required forms (Pre-test, Post-test, and feedback). The game was projected onto the classroom screen, enabling the entire class to participate together, with me serving as the facilitator, guiding the activity much like an MC. The response was unexpectedly positive and highly engaging. Like, there were moments when the entire class raised their hands with enthusiasm, eager to take part in the game. Some students, filled with curiosity, asked questions such as, "Teacher, what would happen if we chose the other option?"—a clear sign they were invested and did not want to miss any part of the game's narrative slides. In one particularly memorable session, a student shared, "If you taught using games like this, I'd happily retake this course!"—a striking comment, considering I was only substituting for a colleague for that single lesson. This interactive approach proved to be highly effective in engaging the students. Although the narratives within the game are lengthy, in this context, they successfully served their intended purpose – fostering a sense of intrigue and exploration among the students: "The purposes of plot hooks are to arouse curiosity and create intrigue, all of which leads the player to ask, 'What is going to happen next?'... Stories are enjoyable and allow users to explore new places, situations, and people (Dickey, 2015)".

Besides, attention should be paid to the diverse learning needs and preferences among students: The current survey revealed that 40.6% of students are uninterested in designing serious or educational games, while 59.4% express enthusiasm. As seen in the data above, students have highly varied preferences. Some dedicate hours daily to gaming, while some spend nearly zero minutes playing games.

Disciplinary needs also shape students' expectations. For example, journalism students use AI to "generate ten headline titles or create visualisations for news articles". Fast speed and continuous output are prioritised. In contrast, developing AI-based games or videos is time-consuming: "Making a game takes so long, teacher. That day, we only managed two AI-generated pages, but we went through over ten to twenty coding iterations, taking about four hours (student feedback)".

Students' preferences in assignments are different, too. In the same class (Introduction to Sociology Module), some enjoy using AI to create videos presenting sociological issues, while others favour traditional methods like in-depth interviews: "I'm a student who prefers reading and researching documents (student feedback)".

Last but not least, the learning pace and self-learning abilities are varied. While many are accustomed to short-form content, others seek lessons with deeper intellectual engagement:

Student 1: "The game you shared, I actually played it, but I found it a bit hard to understand. The text was too long. For me, a game should be as short as possible to keep players interested and avoid boredom. How can I read a whole long paragraph right when I start? So, I just picked an option randomly. After choosing, another long chunk of text appeared, and I wondered, 'Why is it analysed like that?' I had to go back to the previous part.

In class, the diagram you showed helped me visualise the concepts somewhat. But at home, I sent it to ChatGPT and told it to give me just keywords. It gave us only two keywords per topic, and with those, I could distinguish four or five concepts clearly".

Student 2: "I understand your intention was for us to absorb knowledge through the game. When I entered your game and saw all that text, my first action was to take screenshots. After playing, I wrote everything down. So, before that class, I had already figured out what we'd learn. But I'm sure not every classmate would do what I did or care about all that text because it's pretty long. Honestly, I played your game four times to screenshot the theory and read it beforehand. I really enjoy the feeling of reading something and understanding how it relates to social issues. I like how it unfolds layer by layer, like when you play the game, make a choice, and learn, 'Oh, for this theory, it's abcxyz".

Some first-year students struggle to keep up with academic content: "You lecture quickly with dense information, so I sometimes feel overwhelmed (student feedback)". Conversely, those who are seeking scholarly depth will find AI lacking: "I always feel, teacher, that you leave out 'something,' as if it's too complex or you don't explain it fully. It's like we never reach the deepest level of knowledge. Is it because this is a general education course that the content stops there? (student feedback)".

Comments:

It is evident that AI is not a one-size-fits-all solution. Therefore, in response to the question, "As a teacher, do I feel fear of being replaced by AI?" I can confidently say that I do not harbour such fears. Some reasons can be listed as:

- **Irreplaceable Human Interaction**: The interactions between instructors and students, as well as among learners themselves, are elements that cannot be replicated by technology. Teachers possess a unique sensitivity in orchestrating classroom activities - knowing which activity should come first, what should follow, and how different interactions (whether human-to-human or human-to-content) influence the classroom atmosphere.
- **The Art of Teaching and Learning**: The allure of teaching and learning stems from a variety of factors that cannot be achieved through purely mechanical means. The human touch - empathy, creativity, and adaptability - brings a depth to education that technology alone cannot provide.
- **AI's Limitations and Human Strengths**: AI still has its flaws. The professional expertise and sharp, nuanced thinking of humans remain unmatched. As educators, the AI era provides us with the opportunity to refine our skills, deepen our critical thinking, and nurture the heart of our profession, breathing life into the teaching and learning process.

I firmly believe that when art, technology, and science converge, the future of education will hold immense promise. Like, by personalization (such as in my own experience of being guided by AI in coding) AI will certainly be able to assist those lacking foundational knowledge in exploring the social sciences, and serve as a personal tutor for students struggling to keep pace, whilst allow teachers more time to instruct deep critical thinking in other students. When paired with the expertise of educators, AI will become a remarkable companion, igniting imagination and transforming the ways we learn in the future. This vision echoes the introduction of Microsoft Copilot: “Your AI companion to inform, entertain, and inspire”.

As a concluding remark, the Figure 11 below exemplifies this promising human–AI collaboration:

Figure 11. The design process of a bureaucracy maze mini-game with AI collaboration

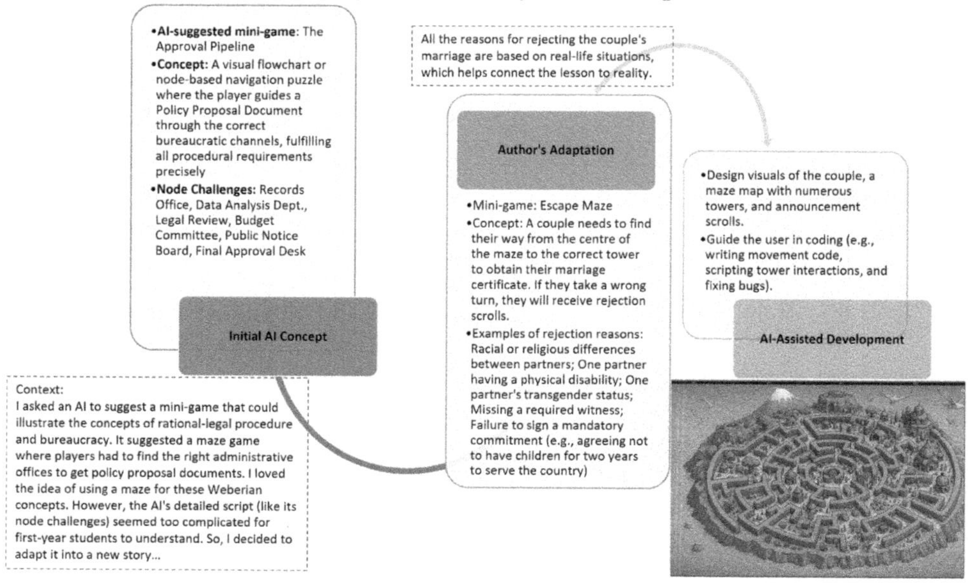

Note. The image of the maze game is a direct AI output.

REFERENCES

Antony, O. (2005). *Aristotle's poetic concept: An analysis of poetry*. SparkNotes Editors. https://www.sparknotes.com/philosophy/poetics/section1/

Banks, N. (n.d.). *AI prompting techniques: Why prompting matters*. Retrieved October 4, 2024, from https://www.thisisdefinition.com/insights/prompting-techniques

Briggs, S. M., & Friedman, J. (2009). *Criminology for dummies*. Wiley.

Clement, J. (2024). *U.S. daily time spent playing games/computer use by age 2023*. Statista. https://www.statista.com/statistics/502149/average-daily-time-playing-games-and-using-computer-us-by-age/

DAIR.AI. (n.d.). *Prompting techniques*. Retrieved October 4, 2024, from https://www.promptingguide.ai/techniques

Dickey, M. D. (2015). *Aesthetics and design for game-based learning*. Routledge.

Greyling, C. (2023, August 2). *12 Prompt engineering techniques*. https://cobusgreyling.medium.com/12-prompt-engineering-techniques-644481c857aa

Husain, M. (2002). *Ontology and the art of tragedy: An approach to Aristotle's poetics*. State University of New York Press.

Monami. (2017). *Things you must know about Aristotle's theory of drama in poetics*. Owlcation. https://owlcation.com/humanities/Aristotle-Theory-Drama-poetics

Nickerson, C. (n.d.). *Social action theory (Weber): Definition & examples*. Simply Psychology. Retrieved May 1, 2025, from https://www.simplypsychology.org/social-action-theory.html

Ninh. (2020). SOC 300: Introduction to sociology (Ninh) (3.4.2: Power and authority). Social Sci LibreTexts. https://socialsci.libretexts.org/Courses/Cosumnes_River_College/SOC_300%3A_Introduction_to_Sociology

Takeuchi, L. M., & Vaala, S. (2014). *Level up learning: A national survey on teaching with digital games*. The Joan Ganz Cooney Center at Sesame Workshop.

Todd, M., Weeks, M., Hobbs, M., & Tomley, S. (2015). *The sociology book (C. Thorpe & Yuill, Christ* (Publishing, D. K., Ed.).

Utts, J. M., & Heckard, R. F. (2007). *Mind on statistics* (3rd ed.). Thomson Learning.

Yasar, K. (2023, September). *Definition: AI prompt*. https://www.techtarget.com/searchenterpriseai/definition/AI-prompt

ENDNOTES

1 I intentionally did not provide any document defining this term to observe how the AI would interpret and learn from its available sources.

2 ΔM (where Δ is the Greek letter "delta") indicates the change or difference in the mean scores between two measurements.

3 Rated on a scale from 0 ("I was distracted, absent-minded to the point of not being aware of what was happening in class") to 6 ("I concentrated and understood all the knowledge the teacher conveyed").

4 Rated on a scale from 0 ("I had a completely negative evaluation of the lecturer") to 6 ("I appreciated the effort the lecturer put into preparing the lesson").

5 Rated on a scale from 0 ("I had no interest at all") to 6 ("I wanted to learn a lot more about Sociology").

6 Rated on a scale from 0 ("Feeling extremely interested and inspired") to 6 ("Tired, stressed, just want to go home right away").

Chapter 15
Artificial Intelligence in Academic Research: Applications, Challenges, and Future Directions

Pi-Chi Han
https://orcid.org/0000-0001-9429-4967
National Kaohsiung Normal University, Taiwan

ABSTRACT

Artificial Intelligence (AI) is rapidly transforming academic research by streamlining literature reviews, data collection, statistical analysis, and academic writing. This chapter traces the evolution of AI in research, from early rule-based systems to current machine learning and deep learning applications. It explores key areas where AI enhances research productivity and insight, while also addressing pressing ethical and methodological concerns such as algorithmic bias, data privacy, transparency, and authorship accountability. The chapter argues that while AI holds great potential to augment scholarly inquiry, its integration must be guided by rigorous ethical standards and human oversight to preserve the integrity, equity, and creativity central to academic work.

INTRODUCTION

The integration of Artificial Intelligence (AI) into academic research has ushered in a transformative era, redefining research methodologies, enhancing efficiency, and expanding the boundaries of scholarly inquiry. AI technologies – ranging from machine learning and natural language processing to robotics and automated data analysis – are revolutionizing research processes across virtually all disciplines. Early

DOI: 10.4018/979-8-3373-2397-8.ch015

implementations of AI in academia demonstrated its potential for automating complex tasks, and recent advancements have greatly amplified that impact. Researchers now leverage AI to sift through vast bodies of literature, analyze large datasets, and even generate novel insights that would be onerous or impossible to obtain through traditional means. By examining key applications of AI in the research lifecycle, along with the ethical considerations and future prospects of these technologies, this chapter provides a comprehensive overview of AI's growing role in academic research. The discussion spans multiple fields – from medicine and engineering to education and agriculture – reflecting AI's pervasive influence on knowledge creation (Taneja et al., 2023). Ultimately, the chapter highlights both the innovative contributions of AI and the challenges of ensuring that its adoption in academia aligns with principles of rigor, ethics, and scholarly integrity (Pigola et al., 2023).

THE EVOLUTION OF AI IN ACADEMIC RESEARCH

AI's trajectory within academic research can be traced back to the mid-20th century, with early computational models laying the groundwork for what would become a transformative scholarly tool (Ekundayo et al., 2024). The earliest forays into AI were characterized by rule-based expert systems designed to mimic human decision-making processes. These nascent AI tools found applications in areas such as symbolic computation and early natural language processing (Tobin et al., 2019). By the 1980s, the rise of expert systems demonstrated how encoding human knowledge into intricate "if–then" rules could aid domains like medical diagnostics and financial analysis. However, these rule-based systems proved brittle, struggling to handle uncertainty or adapt beyond their predefined rules. Their limitations became apparent as they often failed when confronted with scenarios not anticipated by their creators.

A significant turning point came with the transition from purely rule-based approaches to machine learning algorithms capable of learning from data without explicit programming (Otero et al., 2023). Early machine learning methods such as decision trees and support vector machines provided researchers with new tools to identify patterns and make predictions from empirical data. This shift opened up avenues in data mining and pattern recognition that were previously impractical. Concurrently, developments in statistical methods enriched the analytical toolkit of researchers, enabling them to quantify uncertainty and draw inferences from complex datasets – an essential aspect of rigorous academic inquiry.

The emergence of deep learning in the early 21st century further propelled AI's capabilities, inspired by the multi-layered neural networks of the human brain. Deep learning algorithms excel at extracting intricate features from large, complex datasets, driving breakthroughs in tasks such as image recognition, natural language understanding, and predictive modeling (Khodayar & Regan, 2023). This deep learning revolution enabled researchers to tackle problems of unprecedented complexity and scale with remarkable accuracy and efficiency. The evolution of AI has been punctuated by landmark achievements that illustrate its progression from theory to application. For example, the development of *Unimate* in 1961 (an industrial robotic arm) and *ELIZA* in 1964 (an early conversational chatbot) showcased the tangible possibilities of AI beyond theoretical concepts (Thakkar et al., 2024). Over the decades, AI's growing sophistication has continuously expanded what scholars can achieve, from automating routine tasks to providing intelligent support in experimental design and analysis.

Crucially, this technological evolution has directly impacted academic research practices. The progression from rule-based systems to advanced machine learning and deep learning techniques has facilitated improvements in every stage of research, including literature reviews, data collection, hypothesis testing, and result analysis. Studies note that modern AI techniques have become integral to research workflows, enabling more thorough literature surveys and more complex data analyses than were previously feasible (Geffner, 2018; Jantakun et al., 2021; Taneja et al., 2023). In essence, AI has evolved from a niche computational curiosity into a cornerstone of contemporary academic research methodology. Today's researchers operate in an era where AI-driven tools augment human intelligence, allowing scholars to probe deeper questions, analyze data at greater scale, and explore interdisciplinary frontiers with enhanced precision. This historical journey sets the stage for understanding the specific applications of AI that are now transforming how research is conducted.

KEY AI APPLICATIONS IN ACADEMIC RESEARCH

Integrating AI into academic research has catalyzed a paradigm shift in how scholars approach various research activities. From accelerating literature reviews to improving data analysis and enhancing collaboration, AI-driven tools are reshaping traditional methodologies. In particular, several key applications of AI in the research process can be identified as follows:

Automated Literature Reviews

AI-powered tools such as semantic search engines and citation analysis platforms greatly expedite the process of surveying literature. These systems can intelligently search large academic databases to identify relevant publications and even summarize key findings. AI has become indispensable at this stage of research by rapidly scanning the ever-growing scholarly output and highlighting pertinent information for researchers. For instance, advanced natural language processing (NLP) techniques enable a semantic understanding of article content, going beyond simple keyword matching to uncover hidden connections and emerging themes in the literature (Torre-López et al., 2023). This not only saves time but also helps scholars maintain comprehensive and up-to-date awareness of their fields. By automating the search and aggregation of sources, AI tools significantly reduce the time-consuming and repetitive work involved in traditional literature reviews (da Silva Júnior & Dutra, 2021). Studies have found that such tools can regularly update literature searches and even identify gaps in the existing knowledge base. The efficiency gains are substantial: AI-driven searches can filter through thousands of articles in a fraction of the time a manual review would take, ensuring that researchers do not overlook crucial publications. A wide array of AI-based literature review assistants is now available, reflecting a varied landscape of tools each with different strengths (Buetow & Lovatt, 2024). Harnessing these tools offers a transformative approach to scholarship by allowing academics to quickly pinpoint relevant studies and synthesize prior work (DesRoches, 2022). Notably, automated literature review platforms also incorporate machine learning algorithms to extract and organize information from sources, helping to identify prevailing trends and knowledge gaps that might otherwise remain unnoticed. In summary, AI-driven literature review tools greatly enhance the thoroughness and speed of surveying scholarly literature, enabling researchers to ground their work in a more exhaustive understanding of prior research.

Data Collection and Processing

Machine learning algorithms enable researchers to extract, integrate, and preprocess vast datasets from multiple sources, including structured data (e.g. databases, spreadsheets) and unstructured data (e.g. text, images). In many fields, the volume of data available for research has grown exponentially, and AI offers the means to handle this complexity. For example, machine learning excels at aggregating data streams and detecting patterns across large data repositories – capabilities that are invaluable in disciplines ranging from the social sciences to the physical sciences (Strielkowski et al., 2023). By automating data collection (such as web scraping or sensor data acquisition) and data cleaning (through algorithms that normalize or impute missing values), AI tools free researchers from tedious manual data handling and reduce errors in the preliminary stages of research. However, effective application of these methods depends on careful data representation and curation. Studies have shown that many challenges in data-driven research stem from the quality of input data and the preprocessing techniques used (Khodayar & Regan, 2023). Thus, researchers must still apply sound judgment in how data are selected and prepared for AI analysis, ensuring diverse and representative datasets to improve the validity of outcomes. The advantage of AI in data processing is particularly evident in predictive analytics: by assimilating large volumes of historical data, AI models can identify intricate relationships and forecast future trends or outcomes that would be difficult for humans to discern unaided. For instance, in educational research, machine learning has been used to predict student performance and identify at-risk students in need of intervention (Akgun & Greenhow, 2022). Similarly, in sustainability studies, AI systems help analyze complex environmental and educational data to inform sustainable practices (Lin et al., 2023). Across domains – from power systems engineering to higher education – AI-driven data processing expands the scope and scale of research questions that can be tackled. Researchers do need to evaluate and choose appropriate AI tools for data tasks, considering factors like each tool's capabilities, available training support, and cost, to ensure the best fit for their specific research needs (Buetow & Lovatt, 2024). When used adeptly, AI data processing tools can reveal meaningful patterns and insights far more efficiently than traditional manual methods, accelerating the pace of discovery and enabling more complex empirical investigations.

Statistical Analysis and Hypothesis Testing

AI-driven statistical software has become a powerful aid in conducting complex data analyses, identifying patterns, and testing hypotheses with greater accuracy and efficiency. Traditional statistical analysis often relies on model assumptions and human-guided exploration of data, but AI introduces adaptive algorithms that can model nonlinear relationships and high-dimensional data beyond the reach of classical techniques. Machine learning models, including advanced methods like neural networks and ensemble techniques, are now routinely employed to detect subtle patterns, classify observations, and make predictions from research data. These AI-based approaches complement conventional statistical methods by handling large datasets and multiple variables in a more automated fashion, which is particularly useful in fields such as genomics, economics, and engineering. For example, researchers can train AI algorithms on historical or experimental data to predict outcomes or uncover associations – such as forecasting equipment failures from sensor readings or identifying risk factors for diseases from health records (Strielkowski et al., 2023). The ability of AI to learn from data enables a form of hypothesis generation and testing where the algorithm itself may suggest which variables are significant or which patterns merit further investigation. Moreover, AI tools can perform tasks like data cleaning, outlier detection, and model selection automatically, streamlining the analytical workflow. This level of automation reduces the likelihood of human error in analysis and allows researchers to focus more on interpreting results and their theoretical implications. Importantly, studies report that incorporating AI into statistical analysis can enhance the precision of research findings – models can achieve higher predictive accuracy and reveal nuanced effects that simpler statistical tests might miss (Gao & Wang, 2023). However, the use of AI in analysis necessitates careful validation and an emphasis on interpretability. Researchers must guard against overfitting models to data and should use techniques like cross-validation and explainable AI methods to ensure that results are reliable and can be understood in context (Hildt, 2025). In sum, AI has become a valuable partner in the realm of data analysis and hypothesis testing by improving efficiency and expanding analytical capabilities. When appropriately applied, AI-driven statistical tools augment researchers' ability to draw meaningful conclusions from complex data, ultimately strengthening the rigor and reliability of academic research.

Writing and Publishing Assistance

AI-based writing assistants are increasingly used to help researchers prepare and refine scholarly manuscripts. These tools can perform a range of functions to support academic writing: they offer suggestions for improving grammar and style, check for proper syntax and clarity, and even detect potential plagiarism or citation errors. By doing so, AI writing assistants enhance the language quality and overall readability of research papers, which is crucial for effective dissemination of results. For instance, AI-driven grammar and style checkers (advanced forms of proofreading software) can identify convoluted sentences or ambiguous phrasing and recommend clearer alternatives. This capability is particularly beneficial for researchers writing in a non-native language, as the AI can help ensure that scientific content is communicated precisely and professionally (Dong, 2023). Additionally, some AI tools assist in organizing content and maintaining logical flow, which is valuable during manuscript revision. Beyond language polishing, AI can streamline the publication process itself: it can automatically format manuscripts according to specific journal guidelines, suggest relevant journals for submission, or generate summaries and keywords. A notable application is in plagiarism detection – journals and institutions employ AI-based systems to scan submissions for unoriginal text, thereby upholding academic integrity. Researchers similarly can use such tools proactively to ensure their work properly paraphrases and cites sources, avoiding inadvertent plagiarism (Bekbolatova et al., 2024). AI's role in writing extends to idea generation as well: generative AI models (such as large language models) can help authors overcome writer's block by proposing draft text for sections like literature reviews or introductions, which the researcher can then refine. However, the increasing capability of generative AI to produce coherent text brings new ethical considerations. Scholars caution that AI is not a replacement for human authorship or critical thinking; its outputs require careful verification and editing to ensure accuracy and originality (Tomlinson et al., 2023). There are growing discussions about how to appropriately acknowledge AI contributions in authorship and maintain transparency when AI has been used in the writing process. Best practices now suggest disclosing the use of AI in creating content and rigorously checking AI-generated material for factual correctness (Chetwynd, 2024; Khalifa & Albadawy, 2024). Overall, when used responsibly, AI writing and publishing assistants can significantly reduce the time and effort required to prepare scholarly publications, allowing researchers to iterate drafts more efficiently and focus on the substantive aspects of their work. These tools serve as productivity aids that, in collaboration with human expertise, help elevate the clarity and quality of academic writing.

Collaboration and Knowledge Sharing

AI-facilitated platforms are transforming how researchers collaborate and share knowledge. In the digital era, collaborative research often involves geographically dispersed teams, interdisciplinary partnerships, and large-scale data sharing – all areas where AI can provide critical support. Intelligent collaboration platforms employ AI algorithms to connect scholars with complementary research interests or expertise, thereby fostering interdisciplinary dialogue and partnerships that might not have formed otherwise. For example, some academic social networks and conference management systems use recommendation algorithms to suggest potential collaborators or reviewers based on publication histories and research profiles. AI also enhances knowledge sharing by integrating diverse datasets and resources in a unified environment, allowing researchers to easily access and combine data from multiple sources (Mozaffar et al., 2022). This capability is particularly valuable in big-science projects or multi-center studies, where managing and merging data is a complex challenge. Furthermore, AI-driven project management and communication tools help streamline the logistics of collaboration: they can automate version control of documents, coordinate schedules across time zones, and even translate communications in real time for international teams. Virtual research environments equipped with AI enable real-time editing, annotation, and discussion on shared documents or code, thus increasing productivity and coherence in team science efforts. Importantly, AI is playing a growing role in scholarly publishing and open science initiatives, which are extensions of research collaboration. For instance, automated tools can assist in the peer review process by checking manuscripts for compliance with guidelines or by flagging potential statistical issues, thereby aiding editors and reviewers (Dave & Patel, 2023; Razack et al., 2021). AI can also help match manuscripts to suitable reviewers by analyzing the content of submissions and identifying relevant experts, making the peer review system more efficient. In terms of disseminating knowledge, AI-powered recommendation systems on digital libraries help researchers discover relevant work by suggesting articles related to their interests (Glickman & Zhang, 2024). All these AI applications contribute to a more connected and agile research community. However, while AI eases many technical barriers to collaboration, it also raises considerations about ensuring clear communication and maintaining research standards. Scholars must exercise judicious oversight when sharing data and interpretations through AI-mediated platforms to avoid miscommunication or over-reliance on automated summaries. There is consensus that human expertise and judgment remain central to meaningful collaboration; AI is a facilitator, not a substitute for the creative and critical exchange of ideas among researchers (Chandra & Dasgupta, 2023). When leveraged appropriately, AI and human expertise together can elevate the quality and impact of research collaborations, enabling teams to achieve breakthroughs that would be difficult for individuals or single disciplines alone. The scholarly ecosystem is becoming increasingly technology-driven, and AI's contribution to connecting researchers and enhancing reproducibility is gradually increasing (Perifanis & Kitsios, 2023; Razack et al., 2021). In essence, AI is knitting the academic world closer together by providing powerful tools for collaboration and knowledge dissemination, thus accelerating the collective advancement of science.

ETHICAL AND METHODOLOGICAL CONSIDERATIONS

While AI offers significant advantages to academic research, its integration also raises important ethical and methodological concerns. Researchers must navigate these challenges to ensure that the use of AI upholds the integrity and equity of scholarly work. Key issues include:

Bias in AI Algorithms

AI systems can inadvertently perpetuate biases present in their training data or design, leading to skewed or unfair research outcomes. If an AI model is trained on unrepresentative or biased data (for example, a dataset lacking diversity in populations or viewpoints), its predictions and conclusions may reinforce those biases. This is a serious concern, as biased AI outputs could distort research findings or propagate social inequalities under the guise of objectivity. For instance, an AI tool used to screen scholarly literature might underrepresent contributions from certain regions or demographics if it was trained primarily on Western publications. Similarly, AI models in fields like economics or sociology could yield biased insights if the data reflect historical prejudices. Addressing algorithmic bias requires careful attention to data curation and model validation. Researchers need to use diverse and representative datasets and test their AI models for bias during development (Bulut et al., 2024). Techniques such as bias audits, fairness metrics, and the inclusion of counterbalancing data can help mitigate these issues. Moreover, transparency in how AI algorithms make decisions (i.e., the pursuit of explainable AI) is crucial so that any potential bias can be identified and corrected. It is also important to remember that over-reliance on AI without critical scrutiny can amplify bias; human oversight is necessary to interpret AI results in context. The literature emphasizes that algorithmic bias is not just a technical problem but also an ethical one: failing to address it can perpetuate existing societal prejudices and undermine the validity of research conclusions (Ahmed, 2024; Ajani et al., 2024). Researchers must therefore implement robust validation techniques and remain vigilant to ensure that AI tools produce fair and equitable results. By actively working to eliminate bias, scholars can harness AI's strengths without compromising the objectivity and inclusivity of academic research.

Data Privacy and Security

The use of AI in research often involves the collection and analysis of large datasets, some of which may contain sensitive personal or institutional information. Ensuring the privacy and security of these data is paramount for ethical research practice. AI systems, especially those in fields like healthcare, education, or social sciences, may handle data about individuals (patients, students, survey respondents) that are protected by privacy laws and ethical norms. A major concern is that AI's appetite for vast amounts of data could lead to unintended exposure of confidential information if not properly managed. For example, an AI project analyzing student performance data must protect student identities and personal details (Karpouzis, 2024). Similarly, AI-driven analyses of genetic or medical data must comply with regulations like HIPAA or GDPR to safeguard patient privacy. Researchers have the responsibility to implement strict data protection measures such as encryption, secure storage, and controlled access to data. Prior to using such data, ethical approval and informed consent (where applicable) should be obtained, with clear communication about how AI will be utilized in the analysis. Anonymization techniques are often employed so that AI models work on de-identified data, minimizing the risk of tracing results back to individuals. Despite such precautions, the powerful data-mining capabilities of AI raise the risk of re-identification – piecing together anonymized data to reveal identities – which must be guarded against using state-of-the-art privacy-preserving techniques. Data security is equally critical: robust cybersecurity practices are needed to prevent unauthorized access or data breaches, especially when research data are stored in cloud platforms or shared across institutions. The ethical mandate is to comply with data protection regulations and uphold the trust of those who provide data for research (Roshanaei et al., 2023). Notably, educational contexts have highlighted privacy as a primary concern with AI adoption, as increased reliance on digital platforms and data collection could lead to misuse of student or faculty information if safeguards fail (Al-Zahrani, 2024). Researchers must continually update their data privacy protocols to match evolving threats and standards. In summary, maintaining data privacy and security in AI-driven research is non-negotiable: it protects participants from harm, ensures compliance with legal frameworks, and preserves the integrity of the research process. By implementing stringent data protection measures and being transparent about data usage, scholars can uphold ethical standards while benefiting from AI's analytic power.

Transparency and Reproducibility

Ensuring that AI-driven research methodologies are transparent and that results are reproducible is crucial for academic integrity. The complexity of many AI models, especially deep learning networks, often makes them "black boxes" whose internal workings are not easily understood even by experts (Gillani et al., 2023). This opacity can be problematic in a research context: if a study relies on an AI algorithm to generate findings, other researchers need to understand how the algorithm arrived at those findings to trust and build upon them. A lack of transparency can breed skepticism and hinder the scientific process of verification. Therefore, a key methodological consideration is the explainability of AI – developing models and analysis techniques that provide interpretable outputs or rationales (Hildt, 2025). Researchers are encouraged to document their AI methods in detail, including model architectures, training procedures, and parameter settings, so that others can replicate the approach. Whenever possible, open-source code and datasets should be shared alongside publications to enable independent reproduction of results. Reproducibility is a cornerstone of science, and the use of AI does not exempt researchers from this norm. In fact, given the stochastic nature of some machine learning training processes, reproducing results might require additional steps (such as fixing random seeds or sharing pre-trained model weights). Another aspect of transparency is disclosing the role that AI played in the research. For instance, if a section of a paper was drafted with the help of a generative AI system, acknowledging this use is important for clarity and honesty (Jain & Jain, 2024). The academic community is actively discussing guidelines for such disclosures to maintain trust in scholarly communications. Moreover, the integration of AI intersects with issues of academic integrity in new ways. Concerns have been raised that the ease of obtaining AI-generated text or analysis might tempt some to present AI outputs as one's own scholarship without proper attribution, which would be a serious breach of ethics

(Tan & Maravilla, 2024). To guard against this, institutions and journals are beginning to develop policies for the responsible use of AI in research and writing. Overall, fostering transparency and reproducibility in AI-assisted research may involve extra effort – such as providing extensive supplemental material or opting for simpler, more interpretable models when feasible – but these practices are essential. They ensure that the scholarly community can validate and trust AI-augmented findings and that future researchers can learn from and extend those findings. Collaborative efforts among researchers, publishers, and policymakers are underway to establish standards that promote openness and accountability for AI in academia (Alenezi & Akour, 2025; Cordero et al., 2024). Embracing these standards will help maintain the credibility of research in an era increasingly influenced by complex AI systems.

Accountability and Authorship

The use of AI in generating research results or writing raises questions about responsibility and credit. Traditionally, researchers are accountable for all aspects of their work – from data collection to analysis to writing – and they receive authorship or inventor credit for their intellectual contributions. AI complicates this picture by acting as a semi-autonomous agent participating in these tasks. A pressing ethical consideration is how to assign authorship when AI systems significantly contribute to a paper or discovery. For example, if an AI system formulates part of the text of an article or autonomously discovers a pattern leading to a research breakthrough, can or should the AI be considered an "author" or co-creator? The emerging consensus is that AI, as a tool lacking independent agency or accountability, should not be listed as an author on scholarly works. However, human researchers who design or operate the AI are responsible for its contributions. Clear guidelines are needed to define the roles of researchers versus AI in the research process (Balta, 2023). Many journals and academic bodies are now drafting policies: typically, they stipulate that authors must disclose the use of AI in producing any content and affirm that humans take responsibility for the final output. This ensures that accountability remains with researchers, who must verify and stand by the results and text that AI helped produce (Sharma, 2024). Additionally, researchers need to consider the extent to which AI-derived insights can be trusted and how errors made by AI will be handled. If an AI model introduces a flaw – say, a misidentified trend or an incorrect reference – the human researcher is accountable for that error once it appears in their published work. Thus, rigorous validation and proofreading remain essential, even if AI automates parts of the research workflow. Questions of accountability also extend to ethical issues: who is responsible if an AI application in research causes harm or breaches ethics? Is it the developer of the AI, the user (researcher), or an institution? The prevailing view is that human researchers and their institutions retain responsibility for ensuring ethical compliance when using AI tools. As such, they must exercise oversight and not abdicate decision-making entirely to AI systems. In terms of scholarly credit, using AI might change the nature of intellectual contributions – for instance, if an AI conducts data analysis, the researcher's contribution may shift more toward interpretation and study design. This could impact how we evaluate contributions for authorship. Some have proposed new contributorship taxonomies to explicitly acknowledge the use of software tools and algorithms in the research process. What remains clear is that establishing and following guidelines for authorship and accountability in AI-assisted research is essential to maintain fairness and trust in academic work (Tomlinson et al., 2023). By being transparent about AI's role and by ensuring humans remain in control of the research narrative, the academic community can adapt traditional authorship principles to the modern, AI-augmented research environment.

Human-AI Collaboration

The increasing presence of AI in research calls for a careful balance between AI automation and human insight. AI can handle certain tasks with superhuman speed and accuracy – processing data, recognizing patterns, optimizing parameters – yet it lacks the intuition, creativity, and critical reasoning of human researchers. A key consideration is determining which tasks to automate with AI and which to retain under direct human control to maintain research quality and meaningful scientific inquiry. Over-automation can lead to a de-skilling of researchers or an erosion of critical thinking: if scholars become overly reliant on AI outputs, they might accept results uncritically or fail to develop deep expertise in their domain (Ahmed, 2024). It is therefore essential to integrate AI in ways that augment rather than replace human creativity and judgment. For example, an AI might generate a set of potential hypotheses from data patterns, but researchers should evaluate these hypotheses, prioritize them, and design appropriate experiments to test them. In academic writing, AI can suggest improvements or even draft paragraphs, but human authors must curate the content, inject original ideas, and ensure coherence and scholarly tone. Maintaining this balance is also important for educational aspects of academia: emerging scholars need to learn fundamental research skills, and if AI handles all analysis and writing, students may not develop the necessary competencies. From an ethical standpoint, human oversight is crucial to catch AI's mistakes or inappropriate outputs. AI does not understand context or values; it may produce results that are statistically sound yet contextually nonsensical or ethically problematic. Human researchers provide the moral and conceptual compass to interpret AI findings within the broader scope of knowledge and societal norms (Popenici & Kerr, 2017). Additionally, the collaboration between humans and AI should be a partnership in which each side's strengths compensate for the other's weaknesses. Humans can guide AI by asking the right questions and providing high-quality training data, while AI can process information at a scale and speed humans cannot. Success in this symbiosis has been noted in fields like medical research, where doctors and AI systems together achieve better diagnostic accuracy than either alone (Perifanis & Kitsios, 2023). To maximize the benefits of human–AI collaboration, researchers are encouraged to stay informed about how their AI tools work – attaining a level of *AI literacy* (Long & Magerko, 2020) – so they can better steer and interpret the AI's contributions. There is also a need to develop a culture of responsible AI use in academia: guidelines and training that help researchers know when to properly collaborate with AI, when to override it, and how to document this collaboration. By striking an appropriate balance, the research community can leverage AI's capabilities while preserving the essential human elements of scholarly inquiry: curiosity, skepticism, and ethical reflection. In doing so, academics ensure that they benefit from AI's assistance without compromising the creativity, rigor, and critical perspective that drive genuine innovation in research.

In light of these considerations, it is evident that leveraging AI in academic research demands not only technical adjustments but also a strong ethical compass and methodological vigilance. Issues such as bias, privacy, transparency, accountability, and the human–AI interface require proactive management by researchers, institutions, and publishers. Collaborative efforts are underway to develop ethical frameworks and best practices for AI in research (Bjelobaba et al., 2024). For example, universities are instituting guidelines for AI use in data handling and writing, and conferences are hosting panels on AI ethics in academia. By anticipating and addressing these challenges, the academic community can ensure that the adoption of AI technologies bolsters research quality and productivity without eroding ethical standards or public trust. In practice, this means continuously auditing AI systems for fairness, safeguarding data rigorously, being open about AI methodologies, clarifying the role of AI in authorship, and maintaining robust human oversight. Such measures will allow scholars to harness AI's powerful capabilities while upholding the values of integrity, accountability, and critical inquiry that define academia. Ultimately, responsible integration of AI can enable researchers to push the frontiers of knowledge further, so long as they remain conscientious stewards of both the technology and the principles of good science (Dhopte & Bagde, 2023).

THE FUTURE OF AI IN ACADEMIC RESEARCH

Looking to the future, AI is poised to further transform academic research in profound ways. One anticipated development is the advent of real-time data analysis and adaptive experimentation. As AI algorithms become faster and more efficient, researchers will increasingly be able to analyze incoming data on the fly and adjust their experimental or analytical procedures dynamically. For instance, AI-driven technologies are expected to facilitate real-time processing of data from laboratory instruments or sensor networks, allowing researchers to interpret vast datasets with unprecedented speed and accuracy. Such tools can identify hidden patterns and correlations in data streams that might otherwise go unnoticed, potentially leading to new insights and discoveries during the research process itself (Gao & Wang, 2023). An example is in large-scale physics experiments or astronomical surveys, where AI systems could flag anomalous or interesting events in real time, enabling scientists to direct attention to those events immediately. This agility in data analysis will make research more responsive and iterative, blurring the line between data collection and interpretation.

Another emerging trend is the development of AI-generated hypotheses and intelligent research assistants. In the near future, AI systems might not only analyze data but also propose testable hypotheses or design experiments. Early signs of this are already visible in drug discovery research, where AI models suggest candidate molecular compounds and the lab then tests them. We can expect AI "co-researchers" to become more common – software agents that survey literature, integrate findings, and postulate explanations or predictions that human researchers might overlook. These AI assistants could also handle routine tasks in scholarly work: managing citations, drafting sections of grant proposals based on given inputs, or even reviewing literature to produce initial literature review drafts. As such capabilities mature, researchers will be able to delegate more groundwork to AI and devote greater focus to creative design and interpretation. However, this raises questions about how to validate AI-suggested hypotheses and ensure that the scientific method is preserved; human oversight will remain critical to vet ideas before accepting them into the canon of knowledge.

AI is also likely to have a significant impact on peer review and academic publishing practices. We might see AI tools that assist journal editors by automatically evaluating the soundness of submitted manuscripts – checking for issues like statistical errors, adherence to reporting standards, or potential fraud (such as image manipulation or plagiarism). Some journals are already experimenting with AI to screen submissions for basic quality benchmarks, which could speed up the review process and reduce reviewer burden. In the future, more advanced AI might provide meta-reviews, summarizing the consensus of human peer reviewers or highlighting sections of a manuscript that warrant closer scrutiny. Additionally, AI could play a role in matching papers to the best reviewers by analyzing the content of a submission and comparing it to databases of expert profiles (Glickman & Zhang, 2024). In academic publishing, we may also see AI facilitating the creation of enhanced publications: for example, automatic generation of plain-language summaries, infographic abstracts, or even interactive figures that update with new data. These innovations aim to improve the dissemination and accessibility of research findings.

Interdisciplinary research stands to benefit greatly from AI advancements. As AI systems excel at integrating diverse types of data, they will enable collaborations across fields that previously had difficulty interfacing. Enhanced interdisciplinary partnerships are expected as AI platforms provide common ground for, say, a biologist, a computer scientist, and an ethicist to work on a complex problem by pooling their data and methods (perhaps in a shared AI-driven simulation environment). By breaking down technical barriers, AI encourages the synthesis of knowledge across domains, potentially leading to innovative approaches that no single-discipline perspective would achieve. Fostering such convergence science is a priority for many research funding agencies, and AI is a natural catalyst for it.

The future will also see continuous upskilling of researchers in the use of AI. As AI tools become more central to research, scholars must become conversant in computational thinking and data science techniques – a concept referred to as developing *AI literacy* among researchers (Long & Magerko, 2020). Graduate training programs are increasingly incorporating modules on machine learning, coding, and algorithmic ethics to prepare the next generation of academics. Lifelong learning will be essential; established researchers may periodically need to refresh their skills to keep up with new AI tools and paradigms. This cultural shift in academia toward embracing computational methods is likely to deepen, with more researchers able to custom-tailor AI tools for their specific research questions. In tandem, we can expect greater availability of user-friendly AI platforms that do not require deep programming expertise, lowering the barrier for all scholars to utilize AI in their work.

Crucially, discussions about the ethical and societal impact of AI in research will remain front and center. Future studies will likely delve deeper into AI's influence on human cognitive skills and on the research ecosystem itself (Morandini et al., 2023). Open questions remain about how heavy reliance on AI might affect researchers' creativity, critical thinking, and problem-solving abilities in the long term. Some worry about the "black box" effect dampening the drive to deeply understand phenomena if an AI provides answers too easily. Others are concerned about equitability: ensuring that AI research tools are accessible to scientists in developing regions or smaller institutions – not just those at well-funded centers – so that AI does not widen the gap in research capabilities. There is also the issue of maintaining academic integrity in the age of AI. As generative AI becomes more capable of producing text and analyses, the academic community must establish norms to prevent misconduct (such as undisclosed AI-generated writing or data fabrication). Proactive measures – for example, journals implementing checks for AI-authored text or universities updating codes of conduct – will likely become standard (Blau et al., 2024; Tan & Maravilla, 2024). Policymakers and research institutions are expected to collaborate on guidelines that balance innovation with ethical constraints, ensuring that AI is used to advance knowledge responsibly (Perkins & Roe, 2024). Indeed, several international bodies and conferences are already formulating principles for trustworthy AI in research contexts, emphasizing transparency, accountability, and inclusivity.

In the broader academic environment, including education and mentorship, AI's future influence cannot be ignored. In higher education teaching – which complements academic research – AI tools promise personalized learning experiences, automated grading, and intelligent tutoring systems that adapt to student needs (Abbas et al., 2023; Alotaibi, 2024). These applications, while slightly beyond the scope of research per se, will indirectly affect research by shaping better-prepared students and possibly altering how knowledge is disseminated and consumed. However, they also come with challenges such as potential over-reliance on AI by students, educational inequalities in access to AI, reduced human interaction in learning, and new privacy considerations – echoing many themes from the research domain (Gligorea et al., 2023; Singh & Hiran, 2022). Ensuring that the next generation of scholars is adept at using AI but also grounded in critical thinking will be vital.

The convergence of AI and academic research thus paints a picture of a highly dynamic future. Researchers can expect AI to be an ever-present collaborator – one that significantly accelerates the pace of discovery and broadens the horizons of inquiry. Routine tasks will be increasingly automated, freeing scientists to concentrate on creativity and interpretation. New research questions will become approachable as AI breaks through current analytical limitations. At the same time, the human element will remain indispensable: guiding the direction of research inquiries, providing ethical judgment, and contextualizing findings. Maintaining a healthy skepticism and oversight over AI outputs will be crucial to address issues of bias, error, and misuse (Popenici & Kerr, 2017). We will likely see continued emphasis on the motto "augment, not replace," meaning that AI should enhance human research capabilities while humans ensure that meaning and values are preserved in the pursuit of knowledge.

In practical terms, academic research in the coming decades could see scenarios like these: a multidisciplinary team working on climate change uses an AI system to integrate satellite data, climate models, and social science data in real time to propose adaptive policy interventions; a historian employs an AI language model trained on centuries of archival texts to identify shifts in rhetoric or sentiment that signal societal changes, yielding new historical insights; a laboratory scientist partners with an AI that designs and conducts virtual experiments overnight, suggesting the most promising compounds to synthesize the next day; and a global network of researchers collaborates via an AI-managed platform that handles translations, data harmonization, and literature updates seamlessly. Such vignettes illustrate the potential for AI to be woven into the fabric of research in creative and powerful ways.

However, realizing these futures will require careful stewardship. The academic community must proactively shape how AI is used – advocating for open research tools, sharing best practices, and being vigilant about ethical pitfalls. If done well, the future promises a research enterprise that is more efficient, innovative, and inclusive, tackling grand challenges with a combination of human ingenuity and AI's computational might. By leveraging AI responsibly and ethically, researchers can indeed unlock new possibilities, accelerate discoveries, and contribute solutions to some of the world's most pressing problems (Perifanis & Kitsios, 2023). The coming years will be pivotal in setting the norms and infrastructure for this AI-augmented scholarly world.

CONCLUSIONS

AI has become an indispensable tool in academic research, fundamentally enhancing how scholars gather information, analyze data, and disseminate knowledge. Across the research lifecycle, AI-powered systems are streamlining processes that were once labor-intensive and time-consuming. For example, literature reviews – traditionally a daunting task of sifting through mountains of publications – can now be expedited by AI-driven semantic search engines and citation analysis platforms, which quickly identify relevant sources and even summarize their key points. These tools leverage natural language processing and machine learning to scan vast repositories of scholarly articles, books, and patents, enabling researchers to efficiently synthesize existing knowledge and spot gaps in the literature. Machine learning algorithms automate the extraction of relevant information from texts and the aggregation of findings, reducing the likelihood that important prior work is overlooked. Studies have shown that such AI-assisted literature reviews not only save time but can also improve the breadth and depth of reviews by uncovering connections that a manual search might miss (Markowitz et al., 2024). As a result, researchers can build on a more solid foundation of past scholarship when formulating new research questions.

In the realm of data analysis and hypothesis testing, AI's impact has been revolutionary. AI-driven statistical software and machine learning models assist in conducting complex analyses that would be arduous or impractical to do by hand.

They can identify subtle patterns, interactions, or anomalies in data that might elude human analysts, and they can make predictions with a level of precision that improves the reliability of research findings. For instance, by training algorithms on large datasets, researchers can develop predictive models for phenomena ranging from disease outbreaks to material properties, thereby testing hypotheses *in silico* before committing to costly real-world experiments. These approaches enhance both the rigor and efficiency of research: results are derived from robust computational methods, and human researchers can devote more energy to interpreting outcomes and exploring theory. It is important to note, however, that the integration of AI in analysis requires researchers to maintain and develop new skills in data science and AI literacy (Bender et al., 2021). The community increasingly recognizes the need for training and guidelines to ensure that researchers understand their AI tools and can validate their outputs. International efforts are underway to establish standards for transparency, reproducibility, and ethics in AI-assisted analysis and writing (BaHammam, 2023). Adhering to these standards will help safeguard the credibility of findings in this new era of data-centric research.

AI has also made significant inroads into academic writing and publishing. Researchers now frequently use AI-based writing assistants to refine their manuscripts. These tools help polish language, check grammar and style, and ensure that the text meets formal academic standards. They can detect potential plagiarism by cross-referencing text against vast databases (BaHammam et al., 2023) and suggest improvements in clarity or conciseness, which is especially beneficial for authors who are non-native English speakers or early-career scholars honing their academic writing skills. The result is often a clearer, more coherent manuscript and a smoother path through the publication process. Some experiments have even explored AI as a co-author, particularly in educational settings – for example, students using systems like ChatGPT to generate ideas or draft essays, which has sparked conversations about how to incorporate AI into pedagogy and assessment (Jen & Salam, 2024a; 2024b). In research publishing, AI's influence is seen in tools that assist editors and reviewers by automatically evaluating submission quality, as well as in emerging practices like the automated formatting of references and text to meet journal guidelines. While AI can speed up publication workflows and help maintain high writing quality, the academic community is cautious about preserving core values such as originality and proper attribution. Policies now emphasize that AI-generated text or translations must be used responsibly and disclosed appropriately (Tomlinson et al., 2023). These measures aim to prevent issues like undisclosed plagiarism or the dilution of a researcher's authentic voice.

Collaboration in research has been enhanced by AI through platforms that connect scholars and manage knowledge more effectively. AI-facilitated research networks and databases allow for easier sharing of data and methodologies across institutions. They can recommend collaborators or resources, breaking down silos between disciplines and encouraging interdisciplinary endeavors. In fields where research is global and collective, such as genomics or climate science, AI tools help standardize and combine datasets from different groups, enabling large-scale studies that pool knowledge for greater impact (Razack et al., 2021; Cordero et al., 2024). Moreover, by incorporating AI in project management (for scheduling meetings, tracking contributions, handling version control of documents, etc.), teams find it easier to coordinate and maintain momentum. During recent periods when remote collaboration became the norm, AI-powered communication tools (including real-time transcription and translation services) proved invaluable in keeping international research projects active and inclusive. As these technologies mature, we can expect research collaborations to become even more fluid and far-reaching, unconstrained by many traditional logistical barriers. However, as with other areas, human judgment remains critical: AI can facilitate connections and manage routine tasks, but successful collaboration ultimately relies on the creativity, trust, and mutual understanding among human researchers.

At the same time, the adoption of AI in research brings forth new challenges and responsibilities. Researchers now face the imperative of becoming skilled in AI methodologies – not necessarily as developers of AI algorithms, but as informed users who understand the capabilities and limitations of these tools. This might involve learning new programming languages, data analysis techniques, or principles of algorithmic ethics. The concept of AI literacy is gaining prominence, referring to the competencies that enable researchers to effectively and critically use AI (Long & Magerko, 2020). Institutions are responding by updating curricula and offering workshops to ensure scholars are prepared for an AI-rich research environment. Additionally, maintaining ethical integrity is an ongoing concern. The ease of generating text with AI, for instance, has led to debates on academic honesty and the definition of plagiarism in the context of AI assistance (Jen & Salam, 2024b). Ensuring that AI is used as a tool rather than as a shortcut to fabricate results or bypass scholarly effort is key to preserving trust in academic outputs. Consequently, many journals and conferences have issued statements or guidelines on the acceptable use of AI, and some have implemented screening mechanisms to detect AI-written content in submissions. These developments illustrate that the academic community is actively adapting its norms to integrate AI without compromising values such as honesty, accountability, and rigor.

In reflecting on AI's burgeoning role, one must also acknowledge its limitations and the areas where human researchers remain irreplaceable. AI systems, no matter how advanced, operate based on patterns in existing data and predefined objectives; they do not possess genuine understanding or creativity in the human sense. They can err in ways that a human might not – such as confidently producing a subtly flawed analysis or misinterpreting context. Therefore, human oversight and critical thinking are more important than ever when AI is involved. Researchers must not become passive consumers of AI outputs; instead, they should actively interpret and question those outputs. This includes verifying AI-derived results with alternative methods or theoretical expectations and being prepared to override AI suggestions that conflict with expert knowledge or ethical considerations. Maintaining a healthy degree of skepticism toward AI-driven conclusions helps prevent the propagation of errors and guards against the undue influence of algorithmic bias. As one report emphasized, protecting scientific integrity in the age of generative AI requires concerted efforts by scientists, institutions, and policymakers to uphold standards and implement safeguards (Blau et al., 2024).

In conclusion, the integration of AI into academic research is leading to a paradigm shift in how knowledge is discovered, validated, and shared. We are witnessing a research landscape where routine tasks are increasingly automated, complex analyses are made tractable, and collaboration can span the globe with unprecedented ease. When used responsibly, AI has the capacity to amplify human intellect – enabling scholars to analyze more data, consider more hypotheses, and disseminate findings more efficiently than ever before. Indeed, AI has been described as a powerful new paradigm for scientific research (Xu et al., 2021), one that holds the promise of accelerating innovation and addressing intricate questions that were beyond reach in the past. However, realizing this promise relies on researchers embracing AI thoughtfully and ethically. The academic community must continue to establish norms that ensure fairness, transparency, and accountability in AI usage – from mitigating biases to acknowledging AI contributions in research. Investments in education and policy will be crucial to guide AI's development and application in directions that benefit society and expand our understanding of the world.

Ultimately, the symbiosis of human creativity and machine computation can lead to extraordinary advancements. By leveraging AI responsibly and ethically, researchers can unlock new possibilities, test bold ideas, and expedite discoveries that address some of the most pressing challenges in science and humanity (Perifanis & Kitsios, 2023). The responsible adoption of AI is critical for ensuring that the progress it brings does not come at the cost of the core values of academia. As we navigate this transition, continual reflection and adaptation are necessary – the community must remain vigilant about AI's ramifications for scholarly practices and be ready to refine its approaches accordingly (Wei, 2023). The journey is ongoing, but if guided with wisdom, the infusion of AI into academic research will stand as one of the great enablers of scholarly progress in the 21st century, enriching the pursuit of knowledge for generations to come.

REFERENCES

Abbas, N., Ali, I., Manzoor, R., Hussain, T., & Hussaini, M. H. A. (2023). Role of artificial intelligence tools in enhancing students' educational performance at higher levels. *Journal of Artificial Intelligence* [JAIMLNN]. *Machine Learning and Neural Network*, *3*(5), 36–49. DOI: 10.55529/jaimlnn.35.36.49

Ahmed, S. K. (2024). Artificial intelligence in nursing: Current trends, possibilities and pitfalls. *Journal of Medicine, Surgery, and Public Health*, *3*, 100072. DOI: 10.1016/j.glmedi.2024.100072

Ajani, O. A., Gamede, B., & Matiyenga, T. C. (2024). Leveraging artificial intelligence to enhance teaching and learning in higher education: Promoting quality education and critical engagement. *Journal of Pedagogical Sociology and Psychology*, *7*(1), 54–69. DOI: 10.33902/jpsp.202528400

Al-Zahrani, A. M. (2024). Unveiling the shadows: Beyond the hype of AI in education. *Heliyon*, *10*(9), e30696. DOI: 10.1016/j.heliyon.2024.e30696 PMID: 38737255

Alenezi, M., & Akour, M. (2025). AI-driven innovations in software engineering: A review of current practices and future directions. *Applied Sciences (Basel, Switzerland)*, *15*(3), 1344. DOI: 10.3390/app15031344

Alotaibi, N. S. (2024). The impact of AI and LMS integration on the future of higher education: Opportunities, challenges, and strategies for transformation. *Sustainability*, *16*(23), 10357. DOI: 10.3390/su162310357

BaHammam, A. S. (2023). Balancing innovation and integrity: The role of AI in research and scientific writing. *Nature and Science of Sleep*, *15*, 1153–1156. DOI: 10.2147/nss.s455765 PMID: 38170140

Bahammam, A. S., Trabelsi, K., Pandi-Perumal, S. R., & Jahrami, H. (2023). Adapting to the impact of artificial intelligence in scientific writing: Balancing benefits and drawbacks while developing policies and regulations. *Journal of Nature and Science of Medicine*, *6*(3), 152–158. DOI: 10.48550/arxiv.2306.06699

Balta, N. (2023). Ethical considerations in using AI in educational research. *Journal of Research in Didactical Sciences*, *2*(1), 14205. DOI: 10.51853/jorids/14205

Bjelobaba, S., Waddington, L., Perkins, M., Foltýnek, T., Bhattacharyya, S., & Weber-Wulff, D. (2024). Research integrity and GenAI: A systematic analysis of ethical challenges across research phases. *arXiv Preprint arXiv:2412.10134*. https://doi.org//arxiv.2412.10134DOI: 10.48550

Blau, W., Cerf, V. G., Enriquez, J., Francisco, J. S., Gasser, U., Gray, M. L., & Witherell, M. (2024). Protecting scientific integrity in an age of generative AI. *Proceedings of the National Academy of Sciences of the United States of America, 121*(22), e2407886121. DOI: 10.1073/pnas.2407886121 PMID: 38771193

Buetow, S., & Lovatt, J. (2024). From insight to innovation: Harnessing artificial intelligence for dynamic literature reviews. *Journal of Academic Librarianship, 50*(4), 102901. DOI: 10.1016/j.acalib.2024.102901

Bulut, O., Beiting-Parrish, M., Casabianca, J. M., Slater, S. C., Jiao, H., Song, D., . . . Morilova, P. (2024). The rise of artificial intelligence in educational measurement: Opportunities and ethical challenges. *arXiv Preprint arXiv:2406.18900*. https://doi .org//arxiv.2406.18900DOI: 10.48550

Chandra, A., & Dasgupta, S. (2023). Impact of ChatGPT on medical research article writing and publication. *Sultan Qaboos University Medical Journal, 23*(4), 429. DOI: 10.18295/squmj.11.2023.068 PMID: 38090250

Chetwynd, E. (2024). Ethical use of artificial intelligence for scientific writing: Current trends. *Journal of Human Lactation, 40*(2), 211–215. DOI: 10.1177/08903344241235160 PMID: 38482810

Cordero, J., Torres-Zambrano, J., & Cordero-Castillo, A. (2024). Integration of generative artificial intelligence in higher education: Best practices. *Education Sciences, 15*(1), 32. DOI: 10.3390/educsci15010032

Dave, M., & Patel, N. (2023). Artificial intelligence in healthcare and education. *British Dental Journal, 234*(10), 761–764. DOI: 10.1038/s41415-023-5845-2 PMID: 37237212

DesRoches, A. (2022). Harnessing the power of artificial intelligence in scholarly publishing. *Editor Office News, 15*(9), 3. DOI: 10.18243/eon/2022.15.9.3

Dhopte, A., & Bagde, H. (2023). Smart smile: Revolutionizing dentistry with artificial intelligence. *Cureus, 15*(6), e41227. DOI: 10.7759/cureus.41227 PMID: 37529520

Dong, Y. (2023). Revolutionizing academic English writing through AI-powered pedagogy: Practical exploration of teaching process and assessment. *Journal of Higher Education Research, 4*(2), 52–60. DOI: 10.32629/jher.v4i2.1188

Ekundayo, T., Khan, Z., & Nuzhat, S. (2024). Evaluating the influence of artificial intelligence on scholarly research: A study focused on academics. *Human Behavior and Emerging Technologies, 2024*(1), 8713718. DOI: 10.1155/2024/8713718

Gao, J., & Wang, D. (2023). Quantifying the benefit of artificial intelligence for scientific research. *arXiv Preprint arXiv:2304.10578*. https://doi.org//arxiv.2304.10578DOI: 10.48550

Geffner, H. (2018). Model-free, model-based, and general intelligence. *arXiv Preprint arXiv:1806.02308*. https://doi.org/DOI: 10.24963/ijcai.2018/2

Gillani, N., Eynon, R., Chiabaut, C., & Finkel, K. (2023). Unpacking the "black box" of AI in education. *Journal of Educational Technology & Society*, *26*(1), 99–111. DOI: 10.48550/arxiv.2301.01602

Glickman, M., & Zhang, Y. (2024). AI and generative AI for research discovery and summarization. *arXiv Preprint arXiv:2401.06795*. https://doi.org/DOI: 10.1162/99608f92.7f9220ff

Gligorea, I., Cioca, M., Oancea, R., Gorski, A. T., Gorski, H., & Tudorache, P. (2023). Adaptive learning using artificial intelligence in e-learning: A literature review. *Education Sciences*, *13*(12), 1216. DOI: 10.3390/educsci13121216

Hildt, E. (2025). What is the role of explainability in medical artificial intelligence? A case-based approach. *Bioengineering (Basel, Switzerland)*, *12*(4), 375. DOI: 10.3390/bioengineering12040375 PMID: 40281735

Jain, R., & Jain, A. (2024, July). Generative AI in writing research papers: a new type of algorithmic bias and uncertainty in scholarly work. In *Intelligent Systems Conference* (pp. 656-669). Cham: Springer Nature. https://doi.org/DOI: 10.1007/978-3-031-66329-1_42

Jantakun, T., Jantakun, K., & Jantakoon, T. (2021). A common framework for artificial intelligence in higher education (AAI-HE mode). *International Education Studies*, *14*(11), 94–103. DOI: 10.5539/ies.v14n11p94

Jen, S. L., & Salam, A. R. H. (2024a). A systematic review on the use of artificial intelligence in writing. *International Journal of Academic Research in Progressive Education and Development*, *13*(1), 1819–1829. DOI: 10.6007/ijarped/v13-i1/20584

Jen, S. L., & Salam, A. R. H. (2024b). Using artificial intelligence for essay writing. *Arab World English Journal (AWEJ) Special Issue on ChatGPT*, April 2024, 90-99. https://doi.org/DOI: 10.24093/awej/ChatGPT.5

Khalifa, M., & Albadawy, M. (2024). Using artificial intelligence in academic writing and research: An essential productivity tool. *Computer Methods and Programs in Biomedicine Update*, *4*, 100145. DOI: 10.1016/j.cmpbup.2024.100145

Khodayar, M., & Regan, J. (2023). Deep neural networks in power systems: A review. *Energies*, *16*(12), 4773. DOI: 10.3390/en16124773

Lin, C. C., Huang, A. Y., & Lu, O. H. (2023). Artificial intelligence in intelligent tutoring systems toward sustainable education: A systematic review. *Smart Learning Environments*, *10*(1), 41. DOI: 10.1186/s40561-023-00260-y

Long, D., & Magerko, B. (2020, April). What is AI literacy? Competencies and design considerations. In *Proceedings of the 2020 CHI Conference on Human Factors in Computing Systems* (pp. 1-16). https://doi.org/DOI: 10.1145/3313831.3376727

Markowitz, D. M., Boyd, R. L., & Blackburn, K. (2024). From silicon to solutions: AI's impending impact on research and discovery. *Frontiers in Social Psychology*, *2*, 1392128. DOI: 10.3389/frsps.2024.1392128

Morandini, S., Fraboni, F., De Angelis, M., Puzzo, G., Giusino, D., & Pietrantoni, L. (2023). The impact of artificial intelligence on workers' skills: Upskilling and reskilling in organizations. *Informing Science*, *26*, 39–68. DOI: 10.28945/5078

Mozaffar, M., Liao, S., Xie, X., Saha, S., Park, C., Cao, J., & Gan, Z. (2022). Mechanistic artificial intelligence (mechanistic-AI) for modeling, design, and control of advanced manufacturing processes: Current state and perspectives. *Journal of Materials Processing Technology*, *302*, 117485. DOI: 10.1016/j.jmatprotec.2021.117485

Perifanis, N. A., & Kitsios, F. (2023). Investigating the influence of artificial intelligence on business value in the digital era of strategy: A literature review. *Information (Basel)*, *14*(2), 85. DOI: 10.3390/info14020085

Perkins, M., & Roe, J. (2024). Generative AI tools in academic research: Applications and implications for qualitative and quantitative research methodologies. *arXiv Preprint arXiv:2408.06872*. https://doi.org//arxiv.2408.06872DOI: 10.48550

Pigola, A., Scafuto, I. C., da Costa, P. R., & Nassif, V. M. J. (2023). Artificial intelligence in academic research. *International Journal of Innovation*, *11*(3), e25408. DOI: 10.5585/2023.25408

Popenici, S. A., & Kerr, S. (2017). Exploring the impact of artificial intelligence on teaching and learning in higher education. *Research and Practice in Technology Enhanced Learning*, *12*(1), 22. DOI: 10.1186/s41039-017-0062-8 PMID: 30595727

Razack, H. I. A., Mathew, S. T., Saad, F. F. A., & Alqahtani, S. A. (2021). Artificial intelligence-assisted tools for redefining the communication landscape of the scholarly world. *Science Editing*, *8*(2), 134–144. DOI: 10.6087/kcse.244

Roshanaei, M., Olivares, H., & Lopez, R. R. (2023). Harnessing AI to foster equity in education: Opportunities, challenges, and emerging strategies. *Journal of Intelligent Learning Systems and Applications*, *15*(4), 123–143. DOI: 10.4236/jilsa.2023.154009

Sharma, D. N. (2024). Artificial intelligence: Legal implications and challenges. *Knowledgeable Research: A Multidisciplinary Peer-Reviewed. Refereed e-Journal*, *2*(11), 13–32. DOI: 10.57067/220k4298

Singh, S. V., & Hiran, K. K. (2022). The impact of AI on teaching and learning in higher education technology. *Journal of Higher Education Theory and Practice*, *22*(13), 1–10. DOI: 10.33423/jhetp.v22i13.5514

Strielkowski, W., Vlasov, A., Selivanov, K., Muraviev, K., & Shakhnov, V. (2023). Prospects and challenges of machine learning and data-driven methods for the predictive analysis of power systems: A review. *Energies*, *16*(10), 4025. DOI: 10.3390/en16104025

Tan, M. J. T., & Maravilla, N. M. A. T. (2024). Shaping integrity: Why generative artificial intelligence does not have to undermine education. *Frontiers in Artificial Intelligence*, *7*, 1471224. DOI: 10.3389/frai.2024.1471224 PMID: 39512399

Taneja, A., Nair, G., Joshi, M., Sharma, S., Sharma, S., Jambrak, A. R., & Phimolsiripol, Y. (2023). Artificial intelligence: Implications for the agri-food sector. *Agronomy (Basel)*, *13*(5), 1397. DOI: 10.3390/agronomy13051397

Thakkar, A., Gupta, A., & De Sousa, A. (2024). Artificial intelligence in positive mental health: A narrative review. *Frontiers in Digital Health*, *6*, 1280235. DOI: 10.3389/fdgth.2024.1280235 PMID: 38562663

Tobin, S. C., Jayabalasingham, B., Huggett, S., & de Kleijn, M. (2019). A brief historical overview of artificial intelligence research. *Information Services & Use*, *39*(4), 1–6. DOI: 10.3233/ISU-190060

Tomlinson, B., Torrance, A. W., & Black, R. W. (2023). ChatGPT and works scholarly: Best practices and legal pitfalls in writing with AI. *SMU Law Review Forum*, *76*, 108-118. https://doi.org/DOI: 10.25172/slrf.76.1.5

Wei, L. (2023). Artificial intelligence in language instruction: Impact on English learning achievement, L2 motivation, and self-regulated learning. *Frontiers in Psychology*, *14*, 1261955. DOI: 10.3389/fpsyg.2023.1261955 PMID: 38023040

Xu, Y., Liu, X., Cao, X., Huang, C., Liu, E., Qian, S., & Zhang, J. (2021). Artificial intelligence: A powerful paradigm for scientific research. *The Innovation*, *2*(4), 100179. DOI: 10.1016/j.xinn.2021.100179 PMID: 34877560

Chapter 16
Relevance of Artificial Intelligence in Assessment:
A Balanced Approach

Praveen Kumar Dubey
https://orcid.org/0000-0003-1060-2278
Montana State University Northern, USA

Angela Rae Crevar
https://orcid.org/0000-0002-0596-9174
Mercer University, USA

Mattius K. Rischard
Montana State University Northern, USA

ABSTRACT

This chapter explores the integration of Artificial Intelligence (AI) in education for formative and summative assessment. The educational shift from teacher-based assessment to AI-powered assessment tools have evolved to increase the learning outcomes for the students and helped teachers to implement best assessment practices. The relevance of AI in assessment has created a balanced approach to improve assessment in education. Moreover, AI-powered tools have created new landscapes for students' assessment for both formative as well as summative assessments. The chapter discusses the role of AI in student assessment such as formative and summative assessment with AI, personalized learning paths, adaptive learning, instant feedback, tracking progress, Integration of AI in Pedagogy, and Behavioral and Engagement Analytics to improve students learning outcomes. Additionally, it addresses the challenges in implementing AI-powered assessment for efficient

DOI: 10.4018/979-8-3373-2397-8.ch016

resources allocation, and fairness, bias, and ethical consideration in AI algorithms.

INTRODUCTION

Well-designed assessments are the essential elements in determining the learning outcomes for students. Traditional assessments such as multiple-choice questions, essays, and short answer questions have been widely used to evaluate student knowledge. These assessments not only predict students' learning outcomes, but they also help to provide tailored educational approaches for learning. What makes it more challenging is that the assessment is both time consuming and demands effort. The use of artificial intelligence (AI) addresses such issues and reduces the required time and effort. Furthermore, the use of artificial intelligence improves the performance as well as the quality of formative and summative assessments. The use of AI has several implications in education. It has shortened the teachers' correction times with possibility of reduced errors and supported students' problem solving with automated feedback (Vittorini et al., 2021). As generative AI becomes extensively used in education, educators face challenges in designing thoughtful assessments that authentically evaluate student learning goals. To achieve equitable learning, personalized goal setting with resource allocations for tailored learning is needed. Such a learning system offers personalized feedback, facilitates reflective learning experiences through interactive chatbots, and removes the learning gaps or improves students' personal learning growth. Moreover, formative and summative assessments offer personalized feedback, efficiency, and more data-driven insights to meet the overall individual learning needs.

The role of AI in assessment such as formative and summative assessments have been used to improve the students' learning outcomes. Moreover, in recent years, AI has played a similar role in enhancing student assessments and eventually bettering student learning outcomes. Rather than describing AI as an additional tool in education, it has been acknowledged as an innovative tool embedded to increase flexibility as well as a newer version of traditional assessment to achieve higher educational goals. This chapter explores the transformative use of AI in enhancing the significant use of formative and summative assessments in educational settings to offer personalized feedback, efficiency, and data-driven decisions to improve overall student learning outcomes. Additionally, this chapter examines how the balanced approach of using formative and summative assessment not only improves learning outcomes but helps instructional staff to use assessment for best learning outcomes. AI-powered educational assessment tools are transforming education; and the use of AI tools for formative and summative assessments has become essential for teaching and learning. Moreover, AI-powered educational assessment tools provide benefits such as improved accuracy and efficiency of assessments, personalized feedback for student learning, and teachers ability to adopt strategies to meet unique student learning needs. Furthermore, this chapter examines the relevance of AI in assessment for improved student learning outcomes.

THE ROLE OF AI IN STUDENT ASSESSMENT

The role of AI in assessment is considered to improve overall student learning. The arguments are that AI-powered educational assessment tools provide efficiency, accuracy, and personalized feedback to students. AI-powered assessment tools enable teachers with strategies to meet the unique learning needs of students. AI technologies support significant increases in academic performance of students. Furthermore, the use of AI grading systems provides faster, accurate, and more secure feedback for both formative and summative assessments than teachers. The supporting evidence suggests that the AI in education has transformed education by enhancing the learning experiences and enriching the learning resources, it proved a significant enhancement in educational assessment tools for both formative and summative assessments. Empirical evidence supports the balanced approach for the use of AI as an educational tool for student assessment. While discussion surrounding the use of AI in pedagogy, student learning outcomes, and student assessment to explore the best strategies to enhance student learning through well-developed assessments. Thus, to fully utilize the AI-powered assessment tools, it is considered that educators should use a balanced approach in student assessment to evaluate students' learning outcomes.

The recent use of AI in education suggests that it has been integrated in different domains of teaching-learning and assessment is one of them. Use of AI in education advances due to the process involved for learning support, delivery of content, and real-time assessment of the content. Thus, the use of the knowledge of the learning processes is an efficient way to train machines to develop adaptive learning systems where learners are engaged in a small unit with embedded formative assessment to help meet the learning needs of students (Chiu et al., 2023). Moreover, to meet the full potential of assessment using AI, teachers should be professionally trained in pedagogic competence to utilize novel pedagogies and approaches (Sanusi et al., 2022). Such training and professional development would help teachers to gain the required skills to implement AI-powered assessment tools for formative as well as summative assessments. Furthermore, using AI for formative and summative assessment opens the door for teachers to collect real-time student learning data and make informed decisions to provide equitable learning opportunities for all students. Next section discusses the use of AI in formative assessment and summative assessment and its implications in student learning.

Formative Assessment (Ongoing, Diagnostic)

Formative Assessment is a critical part of the learning process that involves a targeted approach to provide ongoing feedback for the learners throughout the instructional period. Formative assessment is diagnostic in nature with added benefit for learners where they identify their strengths, reflect on weaknesses, and implement a targeted effort to improve the learning outcomes. The aim of such an assessment is to enable educators to adjust their instructional strategies to students' learning needs, design personalized learning plans with time and resource-sensitive approaches.

The formative assessment occurs during the course work to measure or verify students' learning progress. What makes it a tedious and error-prone task especially when educators need to provide feedback to students in a timely manner and help them to master the content simultaneously. Considering this, specific problems arise such as- what are the different ways to address such issues effectively and finding reliable ways to exercise the implementation of automated grading systems for quick learning with feedback. Furthermore, the use of automated grading tools can shorten the grading times with the possibility for reduced errors and support students during the learning process through feedback. It not only provides accurate and timely feedback; moreover, increases the overall student learning outcomes. Such approaches include but are not limited to the uses of multiple-choice quizzes based on some available specific instructional materials with a focused approach on the grasp of key concepts.

Formative Assessment and Artificial Intelligence

The students' progress is monitored using formative assessment to provide feedback and guide teachers' instructional practices. To conduct formative assessments, teachers need to know each student's learning style, their learning progress, and ways to support achieving student learning goals (Hopfenbeck et al., 2023). Considering this, in a traditional classroom, teachers are challenged to find ways to help a student or entire class and provide individualized feedback through teacher assessment, peer assessment, self-assessment or any other means of assessment (Double et al., 2020).

The founding principle of formative assessment practices expects self-regulated and proactive student participation with an ideology where students participate in peer-discussions and assessment processes (Hopfenbeck et al., 2023). Such expectations are characterized by accountability systems, purpose driven goals, and shared mutual understanding purposes. To achieve these goals, one teacher is responsible for managing large class sizes, under-resourced classrooms, and building a high degree of trust with learners. In contrast, even in well-supported classrooms with best practices implementing formative assessment, teachers endanger continuous barriers to support such assessment systems. Given the challenges faced to implement formative assessment in the classrooms, AI-powered tools provide opportunities to identify the most significant strategies to overcome assessment hurdles and support teachers to influence the landscape of formative assessment at sustainable scale.

Considering the effectiveness in meeting individualized learning needs, high-quality feedback, and time sensitive learning management; AI stands out as a solution to fully or partially automate assessment procedures in a feasible manner. The AI automated assessment system frees teachers from labor intensive grading processes and allows them to focus on addressing students' fine or extended learning needs. Thus, the use of AI-powered assessment tools in formative assessment imposes its relevance in well planned classroom instruction. Furthermore, AI-powered assessment tools ensure to make the assessment procedures fully or partly automated, feasible for teachers to maintain, and eventually reduce the time burden for teachers (Swiecki et al., 2024). In addition, AI can broadly improve the quality and effectiveness of peer assessment for any class sizes (Hopfenbeck et al., 2023). The AI-powered automated essay grading tools are the typical example of such usage. The automated assessment tools are widely integrated with AI based natural language processing to provide students with timely formative feedback to help them revise and improve their writing (Murphy, 2019).

The AI-powered automated essay grading tool not only demonstrates improvement in quality feedback, but it also improves efficiency and flexibility of formative assessment for the individual student learning. A formative assessment used during the learning process monitors students' progress with improved timely feedback and further guides their instruction. Such customized assessment tools individualize student progress through enabling the most suitable tasks or questions for each student at different points throughout the instruction.

Summative Assessment

Summative assessments are designed to measure students' overall progress in a unit or course against predetermined standards. Such assessments provide a final evaluation of student learning at the end of a learning period, usually a high-stake assessment. Although such exams are typically used to measure student knowledge and skills, it can be used to incorporate student learning opportunities from collected data to make pedagogical decisions for future teaching and instruction. The following section discusses how the use of AI contributes to student individualized learning and enhances the student's performance.

Summative Assessment and Artificial Intelligence

Summative Assessment evaluates student learning outcomes at the end of a course or unit with a goal to measure students' achievement on predetermined learning objectives to enhance or support student learning. The process actively involves students in self-assessment and reflection that builds student understanding and ownership of their own learning (Ali, 2024). The assessment promotes students' demonstration of knowledge and skills to meet their learning goal on the given topic while gathering data that shapes students' future learning. The summative assessment not only assesses students' ability to apply their knowledge on the current topic but inherently narrates the holistic view to further their skills in newer or next contexts. The use of AI-powered tools plays a crucial role in evaluating students' learning through summative assessment with comprehensive measures on students' learning attainment.

Integrating generative AI into summative assessment facilitates the focused approach that meaningfully extracts the data to evaluate through careful measurement of student learning. Student learning is supervised through AI algorithms that have a possibility to adjust different levels of student understanding or learning. It streamlines the assessment process and leverages AI-powered tools to reduce teachers' time and resources on assignments grading. The response is quick and timely. Moreover, generative AI-powered tools enable tailored learning for students with interventions and promotion for improved student learning. The data-driven assessment process encourages continuous improvement for students' learning and program improvements (Ali, 2024). Generative powered AI tools not only support struggling students but also revolves around promoting high achievers to align their progress to meet the learning goals of the next standards. It enhances teacher effectiveness and efficiency by saving time while meeting students' other personalized learning goals.

The idea of summative assessment is based on a holistic approach of prioritizing the content memorization and demonstration of skills through appropriate testing. Moreover, AI in summative assessment helps students carefully personalize their learning with proper assessment tools and framework to achieve their pre-designed goals. In fact, students attest that the inclusion of AI-powered testing tools have positive learning experience on student overall learning where students want to try such testing tools included in their learning (Clift & Petrovska, 2025). Additionally, the inclusion of generative AI tools such as ChatGPT in summative assessment allows for additional learning for its usage. Furthermore, such testing tools create additional learning opportunities where students can explore newer ways to enhance their learning experiences and help improve their focus on complex content. Notably, including generative AI assessment tools have net overall positive effect on student learning and encourage successful implementation of student-centred learning. Overall, students enjoy all the perks offered by AI-powered assessment tools to meet their needs of personalized learning and promote direct student engagement.

Both students' and teachers' view that AI-powered assessment tools have potential for efficiency and personalized feedback but share concern that its usage could take away opportunities of interactions and jeopardize student-teacher connection (Van den Berg & Papadopoulos, 2024). Such opinions have been shared by other stakeholders and increased concerns beyond the use of technology in the classroom. In fact, it is argued that getting direct feedback from teachers helps students adopt several characteristics of learning and decision-making process. However, feedback received from AI-powered tools skips such interactions and removes the benefits of personalized interaction between student and teacher.

We argue that it is important to analyze and evaluate students' and teachers' opinions towards summative assessment and how it is implemented into the learning. As students' and teachers' attitude toward AI-powered assessment tools motivates acceptance and improves the learning outcomes for students. To improve the students' perceptions toward AI-powered assessment tools, the potential lies in prioritizing the adoption of technology with increased students' participation and reducing biases while setting a higher expectation with improved student achievement as an overall goal. Furthermore, teachers can explain the purpose and usage of such assessment tools to alleviate students' concern regarding their connections and interactions with their teachers and how teachers still provide very personalized learning and feedback through constant student-teacher interaction throughout the instructional activities.

Personalized Learning Paths

Self-regulated learning and formative assessment recognizes the students' ability to act as an independent learner with the importance for critical thinking. Moreover, the adoption of AI in education provides quality education, practical teaching and learning opportunities, and better personalized learning tools for student learning (Dubey & Crevar, 2025). As learners, students use necessary skills for reasonable and reflective thinking for their learning goals. To accommodate individual students' learning needs, personalized learning tools pave the path for students to assess their strengths and weaknesses through the use of AI-powered platforms, which provide tailored activities, learning exercises, and aimed resources for improved learning outcomes. The personalized learning paths are built on the idea that each learner is unique in their learning, knows what works best for their learning, and understands self-directed and self-regulated learning processes. The AI-powered personalized learning tools play a role in individualization, differentiation, and personalization of curriculum for individual student learning needs (Bray & McClaskey, 2013).

Personalized learning provides students with an opportunity to control their learning, individualized differentiated instruction, and real-time feedback to fit the learners' strength, weakness, and interests (Shemshack & Spector, 2020). Since the foundation of personalized learning lies in students' learning from previous experiences through language and interaction, the most personalized learning models are built with the integration of technology considering these characteristics. Moreover, personalized learning can be considered as an evidence-based learning model that supports learners' preferences in educational practices. A personalized learning path is designed to recognize and analyze the individual skills, abilities, and/or preferences, and customize the content delivery accordingly (Bhutoria, 2022). Thus, the need to customize, revise, and re-structure curriculum needs a learning system which considers the better understanding of specific problems and derives new learning paths from it. AI-enabled systems are designed to analyze the existing data, identify the behavior patterns of learners, match the learners' skills and knowledge, and predict the next learning step suitably aligned with their learning capabilities. Such AI systems are so synced that it "classify learners on the basis of those factors and recommend suitable learning choices as per the capabilities of any particular learner by predicting their moves" (Bhutoria, 2022, p.7).

Personalized learning integrates the AI-powered tools to promote student-centered learning with preference to promote students' expressions for their choices and interests. Thus, AI-powered personalized learning emerges as an innovative learning system that not only promotes a student-centered learning model but interacts with teachers where they consider their previous knowledge of students and link it to acquire the best learning outcomes for the students. Moreover, AI-powered personalized learning tools provide an opportunity for students to find meaning and personal values in their own learning (Solari et al., 2022). In the end, AI is the driving force that promotes inclusive learning management systems that enables a student-centered learning environment to meet the 21st-century learning needs of all students.

Adaptive Learning

Adaptive learning is a knowledge-based assessment assisted by AI to provide real-world classroom experiences for students. It improves the individual student learning through enhanced personalized learning environments. Research suggests that "adaptive learning technology uses data-driven instruction to create personalized learning experiences for students which is adjusted and tailored to meet the individual learning needs" (Dubey, 2025, p.90). The evidence suggests that adaptive learning is the part of enhanced student learning experiences that is more efficient than traditional learning with educational equity for all students. The quest to support the educational journey of students while supporting cost effective learning, it is so eminent that teachers around the world are inclined to support such learning environments. Such adaptive learning systems are so successful that an extensive number of students are using it for personalized learning goals. An example of such a learning system is Intelligent Learning Systems (ITS). The ITS systems continuously record, interact, and make learning decisions based on student interactions, knowledge gains, and individual students' learning preferences (Minn, 2022). The goal of such a system is to increase students' individual learning gains, mobilize learning goals, and help them to improve their learning by offering tailored learning. The adaptive learning systems use algorithms and student data tracking systems to monitor student learning processes, improves engagement and performance, and then creates an effective and engaging learning process for individual students.

Evidence suggests that AI technologies such as ITS significantly enhance student learning compared to other traditional learning activities (Rose et al., 2019). The students' intrinsic motivation and competence to learn with AI-powered tools depends on teacher support and student expertise with self-regulated learning and digital literacy. Thus, it is important for teachers to support students so that they can learn the required skills and relatedness to digital technology to meet the needs of autonomy of learning. The end goal is to provide a safe and comfortable learning environment for students where they feel connected to their peers and teachers. While using the AI-based tools, teachers should use such tools that support students with high quality learning with motivation.

The growth of online learning has enabled the availability of adaptive learning for students' personalized learning outcomes. The AI-powered techniques have created an ecosystem that works on student knowledge assessment necessary for improved learning with content mastery. Minn (2022) described the adaptive learning environment has requiring the ability to provide highly specific data driven feedback and structure that supports each student's individual learning skill proficiency. The research has been done to deliver ITS that assist students more effectively by seamlessly making complex and time-consuming data mining, and other learning techniques.

Adaptive Testing

Adaptive testing facilitates students' assessments based on selected questions to test learners' knowledge and identify what difficulty level items their knowledge belongs to. The adaptive tests are based on the idea to evaluate students' knowledge on one-time evaluation rather than formative. Some of the examples of such tests are

Graduate Record Examinations (GRE) and Test of English as a Foreign Language (TOEFL). These exams use AI-enabled tools that use algorithms to grade students' responses for accuracy, reduced biases, and judgement errors. Adaptive testing systems are AI-powered tools to adjudicate the difficulty of questions in real time based on how other students responded. The process allows students to measure students' accurate abilities to create customized learning experiences.

The adaptive system motivates students' engagement and reading behavior. It improves students' learning memory cycle through taking practice tests. Thus, to design the adaptive testing systems, it is recommended to include information regarding students' memory retention, and how they engage in learning. To develop adaptive testing, the algorithms are based on Item Response Theory (IRT). The algorithm personalizes the assessment and how an assessment is administered to each student individually. The question item's difficulty is matched to students' ability and designed to stop when certain psychometric criteria are reached.

Instant Feedback

Feedback is an integral part of teaching, learning, and student assessment. In fact, assessment and feedback are tied together with the process of student learning, skills development, and meeting the goals of pre-design curriculum. The purpose of the feedback is to provide continuous improvement and evidence of student learning. Moreover, feedback helps students to identify learning gaps, insight into their strengths and weaknesses, and what strategies to use to fill the skill gaps with an aim to improve student growth and focus on meeting those goals of learning.

Artificial intelligence attempts to simulate human-like learning experiences to its learners with the large language models (LLM) in grading and feedback. These automated AI-powered tools provide extensive feedback and response prompts so that students have an opportunity to improve their learning outcomes. For example, automated evaluations such as Grammarly and Pigai are assisted corrective writing feedback systems that provide learners with identification of errors, spelling and grammar checkers, and suggestions for improvements. These automated evaluation systems rely on natural language processing to identify errors and make appropriate suggestions. Furthermore, companies like OpenAI and Google have developed newer versions of AI-generative systems such as sophisticated generative pretrained transformers (GPT) and *PaLM 2*. These newer AI-automated tools are extremely powerful and use LLMs to provide learners with sophisticated advanced level feedback. The usage of these AI-powered tools made it possible for learners to improve their essay writing skills and disrupted how students experience their educational journey.

Instant feedback capabilities of automated evaluation systems provide several advantages to its users. One advantage is the ability to tailor the learning responses by asking the automated grading systems to reiterate the feedback in easier language so it is easy to understand or to explain it further so that learners can improve their learning outcomes. Utilizing the AI-powered grading system can significantly reduce educators for providing feedback. Additionally, teachers can use that time responding to each student's assignment, improving their learning experiences, and freeing up valuable time for other extremely important tasks for student learning.

Instant feedback supports student learning through continuous learning. Escalante et al. (2023) showed in their research that students who preferred AI-generated feedback stated that it provided the clarity and specificity of the feedback, which helped to improve their writing and overall learning outcomes. Such AI-generated tools suggest the importance of personalized learning through evaluating and providing feedback as a potential to improve student learning. Furthermore, such feedback increases students' motivation, cultivating active student engagement, and improved meta-cognitive skills for better learning outcomes. Thus, we recommend that utilizing AI-powered grading tools provide the opportunities for students to get instant feedback and further their learning by discussing with their teachers through collaboration, follow up questions, interactions and engaging through debate.

Tracking Progress

AI-powered learning tools cultivate the collaborative learning environment with real-time data collection to capture every aspect of student learning experiences. These tools redefine the roles of educators, learners, and policymakers in creating rigorous data driven effective student learning outcomes where students' learning is analyzed through the detailed analysis of specific topics, patterns, or skills growth overtime. Such data analysis identifies the student's learning struggles while pinpointing the improvement of learning strategies or plan and how to earn missing skills to master the content.

The wide use of AI-powered learning tools has opened newer doors that provide an accurate understanding of student learning processes. AI learning analytics helps institutions to effectively and efficiently utilize gathered data to assess the usefulness of pedagogies, instructional design, and detect and monitor learners' behavioral and emotional states (Hooda et al., 2022). Thus, educators can focus on monitoring students for ongoing learning needs and craft pedagogies to meet the learning outcomes. Such interventions not only help teachers quickly analyze students' engagement but also provide instant feedback and remedies to redirect students into newer productive learning goals.

AI- powered automated grading systems use an AI algorithm that not only reduces the grading time for teachers, however; provides an opportunity of robustness for human gradings. Such achievements are made possible due to the exhaustive use of deep learning and natural language processing (NLP) technologies (Yeung et al., 2023). The key idea is for the instructor to switch the curriculum and teaching that makes system students focused, namely, student-centered learning. Now, all the curriculum and pedagogical decisions that a teacher makes is with a compelling idea of meeting the needs of students learning. Empowered by innovative data collection and mining capabilities, AI-powered tracking tools extract valuable information that explicitly structures all the students' learning characteristics and classified to meet the system-wide needs of educational systems. Thus, the automated grading not only analyzes the data, but provides the solutions with proper recommendations for school wide learning. Such systems are not limited to any particular grade-level or subject. In fact, it is available for all with no restriction on grades or subjects. Furthermore, the system's ability to adapt to specific learning requirements and abilities to meet learners' particular learning needs enhance the teachers and students' ability to initiate a path of learning excellence. Additionally, tracking systems have capabilities to provide educators with a system to track student progress so that they can offer targeted personalized learning to support students' improved learning outcomes.

The use of AI in education offers expansion of learning analytics through scalability, data collection systems, and opportunities for enhanced student learning. Moreover, involving stakeholders such as students and teachers can potentially help design AI-powered tools to meet the learning needs of all. AI and the tracking system brings innovation and technology together and improves the current assessment systems to enable newer ways of learning at the same time. Such AI enables systems to offer data-collection processes to meet the intensive learning requirements for students and create the promise of adaptive and personalized learning experiences at large scale.

Considering all the benefits that AI-powered tools provide, we argue that tracking progress helps prevent potential disruptions and apply early intervention so that situations of learning chaos are avoided at all costs. While the spread of mass education always questions the accessibility, affordability, and feasibility of teaching students properly and tracking their progress has always been a concern for teachers, policymakers, and other stakeholders. However, AI-powered learning tools with progress tracking capability provide solutions to such problems. To avoid any implementation related issues, streamlining the biases related to AI algorithms could strengthen any misuses by early detection beforehand and preventive measured solutions.

Integration of AI in Pedagogy

AI is widely recognized as a new technological tool employed to different pedagogical strategies to foster students' learning in different areas such as literacy, math, science, social sciences, and other subject areas. To keep the classroom engaged and focused, the pedagogy should be reconsidered in the AI-embedded classroom. Moreover, pedagogy in a digital classroom should be explored to avoid the difficulties of designing and delivering lessons to keep students engaged and immersed in learning activities. So, it is highly required to rethink and reimagine the use of AI in the classroom. Furthermore, the critical connection between AI technological tools, pedagogy, and content should be the foundation for lesson design and implementation. A similar approach should be used to achieve the goals of personalized learning. Thus, highly effective pedagogical strategies are essential for better student assessment, and eventually higher learning outcomes.

AI in education paired with interactive innovative tools have capabilities to enable pedagogical strategies that make learning engaging and interactive for students (Alfredo et al., 2024). In other words, educational institutes are adopting AI-powered data intense tracking systems to scale, accessible, and personalized learning for students. Such AI-powered tools provide various interfaces to help educators prepare well-versed pedagogical resources to achieve the highest level of support for students. In fact, potential generated by the use of AI in education has created a wider and focused approach for pedagogical systems. The use of algorithms for pedagogy has not only improved the student's involvement but led to a better understanding of technology usage, accountability, transparency, and increased student involvement.

Careful considerations of growing needs for students' learning have challenged the design and approach in which pedagogy has been used in education. Such approaches have deployed AI with the aim of serving students' learning needs, collecting data for data driven decisions, and improving overall learning outcomes for students. So, recognizing that significance lies in achieving the goals of serving students' interest with technological automation, deployment, and recognition for innovative pedagogical approaches. This acknowledgement has removed the normally assumed role of teachers' in creating and delivering pedagogical resources for learning. Now, the use of AI in education has the competence and capabilities of teacher's expertise in subject matters and offers well-designed lessons with accessibility and flexibility. This situation has directly shifted the role of educators as who teaches the lesson to a facilitator. Moreover, one size fits all myth has broken and improved the overall approach with direct implementation on how teachers' workload will be distributed to meet the students' learning and impacted how teachers' see their role in the classroom ecosystem. For better or worse, teachers have more flexibility in how they plan their teaching time that fits the learning needs of students and improves their overall learning outcomes.

Behavioral and Engagement Analytics

Analyzing students' learning behavior is an essential element in evaluating students' classroom performance and predicting their long-term academic achievement while determining teacher quality for student learning growth (s et al. 2024). In a traditional classroom, teachers perform tasks to evaluate student learning to maintain the progress throughout the learning process. Such tasks draw teachers' significant attention towards monitoring students' learning behaviors, appropriateness of the learning assignments, and setting students' future learning goals. Moreover, teachers spent substantial amount of time emphasizing classroom activities that can be managed through some sophisticated AI-powered tools that recognize students' learning behaviors, enabling individualized learning, target-based assessments, and some other ways to effectively manage student learning. Thus, it is important to create such a system, which effectively monitors students' classroom interactions, behaviors, and how they learn in a classroom.

The goal is to create a data-driven system where educators are making well informed decisions to improve student engagement for enhanced student learning outcomes. Thus, the priority should be to help educators effectively and actively participate in improving the learning environment of a classroom with enhanced teaching strategies and increased student achievement. Such goals can be achieved through the deployment of technological tools powered by AI as it brings a novel approach to promote effective learning application. Automated AI- powered tools analyze the students' behaviors to reduce the teachers' workload so that they can focus on other instructional needs of the classroom. The beauty of these systems is that they are designed with sophisticated algorithms to detect the students' learning behaviors and develop a well mapped individualized learning plans for learners. In addition to tracking student progress, such systems determine the patterns and help educational systems perform better through intervention plans, enrichment, and efficiency for student self-growth. On a broader perspective, it provides educational institutions an opportunity to identify students' learning patterns, improved learning outcomes, and effectiveness of teaching.

AI-powered tools have exploited the students' behavioral and analytical data to promote student engagement. For example, adoption of natural language processing (NLP) dominated the processing of textual data in essays and discussion post with systems tendency to capture and analyze non-verbal aspect of students' learning engagement (Chen et al., 2025). Moreover, it reflects the recognition of students' engagement and considers the behavioral and emotional components for multifaceted language recognition (Wong & Liem, 2022). Considering the potential to engage learners from cognitive, behavioral, and emotional perspectives, AI-powered tools have widespread usage for students' learning (Wang & Xue, 2024). Even though systems with AI-powered tools have the potential to transform interactive student learning, it has received limited attention regarding full implementation due to several barriers such as cost, complexity, and usability issues. To resolve such situations, schools should engage students in activities to develop group and classroom interaction. Such activities will promote students' positive conduct, effort, persistence, concertation, attention, and involvement in curricular and extracurricular activities.

CHALLENGES IN IMPLEMENTING AI-POWERED ASSESSMENT

The recent increase in the implementation of AI in educational assessment suggests the popularity of AI-powered tools while fostering improved students' learning outcomes, better time management, and enhanced pedagogical resources. The characteristics are stimulated by human intelligence, and adopting various technological agents such as intelligent tutoring, feedback software, essay grading with NLP, etc. with provided benefits to reduce teacher workload so that teachers can focus on student growth through pedagogical innovations. These AI-powered innovations have offered personalized learning plans for students with continuous assessments and immediate constructive feedback. Even though AI-powered tools bring numerous benefits to educational communities, they are not without concerns, risks, or privacy issues. In fact, the use of AI in education is still struggling with the need for policies, regulations, and guidelines to protect and collect data from threats.

The discussion in this section is beyond the assumptions of right or wrong while providing potential adverse effects that could influence students' learning outcomes widely. The potential of generative AI to disrupt assessment processes through feedback is a creative way to see how it performs, but susceptibility of homework assignments to cheating has made teachers and institutions rethink how assessment processes work in terms of scalability and availability. In response, many educational institutions have either banned or prohibited students from using generative AI for the educational purposes provided researchers claim that assessment might be the area for best opportunity for the use of AI. Such situations arise due the fact that assessment is a fundamental and crucial element for student learning and enhanced learning outcomes.

The students and teachers share similar perspectives regarding the potential impact, and pitfalls of implementing AI for summative assessment due to efficiency, speed, and human bias avoidance (Viberg et al., 2022). In other words, regardless of how much technology advances, its implementation always creates challenges.

It raises concerns about students' privacy and educational data security (Viberg et al., 2022), in addition to the potential of algorithmic biases and discriminating practices (Uttamchandani & Quick, 2022). The concerns have risen due to the lack of involvement of teachers and students in the design and development of AI tools in education which could potentially lead to lack of understanding and trust for the use of AI in education (Shibani et al., 2022). Such a lack of involvement in program design and development raises the accountability and transparency for use of AI at educational institutions.

The problem related to the use of AI in education does not stop at such implications. It goes further with the increased use of AI-powered assessment by making it more complicated as the academic institutions lack a system that creates authentic lines for the best practices. Such situations get worse when students heavily use AI-powered assessment tools with no proper guidelines and regulations. Now, to resolve the situation, it becomes mandatory for AI in education systems to incorporate concerns raised by students and teachers and meet them while creating well-versed learning systems. While developing such systems, it becomes clear that systems design effective, inclusive, and ethical policies for all the stakeholders to follow and to avoid any misuses. Additionally, it is mandatory for institutions to identify and clearly communicate the appropriate necessary ethical procedures for its user. Furthermore, the responsibilities do not end with communicating these guidelines, proper training is necessary for all the AI in education practitioners.

The researchers have mentioned several other challenges in the implementation of AI-powered tools in educational assessment. One way to resolve such issues is with the implementation of high-quality targeted professional development to further teachers' assessment practices (Alfredo et al., 2024). Such assessments require teacher competency in different areas such as pedagogical practices, content knowledge, etcetera, keeping that in mind, Alfredo et al. (2024) suggested that it is evident that provided professional development should be wide in scope and secure highest engaging qualities. For example, professional development should provide teachers with an opportunity to create a mutually respectful environment where teachers practice culturally and linguistically sensitive best practices to promote the highest standard quality of student learning outcomes.

EFFICIENT RESOURCES ALLOCATION

Educational institutes around the globe are facing challenges with growing enrollment, limited budgeting resources, and demands for long term sustainability; and to address such challenges the campus managements are integrating AI and advanced technologies into their day-to-day operations (Koukaras et al., 2025). In other words, the development of effective and smart systems requires technological development aligned with sustainable goals aiming for environmental sustainability, social responsibility, and a comprehensive plan for users (Silva-da Nóbrega et al., 2022). For example, Koukaras et al. (2025) developed a framework designed to collect data using AI-driven analytics that leverages the institute's resources to make informed decisions to forecast different scenarios to present potential benefits while incorporating data privacy, security, and inclusive accessibility. The aim of adopting AI-powered tools is to enable educational institutes management teams to be more responsive, efficient governance, and improve outcomes for students and staff.

For instructional purposes, the use of AI-powered technologies (such as chatbots) is becoming an integral part of education and offering potential to enhance teacher effectiveness, student engagement, and student learning outcomes. The integration of such technologies involves selection of resources to maximize efficiency, effectiveness, and learning opportunities. Moreover, allocation of optimal resources is integral to achieve the goals of maximizing student learning and educational efficacy. The system underpins the security and privacy considerations in their implementation process to meet the overall learning needs of the current student population. Considering the sensitivity and broader use of AI -powered tools in educational excellence, it is recommended the adoption of a framework that implements all the safety, privacy, and vulnerability issues for the betterment of overall student learning achievement.

FAIRNESS, BIAS, AND ETHICAL CONSIDERATION IN AI ALGORITHMS

The wide-spread implementation of AI-powered tools in education has transformed education and provided the tailored approach for learning experiences for students. However, the inherent biases in AI algorithms have caused unintentional prejudice against specific demographics, issues of fairness, and ethical considerations. Lately, in the educational community, discussions among the stakeholders regarding fairness, algorithmic biases, and ethical violations regarding AI-powered tools have been happening. It has been acknowledged around the educational communities how the issues of these violations fundamentally undermining the growth and accomplishments with the use of AI-powered tools; and challenged the educational communities to ensure implementation of ethical and fair practices with collaboration and mutual respect. Furthermore, the issues of fairness, biases, and ethical consideration for AI-powered tools in education have challenged the existing practices to reflect how important it is to improve the overall learning experiences of students from all walks of life. Thus, to mitigate such situations, researchers identify the strategies ranging from fair data-collection to algorithmic fairness interventions to navigate the systems to provide environments to shape more equitable educational settings (Chinta et al., 2024).

The AI in education uses the capabilities of NLP, computer vision, and some other AI tools to assess student learning, growth, and learning experiences. These assessment tools provide consistency, objectivity, and efficiency in assessing students' knowledge, finding learning gaps in content areas, and a personalized learning plan for future improvements. Despite these benefits, AI-powered tools raise critical issues of fairness and bias that are amplified by the historical data these tools are trained on. In fact, some of these AI-powered assessment tools use subjectivity of humans that results in unfair assessment practices for marginalized student populations. Such practices adopted by AI grading tools create a learning gap due to cultural differences that are indulged in educational practices from the past. Thus, ethical considerations play a vital role in determining the accountability and transparency of AI systems in education (Chinta et al., 2024).

To improve the effectiveness and efficiency of AI in education, it is critical to acknowledge the profoundness of fairness, biases, and ethical practices. It is not only important how AI-powered tools help grow educational opportunities for students, but how fairness, biases, and ethical practices are core ideas for the social impacts due to these technologies. Research suggests that AI algorithms can affect societal norms and increase the achievement gaps among different groups if not designed carefully and scrutinized properly. The challenge is not only to provide an advanced learning tool but to develop AI-powered tools that are transparent, explainable, accountable (Chinta et al., 2024). Thus, to achieve such goals it is important to consider how AI in education has evolved and advanced as a learning system. By outlining a comprehensive fairness framework that promotes global cooperation and collaboration, the AI-powered tools can enrich educational opportunities while preventing the disparities (Chinta et al., 2024). Additionally, such a framework advocates collaboration from all stakeholders and demands for continuous innovative solutions.

AI-POWERED TOOLS IN STUDENT ASSESSMENT: A BALANCED APPROACH

The integration of AI in educational assessment has been rapidly transforming the landscape of student assessment and how learning is evaluated to offer new learning possibilities for student learning. For evaluation purposes, formative assessment activity occurs during the lesson to help teachers verify the student progress and adjust the instruction to meet the learning goals, whereas the summative assessments happen at the end of the lesson or unit to determine students' overall learning for that lesson or unit. Moreover, AI-powered tools attempt to stimulate similar evaluation processes for student learning outcomes. The automated assessment tools use the AI algorithms to perform the human-like grading task not only to reduce the assessment time but also provide a robust opportunity for enhanced learning for students. The AI-powered assessment helps students benefit with effectiveness of learning strategies with an aim to pioneer the best learning practices. To fully utilize these advanced AI assessment tools for student learning, teachers should use the combination of formative, diagnostic, and summative assessments to measure how a student has learned during or after the lesson or unit.

Despite the benefits, the AI assessment tools can raise critical issues of fairness, biases, and transparency. Addressing such issues are crucial for creating fair and educational equity in the educational system. If such issues do not translate into student support, it will drastically reduce the educator's approach towards fair assessment and inadvertently perpetuate and amplify the existing unfair practices for historically marginalized student populations. Thus, it is extremely important to deploy the mitigating strategies through teachers analyzing the pre and post test data to make unbiased learning decisions. Additionally, teachers should carefully balance the stakeholders' involvement in designing and deployment of AI assessment tools. The active involvement of target end-users such as students will help explore the safety, reliability, and trustworthiness of AI-powered assessment tools in education. Thus, to achieve the object of fully utilized AI assessment tools, teachers should use a well-oiled assessment system that thoroughly examines the connection between student learning outcomes and fairness, unbiased, and ethical practices with AI assessment tools.

CONCLUSION

AI has been transforming and reshaping the educational landscape and improving teaching and assessment for student learning. Moreover, the AI-powered educational assessment tools provide efficiency, accuracy, and personalized feedback and enabling teachers with the best teaching strategies to meet the unique learning needs of all students. It not only provides faster, accurate, and more secure grading systems (for both formative and summative assessments), but also supports teachers to increase academic performance of students. Furthermore, by exploring the full strength of AI-powered assessment tools, educators can avail personalized and adaptive learning environments to students and ultimately improve students learning outcomes. The implications of AI in education are so imminent that it provides individualized differentiated tailors learning with added benefit of real-time feedback that fits the learners all learning needs to achieve higher learning outcomes.

Adaptive learning technologies are designed to assist students improve their learning outcomes with the creation of personalized learning environments. For example, AI-powered technologies such as ITS enhanced students' learning and provides them with an ability to self-regulate students' learning by enhancing their intrinsic motivation in improving their overall learning outcomes. The AI assessment tools stimulate human-like learning experiences to learners by providing extensive feedback with the extensive use of LLM. The feedback supports students' learning growth through continuous improvement plans. Student learning is tracked with the use of AI-powered tools that expand on learning analytics through scalability, data-collection, and enhanced learning opportunities for students. Such strategies are carefully considered structuring pedagogy with the use of AI. To improve overall learning, these AI tools are aligned with behavioral and engagement analytics to evaluate students' learning performance in predicting long-term academic goals. In the end, AI assessment tools have shown potential to improve students' learning outcomes if it is used with proper considerations for fairness, biases, and implication of ethics.

PRACTICAL IMPLICATIONS

In traditional assessment, the predefined test-items are used to test the student proficiency which represents sparse datasets (Swiecki, 2024). The AI-powered assessment tools have redefined its significance as a whole. The use of AI for assessment in education provides extensive opportunity and resources for teachers in exploring the students' learning outcomes. It provides real-time data to teachers so that they can make instant decisions to meet the learning goals. While implementing AI-powered assessment tools, educators should consider the ethical use of these newly adopted tools, reducing biases, and providing privacy to student personal data.

FUTURE DIRECTIONS

The AI-powered assessment tools have been used for formative and summative assessment in the last several years due to its real-time data collection and decision-making capabilities and providing opportunities for enhanced personalized learning. The current role of AI in assessment is mostly teacher driven to assess students' skills. The future research should investigate the development and use of self-assessment tools for students so that learners can assess their own competence required for future learning tasks or skills.

REFERENCES

Alfredo, R., Echeverria, V., Jin, Y., Yan, L., Swiecki, Z., Gašević, D., & Martinez-Maldonado, R. (2024). Human-centred learning analytics and AI in education: A systematic literature review. *Computers and Education: Artificial Intelligence*, *6*, 100215. DOI: 10.1016/j.caeai.2024.100215

Ali, Q. I. (2024). Towards more effective summative assessment in OBE: A new framework integrating direct measurements and technology. *Discover Education*, *3*(1). Advance online publication. DOI: 10.1007/s44217-024-00208-5

Bhutoria, A. (2022). Personalized education and artificial intelligence in the United States, China, and India: A systematic review using a human-in-The-Loop model. *Computers and Education: Artificial Intelligence*, *3*, 100068. DOI: 10.1016/j.caeai.2022.100068

Bray, B., & McClaskey, K. (2013). A Step-by-step guide to personalized learning. https://files.eric.ed.gov/fulltext/EJ1015153.pdf

Chen, X., Xie, H., Qin, S. J., Wang, F. L., & Hou, Y. (2025). Artificial intelligence-supported student engagement research: Text mining and systematic analysis. *European Journal of Education*, *60*(1). Advance online publication. DOI: 10.1111/ejed.70008

Chinta, S. V., Wang, Z., Yin, Z., Hoanh, N., Gonzalez, M., Quy, T. L., & Zhang, W. (2024). FairAIED: Navigating Fairness, Bias, and Ethics in Educational AI Applications. Computer Science: Machine Learning. https://arxiv.org/abs/2407.18745

Chiu, T. K., Moorhouse, B. L., Chai, C. S., & Ismailov, M. (2023). Teacher support and student motivation to learn with artificial intelligence (AI) based chatbot. *Interactive Learning Environments*, •••, 1–17. DOI: 10.1080/10494820.2023.2172044

Clift, L., & Petrovska, O. (2025). Learning without limits: Analysing the usage of generative AI in a summative assessment. *Proceedings of the 9th Conference on Computing Education Practice*, 5-8. https://doi.org/DOI: 10.1145/3702212.3702214

Double, K. S., McGrane, J. A., & Hopfenbeck, T. N. (2020). The impact of peer assessment on academic performance: A meta-analysis of control group studies. *Educational Psychology Review*, *32*, 481–509. DOI: 10.1007/s10648-019-09510-3

Dubey, P. K. (2025). Personalized Learning and Pedagogy: Harnessing AI for Tailored Education. In Wang, V. (Ed.), *Integrating AI into Pedagogical Education*. IGI Global., https://www.igi-global.com/book/integrating-into-pedagogical-andragogical-education/343053

Dubey, P. K., & Crevar, A. (2025). Integrating Artificial Intelligence in Higher Education: Enhancing Pedagogy, Instruction, and Administration. In Wang, V. (Eds.), Integrating AI into Andragogical Education. IGI Global (In Press). Release Date: Feb 2025. https://www.igi-global.com/book/integrating-into-pedagogical-andragogical-education/343053

Escalante, J., Pack, A., & Barrett, A. (2023). AI-generated feedback on writing: Insights into efficacy and ENL student preference. *International Journal of Educational Technology in Higher Education*, *20*(1). Advance online publication. DOI: 10.1186/s41239-023-00425-2

Hooda, M., Rana, C., Dahiya, O., Rizwan, A., & Hossain, M. S. (2022). Artificial intelligence for assessment and feedback to enhance student success in higher education. *Mathematical Problems in Engineering*, *2022*, 1–19. DOI: 10.1155/2022/5215722

Hopfenbeck, T. N., Zhang, Z., Sun, S. Z., Robertson, P., & McGrane, J. A. (2023). Challenges and opportunities for classroom-based formative assessment and AI: A perspective article. *Frontiers in Education*, *8*. Advance online publication. DOI: 10.3389/feduc.2023.1270700

Koukaras, C., Hatzikraniotis, E., Mitsiaki, M., Koukaras, P., Tjortjis, C., & Stavrinides, S. G. (2025). Revolutionising educational management with AI and wireless networks: A framework for smart resource allocation and decision-making. *Applied Sciences (Basel, Switzerland)*, *15*(10), 5293. DOI: 10.3390/app15105293

Minn, S. (2022). AI-assisted knowledge assessment techniques for adaptive learning environments. *Computers and Education: Artificial Intelligence*, *3*, 100050. DOI: 10.1016/j.caeai.2022.100050

Murphy, R. F. (2019). Artificial intelligence applications to support K-12 teachers and teaching. *Rand Corp.* 10, 1–20. doi: DOI: 10.7249/PE315

Sanusi, I. T., Olaleye, S. A., Agbo, F. J., & Chiu, T. K. (2022). The role of learners' competencies in artificial intelligence education. *Computers and Education: Artificial Intelligence*, *3*, 100098. DOI: 10.1016/j.caeai.2022.100098

Shemshack, A., & Spector, J. M. (2020). A systematic literature review of personalized learning terms. *Smart Learning Environments*, *7*(1). Advance online publication. DOI: 10.1186/s40561-020-00140-9

Shibani, A., Knight, S., & Buckingham Shum, S. (2022). Questioning learning analytics? Cultivating critical engagement as student automated feedback literacy. In *LAK22: 12th international learning analytics and knowledge conference* (pp. 326–335).

Silva-da Nóbrega, P. I., Chim-Miki, A. F., & Castillo-Palacio, M. (2022). A Smart Campus Framework: Challenges and Opportunities for Education Based on the Sustainable Development Goals. *Sustainability, 14*, 9640.

Solari, M., Vizquerra, M. I., & Engel, A. (2022). Students' interests for personalized learning: An analysis guide. *European Journal of Psychology of Education, 38*(3), 1073–1109. DOI: 10.1007/s10212-022-00656-3

Swiecki, Z., Khosravi, H., Chen, G., Martinez-Maldonado, R., Lodge, J. M., Milligan, S., & Thompson, N. (2024, March 10). *Computerized adaptive testing (CAT): An introduction*. Assessment Systems. https://assess.com/computerized-adaptive-testing/

Van den Berg, S., & Papadopoulos, P. M. (2024). Summative assessment with artificial intelligence: Qualitative analysis and comparison of technology acceptance in student and teacher populations. *Innovations in Education and Teaching International*, •••, 1–16. DOI: 10.1080/14703297.2024.2436613

Viberg, O., Mutimukwe, C., & Grönlund, Å. (2022). Privacy in la research: Understanding the field to improve the practice. *Journal of Learning Analytics, 9*, 169–182.

Wang, Y., & Xue, L. (2024). Using AI-Driven Chatbots to Foster Chinese EFL Students' Academic Engagement: An Intervention Study. *Computers in Human Behavior, 159*, 108353.

Wong, Z. Y., & Liem, G. A. D. (2022). Student Engagement: Current State of the Construct, Conceptual Refinement, and Future Research Directions. *Educational Psychology Review, 34*(1), 107–138.

Yeung, W. E., Qi, C., Xiao, J. L., & Wong, F. R. (2023). Evaluating the effectiveness of AI-based essay grading tools in the summative assessment of higher education. *ICERI Proceedings, 1*, 8069-8073. https://doi.org/DOI: 10.21125/iceri.2023.2063

Chapter 17
AI in Education:
Past, Present, and Future

Viktor Wang
https://orcid.org/0000-0001-9557-0054
California State University, San Bernardino, USA

Geraldine Torrisi-Steele
https://orcid.org/0000-0002-6045-4114
Griffith University, Australia

ABSTRACT

This chapter explores the evolution of Artificial Intelligence (AI) in educational technology, tracing its journey from early computational models like computer-assisted instruction (CAI) and intelligent tutoring systems (ITS) in the 1960s and 1970s, which laid the groundwork for AI's current transformative role in classrooms and beyond. Today, AI-powered tools are reshaping personalized learning, automating administrative tasks, and creating immersive learning experiences through virtual and augmented reality. Looking ahead, AI is expected to foster lifelong learning, improve assessment methods, and address equity and accessibility challenges, while also raising ethical concerns around data privacy and algorithmic bias. The chapter emphasizes AI's potential to revolutionize education by making it more inclusive, accessible, and tailored to individual learning needs, ultimately reshaping the way we teach, learn, and engage with knowledge.

INTRODUCTION

Artificial Intelligence (AI) in Education is at the forefront of the discourse of technology in education. There is palpable excitement about the possibilities of AI in education and literature resounds with the promise of 'the great transformation of

DOI: 10.4018/979-8-3373-2397-8.ch017

education'. The excitement is tempered by an increasing number of practitioners and researchers voicing caution that we should not forget that AI technologies, despite their promise, can cause harm and so, it is vital to ensure that AI technologies are ethically designed and implemented with transparency, privacy, and equity always in mind.

From its humble beginnings in computer-assisted instruction in the 1960's and 70's, AI technologies are set to do more than simply 'automate' drill and practice instruction. In the present day, AI is a central component of educational technology. The rapid advancements in machine learning, natural language processing, and data analytics are enabling AI to become more integrated into the classroom, enhancing both teaching and learning experiences. AI-powered tools are capable of providing personalized learning experiences that adapt to the unique needs of each student. These tools analyze vast amounts of student data, including performance metrics and learning patterns, to recommend customized learning paths. This approach shifts education from a one-size-fits-all model to one that values the individuality of each learner, promoting engagement and improving outcomes. Adaptive learning platforms, for instance, adjust the learning experience based on real-time data, ensuring that students are always challenged at the appropriate level. These platforms not only provide personalized content but also offer continuous assessment, allowing for ongoing feedback and intervention when necessary.

Married with other emerging technologies such as Virtual and Augmented Reality, AI technologies are being integrated to provide richer and personalized immersive learning experiences. AI technologies are freeing up teachers from the more mundane classroom tasks to enabling them to focus on what human teachers do best – mentor, establish learning relationships with students and facilitating higher order and complex skills and thinking. Beyond the classroom, AI technologies are being implemented to serve the needs of education administration as well as support leadership and decision making.

Looking to the future, the potential for AI to revolutionize education is will undoubtedly grow. As AI continues to evolve, its role in education is expected to expand and become more integrated into all aspects of the educational experience. In a world where the job market is constantly changing and evolving, there is an increasing need for individuals to engage in continuous learning and skill development throughout their lives. AI-powered platforms can provide learners of all ages with personalized, on-demand learning opportunities, enabling them to acquire new skills and knowledge at their own pace. These platforms could be used to support career development, enable individuals to reskill or upskill, and provide access to learning opportunities for people in remote or underserved areas. By making education more flexible and accessible, AI has the potential to democratize learning and create new pathways for personal and professional growth.

By embracing AI responsibly, we can create an educational system that is better equipped to meet the needs of today's learners and prepare them for the challenges and opportunities of tomorrow. The future of AI in education can be bright.

In this concluding chapter we use the temporal framework of past, present and future to take a 'balcony view' of AI in education. We revisit and emphasize some key themes in the field of AI in education to facilitate reflection and provide a launching point for further exploration in the emergent field of AI in education. D

PAST: THE EARLY BEGINNINGS OF AI IN EDUCATION

The journey of Artificial Intelligence (AI) in education began quite a long time ago although it's rapid evolution in recent years gives the impression that AI in education is completely new. Interestingly, Doroudi (2023) argues that the history of AI is 'intertwined' with education from the beginnings of AI. Doroudi points out that early researchers in AI "saw AI as a tool for thinking about human learning and used their understanding of how people learn to further AI" (Doroudi, 2023, p. 885). The development of AI, Doroudi (2023) argues, was enabled by the models of human knowledge that were built during the cognitive revolution – the same models that inform education today.

In the 1960s and 1970s, the first educational technologies emerged, giving rise to computer-assisted instruction (CAI) and intelligent tutoring systems (ITS). These early systems, while rudimentary by today's standards, laid the groundwork for the integration of AI into education. These tools were designed to help students learn specific skills through repetition and feedback, often in a drill-and-practice format. For instance, the PLATO system, developed in the 1960s, allowed students to interact with computer-based lessons and receive immediate feedback on their progress. While these early systems were not "intelligent" in the sense we understand today, they represented the first steps toward integrating technology into the learning process.

PLATO (Programmed Logic for Automatic Teaching Operations) was a groundbreaking system that allowed students to engage with educational content via a computer. It was one of the first instances of computer-based education, allowing for interactive learning and immediate feedback.

"PLATO is a fast, flexible, and responsive system designed expressly to present interactive instructional lessons attractively and economically. From data collected on three predecessor systems over a period of 15 years, PLATO developers concluded that they would have to make extensive modifications in exiting computer equipment before it would be suitable for delivering the kind of individualized instruction they wanted" stated Hody and Avner in their 1978 paper (p. 143)

Despite limitations of the time, PLATO demonstrated the potential of computers to enhance learning and became a precursor to the more sophisticated systems that would follow in the coming decades.

As the field of AI continued to develop in the 1980s and 1990s, the focus shifted toward creating more sophisticated applications of AI in education. This period saw the rise of expert systems. In a 1987 paper entitled "Artificial intelligence and expert systems in education: Progress, promise and problems", Romiszowski states "The most common application of AI so far is in the form of expert systems. Although not very common there are already many examples in commercial use and the market is estimated to grow exponentially in the next few years" (Romiszowski, 1987, p. 9) Expert systems used knowledge-based approaches to simulate human expertise in specific domains. Expert systems were designed to solve complex problems by applying a set of rules and logic, allowing them to provide personalized learning experiences. These systems became the foundation for intelligent tutoring systems (ITS), which could assess a student's performance and offer tailored feedback based on individual learning needs

Romiszowski, (1987) also observed that intelligent tutoring systems had "not yet left the laboratory stage" (p. 10) at the time. Around a decade later, intelligent tutoring systems, such as the Cognitive Tutor developed by Carnegie Learning in the late 1980s, early 90s, marked a significant step forward in the application of AI in education.

"We developed production system models in ACT [Adaptive Control of Thought] of how students solved problems in LISP, geometry, and algebra. Computer tutors were developed around these cognitive models. Construction of these tutors was guided by a set of eight principles loosely based on ACT theory" (Anderson, Corbett, Koedinger, & Pelletier, 1995, p. 167).

These systems used rule-based algorithms to simulate the process of human tutoring, providing students with immediate feedback on their work. Unlike earlier systems, which simply presented information to students, ITS systems could assess a student's understanding of a topic and adjust the difficulty of the content based on their performance. This allowed for a more individualized approach to learning, as the system could adapt to each student's unique needs. For example, if a student struggled with a particular concept, the system could offer additional practice problems or explanations to help them master the material.

By the turn of the millennium, technology development including AI was surging ahead. AI systems became implemented more widely in intelligent tutoring systems (Guan, Mou, & Jiang, 2020). With the growing computing power and the permeation of the internet and associated communications technology, AI in education began to take on new forms. Increasingly sophisticated machine learning algorithms and the popularization of data analytics (mostly as a result of vast volumes of data generated by internet technologies) enabled educational technologies to become more dynamic and responsive to the needs of learners. In around the 2010's, learning management systems, developed originally for online learning, became part of on-campus education (Lang, 2023) and learning analytics grew in their importance and popularity, becoming routine in education (Axelsen, Redmond, Heinrich, & Henderson, 2020) Although the idea of adaptive learning was present in the 70's in the field of AI, in the second decade of the 2000's the conditions became highly conducive for expansion and increased popularity of adaptive learning platforms, which used AI to provide personalized learning experiences based on real-time data. These platforms analyzed a student's performance and learning patterns, adjusting the content and pace of instruction to match their individual needs. Soon learning management systems (LMS) that incorporated AI-driven features became popular. These systems, such as Blackboard and Moodle, began to integrate AI tools that could track student performance, provide personalized feedback, and suggest learning resources. By analyzing data from student interactions with course materials, AI-powered LMS platforms could identify areas where students were struggling and offer targeted interventions. This not only helped students succeed but also provided instructors with valuable insights into how their students were progressing, allowing them to adjust their teaching strategies accordingly.This shift from one-size-fits-all education to personalized learning was a significant milestone in the integration of AI into education. Personalization and customization in learning has come to the fore of educational technologies, and there's mounting evidence that it can enhance learning and the learning experience (du Plooy, Casteleijn, & Franzsen, 2024) .

Adaptive learning platforms, such as Knewton and DreamBox, became popular in the 2000s and 2010s, offering students customized learning experiences that were tailored to their strengths and weaknesses. These platforms used machine learning algorithms to track a student's progress and adjust the content in real time. For example, if a student struggled with a particular math concept, the platform could present additional practice problems or provide alternative explanations to help the student master the material. This personalized approach allowed students to learn at their own pace, with the system continuously adapting to their evolving needs.

In addition to adaptive learning, in the 2010's AI began to play a significant role in automating administrative tasks within educational institutions. The use of AI to streamline administrative processes, such as grading, scheduling, and attendance tracking, allowed educators to focus more on teaching and less on paperwork. AI-powered tools like grading software and virtual assistants became increasingly common in classrooms, providing teachers with more time to engage with students and personalize instruction. This automation also helped to reduce the administrative burden on teachers, allowing them to devote more time to activities that directly impacted student learning.

As AI technology continued to evolve, the 2010s and 2020s saw the rise of even more sophisticated applications in education. The development of natural language processing (NLP) and machine learning algorithms enabled AI to engage in more complex interactions with students. AI-powered chatbots and virtual assistants, such as IBM's Watson, began to be used in educational settings to provide real-time support to students. These systems could answer questions, provide feedback on assignments, and even simulate one-on-one tutoring sessions. The ability of AI to interact with students in a conversational manner opened up new possibilities for personalized learning and support.

For example, chatbots like Duolingo's language learning assistant use natural language processing to engage students in real-time conversations, providing immediate feedback and helping them practice language skills. Similarly, AI-powered writing assistants like Grammarly offer students personalized feedback on their writing, helping them improve their grammar, style, and clarity. These tools not only assist students in their learning but also provide teachers with valuable insights into student performance, helping them identify areas where students may need additional support.

In addition to enhancing the learning experience, AI has also played a crucial role in improving educational accessibility. AI-powered tools like speech recognition software, text-to-speech programs, and real-time translation services have made education more accessible to students with disabilities and those who speak languages other than the language of instruction. These tools have helped bridge the gap for students who may have previously faced barriers to learning, ensuring that education is more inclusive and equitable.

PRESENT: AI IN EDUCATION TODAY

"Artificial intelligence (AI) seems to offer considerable potential in higher education by offering personalized learning experiences and fostering deeper student engagement" (Ruano-Borbalan, 2025)

The presence of AI in education was spurred on the appearance and accessiblity of generative AI in the public domain (i.e. ChatGPT in November of 2022) Artificial Intelligence is taking the centre stage in education. AI has become a central component of educational technology, already transforming both the classroom experience and administrative processes. AI in education is firmly establishing for the purposes of assessment and evaluation; prediction of learning and academic success, managing student learning, as well as personalized learning and intelligent tutoring systems (Crompton & Burke, 2023). Systematic reviews of literature such as that by Crompton and Burke (2023) reveal that most applications of AI in education are intended for student use, followed by instructor use, and to a lesser extent for use in administration.

The rapid advancements in machine learning, natural language processing, and data analytics have made it possible for AI to support personalized learning, automate administrative tasks, and provide real-time insights into student performance. Today's AI-powered educational tools can adapt to individual learning needs, offering personalized content and feedback based on student performance, and providing teachers with valuable data to inform instructional decisions. These advancements have not only revolutionized how education is delivered but have also created new opportunities for educators and learners alike. Findings of studies are supporting the view that "AI offers significant benefits, including personalized learning, improved academic outcomes, and enhanced student engagement. " (Vieriu & Petrea, 2025, p. 1)

The integration of AI into education ushered in a new era of personalized learning. One of the most significant developments in AI for education has been the rise of adaptive learning platforms. These platforms use AI algorithms to analyze student data and adjust the learning experience based on individual progress. This personalized approach allows each student to receive instruction tailored to their unique strengths, weaknesses, and learning pace. For example, platforms like DreamBox and Knewton offer personalized math and reading lessons that adapt in real-time to the learner's needs. These systems use sophisticated algorithms to monitor a student's progress and adjust the difficulty level of the content, ensuring that students are constantly challenged at the right level. This shift from a one-size-fits-all approach to a personalized model has the potential to greatly improve student engagement and outcomes, particularly for students who may have been left behind by traditional educational methods.

Adaptive learning platforms have been shown to increase student engagement and achievement by providing a learning experience that is both challenging and supportive. In traditional classrooms, students are often expected to learn at the same pace, which can lead to frustration for those who struggle with the material or boredom for those who excel. With AI-powered adaptive learning systems, students can progress at their own pace, receiving targeted interventions when they encounter difficulties. For example, if a student struggles with a particular math concept, the system can offer additional practice problems or provide alternative explanations to help the student understand the material. On the other hand, students who master a concept quickly can move on to more advanced topics, ensuring that they are always learning at an appropriate level. This individualized approach to learning has been shown to improve retention and mastery of content, leading to better long-term academic outcomes.

AI is also playing a crucial role in automating administrative tasks in education. Grading, attendance tracking, and lesson planning are just a few of the time-consuming tasks that AI systems can help streamline. In many educational institutions, teachers spend a significant amount of time on administrative duties, leaving less time for direct interaction with students. AI can help alleviate this burden by automating routine tasks, allowing educators to focus more on teaching and less on paperwork. AI-powered grading systems, for example, can quickly and accurately grade assignments, quizzes, and exams, providing instant feedback to students. This not only saves teachers valuable time but also ensures that students receive timely feedback on their performance, which is essential for effective learning.

Attendance tracking is another area where AI is making a significant impact. AI-powered systems can automatically track student attendance using facial recognition or other biometric technologies, reducing the need for manual record-keeping. These systems can also alert teachers and administrators when students are absent or tardy, enabling them to intervene early and provide support to students who may be struggling. By automating these administrative tasks, AI allows educators to spend more time engaging with students and providing personalized instruction.

In addition to automating routine tasks, AI-driven analytics tools are helping educational institutions make data-informed decisions about resource allocation, student support, and curriculum development. By analyzing large volumes of data, AI can provide valuable insights into student performance, identifying trends and patterns that might otherwise go unnoticed. For example, AI can analyze student test scores, attendance records, and other performance data to identify students who are at risk of falling behind. With this information, educators can intervene early, providing additional support and resources to help these students succeed. AI can also help institutions identify areas where the curriculum may need to be adjusted to better meet the needs of students. By providing real-time insights into student performance, AI allows educators to make informed decisions that can improve learning outcomes for all students.

Moreover, AI is being used to create immersive learning experiences through technologies like virtual reality (VR) and augmented reality (AR). These technologies, when combined with AI, offer students the opportunity to engage with content in a more interactive and dynamic way. Traditional methods of instruction often rely on static materials such as textbooks, which can limit students' engagement and understanding of complex concepts. By contrast, AI-powered VR and AR technologies allow students to interact with the material in a more hands-on, experiential way. For instance, AI-powered VR simulations can immerse students in historical events, scientific experiments, or complex mathematical concepts, providing a hands-on, experiential learning environment that would be impossible with traditional methods. Students can explore ancient civilizations, conduct virtual chemistry experiments, or even visualize mathematical concepts in three dimensions, making abstract ideas more concrete and easier to understand.

The combination of AI and immersive technologies is opening up new possibilities for experiential learning, making education more engaging, interactive, and impactful (Chalkiadakis, et al., 2024). Virtual reality has the potential to transform fields such as science, engineering, medicine, and history by allowing students to explore and interact with content in ways that were previously unimaginable. For example, medical students can use VR simulations to practice surgeries or diagnose patients in a risk-free environment. Similarly, engineering students can use VR to design and test prototypes without the need for expensive physical materials. The ability to engage with content in a fully immersive environment not only enhances students' understanding of the material but also provides them with valuable hands-on experience that can be applied in real-world situations.

Augmented reality, overlays digital content onto the physical world, creating a hybrid learning experience. For example, AR can be used to enhance textbooks by adding interactive elements such as videos, animations, or 3D models that students can explore using their smartphones or tablets. This technology can also be used in the classroom to provide interactive learning experiences that blend the digital and physical worlds. For instance, students can use AR to explore a virtual solar system projected onto the classroom floor, allowing them to interact with the planets and learn about their characteristics in a more engaging way. By combining AI with VR and AR, educators can create dynamic learning environments that capture students' attention and enhance their understanding of complex concepts.

In addition to enhancing the learning experience, AI is also playing a crucial role in improving educational accessibility. AI-powered tools like speech recognition software, text-to-speech programs, and real-time translation services have made education more accessible to students with disabilities and those who speak languages other than the language of instruction. These tools have helped bridge the gap for students who may have previously faced barriers to learning, ensuring that education is more inclusive and equitable. For example, speech recognition software can help students with physical disabilities or learning difficulties, such as dyslexia, by transcribing spoken words into text. Text-to-speech programs can assist students with visual impairments by reading aloud written content, allowing them to access course materials more easily. Real-time translation services can help non-native speakers understand course content in their own language, ensuring that language barriers do not prevent them from fully participating in the learning process.

AI is impacting on the nature of assessment. Traditional assessments, such as standardized tests and essays, have limitations in their ability to measure a student's true understanding and skills. AI-powered assessments can provide a more accurate and comprehensive picture of a student's abilities, considering factors such as problem-solving skills, creativity, and collaboration. These assessments could be used to track a student's progress over time, providing teachers with valuable insights into their development and helping to identify areas where they may need additional support.

AI is transforming the landscape of education in profound ways, enhancing both the learning experience and administrative processes. From personalized learning platforms to immersive technologies and improved accessibility, AI is making education more engaging, efficient, and inclusive. As AI continues to evolve, its potential to reshape education is limitless, providing new opportunities for learners of all ages and backgrounds. By embracing AI in education and addressing the ethical considerations it raises, we can create a more equitable and effective educational system that prepares students for the challenges and opportunities of the future.

FUTURE: THE NEXT FRONTIER OF AI IN EDUCATION

Looking to the future, the potential for AI in education is vast. As AI continues to evolve, its applications in education are expected to become even more sophisticated and widespread. AI technologies may, in the future, evolve beyond what we can imagine today, but for the moment, there are several identifiable themes that are likely to characterize the next frontiers of AI in education.

IMMERSIVE, PERSONALIZED AND EXPERIENTIAL LEARNING

"The advent of AI in educational settings transcends mere technological advancement, reshaping the educational experience at its core" (Walter, 2024, p. 1)

Accompanied by the development ofof immersive learning technologies, such as virtual reality (VR) and augmented reality (AR), AI has the potential to revolutionize the learning experience so it is personalized, immersive and experiential. By combining AI with VR and AR, students could engage in interactive, experiential learning that takes them beyond the classroom. For example, AI-powered VR simulations could allow students to explore historical events, scientific concepts, or even complex mathematical problems in an immersive, hands-on environment. This type of learning has the potential to deepen understanding and improve retention by engaging students in ways that traditional methods cannot.

"The integration of AI with immersive technologies represents a powerful combination for advancing education. AI enhances the interactivity and adaptability of VR/AR environments,while immersive technologies provide the experiential context needed for deeper learning. Together, they hold the potential to revolutionize traditional education systems" (Bekteshi, 2025, p. 23)

AI AND LIFELONG LEARNING

"We suggest that lifelong learning in the 'age of AI' must take into account the complexity of the digital throughout the life course and account for the complex ways technologies are changing the nature of work and other spheres of life." (Palenski, Hills, Unnikrishnan, & Eynon, 2024, p. 1233)

Lifelong learning is recognized as important to individuals, their working lives and to societies (Palenski, Hills, Unnikrishnan, & Eynon, 2024). As the world of work continues to change rapidly, the need for continuous learning and skill development will only grow. The rise of automation, artificial intelligence, and other disruptive technologies means that workers must constantly adapt to new tools, processes, and industries. This shift necessitates an ongoing commitment to learning throughout one's career. The relationships between AI and lifelong learning is two-fold. Firstly, the importance of AI literacy is accentuated since the nature of work and technological society is changing. It is imperative that all members of society have the literacy and skills to work ethically and responsibly with AI technologies. Secondly, AI itself has the potential to as an enabler of lifelong learning.

One of the greatest challenges for fostering lifelong learning is how to "effectively personalize experiences to meet the evolving needs of individuals throughout their lives" (Bayly-Castaneda, Ramirez-Montoya, & Morita-Alexander, 2024, p. 1).AI-powered platforms can offer learners of all ages the opportunity to engage in personalized, on-demand learning, allowing them to acquire new skills and knowledge at their own pace. These platforms can be tailored to meet the needs of individuals in various stages of their careers, from young professionals looking to develop specific skills to older workers seeking to reskill or upskill. With AI, learning becomes more flexible, accessible, and personalized, providing individuals with the tools they need to thrive in a rapidly changing job market.

For example, AI-powered platforms like Coursera and LinkedIn Learning already offer a wide range of online courses that allow users to learn at their own pace. These platforms use AI to recommend courses based on users' interests, past learning behavior, and professional goals, providing a personalized learning experience. As AI continues to improve, these platforms will likely become even more sophisticated, offering more tailored learning paths and real-time feedback that adjusts as learners progress.

Moreover, AI could play a crucial role in providing access to education for people in remote or underserved areas. By offering online, AI-powered learning platforms, individuals who may not have access to traditional educational institutions can still acquire valuable skills and knowledge. This democratization of learning could help bridge the educational gap between developed and developing regions, providing new opportunities for personal and professional growth in areas where educational resources are scarce.

NATURAL LANGUAGE PROCESSING AND CONVERSATIONAL AGENTS

"We're entering a new era where AI education agents are not just digital tools but intelligent, responsive conversational partners. These agents don't just deliver content; they engage learners through context-aware dialogue, adaptive feedback, and personalized pacing" (Frey, 2025, p. para 13)

The future of AI in education will also be marked by the increasing use of natural language processing (NLP) and conversational agents. NLP is a branch of AI that focuses on the interaction between computers and human language, enabling machines to understand, interpret, and respond to natural language input. In education, this technology has the potential to revolutionize how students interact with digital learning tools.

AI-powered chatbots and virtual assistants are already being used to provide students with real-time support and answer questions about course material. These systems can engage in basic conversations with students, helping them navigate course content, clarify concepts, and even provide feedback on assignments. For example, platforms like Duolingo use AI-driven chatbots to help users practice language skills, providing instant feedback and adjusting the difficulty of tasks based on the learner's proficiency level.

In the future, these technologies could evolve to offer more sophisticated interactions, allowing students to engage in deeper conversations with AI systems and receive personalized feedback in real-time. For instance, AI-driven conversational agents could act as teaching assistants, answering students' questions, providing explanations, and offering guidance on assignments. These systems could be available 24/7, bridging the gap between in-class learning and outside-of-class support. This could be especially beneficial for students who may need additional help outside of traditional classroom hours, offering them a more personalized learning experience and improving their chances of success.

Furthermore, AI-powered virtual assistants could be used to help students stay organized and manage their learning. For example, an AI assistant could remind students of upcoming deadlines, suggest study resources based on their performance, and help them set goals for their learning. By offering personalized support in a conversational format, AI could help students become more self-directed and engaged in their learning, leading to improved outcomes.

In the future, it can be expected that chatbots and conversational agents become even more intwined in education, and in daily life (Pereira, et al., 2023).

AI IN ASSESSMENT AND EVALUATION

"AI has significant potential to transform educational assessment, offering more dynamic, efficient, and personalized evaluation methods. Future research should focus on addressing ethical concerns like data privacy and algorithmic bias while enhancing AI-driven assessments' adaptability and scalability to support diverse learner needs". (Saputra, Kurniawan, Yanita, Putri, & Mahniza, 2024, p. 9068)

Assessment has always been at the center of the learning process and the learning experience. Traditional assessments, such as standardized tests and essays, are limited in their ability to measure a student's true understanding and skills. These methods often fail to capture the full range of a student's abilities, particularly in areas such as creativity, problem-solving, and collaboration.

AI-powered assessment tools, on the other hand, can provide more accurate, dynamic evaluations by analyzing a student's performance across a wide range of activities, including projects, discussions, and problem-solving tasks. These tools can track a student's progress over time, offering a more comprehensive view of their abilities and development. For example, AI systems could analyze a student's responses to open-ended questions, evaluate their problem-solving strategies, and provide personalized feedback on their performance.

"AI technologies, like machine learning and natural language processing, are particularly effective in providing real-time feedback and evaluating higher-order competencies, including critical thinking and creativity" (Saputra, Kurniawan, Yanita, Putri, & Mahniza, 2024, p. 9056).

Moreover, AI have potential to reduce bias in assessments. Traditional grading methods, particularly those involving human evaluators, can be subject to unconscious bias, which may unfairly impact students from marginalized groups. AI-powered assessment tools, when properly designed, can offer more objective evaluations, ensuring that all students are assessed fairly and equitably. This could lead to more accurate and inclusive assessments of student learning, helping to identify strengths and weaknesses that may have been overlooked using traditional methods.

AI could also enable more frequent and formative assessments, which provide ongoing feedback to students throughout their learning journey. This could help to identify learning gaps early, allowing teachers to intervene and provide additional support before students fall behind. By offering real-time, personalized feedback, AI-powered assessments could help students take ownership of their learning and make more informed decisions about their academic progress.

ADDRESSING EQUITY AND ACCESSIBILITY

"We believe AI technology has the potential to help the world address these chronic challenges in education relating to equity, learning outcomes, and real world relevance. " (Srinivasan, 2022, p. 1)

One of the most significant challenges in education today is ensuring that all students, regardless of their background or abilities, have access to high-quality education. AI has the potential to help bridge this gap by providing personalized learning experiences that cater to the diverse needs of today's learners.

AI-powered tools can support students with disabilities by offering adaptive learning environments that cater to their specific needs. For example, speech recognition software can help students with physical disabilities or learning difficulties, such as dyslexia, by transcribing spoken words into text (Zhao, Cox, & Chen, 2025). Text-to-speech programs can assist students with visual impairments by reading aloud written content, allowing them to access course materials more easily. Real-time translation services can help non-native speakers understand course content in their own language, ensuring that language barriers do not prevent them from fully participating in the learning process.

By providing personalized support to students with disabilities and those from diverse linguistic and cultural backgrounds, AI can make education more inclusive and equitable. This could help close the achievement gap, ensuring that every student can succeed, regardless of their starting point. Furthermore, AI-powered tools can be used to provide targeted interventions for students who are at risk of falling behind, offering them the support they need to stay on track and achieve their academic goals.

ETHICAL CONSIDERATIONS AND CHALLENGES

"As artificial intelligence (AI) continues to transform the world—including higher education—the need for responsible use has never been more critical. While AI holds immense potential to enhance teaching and learning, ethical considerations

around social inequity, environmental concerns, and dehumanization continue to emerge " (Wargo & Anderson, 2024, p. para 2)

While the potential benefits of AI in education are vast, it is essential to address the ethical challenges that come with its widespread use. As AI becomes more integrated into education, issues such as data privacy, algorithmic bias, and the digital divide must be carefully considered to ensure that AI is used in ways that are fair, transparent, and inclusive.

One pressing ethical concerns surrounding AI in education is data privacy. AI-powered educational tools rely on large amounts of student data to function effectively, including information about students' learning behavior, performance, and personal characteristics. Ensuring that this data is collected, stored, and used responsibly is crucial to maintaining students' trust and protecting their privacy (Reidenberg & Schaub, 2018)Educational institutions and technology providers must implement strong data security measures and ensure that students and parents are informed about how their data will be used. Alongside privacy, issues of data ownership as well as informed consent are persistent but important issues for AI in education. The ongoing lack of legal clarity around issues of data ownership and consent needs attention (Corrin, et al., 2019).

Algorithmic bias is another pressing ethical concern. Bias in AI can be conscious or unconscious and there are multiple forms of bias including program bias, digital biases, gender biases, discrimination biases. Biases may be in the datasets or in the algorithms (Karan & Angadi). AI systems are only as good as the data they are trained on, and if the data is biased, then the AI's recommendations and assessments can also be biased. For example, an AI-powered admissions system that is trained on historical data may inadvertently reinforce existing biases in the selection process, disadvantaging students from underrepresented groups. It is essential to ensure that AI systems are designed to be fair and inclusive, and that they are regularly audited to identify and address any biases that may arise. A failure to address algorithmic bias will hijack the potential of AI for democratize education. Furthermore, the algorithms behind AI technologies are only as inclusive as the data they are trained on. Hence, addressing algorithmic bias includes mechanisms for ensuring the quality and completeness of training data. A range of harms can arise from algorithmic bias including what are termed "allocative harms" – which result from "withholding of some opportunity or resource from a specific group or the unfair distribution of a good across groups" and representational harms – which is the stereotyping of particular groups (Baker & Hawn, 2022).

Accessible and equitable access to AI for all also rests on meeting the challenge of the digital divide.. While AI has the potential to democratize learning, it also has the potential to exacerbate existing inequalities. Students in underserved areas or from low-income backgrounds may not have access to the necessary technology or internet connectivity to benefit from AI-powered learning tools (Kitsara, 2022).. To ensure that AI benefits all students, it is essential to invest in infrastructure and support for underserved communities, ensuring that all learners have access to the tools they need to succeed. Furthermore, even if physical or economic access to technologies is present, there is also a need to ensure opportunities for developing digital and AI literacies. Without such literacies, individuals are not empowered to reap potential benefits of AI in education (Wang, Boerman, Kroon, Möller, & de Vreese, 2024).

CONCLUSION

The future of AI in education is filled with exciting possibilities. From fostering lifelong learning and improving assessment methods to enhancing equity and accessibility, AI has the potential to transform education in profound ways. However, as AI continues to evolve, it is essential to address the ethical challenges that come with its widespread use. By ensuring that AI is used responsibly and inclusively, we can create a more equitable, effective, and personalized educational system that benefits all students, regardless of their background or abilities.

The evolution of AI in educational technology has come a long way, from its early beginnings as a theoretical concept to its current role as a transformative force in the classroom and beyond. In the early stages, AI was largely confined to academic research and discussions, with little practical application in everyday educational settings. The technology was seen as a distant possibility, with questions about its feasibility and potential impact remaining largely unanswered. However, as AI has advanced, it has moved from the realm of theory into practical use, fundamentally changing how education is delivered, accessed, and experienced. Today, AI is a key driver of innovation in education, influencing everything from personalized learning experiences to data-driven decision-making and administrative processes.

As AI continues to develop, it holds the potential to revolutionize education in ways that were once thought impossible. With classrooms that are increasingly diverse in terms of learning styles, backgrounds, and abilities, educators face the challenge of ensuring that every student receives the support and resources they need to succeed. AI can address this challenge by providing personalized learning experiences that cater to each student's unique needs. AI-powered platforms can assess a student's strengths and weaknesses, adjust the pace and difficulty of lessons, and offer tailored resources to help them succeed. This level of personalization ensures that students are not left behind or forced to move ahead at a pace that is too fast for them to keep up with.

Furthermore, AI has the potential to make education more accessible to a wider range of learners. As the demand for education grows globally, the traditional models of face-to-face learning in classrooms may not be able to meet the needs of all students. AI-powered platforms and tools can provide access to high-quality education for students in remote areas, those with disabilities, and those who may not have access to traditional educational institutions due to financial or logistical barriers. AI can help bridge these gaps by offering flexible, on-demand learning opportunities that allow students to learn at their own pace and on their own schedule. For example, online learning platforms powered by AI can offer real-time feedback and personalized recommendations, helping students to stay on track and make progress even when they are not in a traditional classroom setting.

In addition to making education more personalized and accessible, AI can also improve the efficiency of educational systems. Traditional educational models often involve a significant amount of administrative work, from grading assignments to tracking student progress. AI has the potential to automate many of these tasks, freeing up educators to focus more on teaching and less on administrative duties. AI-powered grading systems, for example, can quickly and accurately assess assignments, saving educators valuable time and providing students with immediate feedback. Additionally, AI can be used to analyze large amounts of data to identify trends, assess student performance, and inform decision-making. This data-driven approach can help educators and administrators make more informed decisions about curriculum design, resource allocation, and student support services, ultimately leading to more effective educational outcomes.

As AI continues to evolve, it is essential that we embrace its potential responsibly. While the benefits of AI in education are clear, it is also important to recognize and address the ethical challenges that come with its widespread use. Issues such as data privacy, algorithmic bias, and the digital divide must be carefully considered to ensure that AI is used in ways that are fair, transparent, and inclusive. The use of AI in education relies heavily on the collection and analysis of student data, which raises concerns about privacy and the potential for misuse. It is crucial that educational institutions and technology providers implement strong safeguards to protect student data and ensure that it is used only for the purposes of improving learning outcomes. Additionally, AI systems must be designed to be free from bias, as biased algorithms can perpetuate inequalities in education. Ensuring that AI tools are inclusive and equitable is essential to ensuring that all students, regardless of their background or abilities, can benefit from the opportunities that AI offers.

The future of AI in education is bright, and its impact will be felt across all levels of education, from K-12 schools to higher education and beyond. As AI technology continues to improve, its applications in education will become even more sophisticated and widespread. In K-12 schools, AI has the potential to transform the way students learn, offering personalized learning experiences that cater to each student's needs and abilities. AI-powered tools can help students develop critical thinking, problem-solving, and creativity skills, preparing them for the challenges of the future workforce. In higher education, AI can support students in a variety of ways, from helping them navigate complex coursework to providing personalized career guidance. AI-powered systems can also assist faculty in designing and delivering more effective courses, using data to inform teaching practices and improve student outcomes. Beyond formal education, AI has the potential to support lifelong learning, enabling individuals to acquire new skills and knowledge throughout their careers. AI-powered platforms can provide personalized learning paths, allowing individuals to learn at their own pace and acquire the skills they need to succeed in an ever-changing job market.

As we look to the future, it is clear that AI will play a central role in shaping the next generation of educational technology. The potential for AI to enhance the learning experience, improve educational outcomes, and make education more accessible and inclusive is immense. However, to fully realize the benefits of AI in education, it is essential that we approach its implementation thoughtfully and responsibly. By embracing AI in a way that prioritizes equity, transparency, and privacy, we can create an educational system that is better equipped to meet the needs of today's learners and prepare them for the challenges and opportunities of tomorrow. The future of AI in education is not just about technology—it is about creating a more effective, inclusive, and personalized educational experience for all students, regardless of their background or circumstances. As we continue to explore the possibilities of AI in education, it is important to remember that the ultimate goal is to enhance the learning experience and empower all students to reach their full potential. By doing so, we can ensure that AI becomes a force for good in education, shaping the future of learning for generations to come.

REFERENCES

Anderson, J., Corbett, A., Koedinger, K., & Pelletier, R. (1995). Cognitive tutors: Lessons learned. *Journal of the Learning Sciences*, *4*(2), 167–207.

Axelsen, M., Redmond, P., Heinrich, E., & Henderson, M. (2020). The evolving field of learning analytics research in higher education From data analysis to theory generation, an agenda for future research. *Australasian Journal of Educational Technology*, *36*(2). https://ajet.org.au/index.php/AJET/article/view/6266

Baker, R., & Hawn, A. (2022). Algorithmic bias in education. *International Journal of Artificial Intelligence in Education*, *32*, 1052–1092.

Bayly-Castaneda, K., Ramirez-Montoya, M., & Morita-Alexander, A. (2024). Crafting personalized learning paths with AI for lifelong learning: A systematic literature review. *Frontiers in Education*, *9*, 1–12.

Bekteshi, L. (2025). Education in the Era of AI and Immersive Technologies: A Systematic Review. *Journal of Research in Engineering and Computer Sciences*, *3*(1), 1–14.

Chalkiadakis, A., Seremetaki, A., Kanellou, A., Kallishi, M., Morfopoulou, A., Moraitaki, M., & Mastrokoukou, S. (2024). Impact of Artificial Intelligence and virtual reality on educational inclusion: A systematic review of technologies supporting students with disabilities. *Education Sciences*, *14*(11), 1223. DOI: 10.3390/educsci14111223

Corrin, L., Kennedy, G., French, S., Shum, S., Kitto, K., Pardo, A., . . . Colvin, C. (2019). *The ethics of learning analytics in Australian Higher Education - Discussion Paper.*

Crompton, H., & Burke, D. (2023). Artificial intelligence in higher education: The state of the field. *International Journal of Educational Technology in Higher Education*, *20*. Advance online publication. DOI: 10.1186/s41239-023-00392-8

Doroudi, S. (2023). The Intertwined Histories of Artificial Intelligence and Education. *International Journal of Artificial Intelligence in Education*, *33*, 885–928.

du Plooy, E., Casteleijn, D., & Franzsen, D. (2024). Personalized adaptive learning in higher education: A scoping review of key characteristics and impact on academic performance and engagement. *Heliyon*, *10*(21), e39630. DOI: 10.1016/j.heliyon.2024.e39630 PMID: 39524879

Frey, T. (2025, May 1). *The Future of Education with AI Agents: How Conversational Agents Will Replace Classrooms*. Retrieved May 2025, from Futurist Speaker Thomas Frey: https://futuristspeaker.com/future-of-education/the-future-of-education-with-ai-agents-how-conversational-agents-will-replace-classrooms/#:~:text=We're%20entering%20a%20new,adaptive%20feedback%2C%20and%20personalized%20pacing

Guan, C., Mou, J., & Jiang, Z. (2020). Artificial intelligence innovation in education: A twenty-year data-driven historical analysis. *International Journal of Innovation Studies*, *4*(4), 134–147.

Hody, G., & Avner, R. (1978). The PLATO system: An evaluative description. In E. C. DelLand, *Information Technology in Health Science Education. Computers in Biology and Medicine.* (pp. 143-177). Springer.

Karan, B., & Angadi, G. (n.d.). Potential Risks of Artificial Intelligence Integration into School Education: A Systematic Review. *Bulletin of Science, Technology & Society*, *43*(3-4), 67–85.

Kitsara, I. (2022). Artificial Intelligence and the digital divide: From an innovation perspective. In A. Bounfour, *Platforms and Artificial Intelligence The Next Generation of Competences* (pp. 245–265). Springer.

Lang, S. (2023). Learning Management Systems (LMSs). In O. Kruse, *Digital Writing Technologies in Higher Education.* (pp. https://doi-org.libraryproxy.griffith.edu.au/10.1007/978-3-031-36033-6_11). Springer.

Palenski, T., Hills, L., Unnikrishnan, S., & Eynon, R. (2024). How AI works: Reconfiguring lifelong learning. *Postdigital Science and Education*, *6*, 1216–1238.

Pereira, D., Falcáo, F., Costa, L., Lunn, B., Pégo, J., & Costa, P. (2023). Here's to the future: Conversational agents in higher education- a scoping review. *International Journal of Educational Research*, *122*, 102233. DOI: 10.1016/j.ijer.2023.102233

Reidenberg, J., & Schaub, F. (2018). Achieving big data privacy in education. *Theory and Research in Education*, *16*(3), 263–279.

Romiszowski, A. (1987). Artificial intelligence and expert systems in education: Progress, promise and problems. *Australian Journal of Educational Technology*, *3*(1), 8–23.

Ruano-Borbalan, J. (2025). he transformative impact of artificial intelligence on higher education: A critical reflection on current trends and futures directions. *International Journal of Chinese Education*, *14*(1). https://doi-org.libraryproxy.griffith.edu.au/10.1177/2212585X251319364

Saputra, I., Kurniawan, A., Yanita, M., Putri, E., & Mahniza, M. (2024). The Evolution of Educational Assessment: How Artificial Intelligence is Shaping the Trends and Future of Learning Evaluation. *The Indonesian Journal of Computer Science, 13*(6), 9056–9074.

Srinivasan, V. (2022). AI & learning: A preferred future. *Computers and Education: Artificial Intelligence, 3*, 100062. DOI: 10.1016/j.caeai.2022.100062

Vieriu, A., & Petrea, G. (2025). The Impact of Artificial Intelligence (AI) on Students' Academic Development. *Education Sciences, 15*(3), 343. DOI: 10.3390/educsci15030343

Walter, Y. (2024). Embracing the future of Artificial Intelligence in the classroom: The relevance of AI literacy, prompt engineering, and critical thinking in modern education. *International Journal of Educational Technology in Higher Education, 21*(15). Advance online publication. DOI: 10.1186/s41239-024-00448-3

Wang, C., Boerman, S., Kroon, A., Möller, J., & de Vreese, C. (2024). The artificial intelligence divide: Who is the most vulnerable? *New Media & Society, 00*(0), 1–23.

Wargo, K., & Anderson, B. (2024). Striking a Balance: Navigating the Ethical Dilemmas of AI in Higher Education. *Educause Review*, https://er.educause.edu/articles/2024/12/striking-a-balance-navigating-the-ethical-dilemmas-of-ai-in-higher-education

Zhao, X., Cox, A., & Chen, X. (2025). The use of generative AI by students with disabilities in higher education. *The Internet and Higher Education, 66*, 101014. DOI: 10.1016/j.iheduc.2025.101014

About The Contributors

Viktor Wang is a globally recognized professor and leader in the field of Education in the Department of Educational Leadership and Technology at California State University, San Bernardino. His distinguished career is marked by innovation, scholarship, and mentorship. With more than 240 peer-reviewed publications, Dr. Wang has made transformative contributions to academic research and thought leadership. His work has inspired over 200 scholarly articles and more than 1,500 book chapters contributed to his edited volumes and journals by scholars around the world. His publications are widely respected and housed in top-tier institutions, including Stanford University Libraries and other globally renowned academic collections. Dr. Wang has received numerous prestigious honors, including the 2016 Presidential Award for Exceptional and Innovative Leadership from the American Association for Adult and Continuing Education (AAACE), as well as institutional recognition such as the Distinguished Faculty and Scholarly Achievement Award from CSULB. A dedicated mentor, Dr. Wang has successfully guided more than 80 doctoral students through dissertation completion. His leadership has also driven measurable institutional outcomes, including enrollment growth, the launch of innovative academic programs, and the establishment of international educational partnerships.

***

Andi Asrifan is an accomplished educator and academic leader with a Doctorate in Education, specializing in English Language Education from Universitas Negeri Makassar. With a strong academic foundation, he holds a Master's degree in the same field and a Bachelor's degree in Secondary Education. His dissertation focused on developing bilingual educational materials, reflecting his commitment to enhancing language education. Dr. Asrifan has extensive experience in various educational roles, including serving as the Head of the International Affairs Office at Politeknik

Negeri Nunukan and as the Head of the Institute for Student Development and Alumni at Universitas Muhammadiyah Sidenreng Rappang. He is also an active member of several professional organizations, including the Linguistics Society of Indonesia and TEFLIN. In addition to his administrative roles, Dr. Asrifan is a passionate advocate for educational innovation and has participated in numerous international conferences and webinars, sharing his insights on language teaching and curriculum development. His dedication to professional development is evident through his participation in various training programs.

Eun-Ok Baek is a Professor and the Program Coordinator of Instructional Design and Technology program at California State University, San Bernardino. Her research explores the potential of technology to support learning and performance, focusing on online/mobile learning communities, educational technology integration, AI-enhanced education, STEM teaching, and socio-cultural factors influencing technology adoption.

Mei Rianto Chandra serves as a lecturer in Chinese Literature at Bina Nusantara University in Indonesia. He obtained his doctorate in linguistics from Jinan University in Guangzhou, China. His primary study domains are Chinese linguistics and Learning chinese as a second language.

Angela Crevar serves as an assistant professor at Mercer University. She received her Ph.D. in Educational Leadership and Policy from Texas Tech University. Angela served as a postdoctoral researcher at Texas Tech University, and she served as a high school principal for ten years. Her research is focused on the nexus of high school to college and career readiness with a focus on pathways through education to student success. These pathways include career technical education, hybrid education, and non-traditional pathways. Her work has been published in the Journal of Higher Education and Policy and Leadership Studies and Early Education and Development. Her work has also been presented at the Association for Public Policy Analysis and Management, American Educational Research Association, Association for Education Finance and Policy, University Council for Educational Administration, and the Society for Research on Educational Effectiveness national conferences.

Dang Hoang Thanh Lan is a lecturer in the Faculty of Sociology and Social Works at the University of Social Sciences and Humanities, Vietnam National University, Hanoi. She is currently pursuing a Ph.D. at University College Cork, Ireland, where she developed a passion for comparative sociology. Her research interests centre on the sociology of education, technology, politics, religion, urban, and youth. Signature pedagogy is the philosophy that she is committed to fostering students' "habits of the mind, hands, and heart".

Ashley L. Dockens, PhD, AuD, CCC-A, is a dynamic academic leader serving at Lamar University as the Assistant Provost of Academic Innovation and Quality Assurance, Office of Academic Affairs, and the Associate Dean of Policy and Procedure, College of Graduate Studies. In these roles, she shapes and implements policies to drive academic excellence and compliance. Having previously served as the Director of the Center for Teaching and Learning Enhancement, Dr. Dockens is dedicated to promoting innovative teaching practices and leading all university AI initiatives, ensuring ethical and effective integration into academic programs. As an Associate Professor of Audiology, she shares her passion for the field, having previously directed the Doctor of Audiology program. In higher education, she serves as a regular speaker on the topic of generative AI at state, national, and international venues. Beginning March 2024, Dr. Dockens committed to serve as Chair of the AI Taskforce for the Council of Academic Programs in Communication Sciences and Disorders, an international accreditor for the field. Dr. Dockens' diverse roles reflect her commitment to higher education through leadership, contributing to the overall success of the academic community.

Dubey is an Assistant Professor of Education and Director of Clinical Experiences and Partnerships at Montana State University Northern. His research interest focuses in the areas of Multicultural/Immigrant Education, Diversity, Equity, & Inclusivity, Leadership and Change, Technology in Education (Digital Equity & AI), STEM education, Comparative and International Education, Teacher Quality, and Teacher Choice for diverse classrooms. In his research, he uses the statistical tools of Structural Education Modelling (SEM), Mediation & Moderation, and R programming to address the issues that intersect in improving the learning experiences of diverse student population, immigrant/refugee students, and minority students. He has presented research papers at several national research conferences such as AERA, UCIE, AEFP, SREE, etc. and is currently working on different projects and grants.

Angela Elkordy, PhD, is an Associate Professor in the Educational Leadership Department of the National College of Education, National Louis University. Before transitioning to higher education full-time in 2014, she served in K-12 contexts as a technology teacher, Director of Libraries, and school principal. Dr. Elkordy's research interests focus on the intersection of emerging technologies, research methods, and leveraging findings from the learning sciences for effective teaching and learning.

She teaches graduate and doctoral students various topics in educational leadership, generative AI in education, instructional design, and research methods.

Qi Guo is a Ph.D. student in the Instructional Psychology and Technology program at Brigham Young University. Her research interests center on enhancing online instruction through educational technologies, exploring the integration of artificial intelligence in learning environments, and applying gamification strategies to engage students in STEAM education.

Pi-Chi Han is the Chair and Professor at the Graduate Institute of Adult Education, National Kaohsiung Normal University, Taiwan. Her academic endeavors integrate research, teaching, and consulting, focusing on advancing global talent development across public, private, and non-governmental organizations. Dr. Han is a distinguished Senior Advisor to the Asia-Pacific Economic Cooperation (APEC), contributing to the Human Resources Development Working Group (HRDWG) and the Policy Partnership on Women and the Economy (PPWE). Dr. Han's international academic appointments include serving as a faculty member at the University of Missouri, St. Louis, USA, and as a visiting scholar at the Chinese Academy of Social Sciences, China. Her research portfolio encompasses international active aging and workforce retooling, intercultural competence, female marriage migrants' leadership development, cross-cultural mentoring frameworks, and the application of Confucian leadership principles in contemporary contexts.

Mary A. Hansen, PhD, is a university professor in the Education Department of Robert Morris University in Pennsylvania. Dr. Hansen's research interests lie in the area of educational measurement and assessment. Her classroom-based research focuses on classroom assessment practices and the use of technology and assistive technology in the classroom. She has published on the use of technology to support reflection in pre-service teacher education, the attitudes and experiences of pre-service and in-service teachers towards inclusion, and the use of inclusive practices in business education. Dr. Hansen has also published and presented research related to large scale alternate assessments.

Greg Kaiser, PhD, is a distinguished Professor of Education at Azusa Pacific University, where he has dedicated 29 years to advancing the field of educational leadership. Earning his doctorate from Claremont Graduate University, Dr. Kaiser is recognized for his expertise in systems and school leadership, as well as his deep understanding of organizational structures in schools and the translation of theory into practice. An innovative and creative educator, Dr. Kaiser is known for being at the cutting edge of educational strategies, continually pushing the boundaries of traditional teaching and leadership methodologies to inspire and equip the next generation of educational leaders.

Sue Kaiser, EdD, is a respected faculty member at California State University, San Bernardino, with a doctorate in Educational Administration from the University of Southern California. With over 40 years of experience in education, Dr. Kaiser has held numerous leadership roles, including teacher, administrator, and consultant. Her expertise lies in leadership development, organizational change, and educational equity, making her a sought-after authority in the field. Dr. Kaiser is deeply committed to mentoring future educational leaders, contributing significantly to both the academic and practical aspects of educational leadership through her teaching, research, and extensive consulting work.

Dra. Clara Herlina Karjo, M.Hum., is a prominent professor at Bina Nusantara University (BINUS) in Indonesia, with a focus on applied linguistics. She obtained her master's and PhD degrees in applied English linguistics from Atma Jaya University, Jakarta.

Ruchika Katariya is an experienced academic professional with over Ten years in teaching and research in Computer Science & Engineering. I am pursuing a Ph.D. from Sage University, Indore, and holds an M.Tech in Computer Science & Engineering. My expertise includes Database Management, Machine Learning, and Data Analytics. Currently working as an Assistant Professor in the Artificial Intelligence & Data Science Department Has published research papers in international journals and earned certifications in Data Science. Passionate about education and innovation, I actively organizes workshops and academic events, fostering a dynamic learning environment.

Qian Kun is associated with Jiangsu University in Zhenjiang, China. He obtained his doctorate in linguistics from Jinan University in Guangzhou, China. His primary research domains include Chinese linguistics.

Aida Leyton, An educational leader with 25 years of experience transforming learning through innovative programs in science, technology, and innovation. She has trained over 1,000 professionals across Latin America, developed more than 30 educational programs, and created methodologies blending neuroscience and experiential learning. A specialist in 21st-century skills, women's leadership, and learning outcomes assessment, her work impacts educational communities and organizations through scalable and measurable solutions.

Michael McVey, EdD, is a tenured faculty member in the Department of Teacher Education at Eastern Michigan University. He began his career as a high school Special Education and English Literature teacher before transitioning to higher education in 1999. After several years at the University of Arizona, he joined EMU, where his work focuses on emerging educational technologies and teacher preparation. Michael presently serves as a Trustee on a Board of Education in Saline, Michigan, and was a Director for the International Society for Technology in Education (ISTE) for six years.

Tracy Medrano is a Lead Instructional Designer and Lecturer at California State University, San Bernardino (CSUSB). As a Lecturer, she teaches graduate-level courses in instructional design and technology. In her role as Lead Instructional Designer, she oversees campus-wide quality assurance initiatives, leads faculty development workshops, and supports the design and certification of online and hybrid courses. She also serves as the systemwide Quality Learning & Teaching (QLT) Course Manager for the California State University Office of the Chancellor. Her combined roles support an applied research perspective, allowing her to translate real-world instructional design and teaching challenges into forward-thinking, research-informed practices. In particular, some of her research focuses on the intersection of artificial intelligence (AI) and instructional design, particularly how educators and AI tools can ethically co-create inclusive, engaging learning experiences that align with course outcomes and reflect human-centered design principles. Her work aims to advance innovative design and teaching practices that meet the demands of evolving educational environments.

María Carolina Órdenes Guzmán is a tutor teacher and teacher educator at Pontificia Universidad Católica de Chile, where she specializes in the methodology of English language teaching for primary education. She brings over 15 years of extensive experience in teaching English as a foreign language across both primary and secondary levels. Her expertise extends to the preparation of students for international examinations. Carolina holds a Master of Arts in Teaching English as a Foreign Language from Universidad Alberto Hurtado. She has also completed one diploma in school leadership and a diploma in pedagogical mentoring for initial teacher training. Her scholarly interests lie in the realm of English language teacher education, with a particular emphasis on core teaching practices, assessment for learning, AI in education, and educational technology.

Prakasha G S is an Associate Professor at School of Education, Christ University Central campus, Bangalore, India. He has 21+ years of teaching and research experiences in Education. His research interest areas are Teacher-education,

Educational-technology, Teaching-learning, Assessment-evaluation, and Higher education. He has published research articles in peer-reviewed journals indexed in Scopus and web of science. He conducts Quantitative data-analysis workshops and delivers lectures on Research and Publication. He is an active editorial board member for Sage Open, Springer Nature, Tylor & Francis, and IGI Global. He is actively involved in research activities, which have national and international importance.

MattiusRischard is an Assistant Professor of English at Montana State University-Northern. He received his MA and PhD at the University of Arizona from the Department of English and Social, Cultural, and Critical Theory Programs. He has taught writing, literature, and digital/visual culture and methods for the University of Arizona, Pima Community College, and as a Writing Assessment Specialist for the University of Texas. He is the author of Street, Text, and Representation in African American Literature (Routledge, 2024), and publishes and presents on sociohistorical, phenomenological, and computational methods of literary and cultural analysis. Winner of the 2020 New Directions in the Humanities International Award, he has written widely in the fields of writing pedagogy, assessment, and digital humanities research for journals including Writing Spaces, Texas Studies in Literature and Language, and The International Journal of Critical Cultural Studies.

Rismawati Sudirman is a distinguished academic and consultant with a robust focus on sustainability reporting. She currently holds the position of lecturer and Head of the Quality Assurance Institute at Universitas Muhammadiyah Palopo, where she has been pivotal in ensuring the quality of university processes and outputs since February 2020. Additionally, she serves as an Assurer for Sustainability Reporting at the National Center for Sustainability Reporting in Jakarta, specializing in the evaluation of sustainability reports for mining companies across Indonesia. Her academic qualifications are extensive, comprising a Bachelor's degree in Economics and Accounting, a Master's degree in Accounting Science, and a Doctorate in Accounting from Universitas Brawijaya, Malang. Rismawati is also a certified specialist in sustainability reporting, risk management, and tax planning, holding several prestigious certifications including Certified Sustainability Reporting Specialist (CSRS) and Certified Risk Management Practitioner (CRMP). In her professional capacity, she has provided consultancy services in financial management and tax compliance for companies such as PT. Reski Barito Timur and PT. Helay Raya. Furthermore, she has authored multiple publications on taxation and management, contributing significantly to the academic community. Her interests in reading, writing, and travel reflect her commitment to lifelong learning and professional growth in her field.

Vivit Rosmayanti, S.Pd.I., M.Pd was born in Botta on June 26, 1987. She has over 10 years of experience teaching at the University. She obtained a bachelor's degree in English Education from Alauddin State Islamic University. She completed her master's and doctoral degrees in English Education from Makassar State University. She is currently a lecturer in the Post Graduate Program, Department of English Education at Makassar State University, South Sulawesi, Indonesia. She is also actively writing research articles to be published in nationally and internationally accredited journals. She has written in some chapter books, monographs, and reference books. She is interested in teaching methods for teaching English. Her research interests include language teaching methodology, ICT instruction, and ESP teaching. She can be contacted at email: rosmayantivivit@gmail.com

Kaye Shelton is a University Professor of Educational Leadership at Lamar University in the Center for Doctoral Studies. In this role, she teaches doctoral courses and chairs dissertation studies. She has chaired more than 100 completed dissertation studies since 2011. Previously, as Dean of Online Education for Dallas Baptist University, she led the development and ongoing operations of online programs with over 55 majors and degrees offered fully online. She is a certified online instructor and has taught online since 1999. In addition, Dr. Shelton works nationally and internationally with the OLC Quality Scorecard for the Administration of Online Programs. She is also an Online Learning Consortium Quality Scorecard program evaluator and teaches workshops regarding its implementation. Dr. Shelton has been involved with research in online education since 1997 and has advised peer institutions regarding the creation of online learning programs and best practices for teaching online and faculty support. An inductee of the Texas Distance Learning Hall of Fame, an Online Learning Consortium Fellow, and winner of both the Blackboard and eLearning exemplary online course awards, she has published articles and book chapters along with An Administrator's Guide to Online Education. Dr. Shelton was awarded a Sloan-C Effective Practice award for her research regarding the Quality Scorecard for the Administration of Online Education Programs and the John R. Bourne award for Outstanding Achievement in Online Education.

Andi Annisa Sulolipu is a lecturer in the Doctoral Program in Economics Education at Universitas Negeri Makassar. She earned her Bachelor’s degree from Universitas Negeri Makassar and completed both her Master’s and Doctoral studies at Universitas Negeri Malang.

Geraldine Torrisi-Steele is an associate professor/deputy head in the School of Information and Communication Technology at Griffith University, Australia. She is a Senior Fellow of the Higher Education Academy (UK). Her interest in learning and teaching, learning theory, technology for learning, human-computer interaction, and leadership distills from her "pre-academia" experiences in secondary school mathematics and physics teaching, and the design, development, and project management of digital interactive media for learning in higher education.

Romina Wilson is a dedicated Instructional Design and Educational Technology professional specializing in generative AI, learning design, and student support systems. She earned her Master's Degree in Instructional Design & Technology from California State University, San Bernardino, where she graduated with distinction and contributed to advancing research on AI integration in education. Romina's work centers on leveraging innovative technologies to enhance learner engagement, promote equity, and transform educational environments. She is poised to further her expertise as an incoming PhD student in Learning, Design, & Technology at the University of Tennessee-Knoxville, beginning in fall 2025. Beyond her academic and professional pursuits, Romina is passionate about creativity and community, finding joy in singing karaoke as a way to connect with others and express herself through music.

Index

A

B

G

H

I

L

M

N

P

Q

R

S

T

U

V

W

www.ingramcontent.com/pod-product-compliance
Ingram Content Group UK Ltd.
Pitfield, Milton Keynes, MK11 3LW, UK
UKHW050949290926
15470UKWH00005B/1731

9 798337 323978